The
Applied Psychology of
Work Behavior
A Book of Readings

The Applied Psychology of Work Behavior

A Book of Readings

Dennis W. Organ
Indiana University

1983   Revised Edition

BUSINESS PUBLICATIONS, INC.   Plano, Texas   75075

© BUSINESS PUBLICATIONS, INC., 1978 and 1983

ISBN 0-256-02436-7
Library of Congress Catalog Card No. 82–73399
Printed in the United States of America

1 2 3 4 5 6 7 8 9 0 ML 0 9 8 7 6 5 4 3

Preface

Two recent trends have exerted strong influences upon the study of behavior at work. One of these developments concerns the role of political processes in organizations: Nowadays one is much more apt than in years gone by to see explicit discussions of politics as an inevitable, often constructive, force in organizational behavior. The second trend to be reckoned with is the maturation of "macro" organizational behavior, with more precisely articulated linkages with the "micro" behavior of individuals and small groups.

Therefore, this revised selection of readings has sought to reflect the trends noted above. Unfortunately, selecting new articles for this purpose meant discarding some from the original edition, in order to keep length and costs to reasonable proportions. Furthermore, since balance across the various topics had to be considered, I could not base my decisions solely on what I regarded as the intrinsic interest of a particular piece. The result is that some of my "favorites" had to go.

Again, I have tried to strike a balance between popular and technical sources, between "classics" and the more timely, up-to-date developments, and between competing philosophies. As before, I have tried to ensure a measure of flexibility so that the book can be used for somewhat different purposes.

I would like to thank all of the authors who have generously consented to allow me to use their work. I am grateful also to colleagues for their feedback from using the first edition and for suggesting selections to include in this revised edition. Finally, I would like to express appreciation to Marcia Martin for her help in typing, correspondence, and organization of the manuscript.

Dennis W. Organ

Contents

section one

Organizational Behavior: Scope and Method

Introduction

In the beginning, there was Management. Those who reflected upon organizational phenomena were bound, however loosely, by one discipline or quasi-discipline which could be identified as the study of administration or management. Anyone who sought to design a task more efficiently, to motivate employees to perform more effectively, to clarify lines of authority, or propose ethical standards for organizations belonged to this quasi-discipline.

The loose bonds of this quasi-discipline endured through most of the first half of this century. Since then, most of the substantive areas within Management have been largely "appropriated" by disciplines outside of Management. Economics, mathematics, psychology, sociology, political science, anthropology, and law, to name a few, have staked the claim of their particular expertise upon topics formerly thought to be the exclusive domain of Management. Instead of one discipline, we now have several, including Organizational Behavior, Organization Theory, Operations Research, Personnel, and Administrative (or Business) Policy. Management, as a discipline, is not so much a distinctive, ongoing enterprise as it is now simply a holding company.[1]

The first two selections in this book should help the reader, first, to understand how organizational behavior stands in relation to the larger sphere of what was once Management, and second, to understand how organizational behavior stands in relation to some of the other disciplines which have emerged from this sphere. The article by Organ notes some of the historically significant events that served as

---

[1] For a more complete account of the fractionation of Management as a discipline, see Charles Perrow, "The Short and Glorious History of Organizational Theory," *Organizational Dynamics*, Summer 1973, pp. 2–15.

1

catalysts to accelerate the process by which organizational behavior became a distinctive discipline. Cummings offers some useful criteria for establishing the boundaries, as well as the linkages, between organizational behavior and related domains.

As other disciplines have preempted the concerns of Management, they have generally sought to impose upon these concerns the philosophy and methods of science. Armchair theorizing from the basis of informal personal observation gave way to the experiment, the survey, the simulation, the mathematical model, multivariate statistical analysis, and life under the rule of the .05 level of significance. Recently, some within our profession have expressed doubts about the value of an unqualified adherence to the natural science model of studying organizational behavior; they fear that a narrowly construed definition of legitimate approaches will constrain us from addressing the more timely and relevant phenomena in organizations. Behling provides a succinct statement of the essential tenets of a natural science approach, addresses the criticisms and the purported limitations of this approach, and states the case for why the scientific method should nonetheless guide our efforts. The concluding article by Scott provides a more detailed description of how rigorous methods of research bear upon the pursuit of knowledge about behavior in organizations.

The reader will probably, and rightfully, conclude from the selections in Section One that organizational behavior as a discipline reflects an ongoing state of *tension*. This tension emanates from many different sources: the tension between description versus prescription; between rigor and relevance; between objectivity and humanism; between the status quo and change. Inevitably, this tension means that unanimity is the exception rather than the rule, and only the most daring of our spokesmen will offer the grandiose, unqualified generalizations that the reader might seek. Yet it is precisely this tension that maintains the interest of its practitioners. And, in the final analysis, it is a tension which faithfully reflects its own subject of discourse: behavior in organizations.

1

Organizational Behavior as an Area of Study: Some Questions and Answers*

DENNIS W. ORGAN

Q: What is "organizational behavior"?

A: The precise answer depends on which specific textbook or authority you consult. The consensual core of most definitions, however, would run something like this: "Organizational Behavior (OB), as a field of study, represents the application of behavioral science concepts and methods to the study of human behavior in the organizational environment."

Q: Is organizational behavior simply the "human" side of management, or a "behavioral approach" to management?

A: No, although it might be fair to say that OB started out that way.

In the late 1920s and early 1930s, some experiments in illumination, pay systems, work breaks, and other job conditions took place at the Western Electric Hawthorne plant near Chicago. The results made little sense, at first, because productivity in an experimental group of female operators seemed to hold steady at a fairly high level regardless of the particular set of working conditions arranged. Finally the experimenters, after bringing in some outside consultants, realized that they had unwittingly altered supervisory styles (toward being more considerate of the individual workers and allowing them to make more job decisions) and allowed the operators to become a cohesive work group. These findings, plus others that emerged from an intensive interviewing program and close observation of a work group in action, made it clear that traditional management thought up to that time was deficient. Previous approaches to administration had concentrated on the mechanics of getting things coordinated and controlled, without due consideration of the complexity of the human element. After the publication of *Management and the Worker* (which reported the Hawthorne findings and probed their implications) in 1938, the "behavioral" aspects of work organization were elevated to a much more serious status. Management thinking began to accord much greater emphasis to worker feelings, motives, and the social forces in the "informal organization" not covered by the organization chart.

While these developments spurred a new interest in the relevance of

---

* Prepared especially for this volume.

behavioral sciences for management, they hardly resulted in a new discipline or field of knowledge. It was sometime later, near the end of the 1950s, that OB began to jell as a discipline.

In 1956, the Ford Foundation commissioned two economists, Professors R. A. Gordon and J. E. Howell, to undertake a comprehensive survey and assessment of business education at the college and university level. In their report, published in 1959, Gordon and Howell stated the view that business administration is the "enlightened application" of the behavioral sciences, among other things, to business problems. They felt, however, that business schools at the time were providing too little exposure in their curricula to basic conceptual material in the behavioral sciences.

Gordon and Howell noted approvingly that, at a number of the leading business schools, psychologists, sociologists, and political scientists were finding full-time positions on the faculty, and encouraged other schools to consider this possibility. They urged, too, more cooperation between business schools and departments of psychology and sociology on behavioral research—basic as well as applied—of interest to the business community and aspiring students of management and administration.

The Gordon and Howell report had an enormous impact on the design of business school curricula and recruitment of faculty in the 1960s. The trickle of behavioral scientists, especially psychologists, into business schools became, if not a flood, certainly a sizable stream. As they increased in numbers, they began to share an emerging professional kinship, developing their own national associations and doctoral programs within business schools. They, along with their intellectual offspring, gradually defined a coalescing discipline of OB. The discipline had reached a stage of considerable maturity by the mid-to-late 1960s, although it is of course still evolving, like all fields of knowledge, and not locked into a rigid scheme of development or a fixed set of topics.

Q: Is OB, then, just the *application* of psychology and other behavioral sciences to the study of behavior in organizations?

A: Not exactly. It is certainly more than the mere mechanical process of fitting known facts, laws, findings, and so forth, from psychology to work organizations. We *have* found it useful not to "reinvent the wheel." Where underlying disciplines such as psychology and sociology offer readily available concepts and methods of study that "fit" the organizational context, we do not hesitate to adopt them. Increasingly, however, we sometimes find it worth our while to develop our own constructs, theories, measuring instruments, and so on, when we address problems or issues unique to the organizational setting that have not been attended to by other behavioral sciences.

In any case, OB is not solely concerned with "application" in the narrow sense of the word. True, much of our effort is guided by the hope that we can contribute to pressing, urgent problems in work organizations, such as increasing the productivity and quality of work life in organizations. However, truly valid and lasting contributions will in some instances have to await a thorough testing and "thinking out" stage of our ideas, theories, and findings. Finally, as an intellectual discipline, OB, like any other, prizes knowledge and understanding as a goal in itself. Ultimately, knowledge is a seamless whole piece, and so any advance in our understanding of work behavior is worthwhile as well as intrinsically gratifying.

Q: How do developments in OB reach the practicing manager?

A: It might help, in answering this question, to look at the accompanying diagram of overlapping circles.

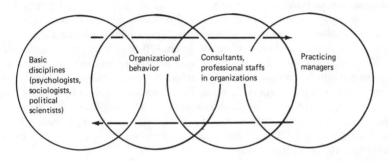

At the far left, we have those behavioral scientists (usually on the faculties of psychology or sociology departments) who teach and do basic research in such areas as human motivation, learning, attitude change, group dynamics, social stratification, and the like. Some of them have particular interests in organizations, most of them do not. Let us say a number of social psychologists conduct research showing that people's attitudes and opinions have little correspondence to their actual behavior. Now, people in OB, most of whom are affiliated with schools of business and administration, find out about this. They find out because many of them keep in touch with what people in the basic disciplines are doing; in fact, since the circles overlap, some of the organizational behavior types may be as much involved in the basic disciplines as anyone else. They ponder the implications of this finding about attitudes not jibing with behavior. Satisfaction with one's job is a type of attitude; productivity is a type of behavior. Maybe job satisfaction and productivity aren't too closely related, then. In any case, it's something to think about and investigate. So research is undertaken by organizational behaviorists, generally confirming that job satisfaction and productivity are not closely correlated. These findings stimulate new thinking about the links between satisfaction and performance (see Section Two-A in this volume). Later it turns up that social psychologists have found that certain factors determine whether attitudes and behavior are related. *If* the attitude is sufficiently specific (not general or vague) and not linked to powerful opposing attitudes, and if the behavior is not constrained by other forces, there may be a reasonably close correspondence between attitudes and behavior. So we may find that certain specific facets of job satisfaction *are* related to certain kinds of performance.

Many of the people who teach, write, and do research in OB also act as consultants to private firms and other organizations. In fact, some of them do part-time work in their own outside consulting firms, and a few do not belong to university faculties, but work full-time on the professional staffs (e.g., in industrial relations, planning, personnel) of corporations. All of these people draw from their expertise and knowledge in teaching students (who later become managers), advising client managers, teaching in management development programs, or writing in popular periodicals, magazines, or trade publications.

Throughout the history of science, lines of influence have sometimes run from the practical problem-solving arena back to basic theory and research, as well as in the other direction. OB is no exception. In the late 1950s, an issue of immediate concern among executives was whether groups made more cautious, conservative decisions than individuals acting alone. A master's thesis (Stoner, 1961) research project by a student in industrial management produced evidence that groups actually make *riskier* decisions. The implications of this finding soon rocked academic social psychology to its foundation and influenced more than a decade of research in social psychology.

Q: Doesn't it take a long time for this communication process to operate?

A: The problem more frequently has been that it operates too quickly. In an address to the Academy of Management in 1974, Professor Lyman Porter reminded the organizational behaviorists that often we have been too quick to offer prescriptions to managers on the basis of premature, tentative, sometimes downright invalid findings. One result is that by promising too much with a hard-sell approach, we have damaged our credibility with practitioners. We have foisted programs upon them that were attractive in package, but weak in substance, and the implied payoffs were not realized.

Part of the problem is that OB, like any science, is a system or collection of "technologies" as well as a field of study. Professor L. L. Cummings (1977) of Wisconsin identifies OB techniques for training leaders, designing tasks, evaluating performance, and designing reward systems. Technologies have their market appeal even when they are based on untested or oversimplified representations of reality.

Q: How can premature prescribing be minimized?

A: Only by the discipline of the scientific method. As Cummings points out, OB is becoming more "influenced by the norms of skepticism, caution, replication of findings, and public exposure of knowledge based on facts."

Q: Doesn't the cold-blooded posture of "scientism" put a damper on the genuine and immediate concern for people?

A: Actually, as Cummings observes, "there is a distinctly humanistic tone within OB." That is, as much as anything else, we want to contribute a knowledge basis for designing organization environments that foster self-development, psychological growth, choice, and fulfillment of individuals—yet do it in a way that also makes organizations more effective in serving the larger society. As Cummings puts it, this is a "humanism without softness." OB is performance-oriented, as well as people-oriented; its orientation toward both is circumscribed by intellectual and scientific honesty, lest we delude ourselves into thinking we have already reached the promised land for which we strive (and will never reach, since it really exists only as a guiding ideal).

Q: What has OB accomplished? What is its track record?

A: To date, our major contribution has been, in a sense, negative. We have been more successful in challenging and overturning previous conceptions about behavior in organizations than we have been creative in providing alternative conceptions. Nowhere is this better illustrated than in the study of leadership. As Professor H. Joseph Reitz (1977) remarks, "the study of leadership is interesting and yet confusing. We seem to have been more proficient at discovering the misconceptions of leadership than the principles of leadership." We realize now that effective leaders cannot be picked on the basis of personality traits, that democratic leadership is not necessarily more effective than autocratic leadership, and leader behavior is as much or more affected by subordinate performance than vice versa.

Q: Isn't this discouraging?

A: It is certainly cause for humility on our part. We realize now that grand theories which will explain any and every thing are not in the offing. If we can't endorse a particular style of leader behavior that is optimal for all situations, maybe we can find a style that at least seems to work reasonably well in a very limited set of situations.

Q: In the final analysis, what does OB have to offer the student?

A: It can help the student become, in the words of Professor R. J. House of the University of Toronto, a "good crap-detector." It can provide a basic framework for evaluating the assertions, conclusions, programs, and slogans that the manager is bombarded with from all sides. It can help the student recognize fallacies in his or her own thinking about work behavior. It can help one avoid painting oneself into a logical corner. It can provide a basis for informal, intelligent observation of behavior in organizations.

REFERENCES

Cummings, L. L. Toward organizational behavior. *Academy of Management Review,* 1977.

Gordon, R. A., & Howell, J. E. *Higher education for business.* New York: Columbia University Press, 1959.

Porter, L. W. Presidential address, Academy of Management meeting, Seattle, 1974.

Reitz, H. J. *Behavior in organizations.* Homewood, Ill.: Richard D. Irwin, Inc., 1977, p. 535.

Roethlisberger, F. J., & Dickson, W. J. *Management and the worker.* New York: John Wiley & Sons, Science Editions, 1964.

Stoner, J. A. F.   A comparison of individual and group decisions including risk. Unpublished master's thesis, School of Industrial Management, Massachusetts Institute of Technology, 1961.

2

Toward Organizational Behavior*

L. L. CUMMINGS

Three bases are analyzed for partitioning organizational behavior (OB) as a field of inquiry from other related fields. OB is characterized by three dimensions and three themes that impact the articulation of these dimensions in teaching, research, and application. Implications are drawn for the evolution of OB as an enacted discipline.

Attempting to describe a field as dynamic and as multifaceted, or even as confusing, as organizational behavior (OB) is not a task for the timid. It may be a task that only the foolish, yet concerned, would even tackle.

What motivates one toward accepting such an undertaking? Two forces are operating. First, there is a clear need to parcel out knowledge into more understandable and convenient packages. Students, managers, and colleagues in other departments request that we respond to straightforward, honest questions like: What is OB? How is OB different from management? How is it different from human relations? It is difficult for students to understand the philosophy or the systematic nature of a program or curriculum if they cannot define the parts. Our credibility with the managerial world is damaged when OB comes out in executive programs as "a little of everything," as "a combination of behavioral jargon and common sense," or as "touchy-feely" without content. The field's lack of confidence in articulating its structure is occasionally reflected in ambiguous and fuzzy suggestions for improvement in the world that managers face.

Second, identification or assertion of the themes and constructs underlying OB, or any other discipline, represents an important platform

* From *Academy of Management Review* 3, no. 1 (1978), pp. 90–98. This article was first developed as a paper for the 1976 National Academy of Management Convention. The author gratefully acknowledges the comments and critiques of: Michael Aiken, Alan Filley, Barbara Karmel, Johannes Pennings, Jeffrey Pfeffer, Donald Schwab, George Strauss, and Karl Weick.

for expanding knowledge. Without assumptions about what is included, excluded, and on the boundary, duplication among disciplines results. The efficiency of knowledge generation and transmission is hampered. Until a field is defined in relation to its intellectual cousins, it may develop in redundant directions. This leads to the usual awakening that parallel, and perhaps even superior, developments already have occurred in adjacent fields about which we are ignorant. Repetition of such occurrences in a field lessens its intellectual credibility among scholars. All of this is not to deny the benefits to be gained from cross-fertilization and exchange across subfields once these are delineated and common concerns and interests are discovered.

These are the forces underlying the concern. What is said here represents an unfinished product—a thought in process—not a finished, static, intellectually frozen definition. In fact, the argument is made that stimulating, dynamic fields are defined *in process* and that the processes of emergence and evolution should never end.

Perspectives on Organizational Behavior

Several partitions have been used in attempting to distinguish OB from related disciplines. Tracing some of these provides perspective on our task and builds a critical platform for appraising where the field is today.

Probably the most common segmentation of subfields relating behavior and organization is based on *units of analysis* where the units are differentiated by level of aggregation. Typically, using this framework, OB is defined as the study of individuals and groups within organizations. The units of analysis are individual and micro (e.g., dyadic) interactions among individuals. Organizational characteristics (e.g., structure, process, climate) are seen either as "givens" which assume a constant state or as independent variables whose variations are assumed to covary with, or cause variations in, the relevant dependent variables. These relevant dependent variables are measures of individual or micro unit affective and/or behavioral reactions.

Organizational theory (OT) is typically defined by its focus upon the *organization as the unit of analysis*. Organizational structure, process, goals, technology, and, more recently, climate are the relevant dependent variables, assumed to vary systematically with variations in environmental characteristics but not with characteristics embedded within systematically clustered individuals. A comparative, cross-organizational framework is essential for development of knowledge in OT. Studies of single organizations add little to understanding of organizations when the unit of analysis and variation is assumed to be the organization itself. This realization is increasingly reflected in the empirical literature of OT.[2]

Some have distinguished the field of inquiry based upon an attribution of *typical or modal methodologies* to the respective subfields. OB is defined as studies utilizing laboratory and, occasionally, field experimentation. OT is identified with the predominant use of survey and, occasionally, case designs. While the simplicity of this methodological distinction is attractive, it does not reflect the current diversity of designs underlying current research on people in organizations and on organizations per se.

The adjective pairs "normative-descriptive" and "empirical-theoretical" are attractive labels for describing *epistomological differences*. Certainly, the two predominant versions of classical OT have been characterized, and criticized, as excessively normative and not descriptive of behavioral and organizational realities. Both Taylor and Fayol on the one hand, and Weber on the other, have provided much of the focus for the normative critics. Some OB scholars view their field's mission as adding descriptive, empirically-based facts to what they see as the essentially normative and theoretical biases of classical OT. With the advent of data among OT scholars and the infusion of organizational development (OD) into the OB tent, these distinctions are no longer descriptive of our domain. Descriptive, empirical, theoretical, and normative can each be used to characterize some work in both OB and OT. Complexity now overshadows the simple straw man of yesterday.

As OD began to emerge a few years ago, the theme of several corridor conversations was that OB *was becoming the applied cousin of OT*. After all, some claimed, OT deals with the theory of organizations by definition. For a moment the distinctions between OB and OD became blurred, and that opaqueness was attractive for some. Reading between the lines, OT was to become the reservoir of accepted and evolving constructs, and OB would emerge as the behavioral engineering function. For managers and consultants we would have OB; for scholars, OT. The largest obstacle to enacting such a distinction is that scholars and appliers do not generally read or listen to one another. The OB people must have their own constructs and theories. The OT people need their own applications, their own means of establishing credibility within the world of action. From this insulation, two OD camps have emerged with their own strategies for change. One focuses on change via the individual and micro unit within the organization and the other on change through structural and environmental

---

[2] Hannan and Freeman (1) have argued quite convincingly that comparative analyses of organizational effectiveness are inappropriate for scientific purposes.

manipulation. Alas, another simple, definitional distinction melts!

My preference among these alternative taxonomic bases is the first. The unit of analysis perspective seems cleanest. The most severe problem with this view is finding intellectual bridges to link the subfields. This linkage is crucial for understanding the way organizations function, the impacts they exert, and the opportunities they provide. Some bridges begin to emerge which are at least suggestive. For example, an organization's structure (i.e., number of levels, average span of supervision, degree of horizontal differentiation) can be viewed as a construct linking OT and OB. In OT, structure is typically positioned in a nomological network as a dependent variable. In OB, structure is typically positioned as an independent variable. This differential positioning of the same construct suggests a possible general role that several constructs might take in linking OT and OB. Structure, climate, task design, reward systems, and leader behavior can each be conceived of as intervening between causal forces in the environment of organizations and the behavior and attitudes of persons within organizations. Each is beginning to be modeled as a dependent variable in one context and an independent variable in another.

This differentiation of subfields by unit of analysis and their integration by intervening constructs is subject to limitations. The boundaries of aggregation between levels of analysis are arbitrary, with no fundamental laws underlying the distinctions. That is a limitation shared with the biological and physical sciences, where subfields have arisen as linking mechanisms (e.g., biophysics, biochemistry, psychopharmacology). The conception also lacks feedback loops with reversible intervening constructs. It is likely that such reciprocal causation reflects reality and that models that omit these loops will not provide a full understanding.

If we were to assume this posture of differentiation, what would be the result? Remembering that the distinctions are based primarily on levels of analysis with a slight nod toward the other distinctions, we can propose the definitions in Figure 1.

A DIMENSIONAL CHARACTERIZATION OF ORGANIZATIONAL BEHAVIOR

I believe that OB is evolving toward the model presented in Figure 2. The field is being enacted, not defined in some a priori sense, by scholars and teachers in ways that imply the dimensional, thematic conception suggested in that figure.

Three dimensions define the conceptual domain of OB. Most disciplines and emerging fields of inquiry that stand at the interface between science and professional practice are describable in terms of

FIGURE 1
Distinctions among Organizational Behavior, Organizational Psychology, Organizational Theory and Personnel and Human Resources

Organizational Behavior–Organizational Psychology (OP)	Both fields focus upon explaining human behavior within organizations. Their difference centers on the fact that OP restricts its explanatory constructs to those at the psychological level. OB draws constructs from multiple disciplines. As the domain of OP continues to expand, the difference between OB and OP is diminishing, perhaps to the point of identity between the fields.
Organizational Behavior–Organizational Theory (OT)	The distinction is based on two differences: unit of analysis and focus of dependent variables. OB is defined as the study of individual and group behavior within organizations and the application of such knowledge. OT is the study of structure, processes, and outcomes of the organization per se. The distinction is neither that OB is atheoretical and concerned only with behavior nor that OT is unique or exclusive in its attention to theory. Alternatively, the distinction can be conceived as between micro and macro perspectives on OB. This removes the awkward differentiation of behavior and theory.
Organizational Behavior–Personnel and Human Resources (P&HR)	This distinction usually depicts OB as the more basic of the two and P&HR as more applied in emphasis. OB is seen as more concept oriented while P&HR is viewed as emphasizing techniques or technologies. The dependent variables, behavior and affective reactions within organizations, are frequently presented as similar. P&HR can be seen as standing at the interface between the organization and the individual, focusing on developing and implementing the system for attracting, maintaining, and motivating the individual within the organization.

these dimensions. The specific articulation of the dimensions depends significantly upon the underlying epistomological themes adopted by the discipline.

A Way of Thinking

OB is a *way of thinking*, a manner of conceiving problems and articulating research and action solutions which can be characterized by five postures. First, problems and questions are typically formulated within an independent variable(s)-dependent variable(s) framework. Recently, OB has begun to incorporate personal and situa-

FIGURE 2
Dimensions and Themes of Organizational Behavior

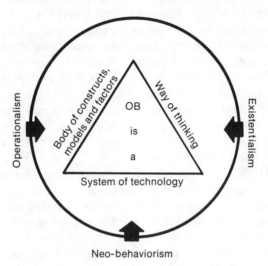

tional moderators into this framework. OB's assertion that behavior within organizations is subject to systematic study is based on conceptualization of the object of study as nonrandom, systematic, and generally purposive. This way of thinking is significantly influencing our methodologies. The field is engaged in a sometimes painful search for cause and effect within our models.

A second component of OB as a way of thinking is its orientation toward change as a desirable outcome for organizations and persons within organizations. Static phenomena possess diminishing prestige as topics of study. Conditions for stimulating change and models for evaluating change are an increasingly important part of the field.

Third, there is a distinctly humanistic tone within OB, reflected in concern for self-development, personal growth, and self-actualization. Although its influence on research and teaching seems to ebb and flow, and its reflection in scholarship and pedagogy varies by school, it is there, and its presence is causing both strain (given its positioning adjacent to scienticism) and excitement, even relevance, within OB. The striving is toward humanism without softness. OB shares this dilemma with most of the person-oriented disciplines that attempt to combine basic, good science with a change orientation. Yet this tone of humanism is only one side of the current, slightly schizophrenic posture of OB. The other side is reflected in a heavy emphasis on operant learning models and behavioral modification techniques, an orientation toward environmental determinism rather than self-actualization.

Fourth, OB is becoming increasingly performance oriented, with more studies including a performance-oriented dependent variable. The field is beginning to capture an important distinction between two types of dependent variables. One perspective focuses on description of a behavior, activity, or outcome, that is, the proper focus for scientific analysis and thinking. The other aims at application of a preference function to these behaviors, activities, or outcomes, resulting in a scaling of effectiveness or success. This is the proper focus for an engineering analysis—a managerial mind set.[3] We are beginning to hear the demands for relevance in our research and teaching. Unless OB can increase its performance payoffs, the field may be in danger of losing some of its hard battles for a niche in the curriculum or a moment in the board room.

Finally, OB uses the discipline imposed by the scientific method. The field is substantially influenced by norms of skepticism, caution, replication, and public exposure of knowledge based on facts. In many ways, this posture of "scientism" confuses some students and clients. It can be seen as the antithesis of several other postures that characterize OB thinking. Yet it is generally accepted as a crucial posture. It helps to keep the field straight, and it is the key ingredient in whatever longevity the field may possess. Scientific method, applied to OB, provides the mechanism for feedback and self-renewal.

A Body of Constructs, Models, and Facts

Even though OB is characterized by some definitional confusion, an implicit agreement is emerging about some of its components. Differences exist concerning the relative weighting of components and the emphasis given to basic science versus application in transmitting the field to others. But most treatments of the field now include coverage of constructs, models, and facts on: motivation, learning or socialization, group structure and process, leader behavior, task design, interpersonal communication, organizational structure, interpersonal change and conflict, and material on relevant dependent variables (e.g., satisfaction, other attitudes, participation measures, performance dimensions, and other behaviors).

This emergence of an identity for the field is evidenced by the second generation of OB textbooks, which are more similar in topical coverage than their ancestors. Some models sell and are thus influential in structuring the introductory level curricula underlying our field. Others stretch the field at its boundaries but do not become a part of

---

[3] My thinking here has been significantly influenced by Robert Kahn of the University of Michigan. His comments at the 1976 Carnegie-Mellon Workshop on Organizational Effectiveness have been particularly helpful.

the core. That core is gradually developing toward an identifiable body of components.

A System of Technology

OB is also a system or a collection of technologies. These have evolved out of the primary areas of study identified as the independent variables of OB. Techniques now exist for: training leaders, designing tasks, designing organizations, evaluating performances, rewarding behaviors, and modeling behaviors.

The uncritical eye might be pleased with OB's tool kit. Superficially, it appears that the field is ready to move into the world of action with vigor and confidence. But our posture of scientism keeps the field honest. These technologies are largely exploratory, unvalidated, and in a few cases, under evaluation. The field has even spawned in occasional technology that has been adopted and later found damaging to an organization and its participants. In most cases, even when the technologies work, the field's theoretical models are not sufficiently developed to explain why they were effective. So, a system or collection of technologies? Yes. A behavioral engineering discipline? No.

THEMES INFLUENCING ORGANIZATIONAL BEHAVIOR

As depicted in Figure 2, three themes span the dimensions defining OB and influence the way each dimension is articulated. The relative emphasis given to each theme over time, by the various schools of thought within OB, determines our ways of thinking, constructs and facts, and development of technologies.

EXISTENTIALISM

The emphasis here is upon the uncertain, contingent environment of people within organizations (and organizations). Existentialism emphasizes that in the face of this type of environment, persons must exercise self-control in pursuit of their own objectives. The ultimate responsibility for designing productive and satisfying organizational environments rests with human beings. It is their responsibility to fashion themselves—to implement self control. This philosophical posture leaves a legacy of concepts within OB—goal, purpose, expectation, expectancy, instrumental, path, and contingency.

This theme is forcing OB to become a more complex discipline. It asserts that no meaning exists in absolutes. All meaning derives from comparison; meaning is always relative. Activities and outcomes within organizations are meaningful only within a context including implicit or explicit statements of purpose. This is at the core of one important, current development in conceptualizing the influence of most of the independent variables treated in OB—the concept of contingency.

With the realization that an independent variable's effects depend, the next logical question becomes: Depends upon what? When? and so forth. *Why* did *who* do *what* with *whom* with what *outcomes*? This seemingly simple question can be applied to most independent-dependent variable linkages currently of concern in OB. The *why* focuses on the causes, the reasons, the antecedents of variance in the dependent variable. The *who* focuses on the initiating party (individual, group, or organization). The *what* requires description of the behavior in question. The *whom* provides the interaction component, adding dimension to the search for meaningfulness. It provides a vertical, horizontal, or diagonal vector to the reality that OB attempts to understand. The *outcomes* provide the ultimate meaning to the field. Existentialism implies that the meaning in any act exists in its consequences, and OB seems to be moving toward this realization.

Operationalism

Operationalism is reflected in three ways. First, the field is searching for theories of the middle range in most of its subareas. The grand, general, abstract models of motivation, leadership, environment-structure interaction, and change are not yielding satisfying, systematic, cumulative data. Some models posit relations between environmental and organizational characteristics and individual attitudes and behaviors. Models are needed to describe the processes through which environment impacts structure and structure impacts attitudes and behavior.

Second, emphasis is being given to the operations or behaviors through which people within organizations function. Whether describing what managers do or analyzing the impact of leaders, the importance of formulating the issue in operational terms is being realized. The literature is beginning to be characterized by questions like:

1. Through what operations is structure actually designed?
2. Through what operations does a leader impact a subordinate?
3. Through what operations do rewards and punishments effect change?
4. Through what operations do groups actually make decisions?

In each case, the field is beginning to examine the physiology of behavior within organizations. The anatomy of OB is important, but its study has not led to understanding the processes through which persons and organizations interact.

Third, measurement issues are impacting the field. Questions of reliability and validity must be faced, and questions of scaling and measurement confronted. We are increasingly anxious about our inability to explain large amounts of variance in dependent variables. Three rather lengthy streams of research have reached the point where lack of early attention to how we operationalized constructs and validated measures has caused major problems for continued, meaningful work. Cases in point are research on: the two-factor model of motivation (with faulty measurement procedures); expectancy formulations of motivation (with testing of inappropriate models); and the impact of organizational design on attitudes and behaviors (with designs that confound independent variables). While not completely pessimistic, I believe that the field has been extremely inefficient and myopic in the research strategies applied in some areas.

Neo-behaviorism

Finally, many causal assumptions and models in OB are moving toward a behavioristic orientation with a cognitive overtone. Motivation theory, under the influence of expectancy models, has moved in this direction. Leadership studies reflect the notion of instrumental, goal-oriented behavior with a significant emphasis on leader behavior being partially a function of the consequences which it produces. The concept of contingency plays a major role in several fields within OB, its general intellectual structure deriving directly from the behavioristic notion of structure and process evolving toward forms that are reinforcing to the organism. The behavioristic perspective also has surfaced in literature dealing with organizational design and organizational control and power. Distributions of influence and power are partially explained by environmental consequences of attempts at influence. The exercise of power generates consequences which, in turn, affect structural configurations of the organization.

Radical behaviorism is not the dominant theme, but rather a combination of general behavioral constructs *and* cognitions. It is not clear what functions are provided by the incorporation of cognitions within OB models. Little research has been addressed to the question of the variance explained in most OB models by cognitions beyond that explained by environmental determinants. Perhaps cognitive concepts do explain added variance, or perhaps they constitute a residual reservoir of unexplained variance to which we inappropriately attribute meaning.

CONCLUSIONS AND IMPLICATIONS

What are the implications of this perspective on the field? First, ultimately the definitions of the domains of OB, OT, OP, and OD are arbitrary. Definitions should be tested by their usefulness in specifying constructs and functional relations. Definitions are needed to guide the field toward middle range and operational theory. Movement toward definition by induction is needed. It may prove fruitful to aim toward definition through describing what is happening in the main streams of research within OB. Definitions established by assertion lead to debate without fruitful results.

Second, realities in organizations change so rapidly that our descriptions (ways of thinking, constructs, and technologies) do not keep pace with the rate of change in the objects of our study.[4] I see two implications of this for OB. First, incredibly long periods of time are needed to assess organizations and to identify the fundamental, underlying nature of the field. Second, increasing energy will be devoted to collapsing the time intervals needed to develop relevant constructs and models and to testing these models. This implies that management, as a general field, will accelerate adoption of both simulation and experimental designs. These designs permit the modeling of time lags. Contrary to the usual evaluation of such designs, they will allow us to become more realistic in our modeling and measurement of OB.

Third, what might this line of reasoning mean for the Academy of Management and its members? The Academy is presently the only camp which attempts to house OB, OT, OD, and P&HR. For the moment, these fields have separate tents within the camp, but I believe that the traditional distinctions are beginning to melt. Several examples illustrate this permeability. The 1976 doctoral consortium conducted at the National Academy Convention included topics from both OT and OB. I suspect it is impossible to talk at an advanced level about one domain without the other. The P&HR division's program at the 1976 National Academy Convention consists of about 40 percent OB material. This reflects a healthy trend for both P&HR and OB. It is naive to deal with many of the important issues in P&HR without incorporating OB models and research. The *Academy of Management Journal*, the *Academy of Management Review, Organizational Behavior and Human Performance*, and *Administrative Science Quarterly* exhibit trends in submissions that reflect an increasing emphasis on *multiple* levels of analysis in both the independent and dependent variable domains.

---

[4] I am indebted to Professor Lou Pondy for stimulating this notion.

I believe we are moving toward an enacted field, perhaps best labeled organizational analysis or organizational science (if we wish to emphasize the scientific lineage of our interests and our aspirations). Basically, we now have five divisions within the Academy, composing organizational analysis or science. These are Organizational Behavior, Organization and Management Theory, Personnel and Human Resources, Organization Development, and Organizational Communication. Such segmentation continues to provide important functions for the Academy and its members, but it remains an open question whether segmentation is the most efficient strategy to advance our common interest in behavior *in* and *of* organizations.

As Thurston said:

> It is the faith of all science that an unlimited number of phenomena can be comprehended in terms of a limited number of concepts or ideal constructs. Without this faith no science could ever have any motivation. To deny this faith is to affirm the primary chaos of nature and the consequent futility of scientific effort. The constructs in terms of which natural phenomena are comprehended are man-made inventions. To discover a scientific law is merely to discover that a man-made scheme serves to unify, and thereby to simplify, comprehension of a certain class of natural phenomena. A scientific law is not to be thought of as having an independent existence which some scientist is fortunate to stumble upon. A scientific law is not a part of nature. It is only a way of comprehending nature.

REFERENCES

1. Hannan, M. T., & J. Freeman. "Obstacles for Comparative Studies," in *New Perspectives in Organizational Effectiveness*, Eds. P. S. Goodman & J. M. Pennings (San Francisco: Jossey-Bass, 1977), pp. 106–31.
2. Thurston, L. S. *Multiple-Factor Analysis* (Chicago: University of Chicago Press, 1947).

3

The Case for the Natural Science Model for Research in Organizational Behavior and Organization Theory *

ORLANDO BEHLING[1]

> Research methods similar to those used in the natural sciences have long been the norm in organizational behavior and organization theory. However, several writers have recently questioned their appropriateness for the study of organizations and the groups and individuals who make them up. In this paper I examine five major objections to the use of such methods in organizational behavior and organization theory and conclude that, while they may indicate a need for more thoughtful application of the natural science approach, they do not rule it out as the primary research strategy for the study of organizations.

One widely accepted view of the role that science plays in organizational behavior and organization theory is that it functions to:

> establish general laws covering the behavior of empirical events or objects with which the science is concerned, and thereby enable us to connect together our knowledge of separately known events and to make reliable predictions of events yet unknown [Braithwaite, 1973, p. 1].

In the tradition of Campbell and Stanley [1963], Cook and Campbell [1976], and Kerlinger [1973], most advocates of this view hold that good research is characterized by careful sampling, precise measurement, and sophisticated design and analysis in the test of hypotheses derived from tentative general laws. Popper [1964] labels this rigorous search for general laws the *natural science model* because it represents a social science approximation of the approach that serves the natural sciences (e.g., physics, chemistry, biology) so well. I will use Popper's label throughout this paper.

---

* From *Academy of Management Review* 5, no. 4, (1980), pp. 483–90. © 1980 by the Academy of Management 0363-7425.

Clearly, the authors of mainstream texts in organizational behavior and organization theory accept the natural science model of good research. Those who include research methods chapters [e.g., Bobbitt, Breinholt, Doktor, & McNaul, 1978; Hamner & Organ, 1978; Jackson & Morgan, 1978] clearly follow this approach and generally appear to owe an intellectual debt to Kerlinger, a strong proponent of the natural science model. Some authors are even more definite in their advocacy of the model. First, Luthans quotes Berelson and Steiner [1964]:

> Organizational behavior should strive to attain the following hallmarks of a science:
>
> 1. The procedures are public.
> 2. The definitions are precise.
> 3. The data collecting is objective.
> 4. The findings are replicable.
> 5. The approach is systematic and cumulative.
> 6. The purposes are explanation, understanding, and prediction [1973, p. 77].

While Berelson and Steiner's points 1, 4, and 6 can be encompassed by all but the most radical definitions of good research, it is clear that 2, 3, and to a certain extent 5, call for application of the natural science approach. Second, Filley, House, and Kerr [1975] have discussed research methods in terms of "levels of rigor." Though they point out the dangers of undervaluing less rigorous research methods for exploratory studies, there is a clear implication in their work that the closer a study approximates the natural science ideal, the better it is. They also organize each of their chapters around a series of "propositions" or tentative general laws.

Recently, however, questions have been raised regarding the appropriateness of the natural science approach for organizational behavior and organization theory research. These questions do not arise from the traditional charges that much research on organizational phenomena merely verifies in elaborate and costly ways things that most managers already know [e.g., Gordon, Kleiman, & Hanie, 1978] or that it simply splits hairs to benefit the egos of theoreticians [e.g., Koontz, 1961]. Rather, the questioners hold that organizations and the groups and individuals who make them up differ from phenomena of interest to the natural sciences in ways that make natural science methods inappropriate for their study.

Some of the apparent dissatisfaction is implicit—for example, the increasing interest in models such as functionalism as replacements for or supplements to the currently dominant causal models [Behling, 1979], and the growing use of intuitive participant-observer methods not merely for exploring new areas but also for drawing conclusions.

But the dissatisfaction has also been made explicit by Behling and Shapiro [1974], Argyris [1976], Lundberg [1976], and most provocatively by Mitroff and Pondy, who write:

> We are conditioned by our scientific training to associate progress with greater rigor, greater precision, disintegrative analysis, more empirical documentation of a phenomenon, and the progressive exorcism of value-laden questions in favor of a purer pursuit of "truth," that is, a closer and closer fitting of our theories to the one objective reality we presume exists. . . . If you are spinning off ideas, you are allowed to be intuitive and nonrigorous, so long as you get scientific again when you begin testing your ideas empirically. But we believe that . . . increased openness toward imprecision extends *beyond* the hypothesis-generation stage. This is not to say that precise, rigorous, empirically testable descriptions and theories are out. But it does mean that looser, nontestable, nongeneralizable descriptions (e.g., poems) of social facts are equally legitimate forms of representation and, perhaps, . . . even more appropriate forms of inquiry than the normal model of science . . . perhaps "science" is the wrong strategy for understanding social phenomena [1978, pp. 145–146].

I share the frustration of Mitroff and Pondy and the other critics with the nitpicking and repeated "back to the drawing board" retrenchments that accompany natural science methods in some areas of organizational behavior and organization theory. I feel, however, that those who argue against the natural science approach should not go unchallenged, for two reasons. First, they typically present only one side of the question. Second, they usually consider only one or two of the important issues bearing on the usefulness of the natural science approach to research. Sociologists [Popper, 1964], social psychologists [Gergen, 1973; Schlenker, 1974], and those in other applied social sciences [Campbell, 1974] have explored a wide range of issues that deserve discussion in organizational behavior and organization theory.

In the following paragraphs, working from Brown [1965], Gergen [1973], Homans [1967], Kaplan [1964], Nagel [1961], Popper [1964], and Schlenker [1974], I identify five key objections to the use of the natural science model raised in other social and behavioral sciences that have been or could be raised in organizational behavior and organization theory, and I explain why they do not rule out attempts to apply the model to solving riddles in the discipline. These objections have been discussed under many different labels; I refer to them as:

1. *Uniqueness.* Each organization, group, and person differs to some degree from all others; the development of precise general laws in organizational behavior and organization theory is thus impossible.
2. *Instability.* The phenomena of interest to researchers in organizational behavior and organization theory are transitory. Not only do

the "facts" of social events change with time, but the "laws" governing them change as well. Natural science research is poorly equipped to capture these fleeting phenomena.

3. *Sensitivity.* Unlike chemical compounds and other things of interest to natural science researchers, the people who make up organizations, and thus organizations themselves, may behave differently if they become aware of researchers hypotheses about them.

4. *Lack of Realism.* Manipulating and controlling variables in organizational research changes the phenomena under study. Researchers thus cannot generalize from their studies because the phenomena observed inevitably differ from their real world counterparts.

5. *Epistemological Differences.* Although understanding cause and effect through natural science research is an appropriate way of "knowing" about physical phenomena, a different kind of "knowledge" not tapped by this approach is more important in organizational behavior and organization theory.

These objections are discussed in greater detail in the following sections.

Uniqueness

This objection holds that the phenomena of concern to organizational behavior and organization theory researchers are specific to the organizations, work groups, or individuals in which they occur. If this is indeed the case, then attempts to generalize from a sample, no matter how carefully chosen, will be futile since no organization, group, or individual can represent any other, much less a broad class. If each case is unique, the idea of general laws is meaningless.

The phenomenological premises underlying Weick's concept of the "enacted organization" [1969] and Pondy and Boje's call for "bringing mind back in" to the study of organizations [1976] lead almost inevitably to the idea that what any one organization, group, or individual has in common with any other exists only in the shared perceptions of the people who interact with them. More directly, Newell and Simon's [1972] and Dawes's [1975] work on individualized processes in decision making represents moves in the direction of substituting appreciation of unique entities for the search for general laws.

Much of the apparent uniqueness of phenomena studied in organizational behavior and organization theory is real, but this fact does not limit the field to the description of singular events. To understand why, it is useful to follow Merton [1949] in differentiating between *empiric generalizations* and *scientific laws.* While both are statements of contingencies of the form "If A, then B," a scientific law is stated in more abstract form than an empiric generalization, permitting the insertion of specific objects, events, and the like as variables and allowing the prediction of specific "events yet unknown" from the abstract statement.

The fact that many works published in organizational behavior and organization theory journals report empiric generalizations (e.g., "matrix organizations work well in aerospace firms" or "urban blue-collar workers are less likely to respond to job enrichment than their rural counterparts") rather than scientific laws does not justify the assertion that the field *cannot* yield scientific laws. (Nor should the statement be interpreted as saying that empiric generalizations are valueless; in fact, they serve as bases for practical decisions in specific situations and also serve as a kind of raw material for builders of scientific laws.)

McKelvey [1975, 1978] points out that the key to the development of meaningful generalizations lies in *taxonomy*, a theory of differences among organizations, together with methods of *classification* derived from it. Such an approach leads to two things. First, McKelvey holds, it permits the development of generalizations about important though relatively narrow populations:

> Narrower, more homogeneous populations would limit the generalizability of any single study, but this would be offset by gains in the definitiveness of the findings, the levels of variance explained, and the applicability of the results to the population. In short, solid findings about a narrower population are better than marginal findings of questionable generalizability to a broadly defined population [1978, p. 1438].

Second, generalizations about narrow populations defined systematically rather than casually can be combined into higher order generalizations. Because such laws must encompass diverse organizations, groups, or individuals, they cannot be as exact or explain as large a portion of the total variance as one might hope. Nevertheless, they represent a form of useful general law.

Instability

The opponents of natural science methods in organizational behavior and organization theory hold that phenomena of concern to researchers in the field change frequently, making it extremely difficult to combine data obtained at different times in order to arrive at general laws, as is commonly done in the natural sciences. Mitroff and Pondy, for example, state:

> The phenomenon will never be completely described or understood before it vanishes and some new phenomenon supplants it. That is the

guts of our conjecture that *science* is the wrong enquiring system for the social "sciences"; it converges too slowly relative to the rate of decay and evolution of social phenomena [1978, p. 147.].

Were this assertion correct, cumulatively developing knowledge about organizations and groups and individuals within them would be well nigh impossible. Instead, organizational behavior and organization theory would be journalism—the recording and explaining of ephemeral phenomena—rather than science.

But this does not appear to be the case, for two reasons. First, as explained in the discussion of the uniqueness objection, scientific research seeks laws that transcend time and place, not empiric generalizations that often are specific to certain situations. Second, as explained by Gergen [1973] and Schlenker [1974] in their discussions of a "continuum of historic durability," to assume that *all* phenomena of interest to organizational behavior and organization theory are ephemeral is as much an error as to assume that even the most specific aspects of them remain constant over long periods. Clearly, some phenomena change more rapidly than others. Relationships with roots in human physiology and those reflecting performance limits of organizational and group forms probably change more slowly than those that are socially determined or simply "common practice." Thus, careful consideration of the likely durability of the phenomena studied should be a necessary part of decisions each researcher makes regarding the appropriateness of methods characterized by varying levels of natural science rigor.

Sensitivity

Opponents of natural science methods in organizational behavior and organization theory charge that awareness of hypotheses in the social sciences inevitably changes the behaviors of the persons involved. These changes take two forms. First, such awareness may create *self-fulfilling prophecies* whereby participants change their behavior to increase the chances of supporting the hypothesis. Behling and Shapiro [1974], for example, point out how researchers' attempts to gain managerial permission to study "need for A" (which could be anything) in an organization can sensitize the managers to its manifestations. This in turn could lead the managers to reinforce "A-seeking" behavior on the part of their subordinates. The research process would thus create rather than measure the importance of "need for A."

Second, such sensitivity may take the form of what Nagel [1961] calls *suicidal predictions*. Nagel points out that predictions of a depression immediately following World War II induced business to cut certain prices, which led to increased demand, which made the prediction incorrect. Similarly, I have observed a case in which participants successfully sabotaged a part of a study performed by a researcher they disliked.

Although the sensitivity of some behaviors to the act of studying them is indisputable, this does not rule out natural science methods in organizational behavior and organization theory for three reasons. First, the sensitivity objection assumes that natural science research is necessarily transparent—that the individuals participating in the study are always aware that they are under study and of the nature of the hypotheses being tested. The need for informed consent in organizational research does undoubtedly restrict the degree to which researchers can keep participants in the dark, but it does not eliminate the use of unobtrusive measures and other means of increasing the chance that the behavior of participants in research studies represents their real world actions.

Second, the sensitivity objection assumes that research participants control all dependent variables of concern to organizational researchers. Obviously, participants can change some things quite easily—for example, where they put a checkmark on an anonymous questionnaire; but the likelihood that they could and would change others in an attempt to support or reject the researcher's hypotheses is small. Work behavior over substantial periods of time, organizational structures, and informal interaction patterns are all examples of important phenomena that probably do not change in response to knowledge of research hypotheses. It seems reasonable to posit a hypothetical "continuum of discretion and control" to parallel Gergen and Schlenker's continuum of historic durability. I suspect that relatively few key dependent variables are close enough to the "immediately and completely responsive" end of the scale to result in the self-fulfilling prophecies or the suicidal predictions the sensitivity critics fear.

Third, the sensitivity criticism holds only if any suicidal and self-fulfilling effects cannot be identified and separated from the "true" effects of the variables of interest. Even though our abilities to tease out these effects are limited, given reasonably sophisticated experimental designs it is usually possible to do so. Moreover, although a "theory of reactions to theories" [Schlenker, 1974] creates the possibility of a mind-boggling progression of theories of reactions to theories of reactions to theories, even greater ability to predict such phenomena could come with a better understanding of the widely recognized but poorly understood "Hawthorne effect" and related phenomena.

Lack of Realism

Critics of natural science methods in organizational behavior and organization theory sometimes hold that the study of social phenomena necessarily changes them to such an extent that the resarcher cannot generalize from such studies to behaviors of organizations, groups, and individuals in the real world. They hold that such studies are, in a word, unrealistic. Stone [1978, pp. 119–20] lists a series of such charges as part of a survey of the pros and cons of various kinds of research methods. Specifically, seven potential threats to realism can be extracted from his list. The first three apply primarily to laboratory experimentation. The remaining four relate to natural science research in the field as well as in the laboratory:

1. The environments in which laboratory studies are performed are often strange and potentially embarrassing. Thus participants may behave differently there than they would in more familiar circumstances.

2. The laboratory environment may be unrealistic because the researcher may not recognize all of the important aspects of the situation under investigation and thus fail to manipulate or control them or to even include them in the research task or situation.

3. Researchers rarely permit participants to show the full range of behaviors open to them in real organizations. Laboratory "employees," for example, are almost never allowed to quit or to form labor unions.

4. It may be practically impossible to control or manipulate some key variables—for example, the economic climate in which the researcher performs the study.

5. It may be ethically unacceptable to manipulate other variables such as emotional stress, even though they may be crucial to the study.

6. For both practical and ethical reasons, research manipulations are rarely as strong as are encountered in actual organizations, even when variables can be manipulated. For example, "pay" is usually a one-shot supplement to the subject's income in research studies, not his or her primary source of support.

7. Dozens of factors may interact in complex patterns to determine the behaviors of individuals, groups, and organizations, but researchers rarely manipulate more than three or four in a single study.

Such criticisms stem in part from a misunderstanding of what a controlled environment for natural science research need be. As Weick points out in regard to laboratory research:

> Because laboratory experimentation is much more flexible than most persons realize, the laboratory can be adapted to exceedingly complex and ambiguous problems. At the same time, many organizational problems are encumbered with extraneous and superfluous details. These details can be removed with little effect on generality [1965, p. 745].

There are, however, two more important reasons why the lack-of-realism criticism is invalid.

First, three of the objections listed above equate the natural science model with the laboratory, when it is in fact possible to do rigorous natural science research in the field as well. Cook and Campbell, building on previous work by Campbell and Stanley [1963], provide a series of research designs capable of minimizing key threats to validity. They point out:

> As the examples in this chapter illustrated again and again, good quasi-experiments and true experiments have been conducted in the field in the past. They have reduced all or most of the threats to internal and statistical conclusion validity, many of the threats to construct validity of effects, and they have even reduced some of the threats to external validity and the construct validity of causes [1976, p. 318].

Second, I believe the criticism is invalid because it assumes that a flawed study—that is, one which does not control all threats to internal and external validity—yields no useful information. In fact, many of the conclusions drawn in the discipline are extracted grudgingly from the weight of evidence from dozens of studies, most of them flawed in one way or another. Campbell has written:

> Too many social scientists expect single experiments to settle issues once and for all. This may be a mistaken generalization from the history of the great crucial experiments in physics and chemistry. . . . Because we social scientists have less ability to achieve "experimental isolation," and because we have good reason to expect our treatment effects to interact significantly with a wide variety of social factors, many of which we have not yet mapped, we have much greater need for replication experiments than do the physical sciences [1969, pp. 427–28].

It is likely to be the weight of evidence, not the crucial study that defines scientific law in organizational behavior and organization theory. Constructive replications, designed not only to verify the results of specific studies within specific contexts but also to test for and overcome threats to internal and external validity, are necessary to establish general laws in organizational behavior and organization theory.

Epistemological Differences

Some opponents of natural science methods in organizational behavior and organization theory argue that understanding in the social sciences should differ from that in the natural sciences and this, in turn, demands different research methods. Advocates of this position hold that natural science strives to generalize about *why* things happen by identifying causes. Social science, on the other hand, seeks to explain the *significance* or *meaning* of phenomena in terms of their implications for the unique social systems in which they occur and as manifestations of important social trends, forces, and conflicts. Max Weber, for example, wrote:

> The analysis of the historically given individual configurations of . . . "factors" and their *significant* concrete interaction, conditioned by their historical context, and especially the *rendering intelligible* of the basis and type of this significance would be the next task to be achieved. . . . "Laws" are obviously of great value as heuristic means—but only as such. Indeed they are quite indispensible for this purpose. But even in this function their limitations become evident at a decisive point. . . . The *significance* of a configuration of cultural phenomena and the basis of the significance cannot, however, be derived and rendered intelligible by a system of analytical laws (*Gesetzbegriffin*), however perfect it may be [1949, pp. 75–76; emphasis in original].

Thus, for example, the events at Lordstown should be studied not simply as a chance to build a data base for generalizing about sources of worker demands for things beyond pay, good physical working conditions, and the like. They have meaning as a milestone in a major shift in expectations regarding work.

Although it is difficult, of course, to argue over the relative merits of different kinds of goals for organizational research, comment should be made regarding the methods normally advocated by those who see the identification of significance as a primary goal of research on organizations. Advocates of this approach argue that the best way to learn about complex social phenomena is to immerse the researcher in the organization under study and allow time for the development of intuitive appreciation of its workings. Unquestionably, since the studies of Roy [1952] and the Hawthorne researchers [Roethlisberger & Dickson, 1964], such in-depth observations have affected the course of thought about organizations. Nevertheless, such methods have important limitations. First, as Campbell [1974] points out, such research, improperly performed, is nothing more than a naive phenomenology that discards objective verification in favor of uncritical acceptance of the observer's experiences as reality. In the face of all we know about biases in the perception and interpretation of complex stimuli [e.g., Tversky & Kahneman, 1974], it would be foolish to contend that any social research, natural science or not, is totally free of systematic bias. But the natural science approach has built in extensive means for protecting the researcher against personal biases and thus such biases affect the outcomes of natural science research less often than they do those of other methods.

Second, such research generates a highly affective kind of knowledge. Although there are notable exceptions [e.g., Leighton's *The Governing of Men*, 1945], the process of conveying this very personal information, no matter how potent, to others can entail substantial loss of both completeness and richness. Researchers often find themselves resorting to the stand-up comic's cliché, "Ya hadda be there."

Conclusion

Numerous objections have been raised to the use of natural science methods in organizational behavior and organization theory. Yet none of the barriers raised is insurmountable. Admittedly imperfect and in need of more thoughtful application, natural science research methods represent an important means of understanding organizations and the behaviors of individuals and groups making them up. My attitude toward the natural science approach can be captured in a paraphrase of Winston Churchill's famous comment on democracy: It is the worst possible way to study organizations—except for all the others.

REFERENCES

Argyris, C.   Problems and new directions for industrial psychology. In M. D. Dunnette (Ed.), *Handbook of industrial and organizational psychology*. Skokie, Ill.: Rand McNally, 1976.

Behling, O.   Functionalism as a base for midrange theory in organizational behavior and organization theory. In C. C. Pinder & L. Moore (Eds.), *Middle range theory and the study of organization*. Leiden, The Netherlands: Martinus Nijhoff, 1979.

Behling, O., & Shapiro, M.   Motivation theory: Source of the solution or part of the problem? *Business Horizons*, 1974, 7, 59–66.

Berelson, B., & Steiner, G. A.   *Human behavior*. New York: Harcourt Brace Jovanovich, 1964.

Bobbitt, H. R., Breinholt, R. H., Doktor, R. H., & McNaul, J. P.   *Organizational behavior* (2d ed.). Englewood Cliffs, N.J.: Prentice-Hall, 1978.

Braithwaite, R.   *Scientific explanation*. Cambridge: Cambridge University Press, 1973.

Brown, R.   *Social psychology*. New York: Free Press, 1965.

Campbell, D. T.   *Qualitative knowing in action research*. Unpublished manuscript, Society for the Psychological Study of Social Issues, 1974.

Campbell, D. T.   Reforms as experiments. *American Psychologist*, 1969, 24, 409–429.

Campbell, D. T., & Stanley, J. C.   *Experimental and quasi-experimental design for research*. Skokie, Ill.: Rand McNally, 1963.

Cook, T. D., & Campbell, D. T.   The design and conduct of quasi-experiments and true experiments in field settings. In M. D. Dunnette (Ed.), *Handbook of industrial and organizational psychology*. Skokie, Ill.: Rand McNally, 1976.

Dawes, R. M.   The mind, the model, and the task. In H. L. Casellon & F. Restle (Eds.), *Proceedings of the seventh annual Indiana theoretical and cognitive psychology conference,* 1975.

Filley, A. C., House, R. J., & Kerr, S.   *Managerial process and organizational behavior* (2d ed.). Glenview, Ill.: Scott, Foresman, 1975.

Gergen, K. J.   Social psychology as history. *Journal of Personality & Social Psychology,* 1973, *26,* 309–320.

Gordon, M. E., Kleiman, L. S., & Hanie, C. A.   Industrial-organizational psychology: Open thy ears O house of Israel. *American Psychologist,* 1978, *33,* 893–905.

Hamner, W. C., & Organ, D. W. *Organizational behavior: An applied psychological approach.* Plano, Tex.: Business Publications, 1978.

Homans, G. C.   *The nature of social science.* New York: Harcourt Brace Jovanovich, 1967.

Jackson, J. H., & Morgan, C. P.   *Organization theory.* Englewood Cliffs, N.J.: Prentice-Hall, 1978.

Kaplan, A.   *The conduct of inquiry: Methodology for behavioral science.* San Francisco: Chandler, 1964.

Kerlinger, F. N.   *Foundations of behavioral research* (2d ed.). New York: Holt, Rinehart & Winston, 1973.

Koontz, H.   The management theory jungle. *Academy of Management Journal,* 1961, *4,* 174–188.

Leighton, A. H.   *The governing of men.* Princeton, N.J.: Princeton University Press, 1945.

Lundberg, C. C.   Hypothesis creation in organizational behavior research. *Academy of Management Review,* 1976, *1,* 5–12.

Luthans, F.   *Organizational behavior.* New York: McGraw-Hill, 1973.

McKelvey, B.   Guidelines for the empirical classification of organizations. *Administrative Science Quarterly,* 1975, *20,* 509–525.

McKelvey, B.   Organizational systematics: Taxonomic lessons from biology. *Management Science,* 1978, *24,* 1428–1440.

Merton, R. K.   *Social theory and social structure.* New York: Free Press, 1949.

Mitroff, I. I., & Pondy, L. R.   Afterthoughts on the leadership conference. In M. W. McCall & M. M. Lombardo (Eds.), *Leadership: Where else can we go?* Durham, N.C.: Duke University Press, 1978.

Nagel, E.   *The structure of science: Problems in the logic of scientific explanation.* New York: Harcourt Brace Jovanovich, 1961.

Newell, A., & Simon, H.   *Human problem solving.* Englewood Cliffs, N.J.: Prentice-Hall, 1972.

Pondy, L. R., & Boje, D. M.   *Bringing mind back in: Paradigm development as a frontier problem in organization theory.* Unpublished manuscript, Department of Business Administration, University of Illinois, Urbana, 1976.

Popper, K. R.   *The poverty of historicism.* New York: Harper Torchbooks, 1964.

Roethlisberger, F. J., & Dickson, W. J.   *Management and the worker.* New York: Wiley, 1964.

Roy, D.   Quota restriction and goldbricking in a machine shop. *American Journal of Sociology,* 1952, *57,* 430–437.

Schlenker, B. R.   Social psychology and science. *Journal of Personality and Social Psychology*, 1974, *29*, 1–15.

Stone, E.   *Research methods in organizational behavior.* Santa Monica, Calif.: Goodyear, 1978.

Tversky, A., & Kahneman, D.   Judgment under uncertainty: Heuristics and biases. *Science*, 1974, *185*, 1124–1131.

Weber, M.   *On the methodology of the social sciences.* New York: Free Press, 1949.

Weick, K. E.   Laboratory experimentation with organizations. In J. G. March (Ed.), *Handbook of organizations.* Skokie, Ill.: Rand McNally, 1965.

Weick, K. E.   *The social psychology of organizing.* Reading, Mass.: Addison-Wesley, 1969.

4

The Development of Knowledge in Organizational Behavior and Human Performance*

W. E. SCOTT, JR.

Within the past few years, researchers have been able to develop useful knowledge about the behavior of individuals in organizations to replace the human relations saws of an earlier time. It is comprised of a body of theory as well as empirical generalizations which possess sufficient reliability and generality to be worthy of critical study. While our knowledge of organizational behavior is incomplete, it is clear that we are no longer required to rely upon anecdotal evidence and speculation as our primary source of information. Rather, it is empirical knowledge based upon systematic study and experimentation which needs to be emphasized. That being the case, it may prove helpful to consider the nature and function of knowledge and the methods by which it is produced.

A number of practical benefits are gained from a study and development of knowledge of organizational behavior and human performance. First, systematic studies of this subject are being conducted at a rapidly increasing rate. Administrators and educators will soon become outdated unless they equip themselves to read, understand,

* Abridged from *Decision Sciences*, 1975, 6, 1, 142–165.

and evaluate the reports of these studies. Second, interest in sponsoring research of all kinds of organizations has been increasing. Specialized research units in many large organizations have presented a number of unresolved, difficult organizational problems. Perhaps, an improved understanding of scientific goals and methods would lead to more satisfactory solutions to these problems. Finally, more interaction between researchers and practitioners is needed. The researcher who seeks to establish relationships between organizational variables and behavior under controlled settings also seeks to apply his findings to an expanding set of conditions. Administrators sensitive to the goals and methods of the behavioral scientist can provide feedback to researchers about the generality of these relationships in complex organizations. This feedback often can raise additional questions which are significant from both a practical and scientific viewpoint. While the popular misconceptions that research is simply a way of solving problems or that the so-called scientific method is applicable to all or most of the complex problems facing the administrator must be rejected, a better understanding of empirical knowledge and its development would enhance the administrator's ability to use and to contribute to the systematic study of organizational behavior.

Characteristics of Knowledge

An individual may acquire knowledge about objects and events in his environment through direct encounter or firsthand experience. Nearly all of us have observed the behavior of others in complex organizations. However, knowledge based solely upon direct encounters with natural phenomena is limited. Some insist that these encounters cannot make the individual knowledgeable at all unless he is able to verbally describe or represent that experience to himself and to others. This is a complex psychological issue not to be pursued here, but raising the issue does provide an opportunity to emphasize two points. First, most of our scientific knowledge is received from significant others by means of conversation, lectures, newspapers, books, and other such media. Second, this process is so ubiquitous that we often forget that verbal symbols, concepts, or terms are different from that to which they refer. The term *organizational behavior,* for example, is a verbal stimulus distinguishable from the phenomena which it signifies. Unfortunately, some concepts from the everyday vernacular signify different meanings to different individuals. To avoid confusion and misunderstanding, the researcher is typically forced to develop a specialized vocabulary which employs precise and invariant meanings, but which lacks appeal until the user gains familiarity with it.

This paper focuses on that knowledge which enables an individual to describe objects and events specifically and to state relationships between objects and events. Several advantages accrue to those who possess this knowledge. First, the knowledgeable individual gains a viewpoint by which to examine and assess behavioral events, especially those in which the significance is not obvious. He is also sensitive to antecedent or causal variables which might not otherwise be perceived either because they are embedded in a complex setting or because they are not a part of the current stimulus field. Second, this kind of knowledge provides the individual with a set of expectancies regarding behavioral outcomes, given the occurrence of or variations in certain environmental and individual difference variables. Therefore, when one has possession of empirical propositions reflecting relationships between antecedent events and behavioral outcomes, that person understands and is able to predict organizational behavior, thereby avoiding uncertainty, surprises, and frustration. Finally, if an individual knows propositions stating relationships between behavior and environmental events which can be changed or varied, then he is able to influence behavior.

Beliefs and Operating Assumptions of the Researcher

The researcher believes in reality. Unlike the solipsist,[1] the scientist assumes that the objects and events which he observes do exist apart from himself.

The researcher also believes that organizational behavior, like other natural phenomena, shows certain consistencies which can be anticipated and explained. He believes that organizational behavior is determined, but he does not assume that there is a single determinant or cause. Rather, he believes that there are multiple determinants which act alone and with other determinants to produce behavior. Yet, he posits *finite* causality. He does not believe that *all* events in nature can influence all other events.

The researcher is an empiricist. He believes reliable knowledge of organizational behavior can best be developed by means of firsthand, controlled observations. He would disagree with the philosophical doctrine which advocates that knowledge may be acquired or developed *solely* through reasoning processes and intuition. For the modern empiricist, reasoning is required for purposes of organizing knowledge and is indispensable to the process of inductive generalization, but the emphasis is upon direct observation and experimentation as the source of knowledge.

---

[1] One who subscribes to the philosophical view that nothing exists or is "real" except the self. [Ed. note]

The researcher has learned to be skeptical, for he has learned that man, as an observer, is subject to error. Consequently, he does not readily agree with a propositional statement simply because it was uttered by a person of recognized status or because it appears intuitively to be true. He does not reject such statements as necessarily false since an empirical test may ultimately lead him to conclude otherwise. He merely asks (1) whether or not they are true, and (2) how could one go about demonstrating their truth or falsity (6, p. 9).

The Researcher and His Language

As stated above, the researcher believes that organizational behavior is a reality apart from himself and that reliable knowledge can be developed about it by means of direct encounter. However, he is aware of the sociolinguistic nature of all scientific endeavor. While linguistic symbols can be distinguished from the objects and events they are meant to represent, few observations of any consequence can be communicated to others without the use of symbols. Direct experience is private and of little social value until it is communicated to others.

The researcher, sensitive to the problems of conceptualization and communication, sets about to construct an objective language which will accurately convey his observations. This language will never be totally independent of the vernacular. Nor should it be. Many terms in the common, everyday language are reasonably precise and unambiguous, in which case they are taken over by the researcher without modification. However, there are also terms in the common language which do not always refer to something out there, or if they do, the "something" is so vague and amorphous that confusion and misunderstanding are rampant. In these cases the researcher is confronted with the necessity of either reconstructing the common language or coining new terms. He will often do both by defining his concepts operationally.

To define a concept operationally means to specify precisely the procedures or operations which are associated with its use. In making a concept synonymous with a set of concrete, reproducible operations, the researcher is able to clarify the phenomenon under investigation and to communicate his observations in an unambiguous manner. For example, to test the proposition that democratic leadership results in (is functionally related to, produces, causes) higher productivity than autocratic leadership, the researcher will have to develop a set of operations defining the terms democratic leadership, autocratic leadership, and productivity. How will the researcher do this?

First of all, the terms are taken from the common language and may require some logical explication[2] before operational definitions can be developed. Upon reflection, the researcher might conclude that the terms *autocratic* and *democratic* leadership refer to specific behavioral patterns exhibited by leaders in formal organizations. But what is the nature of these patterns and how do they differ? Further analysis might lead to the conclusion that autocratic leadership can be characterized by an individual who (1) unilaterally decides what tasks are to be performed by each subordinate, (2) directs subordinates to perform those tasks without deviation, and (3) makes punishment or threats of punishment contingent upon not performing those tasks as directed. The researcher may also decide that democratic leadership can be characterized by an individual who (1) consults with and takes into account the suggestions and preferences of his subordinates in deciding what tasks are to be performed, (2) does not specifically direct his subordinates to perform the tasks, or having elicited task performance, permits deviations in the manner in which they are performed, and (3) makes rewards or promises of rewards contingent upon successful task accomplishment.

If the researcher has not become discouraged at this point, he may attempt to develop a set of operations which he hopes will be somewhat reflective of the explicated concepts. For example, he might develop a behavioral questionnaire which requires organizational leaders to describe how they typically behave with regard to task decisions, methods of eliciting task performance, deviations from task performance, and administration of rewards and punishment. Several analyses and refinements of the questionnaire might enable him to set up a continuum and to classify high scorers on the questionnaire as democratic leaders and low scorers as autocratic leaders. This public and repeatable set of operations is synonymous with and defines the two concepts.[3] After analyzing and defining productivity in the same manner, the researcher is able to investigate the relationship between leadership styles and productivity to be operationally defined in a similar way.

Many concepts in the common, everyday language are rendered less vague and ambiguous by the use of the foregoing procedure. New concepts are also introduced by making them equivalent to a set of operations which others can reproduce. However, the operational

---

[2] Mandler and Kessen (3, pp. 98–104) describe logical explication as a process by which terms in the common language are more precisely defined or redefined.

[3] Perhaps the defining operations should be referred to as a "ZIZ" and "ZAZ." Democratic and autocratic leadership are common terms which have already acquired a variety of meanings. It is doubtful that the reader will readily dismiss those ingrained meanings in favor of the defining operations described here. It is for this reason that it is often a good idea to coin new terms to represent operational definitions.

analysis of the concepts must not be considered a panacea. Spence (9) points out that the formulation of operational definitions is merely one faltering step in building a body of empirical knowledge. If the operationally defined concept is not subsequently found to be related to other concepts, then, it has no scientific significance and should be discarded. The number of digits on the left foot multiplied by the number of freckles on the face divided by two is a perfectly acceptable set of operations defining a concept we shall label Wellcs, but it is highly improbable this would be of any interest to the behavioral scientist.

Another consideration of the researcher is the complexity or "size" of a concept. He may choose to work with concepts referring to a complex of empirical events treated as a syndrome, or he may prefer to work with molecular, unidimensional concepts. Yet, more important than the size or complexity of concepts is the continued persistence of the researcher in conducting research which utilizes a variety of conceptual approaches and which establishes systematic relationships between a syndrome of environmental events and behavioral variables. If these relationships are not found to hold up in every instance, the researcher should break up the syndrome in search of the one or a more limited sub-set of characteristics which may be responsible for the relationship.

Research Variables in Organizational Behavior and Human Performance

Most concepts contained in empirical propositions refer to things which vary or can be varied in amount, degree, or kind. The researcher seeks to establish relationships between *independent* and *dependent variables*.

A dependent variable is anything which is changed or modified as a consequence of a change or a modification in something else. The dependent variable is nearly always some observable aspect of behavior or the consequences of behavior. For example, a researcher may be interested in learning why individuals become members of an organization or *do not* become members, why they remain as members for a long period of time or leave the organization. He may be interested in learning why some individuals or groups are more creative than others, or why some individuals appear to be more satisfied with their jobs than others. He may be interested in learning why some individuals cooperate with each other, while others conflict; why some individuals often contribute far more than is prescribed, while others perform their jobs in the prescribed manner but rarely go beyond that;

and, why some individuals engage in behavior that is judged to be organizationally disruptive.

Obviously, there are a number of dependent variables which are interesting and significant not only because they are functionally related to organizational success, but also because they remain as scientific curiosities, not yet fully explained or predictable. The lives of researchers and managers would be considerably less complicated if they could say that dependent variables were all related and that those factors which lead to high productivity also produce satisfaction, cooperation, and creative contributions. Unfortunately, such is not the case. At least, the relationship between satisfaction and productivity is obscure. Moreover, it is possible that under certain circumstances, such behavior variables as individual productivity and interpersonal cooperation are inversely related. The researcher will frequently direct his attention to these complexities in order to investigate the relationships between behavioral variables or to search for more basic dependent variables.

The independent variable is anything which when changed or modified induces a change or a modification in some aspect of organizational behavior. When a person seeks explanations for turnover, variations in productivity, cooperation, satisfaction, and so on, he is really inquiring about those factors (independent variables) which are functionally related to or cause variations in behavior.

Independent variables in organizational behavior may be viewed as falling into one of two broadly defined classes. There are *environmental* variables, such as task design, magnitude or quality of rewards and punishments and the manner in which they are scheduled, the presence and behavior of significant others, temperature, noise, illumination, group size, and variations in organizational structure. The second class of independent variables is known as *subject* or *individual-difference* variables. These are relatively enduring behavioral characteristics of the individual and include intelligence, aptitudes, propensity to take risks, characteristic energy level, motor skills, and motives.

Observational Strategies

Empirical propositions depend upon firsthand observation for their development, but past experience has made it quite clear that all humans are subject to a variety of observational errors. Consequently, researchers have developed strategies for observing phenomena so that such errors are reduced to a minimum.

Observational strategies may be viewed as falling on a continuum between naturalistic observation and experimentation. As a researcher progresses along the continuum, he exerts increasingly greater control over the phenomena which he is observing.

Naturalistic Observation. Utilizing this strategy, the researcher observes the behavior of individuals as it occurs in a natural setting—namely, in formal organizations. He does not control and manipulate independent variables in order to note their effects on behavior. Rather, he attends to behavior as it ordinarily occurs, watching for apparent covariation between environmental events and behavioral episodes. The researcher may attempt to record those events which seem to be relevant, and he emerges from his study with a verbal description of his observations.

Because naturalistic observation has a number of limitations, a researcher should maintain a cautious attitude toward knowledge based solely upon this strategy. Significant behavioral events may not occur frequently, and since the researcher exerts no control over those events, he may not be prepared to observe them when they do occur. More importantly, the observer makes few attempts to reduce the sources of human error that are attributable to his own act of perceiving. He would not worry much about this source of error if he could depend upon the fact that his sense organs furnish the brain with exact replicas of the real world. However, such is not the case. Illusions are common. Unaided perceptions of physical objects rarely correspond exactly with those resulting from a direct encounter with the object by means of various kinds of measurement techniques.

When the events observed are behavioral, and thus more variable and ambiguous than physical objects, the emotions, expectancies, and past experiences of the observer may become as prominent in determining what is perceived as the behavioral events themselves. Similarly, our perceptions of cause and effect relationships are often inaccurate, especially when the cause and the effect do not always occur together or when the effect does not immediately follow the cause in time (2). Temporal contiguity between events *is* a compelling factor in drawing cause and effect conclusions (11). However, there are a number of events occurring concomitantly with behavior when we observe it in a natural setting. Perhaps the observer could logically dismiss the fly unobtrusively crawling along the sill in another building as a determiner of the behavior of an operative employee on a production line. Yet, which of the several events that are present *will be* selectively attended to? The answer to the question is that the observer will usually arrive on the scene with certain preconceived notions or tentative ideas as to what are the relevant and irrelevant factors, and he will direct his attention to those factors which he believes to be relevant. If he observes a relationship between those events he chooses to concentrate upon, does he do so because there is a relationship which could be confirmed by others, or is the observed relationship attributable to the fact that he expected to find one? Suppose, for example, that the observer suspected that group productivity is higher when the supervisor is physically present than when he is physically absent. Let us further assume (1) that group productivity did not invariably change with the presence or absence of the supervisor, (2) that the supervisor was more often present than absent, (3) that there is *no* inherent relationship between the supervisor's presence and group productivity, and (4) that the observer could accurately discriminate between high and low group productivity and between supervisory presence and non-presence.[4]

Figure 1 shows a record of a series of observations that might have been made under these circumstances.

FIGURE 1
A Record of Observations Made in Organization X Group Productivity

		High	Low	
	Present	10 (a)	5 (b)	15
Supervisor	Absent	4 (c)	2 (d)	6
		14	7	21

The naturalistic observer in this situation might perceive only a limited set of instances which would tend to verify his expectation. For example, Figure 1 shows that group productivity was high during 10 of the 15 times the supervisor was present and that group productivity was low only 5 of the 15 times he was present. Alternatively, the supervisor was present during 10 of the 14 times that group productivity was observed to be high and was absent only 4 times during which group productivity was observed to be high. In the event the observer was astute enough to look for *all* confirming and disconfirming cases during the observational period, he would note that there was a total of 12 confirming cases (cells a and d) and only 9 disconfirming ones (cells b and c). Again, however, the observer might erroneously conclude that the supervisor's presence enhances group productivity since his expectation is verified more than it is not.

---

[4] Point four is not a very valid assumption. Changes in group productivity are not easily discernible, and in the absence of an objective means of assessing significant variations in group output, the observer may "see" changes in the direction of his expectations. Naturalistic observers attempt to sharpen the definitions of the concepts they use in reporting their observations, but they rarely define their dependent and independent variables in terms of a reproducible set of measurement operations. An attempt to develop operational definitions of the terms "supervisory presence" and "group productivity" could prove to be humorous, if not enlightening for the reader.

Only the observer who has an abstract appreciation of correlation (2, pp. 14–15) would come to the correct conclusion. He would do so by comparing the probability of high group productivity given the supervisor's presence (10/15 or .67) with the probability of high group productivity given his absence (4/6 or .67). Since the probabilities are identical, he would conclude that in this situation variations in group productivity appear to be independent of the presence or absence of the supervisor.

Let us assume that all the conditions described above are the same except that the observations were made in a different organization in which there *is* a relationship between supervisory presence and group productivity. An example of a series of observations made under these circumstances is shown in Figure 2.

FIGURE 2
A Record of Observations Made in Organization Y Group Productivity

	High	Low	
Present	10 (a)	5 (b)	15
Supervisor			
Absent	2 (c)	4 (d)	6
	12	9	21

This set of observations would reinforce the observer's expectations in the same manner as those made in Organization X. In this case, however, the probability of high group productivity when the supervisor is present is .67, while the probability of high group productivity when he is not present is only .33.

Although the conclusion that the supervisor's presence caused higher group productivity seems to be supported by the observations made in Organization Y, we must consider the possibility that *other* events were operating in this situation to cause the changes in group productivity. While repeated observations would rule out some of them on the basis that they were never present or always present (and non-varying) when changes in group productivity occurred, perhaps not all of them could be so readily dismissed. Several events may occur together so that it is difficult to say which one is the cause of higher productivity. For example, suppose that the supervisor tended to appear only when production pressure was intense. Then, increased productivity could have resulted because of the varying backlog of visible materials, partially completed assemblies, work orders, etc., rather than the supervisor's presence. The above is an example of *confounding*, a situation in which any variable other than the dependent variable changes along with the independent variable of primary concern. Confounding is always a danger no matter what the observational strategy, but it is most likely to occur when the observer exercises little control over the events he observes.

One often hears that knowledge stemming from naturalistic observation is more relevant to real-life behavior, and hence more valuable to the administrator. But the possibility of confounding places limitations on this knowledge. Different supervisors may not show up only during those times when production pressure increases. Therefore, the results of this study would be of limited generality and quite erroneous if it could be established by more rigorous methods that production pressure rather than supervisory presence was the cause of changes in group productivity.

Despite the limitations of naturalistic observation, a researcher should remain open to knowledge that comes from observers utilizing this strategy. A significant portion of what we know or what we think we know about organizational behavior has been generated by astute individuals who have spent their lives observing behavior as it naturally occurs in formal organizations. Oppenheimer, the physicist, (5) has made a plea not to treat too harshly those who tell a story without having established the completeness or the generality of that story. That plea should not go unheard. In many cases, an observation that has been made in the field has been verified in the laboratory where the observer can exercise the necessary controls over the independent variable and other potentially confounding variables.

Systematic Assessment. In all probability, the individuals in the production departments of organizations X and Y were not responding as one. Some were undoubtedly producing more than others during the presence *and* absence of the supervisors. Furthermore, both the direction and amount of change may have varied from one individual to another as the supervisors were alternately present and absent. Behavioral scientists have grown to expect significant differences in behavior when several individuals are placed in a common environmental setting, and have approached the problem of explaining those differences by postulating that they are attributable to certain enduring characteristics of the individual. This postulate has led to the development of a wide variety of individual-difference measures, the most common of which are standardized tests. Thus, the term "systematic assessment" has come to be applied to that observational strategy in which events existing in varying degrees in nature are operationally defined, and the relationships between events, so defined, are investigated. The observer does not purposefully manipulate the independent variable as in the experimental strategy, but he typically exercises greater control than the naturalistic observer. An example will serve to illustrate the kinds of control that are exercised when the systematic assessment strategy is employed.

Noting that some employees are consistently more productive than others in the same situation, the observer might hypothesize that the differences are due to variations in aptitude.

The first step in testing the hypothesis is to select or construct operational definitions of the aptitudes which are important in determining productivity. In this case, let us assume that a researcher selects rather than constructs a measure of Closure Flexibility.[5] Then, he assembles all the employees in a room in which noise levels, illumination, and other features of the environment are held constant, and administers the test according to the instructions specified by the test manual. Since the observer has controlled environmental stimulation, he assumes that individual scores are representative of the ability which is measured rather than a function of environmental events. If the observer finds reliable differences in scores, he is ready for the next important step. He must now devise an operational definition of productivity so that he might investigate the relationship between the attribute presumably measured by his test and productivity back at the work site. He may decide to define productivity as the number of acceptable units completed by each individual during a specified period of time. He might also choose to introduce some *additional controls* such as having the supervisor always present and holding the quality and quantity of materials constant for each individual during the observing period.

Having observed and recorded the output of each individual, the researcher is now ready to assess the relationship between scores on the Closure Flexibility Test and productivity. A relationship that might have been obtained is depicted by the scatter diagram in Figure 3.

Utilizing the Pearson product-moment correlation coefficient, one of several techniques for assessing relationships between variables, the observer finds a statistically significant correlation of .49. He concludes, therefore, that there is a functional relationship between scores achieved on the Closure Flexibility Test and the level of individual productivity in this situation.

---

[5] The Closure Flexibility Test is a standardized measure of the ability to hold a configuration in mind despite distraction. This aptitude has been found to be related to certain personality traits and has also been found to differentiate among individuals in various occupational groups.

FIGURE 3
The Relationship between Scores on the Closure Flexibility
Test and Individual Productivity

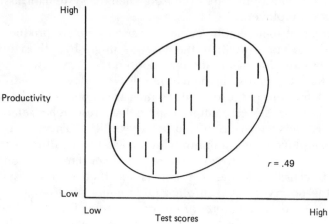

There is a curious mixture of inference and empiricism in this and in all studies utilizing the systematic assessment strategy. It is empirical in the sense that the variables are operationally defined. Since concepts refer to observable events, the observations are capable of being repeated by another individual. Also, the proposition asserting the relationship between Closure Flexibility Test scores and productivity is relatively clear and unambiguous. However, it seems absurd to remain at a strictly empirical level and state that the individual's responses in the test-taking situation caused his subsequent behavior on the production line. Rather, a researcher *infers* some sort of characteristic from the score, and it is that characteristic which is believed to determine the behavioral outcome. In addition to finding that the inferred characteristic is somewhat obscure, a researcher has difficulty specifying and defending the direction of causality. In the above case, it was implicitly assumed that the characteristic measured by the test determined the level of productivity, but variations in task behavior *preceding* the test administration may have determined the score achieved on the test.

The observer utilizing the systematic assessment strategy takes advantage of differences which already exist in nature rather than deliberately creating those differences. As a consequence, the observer does not provide very convincing evidence for causal relationships, whatever the direction. While knowing that individuals differ with regard to closure flexibility, researchers do not know in what other respects the subjects might differ. Perhaps, those who score high on this test also have higher needs for achievement, and the latter characteristic, rather than a high degree of closure flexibility, results in high levels of productivity. The now-familiar problem of confounding is evident here as in every study in which systematic assessment is used.

Nevertheless, functional relationships established by means of systematic assessment can be very useful. Our Closure Flexibility Test, for example, could be used to select from an applicant population those who are most likely to be high producers. However, the possibility of confounding makes it difficult to understand why the relationship exists and places limitations on the generality of the relationship. If the tasks were different and were performed by a different group of individuals in another organization, the same relationship might not hold.

The use of the systematic assessment strategy is not restricted to psychological tests and individual differences. One can also establish operational definitions of organizational characteristics, and then investigate the relationships between differences in those characteristics and behavioral variables. Indik (1), for example, has reviewed a number of studies in which organizational size was found to be related to member satisfaction, absenteeism, and individual output. Size was operationally defined as the number of individuals who are members of the organization, and size was systematically assessed rather than deliberately manipulated as in the experimental strategy. Interestingly enough, Indik offered a set of theoretical postulates to account for the observed relationships between organizational size and behavior (and to account for contradictory findings as well). He speculated that as size increases, communications problems among members tend to increase, task complexity tends to decrease, the need for supervision and coordination increases, and the use of impersonal controls tends to increase. What Indik has done is to ask the reader to consider a variety of *confounding* variables which may be the real causes of dissatisfaction, absenteeism, and productivity. In other words, he seems to be saying that communications problems, task complexity, etc. may often, though not necessarily, vary concomitantly with size to cause the behavior. When they do not vary with size, the relationships will not be observed.

Experimentation. The observer who utilizes the experimental strategy deliberately produces the event he wishes to observe. He systematically varies one event (the independent variable), while controlling the influence of others (potentially confounding variables). Then he notes the effects of the varied event on behavior (the dependent variable). The experimental strategy is by no means a foolproof procedure for producing reliable and generalizable knowledge, but it does provide more convincing evidence for cause-and-effect relationships than other approaches.

Weick (12) prefers to discuss the experimental strategy without reference to a distinction between settings. However, there is some merit in distinguishing between *field experiments* and *laboratory experiments*. The observer may utilize the experimental strategy to study behavior in an ongoing organization, or he may choose to bring behavior into the laboratory where more control can be exercised. Seashore (7) has described the problems which an observer may encounter in conducting a field experiment. They arise primarily because the experiment is incidental to the pursuit of organizational goals and because some loss of control over the appropriate experimental variables is inevitable.

Assume that the observer has decided to conduct a field experiment in order to test the hypothesis that the supervisor's physical presence has a significant effect on group productivity. His first problem is to find an organization which will allow him to conduct the experiment. Having gained entry into an organization, the observer is now faced with a series of experimental design decisions. The experimental strategy, whether employed in the field or in the laboratory, requires at least two different values of the independent variable. Therefore, the observer's first decision is whether to have one group perform the task while the supervisor is present and the other group perform while he is absent (the between-subjects design), or to have *all* employees perform the task under *both* conditions (the within-subjects design). Should the former course of action be chosen, the observer must take care in assigning the subjects to each group so that both groups are approximately equal with respect to confounding variables. He may accomplish this goal by randomly assigning individuals to each group, and then tossing a coin to decide which group will perform with the supervisor present.

A series of observations in which both groups performed the task under identical conditions except the presence and absence of the supervisor may have yielded the data shown in Figure 4.

As the data indicate, the presence of the supervisor seems to affect group productivity. This conclusion assumes that other variables were controlled either by holding them constant or by randomization. If, for example, those who score high on the Closure Flexibility Test are typically the most productive, the random assignment of individuals to the experimental and control groups tends to insure that the average test scores of both groups will be approximately equal before the observations are begun.

The various organizational constraints are likely to prevent the observer from randomly assigning individuals to either the experimental or the control group. Furthermore, it would be nearly impossible to achieve a "pure" condition of supervisory absence for any length of

FIGURE 4
The Relationship between Supervisory Presence and Group Productivity

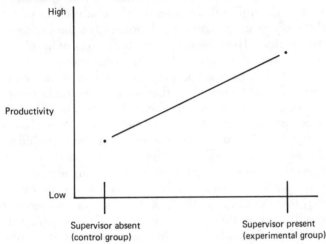

time in a formal organization. A consideration of these and other problems with the implementation of a between-subjects design might have led the observer to adopt the within-subjects design.

The observer is faced with a different kind of problem when he adopts the within-subjects design. He must anticipate the possibility of a progressive error (11, p. 32), a change in behavior that may occur as a function of performing the task over time. In this case, it would not be wise to have the supervisor present during the first four hours of the day and absent during the remaining hours because fatigue effects may confound the results. While there are a number of methods for controlling progressive error, probably the most appropriate one in this experiment would be randomization. The observer would have the supervisor appear at random times throughout the observing period.

The results of the within-subjects experiment may have been quite similar to those obtained from the between-subjects design. However, in both cases, the conclusion that the supervisor's presence enhances group productivity may only hold true in this isolated situation. The observer is dealing with a specific supervisor and a specific work group, and neither is likely to be representative of supervisors and work groups in general. The patterns of interaction between the workers and the relationships between this supervisor and the work group have developed over a period of time. The nature of the interaction history peculiar to this group may be determined by the effects of the supervisor's presence. Moreover, production pressure, which may have affected group productivity and which could not be easily controlled by the observer, may have been significantly higher or lower when the supervisor was present than when he was absent.

The lack of control and the attendant probability of confounding may lead the observer to choose the laboratory as the site for conducting his observations. Here, he might be able to repeat his observations, using different supervisors and different work groups while holding interaction histories, production pressure, and other factors constant. Under these circumstances, the observer is most likely to be able to make a general causal statement about the effect of the supervisor's presence on productivity. However, he is also most likely to be criticized by the laymen on the grounds that the knowledge he has provided is too "theoretical" or has no relevance for the administrator. After all, work groups in organizations have an interaction history. They are not *ad hoc* groups who have never seen each other before, nor are they inexperienced at the task. Furthermore, supervisors come and go at will, and production pressures are variable rather than constant. What the critic really means in this case is that he is not likely to comprehend the influence of the supervisor's presence on behavior in a natural setting because there are other determining factors operating simultaneously there. The effect of the supervisor's physical presence observed in the laboratory may not be observed in the formal organization because that effect is swamped by the effects of other factors which could be controlled in the laboratory. But, a researcher will never know whether a supervisor's presence has an effect on behavior until he observes it when the influences of other factors are controlled. If the effect *is* swamped by other variables in a natural setting, then they too need to be observed under controlled conditions.

As we have seen, the observer, suspecting that production pressure has an effect on behavior, could have controlled its influence either by holding it constant at some value or by allowing it to vary randomly. He could just as well have investigated its effects at the same time that he observed the effects of the supervisor's presence. This possibility brings us to a discussion of the *factorial* experiment in which the simultaneous effects of *two* or *more* independent variables are observed.

If production pressure could be defined in a manner that permitted the observer to systematically vary it from a normal value to a high value, the *main* effects of each of the two independent variables could then be examined. The primary influence of the supervisor's presence could be ascertained by constrasting average group productivity when he is present with average group productivity when he is absent, the average being obtained in both cases by summing across both levels of production pressure. This result is shown in Figure 5.

FIGURE 5
The Main Effect of the Supervisor's Presence on Group Productivity

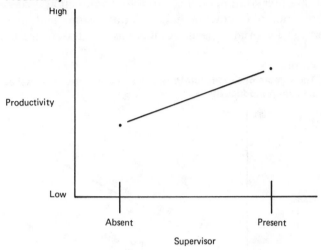

FIGURE 6
The Main Effect of Production Pressure on Group Productivity

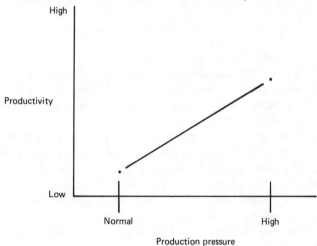

The main effect of variations in production pressure could be examined in a similar fashion, as shown in Figure 6.

The most significant feature of the factorial experiment is that it allows the observer to investigate the *interaction* effects of the independent variables. An interaction effect is said to exist when the relationship between the dependent variable (productivity) and one independent variable (supervisor's presence) varies as a function of the value of another independent variable (production pressure). To clarify the notion of interaction effects, let us assume that the results of the observer's factorial experiment were as illustrated in Figure 7.

FIGURE 7
The Effects of Production Pressure and Supervisor's Presence on Group Productivity

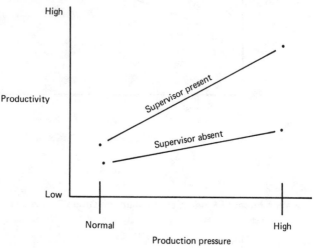

The data suggest[6] that the main effect of production pressure is significant since both curves slope upward. The main effect of the supervisor's presence also appears to be significant since group productivity is generally higher when he is present than when he is absent. However, there appears to be a significant interaction effect as well. That is, the effect of the supervisor's presence on group productivity varies with the value of production pressure. At normal levels of production pressure, the supervisor's presence does not seem to have a large effect on group productivity, but when production pressure is high, his presence has a considerable effect.

One is now able to understand the negative attitude toward knowledge that is produced by the experimental strategy in which the influence of all variables except one is controlled. One observer might have unwittingly or deliberately observed the effects of the supervisor's presence only when production pressure was high, in which case he

---

[6] Needless to say, we cannot discern significant differences in productivity merely by inspection of the data. There are available a number of statistical tests for determining the significance of main and interaction effects.

would have concluded that the physical presence of the supervisor has a very significant effect on group productivity. The response that this bit of knowledge is either irrelevant or theoretical is undoubtedly based upon the subjective feeling that the relationship would only hold under certain conditions which are not typically obtained in nature.

Further observations might support the critic's premise, but such support does not mean that the single factor experiment produced knowledge that is irrelevant or theoretical. That the supervisor's presence has an effect on productivity under certain specifiable circumstances represents a bit of knowledge which we did not possess before the experiment was conducted. Furthermore, researchers seek to extend the generality of their findings by repeating their observations under different conditions. A failure to observe the same relationship under different conditions inevitably stimulates speculation and additional studies until the contradictory findings are resolved. Finally, interaction effects are not always found. If the two productivity curves shown in Figure 7 were parallel or approached that condition, one would have to conclude that the effects of the supervisor's presence were similar whether production pressure was normal or high.

The experimental strategy is most frequently employed by those who seek to establish behavioral propositions which hold for all individuals. Individual differences are deliberately masked or treated as experimental error when changes in behavior, if they occur as a consequence of a change in an environmental event, are shown as changes in group averages. The attempt to establish general behavioral laws is a perfectly legitimate and useful enterprise. However, researchers often observe the behavior of two individuals to be both quantitatively and qualitatively different at the same value of the independent variable. The attempt to explain individual differences in response to constant environmental events and to changes in environmental events has led to the development of a factorial experiment in which at least one of the independent variables is an individual-difference variable systematically assessed (4).

As an example, let us assume that the observer administered the Closure Flexibility Test to his group of subjects and then observed the effects of the supervisor's presence on the productivity of those who scored high and those who scored low on the test. If the observer programmed the supervisor to appear in a randomized sequence, the influence of variations in production pressure would tend to be randomized, and progressive error would similarly be controlled. The results of this hypothetical experiment are shown in Figure 8.

The main effects of both independent variables appear to be significant, but there is also an interaction effect. In this case, the

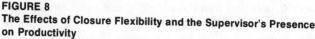

FIGURE 8
The Effects of Closure Flexibility and the Supervisor's Presence on Productivity

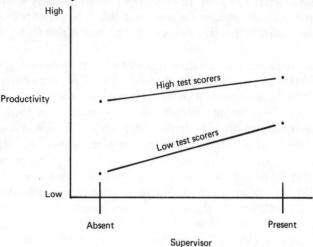

degree to which the supervisor's presence affects productivity depends upon the level of closure flexibility inherent in an individual.

Since behavior is widely held to be a function of the *interaction* between the individual and his environment, the observational approach which combines systematic assessment and experimental manipulation is perhaps the most appropriate one yet devised.

REFERENCES

1. Indik, B. P.   Some effects of organizational size on member attitudes and behavior. *Human Relations,* 1963, *16,* 369–384.

2. Jenkins, H. M., & Ward, W. C.   Judgment of contingency between responses and outcomes. *Psychological Monographs: General and Applied,* 1965, *79,* 1–17.

3. Mandler, G., & Kessen, W.   *The language of psychology.* New York: Wiley, 1959.

4. McGuigan, F. J.   *Experimental psychology: A methodological approach* (2d. ed.). Englewood Cliffs, N.J.: Prentice-Hall, 1968.

5. Oppenheimer, R.   Analogy in science. *American Psychologist,* 1956, *11,* 127–135.

6. Scott, W., & Wertheimer, M.   *Introduction to Psychological Research.* New York: Wiley & Sons, 1962.

7. Seashore, S. E.   Field experiments with formal organizations. *Human Organization* 1964, *23,* 164–170.

8. Skinner, B. F. Are theories of learning necessary? *Psychological Review*, 1950, *57*, 193–216.

9. Spence, K. W. The nature of theory constructions in contemporary psychology. *Psychological Review*, 1944, *51*, 47–68.

10. Turner, M. B. *Philosophy and the science of behavior*. New York: Appleton-Century-Crofts, 1967.

11. Underwood, B. J. *Experimental psychology* (2d. ed.). New York: Appleton-Century-Crofts, 1966.

12. Weick, K. E. Laboratory experimentation with organizations. In J. G. March (Ed.), *Handbook of Organizations*. Skokie, Ill.: Rand McNally, 1965.

13. Zajonc, R. B. Social facilitation. *Science*, 1965, *149*, 269–274.

section two

The Motivational Basis of Behavior in Organizations

Except for the infirm and the heirs to family riches, people obviously have to work in order to attain a standard of living and creature comforts beyond mere survival. And most of these people will have to work in organizations. However, these considerations, at best, suffice only to give us a point of departure for understanding behavior at work. We know that other goals and motives become adjoined to the vocational imperative, but what is the nature of these motives? We know that we work harder and better under some conditions than others, but what accounts for this variability in our performance? Would the answers to these questions enable us to design organizational environments which yield both higher member satisfaction and more effective institutions?

These questions raise theoretical and applied issues. The first five articles in Section Two tackle the conceptual problems attendant to the analysis of motivation at work. These are followed by a description and assessment of several approaches to applying work motivation theory.

A. THEORETICAL ISSUES

Introduction

To seek an understanding of the motivation of behavior at work is to ask "what?" and "how?". The question of *what?* represents a query as to the *content* or substance of motivation. What are the important goals that people seek to attain through work? What are the rewards, incentives, ends, and driving forces? What do people really want—especially once they can take for granted some reasonable satisfaction of material and security needs?

Aronson argues that we strive to maintain and project some semblance of rationality and consistency in both thought and action. Henry Clay once said that he would rather "be right than be President"; most of us would often rather be consistent than be "right." Unfortunately, otherwise astute administrators underestimate and underappreciate the importance of this motive, both in themselves and others, and therein lies the potential for serious misreading of many acts and utterances.

Litwin and Stringer, citing the work of psychologist David McClelland, discuss three enduring motives that govern work behavior: the quest for achievement, affiliation, and power. The differing priorities which people attach to these motives lead to differences in the allocation of effort, different styles of interactions with others, even different meanings attached to organizationally mediated rewards (such as money, recognition, and promotion).

Kerr turns us from the content to the *process* dimension of motivation. Whatever the stated aims of organizations, people pursue those courses of action which provide paths to the goals they seek. Unfortunately, organizations all too often arrange valued goal objects at the ends of paths which run away from, even opposite to, the paths which would lead to officially espoused objectives. Kerr provides several telling illustrations of this phenomenon and offers some explanations of why it occurs.

Lawler and Porter likewise address primarily the process questions of motivation. In particular, they discuss the issue of how performance becomes part of this process. They argue that the process is *not*, as

57

many would like to believe, one of satisfaction giving rise to subsequent performance. Rather, performance enters into the process only if it is conceived by members as the relevant path to extrinsic rewards (such as greater compensation) or more intangible rewards (such as feelings of achievement and pride in work).

Organ states the case that certain forms of satisfaction *can* lead to certain aspects of performance, provided we take account of yet another motive: the need to bring about what we construe as fairness, equity, or social justice in our relationships with each other. This need affects some people more than others; doubtless we all, from time to time, suppress this need when it conflicts with other, more urgently pressing needs; and, in any case, we can exercise considerable ingenuity in distorting our perceptions of what is really fair. Nonetheless, most of us are conditioned from the earliest ages onward to acquire—either as an internalized ethical prerogative or a socially required rule of conduct—the motive of social justice. Failure to incorporate this motive in our analysis is to blind us to the quintessentially humane aspects of organizations.

5

The Rationalizing Animal*

ELLIOT ARONSON

Man likes to think of himself as a rational animal. However, it is more true that man is a *rationalizing* animal, that he attempts to appear reasonable to himself and to others. Albert Camus even said that man is a creature who spends his entire life in an attempt to convince himself that he is not absurd.

Some years ago a woman reported that she was receiving messages from outer space. Word came to her from the planet Clarion that her city would be destroyed by a great flood on December 21. Soon a considerable number of believers shared her deep commitment to the prophecy. Some of them quit their jobs and spent their savings freely in anticipation of the end.

On the evening of December 20, the prophet and her followers met to prepare for the event. They believed that flying saucers would pick them up, thereby sparing them from disaster. Midnight arrived, but no flying saucers. December 21 dawned, but no flood.

What happens when prophecy fails? Social psychologists Leon Festinger, Henry Riecken, and Stanley Schachter infiltrated the little band of believers to see how they would react. They predicted that persons who had expected the disaster, but awaited it alone in their homes, would simply lose faith in the prophecy. But those who awaited the outcome in a group, who had thus admitted their belief publicly, would come to believe even more strongly in the prophecy and turn into active proselytizers.

This is exactly what happened. At first the faithful felt despair and shame because all their predictions had been for naught. Then, after waiting nearly five hours for the saucers, the prophet had a new vision. The city had been spared, she said, because of the trust and faith of her devoted group. This revelation was elegant in its simplicity, and the believers accepted it enthusiastically. They now sought the press that they had previously avoided. They turned from believers into zealots.

* Reprinted from *Psychology Today*, May 1973, by permission of Psychology Today Magazine. Copyright © 1973 Ziff-Davis Publishing Company.

Living on the Fault.   In 1957 Leon Festinger proposed his theory of *cognitive dissonance,* which describes and predicts man's rationalizing behavior. Dissonance occurs whenever a person simultaneously holds two inconsistent cognitions (ideas, beliefs, opinions). For example, the belief that the world will end on a certain day is dissonant with the awareness, when the day breaks, that the world has not ended. Festinger maintained that this state of inconsistency is so uncomfortable that people strive to reduce the conflict in the easiest way possible. They will change one or both cognitions so that they will "fit together" better.

Consider what happens when a smoker is confronted with evidence that smoking causes cancer. He will become motivated to change either his attitudes about smoking or his behavior. And as anyone who has tried to quit knows, the former alternative is easier.

The smoker may decide that the studies are lousy. He may point to friends ("If Sam, Jack, and Harry smoke, cigarettes can't be all that dangerous"). He may conclude that filters trap all the cancer-producing materials. Or he may argue that he would rather live a short and happy life with cigarettes than a long and miserable life without them.

The more a person is committed to a course of action, the more resistant he will be to information that threatens that course. Psychologists have reported that the people who are least likely to believe the dangers of smoking are those who tried to quit—and failed. They have become more committed to smoking. Similarly, a person who builds a $100,000 house astride the San Andreas Fault will be less receptive to arguments about imminent earthquakes than would a person who is renting the house for a few months. The new homeowner is committed; he doesn't want to believe that he did an absurd thing.

When a person reduces his dissonance, he defends his ego, and keeps a positive self-image. But self-justification can reach startling extremes; people will ignore danger in order to avoid dissonance, even when that ignorance can cause their deaths. I mean that literally.

Suppose you are Jewish in a country occupied by Hitler's forces. What should you do? You could try to leave the country; you could try to pass as "Aryan"; you could do nothing and hope for the best. The first two choices are dangerous: if you are caught you will be executed. If you decide to sit tight, you will try to convince yourself that you made the best decision. You may reason that while Jews are indeed being treated unfairly, they are not being killed unless they break the law.

Now suppose that a respected man from your town announces that he has seen Jews being butchered mercilessly, including everyone who has recently been deported from your village. If you believe him, you might have a chance to escape. If you don't believe him, you and your family will be slaughtered.

Dissonance theory would predict that you will not listen to the witness, because to do so would be to admit that your judgment and decisions were wrong. You will dismiss his information as untrue, and decide that he was lying or hallucinating. Indeed, Elie Wiesel reported that this happened to the Jews in Sighet, a small town in Hungary, in 1944. Thus people are not passive receptacles for the deposit of information. The manner in which they view and distort the objective world in order to avoid and reduce dissonance is entirely predictable. But one cannot divide the world into rational people on one side and dissonance reducers on the other. While people vary in their ability to tolerate dissonance, we are all capable of rational or irrational behavior, depending on the circumstances—some of which follow.

Dissonance because of Effort.   Judson Mills and I found that if people go through a lot of trouble to gain admission to a group, and the group turns out to be dull and dreary, they will experience dissonance. It is a rare person who will accept this situation with an "Oh, pshaw. I worked hard for nothing. Too bad." One way to resolve the dissonance is to decide that the group is worth the effort it took to get admitted.

We told a number of college women that they would have to undergo an initiation to join a group that would discuss the psychology of sex. One third of them had severe initiation: they had to recite a list of obscene words and read some lurid sexual passages from novels in the presence of a male experimenter (in 1959, this really was a "severe" and embarrassing task). One third went through a mild initiation in which they read words that were sexual but not obscene (such as "virgin" and "petting"); and the last third had no initiation at all. Then all of the women listened to an extremely boring taped discussion of the group they had presumably joined. The women in the severe initiation group rated the discussion and its drab participants much more favorably than those in the other groups.

I am not asserting that people enjoy painful experiences, or that they enjoy things that are associated with painful experiences. If you got hit on the head by a brick on the way to a fraternity initiation, you would not like that group any better. But if you volunteered to get hit with a brick *in order to join* the fraternity, you definitely would like the group more than if you had been admitted without fuss.

After a decision—especially a difficult one that involves much time, money, or effort—people almost always experience dissonance. Awareness of defects in the preferred object is dissonant with having chosen it; awareness of positive aspects of the unchosen object is dissonant with having rejected it.

Accordingly, researchers have found that *before* making a decision, people seek as much information as possible about the alternatives. Afterwards, however, they seek reassurance that they did the right thing, and do so by seeking information in support of their choice or by simply changing the information that is already in their heads. In one of the earliest experiments on dissonance theory, Jack Brehm gave a group of women their choice between two appliances, such as a toaster or a blender, that they had previously rated for desirability. When the subjects reevaluated the appliances after choosing one of them, they increased their liking for the one they had chosen and downgraded their evaluation of the rejected appliance. Similarly, Danuta Ehrlich and her associates found that a person about to buy a new car does so carefully, reading all ads and accepting facts openly on various makes and models. But after he buys his Volvo, for instance, he will read advertisements more selectively, and he will tend to avoid ads for Volkswagens, Chevrolets, and so on.

The Decision to Behave Immorally.   Your conscience, let us suppose, tells you that it is wrong to cheat, lie, steal, seduce your neighbor's husband or wife, or whatever. Let us suppose further that you are in a situation in which you are sorely tempted to ignore your conscience. If you give in to temptation, the cognition "I am a decent, moral person" will be dissonant with the cognition "I have committed an immoral act." If you resist, the cognition "I want to get a good grade (have that money, seduce that person)" is dissonant with the cognition "I could have acted so as to get that grade, but I chose not to."

The easiest way to reduce dissonance in either case is to minimize the negative aspects of the action one has chosen, and to change one's attitude about its immorality. If Mr. C. decides to cheat, he will probably decide that cheating isn't really so bad. It hurts no one; everyone does it; it's part of human nature. If Mr. D. decides not to cheat, he will no doubt come to believe that cheating is a sin, and deserves severe punishment.

The point here is that the initial attitudes of these men is virtually the same. Moreover, their decisions could be a hair's breadth apart. But once the action is taken, their attitudes diverge sharply.

Judson Mills confirmed these speculations in an experiment with sixth-grade children. First he measured their attitudes toward cheating, and then put them in a competitive situation. He arranged the test so that it was impossible to win without cheating, and so it was easy for the children to cheat, thinking they would be unwatched. The next day, he asked the children again how they felt about cheating. Those who had cheated on the test had become more lenient in their attitudes; those who had resisted the temptation adopted harsher attitudes.

The data are provocative. They suggest that the most zealous crusaders are not those who are removed from the problem they oppose. I would hazard to say that the people who are most angry about "the sexual promiscuity of the young" are *not* those who have never dreamed of being promiscuous. On the contrary, they would be persons who had been seriously tempted by illicit sex, who came very close to giving in to their desires, but who finally resisted. People who almost live in glass houses are the ones who are most likely to throw stones.

Insufficient Justification.   If I offer George $20 to do a boring task, and offer Richard $1 to do the same thing, which one will decide that the assignment was mildly interesting? If I threaten one child with harsh punishment if he does something forbidden, and threaten another child with mild punishment, which one will transgress?

Dissonance theory predicts that when people find themselves doing something and they have neither been rewarded adequately for doing it nor threatened with dire consequences for not doing it, they will find *internal* reasons for their behavior.

Suppose you dislike Woodrow Wilson and I want you to make a speech in his favor. The most efficient thing I can do is to pay you a lot of money for making the speech, or threaten to kill you if you don't. In either case, you will probably comply with my wish, but you won't change your attitude toward Wilson. If that were my goal, I would have to give you a *minimal* reward or threat. Then, in order not to appear absurd, you would have to seek additional reasons for your speech—this could lead you to find good things about Wilson and hence, to conclude that you really do like Wilson after all. Lying produces great attitude change only when the liar is undercompensated.

Festinger and J. Merrill Carlsmith asked college students to work on boring and repetitive tasks. Then the experimenters persuaded the students to lie about the work, to tell a fellow student that the task would be interesting and enjoyable. They offered half of their subjects $20 for telling the lie, and they offered the others only $1. Later they asked all subjects how much they had really liked the tasks.

The students who earned $20 for their lies rated the work as deadly dull, which it was. They experienced no dissonance: they lied, but they were well paid for that behavior. By contrast, students who got $1 decided that the tasks were rather enjoyable. The dollar was apparently enough to get them to tell the lie, but not enough to keep them from feeling that lying for so paltry a sum was foolish. To reduce dissonance, they decided that they hadn't lied after all; the task was fun.

Similarly, Carlsmith and I found that mild threats are more effective than harsh threats in changing a child's attitude about a forbidden object, in this case a delightful toy. In the severe-threat condition, children refrained from playing with the toys and had a good reason for refraining—the very severity of the threat provided ample justification for not playing with the toy. In the mild-threat condition, however, the children refrained from playing with the toy but when they asked themselves, "How come I'm not playing with the toy?" they did not have a super-abundant justification (because the threat was not terribly severe). Accordingly, they provided additional justification in the form of convincing themselves that the attractive toy was really not very attractive and that they didn't really want to play with it very much in the first place. Jonathan Freedman extended our findings, and showed that severe threats do not have a lasting effect on a child's behavior. Mild threats, by contrast, can change behavior for many months.

Perhaps the most extraordinary example of insufficient justification occurred in India, where Jamuna Prasad analyzed the rumors that were circulated after a terrible earthquake in 1950. Prasad found that people in towns that were *not* in immediate danger were spreading rumors of impending doom from floods, cyclones, or unforeseeable calamities. Certainly the rumors could not help people feel more secure; why then perpetrate them? I believe that dissonance helps explain this phenomenon. The people were terribly frightened—after all, the neighboring villages had been destroyed—but they did not have ample excuse for their fear, since the earthquake had missed them. So they invented their own excuse; if a cyclone is on the way, it is reasonable to be afraid. Later, Durganand Sinha studied rumors in a town that had actually been destroyed. The people were scared, but they had good reason to be; they didn't need to seek additional justification for their terror. And their rumors showed no predictions of impending disaster and no serious exaggerations.

The Decision to Be Cruel.   The need for people to believe that they are kind and decent can lead them to say and do unkind and indecent things. After the National Guard killed four students at Kent State, several rumors quickly spread: the slain girls were pregnant, so their deaths spared their families from shame; the students were filthy and had lice on them. These rumors were totally untrue, but the townspeople were eager to believe them. Why? The local people were conservative, and infuriated at the radical behavior of some of the students. Many had hoped that the students would get their comeuppance. But death is an awfully severe penalty. The severity of this penalty outweighs and is dissonant with the "crimes" of the students. In these circumstances, any information that put the victims in a bad light reduces dissonance by implying, in effect, that it was good that the young people died. One high-school teacher even avowed that anyone with "long hair, dirty clothes, or [who goes] barefooted deserves to be shot."

Keith Davis and Edward Jones demonstrated the need to justify cruelty. They persuaded students to help them with an experiment, in the course of which the volunteers had to tell another student that he was a shallow, untrustworthy, and dull person. Volunteers managed to convince themselves that they didn't like the victim of their cruel analysis. They found him less attractive than they did before they had to criticize him.

Similarly, David Glass persuaded a group of subjects to deliver electric shocks to others. The subjects, again, decided that the victim must deserve the cruelty; they rated him as stupid, mean, etc. Then Glass went a step further. He found that a subject with high self-esteem was most likely to derogate the victim. This led Glass to conclude, ironically, that it is precisely because a person thinks he is nice that he decides that the person he has hurt is a rat. "Since nice guys like me don't go around hurting innocent people," Glass's subjects seemed to say, "you must have deserved it." But individuals who have *low* self-esteem do not feel the need to justify their behavior and derogate their victims; it is *consonant* for such persons to believe they have behaved badly. "Worthless people like me do unkind things."

Ellen Berscheid and her colleagues found another factor that limits the need to derogate one's victim: the victim's capacity to retaliate. If the person doing harm feels that the situation is balanced, that his victim will pay him back in coin, he had no need to justify his behavior. In Berscheid's experiment, which involved electric shocks, college students did not derogate or dislike the persons they shocked if they believed the victims could retaliate. Students who were led to believe that the victims would not be able to retaliate *did* derogate them. Her work suggests that soldiers may have a greater need to disparage civilian victims (because they can't retaliate) than military victims. Lt. William L. Calley, who considered the "gooks" at My Lai to be something less than human, would be a case in point.

Dissonance and the Self-Concept. On the basis of recent experiments, I have reformulated Festinger's original theory in terms of the self-concept. That is, dissonance is most powerful when self-esteem is threatened. Thus the important aspect of dissonance is not, "I said one thing and I believe another," but "I have misled people—and I am a truthful, nice person." Conversely, the cognitions, "I believe the task is dull," and "I told someone the task was interesting," are not dissonant for a psychopathic liar.

David Mettee and I predicted in a recent experiment that persons who had low opinions of themselves would be more likely to cheat than persons with high self-esteem. We assumed that if an average person gets a temporary blow to his self-esteem (by being jilted, say, or not getting a promotion), he will temporarily feel stupid and worthless, and hence do any number of stupid and worthless things—cheat at cards, bungle an assignment, break a valuable vase.

Mettee and I temporarily changed 45 female students' self-esteem. We gave one third of them positive feedback about a personality test they had taken (we said that they were interesting, mature, deep, etc.); we gave one third negative feedback (we said that they were relatively immature, shallow, etc.); and one third of the students got no information at all. Then all the students went on to participate in what they thought was an unrelated experiment, in which they gambled in a competitive game of cards. We arranged the situation so that the students could cheat and thereby win a considerable sum of money, or not cheat, in which case they were sure to lose.

The results showed that the students who had received blows to their self-esteem cheated far more than those who had gotten positive feedback about themselves. It may well be that low self-esteem is a critical antecedent of criminal or cruel behavior.

The theory of cognitive dissonance has proved useful in generating research; it has uncovered a wide range of data. In formal terms, however, it is a very sloppy theory. Its very simplicity provides both its greatest strength and its most serious weakness. That is, while the theory has generated a great deal of data, it has not been easy to define the limits of the theoretical statement, to determine the specific predictions that can be made. All too often researchers have had to resort to the very unscientific rule of thumb, "If you want to be sure, ask Leon."

Logic and Psychologic.   Part of the problem is that the theory does not deal with *logical* inconsistency, but *psychological* inconsistency. Festinger maintains that two cognitions are inconsistent if the opposite of one follows from the other. Strictly speaking, the information that smoking causes cancer does not make it illogical to smoke. But these cognitions produce dissonance because they do not make sense psychologically, assuming that the smoker does not want cancer.

One cannot always predict dissonance with accuracy. A man may admire Franklin Roosevelt enormously and discover that throughout his marriage FDR carried out a clandestine affair. If he places a high value on fidelity and he believes that great men are not exempt from this value, then he will experience dissonance. Then I can predict that he will either change his attitudes about Roosevelt or soften his attitudes about fidelity. But, he may believe that marital infidelity and political greatness are totally unrelated; if this were the case, he might simply shrug off these data without modifying his opinions either about Roosevelt or about fidelity.

Because of the sloppiness in the theory, several commentators have criticized a great many of the findings first uncovered by dissonance theory. These criticisms have served a useful purpose. Often, they have goaded us to perform more precise research, which in turn has led to a clarification of some of the findings which, ironically enough, has eliminated the alternative explanations proposed by the critics themselves.

For example, Alphonse and Natalia Chapanis argued that the "severe initiation" experiment could have completely different causes. It might be that the young women were not embarrassed at having to read sexual words, but rather were aroused, and their arousal in turn led them to rate the dull discussion group as interesting. Or, to the contrary, the women in the severe-initiation condition could have felt much sexual anxiety, followed by relief that the discussion was so banal. They associated relief with the group, and so rated it favorably.

So Harold Gerard and Grover Mathewson replicated our experiment, using electric shocks in the initiation procedure. Our original findings were supported—subjects who underwent severe shocks in order to join a discussion group rated that group more favorably than subjects who had undergone mild shocks. Moreover, Gerard and Mathewson went on to show that merely linking an electric shock with the group discussion (as in a simple conditioning experiment) did not produce greater-liking for the group. The increase in liking for the group occurred only when subjects volunteered for the shock *in order* to gain membership in the group—just as dissonance theory would predict.

Routes to Consonance. In the real world there is usually more than one way to squirm out of inconsistency. Laboratory experiments carefully control a person's alternatives, and the conclusions drawn may be misleading if applied to everyday situations. For example, suppose a prestigious university rejects a young Ph.D. for its one available teaching position. If she feels that she is a good scholar, she will experience dissonance. She can then decide that members of that department are narrow-minded and senile, sexist, and wouldn't recognize talent if it sat on their laps. Or she could decide that if they could reject someone as fine and intelligent as she, they must be extraordinarily brilliant. Both techniques will reduce dissonance, but note that they leave this woman with totally opposite opinions about professors at the university.

This is a serious conceptual problem. One solution is to specify the conditions under which a person will take one route to consonance over another. For example, if a person struggles to reach a goal and fails, he may decide that the goal wasn't worth it (as Aesop's fox did) or that the effort was justified anyway (the fox got a lot of exercise in jumping for the grapes). My own research suggests that a person will take the first means when he has expended relatively little effort. But when he has put in a great deal of effort, dissonance will take the form of justifying the energy.

This line of work is encouraging. I do not think that it is very fruitful to demand to know what *the* mode of dissonance reduction is; it is more instructive to isolate the various modes that occur, and determine the optimum conditions for each.

Ignorance of Absurdity.   No dissonance theorist takes issue with the fact that people frequently work to get rewards. In our experiments, however, small rewards tend to be associated with greater attraction and greater attitude change. Is the reverse ever true?

Jonathan Freedman told college students to work on a dull task after first telling them *(a)* their results would be of no use to him, since his experiment was basically over, or *(b)* their results would be of great value to him. Subjects in the first condition were in a state of dissonance, for they had unknowingly agreed to work on a boring chore that apparently had no purpose. They reduced their dissonance by deciding that the task was enjoyable.

Then Freedman ran the same experiment with one change. He waited until the subjects finished the task to tell them whether their work would be important. In this study he found incentive effects: students told that the task was valuable enjoyed it more than those who were told that their work was useless. In short, dissonance theory does not apply when an individual performs an action in good faith without having any way of knowing it was absurd. When we agree to participate in an experiment we naturally assume that it is for a purpose. If we are informed afterward that it *had* no purpose, how were we to have known? In this instance we like the task better if it had an important purpose. But if we agreed to perform it *knowing* that it had no purpose, we try to convince ourselves that it is an attractive task in order to avoid looking absurd.

Man Cannot Live by Consonance Alone.   Dissonance reduction is only one of several motives, and other powerful drives can counteract it. If human beings had a pervasive, all-encompassing need to reduce all forms of dissonance, we would not grow, mature, or admit to our mistakes. We would sweep mistakes under the rug or, worse, turn the mistakes into virtues; in neither case would we profit from error.

But obviously people do learn from experience. They often do tolerate dissonance because the dissonant information has great utility. A person cannot ignore forever a leaky roof, even if that flaw is inconsistent with having spent a fortune on the house. As utility increases, individuals will come to prefer dissonance-arousing but useful information. But as dissonance increases, or when commitment is high, future utility and information tend to be ignored.

It is clear that people will go to extraordinary lengths to justify their actions. They will lie, cheat, live on the San Andreas Fault, accuse innocent bystanders of being vicious provocateurs, ignore information that might save their lives, and generally engage in all manner of absurd postures. Before we write off such behavior as bizarre, crazy, or evil, we would be wise to examine the situations that set up the need to reduce dissonance. Perhaps our awareness of the mechanism that makes us so often irrational will help turn Camus' observation on absurdity into a philosophic curiosity.

6
Motivation and Behavior*

GEORGE H. LITWIN and
ROBERT A. STRINGER, JR.

The Atkinson Model

In his *Introduction to Motivation* (1964), Atkinson presents a formal theory or model of motivated behavior, utilizing a number of principles of motivation which have emerged from the research in this field. We will state the principles embodied in this theory or model, using a simple mechanistic analogy, and then proceed to examine some technical details of the Atkinson model. The basic principles are summarized below:[1]

1. All reasonably healthy adults have a considerable *reservoir of potential energy*. Studies thus far have not indicated that differences in the total amount of potential energy are important determinants of motivation.
2. All adults have a number of basic "motives" or "needs" which can be thought of as valves or outlets that channel and regulate the flow of potential energy from this reservoir.

* Reprinted by permission of Harvard University Press from *Motivation and Organizational Climate* by George H. Litwin and Robert A. Stringer, Jr. Boston: Division of Research, Graduate School of Business Administration, Harvard University. Copyright © 1968 by the President and Fellows of Harvard College. Pp. 10–27.

[1] The mechanical analogy and the language are our own. Neither David McClelland nor John Atkinson should bear any responsibility for this oversimplified description.

3. Although most adults within a given culture may have the same set of motives or energy outlets, they will differ greatly in the relative strength or "readiness" of various motives. A strong motive may be thought of as a valve or energy outlet that opens easily and has a larger aperture for energy flow (due, usually, to frequent use). A weak motive can be thought of as a tight, sticky valve that, even when open, allows only limited energy flow.
4. Whether or not a motive is "actualized," that is, whether energy flows through *this* outlet into behavior and useful work, depends on the specific situation in which the person finds himself.
5. Certain characteristics of the situation arouse or trigger different motives, opening different valves or energy outlets. Each motive or energy outlet is responsive to a different set of situational characteristics.
6. Since various motives are directed toward different kinds of satisfaction, the pattern of behavior that results from arousal of a motive (and the opening of that energy outlet) is quite distinct for each motive. That is, each motive leads to a different pattern of behavior.
7. By changing the nature of the situational characteristics or stimuli, different motives are aroused or actualized, resulting in the energizing of distinct and different patterns of behavior.

In other words, all adults carry around with them the potential energy to behave in a variety of ways. Whether they behave in these ways depends on: *(a)* the relative strength or readiness of the various motives a person has; and *(b)* the situational characteristics or stimuli presented by the situation determine, in large part, which motives will be aroused and what kind of behavior will be generated.

For example, an employee may be used to working in small informal work groups. He is dependent on the group for much of his work satisfaction. We might say that this employee is motivated by a *need for affiliation*. His affiliation energy outlet seems to be wide open when he is allowed to do his job around other people. If the situation was changed, and the worker had to work alone, or if talking was prohibited, or if fellow workers were unfriendly, there would be little opportunity for social interaction. In this new environment, this worker's affiliation energy outlet would not be used. Other motives may be stimulated by the new situation, but we can see how the worker's overall pattern of motivation and behavior would be changed.

Specifically, the Atkinson model holds that *aroused motivation* (to strive for a particular kind of satisfaction or goal) is a joint multiplicative function of *(a)* the *strength of the basic motive* [M], *(b)* the *expectancy* of attaining the goal [E], and *(c)* the *perceived incentive value* of the particular goal [I]. In other words, a person's aroused motivation to behave in a particular way is said to depend on the strength or readiness of his motives, and on two kinds of perceptions of the situation: his expectancies of goal-attainment and the incentive values he attaches to the goals presented. The model can be summarized as follows:

$$\text{Aroused motivation} = M \times E \times I$$

Motives are conceived here as dispositions to strive for general and often internalized goals. They are presumably acquired in childhood and are relatively enduring and stable over periods of time. Expectancies and incentive values depend on the person's experience in specific situations like the one he now confronts, and they change as the person moves about from one situation to another or as the situation itself is altered.

This theory or model of motivation is closely related to the field theory of behavior proposed by Kurt Lewin (1938) and to several other prominent theories of motivation and behavior (see Feather, 1959; Atkinson, 1964, pp. 274–275). These theories all state that the tendency to act in a certain way depends on the strength of the expectancy or belief that the act will lead to a particular outcome or goal and on the value of that outcome or goal to the person.

The Atkinson model was developed to explain behavior and performance related to the *need for achievement* (*n* Achievement), which is defined as a need to excel in relation to competitive or internalized standards. More recently the model has been extended to explain behavior related to the *need for power* (*n* Power), defined as a need for control and influence over others, and the *need for affiliation* (*n* Affiliation), defined as a need for warm, friendly relationships. All these qualities of motivation have been shown to be important determinants of performance and success in business and government organizations (see McClelland, 1961; Vroom, 1964; and Andrews, 1967).

Measurement of Motive Strength

The presence and strength of these motives are assessed through thematic apperceptive methods. This basic method, called the TAT (Thematic Apperception Test), was developed by Murray (1938). Present methods are derivations of the original TAT, aimed at the study of particular motives and suited to particular populations (e.g., college students, businessmen, Negro Americans). The subject is shown a series of pictures, usually of people in fairly ambiguous social and work situations, and he is asked to make up an imaginative story suggested by each picture of the series. These stories are written (by the subject) or recorded (by the experimenter) and analyzed in detail for evidence of the different kinds of imagery associated with various motives.

Such tests are often referred to as projective tests because the subject "projects" into his story his own thoughts, feelings, and attitudes. What the tests actually do is provide us with samples of the kinds of things a person spends his time thinking and daydreaming about when he is not under pressure to think about anything in particular. What do his thoughts turn to when he is by himself and not engaged in a special job? Does he think about his family and friends, about relaxing and watching the Rose Bowl on TV, about getting a particular customer or colleague off his back? Or does he spend his time thinking and planning how he will sell a customer on a new product, cut production costs, or invent a better steam trap, toothpaste tube, or guidance system?

Need for Achievement[2]

If a man spends his time thinking about doing his job better, accomplishing something unusual and important, or advancing his career, the psychologist says he has a high *need for achievement*, often written *n* Achievement—he is concerned with achievement and derives considerable satisfaction from striving for achievement. A man with a strong *need for achievement* thinks not only about the achievement goals, but about how he can attain them, what obstacles or blocks he might encounter, and how he will feel if he succeeds or fails.

What are people with a strong *need for achievement* good for? Evidence indicates that they seek out, enjoy, and do well at jobs that are entrepreneurial in character. They make good business executives, particularly in challenging or developing industries. They enjoy activity and often become salesmen, sales managers, consultants, or fund raisers. Years of careful empirical research have made possible an understanding of why a man with a strong *need for achievement* exhibits such characteristics in his behavior.

1. *He likes situations in which he takes personal responsibility for finding solutions to problems.* The reason is obvious. Otherwise, he could get little personal achievement satisfaction from the successful outcome. Not a gambler, he does not prefer situations the outcome of which depends on chance or other factors beyond his control, rather than on his abilities and efforts. For example:

Some business school students in one study played a game in which they had to choose between two options, each of which afforded only

---

[2] The material in this section is adapted from "Business Drive and National Achievement" by David C. McClelland (1962).

one chance in three of succeeding. For one option they rolled a die, and if it came up at either of two of the six possibilities, they won. For the other option they had to work on a difficult business problem which they knew that only one out of three people on the average had been able to solve in the time allotted.

Under these conditions, the men with high *n* Achievement consistently chose to work on the business problem, even though they knew the odds of success were statistically the same for rolling the die.

To men strong in achievement concern, the idea of winning by chance simply does not produce the same achievement satisfaction as winning by their own personal efforts. Obviously, such a concern for taking personal responsibility is useful in a business executive. He may not be faced very often with the alternative of rolling dice to determine the outcome of a decision, but there are many other ways by which he could avoid taking personal responsibility, such as passing the buck or trying to get someone else (or a committee) to take the responsiblity for getting something done.

The famed self-confidence of the good executive (which, actually, is related to high achievement motivation) is also involved here. He thinks it can be done if he takes responsibility, and very often he is right because he has spent so much time thinking about how to do it that he does it better.

2. *Another characteristic of a man with a strong achievement concern is his tendency to set moderate achievement goals and to take calculated risks.* Again his strategy is well suited to his needs. Only by taking on moderately difficult tasks is he likely to get the achievement satisfaction he wants. If he takes on an easy or routine problem, he will succeed but will get very little satisfaction out of his success, the mere simplicity of the task not affording adequate opportunity to prove his ability and achievement. If he takes on an extremely difficult problem, he is unlikely to get any satisfaction because he may not succeed. Such an eventuality might disprove his ability and frustrate rather than satisfy his need to achieve. In between these two extremes, he stands the best chance of maximizing both his sense of personal achievement and his likelihood of succeeding.

Applying Atkinson's model, it is only the moderate risk situation which simultaneously maximizes his expectancy of success and the incentive value associated with that success, thereby allowing maximal satisfaction of the need. The point can be made with the children's game of ring toss, a variant of which we have used with individuals of all ages, to discover how a person with *high need for achievement* approaches it. To illustrate:

The child is told that he scores when he succeeds in throwing a ring over a peg on the floor and that he can choose to stand anywhere he pleases. Obviously, if he stands next to the peg, he can score a ringer every time, but if he stands a long distance away, he will hardly ever get a ringer. The curious fact is that children with high concern for achievement quite consistently stand at moderate distances from the peg where they are most apt to get achievement satisfaction (or, to be more precise, where the decreasing probability-of-success curve crosses the increasing satisfaction-from-success curve). The ones with low concern for achievement, on the other hand, distribute their choices of where to stand quite randomly over the entire distance. In other words, people with high *need for achievement* prefer a situation where there is a challenge, where there is some real risk for not succeeding, but where that risk is not so great that they might not overcome it by their own efforts.

We waste our time feeling sorry for the entrepreneur whose constant complaints are that he is overworking, that he has more problems than he knows how to deal with, that he is doomed to ulcers because of overwork, and so on. The bald truth is that he has high *need of achievement*—that he lives the very challenges he complains about. In fact, a careful study might well show that he creates most of them for himself. He may talk about quitting business and living on his investments, but if he did, he might then really get ulcers. The state of mind of being a little overextended is precisely the one he seeks, since overcoming difficulties gives him achievement satisfaction. His real problem is that of keeping the difficulties from getting too big for him, which explains in part why he talks so much about them—it is a nagging problem for him to keep them at a level he can handle.

3. *The man who has a strong concern for achievement also wants concrete feedback as to how well he is doing.* Otherwise how could he get any satisfaction out of what he had done? Business is almost unique in the amount of feedback it provides in the form of sales, cost, production, and profit figures. It is no accident that the symbol of the businessman in popular cartoons is a wall chart with a line on it going up or down. The businessman, sooner or later, knows how well he is doing; salesmen will often know their success from day to day. There is a concreteness in this knowledge of results which is by and large missing from the kind of feedback professionals get.

The teacher will serve as a representative example of such a professional. His job is to transmit certain attitudes and certain kinds of information to his students. He does get some degree of feedback as to how well he has done his job, but results are fairly imprecise and hardly concrete. His students, colleagues, and even his institution's administration may indicate that they like his teaching, but he still has no real objective or precise evidence that his students have learned anything from him. Many of his students do well on examinations, but he knows from past experience that they will forget much of what they have written in a year or two. If he has high *need for achievement* and is really concerned about whether he has done his job well, he must be satisfied with sketchy, occasional evidence that his former pupils did absorb some of his ideas and attitudes. Most likely, however, he is *not* a person with high *need for achievement* and is quite satisfied with the affection and recognition that he gets for his work. These feedback measures will gratify needs other than his *need for achievement*.

Obviously not everyone likes to work in situations where the feedback is concrete. It can prove him right, but it also can prove him wrong. The person with high n Achievement has a compelling interest to know whether he was right or wrong. He thrives and is happier when this condition is satisfied by the situation than when it is not, as is usually the case in the professional situation. When an individual with a high *need for achievement* does involve himself in a professional situation, furthermore, he usually seeks out a role where more concrete feedback on performance is provided, such as that of a trial lawyer, a doctor who establishes a clinic, or a professor who becomes a fund raiser.

Need for Power

If a man spends his time thinking about the influences and control he has over others, and how he can use this influence, say, to win an argument, to change other people's behavior, or to gain a position of authority and status, then the psychologist says he has a high *need for power*, often written n Power. He derives satisfaction from controlling the means of influence over others.

Men with a strong need for power will usually attempt to influence others directly—by making suggestions, by giving their opinions and evaluations, and by trying to talk others into things. They seek positions of leadership in group activities; whether they become leaders or are seen only as "dominating individuals" depends on other attributes such as ability and sociability. They are usually verbally fluent, often talkative, sometimes argumentative. Men with a strong *need for power* are seen by others as forceful and outspoken, but also as hard-headed and demanding.

As should be expected, men with a strong concern for power prefer positions which allow the exercise of power. They enjoy roles requiring persuasion, such as teaching and public speaking. In addition, a man with a high concern for power will seek out positions which involve control of the means of influencing others, such as political office or top management slots. Studies of the motivation of managers have shown that although strong achievement motivation distinguishes the successful manager or entrepreneur from other people, the men in top management, and particularly organization presidents, are strongly motivated by the *need for power*.

For the past 20 years, social scientists have been involved in the study of influence and power. Much of this research deals with topics such as "Authoritarian Personality" and "Fascism," and represents largely a kind of social criticism regarding the use of power rather than a genuine scientific exploration of power motivation. In a democracy, matters relating to the accumulation of personal power are inevitably treated with suspicion and dread, and some scientists have been quick to interpret the natural concerns with influence, control, and power which develop in society as a dangerous threat to our democratic institutions and way of life.

What research has been done indicates clearly that men with strong *need for power* do not always gain power and that even when they do, what use they make of this power is determined by *other needs and values*. A man with a strong n Power, little concern for warm, affiliative relationships, and strong authoritarian values would certainly tend toward autocratic and dictatorial action. On the other hand, a man with strong n Power, considerable sensitivity to other's feelings, and a desire to give service to others would probably make an excellent Peace Corps worker or missionary. This polarity in the use of power is illustrated in a study by Andrews (1967) of two Mexican companies. One of these was a dynamic and rapidly growing organization whose employees were enthusiastic about their work; the other organization, despite a large initial investment and favorable market, had shown almost no growth and had serious problems of dissatisfaction and turnover, particularly in the management ranks. Assessment of personnel motivation in both these companies showed that those in the upper management of the more dynamic organization were much higher in n Achievement than either their own subordinates or those in the upper management of the static organization. The presidents of both of these companies were *very high* in the *need for power*. In the case of the dynamic organization, the president's *need for power*, combined with a moderate *need for achievement* and a strong commitment to achievement values, had helped create a thriving, successful business. In the other case, the president's *need for power* and rather authoritarian values led him to dominate every other person in the organization, make all the decisions himself, and leave almost no room for individual responsibility.

Politics as an activity represents one of the clearest theaters for expression of the *need for power*, and men who run for political office characteristically demonstrate very strong power motivation. Here the explicit goal is control of the means of influencing others (e.g., law enforcement, executive position), and this goal can only be reached by influencing many others (e.g., the voters). The various writings on the American Presidency may be the richest literature available on the phenomenology of power, how power is gained, and how it affects men who have it. The following two passages, from Theodore H. White's *The Making of the President 1960,* are very vivid descriptions of the phenomenology of power—how power is experienced by the man who seeks and gains it:

Shortly before he died in 1950, the great Henry L. Stimson was asked which of the many Presidents of his acquaintance had been the best. Stimson, according to the man from whom I heard the tale, reflected a minute or two, for his career stretched over half a century of American history. He had known intimately or served importantly more Presidents, Democratic and Republican, than any other citizen of his age— from Theodore Roosevelt through Taft, Wilson, Coolidge, and Hoover to Franklin D. Roosevelt and Harry S. Truman. After reflection, Stimson replied to his friend:

If, by the phrase "best President," the friend meant who had been the most efficient President—why, of course, the answer would be William Howard Taft. Under Taft, the Cabinet met in order, affairs marched to the agenda of the meeting, responsibility was clearly deputized, and when each man rose from the Cabinet table he knew exactly what he was to do and to whom he was to report. Yes, Taft certainly was the most efficient. If, however, continued Stimson, by the "best President" one meant the "greatest President," then the answer must be different. The name would, without doubt, be Roosevelt—but he was not sure whether the first name was Theodore or Franklin. For both of these gentlemen, you see, not only understood the *use* of power; they knew the *enjoyment* of power, too. And that was the important thing.

Whether a man is burdened by power or enjoys power; whether he is trapped by responsibility or made free by it; whether he is moved by other people and outer forces or moves them—this is of the essence of leadership.

*****

A one-time personal aide of President Truman once put the matter to me in this way: "The most startling thing a new President discovers is that his world is *not* monolithic. In the world of the Presidency, giving an order does *not* end the matter. You can pound your fist on the table or you can get mad or you can blow it all and go out to the golf course. But nothing gets done except by endless follow-up, endless kissing and coaxing, endless threatening and compelling. There are all those thousands of people in Washington working for you in the government— and every one is watching you, waiting, trying to guess what you mean, trying to get your number. Can they fool you? Can they outwait you? Will you be mad when you hear it isn't done yet? And Congress keeps shoving more and more power into the President's lap—the Formosa resolution gives the President power to declare war all by himself; and Congress keeps setting up new regulatory agencies, and you have to hire and fire the men who run them. And they're all testing you. How much can they get away with? How much authority can they take? How much authority do *you* want them to have? And once you choose your men—you have to keep them; which means the endless attrition of *your* will against *their* will, because some of them will be damned good men . . . (White, 1965, pp. 366–367).

Need for Affiliation

If a man spends his time thinking about the warm, friendly, companionate relationships he has, or would like to have, the psychologist says he has a *need for affiliation,* often written n Affiliation. Thoughts about restoring close relationships that have been disrupted, consoling or helping someone, or participating in friendly, companionate activities such as bull sessions, reunions, and parties are regarded as evidence of affiliation motivation.

Since they want others to like them, men with a strong *need for affiliation* are likely to pay attention to the feelings of others. In group meetings they make efforts to establish friendly relationships, often by agreeing or giving emotional support. Men with strong *need for affiliation* seek out jobs which offer opportunities for friendly interaction. In business, these men often take supervisory jobs where maintaining good relationships is more important than decision making. People who have institutionalized helping roles, such as teachers, nurses, and counselors, also demonstrate strong *need for affiliation.*

While strong n Affiliation does not seem to be important for effective managerial performance, and might well be detrimental, recent research has suggested that some minimal concern with the feelings of others and with the companionate quality of relationships is necessary for superior managerial and executive capability. It is reasonable to assume that such basic affiliative concern is critical in understanding others and in building good working relationships with both superiors and subordinates—this affiliative concern is a means to attain other, broader kinds of satisfaction and might well be labeled *interpersonal competence.* Moment and Zaleznik give a graphic description of this kind of behavior:

> People need each other to get work done and to live full lives. The fullness of life is measured by achievements. Communicating with people is the ultimate achievement process. Something new is created through talking and working with people. The ultimate achievement is the creation of new and better resolutions of social and technical problems.

Although there are standards of excellence for individuals' contributions, real resolutions of his problems are tested in the communication process. . . .

. . . his behavior clearly communicates his feelings. He also communicates his confidence in himself; he will unapologetically defend his positions, but he will also change his position in accordance with what he is learning in the process. He acknowledges in his behavior that he is communicating with specific people, rather than thinking out loud about ideas separated from people. His behavior says that the other persons as individuals, as well as sources of ideas, are bound up in the problem-solving process (Moment & Zaleznik, 1963, pp. 120–121).

Compare this with Moment and Zaleznik's description of the "social specialists," which we would characterize as men with strong *need for affiliation:*

People need each other for support. Feeling lonely, disliked, and disrespected by people is the worst thing that could happen to a person. Living together in harmony is the ultimate value. One must work hard and do a good job in order to be accepted by others. But work should not be allowed to interfere with harmony, respect, and affection.

One learns from experience that being close and friendly with people is more important than career success. Having friends and being friendly are necessary to support and encourage a person through periods of disappointment and hardship.

Satisfaction is derived from being liked and accepted in the group. Argument and conflict are frustrating and make for an unhappy experience (Moment & Zaleznik, 1963, pp. 123–124).

Summary

In this chapter a theory of motivation developed out of more than 20 years of laboratory and field research has been presented. Some emphasis was placed on a recent formal model, the Atkinson model, which states that aroused motivation (to strive for a particular goal) is a function of the strength of the basic need and two situationally determined factors, the expectancy of goal-attainment and the perceived incentive value of the goal.

We have tried to describe the three kinds of motivation that we will focus on in this monograph—achievement motivation, power motivation, and affiliation motivation. There are at least three ways of describing these motivational tendencies, all of which we have employed. First, we have tried to define the nature of the basic need or goal, particularly in terms of the kind of satisfaction that is desired. Second, we have described the quality of aroused motivation, in terms of the thoughts and feelings of the motivated person. Third, we have identified patterns of behavior which stem from arousal of the *need for achievement,* the *need for power,* and the *need for affiliation.* It is not always possible to distinguish among these levels of description without being overly tedious. However, the reader should try to keep in mind the very important difference between *motive,* which is a relatively stable personality characteristic, and *aroused motivation,* which is a situationally influenced action tendency. The reader should also keep in mind that aroused motivation can be described in terms of a *pattern of thoughts and feelings,* which is a situationally influenced action tendency. The reader should also keep in mind that aroused motivation can be described in terms of a *pattern of thoughts and feelings,* such as would be revealed in thematic apperceptive stories, or in terms of a *pattern of behavior* which is likely to result from motive arousal.

The specific scoring procedures which are used to analyze thematic apperceptive stories, and which allow us to measure the relative strength of *n* Achievement, *n* Power, and *n* Affiliation have not been dealt with. These scoring procedures are described in detail in Atkinson's *Motives in Fantasy, Action, and Society* (1958). Nonprofessional scorers can use these procedures to derive specific scores which provide objective measures of the strength of aroused motivation. The objectivity of these measures is demonstrated by the high agreement that is possible among scorers working independently. Recent attempts to develop computer programs to do this scoring have been quite successful, providing definite evidence of the objectivity of these scoring procedures (see Litwin, 1965).

The *n* Achievement, *n* Power, and *n* Affiliation scores derived from thematic apperceptive tests through application of the scoring procedures described by Atkinson (1958) are assumed to represent the strength of aroused motivation. That is, they are products of motive strength *and* of situational factors. Under certain circumstances, these scores can also provide a useful index of the strength of the basic motives. When a group of people with similar backgrounds and experiences (and, presumably, perceptions) are in the same constant situation, differences in motivation scores can be assumed to represent differences in the strength of basic motives—the subjective or idiosyncratic elements are assumed to cancel each other out. That is, the situational influences are held constant and relative differences in score represent differences in motive strength.

The administrative implications of the kind of motivation theory we have described are quite dramatic. By identifying and learning to influence particular expectancies and incentives associated with a motive network, it is possible to strengthen the aroused motivation or behavior tendency. Though the role of reinforcement in the Atkinson model has not been clearly specified, the effects of reinforcement on aroused motivation are well established. Using our oversimplified, hydraulic model of the Atkinson theory, reinforcement can be represented as an enlargement of the valve capacity associated with any particular motive. Just as water enlarged the proverbial hole through which the little Dutch boy stuck his finger, so the repeated passage of energy through these motivational valves tends to wear away at their edges, making them larger and more easily opened, increasing their total capacity for energy flow. By tying the expectancies and incentives to as many consistent cues as possible in the business environment, the likelihood of a particular pattern of behavior can be increased.

Since different motives lead to different behavior patterns, it is important that the manager learn to identify, at least in a rough way, different kinds of basic motives or needs. He must also be able to "fit" the demands of a job to a pattern of behavior that will result from and provide satisfaction for the arousal of a given motive. He can create this fit by the selection and appropriate placement of people with different motives, by altering somewhat the demands of a given job, or by *selectively* arousing, satisfying, and thereby reinforcing the kind of motivation that will lead to the most appropriate job behavior. Once he has obtained what he considers a reasonable fit, he can proceed to build into the work situation the kinds of expectancies and incentives that will arouse the desired motivation and assure persistent patterns of behavior.

REFERENCES

Andrews, J.   The achievement motive in two types of organizations. *Journal of Personality and Social Psychology*, 1967, 6, 163–168.

Atkinson, J. W., ed.   *Motives in fantasy, action, and society*. Princeton: D. Van Nostrand Company, 1958.

Atkinson, J. W.   *An introduction to motivation*. Princeton: D. Van Nostrand Company, 1964.

Feather, N. T.   Subjective probability and decision under uncertainty. *Psychological Review*, 1950, 66, 150–164.

Lewin, K.   *The conceptual representation and the measurement of psychological forces*. Durham, N.C.: Duke University Press, 1938.

Litwin, G. H.   The language of achievement: An analysis of achievement-related themes in fantasy using mechanical methods. Unpublished doctoral dissertation, Harvard University, 1965.

McClelland, D. C.   *The achieving society*. Princeton: D. Van Nostrand Company, 1961.

McClelland, D. C.   Business drive and national achievement. *Harvard Business Review*, 1962, 40, July–August, 99–112.

Moment, D., & Zaleznik, A. *Role development and interpersonal compe-tence.* Boston: Division of Research, Harvard Business School, 1963.

Murray, H. A. *Exploration in personality.* New York: Oxford University Press, 1938.

Vroom, V. H. *Work and motivation.* New York: Wiley, 1964.

White, T. H. *The making of the president 1960.* New York: Atheneum, 1965.

7

On the Folly of Rewarding A, while Hoping for B*

STEVEN KERR

Whether dealing with monkeys, rats, or human beings, it is hardly controversial to state that most organisms seek information concerning what activities are rewarded, and then seek to do (or at least pretend to do) those things, often to the virtual exclusion of activities not re-warded. The extent to which this occurs of course will depend on the perceived attractiveness of the rewards offered, but neither operant nor expectancy theorists would quarrel with the essence of this notion.

Nevertheless, numerous examples exist of reward systems that are fouled up in that behaviors which are rewarded are those which the rewarder is trying to *discourage*, while the behavior he desires is not being rewarded at all.

In an effort to understand and explain this phenomenon, this paper presents examples from society, from organizations in general, and from profit-making firms in particular. Data from a manufacturing company and information from an insurance firm are examined to demonstrate the consequences of such reward systems for the organizations involved, and possible reasons why such reward systems continue to exist are considered.

---

* Reprinted from *Academy of Management Journal,* 1975, *18*, 769–783.

SOCIETAL EXAMPLES

Politics

Official goals are "purposely vague and general and do not indicate . . . the host of decisions that must be made among alternative ways of achieving official goals and the priority of multiple goals . . ." (8, p. 66). They usually may be relied on to offend absolutely no one, and in this sense can be considered high-acceptance, low-quality goals. An example might be "build better schools." Operative goals are higher in quality but lower in acceptance, since they specify where the money will come from, what alternative goals will be ignored, etc.

The American citizenry supposedly wants its candidates for public office to set forth operative goals, making their proposed programs "perfectly clear," specifying sources and uses of funds, etc. However, since operative goals are lower in acceptance, and since aspirants to public office need acceptance (from at least 50.1 percent of the people), most politicians prefer to speak only of official goals, at least until after the election. They of course would agree to speak at the operative level if "punished" for not doing so. The electorate could do this by refusing to support candidates who do not speak at the operative level.

Instead, however, the American voter typically punishes (withholds support from) candidates who frankly discuss where the money will come from, rewards politicians who speak only of official goals, but hopes that candidates (despite the reward system) will discuss the issues operatively. It is academic whether it was moral for Nixon, for example, to refuse to discuss his 1968 "secret plan" to end the Vietnam war, his 1972 operative goals concerning the lifting of price controls, the reshuffling of his cabinet, etc. The point is that the reward system made such refusal rational.

It seems worth mentioning that no manuscript can adequately define what is "moral" and what is not. However, examination of costs and benefits, combined with knowledge of what motivates a particular individual, often will suffice to determine what for him is "rational."[1] If the reward system is so designed that it is irrational to be moral, this does not necessarily mean that immorality will result. But is this not asking for trouble?

---

[1] In Simon's (10, pp. 76–77) terms, a decision is "subjectively rational" if it maximizes an individual's valued outcomes so far as his knowledge permits. A decision is "personally rational" if it is oriented toward the individual's goals.

War

If some oversimplification may be permitted, let it be assumed that the primary goal of the organization (Pentagon, Luftwaffe, or whatever) is to win. Let it be assumed further that the primary goal of most individuals on the front lines is to get home alive. Then there appears to be an important conflict in goals—personally rational behavior by those at the bottom will endanger goal attainment by those at the top.

But not necessarily! It depends on how the reward system is set up. The Vietnam war was indeed a study of disobedience and rebellion, with terms such as "fragging" (killing one's own commanding officer) and "search and evade" becoming part of the military vocabulary. The difference in subordinates' acceptance of authority between World War II and Vietnam is reported to be considerable, and veterans of the Second World War often have been quoted as being outraged at the mutinous actions of many American soldiers in Vietnam.

Consider, however, some critical differences in the reward system in use during the two conflicts. What did the GI in World War II want? To go home. And when did he get to go home? When the war was won! If he disobeyed the orders to clean out the trenches and take the hills, the war would not be won and he would not go home. Furthermore, what were his chances of attaining his goal (getting home alive) if he obeyed the orders compared to his chances if he did not? What is being suggested is that the rational soldier in World War II, *whether patriotic or not*, probably found it expedient to obey.

Consider the reward system in use in Vietnam. What did the man at the bottom want? To go home. And when did he get to go home? When his tour of duty was over! This was the case *whether or not* the war was won. Furthermore, concerning the relative chance of getting home alive by obeying orders compared to the chance if they were disobeyed, it is worth noting that a mutineer in Vietnam was far more likely to be assigned rest and rehabilitation (on the assumption that fatigue was the cause) than he was to suffer any negative consequence.

In his description of the "zone of indifference," Barnard stated that "a person can and will accept a communication as authoritative only when . . . at the time of his decision, he believes it to be compatible with his personal interests as a whole" (1, p. 165). In light of the reward system used in Vietnam, would it not have been personally irrational for some orders to have been obeyed? Was not the military implementing a system which *rewarded* disobedience, while *hoping* that soldiers (despite the reward system) would obey orders?

Medicine

Theoretically, a physician can make either of two types of error, and intuitively one seems as bad as the other. A doctor can pronounce a patient sick when he is actually well, thus causing him needless anxiety and expense, curtailment of enjoyable foods and activities, and even physical danger by subjecting him to needless medication and surgery. Alternately, a doctor can label a sick person well, and thus avoid treating what may be a serious, even fatal ailment. It might be natural to conclude that physicians seek to minimize both types of error.

Such a conclusion would be wrong.[2] It is estimated that numerous Americans are presently afflicted with iatrogenic (physician *caused*) illnesses (9). This occurs when the doctor is approached by someone complaining of a few stray symptoms. The doctor classifies and organizes these symptoms, gives them a name, and obligingly tells the patient what further symptoms may be expected. This information often acts as a self-fulfilling prophecy, with the result that from that day on the patient for all practical purposes is sick.

Why does this happen? Why are physicians so reluctant to sustain a type 2 error (pronouncing a sick person well) that they will tolerate many type 1 errors? Again, a look at the reward system is needed. The punishments for a type 2 error are real: guilt, embarrassment, and the threat of lawsuit and scandal. On the other hand, a type 1 error (labeling a well person sick) "is sometimes seen as sound clinical practice, indicating a healthy conservative approach to medicine" (9, p. 69). Type 1 errors also are likely to generate increased income and a stream of steady customers who, being well in a limited physiological sense, will not embarrass the doctor by dying abruptly.

Fellow physicians and the general public therefore are really *rewarding* type 1 errors and at the same time *hoping* fervently that doctors will try not to make them.

GENERAL ORGANIZATIONAL EXAMPLES

Rehabilitation Centers and Orphanages

In terms of the prime beneficiary classification (2, p. 42) organizations such as these are supposed to exist for the "public-in-contact,"

---

[2] In one study (4) of 14,867 films for signs of tuberculosis, 1,216 positive readings turned out to be clinically negative; only 24 negative readings proved clinically active, a ratio of 50 to 1.

that is, clients. The orphanage therefore theoretically is interested in placing as many children as possible in good homes. However, often orphanages surround themselves with so many rules concerning adoption that it is nearly impossible to pry a child out of the place. Orphanages may deny adoption unless the applicants are a married couple, both of the same religion as the child, without history of emotional or vocational instability, with a specified minimum income and a private room for the child, etc.

If the primary goal is to place children in good homes, then the rules ought to constitute means toward that goal. Goal displacement results when these "means become ends-in-themselves that displace the original goals" (2, p. 229).

To some extent these rules are required by law. But the influence of the reward system on the orphanage's management should not be ignored. Consider, for example, that the:

1. Number of children enrolled often is the most important determinant of the size of the allocated budget.
2. Number of children under the director's care also will affect the size of his staff.
3. Total organizational size will determine largely the director's prestige at the annual conventions, in the community, etc.

Therefore, to the extent that staff size, total budget, and personal prestige are valued by the orphanage's executive personnel, it becomes rational for them to make it difficult for children to be adopted. After all, who wants to be the director of the smallest orphanage in the state?

If the reward system errs in the opposite direction, paying off only for placements, extensive goal displacement again is likely to result. A common example of vocational rehabilitation in many states, for example, consists of placing someone in a job for which he has little interest and few qualifications, for two months or so, and then "rehabilitating" him again in another position. Such behavior is quite consistent with the prevailing reward system, which pays off for the number of individuals placed in any position for 60 days or more. Rehabilitation counselors also confess to competing with one another to place relatively skilled clients, sometimes ignoring persons with few skills who would be harder to place. Extensively disabled clients find that counselors often prefer to work with those whose disabilities are less severe.[3]

---

[3] Personal interviews conducted during 1972–73.

Universities

Society *hopes* that teachers will not neglect their teaching responsibilities but *rewards* them almost entirely for research and publications. This is most true at the large and prestigious universities. Clichés such as "good research and good teaching go together" notwithstanding, professors often find that they must choose between teaching and research-oriented activities when allocating their time. Rewards for good teaching usually are limited to outstanding teacher awards, which are given to only a small percentage of good teachers and which usually bestow little money and fleeting prestige. Punishments for poor teaching also are rare.

Rewards for research and publications, on the other hand, and punishments for failure to accomplish these, are commonly administered by universities at which teachers are employed. Furthermore, publication-oriented resumés usually will be well received at other universities, whereas teaching credentials, harder to document and quantify, are much less transferable. Consequently it is rational for university teachers to concentrate on research, even if to the detriment of teaching and at the expense of their students.

By the same token, it is rational for students to act based upon the goal displacement which has occurred within universities concerning what they are rewarded for. If it is assumed that a primary goal of a university is to transfer knowledge from teacher to student, then grades become identifiable as a means toward that goal, serving as motivational, control, and feedback devices to expedite the knowledge transfer. Instead, however, the grades themselves have become much more important for entrance to graduate school, successful employment, tuition refunds, parental respect, etc., than the knowledge or lack of knowledge they are supposed to signify.

It therefore should come as no surprise that information has surfaced in recent years concerning fraternity files for examinations, term-paper writing services, organized cheating at the service academies, and the like. Such activities constitute a personally rational response to a reward system which pays off for grades rather than knowledge.

BUSINESS-RELATED EXAMPLES

Ecology

Assume that the president of XYZ Corporation is confronted with the following alternatives:

1. Spend $11 million for antipollution equipment to keep from

poisoning fish in the river adjacent to the plant; or
2. Do nothing, in violation of the law, and assume a one in ten chance of being caught, with a resultant $1 million fine plus the necessity of buying the equipment.

Under this not unrealistic set of choices it requires no linear program to determine that XYZ Corporation can maximize its probabilities by flouting the law. Add the fact that XYZ's president is probably being rewarded (by creditors, stockholders, and other salient parts of his task environment) according to criteria totally unrelated to the number of fish poisoned, and his probable course of action becomes clear.

Evaluation of Training

It is axiomatic that those who care about a firm's well-being should insist that the organization get fair value for its expenditures. Yet it is commonly known that firms seldom bother to evaluate a new GRID, MBO, job enrichment program, or whatever, to see if the company is getting its money's worth. Why? Certainly it is not because people have not pointed out that this situation exists; numerous practitioner-oriented articles are written each year to just this point.

The individuals (whether in personnel, manpower planning, or wherever) who normally would be responsible for conducting such evaluations are the same ones often charged with introducing the change effort in the first place. Having convinced top management to spend the money, they usually are quite animated afterwards in collecting arigorous vignettes and anecdotes about how successful the program was. The last thing many desire is a formal, systematic, and revealing evaluation. Although members of top management may actually *hope* for such systematic evaluation, their reward systems continue to *reward* ignorance in this area. And if the personnel department abdicates its responsibility, who is to step into the breach? The change agent himself? Hardly! He is likely to be too busy collecting anecdotal "evidence" of his own, for use with his next client.

Miscellaneous

Many additional examples could be cited of systems which in fact are rewarding behaviors other than those supposedly desired by the rewarder. A few of these are described briefly below.

Most coaches disdain to discuss individual accomplishments, preferring to speak of teamwork, proper attitude, and a one-for-all spirit. Usually, however, rewards are distributed according to individual performance. The college basketball player who feeds his teammates instead of shooting will not compile impressive scoring statistics and is less likely to be drafted by the pros. The ballplayer who hits to right field to advance the runners will win neither the batting nor home run titles, and will be offered smaller raises. It therefore is rational for players to think of themselves first, and the team second.

In business organizations where rewards are dispensed for unit performance or for individual goals achieved, without regard for overall effectiveness, similar attitudes often are observed. Under most Management by Objectives (MBO) systems, goals in areas where quantification is difficult often go unspecified. The organization therefore often is in a position where it *hopes* for employee effort in the areas of team building, interpersonal relations, creativity, etc., but it formally *rewards* none of these. In cases where promotions and raises are formally tied to MBO, the system itself contains a paradox in that it "asks employees to set challenging, risky goals, only to face smaller paychecks and possibly damaged careers if these goals are not accomplished" (5, p. 40).

It is *hoped* that administrators will pay attention to long-run costs and opportunities and will institute programs which will bear fruit later on. However, many organizational reward systems pay off for short-run sales and earnings only. Under such circumstances it is personally rational for officials to sacrifice long-term growth and profit (by selling off equipment and property, or by stifling research and development) for short-term advantages. This probably is most pertinent in the public sector, with the result that many public officials are unwilling to implement programs which will not show benefits by election time.

As a final, clear-cut example of a fouled-up reward system, consider the cost-plus contract or its next of kin, the allocation of next year's budget as a direct function of this year's expenditures. It probably is conceivable that those who award such budgets and contracts really hope for economy and prudence in spending. It is obvious, however, that adopting the proverb "to him who spends shall more be given," rewards not economy, but spending itself.

TWO COMPANIES' EXPERIENCES

A Manufacturing Organization

A midwest manufacturer of industrial goods had been troubled for some time by aspects of its organizational climate it believed dysfunctional. For research purposes, interviews were conducted with many employees and a questionnaire was administered on a company-wide basis, including plants and offices in several American and Canadian locations. The company strongly encouraged employee participation in the survey, and made available time and space during the workday for completion of the instrument. All employees in attendance during the day of the survey completed the questionnaire. All instruments were collected directly by the researcher, who personally administered each session. Since no one employed by the firm handled the questionnaires, and since respondent names were not asked for, it seems likely that the pledge of anonymity given was believed.

A modified version of the Expect Approval scale (7) was included as part of the questionnaire. The instrument asked respondents to indicate the degree of approval or disapproval they could expect if they performed each of the described actions. A seven-point Likert scale was used, with 1 indicating that the action would probably bring strong disapproval and 7 signifying likely strong approval.

Although normative data for this scale from studies of other organizations are unavailable, it is possible to examine fruitfully the data obtained from this survey in several ways. First, it may be worth noting that the questionnaire data corresponded closely to information gathered through interviews. Furthermore, as can be seen from the results summarized in Table 1, sizable differences between various work units, and between employees at different job levels within the same work unit, were obtained. This suggests that response bias effects (social desirability in particular loomed as a potential concern) are not likely to be severe.

Most importantly, comparisons between scores obtained on the Expect Approval scale and a statement of problems which were the reason for the survey revealed that the same behaviors which managers in each division thought dysfunctional were those which lower level employees claimed were rewarded. As compared to job levels 1 to 8 in Division B (see Table 1), those in Division A claimed a much higher acceptance by management of "conforming" activities. Between 31 and 37 percent of Division A employees at levels 1–8 stated that going along with the majority, agreeing with the boss, and staying on everyone's good side brought approval; only once (level 5–8 responses to one of the three items) did a majority suggest that such actions would generate disapproval.

Furthermore, responses from Division A workers at levels 1–4 indicate that behaviors geared toward risk avoidance were as likely to be rewarded as to be punished. Only at job levels 9 and above was it apparent that the reward system was positively reinforcing behaviors desired by top management. Overall, the same "tendencies toward conservatism and apple-polishing at the lower levels" which divisional management had complained about during the interviews were

TABLE 1
Summary of Two Divisions' Data Relevant to Conforming and Risk-Avoidance Behaviors (extent to which subjects expect approval)

Dimension	Item	Division and Sample	Total Responses	Percentage of Workers Responding		
				1, 2, or 3 (Disapproval)	4	5, 6, or 7 (Approval)
Risk avoidance	Making a risky decision based on the best information available at the time, but which turns out wrong.	A, levels 1-4 (lowest)	127	61	25	14
		A, levels 5-8	172	46	31	23
		A, levels 9 and above	17	41	30	30
		B, levels 1-4 (lowest)	31	58	26	16
		B, levels 5-8	19	42	42	16
		B, levels 9 and above	10	50	20	30
Risk	Setting extremely high and challenging standards and goals, and then narrowly failing to make them.	A, levels 1-4	122	47	28	25
		A, levels 5-8	168	33	26	41

TABLE 1 (concluded)

Dimension	Item	Division and Sample	Total Responses	Percentage of Workers Responding		
				1, 2, or 3 (Disapproval)	4	5, 6, or 7 (Approval)
		A, levels 9+	17	24	6	70
		B, levels 1-4	31	48	23	29
		B, levels 5-8	18	17	33	50
		B, levels 9+	10	30	0	70
	Setting goals which are extremely easy to make and then making them.	A, levels 1-4	124	35	30	35
		A, levels 5-8	171	47	27	26
		A, levels 9+	17	70	24	6
		B, levels 1-4	31	58	26	16
		B, levels 5-8	19	63	16	21
		B, levels 9+	10	80	0	20
	Being a "yes man" and always agreeing with the boss.	A, levels 1-4	126	46	17	37
		A, levels 5-8	180	54	14	31

	A, levels 9 +	17	88	12	0
	B, levels 1-4	32	53	28	19
	B, levels 5-8	19	68	21	11
	B, levels 9 +	10	80	10	10
Always going along with the majority.	A, levels 1-4	125	40	25	35
	A, levels 5-8	173	47	21	32
	A, levels 9 +	17	70	12	18
	B, levels 1-4	31	61	23	16
	B, levels 5-8	19	68	11	21
	B, levels 9 +	10	80	10	10
Being careful to stay on the good side of everyone, so that everyone agrees that you are a great guy.	A, levels 1-4	124	45	18	37
	A, levels 5-8	173	45	22	33
	A, levels 9 +	17	64	6	30
	B, levels 1-4	31	54	23	23
	B, levels 5-8	19	73	11	16
	B, levels 9 +	10	80	10	10

those claimed by subordinates to be the most rational course of action in light of the existing reward system. Management apparently was not getting the behaviors it was *hoping* for, but it certainly was getting the behaviors it was perceived by subordinates to be *rewarding*.

An Insurance Firm

The Group Health Claims Division of a large eastern insurance company provides another rich illustration of a reward system which reinforces behaviors not desired by top management.

Attempting to measure and reward accuracy in paying surgical claims, the firm systematically keeps track of the number of returned checks and letters of complaint received from policyholders. However, underpayments are likely to provoke cries of outrage from the insured, while overpayments often are accepted in courteous silence. Since it often is impossible to tell from the physician's statement which of two surgical procedures, with different allowable benefits, was performed, and since writing for clarifications will interfere with other standards used by the firm concerning "percentage of claims paid within two days of receipt," the new hire in more than one claims section is soon acquainted with the informal norm: "When in doubt, pay it out!"

The situation would be even worse were it not for the fact that other features of the firm's reward system tend to neutralize those described. For example, annual "merit" increases are given to all employees, in one of the following three amounts:

1. If the worker is "outstanding" (a select category, into which no more than two employees per section may be placed): 5 percent
2. If the worker is "above average" (normally all workers not "outstanding" are so rated): 4 percent
3. If the worker commits gross acts of negligence and irresponsibility for which he might be discharged in many other companies: 3 percent.

Now, since (a) the difference between the 5 percent theoretically attainable through hard work and the 4 percent attainable merely by living until the review data is small and (b) since insurance firms seldom dispense much of a salary increase in cash (rather, the worker's insurance benefits increase, causing him to be further overinsured), many employees are rather indifferent to the possibility of obtaining the extra one percent reward and therefore tend to ignore the norm concerning indiscriminant payments.

However, most employees are not indifferent to the rule which states that, should absences or latenesses total three or more in any six-month period, the entire 4 or 5 percent due at the next "merit" review must be forfeited. In this sense the firm may be described as *hoping* for performance, while *rewarding* attendance. What it gets, of course, is attendance. (If the absence-lateness rule appears to the reader to be stringent, it really is not. The company counts "times" rather than "days" absent, and a ten-day absence therefore counts the same as one lasting two days. A worker in danger of accumulating a third absence within six months merely has to remain ill (away from work) during his second absence until his first absence is more than six months old. The limiting factor is that at some point his salary ceases, and his sickness benefits take over. This usually is sufficient to get the younger workers to return, but for those with 20 or more years' service, the company provides sickness benefits of 90 percent of normal salary, tax-free! Therefore . . . .)

CAUSES

Extremely diverse instances of systems which reward behavior A although the rewarder apparently hopes for behavior B have been given. These are useful to illustrate the breadth and magnitude of the phenomenon, but the diversity increases the difficulty of determining commonalities and establishing causes. However, four general factors may be pertinent to an explanation of why fouled-up reward systems seem to be so prevelant.

Fascination with an "Objective" Criterion

It has been mentioned elsewhere that:

> Most "objective" measures of productivity are objective only in that their subjective elements are (a) determined in advance, rather than coming into play at the time of the formal evaluation, and (b) well concealed on the rating instrument itself. Thus industrial firms seeking to devise objective rating systems first decide, in an arbitrary manner, what dimensions are to be rated, . . . usually including some items having little to do with organizational effectiveness while excluding others that do. Only then does Personnel Division churn out official-looking documents on which all dimensions chosen to be rated are assigned point values, categories, or whatever (6, p. 92).

Nonetheless, many individuals seek to establish simple, quantifiable standards against which to measure and reward performance. Such efforts may be successful in highly predictable areas within an organization, but are likely to cause goal displacement when applied anywhere else. Overconcern with attendance and lateness in the insurance firm and with number of people placed in the vocational rehabilitation division may have been largely responsible for the problems described in those organizations.

Overemphasis on Highly Visible Behaviors

Difficulties often stem from the fact that some parts of the task are highly visible while other parts are not. For example, publications are easier to demonstrate than teaching, and scoring baskets and hitting home runs are more readily observable than feeding teammates and advancing base runners. Similarly, the adverse consequences of pronouncing a sick person well are more visible than those sustained by labeling a well person sick. Team-building and creativity are other examples of behaviors which may not be rewarded simply because they are hard to observe.

Hypocrisy

In some of the instances described the rewarder may have been getting the desired behavior, notwithstanding claims that the behavior was not desired. This may be true, for example, of management's attitude toward apple-polishing in the manufacturing firm (a behavior which subordinates felt was rewarded, despite management's avowed dislike of the practice). This also may explain politicians' unwillingness to revise the penalties for disobedience of ecology laws, and the failure of top management to devise reward systems which would cause systematic evaluation of training and development programs.

Emphasis on Morality or Equity Rather than Efficiency

Some consideration of other factors prevents the establishment of a system which rewards behaviors desired by the rewarder. The felt obligation of many Americans to vote for one candidate or another, for example, may impair their ability to withhold support from politicians who refuse to discuss the issues. Similarly, the concern for spreading the risks and costs of wartime military service may outweigh the advantage to be obtained by commiting personnel to combat until the war is over.

It should be noted that only with respect to the first two causes are reward systems really paying off for other than desired behaviors. In the case of the third and fourth causes the system *is* rewarding behaviors desired by the rewarder, and the systems are fouled up only from the standpoints of those who believe the rewarder's public statements (cause 3), or those who seek to maximize efficiency rather than other outcomes (cause 4).

CONCLUSIONS

Modern organization theory requires a recognition that the members of organizations and society possess divergent goals and motives. It therefore is unlikely that managers and their subordinates will seek the same outcomes. Three possible remedies for this potential problem are suggested.

Selection

It is theoretically possible for organizations to employ only those individuals whose goals and motives are wholly consonant with those of management. In such cases the same behaviors judged by subordinates to be rational would be perceived by management as desirable. State-of-the-art reviews of selection techniques, however, provide scant grounds for hope that such an approach would be successful (for example, see 12).

Training

Another theoretical alternative is for the organization to admit those employees whose goals are not consonant with those of management and then, through training, socialization, or whatever, alter employee goals to make them consonant. However, research on the effectiveness of such training programs, though limited, provides further grounds for pessimism (for example, see 3).

Altering the Reward System

What would have been the result if:

1. Nixon had been assured by his advisors that he could not win reelection except by discussing the issues in detail?
2. Physicians' conduct was subjected to regular examination by review boards for type 1 errors (calling healthy people ill) and to penalties (fines, censure, etc.) for errors of either type?
3. The President of XYZ Corporation had to choose between *(a)* spending $11 million for antipollution equipment, and *(b)* incurring a 50-50 chance of going to jail for five years?

Managers who complain that their workers are not motivated might do well to consider the possibility that they have installed reward systems which are paying off for behaviors other than those they are seeking. This, in part, is what happened in Vietnam, and this is what regularly frustrates societal efforts to bring about honest politicians, civic-minded managers, etc. This certainly is what happened in both the manufacturing and the insurance companies.

A first step for such managers might be to find out what behaviors currently are being rewarded. Perhaps an instrument similar to that used in the manufacturing firm could be useful for this purpose. Chances are excellent that these managers will be surprised by what they find—that their firms are not rewarding what they assume they are. In fact, such undesirable behavior by organizational members as they have observed may be explained largely by the reward systems in use.

This is not to say that all organizational behavior is determined by formal rewards and punishments. Certainly it is true that in the absence of formal reinforcement some soldiers will be patriotic, some presidents will be ecology-minded, and some orphanage directors will care about children. The point, however, is that in such cases the rewarder is not *causing* the behaviors desired but is only a fortunate bystander. For an organization to *act* upon its members, the formal reward system should positively reinforce desired behaviors, not constitute an obstacle to be overcome.

It might be wise to underscore the obvious fact that there is nothing really new in what has been said. In both theory and practice these matters have been mentioned before. Thus in many states Good Samaritan laws have been installed to protect doctors who stop to assist a stricken motorist. In states without such laws it is commonplace for doctors to refuse to stop, for fear of involvement in a subsequent lawsuit. In college basketball additional penalties have been instituted against players who foul their opponents deliberately. It has long been argued by Milton Friedman and others that penalties should be altered so as to make it irrational to disobey the ecology laws, and so on.

By altering the reward system the organization escapes the necessity of selecting only desirable people or of trying to alter undesirable ones. In Skinnerian terms (as described in 11, p. 704), "As for responsibility and goodness—as commonly defined—no one . . . would want or need them. They refer to a man's behaving well despite the absence of positive reinforcement that is obviously sufficient to explain it. Where such reinforcement exists, 'no one needs goodness.' "

REFERENCES

1. Barnard, Chester I. *The functions of the executive.* Cambridge, Mass.: Harvard University Press, 1964.

2. Blau, Peter M., & Scott, W. Richard. *Formal organizations.* San Francisco: Chandler, 1962.

3. Fiedler, Fred E. Predicting the effects of leadership training and experience from the contingency model. *Journal of Applied Psychology,* 1972, *56,* 114–119.

4. Garland, L. H. Studies of the accuracy of diagnostic procedures. *American Journal Roentgenological, Radium Therapy Nuclear Medicine,* 1959, 82, 25–38.

5. Kerr, Steven. Some modifications in MBO as an OD strategy. *Academy of Management Proceedings,* 1973, pp. 39–42.

6. Kerr, Steven. What price objectivity? *American Sociologist,* 1973, 8, 92–93.

7. Litwin, G. H., & Stringer, R. A., Jr. *Motivation and organizational climate.* Boston: Harvard University Press, 1968.

8. Perrow, Charles. The analysis of goals in complex organizations. In A. Etzioni (Ed.), *Readings on Modern Organizations.* Englewood Cliffs, N.J.: Prentice-Hall, 1969.

9. Scheff, Thomas J. Decision rules, types of error, and their consequences in medical diagnosis. In F. Massarik & P. Ratoosh (Eds.), *Mathematical Explorations in Behavioral Science.* Homewood, Ill.: Irwin, 1965.

10. Simon, Herbert A. *Administrative behavior.* New York: Free Press, 1957.

11. Swanson, G. E. Review symposium: Beyond freedom and dignity. *American Journal of Sociology,* 1972, 78, 702–705.

12. Webster, E. *Decision making in the employment interview.* Montreal: Industrial Relations Center, McGill University, 1964.

8

The Effect of Performance on Job Satisfaction*

EDWARD E. LAWLER III and LYMAN W. PORTER

The human relations movement with its emphasis on good interpersonal relations, job satisfaction, and the importance of informal groups provided an important initial stimulant for the study of job attitudes and their relationship to human behavior in organizations. Through the thirties and forties, many studies were carried out to determine the correlates of high and low job satisfaction. Such studies related job satisfaction to seniority, age, sex, education, occupation, and income, to mention a few. Why this great interest in job satisfaction? Undoubtedly some of it stemmed from a simple desire on the

* Reprinted from *Industrial Relations, a Journal of Economy and Society,* vol. 7, no. 1 (October 1967), pp. 20–28.

part of scientists to learn more about job satisfaction, but much of the interest in job satisfaction seems to have come about because of its presumed relationship to job performance. As Brayfield and Crockett have pointed out, a common assumption that employee satisfaction directly affects performance permeates most of the writings about the topic that appeared during this period of two decades.[1] Statements such as the following characterized the literature: "Morale is not an abstraction; rather it is concrete in the sense that it directly affects the quality and quantity of an individual's output," and "Employee morale—reduces turnover—cuts down absenteeism and tardiness; lifts production."[2]

It is not hard to see how the assumption that high job satisfaction leads to high performance came to be popularly accepted. Not only did it fit into the value system of the human relations movement but there also appeared to be some research data to support this point. In the Western Electric studies, the evidence from the Relay Assembly Test Room showed a dramatic tendency for increased employee productivity to be associated with an increase in job satisfaction. Also, who could deny that in the Bank Wiring Room there was both production restriction and mediocre employee morale. With this background it is easy to see why both social scientists and managers believed that if job dissatisfaction could be reduced, the human brake on production could be removed and turned into a force that would increase performance.

Previous Research

But does the available evidence support the belief that high satisfaction will lead to high performance? Since an initial study, in 1932, by Kornhauser and Sharp, more than 30 studies have considered the relationship between these two variables.[3] Many of the earlier studies seemed to have assumed implicitly that a positive relationship existed and that it was important to demonstrate that it in fact did exist. Little attention was given to trying to understand *why* job satisfaction should lead to higher performance; instead, researchers contented themselves with routinely studying the relationship between satisfaction and performance in a number of industrial situations.

---

[1] Arthur H. Brayfield and Walter H. Crockett, "Employee Attitudes and Employee Performance," *Psychological Bulletin*, vol. 52 (September 1955), pp. 396–424.

[2] Ibid.

[3] Arthur Kornhauser and A. Sharp, "Employee Attitudes: Suggestions from a Study in a Factory." *Personnel Journal*, vol. 10 (1932), 393–401.

The typical reader of the literature in the early fifties was probably aware of the fact that some studies had failed to find a significant satisfaction-performance relationship. Indeed, the very first study of the problem obtained an insignificant relationship.[4] However, judging from the impact of the first review of the literature on the topic, by Brayfield and Crockett, many social scientists, let alone practicing managers, were unaware that the evidence indicated how little relationship exists between satisfaction and performance.[5] The key conclusion that emerged from the review was that "there is little evidence in the available literature that employee attitudes bear any simple— or, for that matter, appreciable—relationship to performance on the job." (The review, however, pointed out that job satisfaction did seem to be positively related, as expected, to two other kinds of employee behavior, absenteeism and turnover.)

The review had a major impact on the field of industrial psychology and helped shatter the kind of naïve thinking that characterized the earlier years of the human relations movement. Perhaps it also discouraged additional research, since few post-1955 studies of the relationship between satisfaction and performance have been reported in scientific journals.

Another review, covering much of the same literature, was completed about the same time.[6] This review took a more optimistic view of the evidence: ". . . there is frequent evidence for the often suggested opinion that positive job attitudes are favorable to increased productivity. The relationship is not absolute, but there are enough data to justify attention to attitudes as a factor in improving the worker's output. However, the correlations obtained in many of the positive studies were low."[7] This review also pointed out, as did Brayfield and Crockett, that there was a definite trend for attitudes to be related to absenteeism and turnover. Perhaps the chief reasons for the somewhat divergent conclusions reached by the two reviews were that they did not cover exactly the same literature and that Brayfield and Crockett were less influenced by suggestive findings that did reach statistical significance. In any event, the one conclusion that was obvious from both reviews was that there was not the *strong, persuasive* relationship between job satisfaction and productivity that had been suggested by many of the early proponents of the human relations movement and so casually accepted by personnel specialists.

---

[4] Ibid.

[5] Brayfield and Crocket, "Employee Attitudes and Employee Performance," pp. 396–424.

[6] Frederick Herzberg, Bernard Mausner, R. O. Peterson, and Dora F. Capwell. *Job Attitudes: Review of Research and Opinion* (Pittsburgh: Psychological Service, 1957).

[7] Ibid., p. 103.

A more recent review of the literature by Vroom has received less attention than did the two earlier reviews,[8] perhaps because it is now rather generally accepted that satisfaction is not related to performance. However, before we too glibly accept the view that satisfaction and performance are unrelated, let us look carefully at the data from studies reviewed by Vroom. These studies show a median correlation of +.14 between satisfaction and performance. Although this correlation is not large, the consistency of the direction of the correlation is quite impressive. Twenty of the 23 correlations cited by Vroom are positive. By a statistical test such consistency would occur by chance less than once in a hundred times.

In summary, the evidence indicates that a low but consistent relationship exists between satisfaction and performance, but it is not at all clear *why* this relationship exists. The questions that need to be answered at this time, therefore, concern the place of job satisfaction both in theories of employee motivation and in everyday organizational practice. For example, should an organization systematically measure the level of employee satisfaction? Is it important for an organization to try to improve employee job satisfaction? Is there theoretical reason for believing that job satisfaction should be related to job behavior and if so, can it explain why this relationship exists?

Why Study Job Satisfaction?

There are really two bases upon which to argue that job satisfaction is important. Interestingly, both are different from the original reason for studying job satisfaction, that is, the assumed ability of satisfaction to influence performance. The first, and undoubtedly the most straightforward reason, rests on the fact that strong correlations between absenteeism and satisfaction, as well as between turnover and satisfaction, appear in the previous studies. Accordingly, job satisfaction would seem to be an important focus of organizations which wish to reduce absenteeism and turnover.

Perhaps the best explanation of the fact that satisfaction is related to absenteeism and turnover comes from the kind of path-goal theory of motivation that has been stated by Georgopoulos, Mahoney, and Jones; Vroom; and Lawler and Porter.[9] According to this view, people

---

[8] Victor H. Vroom, *Work and Motivation* (New York: Wiley, 1964).

[9] Basil S. Georgopoulos, G. M. Mahoney, and N. W. Jones, "A Path-Goal Approach to Productivity," *Journal of Applied Psychology*, vol. 41 (1957), 345–53; Vroom, *Work and Motivations;* Edward E. Lawler and Lyman W. Porter, "Antecedent Attitudes of Effective Managerial Performance," *Organizational Behavior and Human Performance*, vol. 2 (May 1967), 122–143. See also Lyman W. Porter and Edward E. Lawler, *Managerial Attitudes and Performance* (Homewood, Ill.: Irwin-Dorsey, 1968).

are motivated to do things which they feel have a high probability of leading to rewards which they value. When a worker says he is satisfied with his job, he is in effect saying that his needs are satisfied as a result of having his job. Thus, path-goal theory would predict that high satisfaction will lead to low turnover and absenteeism because the satisfied individual is motivated to go to work where his important needs are satisfied.

A second reason for interest in job satisfaction stems from its low but consistent *association* with job performance. Let us speculate for a moment on why this association exists. One possibility is that, as assumed by many, the satisfaction *caused* the performance. However, there is little theoretical reason for believing that satisfaction can cause performance. Vroom, using a path-goal theory of motivation, has pointed out that job satisfaction and job performance are caused by quite different things: ". . . job satisfaction is closely affected by the amounts of rewards that people derive from their jobs and . . . level of performance is closely affected by the basis of attainment of rewards. Individuals are satisfied with their jobs to the extent to which their jobs provide them with what they desire, and they perform effectively in them to the extent that effective performance leads to the attainment of what they desire."[10]

Relationship between Satisfaction and Performance

- Vroom's statement contains a hint of why, despite the fact that satisfaction and performance are caused by different things, they do bear some relationship to each other. If we assume, as seems to be reasonable in terms of motivation theory, that rewards cause satisfaction, and that in some cases performance produces rewards, then it is possible that the relationship found between satisfaction and performance comes about through the action of a third variable—rewards. Briefly stated, good performance may lead to rewards, which in turn lead to satisfaction; this formulation then would say that satisfaction, rather than causing performance, as was previously assumed, is caused by it. Figure 1 presents this thinking in a diagrammatic form.

This model first shows that performance leads to rewards, and it distinguishes between two kinds of rewards and their connection to performance. A wavy line between performance and extrinsic rewards indicates that such rewards are likely to be imperfectly related to performance. By extrinsic rewards is meant such organizationally controlled rewards as pay, promotion, status, and security—rewards that

---

[10] Vroom, *Work and Motivation*, p. 246.

are often referred to as satisfying mainly lower level needs.[11] The connection is relatively weak because of the difficulty of tying extrinsic rewards directly to performance. Even though an organization may have a policy of rewarding merit, performance is difficult to measure, and in dispensing rewards like pay, many other factors are frequently taken into consideration. Lawler, for example, found a low correlation between amount of salary and superiors' evaluation for a number of middle and lower level managers.[12]

FIGURE 1
The Theoretical Model

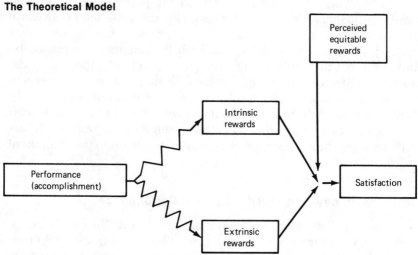

Quite the opposite is likely to be true for intrinsic rewards, however, since they are given to the individual by himself for good performance. Intrinsic or internally mediated rewards are subject to fewer disturbing influences and thus are likely to be more directly related to good performance. This connection is indicated in the model by a semiwavy line. Probably the best example of an intrinsic reward is the feeling of having accomplished something worthwhile. For that matter, any of the rewards that satisfy self-actualization needs or higher order growth needs are good examples of intrinsic rewards.

The model also shows that intrinsic and extrinsic rewards are not directly related to job satisfaction since the relationship is moderated

---

[11] Abraham H. Maslow, *Motivation and Personality* (New York: Harper, 1954). According to Maslow, needs are arranged in a hierarchy with physiological and security needs being the lowest level needs, social and esteem needs next, and autonomy and self-actualization needs the highest level.

[12] Edward E. Lawler, "Managers' Attitudes toward How Their Pay Is and Should Be Determined." *Journal of Applied Psychology*, vol. 50 (August 1966), 273–279.

by expected equitable rewards. This variable refers to the level or amount of rewards that an individual feels he *should* receive as the result of his job performance. Thus, an individual's satisfaction is a function both of the number and amount of the rewards he receives as well as what he considers to be a fair level of reward. An individual can be satisfied with a small amount of reward if he feels that it is a fair amount of reward for his job.[13]

This model would seem to predict that because of the imperfect relationship between performance and rewards and the importance of expected equitable rewards there would be a low but positive relationship between job satisfaction and job performance. The model also leads to a number of other predictions about the relationship between satisfaction and performance. If it turns out that, as this model predicts, satisfaction is dependent on performance, then it can be argued that satisfaction is an important variable from both a theoretical and a practical point of view despite its low relationship to performance. However, when satisfaction is viewed in this way, the reasons for considering it to be important are quite different from those that are proposed when satisfaction is considered to cause performance. But first, let us look at some of the predictions that are derivable from the model and at some data that were collected in order to test the predictions.

Research Data

Usable data were collected from 148 middle and lower level managers in five organizations. One of the organizations was a large manufacturing company; the others were small social service and welfare agencies. As determined from the demographic data collected from each manager, the sample was typical of other samples of middle and lower level managers, with one exception—31 of the managers were female.

Two kinds of data were collected for each manager. Superior and peer rankings were obtained on two factors: (1) how hard the manager worked, and (2) how well the manager performed his job. Since a number of peers ranked each manager, the average peer's rankings were used for data analysis purposes. The rankings by the superiors and peers were in general agreement with each other, so the rankings met the requirements for convergent and discriminant validity. In addition to the superior and peer rankings each manager filled out an attitude questionnaire designed to measure his degree of satisfaction

---

[13] Lyman W. Porter, "A study of Perceived Need Satisfactions in Bottom and Middle Management Jobs," *Journal of Applied Psychology*, vol. 45 (January 1961), 1–10.

in five needed areas. This part of the questionnaire was identical to the one used in earlier studies by Porter.[14] It consists of 13 items in the following form:

The opportunity for independent thought and action in my management position:

(a) How much is there now?
                    (min) 1 2 3 4 5 6 7 (max)

(b) How much should there be?
                    (min) 1 2 3 4 5 6 7 (max)

The answers to the first of these questions (a) for each of the 13 items was taken as the measure of need fulfillment or rewards received. The answer to the second of the questions (b) was taken as a measure of the individual's expected equitable level of rewards. The difference in answers between the second and first of these questions was taken as the operational measure of need satisfaction. That is, the larger the difference between "should" and "is now" in our findings, the greater the *dis*satisfaction.[15]

The 13 items, though presented in random order in the questionnaire, had been preclassified into five types of needs that have been described by Maslow: security, social, esteem, autonomy, and self-actualization.

Predictions and Research Results

Let us now consider two specific predictions that our model suggests. The first is that an individual's degree of need satisfaction is related to his job performance as rated by his peers and by his superior. A second prediction is that this relationship is stronger for managers than for nonmanagers.

The basis for this second prediction can be found in the assumed connection between rewards and performance. It seems apparent that most organizations have considerably more freedom to reward their managers differentially than they do their often unionized rank-and-file employees (unless the latter are on incentive pay plans). Even in a nonunionized organization (such as a governmental unit), management jobs generally offer the possibility of greater flexibility in differential rewards, especially in terms of prestige and autonomy in deci-

---

[14] Ibid.

[15] A third question about the importance of the various types of needs was also included, but the results based on it are not reported in the findings presented in this article.

sion making. Management jobs also typically provide greater opportunities to satisfy higher order intrinsic needs. As the model shows, satisfaction of these higher order needs is more closely tied to performance.

Satisfaction and Performance.   Data collected from our sample of managers generally support the first two predictions. Job satisfaction (the sum of the difference scores for all 13 items) correlates significantly with both the superiors' rankings ($r = 0.32$, $p < 0.01$) and peers' rankings ($r = 0.30$, $p < 0.01$) of performance. Although the correlations are not large, they are substantially larger than the median correlation between satisfaction and performance at the level of rank-and-file workers ($r = 0.14$ as given in Vroom's review). It is possible that this higher relationship came about because we used a different measure of need satisfaction than has been typically used before or because we used a better performance measure. However, our belief is that it came about because the study was done at the management level in contrast to the previous studies which mainly involved non-management employees. Neither our measure of job performance nor our measure of satisfaction would seem to be so unique that either could account for the higher relationship found between satisfaction and performance. However, future studies that use the same measure for both managers and nonmanagers are needed if this point is to be firmly established.

Satisfaction and Effort.   An additional prediction from the model is that satisfaction should be more closely related to the rankings obtained on performance than to the rankings obtained on effort. The prediction is an important one for the model and stems from the fact that satisfaction is seen as a variable that is more directly dependent on performance than on effort. Others have pointed out that effort is only one of the factors that determines how effective an individual's performance will be. Ability factors and situational constraints are other obviously relevant determinants. It is also important to note that if we assume, as many previous writers have, that satisfaction causes performance then it would seem logical that satisfaction should be more closely related to effort than to performance. Satisfaction should influence an individual's performance by affecting his motivation to perform effectively, and this presumably is better reflected by effort than by job performance.

The results of the present study show, in fact, a stronger relationship between the superiors' rankings of performance and satisfaction ($r = 0.32$), than between the superiors' rankings of effort and satisfaction ($r = 0.23$). Similarly, for the peer rankings there is a stronger relationship between performance and satisfaction ($r = 0.30$), than between effort and satisfaction ($r = 0.20$).

Intrinsic and Extrinsic Rewards. The model suggests that intrinsic rewards that satisfy needs such as self-actualization are more likely to be related to performance than are extrinsic rewards, which have to be given by someone else and therefore have a weaker relationship between their reception and performance. Thus, the satisfaction should be more closely related to performance for higher than for lower order needs. Table 1 presents the data relevant to this point. There is a slight tendency for satisfaction of the higher order needs to show higher correlations with performance than does satisfaction with lower order needs. In particular, the highest correlations appear for self-actualization which is, of course, the highest order need, in the Maslow need hierarchy.

Overall, the data from the present study are in general agreement with the predictions based on the model. Significant relationships did appear between performance and job satisfaction. Perhaps even more important for our point of view, the relationship between satisfaction and performance was stronger than that typically found among blue-collar employees. Also in agreement with our model was the finding that satisfaction was more closely related to performance than to effort. The final prediction, which was supported by the data, was that the satisfaction of higher order needs would be the most closely related to performance. Taken together then, the data offer encouraging support for our model and in particular for the assertion of the model that satisfaction can best be thought of, as depending on performance rather than causing it.

Implications of the Findings

At this point we can ask the following question: what does the strength of the satisfaction-performance relationship tell us about an organization? For example, if a strong positive relationship exists we would assume that the organization is effectively distributing differential extrinsic rewards based on performance. In addition, it is providing jobs that allow for the satisfaction of higher order needs. Finally, the poorer performers rather than the better ones are quitting and showing high absenteeism, since, as we know, satisfaction, turnover, and absenteeism are closely related.

Now let us consider an organization where no relationship exists between satisfaction and performance. In this organization, presumably, rewards are not being effectively related to performance, and absenteeism and turnover in the organization are likely to be equally distributed among both the good and poor performers. Finally, let us consider the organization where satisfaction and performance bear a negative relationship to each other. Here absenteeism and turnover

TABLE 1
Pearson Correlations between Performance and
Satisfaction in Five Need Areas

	Rankings by	
Needs	Superiors	Peers
Security	0.21*	0.17†
Social	0.23*	0.26*
Esteem	0.24*	0.16†
Autonomy	0.18†	0.23*
Self-actualization	0.30*	0.28*

* p <0.01
† p <0.05

will be greatest among the best performers. Furthermore, the poor performers would be getting more rewards than the good performers.

Clearly, most organization theorists would feel that organizational effectiveness is encouraged by rewarding good performers and by restricting turnover to poorer performers. Thus, it may be desirable for organizations to develop a strong relationship between satisfaction and performance. In effect, the argument is that the less positive relationship between satisfaction and performance in an organization, the less effective the organization will be *(ceteris paribus)*. If this hypothesis were shown to be true, it would mean that a measure of the relationship between satisfaction and performance would be a helpful diagnostic tool for examining organizations. It is hardly necessary to note that this approach is quite different from the usual human relations one of trying to maximize satisfaction, since here we are suggesting trying to maximize the relationship between satisfaction and performance, rather than satisfaction itself.

One further implication of the model appears to warrant comment. It well may be that a high general level of satisfaction of needs like self-actualization may be a sign of organization effectiveness. Such a level of satisfaction would indicate, for instance, that most employees have interesting and involving jobs and that they probably are performing them well. One of the obvious advantages of providing employees with intrinsically interesting jobs is that good performance is rewarding in and of itself. Furthermore, being rewarded for good performance is likely to encourage further good performance. Thus, measures of higher order need satisfaction may provide good evidence of how effective organizations have been in creating interesting and rewarding jobs, and therefore, indirect evidence of how motivating the jobs themselves are. This discussion of the role of intrinsic rewards and satisfaction serves to highlight the importance of including measures of higher order need satisfaction in attitude surveys. Too often attitude surveys have focused only on satisfaction with extrinsic rewards, such as pay and promotion, and on the social relations which were originally stressed by the human relations movement.

In summary, we have argued that it is important to consider the satisfaction level that exists in organizations. For one thing, satisfaction is important because it has the power to influence both absenteeism and turnover. In addition, in the area of job performance we have emphasized that rather than being a cause of performance, satisfaction is caused by it. If this is true, and we have presented some evidence to support the view that it is, then it becomes appropriate to be more concerned about which people and what kind of needs are satisfied in the organization, rather than about how to maximize satisfaction generally. In short, we suggest new ways of interpreting job satisfaction data.

9

A Reappraisal and Reinterpretation of the Satisfaction-Causes-Performance Hypothesis*

DENNIS W. ORGAN

It would appear that the last nail has been driven into the coffin of the "Human Relations" notion that satisfaction causes performance, insofar as its respectability among theorists and researchers in organizational psychology is concerned. Some impatient critics might remark, as did Charles II of his own imminent surcease, that the beast was "an unconscionable time adying." Nevertheless, after 40 years of empirical studies and reviews (e.g., 4, 7, 12, 16, 17, 19, 20, 28) addressed to the proposition, the notion appears intellectually bankrupt. A newer, tough-minded generation of teachers in organizational behavior seeks to disabuse its charges of the idea that making people happy will make them more productive. One suspects that this task is

---

* Abridged from *Academy of Management Review*, 1977, 2, no. 1, 46–53.

undertaken with gusto, for there is nothing dearer to the behavioral scientist's heart than to demolish with hard evidence a tenet of conventional wisdom; no other activity, it seems, does so much to justify the existence of the occupation.

But it does seem worthwhile to take the widespread *belief* (9) in the satisfaction-causes-performance hypothesis as a datum itself worthy of analysis. What is the unarticulated logic from which the proposition emerged? Perhaps a reconstruction of that logic might show it to be compatible with more current and viable theories, with the satisfaction-causes-performance notion being merely a hasty and imprecise deduction. If the latter could be examined in the context of the intuitive framework which gave birth to it; if, interpreted in terms of current social psychological concepts, that framework could also account post hoc for some reliable empirical generalizations not generally associated with the satisfaction-productivity question; and if the framework, amended by qualifications brought to light in its new context, could specify the boundaries of its own predictive powers (i.e., explain those cases in which satisfaction and performance are more or less unrelated); then the satisfaction-causes-performance position might be seen in a more respectable light.

Unfortunately, explication of the mute logic in question is not found in the literature presumably comprising the "Human Relations" school (e.g., 10, 23, 24); those sources lack any unambiguous declaration that increased satisfaction leads to increased performance. Schwab and Cummings (27) did unearth a 1951 statement: "improve the morale of a company and you improve production." Whether "morale" can be interpreted to mean satisfaction is a moot point, and whether the statement is implied to hold true at the individual level is debatable. In any case, the Human Relations writers as a group have not staked their case on the proposition that happy people consistently outproduce unhappy people. The framework which prompts the lay person to believe in the proposition must be sought in a somewhat speculative fashion.

Reconstructing the Logic behind the Satisfaction-Causes-Performance Hypothesis

The framework in question represents a primitive, vaguely cognized version of the theory of equity in social exchange as articulated by Gouldner (11), Homans (15), Blau (3), Adams (1), and recent contributions by Walster, Berscheid, and Walster (29). A unifying theme to this stream of thought is the assumption that most people expect social justice or equity to prevail in interpersonal transactions. An individual who regards himself or herself as inequitably short-changed will experience resentment and, if the additional costs are not prohibitive, will take aggressive action designed to restore equity (even if the costs *are* prohibitive, the individual may still do so in order to "save face"; e.g., Brown, 6). But an individual accorded some manner of social gift—inequitably in excess of what is anticipated—will experience gratitude and a felt obligation to reciprocate the benefactor. Both Adams' presentation of equity theory (1) and elaborations by Walster et al. (29) recognize alternatives to reciprocation as a means of restoring equity; they include perceptual distortions of the exchange or the parties to the exchange. Nevertheless, their treatment suggests that persons who are inequitably over-rewarded will prefer reciprocation, if possible, as a mode of restoring equity, and research appears to bear this out.

Reciprocal Behavior of Benefactees and the Hypothesis. The underlying premise that individuals seek to reciprocate their benefactors represents a conceptual core from which one might deduce the satisfaction-causes-performance hypothesis. But the deduction rests on two implicit qualifying assumptions: first, that satisfaction results from social gifts which can be personalized in their association with the voluntary actions of official organization representatives; and second, that increased productivity or performance is perceived as a viable and appropriate form of reciprocation to those organizational benefactors. While neither assumption is unreasonable, not all satisfaction results from interpersonal rewards, nor is increased performance the only avenue of reciprocation. Even recognizing these limitations, the proposition that satisfaction causes performance is clearly consonant with the underlying premise. Does the empirical literature justify this extrapolation?

Brayfield and Crockett (4) reviewed studies correlating job satisfaction with performance, concluding that:

> there is little evidence that employee attitudes of the type usually measured in morale surveys bear any simple—or, for that matter, appreciable—relationship to performance on the job.

Vroom's (28) review of 23 studies found a median correlation of .14, echoing the same conclusion. Taken together, these two reviews were thought to have pretty well settled the issue. Nevertheless, several points might temper one's conclusion from those reviews:

1. Of the 23 studies reviewed by Vroom, only three yielded negative correlations, one of which was −.03. In the absence of any functional relationship between satisfaction and performance (ignoring for the moment the direction of causality), the probability of ob-

taining 20 positive correlations by chance out of 23 studies would be only .0002.

2. Correlations in the range of .10–.30, which characterize the majority of the studies reviewed by Brayfield and Crockett and Vroom, are dismissed as insufficient evidence to warrant continued consideration of the satisfaction-performance caused link. Yet anyone who follows the empirical literature knows that correlations of such magnitude dot the landscape of the behavioral sciences. Especially when statistically significant, correlations greater than .20 usually signal the continued exploration and analysis of relationships measured at that level (and, of course, boundary conditions within which the relationship holds). Rarely can researchers account for more than 10 percent of the variance in a criterion by a single variable, except in the testing of propositions that verge on the tautological or that are hopelessly confounded by method variance (e.g., by response set when two or more variables are measured by responses from the same source).

Even if the consistent, albeit small, positive correlations between satisfaction and performance are taken as evidence of a relationship, they do not constitute support for any particular causal interpretation. Lawler and Porter (20) find a more plausible and convincing causal model in a scheme in which satisfaction follows from rewards, which in turn are preceded by performance with varying degrees of fit, depending on how closely rewards are tied to level of performance. Thus, a number of crosslagged correlational studies—taking measures of performance, satisfaction, and rewards at two different points in time—have been conducted in an attempt to sort out the magnitudes of the various causal relationships that might contribute to a single static correlation between satisfaction and performance.

The guiding spirit behind these and similar studies seems to have been to pit competing theories (i.e., satisfaction-causes-performance vs. performance-rewards-satisfaction) against one another, to find which one received the more support, and declare a winner. If one must pick a single theory, a reasonable assessment of the evidence probably tilts more toward the performance-rewards-satisfaction model. But the contention here is that one need not view these contrasting approaches as running a horse race; there is no reason why attraction to either one excludes the other from consideration. *Both* relationships may exist, in varying degrees of mix from one situation to another. And the reference here is not simply to the feedback mechanism by which satisfaction from previously attained performance-contingent rewards increases the likelihood of future performance, but also the situation in which rewards first granted on a "noncontingent"[1] basis evoke desired behavior in the future as a reciprocal exchange for such rewards.

The Exchange Model and the Environment. If a primitive equity-in-social exchange model contains the logic for an assertion that degree of satisfaction (from interpersonal rewards) may cause level of performance (as measured by objective criteria or supervisory ratings), and if a modicum of evidence supports this position, can that same intuitive model account for other consistent findings in the work environment? It is consistent with the finding that satisfaction generally correlates negatively with unexcused absences; regular attendance may represent an aspect of performance which individuals deem an appropriate reciprocal exchange for rewards previously received. Organizational psychologists have been more willing to admit a causal connection between satisfaction and absenteeism than between satisfaction and performance, even though the correlations obtained in testing the former relationship are neither much greater nor markedly more consistent than those found in researching the latter relationship (cf. Vroom, 28, 178–186).

The social exchange framework could also account for the historic findings by Fleishman (8) that consideration in supervisory behavior reliably predicted the number of grievances processed by subordinates. It explains why Patchen (22) found that, on important decisions, participants tend to defer to those *most affected* by the decision—in order to receive similar deference on future decisions with whose consequences *they* must live.

As Herman (13) pointed out in a cogent analysis of job attitude-behavior relationships, measures of satisfaction or other job attitudes are constructed to maximize the amount of variance they permit, while "situational contingencies may restrict the possible variance on the performance measure." In other words, the design of many tasks in organizations reflects an objective of constraining the variability of task performance among individuals. Technology often tends to exert a leveling effect such that the amount of work to be done per unit time and per person holds roughly constant or varies only within a narrow range. When this is the case, performance—in the objective or quantitative sense—is limited in the opportunity it affords participants to reciprocate rewards from organizational officials; participants, to the extent they actually do wish to reciprocate, must choose other types of work behavior.

---

[1] It is doubtful that anyone ever dispenses a reward on a purely "noncontingent" basis; the reward is presumably contingent on some response by the recipient, if nothing other than physical presence. The word "noncontingent" here signifies rewards given in advance of the behavior which they might evoke.

In numerous situations, outstanding performance or productivity, beyond some minimally acceptable level, is of relatively little interest to organizational officials. They may be more desirous of such things as regular attendance, predictability, following the rules, "not making waves," avoidance of hassles, cooperation, and generalized tendencies toward compliance. Certainly such behaviors represent the glue which holds collective endeavors together, and they are the behaviors about which Roethlisberger and Dickson (23) and Gardner (10) seemed more concerned as a function of "sentiments." In short, whoever first voiced agreement with the proposition that satisfaction affects performance might not have been limiting the concept of performance to a narrow definition of the sort usually measured by industrial psychologists.

Social Exchange and Reciprocity. Contemporary theoretical and empirical study of social exchange has identified some limiting conditions under which reward-produced satisfaction generates reciprocity or equity-striving behavior by recipients. If Human Relations thinking is to be faulted it would be for failing to take these boundaries into account. One such boundary condition, identified by Brehm (5), is the perception by recipients that their behavioral freedom has been unreasonably threatened by obligations foisted upon them. In such a case, their response is likely to be psychological reactance–deliberately avoiding, or even behaving contrary to, reciprocity effecting responses. For example, the perception by recipients of benefactors' manipulative intent is likely to evoke psychological reactance. Organ (21) has shown that the degree of surveillance accompanying conferral of social gifts is one determinant of whether reciprocity or reactance characterizes subordinate responses.

Another boundary condition is the recipient's attribution of volition to the giver. Only social gifts which the benefactor is seen as capable of withholding are deemed as mandating reciprocity. Thus, one would expect that in unionized organizations, satisfaction produced by extrinsic rewards would not produce the same degree of reciprocity in behavior as in non-union organizations. Similarly, social rewards under the personal control of superiors would likely effect more reciprocity than those administered by company policy on an impersonal basis.

Furthermore, as Blau (3) notes:

> regular rewards create expectations that redefine the baseline in terms of which positive sanctions are distinguished from negative ones.

That is, rewards which once exerted obligatory holds on persons may do so decreasingly as they begin to be perceived as "rights." A corollary derivable from this principle is that organizational participants may show greater degrees of reciprocity for prior rewards in the early stages of their tenure than in later stages. A study reviewed by Brayfield and Crockett (4) found a significant positive correlation between satisfaction and performance for inexperienced and untrained women, but an insignificant correlation for women with longer tenure. Wanous's (30) finding that extrinsic rewards significantly predicted later performance came from a sample of newly hired telephone operators, and Schiemann's (26) similar findings drew from a sample of management trainees. Schein (25) argued that one mechanism for securing commitment from new organization members is to shower them with such lavish gifts of time and perquisites that they feel guilty if they do not reciprocate with loyalty and hard work.

Ultimately equity in social exchange is a perceptual matter, defined by private and idiosyncratic evaluations of the individual. This consideration complicates formulation of precise behavioral predictions from a social exchange conceptual framework. Individuals differ in what they regard as appropriate repayment of social gifts, in the time horizon appropriate for achieving equity, in their capacity for perceptual distortion of the intents and attributions of the benefactor, and, perhaps even more generally, in sensitivity to social exchange morality. Identification of the personality dimensions which subsume such differences should lend greater predictive power to a social exchange-equity framework and enhance its viability as a general theory of organizational behavior.

Reconsideration of Reciprocity in the Context of the Hypothesis. The satisfaction-causes-performance hypothesis, then, merits reconsideration in the perspective which views reciprocity as a normative determinant of much behavior in organizations. This perspective is not fully developed, either theoretically or empirically. It requires conceptual development and systematic research along several dimensions.

There is a need to know what types of satisfiers evoke feelings of obligation and how these vary as a function of different kinds of organizational environments. In addition, there is a need to identify which behaviors organization officials perceive as appropriate and desirable forms of reciprocation, and how such perceptions are affected by contextual factors—e.g., the range of individual production that is possible due to technological or job design constraints, the costs of absenteeism or turnover, threats posed by powerful unions, the types of pressures exerted on the immediate superior, and so on. Subordinate perceptions of what behaviors qualify as reciprocation are also important; these may not conform to the expectations of superiors due to contextual variables such as group norms, the history of labor-management politics and relationships, the physical or psychological costs of such behaviors, or conflicts with professional credo.

Finally, there is a need to explore the alternatives to reciprocation, especially in the case where a salient mode of reciprocation is not viable. Blau (3) identifies status-enhancement of the benefactor as the most probable consequence. But the aversion of indebtedness may prompt other coping techniques, such as derogation of the value of the benefaction, minimizing the cost to the benefactor of supplying the benefaction, or avoiding as far as possible any future interaction with the benefactor.

Conclusion

The skeptic may contend that any conceptual approach which predicts desired behavior as following from noncontingent rewards is bankrupt from the start, because it flies in the face of known operant principles. But this objection would rest on an unnecessarily narrow and short-sighted application of reinforcement processes. From childhood persons are rewarded by socializing agents for demonstrating equity in interpersonal relationships and often punished (e.g., by withholding of approval) for not so doing. That such conditioning occurs on an aperiodic rather than perfectly consistent basis only strengthens the tendency for such behavior to occur long after it has ceased to generate explicit social rewards. Intermittent schedules of reinforcement produce a resistance to extinction which, even in lower organisms, may endure for years. Of course, individuals differ in the nature of their prior reinforcement histories in this regard.

In summary, the argument here is that the satisfaction-causes-performance notion and the "Human Relations" syndrome which it connotes deserve more judicious consideration than recently accorded it. Results of empirical research, while hardly lending a ringing confirmation, are sufficiently equivocal to justify an open mind on the issue. The proposition can be deduced, with some qualifications, from a respectable and tractable conceptual framework, a crude layman's version of which probably gave birth to the idea. Rather than prematurely burying this idea, one should set it in proper perspective and glimpse whatever truths it might imperfectly reflect.

Scientific inquiry has traditionally been governed, at least in lip service, by the heuristic of conservatism. This principle is interpreted to mean, among other things, that the null hypothesis is given the benefit of a doubt and that we err on the cautious side in endorsing the validity of propositions. In the behavioral sciences, the principle of conservatism might also be taken as putting the burden of proof on the behavioral scientists in their repudiation of folk-style psychology. This is not to say that folk-style psychology itself constitutes scientific knowledge, but rather that it arises from some kind of mute logic and phenomenology. The full understanding of this logic and phenomenology is itself a task of the behavioral sciences.

REFERENCES

1. Adams, J. S.   Inequity in social exchange. In L. Berkowitz (Ed), *Advances in experimental social psychology*, vol. 2. New York: Academic Press, 1965.

2. Alwin, D. F.   Making inferences from attitude-behavior correlations. *Sociometry*, 1973, *36*, 253–278.

3. Blau, P. M.   *Exchange and power in social life.* New York: Wiley, 1967.

4. Brayfield, A. H., & Crockett, W. H.   Employee attitudes and employee performance. *Psychological Bulletin*, 1955, *52*, 396–424.

5. Brehm, J. W.   *A Theory of psychological reactance.* New York: Academic Press, 1966.

6. Brown, B. R.   The effects of effort to maintain face on interpersonal bargaining. *Journal of Experimental Social Psychology*, 1968, *4*, 107–122.

7. Cherrington, D. L., Reitz, H. J., & Scott, W. E., Jr.   Effects of contingent and noncontingent reward on the relationship between satisfaction and task performance. *Journal of Applied Psychology*, 1971, *55*, 531–537.

8. Fleishman, E. A.   Twenty years of consideration and structure. In E. A. Fleishman & J. G. Hunt (Eds.), *Current developments in the study of leadership*. Carbondale, Ill.: Southern Illinois University Press, 1973.

9. Gannon, M. J., & Noon, J. P.   Management's critical deficiency. *Business Horizons*, 1971, *14*, 49–56.

10. Gardner, B. B.   *Human relations in industry*. Chicago: Richard D. Irwin, Inc., 1945.

11. Gouldner, A. W.   The norm of reciprocity: A preliminary statement. *American Sociological Review*, 1960, *25*, 161–178.

12. Green, C. N.   Causal connections among managers' merit pay, job satisfaction, and performance. *Journal of applied psychology*, 1973, *58*, 95–100.

13. Herman, J. B.   Are situational contingencies limiting job attitude-job performance relationships? *Organizational Behavior and Human Performance*, 1973, *10*, 208–224.

14. Herzberg, F. (Ed.).   *Job attitudes: review of research and opinion*. Pittsburgh, Pa.: Psychological Service of Pittsburgh, 1955.

15. Homans, G. C.   *Social behavior: Its elementary forms*. New York: Harcourt, Brace and World, 1961.

16. Katz, D., Maccoby, N., Gurin, G., & Floor, L. G. *Productivity, supervision and morale among railroad workers*. Ann Arbor: University of Michigan Survey Research Center, 1951.

17. Katz, D., Maccoby, N., & Morse, N. *Productivity, supervision and morale in an office situation*. Ann Arbor: University of Michigan Survey Research Center, 1950.

18. Kesselman, G. A., Wood, M. T., & Hagen, E. L. Relationships between performance and satisfaction under contingent and noncontingent reward systems. *Journal of Applied Psychology*, 1974, 59, 374–376.

19. Kornhauser, A., & Sharp, A. Employee attitudes: Suggestions from a study in a factory. *Personnel Journal*, 1932, 10, 393–404.

20. Lawler, E. E., III, & Porter, L. W. The effect of performance on job satisfaction. *Industrial Relations*, 1967, 7, 20–28.

21. Organ, D. W. Social exchange and psychological reactance in a simulated superior-subordinate relationship. *Organizational Behavior and Human Performance*, 1974, 12, 132–142.

22. Patchen, M. The locus and basis of influence on organizational decisions. *Organizational Behavior and Human Performance*, 1974, 11, 195–221.

23. Roethlisburger, F. J., & Dickson, W. J. *Management and the worker*. New York: Wiley, Science Editions, 1964.

24. Saltonstall, R. *Human relations in administration*. New York: McGraw-Hill, 1959.

25. Schein, E. H. Organizational socialization and the profession of management. *Industrial Management Review*, 1968. Reprinted in H. L. Tosi & W. C. Hamner (Eds.), *Organizational behavior and management*. Chicago: St. Clair Press, 1974.

26. Schiemann, W. A. Satisfaction-rewards-performance: Review of the literature a causal analysis. Paper presented at the meeting of the Midwestern Psychological Association, Chicago, April 1975.

27. Schwab, D. P., and Cummings, L. L. Theories of performance and satisfaction: A review. *Industrial Relations*, 1970, 9, 408–430.

28. Vroom, V. H. *Work and motivation*. New York: Wiley, 1964.

29. Walster, E., Berscheid, E., & Walster, G. W. New directions in equity research. *Journal of Personality and Social Psychology*, 1973, 25, 151–176.

30. Wanous, J. P. A Causal-correlational analysis of the job satisfaction and performance relationship. *Journal of applied psychology*, 1974, 59, 139–144.

B. INTERVENTIONS

Introduction

Theoretical models of job motivation have inspired a variety of formal programs aimed at increasing the effectiveness and productivity of employee performance. Of these programs those centered around behavior modification, job redesign, and goal-setting have found widespread application. They have also aroused spirited debates among managers and behavioral scientists who represent competing philosophical and ideological perspectives upon worker motivation.

Lawrence Miller, a consultant who helps organizations design programs of employee behavior modification, provides a brief sketch of the essential steps in such programs. Behavior modification represents a practical application of operant concepts and methods, as found in the writings of B. F. Skinner and the work of other "neo-behaviorist" psychologists influenced by Skinner. The techniques of behavior modification do not presuppose any particular classes of "motives" or other internal psychological states. Rather, they provide a straightforward self-correcting method of arranging the immediate antecedents and consequences of specific behaviors so as to strengthen those behaviors.

The article from *Organizational Dynamics* reports the experience of Emery Air Freight with a behavior modification program. As of the date of this report, the company had a very positive experience using this approach. However, not all instances of behavior modification in work organizations have met with resounding success. Some attempts have proved abortive, not because of any flaw inherent in operant precepts, but due to naive or shortsighted use of these techniques without taking the larger context into analysis.

Programs of job redesign—variously termed "job enlargement" and "job enrichment"—seek to increase the role of "intrinsic" rewards from work. These programs restructure jobs so as to permit greater scope for worker autonomy, responsibility, and sense of achievement. Another selection from *Organizational Dynamics* assesses the practical gains from such approaches, with particular reference to some European firms that have experimented on a large scale with them.

Latham and Baldes report the outcomes of an applied motivational program using a fairly simple method of goal setting. For many years, a number of organizations have used this method for their managerial personnel in the context of a larger program known as management by objectives (MBO); Edwin A. Locke, through laboratory research, has developed the conceptual framework for predicting the effects of different types of goals and goal-setting processes. Increasingly, organizations have sought to exploit the benefits of goal setting at the operative level, in the fashion illustrated by Latham and Baldes.

The reader needs no research reports to know that organizations have tried many schemes of incentive pay based on performance in order to motivate employees. Deci argues that, on some jobs, this may have the unintended effect of simply replacing one form of motivation with another, rather than increasing the total motivational force. His argument comes from a cognitive evaluation approach to task motivation. This approach suggests that intrinsic motivation depends upon our perceptions of whether we act as "origins" or "pawns" in responding to a task. To the extent that we attribute our efforts to external inducements, we regard the task as less appealing. While this theoretical approach has been a matter of much controversy, the experiments inspired by it have fairly consistently shown that, for whatever reason, pay incentive contingent upon performance can have nonobvious and possibly undesired effects in the longer run.

10

Behavior Management

The advantage of the behavior management approach to changing performance is well illustrated by an incident that occurred on an airplane a few years back. One of our consultants sat next to the president of a medium-sized corporation. They began talking, and the consultant described the type of service he performed. The president responded by noting that he could really use some help with his senior vice president. He described this vice president as having a very bad attitude, which had persisted for several months. Our consultant asked "What does this vice president do that causes you to feel that he has a bad attitude?" The president thought for a while and then responded, "Well, whenever I give him a report to read, I never hear back from him. And when I do, he's always so critical." It was agreed that there was nothing else that this vice president did to manifest his bad attitude and that if these behaviors were to change it would indicate an improvement in attitude. Our consultant then made some specific recommendations involving measurement and techniques of feedback that would be likely to alter the rates of the problem behaviors.

The president was able to understand and implement a few relatively quick and simple procedures to alter these specific behaviors. The problem of his vice president's "bad attitude" had become a simple and relatively easy matter to improve. This is the essence of the direct approach to behavior change in the workplace.

DIRECT, EXTERNAL APPROACH TO BEHAVIOR

The direct or external approach to changing behavior has gained increasing acceptance and adherence over the past 10 to 20 years. This direct approach is also referred to as the behavioral model, behaviorism, behavior modification, or behavior management. All these terms refer to the behavior change techniques based on the effects of environmental events, stimuli, without reference to explanations of mental conditions, states, motivations, needs, or drives. Behavior management does not deny that internal states exist. Whether internal states exist or not is irrelevant. The question is can behavior be changed and predicted from changes in the external environment? The research overwhelmingly demonstrates that the answer is affirmative (*Journal of Applied Behavior Analysis*, 1967–1977).

The differences between the direct and indirect approaches to improving human performance in organizations can be summarized in the following four points:

1. The *change in behavior is explained as a direct function of the changes* in the environment, rather than as a change in an internal motivation or need that in turn causes a change in behavior. Behavior management studies the specific conditions that exist in the individual's environment, alters those conditions, and measures the subsequent change in behavior.

2. *Evaluation of the effort to improve performance is based on the direct measurement of behavior and its results.* The indirect approaches have relied heavily on measures of attitude and satisfaction.

These internal conditions are generally assessed by the use of attitude questionnaires. Behavior management does not consider the responses to questionnaires significant when the goal behaviors of concern, such as rates of work, attendance, and on-time arrivals to work, can be measured directly.

Goals for behavior management are stated in terms of increasing or decreasing rates of behavior or the product of behavior. The ongoing measurement of behavior is an essential element of every behavior management effort. Because of this direct measurement and because goals are stated in terms of increasing or decreasing behavior, the evaluation mechanism is built into every project. Economic evaluation of these projects becomes relatively simple and direct.

3. *Behavior management is a technique of management.* Behavior management is not a theory to which managers should attempt to conform because it is a correct theory of human nature. It is a technique designed to assist the manager in achieving his goals and should be applied to aid the organization in accomplishing the specific goals that define its productivity. It may be applied to improve the quality of products, reduce absenteeism or turnover and increase output measures, sales, new business development, and increase other specific contributions of managers and employees. The manager should have specific, measurable objectives in mind before implementing a behavior change effort.

4. *The direct approach is more acceptable and receives a more favorable response from the manager because it is focused on his*

objectives, for it provides him with a procedure for directly affecting the achievement of his objectives and demonstrates observable results in a relatively short period of time. Because of these factors and the compatibility of the direct approach with the "business of managing," the manager is more favorably disposed toward performance improvement efforts.

Behavior management is a nontheory of behavior (Skinner, 1950). It is the study and application of what works. Its development is based on empirical research. It did not start with a grand theory of human nature. Simple questions were asked and tested. Why does one specific behavior increase or decrease? How is a behavior acquired, or why does a behavior decrease? Highly controlled laboratory studies were conducted to answer these questions. As these questions have been answered through data collection and analysis, a set of principles has developed. The goal of behavior management is to discover lawful relationships. Investigation has determined that some lawful relationships between environmental events and behavior do exist, much as the study of physics has determined that larger bodies tend to attract smaller bodies.

Whereas the historical evolution of behavior management is undoubtedly of secondary interest to most managers, a brief review of its development may help in understanding its principles.

The development of the science of behavior involved dozens of individual researchers; however, the work of the following men represents the most essential contributions: John B. Watson, Edward L. Thorndike, and B. F. Skinner.

John B. Watson

John B. Watson, more than any other single individual, is responsible for the initiation of behaviorism and for its first applications to business. Watson believed that all behavior was explainable as a function of stimuli that preceded the behavior. The so-called Stimulus-Response (S–R) model is the result of Watson's work. Watson described the purpose of his work in the following passage:

> Behaviorism, as I tried to develop it in my lectures at Columbia in 1912 and in my earliest writings, was an attempt to do one thing—apply to the experimental study of man the same kind of procedure and the same language of description that many research men had found useful for so many years in the study of animals lower than man. We believed then, as we do now, that man is an animal different from other animals only in the types of behavior he displays (Watson, 1920).

Before Watson psychology had been dominated by the internal approach, and he challenged its advocates to demonstrate the effects of their work and to apply the methods of empirical science. Watson demonstrated that human behavior could be studied scientifically and that it occurred in predictable patterns relative to conditions in the environment.

Perhaps Watson's most famous experiment, the one that led him to some of his conclusions, involved Little Albert, an 11-month-old boy who had become friendly with a white rat (Watson, 1920). Although this experiment was highly questionable from an ethical point of view, it did demonstrate some important principles of behavior. Watson decided that he would try to condition the response of fear in poor Little Albert. He attempted to pair a number of different stimuli with the white rat to condition a fear of the rat. He tried scaring Little Albert with a mask, a dog, a monkey, burning newspapers and other stimuli that might elicit the fear response. Albert was not impressed by any of these. Finally, Watson created a loud noise by hitting an iron bar with a hammer behind Little Albert's head. This succeeded in sending Albert into a screaming fit. Watson then paired the frightening stimulus of the loud noise with the white rat. Every time Albert was permitted to see his little white friend, he was startled by the loud noise. Eventually the sight of the white rat, by itself, created the fear and caused poor Little Albert to cry.

In addition to showing that fears may be caused by conditions of the environment, this experiment demonstrated the principle of generalization. The newly acquired fear of the white rat generalized to other furry objects. Albert was now afraid of a dog, a rabbit, and even a Santa Claus mask. At Albert's expense some of the most basic forms of emotional learning had been demonstrated. (In Watson's defense it must be reported that he demonstrated that Albert could be deconditioned or unlearn these same fears.)

Watson limited his investigation to the relationship between preceding stimuli and subsequent behavior. For this reason the relationship he described is referred to as the Stimulus–Response (S–R) model. He believed that all behavior could be explained in terms of eliciting stimuli that occurred some time before the behavior. Although this explanation is no longer considered sufficient to explain all forms of learning, it did lay the foundation for the empirical investigation of human learning.

Watson defined the "behaviorists' platform":

> The behaviorist asks why don't we make what we can observe the real field of psychology? Let us limit ourselves to things that can be observed, and formulate laws concerning only those things. Now what can we observe? We can observe behavior—what the organism does or says.

And let us point out at once: that saying is doing—that is behaving. Speaking overtly or to ourselves (thinking) is just as objective a type of behavior as baseball (Watson, 1924).

Edward L. Thorndike

While Watson was pursuing the study of the effect of preceding stimuli on behavior, E. L. Thorndike was developing his Law of Effect (Thorndike, 1913). He placed small animals such as cats, dogs, and chickens in "puzzle boxes" from which they learned to escape. There was an exit door to the box that could be opened by manipulating a lever. The animals were deprived of food until they managed to open the door. They obtained food, their reinforcer, after they managed to manipulate the lever and open the door. Thorndike found that the animal's speed of opening the door increased following experience. The animals were learning. From these experiments Thorndike formulated his Law of Effect:

> When a modifiable connection between a situation and a response is made and is accompanied or followed by a satisfying state of affairs, that connection's strength is increased: when made and accompanied or followed by an annoying state of affairs, its strength is decreased.

Thorndike accepted Watson's stimulus–response relationship but added that these relationships are strengthened as a function of the consequences that follow the behavior. Thorndike also argued that the effects or consequences of a behavior are direct and do not need to be explained in terms of mediating processes such as thought. The behavior is increased or decreased as a direct effect of the consequence.

B. F. Skinner

B. F. Skinner has been acclaimed by the American Psychological Association as the most influential living psychologist, and he is without a doubt the most controversial. Skinner's contributions to the development of psychology as a science and as a means of improving human behavior are tremendous but difficult to categorize. Many cannot be as clearly defined as his own science would require. Four of the more significant are (1) his development and articulation of a technology of empirical investigation of behavior, (2) his distinction between operant and respondent behavior, (3) his development of the concept of "contingencies of reinforcement," and (4) his advocacy of behavior change and cultural design based on the empirical analysis of behavior.

Empirical Investigation.   Skinner is the antitheorist. Whereas the results of his research may be termed a theory of behavior, he opposed the formulation of theories of human behavior. Skinner (1950) argues that the empirical data from the direct observation of behavior and its environment are a sufficient source of knowledge and that no interpretative theories are necessary. Skinner defined terms empirically. For example, reinforcement is defined as the presentation or removal of a stimulus, resulting in an increase in the rate of a response. It is defined by its effect on the behavior; reinforcement increases the rate of behavior. It is impossible, therefore, to say that an event is reinforcing unless an increase in the rate of a behavior can be demonstrated.

Skinner developed the language of the empirical investigation of behavior. All sciences require clear definition of terms to enable investigation to proceed in an orderly fashion. The definition of the language of behaviorism is one of Skinner's most significant contributions.

Skinner also provided a framework for behavioral research. He divided his observations into those concerned with independent variables (factors that affect a behavior and that can be managed in such a way as to cause a change in behavior) and the dependent variables (the behaviors affected by the independent variable). Skinner is concerned with discovering the specific relationships or "functional relationships" between the dependent and independent variables.

The essential elements of Skinner's system are summarized in the following table:

Independent Variables

Type of reinforcement or punishment
Schedule of reinforcement or punishment

Dependent Variables

Rate of responding
Rate of acquiring a new response
Rate of extinction

At least as great as any technical innovations Skinner may have contributed is the general approach toward his subject that he promoted. This "attitude of science" is the single most distinguishing feature of the direct approach to behavior change.

> Science is first of all a set of attitudes. It is a disposition to deal with the facts rather than with what someone has said about them. . . . Science is a willingness to accept facts even when they are opposed to wishes. . . . The opposite of wishful thinking is intellectual honesty. . . . Scientists

have simply found that being honest—with oneself as much as with others—is essential to progress. Experiments do not always come out as one expects, but the facts must stand and the expectations fall. The subject matter, not the scientist, knows best (Skinner, 1953).

Operant and Respondent Behavior. Skinner defined types of behavior according to the manner in which they are acquired and maintained. Respondent behaviors are those *elicited* by a stimulus and are acquired through the procedures of "classical conditioning," the pairing of an unconditioned stimulus with a conditioned stimulus. Operant behaviors are those that are *emitted* by the organism and that act on the environment. They result in reinforcement. In other words, in respondent behavior, the organism reacts to the environment, while in operant behavior the response acts on the environment.

Skinner defined and studied operant behavior. He argued that most of the behaviors performed by any organism, human or animal, are operant behaviors and may be explained by an analysis of the reinforcements that have resulted from the operant behavior's acting on the environment. For example, the behavior of coming to work results in social approval, payment of money, and other reinforcers that maintain the performance of this behavior. If the behavior of coming to work did not act on the environment, if there were no consequences resulting from it, the operant of coming to work would extinguish; that is, it would cease to occur.

The "Contingencies of Reinforcement." The relationships between the behavior of an individual and the environment are described by Skinner as the contingencies of reinforcement:

> An adequate formulation of the interaction between an organism and its environment must always specify three things: (1) the occasion upon which a response occurs, (2) the response itself, and (3) the reinforcing consequences. The interrelationships among them are the "contingencies of reinforcement" (Skinner, 1969).

The contingencies between behavior and environment are often stated in terms of an if–then relationship. If *A* occurs, then *B* will follow. If I finish this chapter on time, I can go to the beach this weekend. If you increase the number of customers on whom you call, then you will increase your commissions. If Johnny finishes his homework by eight o'clock, he may watch television for one hour.

Our world is composed of our behavior and the reaction of the environment to our behavior. These contingencies of reinforcement are the structure within which we live, the relationships that may explain our slow rate of learning, our feelings of depression, or our overeating. Skinner laid the foundation for the analysis of the contingencies of reinforcement.

FIGURE 1
The Contingencies of Reinforcement

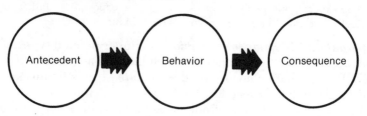

Advocacy of Behavior Change and Cultural Design. Many of Skinner's writings are not scientific. Most notably his well-known novel *Walden II* and his more recent *Beyond Freedom* and *Dignity* have gone beyond his data to propose applications of the science of behavior to social problems. Unfortunately, this advocacy has led to serious misunderstandings of the science of behavior and of his own positions in regard to this science. Skinner has devoted the greatest portion of his most recent book *About Behaviorism* to answering these criticisms and misunderstandings.

Skinner desired to create public debate on the social and cultural application of behavior change, and he has undoubtedly succeeded. If, however, the degree to which his recent writings have been misunderstood is an indication of his success at communicating his ideas, he has not been entirely successful. Perhaps the greatest controversy followed his publication of *Beyond Freedom and Dignity*. Contrary to the misinterpretation of many, Skinner does not argue against freedom. He is very much in favor of freedom and increasing individual freedom. He does, however, argue that the popular comprehension and the literature of freedom have hindered the progress of our culture. Skinner argues that mankind is not free in the sense of being autonomous and free from influence. On the contrary, Skinner argues that mankind's behavior is controlled by his environmental conditioning, and freedom must, therefore, be viewed in the context of this environmental control. He believes that mankind reacts negatively to aversive or negative control such as would be imposed by a dictator. These forms of control characterized by the threat of punishment are the ones we fear. Forms of control based on positive reinforcement are the ones that we least notice and that are most desirable. Skinner argues that these forms, already present in our environment, should be carefully studied and used to create a society that results in the greatest benefit.

Skinner's outspoken advocacy of the application of his techniques to cultural design has created considerable debate because these techniques contradict the popular view and require a reexamination of accepted beliefs and habits. As has been the case at previous periods in human history, positions that contradict popular understandings of the human condition and that are supported by empirically gathered data have resulted in significant changes in the course of human history. The work of Galileo and Darwin resulted in similar controversy, change of traditional views, and eventual progress. Only future generations will be able to assess Skinner's final contribution to the understanding of the human condition.

DOES BEHAVIOR MANAGEMENT WORK IN ORGANIZATIONS?

Behavior management is the result of the trial-and-error applications of operant conditioning principles in the work setting. Does it work? This is the question that Skinner would hope we would ask. Behavior management has been systematically applied in the business and industrial settings only during the past few years. The contingencies of reinforcement have, however, been operating since the first person began working. All work behavior, regardless of the system or philosophy of management in effect, is explainable by analyzing the contingencies of reinforcement and may be changed by altering these contingencies.

The argument is often made that changing behavior in the work setting is not as simple as in the laboratory, classroom, or mental hospital. This is certainly true, and the complexity of the contingencies operating in the workplace is one of the primary reasons why application to organizations has not been more extensive. But behavior management has demonstrated its ability to change behavior, both in the workplace and other settings. It is the task of this book to present some of the results, as well as the principles and techniques of behavior management.

Behavior management systems are currently in use in more than fifty major corporations that I know of, and probably many more. Among the corporations now using these programs are the 3M Corporation, Western Electric, Westinghouse, Airco Alloys, Inc., Milliken & Company, General Mills, AT&T, Dart Industries, Inc., Pennwalt Corporation, Emery Air Freight, Questor Corporation, Ford Motor Company, American Can, Connecticut General Life Insurance Company, General Electric, Weyerhaeuser Company, and numerous others.

The application of behavior management to industrial organizations may be the best kept secret in management today. Most companies have no desire to advertise the techniques they are using or the results they have received. Nonetheless, a sampling of results leaves one wondering why there is not more discussion of these techniques in management publications and why more systematic research has not been conducted. The following are a few of the documented results witnessed during the past few years:

- One of the largest textile firms in the country has reported savings or earnings of approximately $20 million that can be directly attributed to behavior management programs.
- A midwestern plant of one of the major corporations listed in the preceding paragraph has reported that their cost accountants have attributed $600,000 in annual cost reductions to a behavior management effort that cost approximately $700,00 to implement.
- A textile-finishing plant that had been having a number of serious personnel problems implemented a six-month behavior management training program, and a year later the plant set a record for attendance—down to 0.9 percent absenteeism for eight weeks running. This same plant boosted quality, savings to $25,000 per week over the same eight-week period.
- The City of Detroit Garbage Collectors instituted a behavior management program in which efficiency was reinforced with bonuses to the garbage collectors. The city saved $1,654,000 during the first year, after bonuses of $307,000 were paid to the collectors.
- ACDC Electronics Division of Emerson Electronics, instituting a program to improve attendance, met engineering specifications and production objectives. Profits increased 25 percent over forecast; costs were reduced by $550,000, and they received a return on investment, including consultant fees, of 1,900 percent.
- B. F. Goodrich Chemical Company started a program to meet production schedules and increased production by 300 percent.
- Emery Air Freight has instituted numerous programs since 1969 and attributes direct savings of more than $3 million to behavior management.
- Waste in the spinning department of a carpet mill was identified as an area in need of improvement. By posting feedback data and providing verbal reinforcement and small tangible reinforcements, waste variance was reduced from $1,153 per week to $437 per week—an annualized savings of $37,232.
- A thorough analysis of the cost benefit of one behavior management program in one textile plant demonstrated improvements in plant turnover ($102,000 savings); finishing department efficiency ($32,895 savings); attendance ($26,457 savings); quality ($29,725 savings); sewing department efficiency ($15,158 savings); attendance in the sewing department ($27,333 savings); for a total plant-wide annual savings of $233,369.

- A major textile firm began several programs with their trucking operations. One involved reducing the average time that loaded trailers wait for a tractor. The time was reduced from an average 67 minutes to between 35 to 40 minutes. This program is in operation in 42 plants and has reported savings in excess of $1 million.

The results here are only a small sample of those obtained. Each of these programs specified behaviors to be changed, altered specific environmental contingencies, and measured the changes in behavior and corresponding outcomes in terms of productivity, and so forth. In each of these programs environmental contingencies were complex, though the ones changed were relatively simple. While there may be a dozen consequences to our behavior (such as quitting a job or remaining on a job), one consequence may change the course of our actions (such as a raise or a compliment by our boss). It is not necessary to understand all the complexities of environmental influence to put the technology of behavior management to work. It is necessary only to identify clearly the behavior to be changed, the consequence to be altered, and measure the rate of the behavior before and after the consequence is changed. The result, in terms of an increase or decrease in the rate of behavior, indicates whether or not the procedure is working.

More than 20,000 managers and supervisors have been trained in the application of behavior management during the past five years by just one consulting firm specializing in it. All of these managers or supervisors have used behavior change projects as a routine part of their job. Most of these projects have followed a four-step process that has become known as the "cookbook" method of behavior management. This method, while deceptively simple, contains the basic ingredients of operant conditioning as applied to the work situation. These four steps are *pinpoint, record, consequate, evaluate* (Miller, 1974) and include the following:

- *Pinpoint:* The manager must identify and define the specific behavior or behaviors he wishes to change. A behavior is pinpointed when it may be accurately and reliably observed and recorded. For example, "working slowly" is not pinpointed. Completing "43 work units per eight-hour day" is. Similarly, "having a good attitude" is not pinpointed; "smiling at least once during each conversation with another person" is. The ability to specify behavior in pinpointed terms is both a necessary first skill for the manager who wishes to increase his ability to manage his employee's (or his own) behavior and a skill that requires a major change in the behavior pattern of most industrial supervisors.

- *Record:* The manager is asked to count the occurrence of the pinpointed behavior or some result of it. The frequency is to be recorded before any effort is made to change the behavior. This is for establishing baseline data. These data serve as the means of evaluating the behavior change strategy to be implemented after their establishment. The manager generally graphs these data to determine whether the frequency of the behavior is increasing, decreasing, or remaining the same. The establishment of baseline data before the initiation of a change procedure is a fundamental practice of the scientist that has been adopted with no great difficulty by the line manager and supervisor, who often have less than a high school education. The value of knowing where you have been, where you want to get to, and when you have arrived is understood by most individuals of good sense.

- *Consequate:* To consequate a behavior is to arrange for a consequence to follow it. The manager is encouraged to arrange a "reinforcing consequence," one that results in an increase in the rate of the desired performance. The reinforcing consequence most commonly used in behavior management is visualized feedback or knowledge of results. Managers often use the graph of the baseline data they have plotted to illustrate a goal level of performance and either post the graph in a visible location in the work area or personally show it to the worker whose performance is being recorded. The supervisor pairs verbal praise and approval with the visual feedback. This simple procedure has been used literally thousands of times to increase individual workers' productivity. Other reinforcers are raffle tickets, time off, job changes, letters of recognition, or anything else that may prove meaningful to the employee. A consequence may also include a "punisher," an event that results in the decreased rate of behavior. Managers have been taught the empirical meaning and effective use of punishment as a management procedure. Punishment, which is used only when reinforcement does not work, usually involves the least drastic punishing consequence available. A consequence may also involve the removal of a reinforcer that may be maintaining the performance of an undesirable behavior. The emphasis in most behavior management programs is on the use of "social" reinforcement. This includes the recognition by the manager of a job well done. When social reinforcement can be instituted in an organization on an ongoing basis, the organization is most likely to maintain high levels of performance. The use of tangible reinforcement, unless it becomes an institutionalized part of the compensation system, is not likely to be maintained over a long time, and performance is likely to drop as the procedure is discontinued.

• *Evaluate:* Every behavior management project, whether conducted by a consulting psychologist, an inhouse change agent, or the line manager, must include an evaluation procedure if it is to qualify as behavior management. The evaluation of most behavior management projects simply involves the continuation of the counting and recording initiated before the change procedure. Most managers continue to graph the data on the performance with which they are concerned. Behavior management teaches the manager to measure performance on an ongoing basis, even when it is good, so that the conditions affecting it can be studied and managed. One of the primary effects of this evaluation is to provide built-in, or intrinsic, reinforcement for the manager. The manager or supervisor can obtain a great deal of satisfaction from observing the line on a graph go upward or downward as he alters the conditions that he believes affects that performance.

Behavior management is much more than these four simple steps. These steps are one method used to initiate behavior management at the level of the individual supervisor. Behavior management may also involve the alteration of a company-wide system of compensation, objective setting, or information flow. When the principles of behavior management are fully understood by the manager, they become, not a technique to be called upon on difficult occasions, but a "way of life."

REFERENCES

Miller, Lawrence M. *Behavior Management: New Skills for Business and Industry.* Atlanta: Behavioral Systems, 1974.

Skinner, B. F. "Are Theories of Learning Necessary?" *Psychological Review* 57 (1950), pp. 193–216.

Skinner, B. F. *Science and Human Behavior.* New York: Free Press, 1953, pp. 12–13.

Skinner, B. F. *Contingencies of Reinforcement: A Theoretical Analysis.* New York: Appleton-Century-Crofts, 1969, p. 7.

Thorndike, E. L. *The Psychology of Learning.* New York: Columbia University Teachers College, 1913.

Watson, John B. *Behaviorism.* New York: W. W. Norton, 1924, p. ix.

Watson, J. B., & R. Raynor, "Conditioning Emotional Reactions." *Journal of Experimental Psychology* 3 (February 1920), pp. 1–14.

11

At Emery Air Freight:
Positive Reinforcement
Boosts Performance*

At Emery these days, P.R. stands for *positive reinforcement,* not public relations, and the payoffs from applying Skinner's ideas to the motivation of employees exceed the wildest claims ever made by public relations practitioners for the results of their art. One example: Small shipments intended for the same destination fly at lower rates when shipped together in containers rather than separately. By encouraging employees to increase their use of containers (from 45 percent to 95 percent of all possible shipments), Emery has realized an annual saving of $650,000.

"With savings this large we can't afford to worry about charges that we're manipulating our employees," says Edward J. Feeney, Vice-President—System Performance, the man primarily responsible for introducing P.R. at Emery. Continues Feeney: "Actually, the charge that you're manipulating people when you use positive reinforcement—I prefer myself to say that you're shaping their behavior—is a hollow one to start with. People in business manipulate their employees all the time—otherwise they would go bankrupt. The only questions are, how effective are you as a manipulator and what ends do you further with your manipulation? Our end is improved performance, and we've been damned effective in getting it." Feeney emphasizes that his approach and that of Emery's management generally is pragmatic, not doctrinaire. They're sold on the merits of Skinner's ideas, not because of their internal logic or the eloquence with which they are frequently proposed, but because so far at least they have paid off handsomely in each area Emery has seen fit to apply them.

Importance of Performance Audit

Emery has been selective in its application of P.R.; it's a powerful tool that should be employed where it's most needed and where the

* Reprinted by permission of the publisher from *Organizational Dynamics,* Winter 1973 © 1973 by AMACOM, a division of American Management Associations.

potential for improvement is the greatest. These are things that Feeney feels strongly can't be left to intuition or guesswork—hence the necessity for a performance audit before you institute P.R. in a given area. Emery doesn't want to be in the position of the corporation that targeted tardiness reduction as the object of a major effort. Before the drive, tardiness averaged ½ of 1 percent; after the drive ¼ of 1 percent. Big deal! Emery has a different magnitude of payoff in mind.

Take the example of container utilization that we mentioned. Executives at Emery were convinced that containers were being used about 90 percent of the times they could be used. Measurement of the actual usage—a measurement made by the same managers whose guesses had averaged 90 percent—showed that the actual figure was 45 percent, or half the estimate. Feeney saw no reason, given the proper motivational climate, why employees couldn't consistently meet a standard of 95 percent and save Emery $650,000 annually—which, of course, subsequently happened.

The performance audit fulfills two primary purposes. First, it indicates the areas in which the biggest potential profit payoffs exist—the areas in which Emery should focus its attention; second, it convinces previously skeptical managers on quantitative grounds that no words can contravene that there is need for substantial improvement.

The performance audit would be justified for the second effect alone—convincing managers that improvement is needed and persuading them to cooperate with a program designed to bring about the improvement. "Most managers genuinely think that operations in their bailiwick are doing well; a performance audit that proves they're not comes as a real and unpleasant surprise," says Feeney.

We also suspect that an unpleasant surprise of some magnitude is necessary to secure the cooperation of a goodly number of managers in implementing a program that, with its concentration on praise and recognition as motivators and the elimination of censure, runs contrary to the beliefs and practices of a working lifetime.

On the other hand, Feeney emphasizes the importance of cushioning the blow if you want to enlist their cooperation. "We structure the performance audit so that the managers are heroes for making the audits, and we reassure them that irrespective of the current level, they will look good if they can improve."

What about the performance standards set as a part of each performance audit? How are they set? What do they signify? Sometimes, as in the case of the customer service department with its goal of customer call-backs within 90 minutes of the initial telephone query, the department had set the goal in advance of the audit study. On study, it appeared reasonable and it was left unchanged. Sometimes there is no standard, and one has to be set on the basis of observation and common sense.

The latter usually indicates the impracticality of setting perfection or 100 percent performance as your standard. For example, the ideal in answering phone calls from customers would be for the customer never to get a busy signal that might lead him to call one of Emery's competitors. The problem is that studies have shown that in any given hour, five minutes, although not the same five minutes, is always going to account for 35 percent of the calls during the hour. Hence, it's much too costly to staff a switchboard with the number of operators necessary to prevent busy signals during those peak five minutes.

Emery has experimented, with a measure of success, with having employees set the standards for their own jobs. It was done in the customer service office in Chicago. The employees set a higher standard: not just giving customers a progress report within 90 minutes, but having *all* the requested answers to customer queries within that time—and they have presently reached this standard, although they fall short of the 90 to 95 percent achieved on progress reports. The problem, as Feeney sees it, is in giving the employees all the data they need to hit on a reasonable standard—a very time-consuming process. Otherwise, employee-set standards either will be unrealistically high or unacceptably low. Either way, both the company and the employee lose out. The standard that is too low deprives the employee of self-satisfaction and the company of work that it is paying for; the standard that is too high, achievable only once in a while by virtue of extraordinary effort or luck, will leave the employee frustrated and embittered. Sooner or later—and it's usually sooner—his performance will revert to a lower level than before he participated in setting the unattainable standard.

Providing Praise and Recognition—Avoiding Censure

In those areas in which Emery uses P.R. as a motivational tool, nothing is left to chance. Each manager receives two elaborate programmed instruction workbooks prepared in-house and geared to the specific work situation at Emery. One deals with recognition and rewards, the other with feedback. Under recognition and rewards, the workbook enumerates no less than 150 kinds, ranging from a smile and a nod of encouragement, to "Let me buy you a coffee," to detailed praise for a job well done.

Of all forms of praise, the most effective, according to Feeney, is praise for the job well done—expressed in quantitative terms. Not "Keep up the fair work, Murray," as shown on TV, or even "Great going, Joe—keep it up," but "Joe, I liked the ingenuity you showed just now getting those crates into that container. You're running pretty consistently at 98 percent of standard. And after watching you, I can understand why."

In bestowing praise and recognition, Emery follows Skinner pretty closely. There is the same emphasis on reinforcing specific behavior; the same insistence that the behavior be reinforced as soon as possible after it has taken place; the same assertion that you reinforce frequently in the beginning to shape the desired behavior, but that as time goes on, maintaining the desired behavior requires progressively less frequent and unpredictable reinforcement. As Skinner wrote, in reference to Emery's application of his ideas, "You don't need to maintain a system of contrived reinforcers indefinitely. People get the impression that I believe we should all get reinforcers indefinitely. People get the impression that I believe we should all get gumdrops whenever we do anything of value. There are many ways of attenuating a system of reinforcement. . . . But the main thing is to let non-contrived reinforcers take over."

At the gumdrop stage of P.R., Feeney urges supervisors to supply praise and recognition at least twice a week during the early weeks or months of behavior shaping. It's impractical to require them to provide P.R. more frequently—they are too busy, they would forget, etc. Once the desired behavior has been established, managers have more discretion—the key point being the unpredictability of the reinforcement, not the frequency. Keep P.R. coming on a descending scale of frequency—but keep the employee guessing as to when or whether he's going to be praised or recognized.

At least in the early days of shaping behavior, it's difficult to determine which deserves the most credit for the improvement in performance—providing praise and recognition or withholding censure and criticism. Particularly in those cases where the manager seldom praised before—even when he had good reason—the switchover from censure to praise produces instant, almost miraculous results. Performance improves dramatically, and along with it, employee morale and superior-subordinate relations.

What do you do with the employee when praise, recognition, and feedback don't work? Do you contrive to refrain from criticising his or her work? At what point do you throw in the sponge?

Feeney's general answer was that P.R. worked with nine employees out of ten. On those occasions where it appeared not to be working, investigation usually revealed that below-standard performance was not the employee's fault—factors such as the wrong tools or work overload were responsible. And once they were corrected, the employee responded as positively to praise and recognition as anyone else. He cited several instances, not among the rank-and-file, where a custom-tailored program of P.R. salvaged men who were 30 days short of being fired.

Even with the below-par employee, the manager takes the positive note. He would probably ignore a day or a week in which no improvement took place, preferring to wait for a period of even slight improvement—say from 70 to 75 percent. Then he might follow-up his praise of the improvement by asking the man what he thought could be done to improve further. Everything he said from there on would be an attempt to solve the problem and provide the manager with additional opportunities for reinforcement.

All in all, we got the impression of a program that failed, on the few occasions when it did, not because of employee resistance, but because of supervisory intransigence—the boss was unable or unwilling to apply it, especially with the so-called problem employee—and a few supervisors have left Emery in consequence.

Feedback is easier to institutionalize than praise and rewards. A written report is a tangible artifact that you can see. But even with feedback you have occasional lapses, Feeney cautions, in any areas where it isn't mandatory. Some managers loathe paperwork; others are too busy to extend the measure of praise and recognition indicated by the feedback or they don't recognize behavior that deserves positive reinforcement. "The biggest problem with the program occurs," adds Feeney "when managers stop asking for feedback and stop offering recognition and rewards because there's been no recognition of their efforts from above—their boss hasn't asked, 'Why didn't I see your performance report?' or extended any reward or recognition himself. In other words, the program breaks down whenever there are no consequences and no positive reinforcement for the manager who is supposed to implement it."

Beyond Gumdrops—Continuous Feedback

Skinner talks about the necessity of letting the noncontrived reinforcers take over in any program of P.R.—which, in our view, explains the crucial importance at Emery, and probably in any industrial setting, of continuous feedback. Emery, in each area where it has utilized P.R., has required each employee to keep a record himself of what he or she has accomplished each and every day. In customer service, for example, each representative ticked off daily on a sheet how long it had taken to reply to each call. It took no special skill to compare this with the standard of 90 minutes. Similar sheets, all relatively simple and all recorded by the employees themselves, were instituted in all departments covered by P.R.

Noncontrived reinforcers they were not. Emery provided the sheets, gave no option on filling them out, and defined the terms and frequency. But we think this is an example of a contrived reinforcer laying the essential groundwork—providing the time framework for noncontrived reinforcers to mature and take over. Let's postulate three basic stages of development: (1) a period in which frequent P.R. by the supervisor plus continuous feedback leads to rapid progress towards the desired behavior; (2) a period in which infrequent P.R. by the boss is accompanied by continuous feedback—itself, of course, a species of P.R.; (3) a period in which the supervisor is only a very occasional source of P.R. and feedback is overwhelmingly the principal source of contrived reinforcement.

Feeney emphasizes the effect of feedback on improved performance. "We found that when we provided daily feedback only one week out of four or one out of five, performance in the periods without feedback reverted to the previous level or was almost as bad." There's no question that feedback is the critical variable in explaining the success of the program, he adds.

What is continuous feedback, and what is its relation to Skinner's requirement that, in any program of P.R., "The main thing is to let noncontrived reinforcers take over"? The noncontrived reinforcer clearly is the conviction on the employees' part that they are doing a good job, a fair day's work. But how are they to know? Part of the answer is observable—they've been busy, the customers have seemed satisfied, maybe the boss has extended P.R. More conclusive, if they're in doubt, they can look at the sheets and see at a glance exactly how they stand in reference to the standard. In other words, the internal or natural reinforcer—the conviction and satisfaction of a job well done—is corroborated and itself powerfully reinforced by the evidence of a sheet on which the work accomplished is compared daily with the standard for the job.

Feeney tells a story that illustrates both the necessity for continuous feedback and the way in which previous consequences determine present behavior. Emery requires any employee who receives a package damaged during shipment from an airline to fill out a fairly time-consuming form. At a certain installation, he pointed out to the boss that without feedback and P.R. the employees wouldn't bother—the reinforcements they got from filling out the form were all negative. The paperwork was time-consuming and boring, they were likely to get some flack from airline representatives who would in their own good time find ways of hitting back, they were taking time from their number one priority—getting the shipment delivered on time. A check revealed that no damage forms were turned in. However, a physical check of cartons received showed several damaged, one with a hole punched in the side, another that looked as if a hand had reached into the top and taken something out, etc. Feeney feels that his colleague, at this point, got the message. The only way around the problem of getting the damage slips filled out was to (1) specify the desired behavior—i.e., set the standard; (2) require the employee to provide continuous feedback—keep daily records on how many cartons were damaged and submit them to his supervisor; and (3) whenever feasible, positively reinforce the behavior—when the feedback showed that it was justified.

Money and Positive Reinforcement

Skinner includes money in his list of positive reinforcers, as long as it is linked to specific behavior. The weekly paycheck doesn't positively reinforce; it's a negative reinforcer. You work to avoid the loss of the standard of living supported by the paycheck. On the other hand, piece-rate payments geared to specific on-the-job behavior are positive reinforcers; so are commissions paid to salesmen. Just as effective, Skinner argues, would be to take a leaf from gambling and introduce a lottery into industry, with each employee getting a weekly lottery ticket that might pay off in a weekly drawing. Here it's paying off unpredictably but in the long run on a determined schedule that provides the positive reinforcement.

Emery does not use money as a positive reinforcer. Several reasons seem to underly the choice. First, Emery has no employees on incentive payments, not even salesmen; there is therefore no built-in necessity to link dollar payments to improved performance. Second, management holds the belief that performing up to standard is what it has a right to expect from each employee in return for his paycheck. The savings achieved through the program have helped to make it possible for Emery to pay as much or more than its competitors, and offer equal or bigger benefits—facts not lost on its employees. Finally, Emery's experience suggests that praise and recognition, especially self-recognition through feedback, are enough. In some areas, employees have consistently performed up to standard for more than three years. The savings for Emery in consequence have been substantial, despite the omission of money as a positive reinforcer.

At first blush this seems surprising. Interestingly, AT&T had a similar experience with a job-enrichment program that also substantially increased employee productivity and performance. In an AT&T experiment with 120 women answering stockholder inquiries, various measures were taken to give employees more responsibility and control over their jobs. The response was uniformly positive, with one exception—a girl who quit because she wasn't getting more money for a more responsible job. She felt that she was worth more to the company and should be paid more. That only one employee out of 120 expected to get paid more as the consequence of a program that improved the value of their services calls for a little explaining. So does the continuing success of P.R. at Emery.

There are several possible explanations. People know a good thing when they see it. The programs at both AT&T and Emery have improved the intrinsic nature of the job as seen by the employees themselves—that's sufficient reward.

Also, many studies have shown that employees have a crude but keen sense of distributive justice on the job. They may do less than what they themselves consider a fair day's work for a large number of reasons, even though they frequently feel guilty about it. On the other hand, they resent and resist any attempt to exact more than their perception of a fair day's work in return for what they are paid. Improve the job—in Emery's case, provide via praise, recognition, and continuous feedback the evidence of a job well done—and eventually you will develop what Skinner would call the natural reinforcer of job satisfaction. This, in turn, guarantees that the employee will want to live up to his own standard of a fair day's work. In other words, part of the success of P.R. at Emery is that the standards set for employees were seen by them as reasonable to begin with. The missing element was any positive incentive to reach them. The weekly paycheck was ineffective—Skinner is correct—it took praise, recognition, and feedback to do the job. Similarly, at AT&T, job enlargement and job enrichment provided the incentives to improved performance that hitherto were lacking.

A story that Feeney tells illuminates the problem. A Harvard Business School student on a summer assignment with Emery was helping with a performance audit on one of the loading docks. In the process he managed to gain the confidence of a union steward, who told him in so many words that any problems Emery had with the workers were not due to money—they were well paid. The one thing they weren't getting paid was attention. Many of them worked at night with a minimum of supervision and recognition. A situation in which employees feel fairly paid in relation to the work expected of them but in which money is almost the sole recognition received is ripe for improvement via positive reinforcement.

Proof of the Pudding

At present, P.R. is fully operative in three areas at Emery—in sales and sales training, operations, and containerized shipments. The benefits in all three are impressive, and they have been sustained for periods of from three to four years. We can forget about the Hawthorne effect in explaining the success of P.R. at Emery.

In sales training, each salesman completes a programmed instruction course on his own, with plenty of feedback structured into the course to let him know how he is doing. In addition, sales managers apply P.R. in their day-to-day relations with salesmen, and sales reports provide the indispensable feedback. Sales have gained at a more rapid rate since P.R. entered the sales picture, and Feeney feels that it deserves some of the credit for the increased rate.

The relationship between P.R. and improved customer service, part of operations, is undeniable. Before P.R., standards were met only 30 to 40 percent of the time; after P.R., the figure was 90 to 95 percent. Most impressive is the rapidity of the improvement and its staying power. In the first test office, for example, performance skyrocketed from 30 percent of standard to 95 percent in a single day. Staying power? After almost four years, performance in the vast majority of Emery customer service offices still averages 90 to 95 percent.

In containerized shipping operations the story is the same: With P.R., container use jumped from 45 percent to 95 percent—with the increase in 70 percent of the offices coming in a single day.

There were a few cases in which feedback was temporarily interrupted because of managerial changes and other reasons. Whenever this occurred, performance slumped quickly by more than 50 percent, only to return rapidly to the 95 percent level once the feedback was resumed.

All in all, Emery has saved over $3 million in the past three years. No doubt about it: Positive reinforcement pays.

On the basis of this kind of success, Emery has big plans to expand the use of P.R. It's already been extended to overall dock operations. Emery's route drivers are covered and measured on items such as stops per hour and sometimes on shipments brought back versus shipments dispatched. Eventually P.R. will be introduced wherever it's possible to measure work and set quantifiable standards. Feeney and his group will set their priorities, of course, on the basis of what performance audits tell them about the potential for improvement and savings.

When you have scored the kind of success that Emery has you're not quick to innovate. However, thought is being given to the introduction in certain areas of different rewards and schedules, including having the computer acknowledge behavior and even using some kind of financial reward as a positive reinforcer.

What Does Emery Prove?

More precisely, what does Emery prove about the feasibility of behavior modification through positive reinforcement? The question must be asked and answered at several levels. At the first and most apparent level, the answer is easy: In those areas in which Emery has used P.R., behavior modification has been instant, dramatic, sustained, and uniformly in the desired direction. There also seems little doubt that P.R. deserves most of the credit for the dramatic improvement in performance.

A few qualifiers are in order. Positive reinforcement so far has been used selectively at Emery in areas where work could be measured and quantifiable standards set if they didn't already exist, and areas where observation showed that the existing level of performance was far below the standard. This last point applies equally to the customer-service representatives and the dock loaders, but is less true for the salesmen—their performance was lower than Emery felt it should be, but not in the same category as the other two employee groups.

Also Emery has yet to arrive at the point where the natural reinforcers—in this case an internally generated sense of job satisfaction—have taken over. After three to four years of P.R., praise and recognition from the boss is applied infrequently and unpredictably, but the other contrived reinforcer, continuous feedback, is still administered daily. In fact, Emery's past experience has been that whenever it stopped providing continuous feedback, performance rapidly reverted to the previous low levels. On the other hand, this experience occurred during the early days of supplying positive reinforcement. Perhaps now Emery could stop providing continuous feedback and maintain the current high levels of performance. We can only guess.

At another level we have to take into account the context in which P.R. has been used at Emery. We have to consider whether or not special conditions exist at Emery that favor the successful application of positive reinforcement. How far are we justified in claiming that what has worked at Emery will work equally well in a different organization with a different product, a different climate, and different problems?

On the basis of the available evidence, we can't go overboard in generalizing from Emery's undeniable success in applying positive reinforcement to solve its performance problems. That Emery has no incentive programs and is therefore spared the complexity and the conflict habitually generated in manufacturing situations where standards, performance, and earning are inextricably linked; that Emery has so far restricted P.R. to areas in which it has been possible to positively reinforce one employee without producing adverse consequences for any other employee; and that Emery, during the period it has applied P.R., has been a rapid growth organization, able to offer far more than the usual opportunities for growth and promotion are factors that provide a partial measure of the conditions, by no means common in organizations, that have fostered an atmosphere conducive to the application of positive reinforcement.

The second condition we mentioned is something Emery has worked at. Feeney emphasized that Emery was careful not to set individuals or groups competing against each other to see which came closest to meeting the standard. Instead, managers were coached to urge employees to think in terms of what they were doing now compared to what they had done in the past. Comments Feeney, "If you set individuals or teams competing against each other, there's only room for one first—but lots of losers. If you want to know the effect of this kind of competition on performance, all you need is to look at what happens at the end of the baseball season to the performance of the team that's 32 games behind."

Whether the conditions we have described are indispensable to the successful application of P.R. or merely helpful we have no way of determining. The problem is lack of evidence. Emery is the only company to date to have applied P.R. on a fairly broad scale over a fairly long period of time. Even with Emery, neither this report nor a previous article in *Business Week* (December 28, 1971) can claim to be the kind of objective in-depth study that's called for. A few other organizations—among them Cole National in Cleveland, Michigan Bell Telephone, and Ford Motor Co.—are in the early stages of experimenting with positive reinforcement, and more organizations are giving serious thought to using positive reinforcement. More than 200 have contacted Feeney since Emery's work with P.R. received public recognition.

Will positive reinforcement work? Feeney believes that the question has already been answered with a resounding affirmative. He cites upwards of 1,000 case studies involving mental patients, delinquent children, and problem pupils in which P.R. resulted in dramatic improvement in behavior. The only questions remaining, as he sees it, are questions of methodology and application.

Of course, none of these episodes took place in an industrial setting. Until we have a lot more evidence—both from Emery and from other sources—any conclusions about the use of P.R. in industry have to be tentative.

One last level of consideration. Positive reinforcement as the answer to organizational problems of productivity and performance has a plethora of rivals. A generation of theorists and practitioners has systematically overturned stones in the search for a formula or method for converting low-producing groups or individuals into high-producing ones. A partial enumeration would include job enrichment and job enlargement, organization development in all its varied guises. Theory Y, participative management, team development, the Scanlon Plan, autonomous leadership. We could go on—but we won't. How does

P.R. stack up against these other and we think competing approaches to improving productivity and performance?

At this point it's impossible to give a conclusive answer. We have seen the problems with the evidence on the results of positive reinforcement. Similar problems exist with the results of every other technique for improving productivity and performance. There's little objective evidence available, and what evidence there is abounds in caveats—the technique will work under the proper circumstances, the parameters of which are usually not easily apparent.

Take the entire field of organization development. An exhaustive search of the literature on the subject by Professor George Strauss of the University of California Business School at Berkeley turned up exactly three research studies worthy of the name. What did they prove? That under the proper circumstances OD can increase productivity, though perhaps not as much as conventional techniques such as purchasing new equipment, job simplification, and "weeding out" inefficient operators. So far, the search for a sure-fire all-purpose formula for turning low-producing groups into high-producing ones appears to be almost as elusive as the search for the philosopher's stone that would turn everything it touched into gold.

Which leads us to what conclusion as to the merits of positive reinforcement relative to its rivals? With the customary caveats, we feel that P.R. has much to recommend it. As an approach, it deserves more recognition and application than it has hitherto received. It suffers from its sponsorship: Positive reinforcement has a bad name with businessmen and with the general public because of its association with Skinner, his alleged totalitarian leanings, his denial of free will, and the inescapable fact that his theory of human behavior is rooted in his experiments with pigeons. People instinctively resent a theory that seems to suggest that they're not much brighter than pigeons and can be controlled in similar ways.

We understand the problem, but it's unfortunate that it has prevented the more extensive application of positive reinforcement. On the basis of what little we can observe, P.R. is easier, less complex, and less expensive to introduce than most of its rivals, while the results are at least as impressive as those achieved by any of them.

Feeney is probably correct: A lot of managers practice positive reinforcement without knowing it. He cites, for example, Vince Lombardi, who provided endless feedback on performance to his players and who after a really bad defeat never uttered a word of criticism in the locker room. True, but until more organizations consciously and systematically apply positive reinforcement, it will never get the recognition that it appears to deserve.

SELECTED BIBLIOGRAPHY

To anyone who wants to review the evidence that positive reinforcement works, Feeney recommends the following books and articles: Schafer and Martin, *Behavioral Therapy* (McGraw-Hill, 1969); Tharp and Wetzel, *Behavior Modifications of the Natural Environment* (Academic Press, 1969), describe in readable prose how positive reinforcement was used with 150 delinquent children to bring about a remarkable behavior change in 135; Ulrich et al., *Control of Human Behavior* (Scott Foresman), a book described by Feeney as important but highly technical and difficult to read. Finally, the June 1969 issue of *Psychology Today* contains an article, "Smiles, Praise, and a Food Basket," that describes the remarkable improvement positive reinforcement induced in a schizophrenic mental patient.

12

Job Redesign on the Assembly Line: Farewell to Blue-Collar Blues?*

EDITOR, *ORGANIZATIONAL DYNAMICS*

The authors of the much-quoted, much-praised, and much-criticized HEW report *Work in America* wound up their study with a rhetorical bang: "Albert Camus wrote that 'without work life goes rotten. But when work is soulless, life stifles and dies.' Our analysis of work in America leads to much the same conclusion: Because work is central to the lives of so many Americans, either the absence of work or employment in meaningless work is creating an increasingly intolerable situation."

Most who argue that the rhetoric in the report is exaggerated and the thesis overstated would exempt the assembly line, particularly the auto assembly line, from their dissent. The auto assembly line epitomizes the conditions that contribute to employee dissatisfaction: fractionation of work into meaningless activities, with each activity repeated several hundred times each workday, and with the em-

---

* From *Organizational Dynamics*, 1973, 2(2), 51–67. Copyright 1973 by AMACOM, a division of American Management Association. Reprinted by permission.

ployees having little or no control over work pace or any other aspect of working conditions.

Two generations of social scientists have documented the discontent of auto workers with their jobs. Yet the basic production process hasn't changed since Ford's first Highland Park assembly plant in 1913. We read a lot about the accelerating pace of technology: Here's a technology that's stood still for 60 years despite the discontent.

The social explanations are easy. The automakers—when they thought about the problem at all—dismissed it. The economic advantages of the assembly line seemingly outweighed any possible social costs—including the high wages, part of which might properly be considered discontentment pay. In short, the cash register rang more clearly than the gripes.

Recently, the situation has changed. The advent of an adversary youth culture in the United States, the rising educational levels, with a concomitant increase in employee expectations of the job, the expansion of job opportunities for all but the least skilled and the most disaffected, have raised the level of discontent. One of the big three automakers, for example, now has an annual turnover rate of close to 40 percent. G.M.'s famous Lordstown Vega plant, the latest triumph of production engineering—with the average time per job activity pared to 36 seconds and workers facing a new Vega component 800 times in each eight-hour shift—has been plagued with strikes, official and wildcat, slowdowns, and sabotage. At times, the line has shut down during the second half of the day to remedy the defects that emerged from the line during the first half.

IS JOB REDESIGN THE ANSWER?

Much has been written about the two automobile plants in Sweden, Volvo and Saab-Scania, that have practiced job redesign of the assembly line on a large scale. The results, variously reported, have appeared in the world press. Also receiving wide press coverage have been the efforts of Philips N.V. in The Netherlands to redesign jobs on the lines assembling black-and-white and color TV sets. So much for instant history!

We visited the three companies during a recent trip to Europe and shall attempt to evaluate and compare them. But first a caveat: We eschew chic terms, such as job enrichment, autonomy, job rotation, and employee participation, in favor of the drabber *job redesign* for several reasons. First, the other terms have taken on emotional connotations; they've become the rallying ground for true believers who view them as a partial answer or panacea to the problem of employee alienation in an industrial society. The term *job redesign,* by contrast, has no glamor and no followers. Second, most efforts at job redesign, certainly the three we're going to write about, include elements of job enrichment, autonomy, job rotation, and employee participation in varying degrees at different times, but none of the competing terms affords a sufficiently large umbrella to cover what's happened and what's planned in the three organizations. Last, true believers passionately define their faiths differently; using any of the other terms as central would involve us in tiresome and trivial questions of definition. Hence, our choice of job redesign. It's comprehensive, and noncontroversial.

"Job redesign—the answer to what?" might have been a more descriptive subhead than one implying that our sole concern would be the question of employee discontent and its converse, employee satisfaction. Ours is a wider net. We're going to ask and answer (the answers, of course, being partial and tentative) these questions:

1. What conditions on the assembly line are economically favorable to which forms of job redesign?
2. Do many employees resent and resist job redesign? Do they prefer monotonous, repetitious work?
3. Are the "best" results from job redesign obtained when it's at its most thorough (job rotation plus job enrichment plus autonomy plus employee participation)?
4. Is there any single element in job redesign that seems to account for the biggest increase in employee satisfaction?
5. What are the benefits of job redesign—both those we can measure and monetize and those that can only be described?
6. On balance, does management gain as much from job redesign as the employee whose job is redesigned?
7. Last, what's the impact of the overall culture and political system on job redesign? What's the evidence, pro or con, that the success of job redesign at Volvo, Saab-Scania, or Philips—or the lack of it—would be replicated on similar assembly lines in the United States?

A tall order, but remember that we promised only tentative and partial answers to the seven questions.

JOB REDESIGN AT PHILIPS

First Generation, 1960–1965

We start with Philips because, of our three companies, Philips is the pioneer; its experience with job redesign goes back to 1960. We use the terms *first generation, second generation,* and so on to mark the stages of the Philips program because this is Philips's terminology—obviously appropriated from computer lingo.

In the first experiment, concern was more with the deficiencies of long assembly lines than it was with improving job satisfaction. Breaking up the existing line of 104 workers into five shorter assembly lines, installing buffer stocks of components between groups, and placing inspectors at the end of each group instead of the whole assembly line reduced waiting times by 55 percent, improved feedback, and improved the balance of the system—various short chains being stronger than one long chain because the line can never travel faster than the worker with the longest average time per operation.

Almost incidentally, morale also improved: Only 29 percent of the workers on the assembly line responded positively to the survey question "I like doing my job," versus a 51 percent positive response from the test line. Furthermore, when the test line was restructured with half the number of workers, so that each one performed twice the original cycle and workplaces alternated with empty seats, production flowed more smoothly and quality improved. Dr. H. G. Van Beek, a psychologist on the original study team, drew a dual lesson from the experiment: "From the point of view of production, the long line is very vulnerable; from the point of view of morale—in the sense of job satisfaction—downright bad."

Subsequent experiments in several plants involved rotating workers between different jobs on the assembly line, enriching jobs by having employees set their own pace within overall production standards, and enlarging them by making employees responsible for inspecting their own work. Most of the gains from the experiments Philips entered under the heading of "social profit." In other words, morale and job satisfaction improved but bread-and-butter items such as productivity and scrap showed little improvement.

Second Generation, 1965–1968

The key feature of the second phase, a program that involved a few thousand employees scattered over 30 different locations, was the abolition of foremen. With supervisors' enlarged span of control, the men on the assembly line acquired autonomy and more control over their jobs. Even an authoritarian supervisor would find that he was spread too thin to exercise the same amount of control as the previous foreman had.

Once again, the bulk of the profits were social. The bill for waste and repairs dropped slightly, and, of course, Philips pocketed the money that had been paid to the foremen. Otherwise, the gains to Philips were nonmonetary.

Third Phase, 1968

This phase, one that is ongoing, has focused on giving various groups of seven or eight employees total responsibility for assembling either black-and-white TV sets or color selectors for color TV sets, a task equivalent in complexity to assembling a black-and-white set from scratch.

We want to emphasize the word *total:* The group responsible for assembling the black-and-white sets, for example, not only performs the entire assembling task but also deals directly with staff groups such as procurement, quality, and stores, with no supervisor or foreman to act as intermediary or expediter. If something is needed from another department or something goes wrong that requires the services of another department, it's the group's responsibility to deal with the department.

"This third phase has had its problems," concedes Den Hertog, staff psychologist. "Typically, it's taken about six months for the groups to shake down—adjust to the increased pressures and responsibilities." Establishing effective relationships with unfamiliar higher-status employees in staff departments has proved the biggest single problem. On the other hand, anyone in an experimental group can opt out at any time—an option that has yet to be taken up. Of course, it may be the satisfaction of being a member of a select group, even physically separated from other work groups by a wall of green shrubbery, that accounts for no employee's having made a switch. Hertog, however, believes that the increase in intrinsic job satisfactions has more than compensated for any pains of adjustments and accounts for the lack of turnover.

What about results? What's the measurable impact of the program? There have been additional costs, such as increased training costs; more important, small, autonomous groups require new and smaller machines to perform traditional assembly line tasks. On the other hand, there have been measurable benefits. Overall, production costs in manhours have dropped 10 percent, while waiting times have decreased and quality levels have increased by smaller but still significant amounts.

To restructure work and redesign jobs in ways that increase employee job satisfaction at no net cost to the company over the long run is all that Philips, as a matter of policy, requires of such programs. Short-term deficits caused by purchases of new equipment are something it's prepared to live with.

Where is Philips going from here? Obviously, the potential for effective job redesign is large. With 90,000 workers in 60 plants, Philips has barely scratched the surface. Part of the answer would seem to lie in the future strength of the movement for employee participation and power equalization that is particularly strong in Norway and Sweden and is gaining adherents in The Netherlands.

At Philips the primary response has been the establishment of worker consultation in some 20 different departments. Worker consultation is just what it sounds like: Employees meet with first- and second-level supervision to discuss problems of joint interest. Worker consultation exists at different levels in different departments, stresses Hertog, who attributes the difference to the level of maturity of the group itself: "In some groups we're still at the flower pot phase, talking about what should be done to improve meals in the cafeteria, while at other extremes we have departments where we have left the selection of a new supervisor for the group up to the workers."

It's significant that those groups who have considered the question of job redesign consistently have criticized Philips for not doing more of it. The expansion of job redesign, in part, would seem to depend on the expansion of work consultation and the pressures exerted by the workers themselves to get job redesign extended.

JOB REDESIGN AT SAAB-SCANIA

To claim that Saab-Scania has abolished the auto assembly line would misrepresent the facts. Saab-Scania, or to speak more precisely, the Scania Division, has instituted small-group assembly of auto engines—not the whole car—in its new engine plant. Even so, this effort is limited to 50 employees in a plant with a work force of approximately 300, most of whom monitor automatic transfer machines that perform various machining tasks. (See Figure 1.) There's only one manual loading operation in the entire machining process.

More important, the humanization of the auto assembly line is the most dramatic single instance in a series starting in 1969 that Palle Berggen, the head of the industrial engineering department, characterized as "one phase in the development of enhanced industrial democracy."

We won't quarrel with his description, although we think he succumbed to the rhetoric of public relations. Scania, in its actions from 1969 on, has responded to some problems for which the best word is *horrendous*. Employee turnover was running around 45 percent annually, and in the auto assembly plant, 70 percent. Under such conditions, the maintenance of an even flow of production, something crucial in an integrated work system like Scania's, presented insuperable problems. Also, it was increasingly difficult to fill jobs on the shop floor at all. A survey taken in 1969 indicates what Scania was up against:

FIGURE 1
Diagram of Engine Plant, Saab-Scania

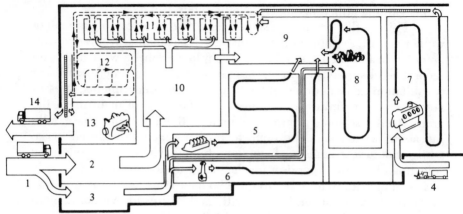

1. Goods reception.
2. Arrival inspection purchased factory parts.
3. Raw material store.
4. Engine blocks (material) from own foundry

5. Machining cylinder heads.
6. Machining connecting rods.
7. Machining engine blocks.
8. Machining crankshafts.
9. Preassembly.
10. Parts store.

11. Group assembly.
12. Engine testing.
13. Ready stock.
14. Engines to Trollhattan and Uusikaupunki.

Only four out of 100 students graduating from high school in Sweden indicated their willingness to take a rank-and-file factory job. In consequence, Scania became heavily dependent on foreign workers—58 percent of the current work force are non-Swedes. This in turn created problems, both expected and otherwise—among the former, problems of training and communications, among the latter, an epidemic of wildcat strikes, previously unknown in Sweden, that largely resulted from the manipulation by extreme left elements of foreign workers ignorant of the tradition among Swedish employees of almost total reliance upon the strong trade union organization to protect their interests.

Any response to these conditions *had* to have as its number-one objective the maintenance of productivity. To assert anything else is window dressing—unconvincing as well as unnecessary. No one can fault an industrial organization for undertaking a program whose primary goal is the maintenance of productivity.

This is not to deny that one byproduct of the program has been "enhanced industrial democracy." What happened is that the pursuit of productivity led to an examination of the conditions that created job satisfactions; these, in turn, suggested the series of actions "that enhance industrial democracy"—a term subject to almost as many definitions as there are interpreters.

Production Groups and Development Groups

Employee representation is nothing new at Scania. Like every company in Sweden with more than 50 employees, it's had an employee-elected Works Council since 1949. However, these bodies have no decision-making function; their role is limited to receiving and responding to information from top management, and their effectiveness depends on the willingness of top management to seriously consider suggestions from the Works Council. David Jenkins, in his recent book *Job Power*, tells of asking a company president if he had ever been influenced by worker suggestions. His reply: "Well, yes. We were going to build a new plant and we showed the workers the plans at one of the meetings. They objected very much to the fact that the plant would have no windows. So we changed the plans and had some windows put in. It doesn't cost much more and, actually, the building looks better. And the workers feel better."

The production and development groups initiated in the truck chassis assembly plant in 1969, by contrast, have real decision-making power. Production groups of five to 12 workers with related job duties decide among themselves how they will do their jobs, within the quality and production standards defined by higher management; they can rotate job assignments—do a smaller or larger part of the overall task. At the same time, the jobs of all members of the production group were enlarged by making them jointly responsible for simple service and maintenance activities, housekeeping, and quality control in their work area, duties formerly performed by staff personnel.

Development groups, a parallel innovation, consist of foremen, industrial engineers, and two representatives of one or more production groups whose function is to consider ideas for improving work methods and working conditions. Representatives of the production groups are rotated in a way that guarantees that every member of a production group will serve each year on a development group.

Employee reception of the production group has been mixed but largely positive. The results appear to be favorable, although Scania has done little or nothing to measure them quantitatively. However, impressions have been sufficiently favorable so that within four years production and development groups have expanded to include 2,200 out of the 3,600 employees in the main plant at Södertälje, and within the year they will be extended throughout the company.

Work Design in the Engine Plant

The four machine lines for the components in the engine factory—the cylinder block, the cylinder head, the connecting rod, and the crankshaft—mainly consist of transfer machines manned or monitored by individual operations. Group assembly is restricted to the seven final assembly stations, each of which contains a team of fitters that assemble an entire engine.

Team members divide the work among themselves; they may decide to do one-third of the assembly on each engine—a ten-minute chore—or follow the engine around the bay and assemble the entire engine—a 30-minute undertaking. In fact, only a minority prefer to do the total assembly job. (Using traditional assembly line methods, each operation would have taken 1.8 minutes.) The team also decides its own work pace, and the number and duration of work breaks within the overall requirement of assembling 470 engines in each ten-day period, a specification that allows them a good deal of flexibility in their pacing. Incidentally, over half the employees in the engine plant are women, while the assembly teams are over 80 percent female. We personally saw four assembly teams with only a single man in the lot.

Benefits and Costs

Kaj Holmelius, who is responsible for planning and coordination of the production engineering staff, ticked off the principal credits and debits, along with a few gray areas in which it would be premature to estimate results. On the plus side, he cited the following:

1. Group assembly has increased the flexibility of the plant, making it easier to adjust to heavy absenteeism.
2. The group assembly concept is responsible for a lower balancing loss due to a longer station time.
3. Less money is invested in assembly tools. Even allowing for the fact that you have to buy six or seven times as many tools, the simpler tools make for a smaller overall cost.
4. Quality has definitely improved, although by how much it's hard to estimate.
5. Productivity is higher than it would have been with the conventional assembly line—although once more, there is no proof. Lower production speed per engine, because it's not economical to use some very expensive automatic tools, is outweighed by higher quality and reduced turnover.
6. Employee attitudes have improved, although there have been no elaborate surveys taken. To Holmelius the best indication of job

satisfaction is that it's impossible to fill all the requests to transfer from other parts of the plant to the assembly teams.

On the negative side, in addition to the reduced production speed, group assembly takes up considerably more space than the conventional assembly line.

In the neutral corner is the impact on absenteeism and turnover. Absenteeism is actually higher in the engine plant—18 percent versus 15 percent for overall plant operations at Södertälje. However, Holmelius attributes the difference to the fact that the engine plant employs a heavier percentage of women. As for turnover, with the plant in operation for a little more than a year, it's too early to tell. Because of an economic slowdown, turnover generally is down from the 45 percent crisis level of 1969 to 20 percent, and it's Holmelius' belief that turnover in the assembly teams will prove significantly lower than average.

What's the Future of Group Assembly?

It's easier to point out the directions in which Scania does *not* plan to extend group assembly. An experiment with having employees assemble an entire truck diesel engine—a six-hour undertaking involving 1,500 parts—was abandoned at the employees' request; they couldn't keep track of all the parts. Similarly, group assembly wouldn't work with the body of the trucks—truck bodies are too complex, and group assembly would require twice the space currently needed. The moot question at the moment is car assembly. So far, group assembly has been applied only to assembling doors. We suspect that in any decision, economic calculations will predominate, including, of course, the inherently fuzzy calculation about the economic value of job satisfaction.

JOB REDESIGN AT VOLVO

Job redesign at Volvo began, almost accidentally, in the upholstery shop of the car assembly plant during the mid-1960s, but a company-wide effort had to wait until 1969, when Volvo faced the same problems that plagued Scania—wildcat strikes, absenteeism, and turnover that were getting out of hand and an increasing dependence on foreign workers. Turnover was over 40 percent annually; absenteeism was running 20 to 25 percent, and close to 45 percent of the employees of the car assembly plant were non-Swedes. One other event in 1971 made a difference: Volvo acquired a young, hard-driving, new managing director, Pehr Gyllenhammar, who developed a keen interest in the new methods of work organization.

Ingvar Barrby, head of the upholstery department, started job redesign by persuading production management to experiment with job rotation along the lines he had read about in Norway. The overwhelmingly female work force complained frequently about the inequity of the various jobs involved in assembling car seats; some jobs were easier than others, while still others were more comfortable and less strenuous, and so on. To equalize the tasks, Barrby divided the job into 13 different operations and rotated the employees among tasks that were relatively arduous and those that were relatively comfortable. Jealousy and bickering among employees disappeared: First, jobs were no longer inequitable; second, employees perceived that they had exaggerated the differences between jobs anyway—the grass-is-greener syndrome. More important, turnover that had been running 35 percent quickly fell to 15 percent, a gain that has been maintained over the years.

Job Alternation and "Multiple Balances"

Volvo uses these phrases instead of the more commonly used *job rotation* and *job enrichment,* but the concepts are the same. In job alternation or job rotation, the employee changes jobs once or several times daily, depending on the nature of the work in his group. Take Line IV A, for example, whose function is to do the external and internal sealing and insulation of car bodies. Because internal sealing is such uncomfortable work—employees work in cramped positions inside the car body—the work is alternated every other hour. The remaining jobs are rotated daily.

"Multiple balances" is our old friend, job enrichment, under another name. One example involves the overhead line where the group follows the same body for seven or eight stations along the line for a total period of 20 minutes—seven or eight times the length of the average job cycle.

Not all employees have had their jobs rotated or enriched—only 1,500 out of 7,000 in the car assembly at Torslanda are affected by the program. Because participation is strictly voluntary, the figures at first glance seem to indicate a massive show of disinterest on the part of Volvo employees. Not so. True, some employees prefer their jobs the way they are. The bigger problem is that Volvo has, to date, lacked the technical resources to closely scrutinize many jobs to determine whether and how they can be enlarged or enriched, or it has scrutinized them and determined that it isn't economically feasible to enlarge or enrich them. A company spokesman gave the job of coating under the car body to prevent rust as an example of a thoroughly unpleasant job that so far has defied redesign.

Production Teams at Volvo Lundbyverken

In the truck assembly plant at Lundbyverken, Volvo has carried job redesign several steps further, with production teams who, in form and function, roughly duplicate the production groups previously described at Scania. The production team, a group of 5 to 12 men with a common work assignment, elects its own "chargehand," schedules its own output within the standards set by higher management, distributes work among its members, and is responsible for its own quality control. In these teams, group piecework replaces individual piecework and everyone earns the same amount, with the exception of the chargehand. Currently, there are 23 production teams involving 100 out of the plant's 1,200 employees. Plans call for the gradual extension of the production team approach to cover most, if not all, of the factory work force.

The Box Score at Volvo

Have the various forms of job redesign, job rotation, job enrichment, and production teams paid off for Volvo? If so, what forms have the payoff taken? Anything we can measure or monetize? Or are we reduced to subjective impressions and interesting although iffy conjectures about the relationship between factors such as increased job satisfaction and reduced turnover?

The two plants deserve separate consideration: Absenteeism and turnover traditionally have been lower at the truck assembly plant than at the car assembly plant. The jobs are inherently more complex and interesting—even before job enrichment, some individual jobs took up to half an hour. The workers, in turn, are more highly skilled and tend to regard themselves as apart from and above the rank-and-file auto worker. They see themselves more as junior engineers. Within this context, it's still true that the introduction of production teams has led to further improvement: less labor turnover, less absenteeism, an improvement in quality, and fewer final adjustments.

At the auto assembly plant the picture isn't clear. Turnover is down from 40 to 25 percent. However, an economic slowdown undoubtedly accounts for some of the decline, while other actions unrelated to job redesign may account for part of the remainder. When Volvo surveyed its employees to probe for the causes of turnover and absenteeism, most of the causes revealed were external—problems with housing, child care, long distances traveling to the plant, and so on. Volvo responded with a series of actions to alleviate these causes, such as extending the bus fleet, together with the community, to transport employees; loaning money to employees to purchase apartments at very favorable rates of interest; putting pressure on the community to expand day-care centers, and so on. Such measures presumably contributed to the decline of turnover. Nevertheless, Gyllenhammar is convinced that "we can see a correlation between increased motivation, increased satisfaction on the job, and a decrease in the turnover of labor." Absenteeism is a sadly different picture: It's double what it was five years ago, a condition that Gyllenhammar attributes to legislation enabling workers to stay off the job at practically no cost to themselves.

As for output in that part of the auto assembly plant covered by job enrichment or job enlargement, there was no measurable improvement. Quality, on balance, has improved, and the feeling is that improved quality and decreased turnover had more than covered the costs of installing the program.

The Future of Job Redesign at Volvo

Despite the relatively ambiguous success of Volvo's job redesign efforts, whatever Volvo has done in the past is a pale prologue to its future plans. In about nine months, Volvo's new auto assembly plant at Kalmar will go on stream. And, for once, that overworked term *revolutionary* would seem justified.

Physically, the plant is remarkable. Gyllenhammar describes it as "shaped like a star and on each point of the star you have a work group finishing a big share of the whole automobile—for example, the electrical system or the safety system, or the interior." Assembly work takes place along the outer walls, while component parts are stored in the center of the building. Architecturally, the building has been designed to preserve the atmosphere of a small workshop in a large factory, with each work team having its own entrance, dressing room, rest room, and so on. Each team is even physically shielded from a view of the other teams. (See Figure 2.)

Each work team, of 15 to 25 men, will distribute the work among themselves and determine their own work rhythm, subject to the requirement of meeting production standards. If the team decides to drive hard in the morning and loaf in the afternoon, the decision is theirs to make. As with production teams in the truck assembly plant, the team will choose its own boss, and deselect him if he turns out poorly.

The new plant will cost about 10 percent more—some 10 million Swedish kroner—than a comparable conventional auto assembly plant. Time alone will tell whether the extra investment will be justified by

FIGURE 2
Diagram of Small Workshop at Volvo Assembly Plant at Kalmar

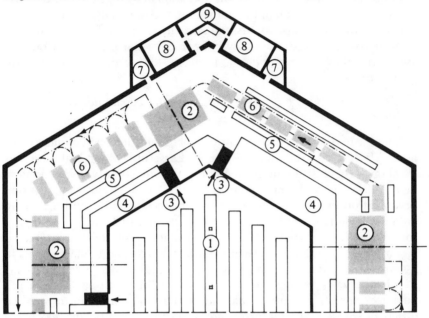

1. Stores.
2. Body buffers.
3. Material intake by electric trucks.
4. Preassembly.
5. Materials.
6. Bodies (on the left, stationary; on the right, moving).
7. Pause area.
8. Toilets, etc.
9. Changing rooms.

the decreased turnover, improved quality, and even reduced absenteeism that its designers confidently expect at the new facility. In announcing the plan for the new factory, Gyllenhammar's economic objectives were modest enough, his social objectives more ambitious. "A way must be found to create a workplace that meets the needs of the modern working man for a sense of purpose and satisfaction in his daily work. A way must be found of attaining this goal without an adverse effect on productivity." With luck, he may achieve both.

WHAT DOES IT ADD UP TO?

On the basis of what we learned at Philips, Saab-Scania, and Volvo, what answers—tentative and partial—do we have to the seven questions that we raised earlier in the article? Or are the results of the programs so ambiguous and inconclusive that, as long as we restrict ourselves to the context of these three companies, we must beg off attempting to answer some of the questions at all? That none of the companies answered all of the questions, and that many of the answers rely on subjective impressions haphazardly assembled, rather than on quantitative data systematically collected, of necessity, limit our answers, but they don't prevent us from presenting them—with the appropriate caveats.

1. *What conditions on the assembly line are economically favorable to which forms of job redesign?*

The basic question here is under what conditions can a man-paced assembly line replace a machine-paced assembly line? Unless this is economically feasible, no form of job redesign is likely to be adopted. Even allowing for rhetoric, none of our three companies—and no other organization of which we are aware—has indicated a willingness to suffer economic losses in order to increase the satisfactions employees might feel if they switched over from machine-paced to man-paced assembly lines. Take the case of manufacturing a pair of man's pants in a garment factory. Give the job to one man and he will take half a day; divide the work among many people on a line with each one using advanced technical equipment, and it takes one man-hour to produce a pair of trousers. The future of job redesign is not bright in a pants factory.

The man-paced assembly line, however, has a couple of widely recognized advantages over the machine-paced line: First, it's much less sensitive to disruption; the whole line doesn't have to stop because of one breakdown—human or technical; second, extensive and costly rebalancing need not be undertaken every time production is increased or decreased. You simply add more people or groups. Of course, there are advantages to machine-paced production, the outstanding one being speed of production, which depends, in turn, on an even flow of production.

There's the rub—and there's the number one cause for job redesign, certainly at Volvo and Saab-Scania. Absenteeism and turnover had risen to the point where they canceled out the economic advantages of machine-paced production. At the same time, evidence had accumulated that job redesign organized around a man-paced assembly line might strike at the root causes of inordinate turnover and absenteeism.

If you look at the design of the new engine plant at Scania, it incorporates Drucker's insight that "the worker is put to use to use a poorly designed one-purpose machine tool, but repetition and uniformity are two qualities in which human beings are weakest. In everything but the ability to judge and coordinate, machines can perform better than man." In the new engine plant, everything that can be automated economically has been—probably 90 percent of the total task—with the final assembly paced by teams on the assumption that the relatively slight increases in production time will be more than compensated for by better balancing and decreased disruption— improvements inherent in the technical change—and improvements in quality, turnover, and absenteeism, the anticipated by-products of job satisfaction.

The results, as you have seen, are sketchy. However, we can affirm that none of the three organizations, by their own testimony, has lost economically by the changeover from a machine-paced to a man-paced assembly line. How much they have gained is decidedly a more iffy question.

2. *Do many employees resent and resist job redesign? Do they prefer monotonous, repetitious work?*

A flip answer might be "God only knows—and he isn't talking." Any answer, at best, is based largely on conjecture. Joseph E. Godfrey asserts that "workers may complain about monotony, but years spent in the factories lead me to believe that they like to do their jobs automatically. If you interject new things you spoil the rhythm of the job and work gets fouled up." As head of the General Motors Assembly Line Division he is qualified, but biased. But even Fred Herzberg, whose bias is obviously in the other direction, concedes that "individual reaction to job enrichment is as difficult to forecast in terms of attitudes as it is in terms of performance. Not all persons welcome having their job enriched." The Survey Research Center at The University of Michigan in a 1969 study concluded that factors such as having a "nutrient supervisor, receiving adequate help, having few labor standard problems all seem to relate at least as closely to job satisfaction as having a challenging job with 'enriching demands.'" One thing does seem clear: Assuming the job level is held constant, education is inversely related to satisfaction. And when Pehr Gyllenhammar foresaw a near future in which 90 percent of the Swedish population would at least have graduated from high school, he was realistically anticipating a situation in which Volvo would become almost entirely dependent on foreign employees unless it found ways of enriching the auto assembly jobs.

3. *Are the "best" results from job redesign obtained when it's at its most thorough (job rotation plus job enrichment plus autonomy plus employee participation)?*

Work in America flatly endorses the thesis that "it is imperative that employers be made aware of the fact that thorough efforts to redesign work, not simply 'job enrichment' or 'job rotation,' have resulted in increases of productivity from 5 to 40 percent. In no instance of which we have evidence has a major effort to increase employee participation resulted in a long-term decline in productivity." Obviously, in this context "best" results means increased productivity.

Before we can answer the question and respond to the claims asserted in *Work in America* a few definitions are necessary. Most descriptions of the elements that enter into a satisfying job concentrate on three: (1) variety, (2) responsibility, and (3) autonomy. Variety defines itself. Responsibility is more complex; it involves both working on a sufficiently large part of the total job to feel that it is a meaningful experience and having a sufficient amount of control over what you are doing to feel personally responsible.

Companies responding to this need for more responsibility may add set-up and inspection to the employee's duties or ask him to assemble one third of an engine instead of a single component—both examples of horizontal job enrichment; and the employee may be permitted to control the pace at which he works—an example of vertical job enrichment. Everything that is subsumed under vertical job enrichment is included in autonomy but it also means something else and something more—giving to the employee himself some control over how his job should be enlarged or enriched—a clear demarcation point between almost all American approaches to job enrichment and some European.

We're describing a circular process; the worker in Sweden and The Netherlands places a higher value on autonomy than the worker in the United States. Therefore, job redesign that incorporates increased autonomy for the employee will be more appreciated and lead to more job satisfaction than comparable efforts would in the United States. Here, Huey Long's concept of a satisfying job, with allowances for the regional overtones, and the hyperbole, still makes sense: "There shall be a real job, not a little old sowbelly black-eyed pea job, but a real spending money beefsteak, and gray Chevrolet Ford in the garage, new suit, Thomas Jefferson, Jesus Christ, red, white, and blue job for every man." The employee did then and still does define, although to a progressively decreasing degree, a satisfying job in terms of how much it pays. For a measure of the difference, take the definition of a dissatisfying job by Malin Lofgren, a 12-year-old Swedish schoolboy: "A bad job is one where others make all the decisions, and you have to do what others say."

Now that the tedious, although necessary, business of definition is out of the way, how do we answer the question with reference to our three companies? Inconclusively. If we define "best" results in terms of gains in productivity, the only certifiable gain occurred with the Philips production groups that scored high on both horizontal and vertical job enrichment, and in which employees were consulted in advance about the ways in which their job should be enriched. In the body of the article, we didn't go into their institutional arrangements, but suffice it to say that both Saab-Scania and Volvo have comparable consultative institutions. Thus, the autonomy factor assumes less significance. The only significant differences would appear to be: (1) The increased status caused by making the production groups at Philips wholly responsible for liaison with other departments, (2) the Hawthorne, or, as the Philips personnel call it, the "Princess" effect—the groups having been visited and complimented by such dignitaries as Queen Juliana and Marshal Tito. On the other hand, the groups at Volvo that chose their own supervisors—certainly a measure of autonomy—have not increased their productivity. Quality, turnover, attendance had improved. But with productivity, there was no measurable impact.

4.   *Is there any single element in job redesign that seems to account for the biggest increase in employee satisfaction?*

In a word—no. But that requires an explanation. Our failure to respond principally reflects lack of evidence; none of the organizations concerned asked themselves the question. None tried on any systematic basis to relate what they were doing in redesigning jobs to what they were accomplishing in increased job satisfaction. Word-of-mouth testimony and more cheerful figures—as in the case of Volvo and Saab-Scania with turnover—seemed sufficient to confirm the efficacy of past efforts and sanction future ones, on similar although expanded lines.

5.   *What are the benefits of job redesign—both those we can measure and monetize and those that can only be described?*

We begin with a proposition shared by a generation of social scientists who have studied the problem and attempted to answer the question: Employee attitudes and job satisfaction are correlated much more clearly wih factors such as absenteeism, turnover, and quality than they are with productivity.

The three companies reinforce this finding. Only one experiment at Philips establishes a positive correlation between job satisfaction and productivity, while several—Philips with productivity groups in Phase III, Saab-Scania in the engine plant and the truck assembly plant, and Volvo in its truck plant—all report improvements in quality, the problem in each case being the absence of quantifiable data. Turnover is another area in which the responses are positive, but suggestive rather than conclusive—"probably lower" in the Scania engine plant; lower in the truck assembly plant; down in both the truck assembly and auto assembly plant at Volvo—but there are no firm figures at the Volvo truck assembly line, while the decrease in turnover at the auto assembly plant is partly attributed to causes unrelated to job redesign. Philips offers no comparisons of absenteeism or turnover before and after job redesign. All we know is that so far no one in the production groups has decided to quit. In short, the evidence—what there is of it—is positive, but fragmented and based more on impressions than on data.

6. *On balance, does management gain as much from job redesign as the employee whose job is redesigned?*

A two-headed question that logically requires both extensive employee attitude surveys before and after job redesign, along with firm measurements that demonstrate the impact of job redesign on factors such as quality, output, absenteeism, and turnover. As we have seen, we have very little of either. The only attitude surveys were, first, the one conducted at the Volvo auto assembly plant to determine the causes of excessive absenteeism and turnover—most of which had nothing to do with job satisfaction and where the subsequent substantial drop in turnover at best could only partially be ascribed to job redesign—and the survey at Philips, where the switchover from machine-paced to man-paced assembly line improved employees' satisfaction with their jobs.

On the balance, as previously stated, management has achieved at least an economic draw from its efforts at job redesign, along with a measure of insurance against a fretful future in which employee expectations will become increasingly difficult to fulfill. The job redesign carried out or contemplated will, it is hoped, help to meet those expectations.

As for the satisfactions the employees have gained from the collective efforts at enlarging and enriching their jobs, we can only guess. We have a few pieces of anecdotal evidence, such as the flood of applications to work in the final assembly at Scania's engine plant, or the absence of turnover among the production groups at Philips. In short, we know too little to generalize.

7. *Last, what's the impact of the overall culture and political system on job redesign? What's the evidence, pro or con, that the success of job redesign at Volvo, Saab-Scania, or Philips—or lack of it— would be replicated in similar assembly lines in the United States?*

Technologically, there are no convincing reasons why assembly lines in new automobile factories or television plants in the United States couldn't be redesigned along lines similar to what has been done at Philips, Saab-Scania, and Volvo. It might prove prohibitively expensive in existing plants—after all, job redesign at Volvo's auto assembly plant was largely restricted, on economic grounds, to job rotation. However, new plants in the United States should present no more inherent problems of job redesign than new plants in Sweden. Yet auto executives in the United States have gone on record as feeling that the situation is hopeless. A 1970 report of the Ford Foundation found that none of the corporation executives interviewed "really believe that assembly line tasks can be significantly restructured," and "no one really believes that much can be done to make the assembly jobs more attractive."

Not that all the features of job redesign at Philips, Saab-Scania, and Volvo are equally exportable. The three companies exist in a different political and social ethos, one in which both management and the workers have gone much further in accepting the idea of employee participation in decision making than all but a handful of managers and a small minority of workers in the United States. A survey of Swedish managers in 1970, for example, showed that 75 percent favored more employee decision making in all departments. Even the idea of replacing the decision of the supervisor with collective employee decisions elicited a favorable response from 11 percent of the managers. Given this different ethos, it is not surprising that all three companies have experimented with what would be in the United States the radical step of either dispensing with first-level supervision or leaving it up to the employees to choose their own supervisor. It is a form of autonomy that few managements in the United States would consider for an instant, and one in which few employees would take much interest.

But why not consider it, as long as management continues to set overall standards of production and quality and to hold the group responsible for meeting them? The experiment of having employees choose their own bosses with the experimental groups in the truck assembly plant at Volvo works so well that it has been incorporated as one of the basic design features in the new auto assembly plant. Employees demonstrated that, given the opportunity, they would choose as leaders men who could organize the work and maintain order and discipline.

Let's indulge in speculation. The single quality that most clearly distinguishes between the efforts at job enrichment here and in the three companies we visited is the emphasis abroad on letting the employees have a part—and sometimes a decisive part—in deciding how their jobs should be enriched. By contrast, most exponents of job enrichment in the United States take the "papa knows best" approach. Fred Herzberg, the best-known work psychologist, asserts that when people took part in deciding how to change their own jobs, "the results were disappointing." We suspect that Herzberg's real objection is not to the results themselves, but to the difficulty of selling most managements on the idea that employee participation should be an integral part of any process of job enrichment. The experiences at Volvo, Saab-Scania, and Philips suggest that the objection to the employee's participating in how his own job should be enriched or redesigned has its roots in symbolism, rather than substance, in the irrational preoccupation with management prerogatives, rather than in any real or potential threat to productivity or profits.

What about the future? Technologically, there seem to be no compelling reasons why Ford, GM, and Chrysler cannot take a lead from Volvo and Saab-Scania. Whether they will is another question. The combination of inertia, custom, and commitment is a formidable one. So far the automakers have chosen to move in the opposite direction: shorter work cycles, smaller jobs, more rapidly moving lines. We should recall that it took a crisis—nothing less than the probability that most people would refuse to work at all or only for uneconomic periods on the jobs the organization had to offer them—to "break the cake of custom" at Volvo and Saab-Scania. Even today, it is clear that there are limits to which auto assembly jobs can be enriched, a limitation obvious in Gyllenhammar's bitter observation that " 'absenteeism with pay' is based on the very utopian hypothesis that people love to work, and no matter what happens they will strive to go to their job every morning." Still, the situation he is in is preferable to the situation he faced. And some of the difference is due to job redesign.

We suspect that it will take a crisis of similar magnitude, together with the belief that they have no choice, to unfreeze the attitudes of automakers in the United States and get them moving in the direction of man-paced assembly lines and the forms of job redesign they facilitate. That such a development, over the long run, is in the cards we strongly believe, but how long it will take for the cards to show up, we leave to the astrologers.

SELECTED BIBLIOGRAPHY

On the general subject of job redesign we strongly recommend three books: The HEW *Work in America* (M.I.T. Press; Cambridge, Mass., 1971) is scarcely unbiased but it pulls together much material in the whole area of employee discontent—what causes it and what can be done about it. David Jenkins' *Job Power: Blue and White Collar Democracy* (Doubleday, New York, 1973) is remarkable for the number of case studies of job redesign both here and in Europe—all based on personal visits to the organizations described. Jenkins, like the various authors of *Work in America,* is convinced of the need for wholesale job redesign as the prime means of alleviating growing employee discontent. Last, *Design of Jobs* (Penguin Books Ltd., Harmondsworth, England, 1972) is a first-rate collection of papers on different aspects of job design. All are worth reading, but of special interest are J. Richard Hackman and Edward E. Lawler III, "Conditions Under Which Jobs Will Facilitate Internal Motivation" (pp. 141–154) and James C. Taylor, "Some Effects of Technology in Organizational Change" (pp. 391–414).

On Philips, there is a suggestive article on the first phase of job redesign that shows clearly that Philips's interest in getting away from the machine-paced assembly line arose mainly from technical and economic dissatisfactions with the line—H. G. Van Beek, "The Influence of Assembly Line Organization on Output, Quality and Morale," *Occupational Psychology,* vol. 38, pp. 161–172. On Scania, there's a section on the company—but not identified by name—in Hans Lindestad and Jan-Peter Norstedt, *Autonomous Groups and Payment by Result* (Swedish Employers Confederation, Stockholm, 1973). The Employers Confederation also has published a detailed account of job redesign at Saab-Scania that is being translated into English but that, unfortunately, was not available at the time this article was written.

13

The "Practical Significance" of Locke's Theory of Goal Setting*

GARY P. LATHAM and J. JAMES BALDES†

Locke's (1968) theory of goal setting has been questioned with regard to its generality to industry (Campbell, Dunnette, Lawler, & Weick, 1970; Heneman & Schwab, 1972). Survey data collected from 292 independent Southern pulpwood producers, however, have shown that goal setting accompanied by the presence of supervision results in high productivity and a low number of injuries (Ronan, Latham, & Kinne, 1973). The results regarding productivity were corroborated through an analysis of variance of data collected from 892 additional producers.

Latham and Kinne (1974) experimentally assessed the effects of a one-day training program on goal setting over 12 consecutive weeks. The results showed that independent producers who set a specific production goal for their crew had higher productivity and lower ab-

* From *Journal of Applied Psychology,* 1975, *60,* 122–124. Copyright 1975 by the American Psychological Association. Reprinted by permission.

† The authors are grateful to E. A. Locke, T. M. Mitchell, and G. A. Yukl for their suggestions in preparing this manuscript.

senteeism than those who were matched and randomly assigned to a control "do your best" condition.

These studies would appear to support the external validity of goal setting from a statistical standpoint. Statistical significance, however, is only one step in probing the external validity of a theory. The crucial consideration is whether or not the application of the theory changes behavior enough to make a difference to an organization's objectives (Campbell et al., 1970).

The purpose of the present article is to describe a time series design that assessed the utility or "practical significance" of Locke's theory on the performance of company logging trucks.[1] The problem investigated was that of increasing the net weight of trucks that transport logs from the woods to the mill. Normally, it takes 60–120 logs/trees for a truck to carry its maximum legal load. Because each tree differs in length and in diameter, it is a matter of judgment as to how many and what type should be carried in a given load.

The hypothesis tested was that the effects of goal setting would appear in the form of an increase in the slope or level of the performance curve, as compared to the baseline performance. Further, it was hypothesized that performance improvement would be evident after the first month of goal setting. This hypothesis was based on the earlier finding by Latham and Kinne (1974) that the effects of goal setting were immediate and consistent over time.

METHOD

Subjects

Six company logging operations in Oklahoma were studied. Each operation consisted of 6 to 10 people who performed one of the following operations: (a) felling a tree, (b) dragging the tree to a landing, (c) loading the tree into a truck, or (d) driving the truck to the mill where it is weighed and unloaded. There were approximately 6 trucks and 6 drivers assigned to each logging operation. The truck drivers differed from previous woods workers who had been studied (Latham & Kinne, 1974; Ronan et al., 1973) in that they were paid by the hour as opposed to piece rate, they were company employees as opposed to independent entrepreneurs, and they were members of a union. Data were collected on the net weights of 36 trucks. This number represented all the company's logging trucks in this area.

---

[1] The two previous studies of independent wood producers were conducted under the auspices of the American Pulpwood Association Harvesting Research Project. Association policy, coupled with the fact that these producers were noncompany employees, prevented the collection of data concerning profits.

Procedure

A detailed analysis of the performance of each logging operation revealed that the trucks were frequently falling far short of their maximum legal net weight. This finding, plus the results of the work previously cited on goal setting, were explained to the timberlands management and union leadership.

A 94 percent truck net weight was decided upon as a "difficult" but attainable performance goal. This goal was assigned to the drivers whose job responsibilities include loading the truck to the maximum legal weight. Prior to establishing a specific goal, these workers had been urged to simply "do their best" in this phase of the operation.

At the onset of goal setting, the drivers were told that this was an experimental program, that they would not be required to make more truck runs, and that there would be no retaliation if performance suddenly increased and then decreased. No monetary rewards or fringe benefits other than verbal praise were given for improving performance. No special training of any kind was given to the supervisors or the drivers.

RESULTS

The close geographical and working relationships of the six logging operations made it impossible to use a control group that would not learn of the goal setting procedure. Thus, a time series design (Campbell & Stanley, 1966) was used to evaluate the results.

Measures of the net weight of all 36 logging trucks were collected for three consecutive months prior to goal setting. In order to be certain that the fluctuations in weather and season would not bias the results favorably, these pre-measures were collected during the summer when logging conditions are optimal, that is, July, August, and September. The results of the goal setting were monitored for nine consecutive months, that is, October–June. The results are shown in Figure 1.

The immediate change in the slope and level of the performance curve supports the hypothesis that setting a specific hard goal versus a generalized goal of "do your best" leads to a substantial increase in performance. Moreover, it is evident that this increase holds across time despite changes in season (fall, winter, and spring). Interviews with drivers concerning the slight decrease in performance during the second month of goal setting revealed that they were testing management's statement that no punitive steps would be taken against them if performance suddenly dropped. No such steps were taken and performance again increased.

FIGURE 1
Percent Legal Net Weight of 36 Logging Trucks across Blocks as a Function of a Specific Hard Goal

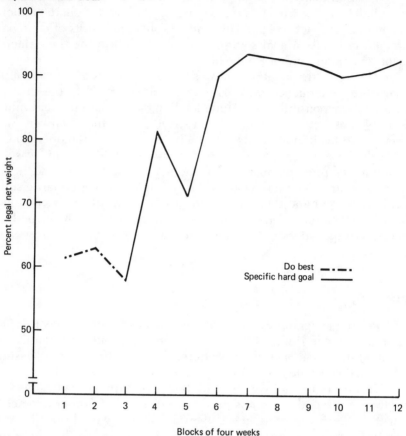

DISCUSSION

The results of this study, when viewed in conjunction with previous work on independent wood producers (Latham & Kinne, 1974; Ronan et al., 1973), lend strong support to the external validity of goal setting theory for the logging industry. Corporate policy prevents a detailed public discussion of the impact of this particular study on the company. However, it can be said that without the increase in efficiency due to goal setting it would have cost the company a quarter of a million dollars for the purchase of additional trucks in order to deliver the same quantity of logs to the mills. This figure does not include the cost for the additional diesel fuel that would have been consumed or the expenses for recruiting and hiring additional truck drivers.

The rival hypothesis that knowledge of results (KOR), rather than goal setting, could have brought about the dramatic increase in performance was ruled out on the grounds that the truck weight had always been available to each individual driver as soon as the truck was weighed in the wood yard. This finding supports Locke's (1968) contention that the mere presence of KOR does not increase performance unless it is used by the individual to set a specific hard goal. It is interesting to note, however, that subsequent to goal setting the drivers began to record their truck weight on a "trip sheet" that had previously been used to record the particular logging site from which the wood had been hauled. Thus, it would appear that goal setting may have led to an increased awareness of KOR.

Similarly, the rival hypothesis that the improvement in performance was due primarily to intergroup competition was ruled out because no special prizes or formal recognition programs were provided for those groups who came closest to or exceeded the goal. No effort was made by the company to single out one "winner." KOR was provided in terms of how well the group, rather than the individual, was doing in terms of meeting or exceeding the goal. More importantly, the opportunity for competition to occur prior to goal setting had always been available to the drivers through their knowledge of the daily and weekly truck weights of each of the other drivers. However, anecdotal information suggests that goal setting did lead to informal competition among drivers. This competition may very well explain why the drivers remained committed to a very difficult goal over the nine-month period.

Finally, the rival hypothesis that the results of this study were due to social facilitation or the pervasive "Hawthorne Effect" was ruled out since the amount of attention and "supervisory presence" given to the drivers before and after goal setting were relatively equal. Latham and Kinne (1974) have shown that woods workers who had a specific production goal had significantly higher productivity than those workers who received only attention and recognition. The only additional instructions given to the supervisors in the present study were to give specific verbal praise to the driver for meeting or exceeding the goal and to withhold negative comments when the goal was not met.

The setting of a goal that is both specific and challenging leads to an increase in performance because it makes clear to the individual what he is supposed to do. This in turn may provide the worker with a sense of achievement, recognition, and commitment in that he can compare how well he is doing now versus how well he has done in the past and, in some instances, how well he is doing in comparison to others. Thus, the worker is not only incited to expend greater effort, but he may devise better or more creative tactics for attaining the goal. In the present study, several drivers on their own initiative made recommendations for minor modifications on their trucks. These modifications included raising the forward stakes in the truck which, in some cases, appeared to enable the driver to increase the accuracy of his judgments as to the weight of the wood that he was carrying.

REFERENCES

Campbell, D. T., & Stanley, J. C. *Experimental and quasi-experimental designs for research.* Skokie, Ill.: Rand McNally, 1966.

Campbell, J. P., Dunnette, M. D., Lawler, E. E., III, & Weick, K. E. *Managerial behavior, performance, and effectiveness.* New York: McGraw-Hill, 1970.

Heneman, H. G., & Schwab, D. P. Evaluation of research on expectancy theory prediction of employee performance. *Psychological Bulletin,* 1972, 78, 1–9.

Latham, G. P., & Kinne, S. B., III. Improving job performance through training in goal setting. *Journal of Applied Psychology,* 1974, 59, 187–191.

Locke, E. A. Toward a theory of task motivation and incentives. *Organizational Behavior and Human Performance,* 1968, 3, 157–189.

Ronan, W. W., Latham, G. P., & Kinne, S. B., III. Effects of goal setting and supervision on worker behavior in an industrial situation. *Journal of Applied Psychology,* 1973, 58, 302–307.

14

Paying People Doesn't Always Work the Way You Expect It to*

EDWARD L. DECI

For many people, the words *money* and *motivation* are nearly synonymous. An abundance of research indicates, however, that this is not the case. Paying workers doesn't necessarily motivate them. Furthermore, money is not the only reward which workers seek to achieve. In order to use money as a motivator, it is necessary that pay be contingent on effective performance. That is, the reward system must be structured so that receiving pay depends on good performance. Money will then motivate performance because performance is instrumental to receiving payments. If money and performance are not tied together, money will not serve as an effective motivator.

Two areas of psychological research have provided support for this assumption about motivation. (1) Behaviorists have substantiated and refined the Law of Effect which states simply that when a response is followed by a reinforcement it will have an increased probability of recurrence. Contingent payments presumably reinforce the response of producing output and should, therefore, strengthen that response. (2) The use of contingent payments can also be defended by cognitive theories of motivation. These theories state that man's behavior is goal-directed; in other words, man will engage in behavior which he believes will lead him to desired goals. Since money is probably one goal all workers accept, cognitive theories would suggest that a worker would produce efficiently in order to get substantial wages, if that was the easiest way he could get them.

One approach to management which has recognized the importance of tying rewards to performance is Scientific Management which was developed by Frederick Winslow Taylor over half a century ago. He used piece-rate payments (i.e., wage incentives) which involve paying people a set rate for each unit of output. Sales commissions and bonus plans work similarly. The motivational assumption

* "Paying People Doesn't Always Work the Way You Expect It to," Edward L. Deci, *Human Resource Management*, Summer 1973, pp. 28–32. Reprinted with permission.

underlying these pay schemes is that a person will perform effectively to the extent that his rewards are made contingent upon effective performance. For this motivational system to work effectively, it is necessary that there be clear standards for performance which the workers understand. Then, performance has to be monitored, and rewards must be administered consistently. Further, the output must be quantifiable so that performance can be measured, and jobs should be relatively independent so that a worker has control of his own production rate.

The rewards in these systems are money, promotions, fringe benefits, etc. These rewards are of course extrinsically mediated, that is, they are given to the employee by someone other than himself. Management administers them to try to control (or motivate) the behavior of the employees. Although this system seems to have advantages for motivating employees, there are also many limitations to it. Perhaps the most serious is that there are many rewards which *cannot* be administered by management. Money is *not* the only reward which workers are looking for. People also need what we call *intrinsic rewards;* that is, internal rewards which the person derives from doing what he likes or meeting a challenge. They give him a feeling of satisfaction and accomplishment. Many studies have reported that employees consider these intrinsic rewards to be important. It follows then that there are many important motivators of human behavior which are not under the direct control of managers and, therefore, cannot be contingently administered in a system such as piece-rate payments.

More recent approaches to management—often referred to as participative management, Theory Y Management, Management by Objectives—have assumed that man can be intrinsically motivated to perform effectively. These approaches focus on structuring jobs so that workers will become ego-involved in their work and committed to doing it well.

There are two essential aspects to motivating intrinsically. The first involves designing tasks which are interesting and which necessitate creativity and resourcefulness. The second involves allowing workers to participate in decisions which concern them so they will feel like they have a say about what they do. The newer participative management theories, then, stress the importance of giving employees a voice in decisions which affect them, and giving them greater latitude in the way they do their jobs. There is less reliance on authority as a control mechanism, and employees are judged by their results. These theories suggest that jobs should be enlarged or enriched so as to be more challenging.

These behavioral scientists believe that participative management is the most effective way of achieving high performance and is also more conducive to satisfied and mentally healthy employees. There are some experimental results which substantiate that organizations which have implemented these practices are more productive and have higher levels of employee satisfaction.

Theories of work motivation which recognize the importance of intrinsic motivation often suggest that work should be structured to elicit this intrinsic motivation and that workers should be rewarded extrinsically for doing well. This presumably has the advantage of motivating employees both intrinsically and extrinsically at the same time, and it assumes that the effects of intrinsic and extrinsic motivation are additive.

It now seems appropriate to ask whether piece-rate payments or other extrinsic reward systems which tie rewards (especially money) to performance are compatible with participative management, which focuses on intrinsic motivation? That is, will a person's intrinsic motivation to do a job remain unaffected by extrinsic rewards?

To investigate this question I have conducted a number of experiments where subjects worked on an intrinsically interesting activity and were given extrinsic rewards for doing so.[1] Then I assessed their intrinsic motivation after their experience with the extrinsic rewards. The hundreds of college students who served as subjects worked on an intrinsically interesting spatial relations puzzle which has seven differently shaped, three dimensional pieces, each of which is made to look like it is composed of three or four one-inch cubes. Subjects used these puzzle pieces to reproduce various configurations which had been drawn on paper for them. Pilot testing showed clearly that subjects found the activity of puzzle-solving highly interesting and enjoyable.

In the experiments to be reported, the experimenter gave each person four configurations to solve and allowed ten minutes to solve each. If a subject were unable to solve one of the puzzles within the ten minutes, he was stopped and shown how to do it. He then proceeded to the next puzzle. At the end of the session with the four puzzles he was left alone in the room to read magazines, solve more puzzles, or do whatever he liked, while the experimenter ostensibly was at a computer terminal.

It was reasoned that subjects were intrinsically motivated if they spent time working on the puzzles when they were alone and when

---

[1] For a fuller presentation of these experiments, see my papers "The Effects of Contingent and Non-Contingent Rewards and Controls on Intrinsic Motivation" in *Organizational Behavior and Human Performance*, vol. 8, 1972, pp. 217–229; and "The Effects of Externally Mediated Rewards on Intrinsic Motivation" in the *Journal of Personality and Social Psychology*, vol. 18, 1971, pp. 105–115.

there were other things they could do such as reading magazines. Hence, the amount of time they spent working on the puzzles while they were alone was a measure of their intrinsic motivation.

Some of the subjects were told at the beginning of the experimental session that they would receive one dollar for each of the four puzzles which they solved within the ten minutes; some were not. Earnings for the puzzle-solving (which took about 20 minutes) ranged from $1 to $4 (average was over $2), and this was paid to subjects in cash at the end of the session. It is important to note that, for those who were promised pay, these money payments were contingent upon performance ($1 per puzzle solved).

Those students who had been paid spent significantly less time working on the puzzles when they were alone in the room than did those who had worked on the same puzzles for no pay. Once subjects began to receive contingent monetary payments for doing an interesting activity their intrinsic motivation to perform the activity decreased. That is, they were less willing to perform the activity in the absence of the external rewards than were subjects who had not been paid. The paid subjects had, to some extent, become dependent on the external rewards (money), and their intrinsic motivation had decreased. Or in other words, the locus of causality of their behavior seems to have shifted from within themselves to the external reward.

In another experiment which Wayne Cascio and I conducted,[2] subjects were told that if they were unable to solve any of the puzzles within the ten minutes, a buzzer would sound indicating that their time on that puzzle had expired. They were then given a short exposure to the buzzer so they would realize that it was truly noxious. Consequently, these subjects were performing the activity because of intrinsic motivation and also because they wanted to avoid a punishment (the buzzer). The results indicate that subjects who had performed under the threat of buzzer condition were also less intrinsically motivated than subjects who had received no threats. Since most subjects were able to solve all or all but one of the puzzles, they received little or no punishment (the buzzer) and they experienced little or no failure in doing the task, so it appears that the threat of punishment was the crucial element in decreasing intrinsic motivation in this experiment.

Their behavior, like the behavior of the paid subjects, had apparently become dependent on the external causes (avoiding punishment), and their intrinsic motivation decreased. In summation, one process by which intrinsic motivation can be affected is to have the

---

[2] Wayne Cascio, now an Assistant Professor of Psychology at Florida International University, assisted me in these experiments while he was my student.

intrinsically-motivated behavior become dependent on external causes such as tangible rewards like money or the avoidance of punishment. The perceived locus of causality shifts from within the person to the external reward and causes a decrease in intrinsic motivation.

In the studies involving money payments, the money was made contingent upon performance ($1 per puzzle solved). In another study, subjects were paid $2 for participating in the experiment regardless of their performance, and they showed no change in intrinsic motivation. This seems consistent with the change in perceived locus of causality proposition mentioned above. With the contingent payments, the subject's performance of the activity is instrumental to his receiving the reward, so he is likely to come to perceive the rewards as the *reason* for his performing the activity. With non-contingent payments, however, the payments are not directly tied to performance, so he is less likely to perceive the money as the reason for his performance. Hence, he is less likely to experience a decrease in intrinsic motivation.

We've said that a change in perceived locus of causality is one process by which intrinsic motivation can be affected; the second process involves feedback. Through this process, intrinsic motivation can either be enhanced or decreased. Subjects in one experiment were males who were reinforced with verbal statements such as "Good, that's very fast for that one," each time they solved a puzzle. The intrinsic motivation in these subjects increased due to the experience with positive verbal feedback. They liked the task more and spent more free time working on it than non-rewarded subjects. To understand why verbal reinforcements increase intrinsic motivation, we need to look at what underlies intrinsic motivation. Being intrinsically motivated involves doing an activity not because it will lead to an extrinsic reward but rather because it will allow a person to have internal feelings of competence and self-determination. Therefore, any feedback which is relevant to the person's feelings of competence and self-determination has potential for affecting his intrinsic motivation. This means, then, that external rewards can have at least two functions. One is a "controlling function" which makes a person dependent on the reward, and the other is a "feedback function" which affects his feelings of competence and self-determination.

Money and threats are commonly perceived as controllers of behavior. As a result, subjects become dependent on these controls and lose intrinsic motivation even though the money or avoided punishment *could* provide them with positive information about their competence and self-determination. On the other hand, a subject is less likely to become dependent on verbal reinforcements because he is less likely to perceive the feedback as the reason for his performance. In fact, the effect of verbal feedback may not be distinguishable from the internal feedback which he gives himself (namely, recognizing that he is competent and self-determining). So, in the experiment described above, the positive feedback would indeed have strengthened the subjects' feelings of competence and self-determination, thereby increasing their intrinsic motivation.

In a replication of the verbal reinforcement experiment we used both male and female subjects and were surprised to find a sex difference. Positive verbal feedback increases the intrinsic motivation of males, but it decreased the intrinsic motivation of females. Apparently, due to socialization processes, females more readily become dependent on verbal praise than males do. For females, we see a change in perceived locus of causality which causes a decrease in intrinsic motivation; however, the same does not happen for males.

Now imagine a situation in which the feedback is negative. It should decrease intrinsic motivation because it decreases the subjects' feelings of competence and self-determination. Wayne Cascio and I did an experiment which utilized a different set of puzzles that were much more difficult. The subjects failed badly in solving these puzzles, and afterward, they were less intrinsically motivated than subjects who had worked on somewhat easier puzzles with a higher success rate. The negative feelings associated with failure had offset some of the internal rewards associated with the activity causing a decrease in intrinsic motivation. Failing at an activity made the people less motivated to do it.

We have seen that intrinsic motivation appears to be affected by two processes: change in locus of causality, and change in feelings of competence and self-determination. Intrinsic motivation decreases when a person's behavior becomes dependent on an extrinsic reward or threat. It also decreases when a person receives negative feedback about his performance on an intrinsically motivated activity. But it increases in males as a result of positive feedback.

To understand the importance of these results for organizations, it is necessary to distinguish between keeping a person on the job and motivating him to perform effectively on that job. To attract and keep a person in an organization, it is necessary to satisfy his needs. He will have to be paid a competitive salary and given other comforts. However, satisfying a worker does not guarantee that he will be motivated to perform well on the job. Let us, therefore, consider how payments and intrinsic factors relate to satisfaction on the one hand and effective performance on the other. Paying workers is necessary to attract them to jobs and keep them satisfied with those jobs. However, in order to use money as a motivator of performance, the performance has to be perceived by the worker as being instrumental to his receiving the money. As we've said, this is generally accomplished by making pay contingent upon performance. In other words, it is not the money *per se* which motivates performance but rather the way that it is administered. To use money as an extrinsic motivator (or controller) of behavior, it has to be administered contingently. However, we've seen that not only are there many difficulties in making such a system work effectively, but also such a system decreases intrinsic motivation.

On the other hand, a system for motivating employees such as participative management, which—through participation and job enlargement—attempts to arouse intrinsic motivation, appears to motivate effective performance at the same time that it satisfies intrinsic needs. Since advocates of participative management stress the importance of intrinsic motivation, the experimental results which demonstrate that money decreases intrinsic motivation have led some antagonists to the conclusion that workers should not be payed. Clearly, such a prescription is absurd. The importance of the non-contingent payment study is that money does not decrease intrinsic motivation if it is paid non-contingently. It is possible to pay workers and still have them intrinsically motivated. So we are left with a dilemma. To use money and other extrinsic rewards as effective motivators they must be made contingent on performance. However, doing this decreases intrinsic motivation.

This suggests then that we must choose between trying to utilize either intrinsic or extrinsic reward systems. I personally favor the prescription that we concentrate on structuring situations and jobs to arouse intrinsic motivation, rather than trying to structure piece-rate and other contingency payment schemes. This preference is based on the evidence which indicates that intrinsic approaches seem to lead to greater productivity and more satisfied workers.

section three

Organizations and People: Patterns of Conflict and Accommodation

Introduction

So far as is known, no work organization to date has provided a means of completely reconciling its goals and operations with the needs and interests of all its members. In part, this statement reflects the inevitable condition that participants have discordant preference orderings among themselves, giving rise to political processes (examined in Section Four) in which trade-offs are made and viable goals are established. Furthermore, the structural devices that create the very condition of organization place constraints upon behavior. And since these devices are both designed and administered by human beings, with all of the limitations and temptations that implies, we know that instances of abuse to some members will occur, whether by accident or plan.

Increasingly, one hears these days of the "stress" suffered by people at work. Organ examines the varying interpretations of what is meant by this term and the implications for health, emotions, performance, and adaptation.

One also hears much about "careers." More and more individuals conceive of their employment, not in terms of day-to-day work experiences, but in long-term career development and personal goals. Most of these careers will unfold within large organizations and will be characterized by distinctive themes and dilemmas at various career stages. A selection from a book on careers by Kotter, Faux, and McArthur discusses these successive problems in career development and how people cope with them.

A defining characteristic of any form of organization is a means of *control*, which in turn requires various schemes of *evaluating* people, their performance, and their potential. Evaluation, more often than not, is subjective in nature and vulnerable to attitudinal and perceptual bias. A study by Rosen and Jerdee illustrates how preconceived notions about older people can distort the perceptions of their abilities and contributions. Of course, older persons are not the only victims of this phenomenon; others who sometimes share this fate are the short, the corpulent, the physically unattractive, not to mention women and minority groups.

Some individuals, whether by temperament or prior conditioning, are predisposed to accept without quarrel the constraints and discipline of work; others are not. Merrens and Garrett empirically assess the notion of the "Protestant Ethic" as a trait which accounts for these differences.

Finally, Lawler presents the case that we can, and must, go further in the direction of fashioning organizational environments to permit individual choice in such areas as job design, work schedules, compensation arrangements, and supervision.

15

The Meanings of Stress*

DENNIS W. ORGAN

Stress has become a modern watchword with a variety of meanings, both popular and scientific. Recent studies in the physiology of stress have important implications for executive behavior.

Everybody knows about it, everyone talks about it, and—judging by the number of paperback books and magazine articles currently devoted to the subject—everyone seems to be interested in it. People complain about the stress of work and the stress of retirement; the stress of poverty and the stress created by fame and riches; the stress of crowding and the stress of isolation; the stress of adolescence and the stress of the midlife crisis. To describe someone as "working under enormous stress" is at once to offer sympathy and to accord a measure of respect. To fail at a task *because* of stress is no shame; to succeed *in spite of* stress renders success all the more glorious. Any behavior, no matter how bizarre, cruel, or apparently irrational, is suddenly understandable if we imagine the behaver as operating under stress. Any act of love or benevolence is somehow tarnished if it did not create stress for the actor or was not born out of the very crucible of stress.

Stress, in sum, has become a watchword of the time, a sibilant one-syllable utterance that comes as close as any one word to expressing the subjective tone of a world view. But the term has developed an elasticity of meaning. The word functions more and more to express rather than to denote. Thus the term becomes more susceptible to usage when it can be neither proved nor disproved, and when it is therefore neither meaningful nor helpful. This would not be cause for concern if stress were merely a vernacular term like *love, anger, ambition*, or *luck*. Certain words are useful precisely because they are preserved for signifying what is, after all, ineffable. *Stress*, however, is also a scientific term. Now there would be no problem if the scientific use of stress were strictly divorced from its vernacular usage; after all, one seldom experiences any problem distinguishing between the ten-

From *Business Horizons* 22, no. 3 (1979), pp. 32–40. Copyright, 1979, by the Foundation for the School of Business at Indiana University. Reprinted by permission.

sion of a wire and the tension of studying for an exam, or between the pressure exerted by a liquid in a container and the pressure experienced when one is working on a tight schedule. In both cases the technical terms are precise, and the nontechnical meanings are vague and inchoate. One will at times belabor the analogies for literary or rhetorical effect, but no one seriously tries to apply the laws of physics to studying for an exam or working under a deadline. Unfortunately, the vernacular and technical meanings of "stress" have become thoroughly confused, possibly because they do overlap to some degree. The confusion has occasioned some serious misunderstanding about the relationships between stress and illness, stress and adaptation, stress and performance, and even stress and life.

VERNACULAR MEANINGS

In everyday discourse, "stress" has a pejorative connotation. If used in reference to something outside us, it generally means something to be avoided or, at best, a necessary evil: a critical, hard-driving boss; congested urban traffic; a final exam; preparing an income tax return on the night of April 14; enduring Howard Cosell's commentary while you watch the Cowboys and the Vikings. If used to describe a subjective feeling, the term is roughly synonymous with tension, dread, anxiety, or worry. Occasionally we do, of course, dilute the pejorative color of the term by associating it with achievements of one sort or another, as when a speaker welcomes the "edge" of stress (tension) before taking the podium, or the stress (pain) of training and preparing for the Boston Marathon. Yet even then the term is used in what is essentially as intrinsically negative sense, "good" only because it is inextricably linked to an eventual outcome (success, victory) which is sought. In brief, we use the term in everyday parlance to mean either a source or cause of discomfort, or the feelings of discomfort itself—that is, "distress."

Now there is nothing wrong or incorrect in using the word in this manner. In fact, the dictionary will confirm that this is a perfectly acceptable form of usage. It is wrong only when one substitutes this definition of stress for the precise technical meaning of stress in statements about relationships between stress and illness, performance, and adaptation. As a technical term in medical science, stress is not something "out there," nor is it a state of mind. Both external circumstances and internal emotional states can be *stressors*, or sources of stress (although neither the circumstances nor the emotion need be unpleasant, undesired, or negative in order to qualify as stressors). But stress itself, as a technical term, refers to a pattern of complex, albeit well-defined physiological reactions.

STRESS AS A PHYSIOLOGICAL STATE

Stress became a scientific construct when it was defined and elaborated in the research and writing of Professor Hans Selye. As a young medical student at the University of Prague in 1925, Selye was struck by the observation that certain symptoms seemed to correlate with illness of all types. A physician could not complete a diagnosis for a patient based on the evidence that he was suffering from headaches, loss of appetite, nausea, and weakness in the muscles; the doctor would need something more "specific" in order to determine what the underlying problem was. Selye wondered if there might not be something of significance to this observation, namely that the body has a stereotyped, nonspecific reaction to any demand placed upon it. He later discovered in experiments with laboratory animals that whether one subjected rats to extreme cold, injected chemical irritants into their tissue, or simply forcefully immobilized them, there were certain common reactions in the animal's physiological processes. Of course, there were specific effects associated with each particular treatment, but Selye was interested in the common denominators—the invariant response of the organism's body to any demand placed upon it. The common features constituted what Selye labelled the general adaptation syndrome, or G.A.S.—the symptoms by which a state of stress is manifested.

Selye's *The Stress of Life*, published in 1956 and written for nontechnically trained audiences, makes it clear that one of the conspicuous agents in this syndrome is the pituitary, a cherry-sized organ resting at the base of the brain. When some external force (a germ, overload on a muscle group, extreme cold) threatens the body, the pituitary signals the alarm stage, the first of the three-stage G.A.S., by sending ACTH (the adrenocorticotrophic hormone) to the endocrine glands, including the adrenals. The adrenals, in response, secrete their hormones (adrenalin and noradrenalin, collectively called the catecholamines) into the bloodstream, and eventually these in collaboration with the sympathetic nervous system trigger a succession of changes in the body chemistry, including changes in the digestive organs, metabolism, and the level of fatty acids and clotting elements in the blood. These effects triggered by the adrenals constitute the second stage of Selye's G.A.S., the stage of resistance, during which the organism seemingly adapts to the demand placed upon it, enabling it to neutralize, isolate, or minimize the damage to the integrity of the organism as a whole. Given sufficiently long exposure to any of the noxious elements (severe cold, chemical irritant, electric shock), the third stage, exhaustion, follows as the adaptive energies of the organism are depleted.

For Selye, then, stress means the common denominator of all adaptive reactions by the body to stressors placed upon it. While Selye means demands of any kind, his interest is clearly in those demands which are clearly physical in nature. Psychologists have, on the other hand, been more interested in demands which are more subtle—demands originating from the social environment, demands cued by symbols, or demands exerted by the emotions and the psyche. Such demands are quite relevant to the concept of stress as defined by Selye because of the mediating role played by the hypothalamus, one of the lower centers of the brain. The hypothalamus regulates many functions of the body, including hunger and temperature; it regulates emotions; and, under conditions of emotional arousal (fear, anger, even ecstasy), sends messages to the pituitary which trigger the sequence of events described in Selye's endocrine studies. It is important, however, to note that any strong emotional response—whether interpreted as "good" or "bad," or even whether a person is consciously aware of or attending to the emotion—results in stress as defined by Selye.

But the emotion is the stressor, not the stress itself; the emotion is the source of the demand which triggers the stress response. The demand need not be emotional in nature to evoke the stress response. So when we speak of *psychological stress* in a way which is at all faithful to the technical meaning of stress, we mean demands or sources of stress that are psychological in nature—for example, anxiety, frustration, or approach-avoidance conflict. There are other demands on the body which evoke the stress response yet arouse no strong feelings at all, and we find that many instances of emotional arousal not ordinarily thought of as "stressful" (in the vernacular) do in fact lead to stress as defined by Selye.

STRESS AND FEELINGS

Consider the results of an experiment conducted by Dr. Lennart Levi of the Karolinska Institute in Stockholm.[1] On successive evenings he arranged for 20 female clerical workers to see four films. The first of these was a bland movie about the Swedish countryside. The other movies were selected for their presumed ability to arouse some strong emotion: "Paths of Glory," a movie about the arbitrary execution of three men as scapegoats following a breakdown of a French army unit in World War I, was considered to be anger-provoking; "Charley's Aunt," a comedy, was expected to induce a pleasant emotional arousal; and "The Mask of Satan," a horror film, was selected to

---

[1] Lennart Levi, *Stress and Distress in Response to Psychosocial Stimuli* (New York: Pergamon Press, 1972), pp. 55–73.

arouse fear and anxiety. The films had their intended effects, as shown by the subjects' ratings and descriptions of the movies as well as their reports of their own reactions. The natural scenery film they judged to be rather boring; they felt aggressive and angry watching "Paths of Glory"; amused, happy, and laughing at "Charley's Aunt"; and frightened by "Mask of Satan." In other words, subjects "felt" different emotions for the different movies. Levi found, however, in an analysis of subjects' urine samples following each movie, that except for the dull scenery film the movies were equally stressful, regardless of whether the film provoked a "pleasant" or "unpleasant" emotion. All three of the movies inducing emotional arousal were associated with increased levels of adrenalin and noradrenalin in the urine, a tell-tale indicator of the stress syndrome defined by Selye.

STRESS AND ILLNESS

The accompanying table shows a list of changes or events that can occur in a person's life. With each event a number is associated that serves as a rough index of the relative degree of adjustment demanded by the event. The weighting scheme was derived through studies by Professors T. H. Holmes and R. H. Rahe and their colleagues at the University of Washington.[2] Their studies asked people of varying ages and from several different cultures to compare each event with each other in terms of the degree of adjustment required. It seems to be universally agreed that the death of a spouse requires more adjustment on the part of the surviving spouse than any other single event. The table provides a rough measure of the degree of adjustment required of a person by totaling the number of points associated with each change in a given period.

Holmes and his co-workers find that once a person "earns" 200 or more points in a single year, there is at least a 50–50 chance of experiencing a fairly serious breakdown in health in the following year. One who totals up 300 or more points in a year runs that risk factor up to a 75–80 percent chance. The illness brought on by such demands for adjustment can appear in almost every specific form: digestive ailments, respiratory problems, back trouble, kidney malfunction, injuries to the bones or muscles, almost any breakdown in the body's economy. What is the explanation for this relationship? Significant changes in one's immediate life environment trigger a rapid succession of new situations with which one has to cope. The endocrine system—the intricate collaborative workings of the pituitary, the adre-

---

[2] T. H. Holmes and R. H. Rahe, "The Social Readjustment Rating Scale," *Journal of Psychosomatic Research*, November 1968, pp. 213–218.

Social Readjustment Rating Scale

Life Event	Scale Value
Death of spouse	100
Divorce	73
Marital separation	65
Jail term	63
Death of a close family member	63
Major personal injury or illness	53
Marriage	50
Fired from work	47
Marital reconciliation	45
Retirement	45
Major change in health of family member	44
Pregnancy	40
Sex difficulties	39
Gain of a new family member	39
Business readjustment	39
Change in financial state	38
Death of a close friend	37
Change to a different line of work	36
Change in number of arguments with spouse	35
Mortgage over $10,000	31
Foreclosure of mortgage or loan	30
Change in responsibilities at work	29
Son or daughter leaving home	29
Trouble with in-laws	29
Outstanding personal achievement	28
Wife begins or stops work	26
Begin or end school	26
Change in living conditions	25
Revision of personal habits	24
Trouble with boss	23
Change in work hours or conditions	20
Change in residence	20
Change in schools	20
Change in recreation	19
Change in church activities	19
Change in social activities	18
Mortgage or loan less than $10,000	17
Change in sleeping habits	16
Change in number of family get-togethers	15
Change in eating habits	15
Vacation	13
Christmas	12
Minor violations of the law	11

Source: L. O. Ruch and T. H. Holmes, "Scaling of Life Change: Comparison of Direct and Indirect Methods," *Journal of Psychosomatic Research,* June 1971, p. 224.

nals, the extra doses of hormones—provides the means for borrowing from the long-term store of adaptation energy in order to provide the sustained arousal and vigilance needed to cope with the novelty, uncertainty, or conflict occasioned by the new situations. But remember it is this encodrine system which provides the basis for resistance to any agent which threatens the body. We are constantly exposed to, even constantly transporting within us, microbes that can do damage to body tissues. Usually a healthy, immune system defends against such bacteria. But if the endocrine system is constantly marshaling the body's energy for adjustment, the capacity for resisting those lurking microbes will be exhausted. Thus wherever the body is most vulnerable, a breakdown can occur after a period of sufficiently great demands for social or psychological adjustment.[3]

One should take note of the fact that a number of events in the table are "positive"; one ordinarily thinks of them as occasions for pleasure or celebration. The layman's definition of "stress" as something to be avoided, something not preferred, hardly seems to apply to events such as marriage, birth of a child, promotion, outstanding personal achievement, sudden drastic improvement in financial position, moving to a bigger home in a better neighborhood, or graduation from college. Yet, to the extent that these events pose demands for adjustment, they are stressful in Selye's sense; and, if enough of these changes are bunched together, they can produce health problems.

One can also see in the "Type A" coronary-prone behavior pattern, described by Meyer Friedman and Ray H. Rosenman, how the linkage between stress, technically defined, and illness is somewhat different from the relationship involving the vernacular meaning of stress as distress. The Type A pattern is one of struggle against the limitations of time; of poised, combative, even hostile striving to compete against other people; of stretching one's self incessantly against self-imposed goals in leisure as well as work.[4]

In *The Hurricane Years*, Cameron Hawley has given us a personification of the Type A executive in the character of Judd Wilder. In the opening pages of the novel, Wilder, an advertising and promotion executive for a carpet company, is leaving the Pennsylvania turnpike and trying to return from New York with the proofs of the stockholders' report before 8:30 that evening. There is no particular urgency in getting the report back by that time; it is simply a goal Wilder has set for himself. Behind the wheel, he experiences a massive heart attack and is rushed to a county hospital. There he comes under the care of

---

[3] For a readable account of the effect of life changes on illness, see Alvin Toffler, *Future Shock* (New York: Random House, 1970), pp. 289–304.

[4] Meyer Friedman and Ray H. Rosenman, *Type A Behavior and Your Heart* (New York: Alfred A. Knopf, 1974).

Dr. Aaron Kharr, who soon recognizes the behavior pattern characteristic of men like Wilder: ". . . inherently aggressive, competitive, en-
ergetic, and ambitious . . . naturally geared to operate at a high
adrenaline level."

The incessant process of struggle provokes a chronically fast-paced
tempo of the endocrine system with consequent chronically high levels of adrenal hormones in the blood. These hormones, which cannot
be metabolized in the overt fight-or-flight response for which they
were designed by evolution, cause clotting elements in the blood
which speed up the formation of plaques in the arterial walls. Thus
Type As have a much higher than average risk of premature coronary
artery disease, even when other risk factors (such as high blood pressure, cigarette smoking, high-fat diet) are held constant.

Curiously, though, the Type A does not think of himself as "nervous," "under stress," or in any sense crippled by anxiety. Indeed,
according to Friedman and Rosenman, anxiety is an unfamiliar state of
mind to the extreme Type A. Also, Type As seldom experience the
subjective sense of fatigue.[5] The stress which is the bane of Type As is
not conscious discomfort or distress on an emotional dimension, but
rather the response of the endocrine system to the unreasonable succession of demands they place upon themselves as they, like Judd
Wilder, become "hooked on adrenaline."

STRESS AND PERFORMANCE

An issue long of interest to layman and scientist alike concerns the
effect of stress on job performance. Some people believe that a lapse in
performance is itself evidence of unusual stress experienced by the
performer; others believe that stress is a direct contributor to improved, more effortful work on a job. Certainly stress, in the vernacular
sense, is likely to impair performance of a complex task because of the
distractions produced by worry or fear or other connotations inherent
in the layman's definition of stress. However, if we define stress in the
more precise, scientific manner as intended by Selye, we can discern
no general relationship in the empirical data between stress and quality of performance. The reason for this is that the stress syndrome is in
response to the total demand from all sources placed on the person.
Part of that demand may be the very effort to maintain performance in
the presence of simultaneously competing demands from the environment, such as unpredictable noise, information overload, fatigue from
illness, or even distractions by sexually arousing stimuli.

---

[5] See David C. Glass, *Behavior Patterns, Stress, and Coronary Disease* (Hillsdale,
N.J.: Lawrence Erlbaum Associates, 1977), pp. 42–50.

Studies by Professor David Glass and his colleagues at Rockefeller University show that subjects working on a clerical task under conditions of randomly intermittent, irritating noise were able to stabilize at a performance level equivalent to subjects working under less adverse conditions.[6] The evidence of stress induced by the noise came not in any differences in quantity or quality of work between groups, but later, *after* the noise ended. Subjects who had coped with the simultaneous demands of performing as well as coping with the noise later showed less tolerance for the frustration of trying to solve what was (unbeknownst to them) actually an insoluble puzzle. Glass was not willing to go so far as to say that the stress of adaptation had *caused* the subsequent decline in frustration tolerance, but the link certainly suggests that stress is more often behaviorally reflected in situations temporally and spatially removed from the original sources of demand than it is shown directly or immediately in "performance." The adaptation energy extracted by a higher than normal level of endocrine activity must be replenished sooner or later, and the involuntary "letdown" which seems to be necessary for such replenishment may show up in such trivial, apparently unrelated symptoms as forgetting to lock the garage door, injuring oneself with a power saw, or inadvertently dumping cigarette ashes into one's full cup of coffee.

STRESS AND ADAPTATION

Actually, the replenishment of adaptation energy referred to above is illusory, according to Selye. Selye believes that each person has a fixed, finite reservoir of adaptation energy to feed the endocrine system. One cannot increase this amount; all one can do is occasionally transfer some from long-term reserves to a smaller but more immediately available status—much like depositing some of your life's savings into current withdrawal accounts. That transfer, it appears, does require some temporary lapse in the form of rest or even "depression." But it is nonetheless a borrowing which can never be repaid.

Thus "adaptation" is costly. To the layman, someone adapting to a stressful condition is functioning in the condition so that it is no longer stressful; one "is getting used to it so it doesn't bother him anymore." For Selye, however, adaptation is the very stuff of which stress is made. It is precisely the process of getting used to it—whether "it" be cold temperatures, muscular strain, or a critical boss—which uses up some of the fixed store of adaptation energy.

---

[6] David C. Glass and Jerome E. Singer, *Urban Stress: Experiments in Noise and Social Stressors* (New York: Academic Press, 1972).

IMPLICATIONS FOR MANAGERS

To eliminate stress means to eliminate all things which require adaptation, and that virtually means to eliminate life itself. Even to reduce stress to minimal practical levels means never to visit a stimulating city, never to gaze at an attractive woman, never to take up new activities, never to pursue one's dreams—if possible, even never to dream. Surely, such a life is hardly worth living, whatever it might promise in the form of longevity. As Selye puts it,

> Vitality is like a special kind of bank account which you can use up by withdrawals but cannot increase by deposits. Your only control over this most precious fortune is the rate at which you make your withdrawals. . . . The intelligent thing to do is to withdraw generously but never expend wastefully.

Selye concedes that there are probably vast differences among individuals in the amount of adaptation energy given to them to draw upon. And even his basic premise, that the amount of adaptation energy available to a person is a genetically predetermined constant, is a theoretical supposition not shared by all other experts. Nevertheless, his point of view is worth pondering, for it poses some serious philosophical implications.

Consider, for example, the adage that "anything worth doing at all is worth doing well." Quite a few people, many successful managers among them, seem to live and work implicitly by this principle. Yet managers often seem to agree with another notion that "80 percent of your success is determined by 20 percent of what you do." Selye's position would be that the crucially important 20 percent may be well worth the extravagant stores of endocrine-derived adaptation energy necessary to meet the demands posed by that 20 percent. For the remaining 80 percent, however, it would be wasteful, uneconomical, and downright inefficient to place the same demands upon one's self or upon others. The 80 percent is worth doing, and perhaps has to be done in some fashion in order for the other 20 percent to mean anything; but it does not necessarily have to be done immediately, perfectly, or even well. Yet it is curious that many managers who seem to be so judiciously and expertly selective in the expenditure of money and other finite physical resources can be so indiscriminate in disbursing the most precious finite resource of all—vitality.

16

Self-Assessment and Career Development

JOHN P. KOTTER, VICTOR A. FAUX, and
CHARLES McARTHUR*

THE FIRST YEAR OUT†

For many people the first year of work after graduating from school
is a period of great challenge and excitement. It is a time characterized
by considerable changes—a new job, new work associates, a new
dwelling, a new city.

The first year out can also be a difficult period. In a recent survey of
MBAs six months after graduation, 62 percent reported that they were
less than happy with either job, employer, career progress, or lifestyle.
Only 5 percent of those sampled reported no real problems since graduation.

Those who have studied the experiences of recent graduates have
concluded that people who have a relatively trouble-free first year out
tend to be systemically different from those who experience some
difficulty. Specifically, those students who make more personally appropriate job choices, who start work with realistic expectations concerning what will follow, and who take an active role in managing
their own "joining-up" process, seem to experience significantly fewer
problems during their first year out than those students who don't. In
this chapter we explore the nature and consequences of each of these
patterns of differences.

The Impact of Job Choice (and Related Decisions)

As one might expect, many of the problems reported by people
during their first year out can be traced directly to an inappropriate job

* From John P. Kotter, Victor A. Faux, and Charles McArthur, *Self-Assessment and
Career Development: A systematic approach to the selection and management of a
career,* © 1978, pp. 177–80 and 185–87. Reprinted by permission of Prentice-Hall, Inc.,
Englewood Cliffs, N.J.

† The first part of this reading is taken from a note, "The First Year Out," by
Professor John P. Kotter. Copyright © 1975 by the President and Fellows of Harvard
College. Reprinted by permission of the Harvard Business School.

selection. For a variety of reasons, some people make job decisions based on an incomplete or inaccurate understanding of themselves, the job, or both. These kinds of decisions invariably lead to problems and often to a change of jobs within a year of graduation.

The same underlying causes that lead people to poor job decisions often lead them to poor decisions in other important areas of their lives. Recent graduates sometimes make inappropriate decisions regarding how to approach a new job, where to live, how to allocate their income, and so on. Again, an incomplete or inaccurate understanding of themselves, the option they are choosing, or both, creates first-year-out problems for them.

Underestimating how much he depends on the proximity of friends for relaxation and support, Bill Jones takes an apartment by himself in an area where he knows no one. Within three months his loneliness seriously affects his work. Helen Johnson, who never commuted more than a few miles to work or school before, finds exactly what she wants in a house about 25 miles from work. After moving in, she finds that it takes one hour to drive to or from work. The 10-hours-a-week commute eats into both her work and nonwork activities, creating a variety of problems for her. Herb Palmer is not really aware of how slowly he gets up to speed in a new situation, so he bases his decision to "not even think about work" after accepting the job offer on other considerations. The same is the case with his decision to take a six-week vacation and start work on August 1. When October 1 comes, all of Herb's contemporaries are well settled in their jobs and Herb's continuing awkwardness stands out like a sore thumb to him and others, including his boss.

As the above examples suggest, virtually none of the important individual decisions made just before or during one's first year of work are independent of the other decisions. Each decision tends to affect other parts of one's life in small and large ways, now and in the future. Insensitivity to the interdependence among decisions and their consequences inevitably leads to problems for many recent graduates.

Pete and Pam Marsh, for example, really wanted to return to a less urban part of the Midwest after graduation. Their families and many of their old friends were still there. Pete carefully looked for jobs in that area but found nothing really appealing. Bit by bit, he began to search in a wider area and he eventually landed a job, enviously considered by his friends to be "a find." The starting salary was good and the company would allow a long vacation period and pay moving expenses—to New York City! After a tense and anxiety-producing process, the Marshes agreed to accept the job. They found a decent apartment and put their six-year-old in school. Pam made some friends and so did their four-year-old. Pete threw himself into the job. Next came another "find"—a great house, close to the apartment, and at a good price. They moved. But after eight months Pete became increasingly frustrated. The job was not developing, and the company seemed less than supportive as time wore on. After 10 months he left. He wanted once again to look for jobs in the less urban part of the Midwest. But what of the child in school, the other child's friends. Pam's attempts to dig in, and the house? He ended up taking another job in the city. Their big-city lifestyle in a short time quite subtly had become the constraint affecting Pete's job choice. It didn't start out that way.

Operationally, this means that in making important job and nonjob decisions one needs to take into account *all* aspects of one's life. The relevant system to analyze when making a job decision or lifestyle decision is one's entire life system (see Figure 1).

People occasionally like to deny that these decisions are interdependent. They want to believe that why they do at work and what they do out of work can be totally separated. They want that "freedom." As they soon learn, the world as we experience it today is one big interdependent mass, and the interdependencies are growing, not shrinking. And those who do not understand that, or who refuse to accept it, are in for a tough time.

The change from student to employee is, in most instances, a very

FIGURE 1
A Life System

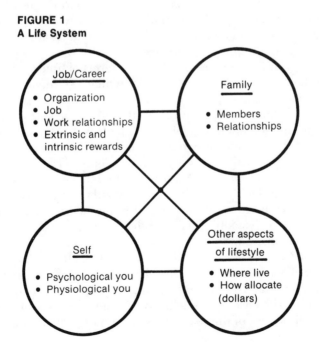

large change. Many people, especially those with little or no full-time work experience, tend to underestimate the size and nature of this change. They enter their job with very unrealistic epectations, based mostly on their student experiences. This leads to inappropriate behavior, which sometimes alienates others or is just ineffective at accomplishing given tasks. The end result for the individual is frustration and disappointment.

Consider for a moment a few of the major ways in which the environment of a student and that of a full-time employee differ:

1. *Bosses.* A student at any one point in time will have four, five, or six "bosses" (teachers), who usually change every four months, and who are often selected by the student. An employee usually has one boss, sometimes for years, with little if any influence over the choice of that superior. These different situations make for very different superior/subordinate dynamics. New workers sometimes continue to behave as if their boss were a professor whom they could ignore, or at worst, get rid of in a few months. Such behavior causes obvious problems.

2. *Feedback from Superiors.* A student learns to expect brief, quantitative performance evaluations (grades) on numerous specific occasions throughout the year. Such a person will often get written feedback on his or her work also. An employee, on the other hand, may *never* get any concrete feedback from superiors outside of pay raises or promotions. It is not unusual for new workers to feel that they are working in a vacuum and that the organization is at fault for not giving them more feedback.

3. *Time Span.* A student learns to think in terms of time cycles of one or two hours (a class), one week (after which a sequence of classes repeats itself), and four months (a semester, when classes change). The time span of an employee can be as short as a few hours (in some production/operating jobs) or as long as many years (in some planning jobs). More importantly, the time cycle can change on the job, often leaving the new employee confused and disoriented.

4. *Magnitude of Decisions.* A business student often gets used to making a number of major decisions (hypothetically) every day. At least at first, the new employee will rarely make any major decisions in his or her job. This often leads to feelings of being underused or ignored.

5. *Speed of Change.* Because of the pace of academic life and the number of major innovations and changes students are encouraged to consider, they often develop highly unrealistic expectations concerning the ease and quickness of making changes in the real world. Discovery of the realities is often quite frustrating and depressing.

6. *Promotion.* A student with a master's degree and no full-time work experience has lived in an environment where promotion occurred once every 12 months—19 promotions in 19 years. It is no wonder that when a student takes a job five levels below the president, others often complain that "the young hot-shot seems to want to be president in just a few years."
7. *The Nature of Problems.* Schools often carefully select problems that can be solved in a short period of time using some method or theory that is being taught. Such a process is "efficient" by many educational standards. New workers often find it incredibly frustrating when the problems they are given aren't as neat and solvable and the information needed for a decision isn't available.

And we could go on, but the point should be clear by now.

Individuals also create a slightly different kind of unrealistic expectation through a poor assessment of themselves and the job while job hunting. The benefits of the self-assessment, opportunity-assessment, and job-assessment processes, described earlier in the book, go far beyond the job-offer decision. The very process of systematically assessing yourself, your future organization, and your job helps create more realistic expectations about what your initial experiences will be like in that job. More realistic expectations lead to fewer disappointing surprises and to more intelligent, adaptive, problem-solving decisions on your part.

Phil Hammer, for example, learned through his self-assessment how much he tended to overlook detail. He learned through his job assessment that his new job would require some (not a lot of) attention to certain types of detail. When he started work in his new job, he took specific actions to avoid a potential problem. First, he managed to rearrange his secretarial assignment so that he was assigned a person who was very detail oriented. Second, he explained his "problem" to his secretary, whom he requested as a major aspect of secretarial responsibility to keep track of details for him. Finally, he made it a habit to carry a note pad with him at all times and forced himself to make himself notes so that he wouldn't overlook things. After 12 months on the job, Phil had not created one single significant problem because of his personal "weakness."

Regardless of the source, inaccurate expectations cause problems for recent graduates. They cause poor performance, disappointment, frustration, and low morale. In some cases the organization concludes that the inappropriate behavior reflects a poor employee selection on their part, and the person is let go. In some cases, feeling "had" by the organization for not being warned about what was to come, the employee quits. In still other cases the problems are overcome, but seldom without leaving some bad feelings all around.

Managing One's Own "Joining Up"

Perhaps one of the most lethal expectations of recent graduates is that, in effect, "It is the organization's responsibility to make sure that the new employee gets the orientation and training needed to be able to do his or her job." Some organizations do try to systematically and quickly help all new employees get "up to speed." They have orientation programs, training programs, and special first assignments. But very few companies do even a fair job of making sure that all new people get the specific orientation, training, and help they need to get up to speed quickly and efficiently.

Most people who have an effective, relatively trouble-free year after leaving school, explicitly or implicitly take responsibility for their own "joining up." Regardless of whether their organization has "programs" for new people, these people systematically take actions to help themselves get "on board." They recognize that if they don't take the initiative, and something goes wrong, they will probably have to suffer the consequences.

In assuming responsibility for their own joining up, people typically take a variety of actions both before they start work and immediately afterward (see Figure 2). While most students do virtually nothing between the day they accept a job offer and the day they show up for work to help their period of adjustment from school to work, others do a number of useful and practical things. By requesting an organization chart and a book of employee pictures (if available), for example, you can start to learn the names and faces of people you will be working with on your new job. Knowing who's who, of course, can be enormously helpful to a new employee. It's much easier for most people to do this in a leisurely way over a two- or three-month period instead of trying to intensely learn names and faces the first few weeks of work, when you are trying to learn so many other things too. As a general rule, the more that you can do before starting work to relieve the burden of your first few weeks on the job, the fewer problems you will face in your first year out.

A variety of actions that people sometimes take once they start work are designed primarily to assist their joining up. By sitting down and having a fairly long and detailed talk with one's boss, for example, regarding what he or she expects, you can help minimize the probability that you will inadvertently violate those expectations. Disappointing, surprising, or annoying your new boss during your first few months on the job can prove to be a major impediment to your joining up, since your boss is usually the key person who can help you during that period, or block your way.

Different people will no doubt prefer different specific tactics to help them once they have started work. However, two general rules of

FIGURE 2
Examples of Actions That Can Help a Person Get Up to Speed in a New Job

Before Starting Work
1. Get on the organization's mailing list.
2. Get your new boss's secretary to send you copies of memos, etc., that you would receive if you had already started work.
3. Request an organization chart and a book of pictures of employees (if one exists) and start learning names and faces.
4. Subscribe to the local paper in the town or city where you will be working.
5. Write to the Chamber of Commerce and real estate agents for information on housing, schools, etc.
6. Open a local bank account.

After Starting Work

1. Invite people to lunch to get to know them.
2. Get to know the secretaries (great sources of information).
3. If athletically inclined, join some of the organization's teams (a good way to form relationships informally).
4. Sit down and have a long talk with your boss regarding what he or she expects of you.

---

thumb seem to be universally applicable to aid the recent graduate. We'll end this discussion of the first year out by passing this sage advice on to you: (1) a modicum of humility usually helps and (2) so does listening very carefully.

THE EARLY CAREER

In the early phase of a career, usually between ages 20 and 35, people make and deepen initial commitments to a type of work, an organization, and a nonwork lifestyle. Professionals, in particular, expend considerable energy to become competent (and recognized as such by others) in their chosen trade. It is usually an exciting period, in which one begins to try to fulfill expectations about the "professional me" that have been developing (through education) for two decades.

Four general sets of issues seem to be particularly important if one is to try to understand this early phase, the obstacles encountered, and the methods typically used to deal with them. One set of issues relates to adapting to being an employee in a complex human organization. A second has to do with getting established in one's work or organization and achieving some initial success. A third has to do with establishing some type of a workable relationship between one's career and the nonwork aspects of life. The fourth relates to a period of questioning of initial career and noncareer choices, which most people go through around age 30.

Adapting to the Realities of Complex Organizations

Most professionals start their careers within an established organization. Having been students in an educational setting for anywhere from 16 to 22 years, they suddenly become employees inside what are usually noneducational organizations . . . this change can create some serious problems for people in their first year of work. Beyond that, the ability to grasp quickly the more subtle realities associated with human organizations often makes the difference between a very successful and an ordinary early career. Some of the more important of these realities are discussed below.

Distribution of Rewards

Simply doing what you think is a good job, or even a very good job, is no guarantee that you will receive the rewards you desire.

For a number of complex reasons, most established organizations do not have performance evaluation systems that (1) completely define what "good performance" is for each job, (2) make sure that employees are aware of those performance criteria, (3) systematically collect data on employees' performances, (4) feed those data back to employees so they can monitor how they are doing, and (5) use those data as the basis for distributing rewards (such as interesting assignments, promotions, money, discretion, etc.). Considerable evidence exists that such a system would be very beneficial for employees, especially during the early career. But because "good" performance is often difficult and expensive to define and measure, and because creating such systems where they don't exist is expensive and time consuming, good performance appraisal systems are very seldom found in organizations.

Instead, rewards are distributed in most organizations based on the judgments of a number of people (a person's immediate superior is usually the key judge), some of whom may have only secondhand information on many of the people they are asked to judge. People who are successful in their initial careers are those who perform well on the criteria used by the judges, and whose performance record is known by the judges. It is for these reasons that the better "how to" books on building a successful career stress (a) learning what your bosses' expectations are concerning your work and (b) getting involved in some highly visible projects.

Development of Potential

Most organizations have no coherent system to make sure that people, in their early careers, get the experience, training, and human contacts needed to really develop their potential for their own benefit and the organization's.

Although the development of people is an important goal for most organizations, it is a *long-range goal*. In most organizations, long-run objectives receive a priority lower than short-run concerns. For this and other reasons (e.g., expense) employee development is seldom given anything close to the resources needed to do a uniformly good job. Even in companies where resources have been allocated to employee development, and where training programs and job rotation systems have been created, numerous individuals seem to end up coping with short-run demands at the expense of their future development.

We have seen many former students who seem to learn more in their first five years of work than others learn in 15 years or more. The fast-learning group appear to be different from others in that they proactively take responsibility for their own learning. They seek out role models and mentors, recognizing that one relationship with a highly talented and successful senior person can be enormously instructive. They don't stay in any one job for more than a few years, taking advantage of the fact that almost all the learning associated with most jobs comes in the first two years. They don't wait to be assigned to new projects and jobs by others; they nominate themselves. In this and other ways they actively manage their own careers.

Dependency on Others

Most professional jobs in organizations, especially managerial jobs, make an individual dependent on numerous others, who often have different or conflicting objectives. Complex interdependencies and conflict are facts of life in most organizations. Individuals who cannot (or will not) find a way to effectively manage their own dependencies are in for a hard time.

Younger people in particular often feel their dependence on others who know more than they do about the job, the organization, the people, and how to get things done. Young managers will often find themselves dependent on the cooperation of subordinates, a boss, other senior officials, various service departments, and possibly even outside suppliers, customers, and regulators. All of these individuals and groups have limited time and talent, and their objectives sometimes clash with cooperation. Students are seldom if ever trained in how to manage this type of dependence network.

Managers use a wide variety of techniques to cope with their complex dependencies. Their techniques are sometimes aimed at reducing dependence, sometimes at influencing those on whom they are dependent to cooperate in certain ways, and sometimes at gaining power over the dependencies (which makes influencing them much easier). The faster a young employee learns to use these techniques effectively, the more successful he or she will generally be in the early career.

The larger and more complex the organization, the more time people end up having to spend managing interdependencies. For example, the following is excerpted from a 29-year-old manager's description of what he does in a typical day at a moderately large manufacturing company:

> When I arrive in the morning I normally read the paper for 15 minutes or a half hour to catch up on the latest news. Randomly throughout the month I will call my boss before working hours actually begin, to let him know that I'm there and on the job, and he can reach me whenever he wants me. This is an important game to play in my situation, because he is located in a different building eight miles away, and sometimes he feels a little insecure as to whether all of his people are working full time and are doing the kinds of things he would like to have done.
>
> I spend about one fourth of the day actually here in my office. The table in the center of the office is the major working area, and it's round. I don't have a standard desk. This was something that I designed when I was promoted six months ago. The average age of my direct reports was about 47–48 years old, and I felt that it would be very difficult for me, being only 28 at the time, to sit behind a big desk and give these guys orders. They had 20 years of experience and knew the company backward and forward. There wasn't any way I could effectively tell them what to do. So I decided to get in a round table and to make sure that all the chairs around the table were of the same type and description so there wouldn't be any overt status difference between anyone in the office, so that we could build a teamwork relationship among all members of the group.
>
> After reading the morning paper I would normally attend several meetings. I spend almost 70 percent of my normal day in meetings. By the way, that drives a lot of people nuts, and it bothers me too, but most of our meetings really are necessary. My peers and I have got to know what each other and top management are doing or we trip all over each other. Meetings are often the best way to get the information across. Meetings are also useful when I need the commitment from other divisions for some action, and when we have a problem but not all the expertise to solve it.

This would take me normally till about 10:30 or 10:45, at which point I would come back to the office and handle the mail. The mail comes in a stack of about 4 to 6 inches each day. I would quickly sort it and deliver messages to my staff to work on the projects and various assignments that came through the mail. I would delegate all the assignments with the exception of *politically* sensitive issues. Those I would discuss with the appropriate manager and handle them together with him. Normally it would take me 10 or 15 minutes to sort the mail and another 15 to 20 discussing the various sensitive issues.

This would bring me to around 11:30–11:45, where I would work on my personal mail, which includes salary and merit reviews, expense accounts, purchase requisitions, etc. This would take me right up to lunch.

After lunch, the schedule of activities changes, depending on what part of the year it is. During the first half of the year the work load is not as heavy as during the last half. During the first half of the year I would spend most of the afternoon in meetings of the type described earlier. In the latter part of the year I spend a great deal of time working on the annual long-range plan. This is a very extensive effort and requires hundreds and hundreds of man-hours of work to put together the details, schedules, and plans that support the strategies of this division. One of the reasons that this effort takes such a great deal of my personal time is that my boss' incentive salary depends on the achievement of many specific goals.

Parenthetically, this young man has had a very successful and satisfying early career.

Achieving

For most professionals, the early career is a period directed toward personal achievement. Considerable time and energy are invested in work and in establishing themselves as credible professionals with proven "track records."

In most of the cases we have observed personally, or heard others report, those people who achieved the most professionally in their early careers were people who were able to generate what Doug Hall has called a "success syndrome."[1] As we have observed it, this process can be described as follows:

1. The new employee does not usually have a traumatic first year and is able to adjust rather quickly to organizational realities. As a result of careful selection or luck, the individual fits well with the organization and its work.

---

[1] Douglas T. Hall, *Careers in Organizations* (Pacific Palisades, Calif.: Goodyear Publishing, 1976).

2. The individual gets some challenging initial assignments which, because of the lack of adjustment problem and the generally good fit, he or she performs well on.
3. This initial success bolsters the individual's self-confidence and helps him or her get challenging, more important (and visible) assignments.
4. The person's self-confidence, on top of everything else, helps him or her to do well in these next assignments.
5. These successes continue to bolster the individual's self-confidence and provide access to additional human and technical resources that are needed to continue to quickly grow and handle more important work.
6. The cycle continues, more or less dramatically, throughout the early career period. Success continues to breed success.

The "high flyers"—those who achieve more success in less time than 95 percent of their peers—seem to be people who position themselves to have opportunities come their way, and then take advantage of most of these opportunities. Eugene Jennings had studied this process in managerial careers,[2] which he calls developing mobility, and has identified the types of underlying rules associated with it. Those rules are:

1. Never become overspecialized. Get broad experience in a number of areas and always maintain your options.
2. Become a "crucial" subordinate to a very mobile and successful boss. If you find yourself working for an immobile superior, move.
3. Make yourself highly visible. Make sure your superiors know about your accomplishments and your ambitions.
4. If you are blocked and can't find a way out, leave the organization, but do it in a way that allows you to part as friends. Never allow a showdown to occur, and don't quit work with an emotional parting shot.

Both moderately and very successful people seem to reach a point late in the early career period where continued growth in their achievements requires that they be put "in charge." It is not unusual for professionals around age 35 to abandon their mentors and begin to feel frustrated because they don't have the power to continue producing even larger achievements. For many, this period doesn't last long, because they are soon put in charge.

---

[2] Eugene Jennings, *The Mobile Manager* (New York: McGraw-Hill, 1967).

Establishing a Workable Relationship between a Job and Other Aspects of One's Life

Most professionals develop two key commitments during their 20s—a commitment to get a job (or organization) and a commitment to an off-the-job lifestyle (with or without a spouse, with or without children). The demands made on an individual by these two commitments periodically change in ways that conflict and put strain on the individual.

The following example, reported by a 28-year-old man who had established a successful initial career at a bank, is not atypical:

> I usually get home by 6:00 P.M. My wife and I have got until at least 7:30 P.M. before we really have any time to exchange more than a "Hi, how are you?" By 7:30 we get the kids to bed. Sometimes we eat with Bobby, sometimes we don't. After dinner we do get some time together, even though we're both a little bit tired. Alice complains, with some reason, that I read magazines and newspapers during the little free time that we have together. We find that time is more precious than it was before. Ever since the baby came, we haven't been able to go to bed before 11 P.M. because that's when Alice completes her last nursing. Normally, we would try to get to bed earlier than that. We hope to resume our normal schedule as soon as the baby starts sleeping through the night.
>
> We're thinking of moving out to the suburbs soon. There's not much for kids to do in the city. There are a lot of other reasons, though. One of our biggest problems is that it is just too damn expensive to live in the city. So we might buy a house—we're really looking into it now—but with a lot of mixed feelings.
>
> Kids, I don't know, we didn't realize until after we had them how much time they require of you. They are just so damn dependent upon you. There's so much work involved with younger children that you've just got to reorder your life a bit. We found the change from being young marrieds without kids to being young marrieds with kids to be something more than we expected.
>
> We have no real desire to go to the suburbs. It's just that it costs so much less to live in the suburbs than in the city. We can own a house, save money, and build up equity at the same time. But in the suburbs I would have a 45-minute commute. I don't like the thought of that very much. On the other hand, I should get to play a little more tennis out there. I have let myself go; I've gotten a little soft. The extra commuting will make time even more precious than it was before though. It's a rough choice. . . .

Young professionals whose spouses also are pursuing careers often find it even more difficult to establish and maintain a workable relationship between their two jobs and an off-the-job lifestyle. "Dual-career" couples who also have children usually find that their time and energy are very scarce resources. The work versus off-the-job strains that develop during the early part of a career are not confined to married couples or couples with children. Single people often run into difficulties, too. Witness the comments of these two young men:

> We're having a meeting next week out at St. Georges. This is the fifth week out of the last eight that I have been at one of these conventions. Many of these conventions are executive oriented, and many of the executives bring their wives. This creates an interesting situation for a bachelor like myself, particularly when most of the women are middle-aged and older. You see, they don't appreciate seeing me show up at each convention with a different attractive young woman.

> I'm in a rather tough situation right now, and I don't see any relief in sight. I was given a promotion six months ago, and at 31 I am now the company's youngest plant manager—which, of course, is terrific. But, the promotion moved me from Chicago to Panto Flats, Texas, which has a population of about 6,000. I would like very much to establish a permanent relationship with a woman, but unlike in Chicago, there just aren't many unmarried women around here. My nonwork lifestyle, at this point, is very unsatisfactory.

There are three ways in which people generally deal with a work/nonwork conflict. Some people make changes in their nonwork lives that, in effect, reduce their commitment there. Many successful young executives take this option. One *New Yorker* cartoon captures this response well. A 30- to 35-year-old manager in a posh office holds a phone in his hand and displays a very annoyed expression. The caption reads: "Martha, how many times have I told you not to bother me while I'm on the way up?"

A second option some people choose is to take actions that reduce their commitment to work. Individuals who receive a great deal of satisfaction from their nonwork lives, and individuals who are disappointed in the amount of satisfaction they are getting from their work, both often select this option.

A third option people sometimes choose attempts not to reduce the commitment to either work or other activities, but simply to allow the conflict to exist and to personally absorb the strain. The young plant manager from Panto Flats solved his problem by jetting to Houston and back an average of two to three nights per week, where he eventually did meet a young woman and got engaged. In the interim, he lived with less sleep and a special variety of jet lag.

Not everyone, of course, experiences the same amount of work/nonwork conflict during the early career. The people we have observed who have experienced the most conflict, and who tend to "solve" this problem in ways that eventually create even more conflicts and problems, make decisions in one aspect of their lives without considering the implications for the other parts. That is, they ignore, to some degree, the interdependence that exists between the various aspects of a life. We have even seen people who tend to be planning oriented create problems for themselves by planning only *within* their careers. People who behave this way are often able to survive during their early career, but the lack of total-life planning and decision making eventually catches up with most of them—often in the midlife period between 35 and 45.

Questioning Initial Choices

Most professionals seem to go through a period of questioning their initial work, organization, family, and lifestyle choices after about 5 to 10 years. For some this is a mild period, while for others it can be fairly difficult and traumatic. As a result, some people abandon their initial commitments and make new ones; they sometimes change organizations, go back to school, start over in a new line of work in a new city, or get married or divorced.

People who make poor initial decisions—who start work with very unrealistic expectations, or who have serious problems adapting to their new environments, or who have trouble creating a workable arrangement between their work and nonwork lives—often find around age 30 that the satisfaction they are getting from the various aspects of their lives is less than they expected or desired. This leads them to a period of reexamination. A few are forced into reexamination and change. Some are fired. Others lose a key promotion they expected. The spouses of a few walk out on them. Even people who are fundamentally satisfied with their lives seem at least to pause and ponder their life situation around age 30. Is this what life is really all about? Have I really made the right choices? Am I responding too much to what I think I "should" do?

Those who actually make major changes as a result of this period of questioning are a minority, no doubt partly because of the difficulties associated with change. Unless one is in a highly unsatisfying position, change usually increases the pain one feels in the short run. Finding a new job, or breaking off a marriage relationship, can be a traumatic experience.

After the period of questioning is over, or after a change has been made, people generally plunge back into their careers with increased dedication and energy. For 5 to 10 years they focus again on achievement in their chosen profession.

MID- AND LATE CAREER

Problems at Midlife

Between the ages of approximately 35 and 45, many people experience a difficult period associated with career, physical well-being, family, or the like, that can range in intensity from mild to very severe. During this period people often get divorced, change jobs, or significantly alter their relationships with their families and their work. On the average, this period is more unsettling, and lasts longer, than the time of questioning that occurs for many around age 30.

The severity of the so-called midlife crisis—if, indeed, one experiences it at all—seems to be a function of how many problems converge with what intensity on a person's life at the same time. A person who experiences each of the common midlife problems mildly but at different times—may wonder what all the talk about a midlife crisis is about. Another who simultaneously experiences each of these problems in a powerful way might change careers, have an affair, move to an entirely new place to live, or even commit suicide.

To understand why some people experience a major crisis at midlife, while others do not, we need to see how and why these problems develop.

Career Problems

By age 35 to 40 most professionals know whether they will achieve the vague and specific career objectives that they have set for themselves. For many, the answer is that they will not. The evidence piles up that they will never become a company president, or a U.S. Senator, or a Pulitzer Prize-winning writer, or even the key person in the X Division of Company Y; it becomes clear that they will never have much, if any, impact on the automobile industry, or U.S. housing policy, or the next generation of computers. The more such a person, consciously or unconsciously, wanted to achieve these career goals, the greater the loss, and the more intense this component of the potential crisis.

Somewhat ironically, not only does career "failure" often produce a problem at midlife, so does "success." People who have worked for years toward a single goal or set of goals often find themselves feeling very uncomfortable and disoriented after achieving the goal. The drive that for years has provided a key part of the structure for their lives is suddenly gone. The striving behavior that they have become so accustomed to, and often received great satisfaction from, is suddenly inappropriate. Having reached the top of the mountain, they find that there is nothing really there and they don't like just taking in the view. Moreover, they miss the climb.

The problem of career success and failure is rooted in the early career, when adult life goals are initially established. It would seem that the narrower a person's definition in career-oriented terms of success in life is, the greater are the chances that he or she will experience this component of the midlife crisis. Likewise, the person who defines success in broader terms—that is, with multiple career, family, and personal objectives that have different time horizons—seems to be less susceptible to this problem.

Physical Problems

Many people become increasingly aware of their physical aging at midlife.[3] And for some this awareness comes as an unwanted shock of serious proportions.

At midlife people often find that they are physically unable to do some things anymore; they can no longer read without glasses, play touch football effectively, or work for 20 straight hours. They sometimes find that on their jobs they are no longer treated as a young, "up-and-coming" star; new employees even treat them as members of the old guard. And suddenly the prospect of death becomes a reality; startlingly, over a period of just a few years, both parents may die, and friends of their own age are killed or have premature coronaries. These losses, combined with the recognition that at 40 they are probably in the second (and *last*) half of their lives, hit some people like an unexpected fist in the face.

Again, it is easy to see how this problem has roots earlier in life. People who develop self-concepts during their adolescence and early careers that include as central elements ideas such as "I am a young star" or "I am physically able to do" this or that are much more likely to experience this part of the midlife crisis than other people. The same is true for people who have not experienced the loss of a friend through death, or have just refused to think about death as an issue.

Family Problems

A person's family can, and often does, also contribute to a crisis at midlife. Those with teenage children must often put up with the younger generation's need for authority figures to rebel against. If such a parent has previously gained considerable satisfaction from relating to the children, and if all his or her children reach adolescence simultaneously, this too can be a very unsettling change.

---

[3] For an informative and highly readable discussion of the aging process, see Margaret Huyck, *Growing Older* (Englewood Cliffs, N.J.: Prentice-Hall, 1974).

Relationships between husband and wife sometimes explode at midlife. During the early career, goals of spouses often are focused heavily in very different worlds; traditionally the male has lived with his career while the woman raised a family. Under these conditions it is easy for people to grow apart. And at midlife, they sometimes suddenly find they no longer meet each other's needs.

A common contemporary pattern that leads up to such difficulties is shown in Figure 3. Here the seeds of problems felt at midlife are again sown long before. The very contract that is the basis of the marriage during the early career helps create the explosion at midlife. Many professionals make it through this difficult period only because the alternatives—divorce primarily—seem equally cumbersome and onerous.

Coping with the Crisis

"Making it through" the midlife crisis can be a difficult experience for an individual and all those close to him or her. The changes people make—in their work and family lives—sometimes are impulsive and not at all helpful. But sometimes the crisis, and whatever adjustments people do make in response to it, lead to a very happy and productive period in their lives. Indeed, some who have looked into this subject would go so far as to say that unless one experiences a crisis of some intensity and then comes to terms realistically with the forces creating it, it isn't possible to lead a really fulfilled life afterwards.

How well one copes with a crisis in midlife is undoubtedly a function of many factors. One in particular is worth noting; we will call it *personal support systems*. It has often been said that "no man is an island." This is particularly true in times of personal crisis. We need the understanding, the empathy, the sympathy, and the support of other human beings to help us keep things in perspective and to help us move toward a realistic resolution of our problems. And whether one gets this support in a time of crisis is very much a function of whether one has previously developed the needed system of personal relationships.

In this highly mobile world in which we live, it takes a conscious effort to build and maintain a personal support system. Without the effort, our own movement across the country and up in organizations will automatically break personal supportive relationships but not build them. And that can leave us in the position of one very successful executive who at age 40 found that "there is not one single person in my life that I feel I can discuss a personal problem with."

FIGURE 3
One Typical Form of a Marriage Crisis at Midlife

Ages	Wife	Husband
25-37	Vicariously enjoys husbands' career and its rewards, while providing support. Suppresses feelings and:	Suppresses feelings and focuses energy on career achievement.

Gives   Gets

Emotional, $, Status,
Housekeeping,   Security,
Maternal, and   Children
Sexual Support

Ages	Wife	Husband
38-40	Kids grow up. She decides vicarious rewards aren't really worth it and begins to feel "had." She withdraws support and puts energy into personal growth and achievement for herself.	He has either accomplished all his goals or discovers he can't; in either case he ends up saying, "Is there nothing more? Gasp!" His suppressed feelings explode. His need for support skyrockets. Leads him to think: "What the hell is she doing running off in other directions while I'm falling apart?"
At age 41-45 leads to:	Leads her to think: "Why can't he hold together like a good husband so I can go out and grow without feeling guilty?"	

EXPLOSION
in the marriage

Generativity

A major theme in the mid- (and late) careers of most healthy, happy, and successful people is generativity. Eric Erikson, who first identified this theme in people's lives, has defined it as "the concern in establishing and guiding the next generation." Erikson postulated that all adults had to come to grips with this development issue in their lives or face psychological stagnation.

The most direct way in which adults concern themselves with establishing and guiding the next generation is by bearing and raising children. There are, however, other ways that people deal with this concern. Professional people, in particular, often seem to do it through their careers.

Managers achieve generativity by building organizations, by coaching younger managers, and by serving as mentors to still others. It is not uncommon for a successful business person to spend the early career involved in personal achievement, to get to the point where he or she is running the business around age 40, and then after a mild to moderately intense crisis period shift activities more and more to developing and managing others who in turn run the business. This type of activity often peaks around age 50–55 and then lets up as the person begins to disengage from work in anticipation of retirement.

By taking advantage of the generativity period in people's lives, some organizations gain a very important and valuable resource. All organizations need to somehow continuously acquire and develop employees. They need some mechanism to help attract new employees, to help new employees "join up," and to aid young employees in adapting to the realities of organizational life. Professional recruiters, formal orientation courses, and the like, are expensive. Middle-aged and older professional employees can often perform these functions in a way that gives them considerable personal satisfaction while saving the organization a lot of money.

Retirement

Retirement, whether it comes at age 60, 62, 65, or 70 or whenever, can be a big shock for people, especially those who are heavily invested in their work and career. Numerous cases have been reported of people who retire from their work and soon afterward die. Suddenly stripped of a large portion of their lives and the satisfaction they derived from it, they just wither away.

People who go through this phase in the late career with the least trauma and problems seem to be those who have consciously or intuitively prepared for it well in advance. For people who successfully retire at age 65, the three to five preceding years tend to be a period of disengaging and planned adjustment. Such people often systematically develop multiple sources of satisfaction and fulfillment that do not depend on their full-time job. They begin to participate more in activities that they like but have never had the time to pursue. They find ways to do voluntary work in their profession. In the final year before retirement they often cut down the number of hours a week they spend at their job. As a result, retirement for them, although sometimes a fairly large change in their activities, does not represent a large shift downward in the total satisfaction they receive from living. Retirement is not then a gigantic, sometimes lethal, loss.

Successful managers often take on more and more civic, charitable, and government tasks between 60 and 65. Some "retire" into a full-time portfolio of interesting and exciting part-time jobs. Others rely more and more on their spouse and families as sources of satisfaction by taking vacations, improving the home, and looking after the grand-children.

As modern medicine continues to lengthen life expectancy and as pressures for earlier and earlier retirement continue, we are moving into a period of history in which more and more people will experi-ence a large part of their lives after retirement. The implications of these changes are not entirely obvious yet. It is clear, however, that until our social institutions adjust to these changes, the burden is on the individual to plan carefully for his or her retirement.

17

The Influence of Age Stereotypes on Managerial Decisions*

BENSON ROSEN AND THOMAS H. JERDEE

Until recently the problem of age discrimination in employment practices has been overshadowed by the problems of race and sex discrimination. However, there are now several indications that gov-ernment agencies intend to enforce vigorously the 1967 Age Discrimi-nation in Employment Act. For example, in 1974 the U.S. Department of Labor won an agreement from Standard Oil of California to pay $2 million in back wages to 160 employees over the age of 40 who had been victimized by discriminatory managerial practices. In a recent interview, a Labor Department official stated that over 400 cases in-volving alleged age discrimination were in preparation ("Age Dis-crimination Moves into the Limelight," 1974).

* From *Journal of Applied Psychology* 1976, vol. 61, no. 4, 428–432. Copyright 1976 by the American Psychological Association. Reprinted by permission.

In many instances of age discrimination, it is quite likely that managerial bias against older workers is based on age stereotypes, that is, widely held beliefs regarding the characteristics of people in various age categories. Research by Aaronson (1966) suggests that increasingly negative stereotypes are associated with increasing age. However, a Louis Harris poll indicated that public expectations concerning the problems of old age were exaggerated compared to the actual experiences reported by the elderly (Harris, 1975).

In a recent study (see Rosen & Jerdee, 1976) we examined differences in evaluations of the average younger and the average older person on 65 job-related traits. We found that respondents viewed older persons, compared to younger persons, to be deficient in on-the-job performance, potential for development, certain interpersonal skills, vitality, and propensity for risk taking. Older persons were rated higher than younger persons on integrity. These perceptions of age differences in job-related characteristics were held by respondents of all ages.

The effects of these age stereotypes on managerial decision making were studied in the present investigation. Participants were presented with a series of six hypothetical administrative incidents in which an employee's age might be expected to have an influence on a managerial decision. We then compared the administrative evaluations and actions recommended for use with younger and older employees in identical circumstances. For each of the incidents, we hypothesized differential administrative evaluations reflecting the aforementioned age stereotypes. We also hypothesized administrative actions indicating less organizational concern and support for the older employee.

THE STUDY

Method

Subjects. The subjects were 142 undergraduate business students (115 males and 27 females) attending the University of North Carolina; 99 percent of the participants were between the ages of 21 and 29.

Procedure. Experimental materials were embedded in an in-basket exercise. Participants were asked to assume the role of a division manager and to react to a series of six in-basket items presented in memo or letter form, each dealing with a different incident. Each incident depicted a different type of managerial problem and was presented in two versions, so as to manipulate the age of the focal person depicted in the memo or letter.

In each of the incidents, age was manipulated by specifying the focal employee's age or describing the focal employee as an "older" or "younger" person. In addition, to enhance the realism of the experimental task and to strengthen the age manipulation, four of the memos included personnel forms with pictures of the focal employees. The pictures were of younger or older men dressed in business attire and were preselected and matched by a three-judge panel to ensure uniformity of physical attractiveness. To control for a possible "specific picture" effect (in which age might be confounded with non-age-related qualities), three different pictures of older men and three different pictures of younger men were used in each of these four incidents. This also permitted separate estimation of the specific picture effect for each of the four incidents.

For each item, participants indicated on fixed response scales their evaluations and the extent to which they would find certain administrative actions appropriate for dealing with the managerial problem. Since each participant received only one version of each of the experimental items, manipulation of the age variable was unobtrusive. The design can best be conceptualized as a series of six separate experiments with random assignment of treatments to participants within each experiment.

The six incidents were as follows:

1. *Resistance to change.* The first incident was concerned with the stereotype that older workers are rigid in their work attitudes and resistant to change. This incident was in the form of a memo from a foreman about a shipping room employee who appeared unresponsive to customer calls for service. The employee was described as either a younger or an older employee, in either case with only 3 months' experience in his present position. Participants indicated the difficulty anticipated in getting the employee to change his behavior and selected one of five possible alternatives for resolving the problem.

2. *Lack of creativity.* In this incident, participants evaluated a candidate for promotion to a marketing position that required "fresh solutions to challenging problems" and "a high degree of creative and innovative behavior." Participants made a promotion decision for a 61-year-old or a 32-year-old candidate with identical qualifications.

3. *Cautiousness and slowness of judgment.* This position was described as requiring a person "who not only knows the field of finance, but who is capable of making quick judgments under high risk." Subjects evaluated either a 29-year-old or a 58-year-old applicant with identical backgrounds and experience.

4. *Lower physical capacity.* The next incident examined stereotypes reflecting diminished physical capacities of older workers. This item was written in letter form and depicted a request from a

clerical employee to be reassigned to a higher paying, but physically demanding, truck loader position. The employee was described as either 52 years old or 23 years old, slender, and in good condition. Participants evaluated the desirability of rejecting the request.

5. *Disinterest in technological change.* The next case concerned perceptions about older employees' desire and ability to keep up with technical change. Participants evaluated a request from a production staff employee asking permission and financial support to attend a conference devoted to "new theories and research relevant to production systems." The employee was described as either 62 years old or 34 years old with 10 years of production experience. Participants evaluated the employee's motives and the desirability of approving the request.

6. *Untrainability.* This item depicted a computer programmer whose technical skills had become obsolete as a result of changes in computer operations. The programmer was described as either 30 years old or 60 years old and of average ability. Participants evaluated the desirability of terminating the programmer and the desirability of retraining him.

Results

Two preliminary analyses were made prior to testing for age effects. The first analysis tested for specific picture effects within the three pictures of older persons and within the three pictures of younger persons, for each of the in-basket incidents that included photographs as part of the age manipulation. Picture effects were not significant for any of the cases. Therefore, data from the specific picture subgroups within older and younger age categories were pooled.

In the second preliminary analysis, comparisons were made between male and female subjects for each of the incidents. Sex effects were not significant. Accordingly, the major analyses are based on responses from both male and female participants.

Resistance to Change. The first incident tested the hypothesis that older employees are seen as more resistant to change. We also hypothesized that people are less likely to decide on positive corrective action when confronted with an older "problem" employee. Age stereotype effects were found on the question "How much difficulty would you anticipate in getting the shipping employee to change his behavior?" The mean difficulty rating for the older worker was 3.13 compared to a mean rating of 2.76 for the younger worker ($t = 2.41$, $p < .05$). Participants also recommended different ways of dealing with the older and younger employee. A positive corrective strategy, "a talk in which the employee is encouraged to change his behavior," was recommended by 65 percent of the participants who read the younger version, but this alternative was recommended by only 42 percent of the participants who read the older version. On the other hand, the alternative, "find someone else to handle customer complaints," was endorsed by 55 percent of the respondents to the older version, compared to only 32 percent of the respondents to the younger version ($\chi^2 = 9.84$, $p < .05$).

Clearly, the older employee was seen as more resistant to managerial influences. Thus, rather than attempt to encourage an older worker to improve his performance, a majority of participants recommended avoiding a confrontation and reassigning the older employee.

Lack of Creativity. We hypothesized that older employees are seen as less promotable to a position requiring creativity and innovative thinking. Among participants who reviewed the record of the older candidate, 25 percent recommended promotion, compared to 54 percent of participants who reviewed the identical qualifications, but for a younger candidate ($\chi^2 = 9.75$, $p < .01$).

Cautiousness. We hypothesized that there is a bias against older applicants for positions requiring financial risk taking. Findings supported the hypothesis. The mean rating on "suitability for the job" was 3.46 for the young applicant compared to a mean rating of 2.97 for the older applicant ($t = 2.91$, $p < .01$). Among participants who reviewed the qualifications of the younger applicant, 25 percent recommended selection, compared to 13 percent of respondents who reviewed an identically qualified older applicant ($\chi^2 = 3.48$, $p < .06$).

Results of these two selection and promotion incidents clearly reflect discrimination against older employees. It appears that when job demands such as innovative thinking, creativity, and risk taking are inconsistent with widely held stereotypes about the characteristics of older people, the potential for discriminatory managerial decisions is quite high.

Lower Physical Capacity. This incident tested the hypothesis that people are less likely to approve an older employee's request for a transfer to a job requiring strenuous physical activity. Again, findings strongly supported the hypothesis. Participants rated the administrative action "persuade the employee to withdraw the transfer request" significantly higher for the older worker ($M = 4.38$), compared to the younger worker ($M = 3.46$; $t = 3.42$, $p < .01$). In addition, a decision to reject the transfer request was evaluated significantly higher for the older worker compared to the younger worker (M older = 3.35, M younger = 2.57; $t = 2.95$, $p < .01$). In this instance, it appears that general stereotypes about the decline of physical strength with age had more influence on managerial judgments than our statement that the 52-year-old employee was in "good physical condition." We now turn to results concerning the influence of age stereotypes on training and development decisions.

Disinterest in Technological Change. This incident tested the hypothesis that older workers are seen as less interested in learning about new technical developments relevant to the job, and the hypothesis that people are less likely to recommend financial support for the development of an older worker. Both hypotheses were strongly supported.

Participants perceived that an older employee was significantly less motivated to keep up to date compared to a younger employee (M older = 4.35, M younger = 4.97; $t = 3.79$, $p < .01$). The decision to allocate funds so that the employee could attend a training seminar was also influenced by the requester's age. A decision to deny the request for company sponsorship of additional training was more strongly recommended for an older employee compared to a younger employee (M older = 3.49, M younger = 2.38; $t = 5.01$, $p < .01$).

Untrainability. With the final incident, we tested the hypothesis that older employees whose skills have become obsolete are viewed as less suitable for retraining and are considered expendable. Participants evaluated the desirability of a company-sponsored refresher course significantly lower for a 60-year-old computer programmer compared to a 30-year-old programmer. Mean desirability of organizational support for retraining was 2.95 for the older employee compared to 3.63 for the younger employee ($t = 2.52$, $p < .05$).

The administrative action "terminate the employee whose skills have become obsolete and hire a fully qualified replacement" was evaluated more favorably for an older employee ($M = 3.21$) compared to a younger employee ($M = 2.53$; $t = 2.40$, $p < .05$).

When considered together, findings from the last two incidents suggest that people are less likely to recommend organizational support to maintain and develop the skills of older employees, and are also strongly opposed to providing retraining opportunities for older employees who no longer possess the job knowledge to carry out their job assignments effectively. In these instances, older workers become the double victims of age stereotypes.

Discussion

At a time when increased organizational attention is focused on the career progress of women and minority employees, the plight of older workers has been relatively ignored. Despite legislation prohibiting age discrimination, there is evidence that older workers may be even more subject to unjust treatment than other clases of employees (Palmore & Manton, 1973).

In a previous study, we found that negative job-related characteristics are attributed to older workers (see Rosen & Jerdee, 1976). We hypothesized that when these negative stereotypes are relevant to a work situation, older workers are potential victims of discriminatory managerial decisions. Our findings consistently support this hypothesis. Participants' assumptions about the physical, cognitive, and emotional characteristics of older employees accompanied a series of administrative actions that were clearly damaging to the well-being and career progress of older workers.

In several incidents, assumptions about the decline in mental and physical capacities of older workers were associated with bias against older employees in personnel decisions. However, denying selection, promotion, and training opportunities on the basis of an employee's age is prohibited by the Age Discrimination in Employment Act (Lundquist, 1968).

In another incident, age stereotypes that depict older workers as rigid and resistant to change accompanied a decision to avoid efforts to correct an older employee's performance. The managerial decision to reassign an older employee who is unresponsive to customer complaints deprives that employee of an opportunity to improve his performance. In instances such as this, managerial actions based on age stereotypes are extremely resistant to change. By transferring the older employee, the manager avoids a direct test of his assumptions about the worker's rigidity and resistance to change and, in so doing, precludes the possibility of learning that the age stereotype is not valid.

In other incidents, assumptions about the decline among older workers of the interest, motivation, and ability to improve their job-related skills were reflected in decisions to avoid investments in the continued development of older employees. However, when the older employee's skills become outdated, as depicted in the final incident, the decision to terminate the employee rather than invest in his retraining is favored.

The present study demonstrates the influence of work-related age stereotypes on managerial decisions. These findings are based on the perceptions of undergraduate business students, and generalizations about potential age bias among older respondents must be made with caution. Whether similar biases would be found among personnel administrators and executives remains to be demonstrated.

It should also be noted that an older worker's opportunity for career advancement and job satisfaction is further affected by mandatory retirement policies. In instances where mandatory retirement restricts the potential tenure of older employees, administrators may view investments in the development or promotion of older employees as yielding less organization benefit, compared to similar expenditure for the development or promotion of younger employees. Whether these administrative assumptions are valid depends to some extent on factors such as the turnover rates among younger and older employees. Nevertheless, mandatory retirement tends to work against the career progress of the older worker.

When taken together, our results provide insights about another age stereotype, the commonly accepted belief that older employees reach a time in their careers when motivation significantly declines and they merely "go through the motions" until retirement. The implicit assumption in this belief seems to be that aging produces a decline in motivation. An alternative explanation for the relationship between age and motivation can be deduced from our findings. It is possible that a pattern of discriminatory managerial decisions based on age stereotypes may significantly influence the motivation of older workers during the last 10–15 years of employment. To the extent that an older employee perceives that his actions are no longer instrumental for career advancement because of managerial biases against older workers, his motivation may gradually be lowered. Limited opportunities for development and lack of feedback for ineffective performance further reduce the older employee's work motivation. Thus, it is quite likely that lowered motivation is not a direct result of aging, but a result of changes in managerial attitudes and treatment of older employees.

REFERENCES

Aaronson, B. S.   Personality stereotypes of aging. *Journal of Gerontology,* 1966, *21*, 458–462.

Age discrimination moves into the limelight. *Business Week,* June 15, 1974, p. 101.

Harris, L.   *The myth and reality of aging in America.* New York: The National Council on Aging, 1975.

Lundquist, T.   The age discrimination in employment Act. *Monthly Labor Review,* 1968, *91*, 48–50.

Palmore, E. B., & Manton, K.   Ageism compared to racism and sexism. *Journal of Gerontology,* 1973, *28*, 363–369.

Rosen, B., & Jerdee, T. H.   The nature of job-related age stereotypes. *Journal of Applied Psychology,* 1976, *61*, 180–183.

18

The Protestant Ethic Scale as a Predictor of Repetitive Work Performance*

MATTHEW R. MERRENS and
JAMES B. GARRETT

The influence of the Protestant ethic in relation to the development of capitalism and western society has been widely discussed (Fullerton, 1959; Weber, 1958). However, until recently the Protestant ethic has not been conceptualized as a personality variable. Through efforts of Mirels and Garrett (1971) a scale was constructed to assess the Protestant ethic as a major personality construct. Their initial investigation firmly established the internal consistency of the Protestant Ethic Scale and also reported a number of relevant correlations with other established measures. Significant positive correlations were found with the Mosher Sex Guilt ($r = .29$, $p < .01$) and Morality Conscience Guilt Scales ($r = .30$, $p < .01$), as well as with the California F Scale ($r = .51$, $p < .001$). A significant negative correlation was obtained in relation to Rotter's Internal-External Scale ($r = .30, p < .01$). Nonsignificant correlations were found in relation to the Marlowe-Crowne Social Desirability Scale ($r = -.10$) and the Sensation Seeking Scale ($r = -.06$). In two later investigations by MacDonald (1971, 1972), further correlational exploration of the Protestant ethic was undertaken. In his investigations high Protestant ethic scores were significantly related to negative attitudes toward the poor and opposition to a guaranteed minimum annual income. In addition, MacDonald reported that values such as comfortable life, equality, exciting life, and pleasure were negatively related, while ambition, self-control, salvation, and social responsibility were positively related to Protestant ethic endorsement. As the brief review above indicates, the research to date used a correlational strategy and disclosed several interesting relationships with more established scales and variables.

* From *Journal of Applied Psychology*, 1975, 60, 125–127. Copyright 1975 by the American Psychological Association. Reprinted by permission.

One of the most basic elements of the original conception of the Protestant ethic concerned work behavior (Weber, 1958). The quote "He who will not work, neither shall he eat" summarizes the essential point that hard and steady work is valued, while unwillingness to work is a symptom of absence of grace and a great sin. Since the work component was an important element in Weber's conception of the Protestant ethic—capitalism relationship, the same component may be an important element of the Protestant ethic now conceived as a personality variable. Therefore, the purpose of this study was to experimentally determine the work styles of high and low Protestant ethic individuals in a task designed to provide low motivation and interest levels. In this investigation a departure from previous studies was the use of an experimental strategy in which the Protestant ethic is related to independently measured nontest behavior. A similar approach was taken by Crowne and Marlowe (1964) in exploring the social desirability variable.

METHOD

Subjects

The Protestant Ethic Scale was administered as part of a large test battery to 333 introductory psychology students with a resultant mean of 86.57 and a standard deviation of 13.55. The 40 male and female subjects in this study were drawn from that population. The high Protestant ethic group was composed of 20 subjects scoring at least one standard deviation above the mean of the Protestant Ethic Scale, and the low Protestant ethic group was composed of 20 subjects scoring at least one standard deviation below the mean on the Protestant Ethic Scale.

Procedure

To eliminate the possible influence of any demand characteristics for specific work performance resulting from the administration of the Protestant Ethic Scale:

1. The Protestant Ethic Scale (19 items) was administered as a small segment of the total test battery.
2. The assessment of work behavior occurred at least seven weeks after the Protestant ethic assessment.
3. The Protestant Ethic Scale and the assessment of work behavior were administered by different experimenters.
4. The 40 subjects chosen for the work behavior task were told that

their names were selected *at random* to participate in a psychology experiment for which they would receive extra credit.

Subjects were seated alone at a table in a small room. Neatly stacked on a table in front of each subject were 100 sheets of 8 × 10-inch paper. On each sheet were printed 25 rows of 10 circles, a total of 250 circles. The subject was given the following directions:

> This is an experiment testing eye-hand coordination. I would like you to draw an "X" in the circles on the sheets in front of you with your non-preferred hand. If you are right-handed, use your left hand. Complete as many as you are able until you become tired. When you are finished, open the door and I will collect your completed sheets.

For each subject the time spent in the room and the number of circles marked served as the dependent measures of work behavior. If the subject did not leave the room after 30 minutes, the experimenter entered the room and told the subject the experiment was over. For such subjects a time of 30 minutes was recorded. All subjects were debriefed upon completing the experimental task.

RESULTS AND DISCUSSION

Table 1 presents the means and standard deviations for both high and low Protestant ethic groups on the two dependent measures. On both dependent measures a significant difference was found between

TABLE 1
Work Behavior of High and Low Protestant Ethic Groups

Protestant Ethic Group	M	SD	df	t
	Time spent (in minutes)			
High	23.00	6.25		
			38	3.49*
Low	16.85	4.80		
	Sheets completed			
High	4.10	.72		
			38	4.98†
Low	2.55	1.19		

Note: For each group, n = 20.
* p < .01.
† p < .001.

the Protestant ethic groups, with high Protestant ethic subjects spending more time working and also producing more output.

The results provide support for the contention that type of work behavior is clearly a component of the Protestant ethic personality variable as measured by the Protestant Ethic Scale. A replication of these findings was obtained with a different population of students ($N = 20$) at another institution with similar results, thus providing additional support of generality and reliability.[1] Since work behavior is a very important and relevant aspect of many human experiences (e.g., academic achievement and occupational success), a paper-and-pencil predictive measure should have wide utility for applied as well as research purposes.

The authors are presently investigating various types of work activities with various interest and motivational levels in relation to the Protestant ethic personality variable.

REFERENCES

Crowne, D. P., & Marlowe, D.   *The approval motive.* New York: Wiley, 1964.

Fullerton, K.   Calvinism and capitalism: An explanation of the Weber thesis. In R. W. Green (Ed.), *Protestantism and capitalism: The Weber thesis and its critics.* Boston: Heath, 1959.

MacDonald, A. P., Jr.   Correlates of the ethics of personal conscience and the ethics of social responsibility. *Journal of Consulting and Clinical Psychology,* 1971, 37, 443.

MacDonald, A. P., Jr.   More on the Protestant ethic. *Journal of Consulting and Clinical Psychology,* 1972, 39, 116–122.

Mirels, H. L., & Garrett, J. B.   The Protestant ethic as a personality variable. *Journal of Consulting and Clinical Psychology,* 1971, 36, 40–44.

Weber, M.   *The Protestant ethic and the spirit of capitalism* (Trans. by Talcott Parsons). New York: Scribner's, 1958.

---

[1] Matthew R. Merrens, "The Protestant Ethic Scale and Work Behavior: A Replication." Unpublished paper, 1974. The findings were replicated at the State University of New York, Plattsburgh, with 10 high and 10 low Protestant Ethic Scale subjects.

19

For a More Effective Organization—Match the Job to the Man*

EDWARD E. LAWLER III

> Of all the ways society serves the individual, few are more meaningful
> than providing individuals with decent jobs. And it is not likely to be a
> decent society for any of us until it is for all of us.—John Gardner, 1968.

Work can be made a more rewarding place to be and organizations
can be made more effective if approaches to organizational design
treat employees as individuals. This important and optimistic statement is supported by a number of recent studies; however, it is often
overlooked in the national debate over employee alienation and job
satisfaction, a debate that has been preoccupied with what in many
ways is the least important issue: whether job dissatisfaction and alienation are increasing.

Twenty, thirty, even forty years ago, social scientists were pointing
out that the way organizations and jobs are designed frequently
creates dissatisfying and alienating work experiences. They were also
noting such serious social consequences of work alienation and job
dissatisfaction as physical illness, mental illness, alcoholism, drug
abuse, and shorter life spans. A more recent concern has been that
when job dissatisfaction is high, individuals do not grow and develop.
And there is no doubt that because work is still dissatisfying for many,
everyone in our country is worse off. Thus, we need to concentrate our
energies on searching for better ways to design work organizations,
rather than on debating whether the situation is worsening.

The research that I have been involved in over the past ten years on
organization and job design suggests a number of approaches that
organizations can take to make work more satisfying, interesting, involving, and sometimes more motivating. All of these efforts have a

* Reprinted by permission of the publisher from *Organizational Dynamics* (Summer
1974). © 1974 by AMACOM a division of American Management Associations.

common aspect: They all recognize that for the work experience to be a positive, growth-producing one, the work situation must be designed to fit the differences that exist among people in their skills, needs, and abilities.

Unfortunately, many organization theorists have argued for the principle of standardization in the design of organizations. Inherent in the concept of standardization is the view that everyone should be treated the same, but treating everyone the same inevitably leads to treating some people in ways that are dissatisfying, dehumanizing, and ineffective. The reason for this is simple: Because of the differences among people, no single way of dealing with individuals is ever the best way to deal with all or even most individuals. Further, the whole concept of treating people in a standardized, homogeneous manner runs counter to the need of many people to be treated as individuals. We know from the research that one of the greatest contributors to alienation is the collective treatment of individuals without regard for their distinctiveness and sense of unique identity. Work organizations are given to this collective treatment because they mass-produce products and frequently handle their employees in a standardized, mass-production way designed to deal with the "average" person. Dissatisfaction is an inevitable result, since very few people are average.

What we need, then, are ways of running organizations that recognize the importance of treating people differently and placing them in environments and work situations that fit their unique needs, skills, and abilities. How can this be done? It isn't easy, because the more people are treated as individuals, the more complex organizations become. But according to the data I and others have collected, there are some approaches that have already been tried and that seem to work well. I should like to share the results of this research and give some examples of how an organization can structure its practices and policies to fit the important differences that exist among individuals.

In considering ways that make work more satisfying, we must not forget that society cannot tolerate approaches that will seriously undermine the economic effectiveness of organizations in order to increase employee satisfaction. Psychologists used to believe that job satisfaction was capable of causing employees to perform better. If this were true, there would be no problem finding new work designs that would increase job satisfaction without harming organizational effectiveness. Unfortunately, my own research and that of many other psychologists shows that satisfaction does not cause employees to work harder. In fact, it has a very low relationship to performance and is probably best thought of as a consequence of performance. Despite this, there is evidence that increasing the job satisfaction of employees can increase the effectiveness of organizations. Why is this so? Satisfied employees are absent less, late less, and less likely to quit. Absenteeism, turnover, and tardiness are very expensive—more costly than most realize. Recent research, for example, shows that the loss of an employee usually costs an organization ten times his or her monthly salary. Thus, because increases in employee satisfaction result in decreases in turnover, absenteeism, and tardiness, organization changes that increase job satisfaction can increase the economic effectiveness of organizations even though they do not increase motivation.

Job Design

One of the most commonly suggested cures for worker alienation and job dissatisfaction is job enrichment. It has been suggested that if we enrich people's jobs, the result will be lower absenteeism, lower turnover, less tardiness, higher productivity, higher job satisfaction, and less alienation. We now have a considerable amount of research data on the effect of job enrichment. It does, indeed, show that the average person is both happier and more effective working on an enriched job than he or she is working on the traditional, standardized, specialized, repetitive, routine job. However, as I remarked before, not everyone is average.

There are many people (at this point, we are not sure how many) who are happier working on repetitive, monotonous, boring jobs. In a recent study, for example, I found a number of telephone operators who did not react favorably to enriched jobs. The older employees, in particular, tended to prefer the more repetitive jobs because they had adjusted to them and knew how to do them well. In addition, the new design threatened to disrupt some of the comfortable interpersonal relationships they had established. Thus, any job enrichment effort that enriches the jobs of everyone in a work area or of everyone doing a particular type of work is bound to make some people less happy and less productive. Admittedly, as a rule, performance and satisfaction go up, but can we afford to engage in work redesign practices that make the work experiences of some people more negative? I don't think we can, when there is an alternative available, and in this case there often is an alternative.

The idea of an alternative is nicely illustrated by the job design approach taken in a Motorola plant where the same product is produced in two different ways—on an assembly line and on a bench where one worker puts the entire product together. This particular version of job design allows people to work on the kind of job that they are most comfortable with. Those people who prefer routine, repetitive jobs have them; those people who prefer enriched jobs have them.

Originally, only a few employees chose to work on the enriched jobs; eventually, about half of the 60 workers decided to work on them. Individualizing jobs to meet the needs and abilities of the employees seemed to result in both the individual's and the organization's being better off, for absenteeism and turnover went down, while product quality went up.

A similar approach has been tried out at Non-Linear Systems with good results. There, however, the employees were allowed to share the work among the members of their teams. Some teams chose to have each member produce the whole product, while others decided to have different people work on different parts of the assembly process. The result was a high degree of individualization.

My own research suggests that the kind of a solution arrived at in Motorola and Non-Linear Systems can be applied in many other situations. Job enrichment can be selectively done and can be limited to only those people who will respond positively to an enriched job. There are, however, many practical problems involved in giving individuals jobs that involve the optimal degree of enrichment for them. For example, there is the problem of who is to decide how much a given job should be enriched. Many social scientists suggest that these decisions should not be made by the individual workers and go on to suggest that individuals should be "coerced" to experience situations where higher-order needs can be satisfied (for example, enriched jobs), because unless they experience them, they won't know what they are missing. I don't think, however, that this position is correct. Our responsibility as social scientists is to provide valid data to individuals about the results of doing certain things. It is not to coerce people into certain actions that we feel are "good" for them. Forcing someone to try an enriched job is somewhat akin to arguing that a virgin should be raped because otherwise he or she cannot know what is being missed. Thus, I don't think that organizations should be defined as providing a high quality of working life only if everyone has his higher-order needs satisfied. Instead, they should be defined as providing a high quality of working life if everyone has a realistic opportunity to satisfy his higher-order needs if he wants to.

The use of work modules represents one approach to giving individuals a greater opportunity to determine the nature of their jobs. As proposed, it would divide up tasks into modules of work, each of which would last for several hours. Employees would then ask to work on a set of modules that together would constitute a day's work. So far this approach has not been tried anywhere, so it is difficult to spell out the details of how it would work. Probably the closest approximation of it that is presently operational is in the airline industry, where pilots and stewardesses request different flights and thus have some control over when and on what they work. To be effective, the use of a work module approach would have to take place in conjunction with some job enrichment activities. Otherwise, employees might be faced with choosing among modules that were all made up of simple, repetitive tasks, so that they would have no real choice. Using work modules has the very distinct advantage of letting individuals pick their work settings, thus taking into account individual needs and preferences. It also recognizes that different individuals prefer different tasks and facilitates the matching of individuals with tasks.

Fringe Benefits and Pay Systems

A clear example of where research suggests organizations can and should treat everyone in a different manner is in the area of fringe benefits. At the present time, regardless of their marital status, age, education, and so on, employees receive the same fringe benefits package—one that is designed for the hypothetical average employee. A considerable amount of research shows that the fringe benefits packages offered by most organizations are favored by only 10 percent of their employees, because, again, there are few "average" employees. To put it in a different way, given the opportunity, 90 percent of the employees would choose different fringe benefits. Despite this, most organizations continue giving everyone the same benefits. Thus, inevitably some employees receive unwanted and inadequate fringe packages, and further, they are denied the opportunity to improve them. Can this situation be changed?

Yes. People can be given the opportunity to choose fringe benefits that fit their own set of needs. Employees can be given the amount of money the organization is presently spending on their pay (salary plus fringes) and they can divide it up themselves among cash and a large number of fringe benefits. This "cafeteria" kind of plan allows the organization to control its costs, so that it ultimately spends the same amount of money as it would in the standardized fringe benefits plan. Both the organization and its employees stand to benefit if the employees receive only those fringe benefits that they desire.

First, the employees will feel that they are being paid more, because they will realize for the first time the value of the benefits they receive and will receive only those that they value. Second, working for the organization should become more attractive, because the employees will be receiving a more highly valued reward package, and this should reduce turnover and make recruiting easier. The systems division of TRW and the Educational Testing Service are among the companies that are experimenting with these flexible benefits.

It would be foolish, however, to overlook the technical problems that are involved in implementing a cafeteria plan. It is not simple to work out a choice system; there are various tax and insurance problems involved. But the experience so far of organizations that have tried it shows that these problems are solvable and worth solving. They are worth solving because this is an area where an organization can design its policies to fit the needs and desires of its employees.

It is also interesting to note that when given the chance, employees do seem to make responsible choices. Older people invest more in retirement, younger people with families get good medical protection, and so on. This finding is in notable contrast to the common but fallacious notion that if employees are given the opportunity for decision making in this area, they will make unwise choices, and therefore, organizations need to protect their employees by choosing the fringe benefits packages that are best for them.

There is another way in which pay systems can be individualized. Most organizations pay people according to the jobs they perform; thus, all people who do the same job receive the same basic pay, regardless of their skills and abilities. In short, the job is paid, rather than the person. On the other hand, several plants, including the General Foods plant at Topeka, Kansas, have successfully experimented with a way of paying people that recognizes differences among individuals in terms of their skills and abilities, that pays the person, not the job. It recognizes that the kind of work an individual may be doing at the moment does not necessarily reflect his abilities and knowledge. Thus, these companies pay people in terms of the number of jobs they are capable of doing, rather than in terms of the job they may be doing at the time. In this system, employees can increase their pay as they become able to do other jobs. An active training and job rotation plan is offered to help individuals learn new jobs and thereby increase their pay.

Although the results are just coming in, they are encouraging. First, it seems that individuals feel more fairly treated because now their individual skills and abilities are recognized and rewarded. Second, the organizations gain employees who are more versatile. The capacity to transfer employees easily allows the organization unprecedented flexibility in adjusting to market demands and to problems of absenteeism, tardiness, and turnover. It also solves some of the difficult problems that are involved when an employee must be shifted from a higher-paying job to a lower-paying job or the reverse.

Even if an organization does not go to a skill-based pay plan, it can depart from the established practice of paying all employees on the basis of the same job evaluation system. As part of a recent study of mine, employees in four work groups were given the opportunity to design their own pay plans. The result: Each group designed slightly different plans, because each had somewhat different needs. All groups decided to operate with a three-pay-grade system, but since the groups differed in the skill levels their jobs needed, they set different minimum time periods for reaching the higher pay grades. The impact of this process on the employees was very positive. Satisfaction went up because the employees had a chance to design a plan that fitted their individual needs. Incidentally, the employees behaved very responsibly when given the opportunity to design their pay system. They set pay rates for themselves that were in line with the market and that management felt were fair.

Selection

There is one area in which organizations make a conscious, research-based, and often effective attempt to assure that individuals fit into the jobs and job situations where they are placed: Most organizations conduct lengthy and often well-researched selection and placement programs. They typically measure the employee's ability, background, and so on and then decide whether or not the individual can handle a particular job. This is an important process and one that often does ensure that individuals will fit and perform well in the jobs that they take. Two practices are noticeably missing, however, in the selection programs of most organizations, and as a result, misplacement and/or unsatisfying job placement frequently occurs.

First, most selection procedures ignore the issue of whether the individual will be satisfied in the job. Instead, they emphasize ability assessment in an attempt to determine whether the person can do the job. This is a serious omission in most selection programs and often leads to unsatisfying job placement and high turnover, and it subverts both organizational effectiveness and the quality of individual life.

Second, most selection programs leave out information designed to help the job applicant decide whether he can perform the job and will find it satisfying. Organizations typically place great emphasis on attracting people to apply for job openings, because they realize that only if a large number of applicants appear for a job can their selection program operate effectively. However, in their attempt to attract many applicants, they often fail to give a realistic picture of what the jobs will be like. Because the individuals do not have a good picture of what their jobs are like, they start work with unrealistic expectations and are often quickly disillusioned. The result is rapid turnover.

Several research studies have shown that this is a problem that can be solved to the benefit of all by giving individuals accurate information about the nature of the jobs. For example, one study with life insurance salesmen showed that when the applicants were given an accurate picture of all aspects of prospective jobs, they seemed to make good choices about whether to go to work for the company. They were less likely to quit and more effective than were employees who decided to come to work as life insurance agents without accurate pictures of their jobs. Another study has shown that telephone operators who were given accurate pictures of their prospective jobs were less prone to quit than those who were not and also tended to be more satisfied once they began work.

What kind of information should individuals receive? In addition to simple descriptive information about the nature of the prospective jobs and job situations, my research suggests that applicants should be supplied with: the results of job satisfaction surveys, employee descriptions of prospective supervisors, and data on turnover and grievance problems associated with a particular work setting. In addition, employers could aid the individual's decision process by feeding back the results of any psychological tests that were administered. The results of such tests are typically retained for company use to aid the organization in the selection process, but there is no reason why the results of these tests and an explanation of their implications cannot be shown to the applicant, to give him individualized information about the nature of his fit with the job environment.

Why does a realistic job preview tend to produce more satisfaction and lower turnover? The answer seems quite simple. Given accurate information, people are able to determine with some precision whether particular job situations will fit their needs and abilities. Further, they develop realistic expectations about the nature of the job and disappointment is minimized. This helps both the individual and the organization, since it reduces turnover and increases satisfaction.

Leadership

Most organizations spend considerable amounts of money training managers to use particular leadership styles. Psychologists have been active in this kind of training and have argued that more democratic and participative leadership will increase employee satisfaction and performance. This view has been accepted by many organizations, and they have invested considerable amounts of money in training supervisors to be more democratic in their leadership styles.

The issue of how democratic management affects employees is not a new one, and there is a great deal of data about it. As a rule, participative management is more likely to produce high levels of satisfaction and motivation than is authoritarian management. Thus, when organizations change the leadership styles of their managers from highly authoritarian to more democratic, they often improve the performance and motivation of their employees. However, they do not improve the satisfaction and motivation of all their employees. Again, the problem is that not everyone is average.

To put the issue quite simply, our research at Michigan shows clearly that some people prefer to be directed and ordered, while others prefer self-direction and self-control. Young, well-educated employees who work on technical and high-level jobs are particularly likely to want to exercise self-control. The desire of employees to participate in decision making varies according to the type of decision. For example, most employees simply are not interested in participating in decisions that involve corporate finance, such as what kinds of bonds to issue. Individuals also differ in their abilities to participate in decision making. Some lack the mental abilities and education required to understand certain types of problems. Frequently, organizations fail to recognize these facts, and in their leadership training programs and their leadership practices an inordinately high value is placed on leaders who consistently "treat everyone the same." The concept of equal treatment is usually equated with fair and good supervision, but the research evidence suggests just the opposite. It shows that effective leadership involves individual treatment, in which the supervisor recognizes individual differences and alters his behavior accordingly. For this to be done well, supervisors must be able to diagnose situations and individuals and use the resulting information in selecting their leadership styles. Admittedly, it is not easy to do this kind of diagnosis, but it is a skill that can be developed and one that must be developed if leaders are to become more effective.

Hours of Work

One of the traditional assumptions about how organizations are best run is that everyone should come to work at the same time and leave at the same time. This assumption is congruent with the idea that standardization is important and that everyone should be treated in the same way. It is inconsistent, however, with the fact that people have different preferences about when they want to come to work and when they want to leave work. It also ignores the fact that people find themselves in different family situations, that transportation is not equally available for everyone, and that there are a number of disadvatages in having everyone arrive simultaneously, namely, overcrowding, transportation problems, and so on.

Some have suggested the four-day, 40-hour workweek as a way of improving the quality of life in organizations, but in terms of treating people as individuals, it is equally as bad as the five-day, 40-hour workweek. It, too, ignores the differences among individuals. Some people prefer the four-day, 40-hour week to the five-day, 40-hour week, but many do not. Thus, a change from the five-day, 40-hour workweek to the four-day, 40-hour workweek helps some and harms others. Again, we have the fact that many people are not average.

There is now an encouraging trend with respect to hours of work. More and more organizations are adopting flexible work hours that allow some people to come to work early and leave early and others to come late and leave late. Admittedly, there are a number of complexities in getting the approach operational. By and large, however, the companies that have tried it have found that the problems are soluble and have developed practical mechanisms for resolving them.

For example, a number of companies work with a set of core hours, perhaps four a day, when everyone is present, so that necessary meetings, communications, and so on can take place. Others have developed log books in order to tell when people will be at work so that events can be scheduled accordingly. The idea of flexible work hours can also be extended to include having individuals work weeks of different lengths. For example, some employees could work 40-hour weeks while others worked 20- or even 10-hour weeks. This would make it possible for husbands and wives to share a job, and it would recognize that while the 40-hour week is accepted by most, it certainly doesn't fit everyone's needs. Installation of the module concept, incidentally, could make it much easier to vary working hours, since individuals could sign up for as many modules as they wanted.

Flexible work hours and similar experiments will undoubtedly spread, because not only do they cater to individual preferences with regard to hours of work, but they also do much to eliminate tardiness—a continual headache in most organizations. In short, many organizations can individualize their employees' work hours. This is not a panacea for all the problems of job satisfaction and alienation, but it is one more way that organizations can adapt themselves to the needs and desires of individuals.

Summary and Conclusions

Organizations can change their job designs, selection, evaluation, pay, work hours, and leadership styles in order to adapt to the needs of individuals and thereby create working environments that will be more effective, satisfying, motivating, and less alienating. Of course, not all organizations can change all of these aspects in order to create better individual-organization fits. It is also clear that not one of these practices in and of itself is going to solve the problems of alienation, dissatisfaction, and low motivation. Taken together, though, and combined with a real concern for the individuality of each employee, they can make a contribution.

It is to be hoped that the practices suggested here are just the forerunners of other, soon to be articulated, practices that will allow further individualization. In my view, it is crucial that we develop more ways for organizations to adapt to the unique needs of each employee, to provide more acceptable job situations and thereby reduce organizational ineffectiveness. It should also help make work a place where people can grow and develop. If our sense of social responsibility is not sufficient to prompt us to action, simple self-interest should be, for making work better for some can make society better for all.

SELECTED BIBLIOGRAPHY

A new book of mine, *Behavior in Organizations* (McGraw-Hill, 1975), with L. W. Porter and J. R. Hackman, extensively considers the role of individual differences in determining behavior in organizations. It is a general text that is written for beginning students and managers.

The best summary of the work on job design that is available is a book by Louis Davis and James Taylor, *The Design of Jobs* (Penguin, 1972). It contains most of the important articles that have been written on job design. Robert Kahn described the work module approach in a recent *Psychology Today* article ("The Work Module—A Tonic for Lunchpail Lassitude," 1973, vol. 6, no. 44).

Most of the behavioral research on pay is reviewed in my book *Pay and Organizational Effectiveness* (McGraw-Hill, 1971). This book considers the relevant theory research and practice and can be read by a manager who has a background in either pay administration or behavioral science. A classic book in this area is W. F. Whyte's *Money and Motivation* (Harper, 1955). It does a nice job of highlighting how individuals differ in their reactions to pay.

Marvin Dunnette's book *Personnel Selection and Placement* (Wadsworth, 1966) presents a good discussion of the issues involved in dealing with individual differences in the selection process. An article by J. Wanous, "Effects of a Realistic Job Preview on Job Acceptance, Job Attitudes, and Job Survival" (*Journal of Applied Psychology*, vol. 58, no. 3), provides a good discussion of the use of realistic job previews.

A recent book by Victor Vroom and P. Yetton, *Leadership and Decision Making* (University of Pittsburgh Press, 1973), deals with how and why leadership styles should be varied according to situations. It is research-oriented but can be read by the nonprofessional.

section four

Groups and Social Influence Processes in Organizations

Introduction

Very little of significance occurs in organizations on a purely individual basis. The respective participants, whatever their rank, almost always confront the fact of their dependence upon others.

Kotter stresses that the sensitivity to this dependence is the beginning of managerial wisdom; the awareness of the need to cope with dependence becomes the stimulus for involvement in the political process. Kotter identifies a number of methods by which effective managers influence those on whom they are dependent.

Kanter, in a selection from her book *Men and Women of the Corporation,* discusses the meaning of power for those whom she observed in a large industrial firm. Their conception of power had little to do with formal authority over a group of subordinates; rather, power inhered in the ability to influence people and events *outside* of one's formally designated responsibilities. Kanter notes how the successful careerists acquire this ability and comments on the counterproductive behavior syndrome of those who lack external clout.

Patchen reflects upon the dynamics of social influence as revealed in his study of decision making. Patchen found little evidence to indicate that important decisions were reached simply on the basis of facts or official authority to make a decision. Quite simply, organizations do not make "optimal" decisions, they make decisions people can live with. Thus, decision making becomes an intricate, ungainly enterprise in which the various parties assess the personal stakes of each other in the outcome, anticipate their reactions, and use the occasion for either amassing or cashing-in credits.

Groups in organizations not only seldom make optimal decisions; occasionally they make very bad decisions that no one individual would have made or wanted to make. Harvey terms this the "Abilene Paradox" (so named after one of his personal experiences used to illustrate the phenomenon). The forces unleashed by group dynamics may, ironically, prevent a group from expressing and managing the areas of agreement which the parties actually share. Harvey recounts some of the corporate and government fiascos attributable to the Abilene Paradox and offers suggestions for how to prevent it.

Whatever the potential risks in group decision making, the fact remains that often there is no real alternative. Thus, we must try to capitalize as much as possible on the advantages of groups, while minimizing the disadvantages. Van de Ven and Delbecq review these respective assets and liabilities and suggest a format—the Nominal Group Technique—for using the potential resources of the group in problem solving and decision making.

20

Power, Dependence, and Effective Management*

JOHN P. KOTTER

Americans, as a rule, are not very comfortable with power or with its dynamics. We often distrust and question the motives of people who we think actively seek power. We have a certain fear of being manipulated. Even those people who think the dynamics of power are inevitable and needed often feel somewhat guilty when they themselves mobilize and use power. Simply put, the overall attitude and feeling toward power, which can easily be traced to the nation's very birth, is negative. In his enormously popular *Greening of America,* Charles Reich reflects the views of many when he writes, "It is not the misuse of power that is evil; the very existence of power is evil."[1]

One of the many consequences of this attitude is that power as a topic for rational study and dialogue has not received much attention, even in managerial circles. If the reader doubts this, all he or she need do is flip through some textbooks, journals, or advanced management course descriptions. The word *power* rarely appears.

This lack of attention to the subject of power merely adds to the already enormous confusion and misunderstanding surrounding the topic of power and management. And this misunderstanding is becoming increasingly burdensome because in today's large and complex organizations the effective performance of most managerial jobs requires one to be skilled at the acquisition and use of power.

Author's note: This article is based on data from a clinical study of a highly diverse group of 26 organizations including large and small, public and private, manufacturing and service organizations. The study was funded by the Division of Research at the Harvard Business School. As part of the study process, the author interviewed about 250 managers.

[1] Charles A. Reich, *The Greening of America: How the Youth Revolution is Trying to Make America Liveable* (New York: Random House, 1970).

From my own observations, I suspect that a large number of managers—especially the young, well-educated ones—perform significantly below their potential because they do not understand the dynamics of power and because they have not nurtured and developed the instincts needed to effectively acquire and use power.

In this article I hope to clear up some of the confusion regarding power and managerial work by providing tentative answers to three questions:

1. Why are the dynamics of power necessarily an important part of managerial processes?
2. How do effective managers acquire power?
3. How and for what purposes do effective managers use power?

I will not address questions related to the misuse of power, but not because I think they are unimportant. The fact that some managers, some of the time, acquire and use power mostly for their own aggrandizement is obviously a very important issue that deserves attention and careful study. But that is a complex topic unto itself and one that has already received more attention than the subject of this article.

RECOGNIZING DEPENDENCE IN THE MANAGER'S JOB

One of the distinguishing characteristics of a typical manager is how dependent he is on the activities of a variety of other people to perform his job effectively.[2] Unlike doctors and mathematicians, whose performance is more directly dependent on their own talents and efforts, a manager can be dependent in varying degrees on superiors, subordinates, peers in other parts of the organization, the subordinates of peers, outside suppliers, customers, competitors, unions, regulating agencies, and many others.

These dependency relationships are an inherent part of managerial jobs because of two organizational facts of life: division of labor and limited resources. Because the work in organizations is divided into specialized divisions, departments, and jobs, managers are made directly or indirectly dependent on many others for information, staff services, and cooperation in general. Because of their organization's limited resources, managers are also dependent on their external environments for support. Without some minimal cooperation from suppliers, competitors, unions, regulatory agencies, and customers, managers cannot help their organizations survive and achieve their objectives.

Dealing with these dependencies and the manager's subsequent

---

[2] See Leonard R. Sayles, *Managerial Behavior: Administration in Complex Organization* (New York: McGraw-Hill, 1964); as well as Rosemary Stewart, *Managers and Their Jobs* (London: Macmillan, 1967); and *Contrasts in Management* (London: McGraw-Hill, 1976).

vulnerability is an important and difficult part of a manager's job because, while it is theoretically possible that all of these people and
organizations would automatically act in just the manner that a manager wants and needs, such is almost never the case in reality. All the
people on whom a manager is dependent have limited time, energy,
and talent, for which there are competing demands.

Some people may be uncooperative because they are too busy elsewhere, and some because they are not really capable of helping. Others may well have goals, values, and beliefs that are quite different
and in conflict with the manager's and may therefore have no desire
whatsoever to help or cooperate. This is obviously true of a competing
company and sometimes of a union, but it can also apply to a boss who
is feeling threatened by a manager's career progress or to a peer whose
objectives clash with the manager's.

Indeed, managers often find themselves dependent on many people (and things) whom they do not directly control and who are not
"cooperating." This is the key to one of the biggest frustrations managers feel in their jobs, even in the top ones, which the following
example illustrates:

> After nearly a year of rumors, it was finally announced in May 1974 that
> the president of ABC Corporation had been elected chairman of the
> board and that Jim Franklin, the vice president of finance, would replace
> him as president. While everyone at ABC was aware that a shift would
> take place soon, it was not at all clear before the announcement who
> would be the next president. Most people had guessed it would be Phil
> Cook, the marketing vice president.
>
> Nine months into his job as chief executive officer, Franklin found
> that Phil Cook (still the marketing vice president) seemed to be fighting
> him in small and subtle ways. There was never anything blatant, but
> Cook just did not cooperate with Franklin as the other vice presidents
> did. Shortly after being elected, Franklin had tried to bypass what he saw
> as a potential conflict with Cook by telling him that he would understand
> if Cook would prefer to move somewhere else where he could be a CEO
> also. Franklin said that it would be a big loss to the company but that he
> would be willing to help Cook in a number of ways if he wanted to look
> for a presidential opportunity elsewhere. Cook had thanked him but had
> said that family and community commitments would prevent him from
> relocating and all CEO opportunities were bound to be in a different
> city.
>
> Since the situation did not improve after the tenth and eleventh
> months, Franklin seriously considered forcing Cook out. When he
> thought about the consequences of such a move, Franklin became more
> and more aware of just how dependent he was on Cook. Marketing and
> sales were generally the keys to success in their industry, and the compa-
> ny's sales force was one of the best, if not the best, in the industry. Cook
> had been with the company for 25 years. He had built a strong personal
> relationship with many of the people in the sales force and was univer-
> sally popular. A mass exodus just might occur if Cook were fired. The

loss of a large number of salesmen, or even a lot of turmoil in the department, could have a serious effect on the company's performance.

After one year as chief executive officer, Franklin found that the situation between Cook and himself had not improved and had become a constant source of frustration.

As a person gains more formal authority in an organization, the areas in which he or she is vulnerable increase and become more complex rather than the reverse. As the previous example suggests, it is not at all unusual for the president of an organization to be in a highly dependent position, a fact often not apparent to either the outsider or to the lower level manager who covets the president's job.

A considerable amount of the behavior of highly successful managers (that seems inexplicable in light of what management texts usually tell us managers do) becomes understandable when one considers a manager's need for, and efforts at, managing his or her relationships with others.[3] To be able to plan, organize, budget, staff, control, and evaluate, managers need some control over the many people on whom they are dependent. Trying to control others solely by directing them and on the basis of the power associated with one's position simply will not work—first, because managers are always dependent on some people over whom they have no formal authority, and second, because virtually no one in modern organizations will passively accept and completely obey a constant stream of orders from someone just because he or she is the "boss."

Trying to influence others by means of persuasion alone will not work either. Although it is very powerful and possibly the single and most important method of influence, persuasion has some serious drawbacks too. To make it work requires time (often lots of it), skill, and information on the part of the persuader. And persuasion can fail simply because the other person chooses not to listen or does not listen carefully.

This is not to say that directing people on the basis of the formal power of one's position and persuasion are not important means by which successful managers cope. They obviously are. But, even taken together, they are not usually enough.

Successful managers cope with their dependence on others by being sensitive to it, by eliminating or avoiding unnecessary dependence, and by establishing power over those others. Good managers then use that power to help them plan, organize, staff, budget, evaluate, and so on. *In other words, it is primarily because of the depen-*

---

[3] I am talking about the type of inexplicable differences that Henry Mintzberg has found; see his article, "The Manager's Job: Folklore and Fact," *Harvard Business Review*, July–August 1975, p. 49.

dence inherent in managerial jobs that the dynamics of power neces-
sarily form an important part of a manager's processes.

An argument that took place during a middle management training seminar I participated in a few years ago helps illustrate further this important relationship between a manager's need for power and the degree of his or her dependence on others:

> Two participants, both managers in their 30s, got into a heated disagreement regarding the acquisition and use of power by managers. One took the position that power was absolutely central to managerial work, while the other argued that it was virtually irrelevant. In support of their positions, each described a very "successful" manager with whom he worked. In one of these examples, the manager seemed to be constantly developing and using power, while in the other, such behavior was rare. Subsequently, both seminar participants were asked to describe their successful managers' jobs in terms of the dependence *inherent* in those jobs.
>
> The young manager who felt power was unimportant described a staff vice president in a small company who was dependent only on his immediate subordinates, his peers, and his boss. This person, Joe Phillips, had to depend on his subordinates to do their jobs appropriately, but, if necessary, he could fill in for any of them or secure replacement for them rather easily. He also had considerable formal authority over them; that is, he could give them raises and new assignments, recommend promotions, and fire them. He was moderately dependent on the other four vice presidents in the company for information and cooperation. They were likewise dependent on him. The president had considerable formal authority over Phillips but was also moderately dependent on him for help, expert advice, the service his staff performed, other information, and general cooperation.
>
> The second young manager—the one who felt power was very important—described a service department manager, Sam Weller, in a large, complex, and growing company who was in quite a different position. Weller was dependent not only on his boss for rewards and information, but also on 30 other individuals who made up the divisional and corporate top management. And while his boss, like Phillips's was moderately dependent on him too, most of the top managers were not. Because Weller's subordinates, unlike Phillips's, had people reporting to them, Weller was dependent not only on his subordinates but also on his subordinates' subordinates. Because he could not himself easily replace or do most of their technical jobs, unlike Phillips, he was very dependent on all these people.
>
> In addition, for critical supplies, Weller was dependent on two other department managers in the division. Without their timely help, it was impossible for his department to do its job. These departments, however, did not have similar needs for Weller's help and cooperation. Weller was also dependent on local labor union officials and on a federal agency that regulated the division's industry. Both could shut his division down if they wanted.

Finally, Weller was dependent on two outside suppliers of key materials. Because of the volume of his department's purchase relative to the size of these two companies, he had little power over them.

Under these circumstances, it is hardly surprising that Sam Weller had to spend considerable time and effort acquiring and using power to manage his many dependencies, while Joe Phillips did not.

As this example also illustrates, not all management jobs require an incumbent to be able to provide the same amount of successful power-oriented behavior. But most management jobs today are more like Weller's than Phillips's. And, perhaps more important, the trend over the past two or three decades is away from jobs like Phillips's and toward jobs like Weller's. So long as our technologies continue to become more complex, the average organization continues to grow larger, and the average industry continues to become more competitive and regulated, that trend will continue; as it does so, the effective acquisition and use of power by managers will become even more important.

ESTABLISHING POWER IN RELATIONSHIPS

To help cope with the dependency relationships inherent in their jobs, effective managers create, increase, or maintain four different types of power over others.[4] Having power based in these areas puts the manager in a position both to influence those people on whom he or she is dependent when necessary and to avoid being hurt by any of them.

Sense of Obligation

One of the ways that successful managers generate power in their relationships with others is to create a sense of obligation in those others. When the manager is successful, the others feel that they should—rightly—allow the manager to influence them within certain limits.

Successful managers often go out of their way to do favors for people who they expect will feel an obligation to return those favors. As can be seen in the following description of a manager by one of his subordinates, some people are very skilled at identifying opportunities for doing favors that cost them very little but that others appreciate very much:

---

[4] These categories closely resemble the five developed by John R. P. French and Bertram Raven; see "The Base of Social Power" in *Group Dynamics: Research and Theory*, ed. Dorwin Cartwright and Alvin Zandler (New York: Harper & Row, 1968), chap. 20. Three of the categories are similar to the types of "authority"-based power described by Max Weber in *The Theory of Social and Economic Organization* (New York: Free Press, 1947).

Most of the people here would walk over hot coals in their bare feet if my boss asked them to. He has an incredible capacity to do little things that mean a lot to people. Today, for example, in his junk mail he came across an advertisement for something that one of my subordinates had in passing once mentioned that he was shopping for. So my boss routed it to him. That probably took 15 seconds of his time, and yet my subordinate really appreciated it. To give you another example, two weeks ago he somehow learned that the purchasing manager's mother had died. On his way home that night, he stopped off at the funeral parlor. Our purchasing manager was, of course, there at the time. I bet he'll remember that brief visit for quite a while.

Recognizing that most people believe that friendship carries with it certain obligations ("A friend in need. . . ."), successful managers often try to develop true friendships with those on whom they are dependent. They will also make formal and informal deals in which they give something up in exchange for certain future obligations.

Belief in a Manager's Expertise

A second way successful managers gain power is by building reputations as "experts" in certain matters. Believing in the manager's expertise, others will often defer to the manager on those matters. Managers usually establish this type of power through visible achievement. The larger the achievement and the more visible it is, the more power the manager tends to develop.

One of the reasons that managers display concern about their "professional reputations" and their "track records" is that they have an impact on others' beliefs about their expertise. These factors become particularly important in large settings, where most people have only secondhand information about most other people's professional competence, as the following shows:

Herb Randley and Bert Kline were both 35-year-old vice presidents in a large research and development organization. According to their closest associates, they were equally bright and competent in their technical fields and as managers. Yet Randley had a much stronger professional reputation in most parts of the company, and his ideas generally carried much more weight. Close friends and associates claim the reason that Randley is so much more powerful is related to a number of tactics that he has used more than Kline has.

Randley has published more scientific papers and managerial articles than Kline. Randley has been more selective in the assignments he has worked on, choosing those that are visible and that require his strong suits. He has given more speeches and presentations on projects that are his own achievements. And in meetings in general, he is allegedly forceful in areas where he has expertise and silent in those where he does not.

Identification with a Manager

A third method by which managers gain power is by fostering others' unconscious identification with them or with ideas they "stand for." Sigmund Freud was the first to describe this phenomenon, which is most clearly seen in the way people look up to "charismatic" leaders. Generally, the more a person finds a manager both consciously and (more important) unconsciously an ideal person, the more he or she will defer to that manager.

Managers develop power based on others' idealized views of them in a number of ways. They try to look and behave in ways that others respect. They go out of their way to be visible to their employees and to give speeches about their organizational goals, values, and ideals. They even consider, while making hiring and promotion decisions, whether they will be able to develop this type of power over the candidates:

> One vice president of sales in a moderate-size manufacturing company was reputed to be so much in control of his sales force that he could get them to respond to new and different marketing programs in a third of the time taken by the company's best competitors. His power over his employees was based primarily on their strong identification with him and what he stood for. Emigrating to the United States at age 17, this person worked his way up "from nothing." When made a sales manager in 1965, he began recruiting other young immigrants and sons of immigrants from his former country. When made vice president of sales in 1970, he continued to do so. In 1975, 85% of his sales force was made up of people whom he hired directly or who were hired by others he brought in.

Perceived Dependence on a Manager

The final way that an effective manager often gains power is by feeding others' beliefs that they are dependent on the manager either for help or for not being hurt. The more they perceive they are dependent, the more most people will be inclined to cooperate with such a manager.

There are two methods that successful managers often use to create perceived dependence.

Finding and Acquiring Resources. In the first, the manager identifies and secures (if necessary) resources that another person requires to perform his job, that he does not possess, and that are not readily available elsewhere. These resources include such things as authority to make certain decisions; control of money, equipment, and office space; access to important people; information and control of information channels; and subordinates. Then the manager takes action so that

the other person correctly perceives that the manager has such resources and is willing and ready to use them to help (or hinder) the
other person. Consider the following extreme—but true—example.

> When young Tim Babcock was put in charge of a division of a large
> manufacturing company and told to "turn it around," he spent the first
> few weeks studying it from afar. He decided that the division was in
> disastrous shape and that he would need to take many large steps
> quickly to save it. To be able to do that, he realized he needed to develop
> considerable power fast over most of the division's management and
> staff. He did the following:
>
> He gave the division's management two hours' notice of his arrival.
>
> He arrived in a limousine with six assistants.
>
> He immediately called a meeting of the 40 top managers.
>
> He outlined briefly his assessment of the situation, his commitment to
>   turn things around, and the basic direction he wanted things to move
>   in.
>
> He then fired the four top managers in the room and told them that they
>   had to be out of the building in two hours.
>
> He then said he would personally dedicate himself to sabotaging the
>   career of anyone who tried to block his efforts to save the division.
>
> He ended the 60-minute meeting by announcing that his assistants
>   would set up appointments for him with each of them starting at 7:00
>   A.M. the next morning.
>
> Throughout the critical six-month period that followed, those who re-
> mained at the division generally cooperated energetically with Mr. Bab-
> cock.

Affecting Perceptions of Resources. A second way effective managers gain these types of power is by influencing other persons' perceptions of the manager's resources.[5] In settings where many people
are involved and where the manager does not interact continuously
with those he or she is dependent on, those people will seldom possess
"hard facts" regarding what relevant resources the manager commands directly or indirectly (through others), what resources he will
command in the future, or how prepared he is to use those resources to
help or hinder them. They will be forced to make their own judgments.

Insofar as a manager can influence people's judgments, he can generate much more power than one would generally ascribe to him in
light of the reality of his resources.

---

[5] For an excellent discussion of this method, see Richard E. Neustadt, *Presidential
Power* (New York: John Wiley, 1960).

In trying to influence people's judgments, managers pay considerable attention to the "trappings" of power and to their own reputations and images. Among other actions, they sometimes carefully select, decorate, and arrange their offices in ways that give signs of power. They associate with people or organizations that are known to be powerful or that others perceive as powerful. Managers selectively foster rumors concerning their own power. Indeed, those who are particularly skilled at creating power in this way tend to be very sensitive to the impressions that all their actions might have on others.

Formal Authority

Before discussing how managers use their power to influence others, it is useful to see how formal authority relates to power. By *formal authority*, I mean those elements that automatically come with a managerial job—perhaps a title, an office, a budget, the right to make certain decisions, a set of subordinates, a reporting relationship, and so on.

Effective managers use the elements of formal authority as resources to help them develop any or all of the four types of power previously discussed, just as they use other resources (such as their education). Two managers with the same formal authority can have very different amounts of power entirely because of the way they have used that authority. For example:

1. By sitting down with employees who are new or with people who are starting new projects and clearly specifying who has the formal authority to do what, one manager creates a strong sense of obligation in others to defer to his authority later.
2. By selectively withholding or giving the high-quality service his department can provide other departments, one manager makes other managers clearly perceive that they are dependent on him.

On its own, then, formal authority does not guarantee a certain amount of power; it is only a resource that managers can use to generate power in their relationships.

EXERCISING POWER TO INFLUENCE OTHERS

Successful managers use the power they develop in their relationships, along with persuasion, to influence people on whom they are dependent to behave in ways that make it possible for the managers to get their jobs done effectively. They use their power to influence others directly, face to face, and in more indirect ways.

Face-to-Face Influence

The chief advantage of influencing others directly by exercising any of the types of power is speed. If the power exists and the manager correctly understands the nature and strength of it, he can influence the other person with nothing more than a brief request or command:

> Jones thinks Smith feels obligated to him for past favors. Furthermore, Jones thinks that his request to speed up a project by two days probably falls within a zone that Smith would consider legitimate in light of his own definition of his obligation to Jones. So Jones simply calls Smith and makes his request. Smith pauses for only a second and says yes, he'll do it.

> Manager Johnson has some power based on perceived dependence over manager Baker. When Johnson tells Baker that he wants a report done in 24 hours, Baker grudgingly considers the costs of compliance, of non-compliance, and of complaining to higher authorities. He decides that doing the report is the least costly action and tells Johnson he will do it.

> Young Porter identifies strongly with Marquette, an older manager who is not his boss. Porter thinks Marquette is the epitome of a great manager and tries to model himself after him. When Marquette asks Porter to work on a special project "that could be very valuable in improving the company's ability to meet new competitive products," Porter agrees without hesitation and works 15 hours per week above and beyond his normal hours to get the project done and done well.

When used to influence others, each of the four types of power has different advantages and drawbacks. For example, power based on perceived expertise or on identification with a manager can often be used to influence attitudes as well as someone's immediate behavior and thus can have a lasting impact. It is very difficult to influence attitudes by using power based on perceived dependence, but if it can be done, it usually has the advantage of being able to influence a much broader range of behavior than the other methods do. When exercising power based on perceived expertise, for example, one can only influence attitudes and behavior within that narrow zone defined by the "expertise."

The drawbacks associated with the use of power based on perceived dependence are particularly important to recognize. A person who feels dependent on a manager for rewards (or lack of punishments) might quickly agree to a request from the manager but then not follow through—especially if the manager cannot easily find out if the person has obeyed or not. Repeated influence attempts based on perceived dependence also seem to encourage the other person to try to gain some power to balance the manager's. And perhaps most important, using power based on perceived dependence in a coercive way is very risky. Coercion invites retaliation.

For instance, in the example in which Tim Babcock took such extreme steps to save the division he was assigned to "turn around," his development and use of power based on perceived dependence could have led to mass resignation and the collapse of the division. Babcock fully recognized this risk, however, and behaved as he did because he felt there was simply *no other way* that he could gain the very large amount of quick cooperation needed to save the division.

Effective managers will often draw on more than one form of power to influence someone, or they will combine power with persuasion. In general, they do so because a combination can be more potent and less risky than any single method, as the following description shows:

> One of the best managers we have in the company has lots of power based on one thing or another over most people. But he seldom if ever just tells or asks someone to do something. He almost always takes a few minutes to try to persuade them. The power he has over people generally induces them to listen carefully and certainly disposes them to be influenced. That, of course, makes the persuasion process go quickly and easily. And he never risks getting the other person mad or upset by making what that person thinks is an unfair request or command.

It is also common for managers not to coercively exercise power based on perceived dependence by itself, but to combine it with other methods to reduce the risk of retaliation. In this way, managers are able to have a large impact without leaving the bitter aftertaste of punishment alone.

Indirect Influence Methods

Effective managers also rely on two types of less direct methods to influence those on whom they are dependent. In the first way, they use any or all of the face-to-face methods to influence other people, who in turn have some specific impact on a desired person.

> Product manager Stein needed plant manager Billings to "sign off" on a new product idea (Product X) which Billings thought was terrible. Stein decided that there was no way he could logically persuade Billings because Billings just would not listen to him. With time, Stein felt, he could have broken through that barrier. But he did not have that time. Stein also realized that Billings would never, just because of some deal or favor, sign off on a product he did not believe in. Stein also felt it not worth the risk of trying to force Billings to sign off, so here is what he did:
>
> On Monday, Stein got Reynolds, a person Billings respected, to send Billings two market research studies that were very favorable to Product X, with a note attached saying, "Have you seen this? I found them rather surprising. I am not sure if I entirely believe them, but still. . . ."
>
> On Tuesday, Stein got a representative of one of the company's big-

gest customers to mention casually to Billings on the phone that he had heard a rumor about Product X being introduced soon and was "glad to see you guys are on your toes as usual."

On Wednesday, Stein had two industrial engineers stand about three feet away from Billings as they were waiting for a meeting to begin and talk about the favorable test results on Product X.

On Thursday, Stein set up a meeting to talk about Product X with Billings and invited only people whom Billings liked or respected and who also felt favorably about Product X.

On Friday, Stein went to see Billings and asked him if he was willing to sign off on Product X. He was.

This type of manipulation of the environments of others can influence both behavior and attitudes and can often succeed when other influence methods fail. But it has a number of serious drawbacks. It takes considerable time and energy, and it is quite risky. Many people think it is wrong to try to influence others in this way, even people who, without consciously recognizing it, use this technique themselves. If they think someone is trying, or has tried, to manipulate them, they may retaliate. Furthermore, people who gain the reputation of being manipulators seriously undermine their own capacities for developing power and for influencing others. Almost no one, for example, will want to identify with a manipulator. And virtually no one accepts, at face value, a manipulator's sincere attempts at persuasion. In extreme cases, a reputation as a manipulator can completely ruin a manager's career.

A second way in which managers indirectly influence others is by making permanent changes in an individual's or a group's environment. They change job descriptions, the formal systems that measure performance, the extrinsic incentives available, the tools, people, and other resources that the people or groups work with, the architecture, the norms or values of work groups, and so on. If the manager is successful in making the changes, and the changes have the desired effect on the individual or group, that effect will be sustained over time.

Effective managers recognize that changes in the forces that surround a person can have great impact on that person's behavior. Unlike many of the other influence methods, this one doesn't require a large expenditure of limited resources or effort on the part of the manager on an ongoing basis. Once such a change has been successfully made, it works independently of the manager.

This method of influence is used by all managers to some degree. Many, however, use it sparingly simply because they do not have the power to change the forces acting on the person they wish to influence. In many organizations, only the top managers have the power to

EXHIBIT 1
Methods of Influence

	What They Can Influence	*Advantages*	*Drawbacks*
Face-to-Face Methods:			
Exercise obligation-based power.	Behavior within zone that the other perceives as legitimate in light of the obligation.	Quick. Requires no outlay of tangible resources.	If the request is outside the acceptable zone, it will fail; if it is too far outside, others might see it as illegitimate.
Exercise power based on perceived expertise.	Attitudes and behavior within the zone of perceived expertise.	Quick. Requires no outlay of tangible resources.	If the request is outside the acceptable zone, it will fail; if it is too far outside, others might see it as illegitimate.
Exercise power based on identification with a manager.	Attitudes and behavior that are not in conflict with the ideals that underlie the identification.	Quick. Requires no expenditure of limited resources.	Restricted to influence attempts that are not in conflict with the ideals that underlie the identification.
Exercise power based on perceived dependence.	Wide range of behavior that can be monitored.	Quick. Can often succeed when other methods fail.	Repeated influence attempts encourage the other to gain power over the influencer.
Coercively exercise power based on perceived dependence.	Wide range of behavior that can be easily monitored.	Quick. Can often succeed when other methods fail.	Invites retaliation. Very risky.

Method	Range	Advantages	Disadvantages
Use persuasion.	Very wide range of attitudes and behavior.	Can produce internalized motivation that does not require monitoring. Requires no power or outlay of scarce material resources.	Can be very time-consuming. Requires other person to listen.
Combine these methods.	Depends on the exact combination.	Can be more potent and less risky than using a single method.	More costly than using a single method.
Manipulate the other's environment by using any or all of the face-to-face methods.	Wide range of behavior and attitudes.	Can succeed when face-to-face methods fail.	Can be time-consuming. Is complex to implement. Is very risky, especially if used frequently.
Change the forces that continuously act on the individual: Formal organizational arrangements. Informal social arrangements. Technology. Resources available. Statement of organizational goals.	Wide range of behavior and attitudes on a continuous basis.	Has continuous influence, not just a one-shot effect. Can have a very powerful impact.	Often requires a considerable power outlay to achieve.

change the formal measurement systems, the extrinsic incentives available, the architecture, and so on.

GENERATING AND USING POWER SUCCESSFULLY

Managers who are successful at acquiring considerable power and using it to manage their dependence on others tend to share a number of common characteristics:

1.   They are sensitive to what others consider to be legitimate behavior in acquiring and using power. They recognize that the four types of power carry with them certain "obligations" regarding their acquisition and use. A person who gains a considerable amount of power based on his perceived expertise is generally expected to be an expert in certain areas. If it ever becomes publicly known that the person is clearly not an expert in those areas, such a person will probably be labeled a "fraud" and will not only lose his power but will suffer other reprimands too.

A person with whom a number of people identify is expected to act like an ideal leader. If he clearly lets people down, he will not only lose that power, he will also suffer the righteous anger of his ex-followers. Many managers who have created or used power based on perceived dependence in ways that their employees have felt unfair, such as in requesting overtime work, have ended up with unions.

2.   They have good intuitive understanding of the various types of power and methods of influence. They are sensitive to what types of power are easiest to develop with different types of people. They recognize, for example, that professionals tend to be more influenced by perceived expertise than by other forms of power. They also have a grasp of all the various methods of influence and what each can accomplish, at what costs, and with what risks. (See Exhibit 1). They are good at recognizing the specific conditions in any situation and then at selecting an influence method that is compatible with those conditions.

3.   They tend to develop all the types of power, to some degree, and they use all the influence methods mentioned in the exhibit. Unlike managers who are not very good at influencing people, effective managers usually do not think that only some of the methods are useful or that only some of the methods are moral. They recognize that any of the methods, used under the right circumstances, can help contribute to organizational effectiveness with few dysfunctional consequences. At the same time, they generally try to avoid those methods that are more risky than others and those that may have dysfunctional consequences. For example, they manipulate the environment of others only when absolutely necessary.

4. They establish career goals and seek out managerial positions that allow them to successfully develop and use power. They look for jobs, for example, that use their backgrounds and skills to control or manage some critically important problem or environmental contingency that an organization faces. They recognize that success in that type of job makes others dependent on them and increases their own perceived expertise. They also seek jobs that do not demand a type or a volume of power that is inconsistent with their own skills.

5. They use all of their resources, formal authority, and power to develop still more power. To borrow Edward Banfield's metaphor, they actually look for ways to "invest" their power where they might secure a high positive return.[6] For example, by asking a person to do him two important favors, a manager might be able to finish his construction program one day ahead of schedule. That request may cost him most of the obligation-based power he has over that person, but in return he may significantly increase his perceived expertise as a manager of construction projects in the eyes of everyone in his organization.

Just as in investing money, there is always some risk involved in using power this way; it is possible to get a zero return for a sizable investment, even for the most powerful manager. Effective managers do not try to avoid risks. Instead, they look for prudent risks, just as they do when investing capital.

6. Effective managers engage in power-oriented behavior in ways that are tempered by maturity and self-control.[7] They seldom, if ever, develop and use power in impulsive ways or for their own aggrandizement.

7. Finally, they also recognize and accept as legitimate that, in using these methods, they clearly influence other people's behavior and lives. Unlike many less effective managers, they are reasonably comfortable in using power to influence people. They recognize, often only intuitively, what this article is all about—that their attempts to establish power and use it are an absolutely necessary part of the successful fulfillment of their difficult managerial role.

Author's note: This article is based on data from a clinical study of a highly diverse group of 26 organizations including large and small, public and private, manufacturing and service organizations. The study was funded by the Division of Research at the Harvard Business School. As part of the study process, the author interviewed about 250 managers.

---

[6] See Edward C. Banfield, *Political Influence* (New York: Free Press, 1965), chap. II.

[7] See David C. McClelland and David H. Burnham, "Power Is the Great Motivator," *Harvard Business Review*, March–April 1976, p. 100.

21

Power*

ROSABETH MOSS KANTER

> The level of decision-making is way up. The level of accountability is
> way down. That's a problem.
> —First line manager at Industrial Supply Corporation

> Powerlessness corrupts. Absolute powerlessness corrupts absolutely.
> —Variation on Lord Acton's comment

Organizational politics was an endlessly fascinating topic of conversation for the people who carried out the day-to-day administration of Industrial Supply Corporation. They watched for the signs of favor and inclusion. They talked over the interesting new people. They speculated about the effects of changes in senior management. They chuckled over the real story behind certain decisions (but were never sure of the truth). A young manager amused himself by starting a rumor about the name of the replacement for a fired vice president, and then heard the word come back to him "on substantial authority." One day, a fairly new sales worker from the field went into the cafeteria at headquarters, and, because all the other tables were filled, he sat down at one where an older man was eating alone. He introduced himself, but the other's name did not register. It was the corporate president. All heads turned. The talk started: "Who's that young guy with Peter Farrell?"

Somewhere behind the formal organization chart at Indsco was another, shadow structure in which dramas of power were played out. An interest in corporate politics was a key to survival for the people who worked at Indsco. This had both a narrower, more personal meaning (how individuals would do in the striving for hierarchical success) and an important job-related meaning (how much people could get done and how satisfying they cold make their conditions of work). First, individual careers rose and fell, and people found the "top" more or less open to them, through dealings in power. Sometimes, crossing the wrong person could be dangerous. There was the story of

---

* From Rosabeth Moss Kanter, *Men and Women of the Corporation*, copyright ©
1977 by Rosabeth Moss Kanter. Reprinted by permission of Basic Books, Inc.,
Publishers, New York.

the powerful executive who was angry at the president of a supplier and wanted to make it difficult for that supplier to sell to Indsco, even though its products were an important manufacturing component. A slightly junior manager—let's call him X—created an arrangement for buying from the supplier that was acceptable to the executive, and that firm's dealings were processed separately. Then another manager—Y—looked over the figures with his subordinate and asked why things were done differently. The subordinate replied, "It's always been like that. That's how it comes down from X." Y said he didn't understand it and asked the subordinate to check into it. The subordinate came back with the story and the word that the arrangement could not be changed, but Y had the manufacturing area in his business plan and wanted to change the situation. He elected to fight, against the advice of his subordinate. Y lost. The situation stayed the same, and he was pushed out of the line of ascent. For the next four or five years, he remained in limbo in a dead-end job. As an observer commented, "He blew it with one move."

However, it was not only individual competition and jockeying for position that made power dynamics important. Sometimes, people could only do their work effectively and exercise whatever competence gave them personal satisfaction if they knew how to make their way through the more cumbersome and plodding official structure via the shadow political structure underneath. Since the labyrinthine complexities of the large, fairly centralized organization reduced everyone's autonomy of action and made every function dependent on every other, politics was automatically necessitated by the system in order for people to gain some control over the machine. Politics was a way of reducing something too large, incomprehensible, and unmanageable to something smaller, more human, and more familiar. For some people, certainly, the concern with power represented individualistic striving for competitive advantage and a lion's share of scarce resources. For others, however, power was a necessary tool for living or surviving in the system at all, and they cared primarily about having a share (a sphere of autonomy and a right to call on resources) rather than monopolizing it.

For the people called "leaders," power was supposedly an automatic part of their functioning. They were given the formal titles of leadership (director, manager, supervisor), and they were expected to aid the mobilization of others toward the attainment of objectives. They had responsibility for results, and they were accountable for what got done; but as everyone knew, power did not necessarily come automatically with the designation of leaders, with the delegation of formal authority. People often had to get it not from the official structure but from the more hidden political processes.

A DEFINITION OF POWER

Power is a loaded term. Its connotations tend to be more negative than positive, and it has multiple meanings. Much has been written in the attempt to distinguish power from related concepts: authority, influence, force, dominance, and others. William Gamson has differentiated the forms of power that contribute something to another person in exchange for compliance (inducements) from those that only remove a threat (constraints).[1] There have been many debates about whether power exists in fixed quantities, in a zero-sum sense, so that one person's amount of power inherently limits another person's, or whether power refers to expansible capacities that could grow, synergistically, in two people simultaneously. Because the hierarchical form of large organizations tends to concentrate and monopolize official decision-making prerogatives and the majority of workers are subject to "commands" from those above, it would be natural to assume that any use of the term *power* must refer to this sort of scarce, finite resource behind hierarchical domination.

However, I am using power in a sense that distinguishes it from hierarchical domination. As defined here, power is the ability to get things done, to mobilize resources, to get and use whatever it is that a person needs for the goals he or she is attempting to meet. In this way, a monopoly on power means that only very few have this capacity, and they prevent the majority of others from being able to act effectively. Thus, the *total* amount of power—and total system effectiveness—is restricted, even though some people seem to have a great deal of it. However, when more people are empowered—that is, allowed to have control over the conditions that make their actions possible— then more is accomplished, more gets done. Thus, the meaning of power here is closer to "mastery" or "autonomy" than to domination or control over others. Power does refer to interpersonal transactions, the ability to mobilize other people; but if those others are powerless, their own capacities, even when mobilized, are limited. Power is the ability to *do*, in the classic physical usage of power as energy, and thus it means having access to whatever is needed for the doing. The problems with absolute power, a total monopoly on power, lie in the fact that it renders everyone else powerless. On the other hand, empowering more people through generating more autonomy, more participation in decisions, and more access to resources increases the total capacity for effective action rather than increases domination. The powerful are the ones who have access to tools for action.

---

[1] William A. Gamson, *Power and Discontent* (Homewood, Illinois: Dorsey Press, 1968).

THE IMPORTANCE OF POWER FOR
LEADERSHIP FUNCTIONS

What makes leaders effective in an organization? What transforms people into effective bosses, managers, supervisors, team leaders? Trying to answer these questions has, of course, long engaged the energies of a large number of social scientists, especially psychologists, and their answers have filled volumes. After an early emphasis on leader "traits," stemming from characteristics of individuals, a more social perspective took hold, one that saw leadership as consisting of transactions between leaders and followers. The leader was presented as a kind of "super-follower," serving through follower designation and follower consent, and able to inspire because first able to respond to the needs, concerns, wishes, and desires of the group. Attention shifted away from the cataloging of individual attributes to the cataloging of behaviors and resources: a series of functions needed by a group that could be called *leadership*, a series of resources useful in interpersonal exchanges. Tuning in to other people was considered very important. For a time in the 1960s, in fact, the belief that sensitive human relations skills held the key to success as a leader achieved almost cult-like proportions in American organizations, and Industrial Supply Corporation was no exception in instituting sensitivity training for managers—made acceptable under such bland labels as "organizational skills" or "management awareness."

Yet research attempts to distinguish more effective and less effective leadership styles based on a human relations emphasis have generally failed, in part because there are trade-offs associated with one or another form of supervision. As early studies comparing authoritarian, democratic, and laissez-faire leaders showed, there were advantages and disadvantages in group productivity and morale associated with each emphasis. Although most theorists today would conclude that human relations skills are important if coupled with a production emphasis, the evidence is mixed enough to permit few conclusions about leader behaviors alone.[2] Two researchers tried to differentiate instrumental and expressive exchanges between superiors and subordinates in several Michigan businesses as a way to predict interactions and group process. The distinction was ultimately not very useful. Subor-

---

[2] See Arnold S. Tannenbaum, *Social Psychology of the Work Organization* (Belmont, Calif.: Wadsworth, 1966), pp. 78–79. After a computerized review of a large number of studies, Suresh Srivastva and colleagues concluded that different ways of supervising do affect subordinates' performance and internal states but that the results seem context-determined; in other words, no conclusions can be drawn about style in the absence of situation. Srivastva, et al., *Job Satisfaction and Productivity* (Cleveland: Department of Organizational Behavior, Case Western Reserve University, 1975), p. 44.

dinates reported getting about equally as much job-related information, whether the leaders emphasized task or human relations matters, and the researchers found very little relationship between style of leadership behavior and subordinate group process.[3] This is one of a number of studies demonstrating that choices about how to relate to other people (listen to their problems? offer praise?) fail to make much, if any, difference in effective management—at least by themselves.

What does make a difference is *power*—power outward and upward in the system: the ability to get for the group, for subordinates or followers, a favorable share of the resources, opportunities, and rewards possible through the organization. This has less to do with how leaders relate to followers than with how they relate to other parts of the organization. It has less to do with the quality of the manager-subordinate relationship than with the structure of power in the wider system. Early theory in organizational behavior assumed a direct relation between leader behavior and group satisfaction and morale, as if each organizational subgroup existed in a vacuum. However, Donald Pelz, in a study at Detroit Edison in the early 1950s, discovered that perceived influence *outside* the work group and upward in the organization was a significant intervening variable. He compared high- and low-morale work groups to test the hypothesis that the supervisor in high-morale groups would be better at communicating, more supportive, and more likely to recommend promotion. Yet when he analyzed the data, the association seemed to be nonexistent or even reversed. In some cases, supervisors who frequently recommended people for promotion and offered sincere praise for a job well done had *lower* morale scores. The differentiating variable that Pelz finally hit upon was whether or not the leaders had power outside and upward: influence on their own superiors and influence over how decisions were made in the department as a whole. The combination of good human relations *and* power produced high morale. Human relations skills coupled with low power sometimes had negative effects on morale.[4] What good is praise or a promise if the leader can't deliver? As other research discovered, both women and men attach more importance to having a competent, rather than a nice, boss—someone who gets things done. A classic study of first-line supervisors showed that more secure (and hence effective) foremen were those who had closer relationships up-

---

[3] Philip M. Marcus and James S. House, "Exchange Between Superiors and Subordinates in Large Organizations," *Administrative Science Quarterly* 18 (1973), pp. 209–22.

[4] Donald C. Pelz, "Influence: A Key to Effective Leadership in the First-Line Supervisor," *Personnel* 29 (1952), pp. 3–11.

ward in the hierarchy; they had the most frequent exchanges with superiors.[5]

Power begets power. People who are thought to have power already and to be well placed in hierarchies of prestige and status may also be more influential and more effective in getting the people around them to do things and feel satisfied about it. In a laboratory experiment, subordinates were more likely to cooperate with and to inhibit aggression and negativity toward leaders of higher rather than lower status. In a field study of professionals, people who came into a group with higher external status tended to be better liked, talked more often, and received more communications. The less powerful, who usually talked less, were often accused of talking *too much*. There was a real consensus in such groups about who was powerful, and people were more likely to accept direct attempts to influence them from people they defined as among the powerful. Average group members, whether men or women, tended to engage in deferential, approval-seeking behavior toward those seen as higher in power.[6] Thus, people who look like they can command more of the organization's resources, who look like they can bring something that is valued from outside into the group, who seem to have access to the inner circles that make the decisions affecting the fate of individuals in organizations, may also be more effective as leaders of those around them—and be better liked in the process.

Twenty Indsco executives in a sample of managers reached the same conclusion when asked to define the characteristics of effective managers. The question of the relative importance of "people sensitivity," as they put it, provoked considerable debate. Finally, they agreed that credibility was more important than anything else. *Credibility* was their term for competence plus power—the known ability to get results. People with credibility were listened to, their phone calls were answered first, because they were assumed to have something important to say. People with credibility had room to make more mistakes and could take greater risks because it was believed that they would produce. They were known to be going somewhere in the orga-

[5] Joan E. Crowley, Teresa E. Levitan, and Robert P. Quinn, "Seven Deadly Half-Truths About Women," *Psychology Today* 7 (March 1973); William F. Whyte and Burleigh Gardner, "The Man in the Middle," *Applied Anthropology* 4 (Spring 1945), pp. 1–28.

[6] The study of negativity: John W. Thibaut and Henry W. Riecken, "Authoritarianism, Status, and the Communication of Aggression," *Human Relations* 8 (1955), pp. 95–120. The study of professionals: Jacob I. Hurwitz, Alvin F. Zander, and Bernard Hymovitch, "Some Effects of Power on the Relations among Group Members," in *Group Dynamics*, ed. D. Cartwright and A. Zander (New York: Harper & Row, 1968). See also R. Lippit, N. Polansky, and S. Rosen, "The Dynamics of Power," *Human Relations* 5 (1952), pp. 44–50; this is a classic study.

nization and to have the ability to place their people in good jobs. They could back up their words with actions. Thus, the ultimate in credibility in the corporate bureaucracy was "the guy who doesn't have to make recommendations; he comes out with a *decision* and all supporting material. Everyone else just says yes or no. . . ."

Credibility upward rather than downward—that is, wider-system power—rendered managers effective, they thought. To have it downward, with subordinates, they must first have it upward, with their own superiors and the people with whom their tasks were interwoven in the matrix. Credibility downward was based on subordinates' belief in their managers' importance, which in turn was based on their political position. People-sensitivity could be an added bonus, but it was considered much less important than power. "Some managers are very successful and very tough," an executive commented. "John Fredericks is as tough as they come but also sensitive to people. His people have gone far, but is that because he's sensitive or because he has clout? It's impossible to untangle." "You can get people to do nearly anything for you if they think you have their interest at heart and will fight for them. They must see that you can produce for them, that the fighting will pay off." And lack of system power could undermine the best of human relations: "Fred Burke came in as an outsider to manage his department, so he didn't know the business and he didn't have the right connections in the company. When he tried to get things from headquarters, he had no clout. Headquarters wanted to talk to the people *under* him because they knew the answers. But sensitive, yes! Christ, I don't know anyone more sensitive than Fred Burke. You've never seen a more sensitive guy; but his people turned against him anyway. They had no respect for him." "What we're saying, I guess," someone tried to summarize the discussion, "is that you need a combination of both—people-skills and credibility." "No," others disagreed. "It's the need to take action that distinguishes effective managers. Having some results at the end of all that people-sensitivity. What good is it if you can't get anything done in Indsco?"

The preference for association with the powerful and the degree to which this preference motivates member of organizations is a function of the degree of dependency built into the organization itself. Where people can do their work rather independently, where they can easily get the things they need to carry out their tasks, where they have a great deal of latitude in decision making, and where rewards are not so contingent on career mobility, then there need not be the same concern with appropriate political alliances. However, the large, complex hierarchical corporation fosters dependency. Emile Durkheim, in *The Division of Labor in Society*, called this "interdependence": the way specialization had created bonds of "organic solidarity" between people who needed each other for the completion of complex tasks. However, an uncomfortable feeling of *dependency* is often the psychological result when the problems of getting approval, being recognized, or moving resources through multiple checkpoints make people see one another as threats, roadblocks, or hindrances rather than as collaborators. A manager known as highly competent made these revealing comments about himself: "I had psychological tests a few years ago. They showed that the weakest point I had was lack of independence, inability to make independent decisions. I bet it would be true of a lot of people in this company. We don't make a decision alone; we are always consulting other people. Because we are not allowed to make decisions without going through too many channels. And that's the other problem as a manager in this company. You don't really have a lot of authority when you come right down to it." In the context of such organizationally fostered dependency, people seem willing to work very hard to reduce it. One way to do this is by allying themselves with the powerful, with people who can make them more independent by creating more certainty in their lives.

Power in an organization rests, in part, on the ability to solve dependency problems and to control relevant sources of uncertainty.[7] This can be true with respect to the system as a whole as well as around individuals. For the system, the most power goes to those people in those functions that provide greater control over what the organization finds currently problematic: sales and marketing people when markets are competitive; production experts when materials are scarce and demand is high; personnel or labor relations specialists when labor is scarce; lawyers, lobbyists, and external relations specialists when government regulations impinge; finance and accounting types when business is bad and money tight.[8] There is a turning to those elements of the system that seem to have the power to create more certainty in the face of dependency, to generate a more advantageous position for the organization.

There is a wide range of dependencies faced by individuals in large corporations, varying in kind and degree with specific organizational location. Weber considered a virtue of rationalized bureaucracies that they rendered power impersonal through the development of rules,

---

[7] Michel Crozier, *The Bureaucratic Phenomenon* (Chicago: University of Chicago Press, 1964), p. 164.

[8] Charles Perrow has also analyzed the ways in which changing technical requirements affect organizational authority structures in his studies of hospitals. See Perrow, "Hospitals: Technology, Structures, and Goals," in *Handbook of Organizations*, ed. J. G. March (Skokie, Ill.: McNally, 1965), and Perrow, "The Analysis of Goals in Complex Organizations," *American Sociological Review* 26 (1961), pp. 854–66. James Thompson made a similar point with respect to businesses in *Organizations in Action* (New York: McGraw-Hill, 1967).

thereby reducing one sort of uncomfortable dependency: the need to be subject to the arbitrary and unpredictable whim of rulers. Michel Crozier echoed the Weberian proposition: bureaucracies are built because people are "trying to evade face-to-face relationships and situations of personal dependency whose authoritarian tone they cannot bear."[9] However, ironically, as one source of dependency on other people is reduced, others spring up. People become dependent on those who can help them make their way through the system or who provide the means to bypass rules that are behaviorally constraining or inappropriately applied. They become dependent on those with discretion over necessary resources; and to the extent that the system cannot be perfectly rationalized, with pockets of uncertainty remaining, those who control important contingencies retain a strong basis for personal power.

The uncertainty inherent in managerial roles has already been discussed. This uncertainty makes pre-selection and automatic movement in careers, or reduced discretion in performance, highly unlikely. It means that people who can influence promotion and placement decisions have a source of power to the extent that people feel dependent because of the uncertainties in their careers. Other sources of dependency derive from the size of giant corporations like Indsco. Beyond the people in the most routine of functions, no one has within a small domain all of the things he or she needs to carry out his or her job. Everyone must get things done through others who are not part of the same face-to-face group in which personal agreements and informal understandings develop. There must be power tools to use in bargaining with those others who are not bound with the person in any form of communal solidarity, or else those others can keep the person in a state of dependency that renders both planning and autonomous action impossible. What makes this more bearable is that others are in the same situation, equally dependent. So as long as dependencies are relatively symmetrical, people can agree to cooperate rather than trade on each other's vulnerabilities. Problems arise as asymmetry grows.

James Thompson developed a set of propositions about the kinds of political processes that develop when organizations contain interdependencies among discretionary jobs; that is, positions that are not completely routinized, where decisions are possible and can affect outcomes: (1) Individuals in highly discretionary jobs seek to maintain power equal to or greater than their dependence on others in the organization. (2) When power is less than dependency, people seek a coalition. Depending on the function, the coalition may be formed

---

[9] Crozier, *Bureaucratic Phenomenon*, p. 54.

inside or outside of the organization. Coalitions with people in the external environment that is relevant for the organization's success may increase power. (3) The more sources of uncertainty or contingency for the organization, the more bases there are for power and the larger the number of political positions in the organization.[10] Thus, more complicated organizations have more politics than less complicated ones, and power is a much more relevant concern for the people who must function within large, complex, hierarchical systems.

To see power as a dominant issue around people in leadership positions in organizations, then, is not the same as positing individual motives such as "needs for power" or "achievement motivation." It is not a characterological but a social structural issue. Critics sometimes assume that a defect in the American character makes people (such as followers or subordinates) prefer winners to losers, or that some excessive striving for status makes people seek vicarious identification with success. However, this should also be seen as a survival mechanism for people who live in the typically American organizational worlds created in the 20th century: to know that one is better off, less dependent and uncertain, when in league with people who are powerful in the dependency-creating systems that one must somehow make one's way through. There are real as well as symbolic payoffs in working for someone who is powerful in systems where resources are scarce and there is constant scrambling for advantage. Powerful authorities can get more for their subordinates. They can more effectively back up both promises and threats; they can more easily make changes in the situation of subordinates. They offer the possibility of taking subordinates with them when they move, so that the manager's future mobility may help others' prospects. Subordinates as well as peers may indeed capitalize on the success of a "comer" in the organization, as Barry Stein has pointed out.[11]

That is not all. There can also be something more immediately empowering about working under a powerful person. Opportunity and power both have structural impact on managers' authority styles. Bernard Levenson suggested that the fact of promotability itself shapes style of supervision. Mobile managers are likely to behave like "good" leaders *because* of their opportunity, whereas nonmobile managers behave in the rigid, authoritarian way characteristic of the powerless, as I show later. *Promotable* supervisors, he argued, are more likely to adopt a participatory style in which they share information, delegate authority, train subordinates for more responsibility, and al-

---

[10] Thompson, *Organizations in Action*, pp. 125–29.

[11] Barry A. Stein, "Getting There: Patterns in Managerial Success," working paper, Center for Research on Women, Wellesley College, 1975. Available through Center for Social and Evaluation Research, University of Massachusetts, Boston.

low latitude and autonomy. They do this, first, to show that they are not indispensable in their current jobs—to show that someone else could indeed take over when they advance. They also find it in their political interest to delegate control as a method of training a replacement, so that the vacancy created by their promotion will be filled with someone on their team. Unpromotable supervisors, on the other hand, may try to retain control and restrict the opportunities for their subordinates' learning and autonomy. The current job is their only arena for power, and they anticipate no growth or improvement for themselves. Moreover, they have to keep control for themselves, so that it will be clear that no one else could do their job. Subordinates must be forced to exercise their skills as narrowly as possible, for a capable subordinate represents a serious replacement threat.[12]

For people at Indsco, having a powerful boss was considered an important element in career progress and the development of competence, just as lack of success was seen as a function of working under a dead-ender. People wanted to work for someone on the move who had something to teach and enough power to take others along. A secretary recalled, "I came in looking for a place to stake out my career. I was first assigned to work for a man who was a dowdy dresser and never cleaned his shoes. (I have a thing about men and shoes. How they take care of their shoes is a good sign of other things.) The whole atmosphere in the group made it clear that people were going nowhere. It was not businesslike. So I said to myself, 'He's going nowhere. I'd better change.' And he did go nowhere." One of Indsco's highest ranking women said, "I had to learn everything myself. So did men. Lots of people go into managerial jobs without any training. I had to model myself after my boss. If the boss is good, okay. If not, that can be terrible. It's better to get a boss who is successful in the organization's terms." In response to a question about what is "helpful" in a manager, a sales worker wrote, "He sees a subordinate's growth as in his interest. He is confident, capable, and conveys a sense that he will be promoted. Clichés like 'being on a winner's team' have taken on new meaning for me. . . . Unhelpful managers are uncertain of themselves, their abilities, present position, or future." An older executive commented, "It's a stroke of luck to get an opportunity to work for someone who's a mover and demonstrate performance to him because astute managers look for good workers and develop them." There was much agreement among managers that people were more likely to emerge with "manager quality" if they worked for the right boss. "Right" meant high credibility. Credibility meant power.

---

[12] Bernard Levenson, "Bureaucratic Succession," in *Complex Organizations: A Sociological Reader*, ed. Amitai Etzioni (New York: Holt, Rinehart & Winston, 1961), pp. 362–75.

ORGANIZATIONAL POLITICS AND THE SOURCES OF POWER

There have been a number of useful classifications of the bases of social power. John R. P. French and Bertram Raven proposed five: reward power (controlling resources that could reward), coercive power (controlling resources that could be used to punish), expert power (controlling necessary knowledge or information), reference power (being personally attractive to other people, so that they are likely to identify or seek a relationship), and legitimate power (authority vested in a position or role and accepted by others as appropriate).[13] Each of these certainly plays a part in determining who becomes powerful in an organization; personal characteristics and background combine with the way an organization distributes scarce resources through positions to give people differential opportunities to become influential.

However, there are also a number of bases of power that are specifically organizational. The French and Raven typology and others of its kind are most useful for understanding one-on-one exchanges or the exercise of influence in rather small-scale interpersonal situations. The politics of a large-scale system are more complex and often do not seem reducible to such simple elements, even though the actual wielding of influence in any one instance may seem to rest on one or another of those five bases of power. This is the familiar problem of system levels in social science. Whereas there are many ways in which human systems are similar, regardless of level, more complex systems also add elements and problems not characteristic of simpler systems. However, social psychology has often treated power as though its operation in the small group were directly analogous to its operation in the large organization, thereby missing some of the more important dynamics of the latter.

The accumulation of power in a corporation is closely tied to the overall state of the system. At Indsco, formal position in the hierarchy was very important, and competence within the position was also a major factor. (Competence, indeed, is often a neglected side of power.) However, rank and decision-making authority alone were sometimes no more than a formal confirmation of already accumulated power; and getting into such a position was not enough to keep a person there, even though the position often provided the means for the consolidation of power. The size of the system and the complexity of its prob-

---

[13] John R. P. French, Jr., and Bertram H. Raven, "The Bases of Social Power," in *Studies in Social Power*, ed. D. Cartwright (Ann Arbor, Michigan: Institute for Social Research, 1959), pp. 150–67.

lems meant that even those with advantageous formal positions had to work with and through many others who had similar bases for power— what Thompson signified when he proposed that the number of power bases in an organization increase with the number of uncertainties or contingencies it faces. Finally, as I have already argued, the relative importance of functions reflected in formal positions shifted with shifting organizational problems and priorities. Though up-the-ladder managerial jobs supposedly became less tied to function, in reality, identification in terms of functional specialties remained. This was even truer lower down the management hierarchy, where people often promoted their function in order to promote themselves and could get trapped when their function was suddenly seen as less critical to financial success or other goals than some other one. A changing business climate was known to shift the relative position of functions with respect to one another and to account for the balance of power between people who depended on each other across functions. The relative centralization or decentralization of decision-making within each function and product area accounted for the relative power that lower-level representatives of an area brought to their task interactions with each other. In addition, whether a person was one of few or one of many in a position to bring pressure on a worker in a related function also affected relative amounts of power.

These abstractions came to life at Indsco in the relationships of field sales managers to product line managers in headquarters. Field sales managers directed the activities of sales workers over a number of product lines in a specific geographic territory; they were concerned with the performance of their people and the kinds of deals that could be made with customers. They responded to the exigencies of a competitive market situation and wanted to be in a favorable position on such things as price, quantity (especially during a time of material shortages), and shipping arrangements. Product line managers had a different set of priorities; they were the "business types" with responsibility, responsible for the profitability of their products across all geographic areas. They controlled price and allocation of product lines. The arrangements actually offered to customers were derived from the negotiations of sales people and line managers. There could be a great deal of tension between the people in these two positions. They had few face-to-face contacts, relating primarily by telephone or by telegram and mail, and their views from their locations differed. Field sales managers would insist that the product people were out of touch with the market, that they had no idea of the competitive scene out there, that they didn't know the customers. Product line managers, on the other hand, complained that the sales force was parochial and lacked knowledge of the overall business picture, that salespeople became too involved with their own special customers and forgot about the fate of Indsco as a whole.

The relative power of the people in these two jobs was determined by a number of system issues. In a growing economy several years earlier, when the corporation was also more decentralized, field managers were considered very powerful, running their "own little business." As the recession emerged and business fell off, and as the corporation began to centralize more and more decisions, the importance of the product line managers grew. Hierarchical position and departmental organization also had an effect. Depending on the department, many of the product managers held grade 16 positions; field managers were more typically at grade 12 or 14. Where this discrepancy in rank occurred, the field managers felt more dependent on the evaluations of product managers for their own career progress, and winning credibility with product managers was more important than the reverse ("They have the power to make or break our careers"), creating an asymmetry in power when the time for negotiations occurred. This asymmetry was reinforced by the typical form of interactions: field managers requested, product managers responded. If a product manager could not be reached by phone, field managers often could not act because they lacked important information. This infuriated them, but often there was nothing they could do without jeopardizing their relationship with the product manager. (A field manager once became so frustrated when he called a product manager several times one day, only to be told that he was in a meeting, then at lunch, then at another meeting, that he finally called the other's boss to say that he was needed right away. "He'll return my messages faster next time." However, he knew that this "kamikaze move" was risky. "With credibility you can get away with it. It depends on your relative position.") So field managers were generally much more concerned with winning favor with product managers, since they were functionally often more dependent, and they were much more effective managers of their own people when they had credibility with headquarters people. Finally, the relative numbers of field managers or product managers interfacing with each other could also affect the balance of power. Dealing with many made it easier for a person to retain some independence and to play them off against one another. One field sales manager related to seven different product line managers, and "with that many, there's no way I'm going to see them as my boss. If one isn't responsive, we'll just work harder on the other products, that's all."

There was thus a formal organizational component of power that was often out the hands of individuals to determine. However, there were also a number of ways in which people could use the organization or operate through it that could increase the power available to them. These involved both activities and alliances.

ACTIVITIES AS A ROUTE TO POWER

Power could be accumulated as a result of performance—the job-related activities people engaged in. The organization itself could be used as a source of power. (This is a side of power that political scientists consider more often with respect to the public arena than do social psychologists and sociologists of organizations.) However, for activities to increase the power of the persons engaging in them, they have to meet three criteria: (1) they are extraordinary, (2) they are visible, and (3) they are relevant—identified with the solution to a pressing organizational problem.

Extraordinary Activities

Not everyone in an organization is in a position to accumulate power through competent performance because most people are just carrying out the ordinary and the expected—even if they do it very well. The extent to which a job is routinized fails to give an advantage to anyone doing it because "success" is seen as inherent in the very establishment of the position and the organization surrounding it. Neither persons nor organizations get "credit" for doing the mandatory or the expected. Excellent performance on tasks where behavior is more or less predictable may be valued, but it will not necessarily add to power. Most factory workers and lower participants in organizations have been rendered powerless not only by the managerial monopoly on decision making but also by the routinization of tasks that reduces, if not eliminates, the opportunity to show enterprise or creativity, or ever do anything out of the ordinary or larger than life. This is a stronger and obverse version of Thompson's proposition that performance requiring discretion is more likely to be noticeable, and noticeability increases power. Crozier, too, theorized that the edge in a bargaining relationship is held by the person whose behavior is not predictable.[14]

There were several ways people at Indsco did something extraordinary: by being the first in a new position, by making organizational changes, or by taking major risks and succeeding. The rewards go to

---

[14] Thompson, *Organizations in Action*, pp. 107–9; Crozier, *Bureaucratic Phenomenon*, p. 158. Thompson also proposed that since highly routinized jobs are protected from the environment and employ skills commonly available, they cannot easily become visible outside the organization.

innovators, not to the second ones to do something; "the first to volunteer for extra work exhibits 'leadership,'" a quality anyone after that seems to lack.[15] A cycle could be observed around new functions and new positions in the corporation. The first time certain jobs were filled, fast track people were attracted. One of the inducements was the chance to step out of the ordinary and to participate in the development of a new function. The second cycle of people started to get trapped, and in one case a job that had been given a high grade when it was new (and required a person with sophisticated skills) was downgraded on the five-year reviews, so that it was seen to require a less senior manager. It became more and more difficult to fill the job as the function became more and more established. It was almost paradoxical: the success of the function as a whole made it less and less possible for the people running it to seem successful as individuals.

It becomes clear why some organizations seem to be continually changing, why new proposals and procedures are always under development. New managers must make changes or handle crises to demonstrate their abilities. If everything was running smoothly before and continues to run smoothly along the same track, what has the leader done? The "builder's complex" may emerge. Each leader needs his or her monument, which can be a physical structure or a redesigned organization chart. Crozier wrote about the plant directors whose ability to initiate action was curtailed by routinization of their functions—except in the case of planning and guiding the construction of new buildings or new physical layouts for shops. So people had a stake in finding reasons to undertake construction.[16] Very top executives at Indsco similarly became identified with the building of new field offices or proposed corporate moves. They would look for businesses to acquire or businesses to divest. They would have pet projects with which they were heavily identified, especially sweeping proposals such as taking the entire sales force off for a week-long meeting. There were definite costs if such plans did not work well—such single events were behind a number of firings—but enhanced power if they did.

Reorganizations were a common way to manipulate the structure to increase power. One new top executive at Indsco quickly established his position by making two power plays: firing the person in a key position under him and bringing in someone from outside the organization to fill the post, and creating a new division from a subgroup of the largest division, putting in someone he had worked with as its

[15] Wilbert Moore, *The Conduct of the Corporation* (New York: Random House, 1962), Vintage Books, p. 115.

[16] Crozier, *Bureaucratic Phenomenon*, pp. 155–56.

general manager. Another head of a function removed levels of the hierarchy; when he was promoted, his replacement put it back in. On a smaller scale, the manager of a personnel staff unit created two new levels of hierarchy in his nine-person group, putting in an assistant and developing two levels of the remaining people by upgrading some. (The people left on the lowest rung maintained their former position in the organization, retaining their "downward anchoring" and distance from the bottom, but they suddenly felt less powerful because when they looked up, they felt more junior.) Reorganizations were a frequent and important power move, for they served several functions at once. They ensured leaders that their own teams were well placed; opposition could be removed or rendered less effective. They provided leaders with rewards to dole out in the form of new opportunities and job changes. They enhanced the leader's power by creating new uncertainties in a situation that had been relatively routinized, making people more dependent on central authorities while they learned the new system. They were highly visible and difficult not to notice. In addition, because the question of the "best way to organize" was always relevant at Industrial Supply Corporation, reorganizations could always be presented as a problem-solving innovation.

Pulling off extraordinary risks was also power-enhancing—a classic source of the awe inspired by charismatic leaders. Very few people dared, but those who did became very powerful, for both organizational and social reasons. Organizationally, they had indicated their task-related value: they could perform in the most difficult of circumstances. Socially, they developed charisma in the eyes of the less daring. This was true of Indsco's most noted charismatic leader, an executive who had died prematurely, in Kennedy-like fashion. I heard about the devotion he inspired at many different levels of the organization and from many different kinds of people: "If we had him still with us, he'd shoot from the hip and say, 'Do it.' We'd all fall all over ourselves to do it, no matter whether it was logical or not. Unfortunately, he's gone; but where this thing might be were he still here! . . ." It was assumed that he could do anything, that no problem would be as bad if he were in charge. His rise to the top and the power he consolidated once he got there, was based almost entirely on one extraordinary risk: he took over a very unproductive plant and turned it around, staking his career on the outcome. When he finally became a division president, he continued to assume personal responsibility for events, to seek relationships and information far down the line, and to make himself available for criticism or blame if employees were unhappy with company decisions.

Visibility

For activities to enhance power, they have to be visible, to attract the notice of other people. Jobs that straddle the boundaries between organizational units or between the organization and its environment tend to have more noticeable activities, for example, than those that are well within a unit. These often become "power positions" because of their visibility. The chance to be noticed is differentially distributed in organizations, especially one that is so large that personal knowledge of everyone in even one's own function is impossible. It was also possible to gain visibility through participation on task forces or committees.

People who looked like "comers" seemed to have an instinct for doing the visible. A new marketing manager found that there was a communications gap around his function; no one seemed to know what was going on in other relevant corners of the unit, so he put out a report every other week. He netted a great deal of appreciation—and visibility. However, in other cases the things that were done for the sake of visibility seemed less beneficial. There were numerous complaints about certain managers who were more interested in choosing those programs that would be visible than those that represented high priorities to other people for reasons of organizational effectiveness or social value.

There were also some games played around "risks" because of the high costs of failure in an organization not set up to reward innovation: "Here when someone takes a chance, he strikes out on his own. If that sucker fails, he's got no place back at home. Nobody's got a string on my ass that's going to pull me back into this thing if I take a chance and try something new. Even the vice president of the new business department says, 'If you come into this department, I can't give you a string to get back with. I don't have that much authority yet.' So we're saying to that guy that it's a total-risk, no-win situation. It's safer to be part of a group. The whole group can't fail. You learn to take a calculated risk, to be 90 percent sure. That's the game to play. The thing to do is to make it *look* like a risk but have it in your back pocket. You need the attention that comes from taking a risk but the security of knowing you can't fail." In short, public appearance was more important than substance.

Relevance

Finally, even extraordinary and visible activities would not necessarily build power if they failed the relevance test: whether or not they could be identified with the solution to pressing organizational problems. Relevance is similar to what other theorists have termed *immediacy*.[17] As I have indicated, reorganizations can always demonstrate some relevance in systems where there can be no such thing as the "perfect" way to organize, but the relevance of other kinds of activities will be dependent on larger system issues, such as a current set of pressures upon the organization, and on how the actor presents his or her activities. Activities could not be engaged in for their own sake, even if brilliantly performed; wider system goals and ideology always had to be honored.

The importance of relevance in organizational politics was made very clear at Indsco in the case of a highly talented and very promising executive who became involved with the design of some new programs for employee relations. He was personally charismatic, and the people under him were highly devoted. He was also highly innovative; the programs he developed were very successfully received, and the organizational model he built represented a highly effective use of resources. His strategy for extending the applicability of his programs ran from the bottom up: first junior people would be involved, then they would pass the word on to their bosses, who would get a personal invitation to attend "briefing sessions" to learn what their subordinates were getting. All of this fit the organization development textbook picture of how to develop a new program. However, the manager became trapped in his own over-investment in his territory; his primary interest was in "drumming up business" so that he could create an even larger and more widespread set of programs. He was such a zealous advocate of his programs and his function that at a time when the company was having financial trouble, he began to be seen as "out to lunch." Questions were raised about his business sense, if he was still pushing development of people when the company might have to lay off people. Those who were against such activities in the first place found their excuse for criticism in declaring them irrelevant or saying that they might be a good thing but that the timing was off. Then the manager also had problems with his own alliances. The people who usually backed him were no longer in positions of power. He had one strong supporter at a high corporate level who saw that his next job was at least a lateral move, but developing the new function did not produce the career advance the manager had originally anticipated and seemed to decrease rather than increase his power.

Another staff unit was more aware of the relevance problem, if less

---

[17] One group which used the concept of immediacy proposed that activities generate power when their consequences are close to, rather than remote from, goals. C. R. Hinings, D. J. Hickson, D. M. Pennings, and R. E. Schneck, "Structural Conditions of Intraorganizational Power," *Administrative Science Quarterly* 19 (March 1974), pp. 22–44.

creative in its programs. There the major strategy was to "sell things by finding an already acceptable label and an organization need to hang it on."

ALLIANCES: POWER THROUGH OTHERS

The informal social network that pervades organizations can be very important, as many theorists have pointed out. In a large, complex system, it is almost a necessity for power to come from social connections, especially those outside of the immediate work group. Such connections need to be long-term and stable and include "sponsors" (mentors and advocates upward in the organization), peers, and subordinates.

Sponsors

Sponsors have been found to be important in the careers of managers and professionals in many settings. In the corporation, "sponsored mobility" (controlled selection by elites) seems to determine who gets the most desirable jobs, rather than "contest mobility" (an open game), to use Ralph Turner's concepts.[18] At Indsco, high-level sponsors were known as "rabbis" or "godfathers," two colorful labels for these unofficial bestowers of power.

Sponsors are often thought of as teachers or coaches whose functions are primarily to make introductions or to train a young person to move effectively through the system. However, there are three other important functions besides advice that generate power for the people sponsored. First, sponsors are often in a position to *fight* for the person in question, to stand up for him or her in meetings if controversy is raised, to promote that person for promising opportunities. When there are large numbers of personnel distributed across wide territories, as in Industrial Supply Corporation, there was much advantage to being the favorite of a powerful person who could help distinguish a person from the crowd and argue his or her virtues against those of other people. ("They say the rabbi system is dead," commented a young manager, "but I can't believe we make promotion decisions without it.") Despite a rating system that tried to make the system more open and equitable at lower levels, sponsors could still make a difference. Indeed, one of the problems with not having a powerful manager, Indsco workers thought, was that the manager would not be strong

---

[18] In a system of sponsored mobility, elites or their agents choose recruits early and then carefully induct them into elite status. Ralph H. Turner, "Sponsored and Contest Mobility in the School System," *American Sociological Review* 25 (December 1960), pp. 855–67.

enough to stand up and fight for subordinates in places where they could not fight for themselves.

Second, sponsors often provided the occasion for lower-level organization members to *bypass the hierarchy:* to get inside information, to short-circuit cumbersome procedures, or to cut red tape. People develop a social relationship with a powerful person which allows them to go directly to that person, even though there is no formal interface, and once there, a social interchange can often produce formal results. This could be very important to formal job success in Indsco, to the ability to get things done, in a system where people could easily get bogged down if they had to honor official protocol. One salesman with a problem he wanted to solve for a customer described Indsco as "like the Army, Air Force, and Navy—we have a formal chain of command." The person who could make the decision on his problem was four steps removed from him, not in hierarchical rank but according to operating procedure. Ordinarily, he would not be able to go directly to him, but they had developed a relationship over a series of sales meetings, during which the more powerful person had said, "Please drop by anytime you're at headquarters." So the salesman found an occasion to "drop by," and in the course of the casual conversation mentioned his situation. It was solved immediately. A woman manager used her powerful sponsors in a similar way. Whenever her boss was away, she had lunch with her friends among the corporate officers. This provided an important source of information, such as "secret" salary information from a vice president. In fact, the manager revealed, "much of what I get done across groups is based on informal personal relations through the years, when there is no formal way to do it."

Third, sponsors also provide an important signal to other people, a form of *reflected power.* Sponsorship indicates to others that the person in question has the backing of an influential person, that the sponsor's resources are somewhere behind the individual. Much of the power of relatively junior people comes not from their own resources but from the "credit" extended to them because there appears to be a more powerful set of resources in the distance. This was an important source of the power of "comers" at Indsco, the "water walkers" and "high fliers" who were on fast tracks because they were high performers with powerful backing. A manager in that position described it this way: "A variety of people become impressed with you. You see the support at several levels; someone seems comfortable with you although he's a vice president, and he looks you in the eye. You get offered special jobs by powerful people. You're pulled aside and don't have to go through channels. If you can sustain that impression for three to four years, your sphere of influence will increase to the point where you have a clear path for a few miles. You can have anything you want up to a certain level, where the power of the kingpins changes. Here's how it happens. A manager who is given a water walker, knowing that the person is seen as such from above and from below, is put in a no-win situation. If the person does well, everyone knew it anyway. If the person doesn't do well, it is considered the manager's fault. So the manager can only try to get the star promoted, move him or her out as fast as possible; and the manager wants to help accelerate the growth of water walkers because someday the manager might be working for them. All of this promotes the star's image." Another rising executive commented, "Everyone attempts to get on the heels of a flier. Everyone who does well has a sponsor, someone to take you on their heels. In my case, I had three managers. All of them have moved but continue to help me. A vice president likes me. I can count on getting any job up a level as long as he remains in favor."

Those seen as moving accumulated real power because of their connections with sponsors, but they also had to be careful about the way they used the reflected power of the sponsor: "It's an embryonic, gossamer-type thing because four levels up is *far* away, and the connection is very tenuous. It's only a promise of things to come. You can't use it with your own manager, or you get in trouble. The rabbis are not making commitments right now. One guy tried to use his connections with his manager, to cash in his chips too early. The axe fell. He had to go back to zero." Handling relationships with sponsors could be tricky, too. "It's scary because you have to live up to others' expectations. There is great danger if you go up against a godfather. It becomes a father/son issue as well as business. God help you if you are not grateful for the favors given." And, of course, fast trackers can also fall when their sponsors fall if they have not developed their own power base in the interim.

If sponsors are important for the success of men in organizations, they seem absolutely essential for women. If men function more effectively as leaders when they appear to have influence upward and outward in the organization, women need even more the signs of such influence and the access to real power provided by sponsors. Margaret Cussler's and Margaret Hennig's studies of those few women in top management positions in U.S. corporations showed dramatically the importance of sponsorship. A British study concluded that "office uncles" were important in the careers of women in organizations because they offered behavioral advice and fought for the women to be promoted.[19] Ella Grasso, the first woman elected to a state governorship

---

[19] Margaret Cussler, *The Woman Executive* (New York: Harcourt Brace, Jovanovich, 1958); Margaret Hennig, *Career Development for Women Executives.* unpublished doctoral dissertation, Harvard Business School, 1970; Michael Fogarty, A. I. Allen, Isobel Allen, and Patricia Walters, *Women in Top Jobs: Four Studies in Achievement* (London: George Allen and Unwin, 1971).

on her own, had a sponsor in John Bailey, who was chairman of the Democratic National Committee from 1961 to 1968. He first spotted her as a political "comer" in the 1950s. Since then he has provided advice, campaign help, and introductions to certain circles.[20] At Indsco the same pattern emerged. One woman was brought into her management position at Indsco by a sponsor, a vice president for whom she had worked as an executive secretary. Her relation to him and the connections she had already made through him made her reception into management quite different from that of other former secretaries. Another secretary who was promoted without sponsorship felt ignored, isolated, and resented after her move, but the first woman's experience was different. Male peers immediately made her one of the gang. During her first week in the new position, she remembered, she was deluged with phone calls from men letting her know they were there if she had any questions, making sure she had a lunch date, and inviting her to meetings.

If sponsors are more important for women, they can also be harder to come by. Sponsorship is sometimes generated by good performance, but it can also come, as one of Indsco's fast trackers put it, "because you have the right social background or know some of the officers from outside the corporation or look good in a suit." Some people thought that higher-ups decided to sponsor particular individuals because of identification and that this process almost automatically eliminated women. (There is, indeed, much research evidence that leaders choose to promote the careers of socially similar subordinates.)[21] Men could not identify with women, and very few women currently held top positions. Identification was the issue in these remarks: "Boy wonders rise under certain power structures. They're recognized by a powerful person because they are very much like him. He sees himself, a younger version, in that person. . . . Who can look at a woman and see themselves?" This was a good question. When women acquired sponsors, the reasons were often different from the male sponsor-protégé situation. In one case, officers were looking for a

---

[20] Paul Cowan, "Connecticut's Governor Grasso Remembers How She Made It," *New York Times*, May 4, 1975.

[21] The evidence that social similarity and compatibility affects a leader's evaluation of followers or subordinates comes from a variety of situations. Borgatta found that high acceptability to a supervisor at the social level was associated with receiving high ratings from him, in an all-male sample. Edgar Borgatta, "Analysis of Social Interaction and Socio-metric Perception," *Sociometry* 17 (February 1954), pp. 7–32. A study of staff nurses and their supervisors in three hospitals discovered that friendship with supervisors was a greater determinant of high evaluations than shared work attitudes and values. Ronald Corwin, Marvin J. Taves, and J. Eugene Haas, "Social Requirements for Occupational Success: Internalized Norms and Friendships," *Social Forces* 39 (1961), pp. 135–40. The cause-effect relationship is not clear in these studies, of course.

high-performing woman they could make into a showpiece to demonstrate the organization's openness to good women. In another instance, an executive was thought to have "hung his hat on a woman" (decided to sponsor her) to demonstrate that he could handle a "tricky" management situation and solve a problem for the corporation.

Peers

More often neglected in the study of the accumulation of organizational power is the importance of strong peer alliances, although Barry Stein has written about the ways groups can capitalize on the success of a "comer."[22] At Indsco high "peer acceptance," as managers put it, was necessary to any power base or career success. "Individual performers" found their immediate accomplishments rewarded, but their careers stuck . . . because they had not built, nor were seen as capable of building, the kinds of connections necessary for success in ever more interdependent higher-level jobs. "The group needs each other," a sales manager remarked. "To become powerful, people must first be successful and receive recognition, but they must wear the respect with a lack of arrogance. They must not be me-oriented. Instead of protecting their secrets in order to stand taller than the crowd, they are willing to share successes. They help their peers. . . . This is 'leader quality.' "

Strong alliances among peers could advance the group as a whole, as Stein noted in commenting on the fact that certain cohorts sometimes seem to produce all of the leaders in an organization.[23] However, a highly competitive situation could also imbue peer relations with politics and pitfalls. A star performer just promoted to his first management position told me quite proudly how he had just handled his first political battle with a counterpart in his position. One reason he was telling me at such length, he explained, was because he had no one he could tell within the organization. He had decided to take care of the issue by going directly to the other man and working it out with him, then promising him it would go no further. My informant had been the one who was wronged, and he could have gone to his boss or the other person's boss, but he decided that in the long run he was wiser to try to honor peer solidarity and try to build an ally out of the person who had hurt him. "I didn't want to create enemies," he commented. "Some peers look to you for help, to work with you for mutual gain, but others wait for you to stumble so they can bad-mouth you: 'Yeah, he's a sharp guy, but he drinks a lot.' If I had gone against the other guy now, even

[22] Stein, "Getting There: Patterns in Managerial Success."
[23] Ibid.

if I had won, he would have had a knife out for me sometime. Better to do him a favor by keeping quiet, and then he'll be grateful later."

Peer alliances often worked through direct exchange of favors. On lower levels information was traded; on higher levels bargaining and trade often took place around good performers and job openings. In a senior executive's view, it worked like this: "A good job becomes available. A list of candidates is generated. That's refined down to three or four. That is circulated to a select group that has an opportunity to look it over. Then they can make bargains among themselves." A manager commented, "There's lots of 'I owe you one.' If you can accumulate enough chits, that helps you get what you need; but then, of course, people have to be in a position to cash them in."

Subordinates

The accumulation of power through alliances was not always upward oriented. For one thing, differential rates of hierarchical progress could mean that juniors or peers one day could become a person's boss the next. So it could be to a person's advantage to make alliances downward in the hierarchy with people who looked like they might be on the way up. There was a preference for "powerful" subordinates as well as powerful bosses. Just in the way Bernard Levenson proposed, a manager on the move would try to develop subordinates who could take over, keeping a member of "his team" in place. Professionals and executives needed more junior people loyal to them as much as they needed the backing of higher-level people. Especially higher up, the successful implementation of plans and policies depended heavily upon the activities of those people lower down in the hierarchy who were responsible for the carrying out of day-to-day operations or the translation into specifics of general guidelines. So alliances with subordinates often developed early in careers, anticipating the time when managers would need the support of "their team." There was often a scrambling by managers to upgrade the jobs reporting to them so that they could attract more powerful subordinates. Also, as I have indicated, managers could benefit from speeding up the career of a person already on a fast track.

However, if power was something that not everyone could accumulate, what happened to the powerless?

ACCOUNTABILITY WITHOUT POWER: SOURCES OF BUREAUCRATIC POWERLESSNESS

People who have authority without system power are powerless. People held accountable for the results produced by others, whose formal role gives them the right to command but who lack informal political influence, access to resources, outside status, sponsorship, or mobility prospects, are rendered powerless in the organization. They lack control over their own fate and are dependent on others above them—others whom they cannot easily influence—while they are expected by virtue of position to be influential over those parallel or below. Their sense of lack of control above is heightened by its contrast with the demands of an accountable authority position: that they mobilize others in the interests of a task they may have had little part in shaping, to produce results they may have had little part in defining.

First-line supervisors in highly routinized functions often are functionally powerless. Their situation—caught between the demands of a management hierarchy they are unlikely to enter because of low opportunity and the resistance of workers who resent their own circumstances—led classic writers on organizations to describe them as "men in the middle."[24] (However, they are also often "women in the middle.") They have little chance to gain power through activities, since their functions do not lend themselves to the demonstration of the extraordinary, nor do they generate high visibility or solutions to organizational problems. They have few rewards to distribute, since rewards are automatically given by the organization; and their need for reliable performance from workers in order to keep their own job secure limits the exercise of other forms of power. "I'm afraid to confront the employees because they have the power to slack, to slouch, to take too much time," a supervisor of clerical workers said, "and I need them for results. I'm measured on *results*—quantitative output, certain attendance levels, number of reports filed. They have to do it for me." Another one said, "When I ask for help, I get punished because my manager will say, 'But it's your job. If you can't do it, you shouldn't be in that job.' So what's *their* job? Sending me notes telling me it's unacceptable? They're like teachers sending me a report card." First-line supervisors also felt powerless because their jobs were vulnerable during times of recession, while people farther up in the hierarchy seemed secure. They resented the fact that their peers were let go, while higher managers were not. "Why us? Aren't they running the show? Shouldn't they be the ones to suffer if business isn't going well?" And supervisors of secretaries . . . were also rendered powerless by the secretary's allegiance to a boss with more status and clout in the organization.

Occupants of certain staff jobs were similarly organizationally powerless.[25] They had no line authority and were dependent on managers

---

[24] Whyte and Gardner, "Man in the Middle." See also Donald R. Wray, "Marginal Men of Industry, the Foremen," *American Journal of Sociology* 54 (January 1949), pp. 298–301.

[25] See Melville Dalton, "Conflicts between Staff and Line Managerial Officers," *American Sociological Review,* 21 (June 1950), pp. 342–51.

to implement their decisions and carry out their recommendations. Staff programs that managers saw as irrelevant to their primary responsibilities would be ignored. Affirmative action and equal employment opportunity officers often found themselves in this position. Their demands were seen by line people as an intrusion, a distraction from more important business, and the extra paperwork that EEO entailed was annoying. Personnel staff who tried to introduce more rational, universalistic, and equitable systems for job placement for nonexempts also had difficulty selling their programs. These staff activities were seen as destroying a managerial prerogative and interfering with something managers preferred to do for themselves. The aims of personnel people in sending out certain candidates for jobs could conflict with the desires of the manager who would be using the candidate and when battles resulted, it was often the more prestigious line manager who prevailed.

Regardless of function, people could also be rendered powerless if their own management did not extend opportunities for power downward—if their situations did not permit them to take risks, if their authority was undercut, or if their sphere of autonomous decision making was limited. There seemed to be a consensus at Indsco that superiors who solved problems themselves or tried to do the job themselves disempowered the managers or professionals under them. Considered ideal, by contrast, was the manager who "never gave anyone an answer; but when you walked out of his office, you had it because he asked you the questions that made you think of it." Many women thus objected to the "protectiveness" that they perceived in their managers, protection that "encased them in a plastic bubble," as one put it, and rendered them ineffectual. Anyone who is protected loses power, for successes are then attributed to the helpful actions of others, rather than the person's own actions. Women complained about the "people who want to move walls for me instead of saying, 'Hey, here's a wall. Let's strategize working through it.' " Another said, "You need a lot of exposure to get ahead, a broad base of experience. I don't want to be protected, given the easy management situations, the easy customers, the sure-fire position." And being in a position where decisions were reviewed and authority could be undercut also created powerlessness. A customer service representative faced a situation where she had to tell a customer that she couldn't ship to him because the materials were not available; this was an order that had come down to her. The customer said he would call the immediate manager. The manager backed up the representative, indicating that he would call headquarters but that the rep was right and had the information. So the customer went one step higher in the hierarchy, calling headquarters himself. This time he managed to get a change. Everyone lost credibility, but espcially the woman. Nothing diminishes leaders' power more than subordinates' knowledge that they can always go over their heads, or that what they promise has no real clout. A management recruiter advised companies that wanted to ensure the success of new women managers not to inadvertently encourage resistance to the new manager; even seemingly innocuous requests, such as a higher manager asking to be kept informed, could encourage subordinates to bypass the woman and do their reporting higher up.[26]

Powerlessness, finally, was the general condition of those people who could not make the kinds of powerful alliances that helped to manage the bureaucracy. People without sponsors, without peer connections, or without promising subordinates remained in the situation of bureaucratic dependency on formal procedures, routine allocations of rewards, communication that flowed through a multi-layered chain of command, and decisions that must penetrate, as Robert Presthus put it, "innumerable veto barriers."[27] People who reached dead ends in their careers also rapidly lost power, since they could no longer promise gains to those who followed them and no longer had the security of future movement. Powerlessness was also the psychological state of people who, for whatever reason, felt insecure in their functioning as leaders and anticipated resistance rather than cooperation from those whom they were to lead. Indeed, the structural characteristics of modern organizational life tend to produce the symptoms of powerlessness in more and more lower-to-middle managers, supervisors, bureaucrats, and professionals. The chance to engage in the nonroutine, to show discretion, to take risks, or to become known, are all less available in the large bureaucracy.

BEHAVIORAL RESPONSES TO POWERLESSNESS

Controlling Behavior and Close Supervision

Psychoanalyst Karen Horney, in *The Neurotic Personality of Our Time*, described people's neurotic attempt to dominate when they feel anxious or helpless, inferior or insignificant. As a protection and a defense, the psychologically powerless turn to control over others. They want to be right all the time and are irritated at being proven wrong. They cannot tolerate disagreement.[28] In short, they become critical,

---

[26] Sidney Reynolds, "Women on the Line," *MBA* 9 (February 1975), pp. 27–30.

[27] Robert Presthus, *The Organizational Society* (New York: Alfred A. Knopf, 1962), p. 35.

[28] Karen Horney, *The Neurotic Personality of Our Time* (New York: W. W. Norton, 1937), pp. 163–70.

bossy, and controlling. Some degree of power, in the sense of mastery and control over one's fate, is necessary for feelings of self-esteem and well-being, as Rollo May has indicated.[29] When a person's exercise of power is thwarted or blocked, when people are rendered powerless in the larger arena, they may tend to concentrate their power needs on those over whom they have even a modicum of authority. There is a displacement of control downward paralleling displacement of aggression. In other words, people respond to the restrictiveness of their own situation by behaving restrictively toward others. People will "boss" those they can, as in the image of the nagging housewife or old-maid schoolteacher or authoritarian boss, if they cannot flex their power muscles more constructively and if, moreover, they are afraid they really are powerless.

One example of this syndrome comes from research on the leadership style of low-power male Air Force officers. Officers of lower status and advancement potential favored more directive, rigid, and authoritarian techniques of leadership, seeking control over subordinates. Subordinates were their primary frame of reference for their own status assessment and enhancement, and so they found it important to "lord it over" group members. They also did not help talented members of the group get ahead (perhaps finding them too threatening) and selected immediate assistants of mediocre rather than outstanding talent.[30] Similarly, in a French bureaucracy technical engineers in an isolated position with low mobility and low power with respect to directors were, in turn, extremely authoritarian and paternalistic with *their* subordinates.[31]

When people expect to be successful in their influence attempts, in contrast, they can afford to use milder forms of power, such as personal persuasion. Even a little bit of influence is likely to work, and it is so much more pleasant to avoid conflict and struggle. But when people anticipate resistance, they tend to use the strongest kind of weapon they can muster. As Frantz Fanon proposed in *The Wretched of the Earth*, the powerless may come to rely on force, first and foremost.[32] In a series of laboratory studies simulating supervision of three production workers, male subjects who lacked confidence in their own abilities to control the world or who thought they encountered resistance from the mock subordinates used more coercive than persuasive power, especially when resistance stemmed from "poor attitude" (a

---

[29] Rollo May, *Power and Innocence* (New York: W. W. Norton, 1972).

[30] Stanley A. Hetzler, "Variations in Role-Playing Patterns Among Different Echelons of Bureaucratic Leaders," *American Sociological Review* 20 (December 1955), pp. 700–6.

[31] Crozier, *Bureaucratic Phenomenon*, pp. 122–23.

[32] Franz Fanon, *The Wretched of the Earth* (New York: Grove Press, 1965).

direct threat to their power) rather than ineptness.[33] We know from other laboratory studies that people are more automatically obedient toward the organizationally powerful than the powerless, regardless of formal position. Subordinates inhibit aggression in the face of power, but they direct more intense aggression to the relatively powerless. Indeed, it can be argued, as a number of other theorists have also done, that a controlling leadership style is a *result* rather than a *cause* of hostile, resistant, or noncompliant behavior on the part of subordinates.[34]

Thus, the relatively powerless in positions of organizational authority also have reason to be more controlling and coercive. If they have less call on the organization's resources, less backup and support from sponsors and managers, less cooperative subordinates, and less influence in the informal power structure, people can only use the strongest tools at their disposal: discipline or threats or maintaintaining tight control over all of the activities in their jurisdiction. If managers or supervisors who encounter resistance from those they are trying to direct tend to become more coercive in their power tactics, it is a vicious cycle: powerless authority figures who use coercive tactics provoke resistance and aggression, which prompts them to become even more coercive, controlling, and behaviorally restrictive.

At Indsco relatively powerless managers who were insecure about their organizational status tended to give the least freedom to subordinates and to personally control their department's activities much more tightly. (I used formal job characteristics, other people's perceptions, and my own observations to decide who was relatively powerless.) These managers made all of the decisions, did an amount of operating work themselves that others in the organization would consider "excessive," and did not let subordinates represent them at meetings or on task forces. They tried to control the communication flow in and out of their department, so that all messages had to pass through them. One manager in a low-power situation, who was consid-

---

[33] B. Goodstadt and D. Kipnis, "Situational Influences on the Use of Power," *Journal of Applied Psychology* 54 (1970), pp. 201–7; B. Goodstadt and L. Hjelle, "Power to the Powerless: Locus of Control and the Use of Power," *Journal of Personality and Social Psychology* 27 (July 1973), pp. 190–96.

[34] Thibaut and Riecken, "Authoritarianism, Status, and the Communicaton of Aggression." Chow and Grusky, in a laboratory simulation with complicated results, found that worker compliance (the degree of productivity and the degree of aggressiveness) shaped supervisory style, especially closeness of supervision and adoption of a punitive style; there were complex interaction phenomena in the data. Esther Chow and Oscar Grusky, "Worker Compliance and Supervisory Style: An Experimental Study of Female Superior-Subordinate Relationships," paper presented at the 1973 meeting of the American Sociological Association. Blau and Scott also pointed out that a group's low productivity may be a cause of supervisory style, as well as a result. Peter M. Blau and W. Richard Scott, *Formal Organizations* (San Francisco: Chandler, 1962), p. 50.

ered "tough to work for—too tight," jumped on a subordinate for calling a vice president directly to ask a question, saying "*I'm* the one who represents this function to v.p.'s." Another manager with good people working for him wanted to see that all the credit went to him. He wrote a report of his unit's activities that made it seem as though he, and not the salespeople involved, had generated an increase in sales: "By negotiating with the profit center, I saw to it that. . . ."

Sometimes low-power managers and supervisors took over the task and tried to do or direct closely the work of subordinates instead of giving them a free hand, because technical mastery of job content was one of the few arenas in which they *did* feel powerful. Often people get to first-line managerial jobs, for example, because they are good at the operating tasks. Trying to do the job themselves or watching over subordinates' shoulders to correct the slightest deviation from how the supervisors themselves would do it represents a comfortable retreat into expertise from the frustrations of trying to administer when organizational power is low. People can still feel good knowing that they could do the job well—or better than their subordinates. Thus, they are tempted to control their subordinates, keep them from learning or developing their own styles, jump in too quickly to solve problems, and "nitpick" over small things subordinates do differently. All of these things were considered characteristics of ineffective managers at Indsco. However, the temptation to take over the work of the next level down instead of engaging in more general leadership—a temptation that always existed, even for people at the very top, as one of them told me—was succumbed to especially by the powerless.

Conditions of work could intersect with low organizational power to reinforce a tendency toward closeness of supervision. Departments of women clerical workers run by powerless women managers were a case in point. The supervisors were, in turn, managed by men, who gave them detailed orders and little discretion, and the supervisors tended to be in a terminal job and poorly connected to informal power alliances. At the same time, the office setup encouraged a restrictive, controlled atmosphere. The clerical workers were confined to banks of desks in large offices virtually under the nose of the supervisor. These departments were considered among the most tightly run in the corporation. They had the least absenteeism and a decided "schoolroom" atmosphere. In contrast, the conditions of work in sales made it more difficult for even the most control-prone manager to supervise as tightly, since salespeople under one manager were often scattered throughout several field offices, and sales workers were legitimately out of the office a great deal of the time. Field sales managers, similarly, operated away from the direct view of their own managers. So the greater freedom of the sales function was empowering all down the line. However, the setting for clerical workers and their bosses made it easier for them to remain powerless.

Rules-Mindedness

The powerless inside an authority structure often become rules-minded in response to the limited options for power in their situation, turning to "the rules" as a power tool. Rules are made in the first place to try to control the uncontrollable; invoking organization rules and insisting on careful adherene to them is a characteristic response of the powerless in authority positions. For one thing, "the rules" represent their only safe and sure legitimate authority, the place where higher-ups are guaranteed to give them backing, because higher-ups wrote or represent the rules. They have few other means to use in bargaining with subordinates for cooperation. As Crozier wrote, "If no difference can be introduced in the treatment given to subordinates, either in the present definition of the job or in the fulfillment of their career expectations, hierarchical superiors cannot keep the power over them. Superiors' roles will be limited to controlling the application of rules."[35]

Second, powerlessness coupled with accountability, with responsibility for results dependent on the actions of others, provokes a cautious, low-risk, play-it-safe attitude. Getting everything right is the response of those who lack other ways to impress those above them or to secure their position; and in turn they demand this kind of ritualistic conformity from subordinates, like schoolteachers more concerned about neatness of a paper than its ideas. Secretarial supervisors at Indsco tended to be known for these traits: a concern with proper form rather than a good outcome. Or, as someone else said, "You don't give freedom or experiment with procedure when you're a first liner. You try to cover your ass and not make a mistake they can catch you on."

Overconformity to the rules and ritual concern with formalities are characteristics of the "bureaucratic personality" identified in Robert Merton's classic essay. Bureaucratic organizations, by their very structures, exert constant pressures on employees to perform reliably within prescribed and predictable behavioral limits. At the same time, routinization of careers within a bureaucracy—the provision of planned, graded, incremental promotions and salary increases—offers incentives for disciplined action and conformity to official regulations. These features taken together, Merton concluded, produced the bureaucrat's substitution of means (the rules, the forms, the procedures) for ends (goals, purposes, underlying rationales).[36]

---

[35] Crozier, *Bureaucratic Phenomenon*, p. 188.
[36] Robert K. Merton, "Bureaucratic Structure and Personality," in *Social Theory and Social Structure*, rev. ed. (Glencoe, Ill. Free Press, 1957).

Melville Dalton also recognized that the powerless hang on to rules, contrasting the "strong" and the "weak" as models of managerial tendencies.

> The weak are fearful in conflict situations and absorb aggressions to avoid trouble. . . . They hesitate to act without consulting superiors and take refuge in clearly formulated rules, whether adequate or not for their footing at the moment. Following their fairy-tale image of the organization as a fixed thing, they suffer from their experience that it is not. This, of course, aggravates their difficulty in grasping the tacit expectations that associations do not want to spell out, when events are troublesome. . . . As they seek to escape dilemmas, their unfitness to act outside the haven of understood rules invites aggression from the strong who are searching for shortcuts in the network of official routes.[37]

Thus, it is those lower in power who become rules-minded, but it is a bit too simple to attribute the concern with rules only to a reactive stance—a general bureaucratic world view. For those with relatively little organizational power but who must lead or influence others, *their control of "the rules" can represent one of their few areas of personal discretion.* They can exchange a bending of the rules for compliance; they can reward their favorites with a lighter application of the rules. However, first the rules must be experienced and honored. Subordinates or clients or workers must know what the formalities are like before they can be grateful for a bit of special treatment. They must see that the manager or supervisor or official has the right to invoke the full measure of the rule. So the persons who concern themselves with the rules both have something that *must* command obedience and have the basis for a form of power through differential application of those same rules. Staff officials without the power or credibility to persuade people to other departments to carry out the *spirit* of new programs (like affirmative action or centralized secretarial hiring) could fall back on their *letter,* buying uncooperative departments in mounds of paperwork.

One Indsco manager who was particularly concerned about protocol, formalities, and proper procedure had come up the ranks the hard way and was still not in a very influential position. He was upset that perquisites and privileges that had taken him long to earn were now automatically given out to younger people. He felt that they took liberties and behaved much too casually. One time, a young person introduced himself to the manager at a company function and then called to make a lunch date. The manager turned him down and then phoned his boss to complain that the young person was trying to get into the executive dining room. However, there were hints of the true

---

[37] Melville Dalton, *Men Who Manage* (New York: John Wiley & Sons, 1959), p. 247.

feelings behind the manager's complaints. The manager was someone whose only source of power and respect came through the organizational formalities. He counted on being able to control his subordinates by carefully doling out privileges or offering small deviations from the formal rules. If the rules did not mean much anymore, what did he have left?

Territoriality and Domain Control

Merton went on to argue that bureaucrats adopt a domineering manner because whenever they use the authority of their office with clients or subordinates, they are acting as representatives of the power and prestige of the entire structure.[38] Vicarious power—power through identification—Merton seemed to say, breeds bossiness. However, if we look more closely at the organizational structures he described, we can see that this aspect of the "bureaucratic personality" reflects a response to *powerlessness* rather than to power, delegated or otherwise. The organization's concern with regulations reduces administrators' spheres of autonomy, limits their influence and decision-making power. The very provision of graded careers stressing seniority, in which incremental advances are relatively small and all must wait their turn, fosters dependency on the organization, which always holds back some rewards until the next advance. It removes incentives for assertion and reduces people to a common denominator—one in which they did not participate in defining. Unless people can accumulate power through activities or alliances, they face a sense of helplessness and insignificance.

In response to organizational insignificance, officials turn to their own small territory, their own little piece of the system—their subordinates, their function, their expertise. They guard their domain jealously. They narrow their interests to focus exclusively on it. They try to insulate and protect it and to prevent anyone else from engaging in similar activities without their approval or participation as "the experts." Another organizational cycle is set in motion. As each manager protects his or her own domain, the sense of helplessness and powerlessness of other administrators in intersecting units increases. They, in turn, may respond by redoubling their domination over their territory and their workers. The result can be "suboptimization": each subgroup optimizing only its own goals and forgetting about wider system interests. For example, a worker in Crozier's clerical agency described this territoriality of supervisors. Supervisors were squeezed by higher management, which blamed them for poor morale and deliv-

---

[38] Merton, "Bureaucratic Structure and Personality."

ered speeches and written instructions advising them to pay more attention to leadership. In the worker's view, "They worry too much about their career and the possibility of promotion. They are jealous and awfully competitive. They are also sectarian. Often there is a lot of hostility between sections. . . . Each one of them wants to have his little kingdom."[39]

At Indsco, territoriality seemed more often a response of relatively powerless staff than of line officials. Line officials could turn to close supervision or rules application, but staff had only whatever advantage they could gain through specialized knowledge and jurisdiction over an area of expertise. This was especially clear around personnel functions. The organization was so large that personnel training, management development, and organization development responsibilities were divided up among many different units, some attached to divisions, some attached to the corporation, and some attached to specific functions. Such units often prevented each other from acting by claiming territorial encroachments. The result was that nearly all of them remained narrowly specialized and highly conservative. It was enough to kill a proposal with which other units would have to cooperate if the idea originated in one that was looking temporarily more powerful. There was a parallel problem on the wider system level, where one division was much larger and more powerful than others. Organizational and personnel innovations developed by the major division were rarely adopted by any of the others, even if they proved highly effective, because the other units were trying to protect their own territory as an independent domain.

There were also reflections of territoriality among low-power staff people on the individual level. The tendency was to hang on to a territory that provided legitimacy, even when inappropriate. One staff woman, hired to run affirmative action programs, tended to bring up the women's issue wherever she was, as though she would have no right to participate unless she dragged in her "expertise." Yet, on one occasion she had been invited to join a group of managers because of what she might contribute to general discussions of organizational issues. But she could not let go of her domain, and the managers were sorry they had included her. Similarly, sometimes staff people clung to whatever might help solve their future power issues, regardless of its relevance to present tasks. One manager asked a personnel staff official to send him an older, experienced woman for a position as his administrative assistant. Instead, the man in the personnel department insisted on sending him three ambitious, rather inexperienced younger women, making it clear that personnel matters, such as the deci-

---

[39] Crozier, *Bureaucratic Phenomenon*, pp. 40–42.

sion about which candidates were appropriate, were his domain. However, perhaps there was something else underneath. The three women were ambitious and on the move. If he placed them fast, they owed him a favor, and because they were going to seek to move, they would have to keep coming back to him. Therefore, they were "his" candidates and represented possible future alliances.

Territorial control and domain concerns were also behind much of the treatment of secretaries at Indsco; but now it also becomes clear that relatively powerless bosses are likelier to be the ones who try to keep strong personal control over secretaries. Those secretaries who were encouraged by their bosses to seek promotions out of the secretarial ranks tended to work for the more powerful bosses.

The behavioral responses of powerless "leaders" to their situations, then, in controlling behavior, rules-mindedness, and territoriality, could make the conditions of work less satisfying for subordinates. To seek a more powerful leader could also be a way of seeking a more empowering, freedom-enhancing environment.

CYCLES OF POWER AND POWERLESSNESS

Power rises and falls on the basis of complex exigencies: the organizational situation, environmental pressures, the simultaneous actions of others. However, in terms of individual behavior at least, power is likely to bring more power, in ascending cycles, and powerlessness to generate powerlessness, in a descending cycle. The powerful have "credibility" behind their actions, so they have the capacity to get things done. Their alliances help them circumvent the more restricting aspects of the bureaucracy. They are able to be less coercive or rules-bound in their exercise of leadership, so their subordinates and clients are more likely to cooperate. They have the security of power, so they can be more generous in allowing subordinates power of their own, freedom of action. We come full circle. The powerful are not only given material and symbolic advantage but they are also provided with circumstances that can make them more effective mobilizers of other people. Thus they can accomplish and, through their accomplishments, generate more power. This means they can build alliances, with other people as colleagues rather than threats, and through their alliances generate more power.

The powerless are caught in a downward spiral. The coping mechanisms of low power are also those most likely to provoke resistance and further restriction of power. The attitudes of powerlessness get translated downward, so that those under a low-power leader can also become ineffective. There was this vicious circle at Indsco: A young trainee was assigned to a "chronic complainer" of a manager, who had

had organizational problems and had fallen well below the level of peers in his cohort. The trainee was talented but needed to be channeled. The manager's negativism began to transfer down to the trainee, and the young man started to lose his motivation. Nothing was done to correct the atmosphere. He became less motivated and more critical of the organization. He vented his hostility in nonconformist ways (long hair, torn clothes, general disrespect for people and things). Then people began to reinforce his negativity by focusing on what they observed: he's a "wise guy." They observed the symptoms but never looked at the real problem: the manager's situation. Finally, the trainee resigned just before he would have been terminated. Everyone breathed a sign of relief that the "problem" was gone. The manager lost even more credibility. This just reinforced his negativity and his coerciveness.

Since the behavioral responses of the powerless tend to be so ineffective as leadership styles, it would be the last rather than the first solution of most organizations to give such ineffective people more power or more responsibility. Yet all the indicators point to the negative effects of behavior that come from too little power, such as rules-mindedness and close supervision. Chris Argyris has noted that alienation and low morale accompany management's praise for the reliable (rules-obedient) rather than the enterprising (risk-taking) worker. Studies have shown that turnover varies with the degree to which supervisors structure tasks in advance and demand compliance, absenteeism with the tendency of supervisors to be "directive" and maintain close and detailed control. Yet when supervisors at Sears Roebuck had responsibility for so many people that they could not watch any one person closely, employees responded to this greater latitude with greater job satisfaction.[40] So perhaps it is meaningful to suggest interrupting the cycle of powerlessness: to empower those in low-power situations by increasing their opportunities and their latitude rather than to continue to punish them for their ineffectiveness, reinforcing their powerless state of mind.

Power in organizations, as I am using the term, is synonymous with autonomy and freedom of action. The powerful can afford to risk more, and they can afford to allow others their freedom. The bureaucratic machinery of modern organizations means that there are rather few

---

[40] Chris Argyris, *Integrating the Individual and the Organization* (New York: John Wiley & Sons, 1964); M. Argyle, G. Gardner, and I. Cioffi, "Supervisory Methods Related to Productivity, Absenteeism, and Labor Turnover," *Human Relations* 11 (1958), pp. 23–40; study by E. Fleishman and E. Harris cited in Charles Hampden-Turner, "The Factory as an Oppressive Environment," in *Worker's Control: A Reader on Labor and Social Change,* ed. G. Hunnius, G. D. Garson, and J. Case, (New York: Vintage, 1973), pp. 30–44. The Sears study was James Worthy, "Organizational Structure and Employee Morale," *American Sociological Review* 15 (1950), pp. 169–79.

people who are really powerful. Power has become a scarce resource that most people feel they lack. Although the scramble for political advantage still distinguishes relative degress of power, the organization places severe limits on everyone's freedom of action. The powerful get more, but they still share some of the mentality of powerlessness.

22

The Locus and Basis of Influence on Organizational Decisions*

MARTIN PATCHEN

A number of recent writers have emphasized that the process of decision-making within organizations is a group process involving some kind of accommodation among individuals and units. This accommodation has been variously discussed in terms of such processes as resolving conflict (March & Simon, 1958), mutual adjustment (Lindblom, 1968), forming a winning coalition (Bauer, 1968; Thompson, 1967), and of both conflict and consensus-building (Hilsman, 1959).

Given that decision-making in organizations is a process of accommodation among individuals and units, it is important to know the basis on which given individuals or units exert more or less influence on the final decision. Who is influential and why? This paper discusses the basis of interpersonal influence and reports the results of a study which focuses on the bases of influence on organizational decisions.[1]

THE BASES OF INFLUENCE

On the subject of the bases of influence, the work of French and Raven (1959) has been widely cited. However, while French and

* Abridged from *Organizational Behavior and Human Performance*, 1974, *11*, pp. 195–221. Copyright © 1974 by Academic Press, Inc.

[1] The study reported here was conducted by the Survey Research Center of the University of Michigan under the direction of the author. Interviewing was done by the field staff of the National Opinion Research Center under the immediate supervision of Eve Weinberg and Jean Schwartz. The study was sponsored by Time, Inc. Arnold Tannenbaum and Robert Perrucci made helpful comments on an earlier version of this paper.

Raven have pointed to some important aspects of influence, their classification is limited in important ways.

French and Raven define the basis of power in terms of "the relationships between O and P which is the source of that power" and then discuss five bases of power. Two of these (reward power and coercive power) are defined in terms of *resources* available to the influencer, i.e., "reward power is defined as power whose basis is the ability to reward" and coercive power is "similar to reward power in that it also involves O's ability to manipulate the attainment of valences" (French & Raven, 1959, p. 157).

However, referent power is said to have "its basis in the identification of P (target) with O (influencer)—a feeling of oneness of P with O, or a desire for such an identity" (French & Raven, 1959, p. 161). Thus, referent power is described not in terms of the resources of the influencer but in terms of the *characteristics and motivations* of the target. Similarly, legitimate power is defined in terms of the target person's characteristics and motivations, i.e., "as that power which stems from internalized values in P which dictate that O has a legitimate right to influence P and that P has an obligation to accept this influence" (French & Raven, 1959, p. 159). Finally, "expert power" is discussed in terms which appear that it in part depends on certain characteristics of the influencer (e.g., his credibility) and in part on certain resources he possesses (e.g., facts). It appears, then, that the five "bases of power" distinguished by French and Raven are not described in a conceptually parallel way. Instead, for different types of power, different aspects of the process underlying successful influence are highlighted.

Table 1 presents a conceptual framework for analyzing social influence which is intended to consider more systematically the various components of the influence process. Looking first at the person exerting influence, the scheme directs the investigator's attention to the relationship between his characteristics, the resources available to him, and his role in the decision process. Thus, for example, the person with the characteristic of specialized training and experience has information resources and may, because of his expertise, conduct certain investigations or tests relevant to the decision. Similarly the scheme draws attention to the relation between the characteristics, needs, and decision-making role of those who are the targets of influence.

Most important, the scheme directs attention to the degree of correspondence between the resources of the influencer and the needs of the target, as well as to the types of communication between them following from their respective decision-making roles. Thus, for example, the person with information about the consequences of possible decisions has an important resource which meets the needs of the target person who has a need for such information. The person exerting influence may have the role of giving relevant information to the target person whose role may be to review such information from this and other sources. The interaction between these persons is likely to have an effect on the target person, by making certain options seem more or less desirable and perhaps by indicating new options not considered previously.

The five rows of Table 1 correspond to the five bases of power discussed by French and Raven, i.e., expert power, reward power, coercive power, referent power, and legitimate power. (The sixth row will be discussed later.) Note that more explicit recognition of these separate aspects calls attention to some possibly important features of the influence process which might otherwise be overlooked. For example, in considering referent power (defined by French and Raven in terms of characteristics of the target person), one is led to look also for characteristics and resources of the influencer which may lead the target person to conform because of a desire to be similar to, or to be approved by, the influencer (see the fourth row of Table 1).

Though the examples in Table 1 are intended to mirror the five bases of power discussed by French and Raven, there is no necessary implication that these are the only five types of power that could be distinguished. A listing of types of power would probably depend on a categorization of the needs of the target person and/or the resources controlled by the influencer.

The conceptual framework outlined in Table 1 suggests a number of empirical questions. What types of characteristics will influential persons be found to have in various types of situations? What types of resources will they be found to command? In what types of activities will they be found to engage? Similar questions may be asked about the characteristics of targets of influence, their needs and their activities, as these relate to the characteristics, resources, and activities of influencers.

With respect to influence on organizational decisions, the writings of a number of theorists suggest some answers to these questions. A number of writers have stressed the importance of specialized knowledge in gaining organizational influence (Thompson, 1967, chap. 10; Lawrence & Lorsch, 1967). March and Simon (1958, chap. 5) have discussed the problem-solving process as one of the fundamental ways of resolving conflict in organizations. These writings would lead us to expect influentials in organizations often to have the characteristics, resources, and activities which are consistent with expert power.

Many discussions of decision-making and influence in organizations have stressed bargaining as a key process by which accommodation is reached in organizations (March & Simon, 1959; Bauer, 1968;

TABLE 1
A Framework for Analyzing Social Influence,* with Some Examples

Person Exerting Influence			Target(s) of Influence			
Characteristics	Resources	Decision Role with Respect to Target	Characteristics	Needs	Decision Role with Respect to Influencer	Effect of Influencer on Target
Expertise: special training, special experience, etc.	Knowledge about how to reach certain goals	Investigates, makes tests, gives information to others	Unexpert	Wants to find best ways to reach goals	Reviews information presented by experts	Sees new options; sees new favorable or unfavorable consequences following various actions
Occupies important position in hierarchy	Control over material rewards (money, promotion, etc.)	Makes request, coupled with promise of reward for compliance	Occupies less important position in hierarchy	Wants rewards controlled by influencer	Decides whether to accede to request of others	Compliance seen as means to rewards
Occupies important position in hierarchy	Control over material penalties (fines, demotions, etc.)	Gives order, coupled with threat of punishment for non-compliance	Occupies less important position in hierarchy	Wants to avoid punishment but maintain self-esteem	Decides whether to accede to order	Compliance seen as way of avoiding penalty but may be seen as blow to self-esteem
Strong; successful; has attractive qualities	Approval	States own opinions, preferences	Less strong, less successful	Wishes to be similar to, approved by, influencer	Hears opinions, preferences of influencer	Sees compliance as way of being similar to, approved by, influencer

Occupies legitimate position of authority; secured position by legitimate methods	Symbols of legitimacy; label of others' action as right or wrong	Announces decision; asks for support	Occupies position of subordination; accepts legitimacy of other's position	Wishes to fulfill moral obligations	Gets request from authority	Sees conformity to requested action as morally correct
Is affected by certain decisions (by virtue of work needs, responsibilities, etc.)	Own cooperation; (may also have some resources listed in other rows)	Vigorously makes preference known to others	Peers or final decision-making authority	Want high level of cooperation from influencer	Decide whether to accept recommendation	See accepting recommendation as leading to future cooperation by influencer

* This framework may be expanded to include (a) the motivation of the influencer to use his resources and (b) the perception by the target that the influencer will use his resources.

Lindblom, 1968; Hilsman, 1959). As Lindblom points out, discussions of bargaining are concerned essentially with "the play of power." They are, thus, emphasizing the importance of reward power and coercive power in organizations. This line of theoretical work would lead us to expect influentials (and targets of successful influence) to often have the characteristics, resources, and activities which characterize reward power and coercive power. On the basis of Weber's classical work (Weber, 1947) and our knowledge of bureaucracies, we also would expect influentials often to have the characteristics, resources, and activities which typify legitimate power. (Referent power has received less theoretical attention as a basis of power in organizations.)

However, although there has been some research on the bases of supervisory influence over subordinates in organizations (Bachman, Bowers, & Marcus, 1968), there is little empirical evidence concerning the bases of influence in organizational decision-making.

The rest of this paper presents a report of a study which provides descriptive data on this topic. That portion of the data which concerns the characteristics, resources, and activities of influential persons suggest certain bases of influence not covered by the French and Raven schema. The data also raise some important methodological questions about the measurement of influence in organizations. (A descriptive account of each case is available elsewhere [Patchen, 1969].)

DESCRIPTION OF THE STUDY

The study concerned decisions by business firms to make specific purchases. Thirty-three such decisions in 11 firms were studied. Most of these decisions (e.g., to use hydrochloric acid instead of sulfuric acid for steel producing) were of considerable importance to the companies, as judged by their possible effects on company operations, although some decisions (e.g., to purchase a pick-up truck) were of more minor import.

Information Obtained

Each person involved in the decision was asked about a variety of relevant matters, including the following:[2] (1) Who brought the problem to his attention and with whom he discussed the problem; (2) his

---

[2] Other questions asked in the interview concerned the reasons for the decisions which were made, sources of relevant information, personal contact with suppliers, satisfaction with the decision, and a few basic personal facts about the respondent.

role in the decision; (3) who was involved at any stage of the decision; (4) any differences of opinion within the company; (5) how differences of opinion were resolved; (6) whom he judged to have had most influence on the decision and why this person exerted such great influence.

RESULTS

People Involved in Decisions

For all 33 decisions in 11 companies, an average of 15.0 persons were mentioned by respondents as having been involved in any way in each decision. Typically, especially for the more important purchases, the persons involved in each decision represented a variety of types of organizational units and specialties. For example, in a company which makes automobile parts, a decision to use zinc rather than aluminum for one of their products involved engineering, sales, manufacturing, and purchasing, as well as some other units. In some cases, men at several levels of company structure (i.e., local plant and corporate office) were involved in a decision. In one such case, a respondent, describing the decision to purchase a new piercing press, quipped "They have everybody but the Pope in on a decision like this."

The number of participants in a decision varied more by the magnitude of the decision involved than by company. For 20 decisions rated by the researcher as being of moderate or major importance, an average of 19.8 persons were mentioned while for 13 more minor decisions, an average of 7.9 persons were mentioned. Since we may not have identified some of the people involved in each decision (especially those with more peripheral involvement), these figures are clearly not precise, but they should serve to give at least a rough estimate of the number of persons with some involvement.

These figures give very conservative estimates of the actual numbers with an important part in the decision since they are based only on the number of persons interviewed; in some cases, one or more persons with an important role in these data indicate that the decisions studied were typically made by a group of people and not by just one or two persons. Additional confirmation that a number of people typically had important roles in the decision comes from the data, to be discussed later, concerning the identity of those who had greatest influence on each decision.

Resolving Differences of Opinion

After asking about the respondent's role in the decision to get a product in the general category, we asked: "When the subject was first discussed, were there any differences of opinion within the company about the desirability of making this purchase (rental)?" Later in the interview we asked a similar question concerning possible differences of opinion in choosing a particular type of product or a particular supplier.

With respect to the basic decision to buy, there was at least some evidence of differences of opinion (one or more reports) in 22 out of the 33 cases and considerable evidence of disagreements (reports by half or more of the respondents) in 13 cases. With respect to the decision about what specific product to buy, there was at least some evidence of differences of opinion in 18 cases and considerable evidence in 9 cases.[3] Taking the cases as wholes, in 27 of the 33 cases at least one person reported a disagreement within the company at some point during the decision-making process. In 19 cases, half or more of the respondents reported a disagreement at some point.

When a disagreement was mentioned, the respondent was asked the reasons for this difference of opinion and then was asked "How were the differences resolved?" Table 2 shows a tabulation of answers given to this question.[4] The answers are shown separately for resolution of differences concerning whether to make a purchase of the general type and for resolution of differences concerning the specific type of purchase. The table shows the number of *cases* in which a given method was mentioned one or more times as a method used to resolve differences and also shows the total number of mentions for each method.

The data show that getting more information (or further analyzing information) was the method most frequently reported as the way in which differences were resolved. For example, describing the resolution of initial differences over what computer would best fill their needs, an executive of one firm said "We brought in all known computer manufacturers and requested an exact explanation of price, work, etc." An engineer in another company, describing the resolution of differences concerning whether a certain type of laminate should be used in cabinet manufacture, said "Sales dropped their opposition when they saw a sample of a cabinet which was made up."

Meetings or discussions were mentioned with second greatest fre-

---

[3] The decision to buy a product in a certain category and the decision about the specific type to buy were separate decisions in some cases but were closely intertwined in other cases.

[4] Reliability between two coders (the study director and an assistant) in coding these responses was .76. Reliability was computed by dividing the number of coding agreements by the sum of agreements plus disagreements. The "don't know" category was omitted and categories considered subcategories of "problem solving" (1, 2, and 3 in Table 2) were combined for this computation. (If the three problem-solving subcategories are considered separately, the reliability is .73.) Differences between codings were resolved by the study director.

TABLE 2
Reported Ways in Which Differences of Opinion Were Resolved

Method of Resolving Differences*	Differences about Getting Product of General Type (N = 22 cases)		Differences about Specific Product to Get (N = 18 cases)		All Differences
	Number of Cases Where Method Mentioned	Total Number of Mentions	Number of Cases Where Method Mentioned	Total Number of Mentions	Total Number of Mentions
1. Getting more information, or further analyzing information	16	29	11	18	47
2. Finding new solution to problem	7	8	2	2	10
3. Further defining, specifying goals	1	1	2	2	3
4. Discussions or meetings	5	6	10	14	20
5. Persuasion	4	5	3	3	8
6. Vote or survey of opinion taken	0	0	3	3	3
7. Agreement or consensus reached	4	5	2	2	7
8. Decision made by person in position of higher authority	1	2	2	3	5
9. Decision made or most influenced by person not in position of higher authority	3	3	3	3	6
10. By negotiations, bargaining	1	1	0	0	1
11. Reason(s) for decision given without telling how difference resolved	2	2	1	2	4
12. Other answers					
a. Relevant to how differences resolved	2	2	1	1	3
b. Not relevant to question	4	4	1	1	5
13. Don't know	2	2	3	3	5

* More than one method could be mentioned by any respondent.

quency as the way in which differences were resolved. Also mentioned with moderate frequency were finding a new solution to the problem which apparently satisfied everyone (e.g., "We decided to carry only stress-proof (material) which got rid of the increase in inventory problem"); persuasion (e.g., "After a long slow process, they (division heads) were convinced"); and getting consensus (e.g., "an agreement was made by consensus of opinion"). Resolution of a dispute by a person in higher authority was mentioned in only a few cases while mention of a decision being made (or most influence being exerted) by a person not in higher authority was slightly more frequent.

Other methods of resolving differences which were mentioned only rarely were: conducting a vote or survey of opinion within the company; further defining or specifying goals; and negotiations or bargaining (only one mention). No mention at all was made of differences being resolved in ways which could be coded as "rewards promised or expected" for giving in or as "threat or expectation of penalties" for not giving in.

In general, the picture that emerges from these data is that differences of opinion concerning these company purchases seem to be resolved with a heavy emphasis on problem-solving, especially by getting more information and devising new solutions and occasionally by further defining goals. The data also suggests a frequent emphasis on reaching consensus, as indicated especially by the references to meetings and discussions, persuasion, and getting consensus. Even the few references to taking a poll or vote seem to reflect a concern with getting widespread agreement, if not total consensus. Also, the method of devising a new solution, which is in part problem-solving, may sometimes be used to help reach consensus.

JUDGING WHO IS MOST INFLUENTIAL

So far the data have indicated that a group of people were usually involved in making most purchase decisions and that when disagreements arose, as they frequently did, they tended to be resolved by further information-seeking and by a process of reaching consensus. But we have not yet considered who was most influential in this process of accommodation nor why certain persons were particularly influential.

After each respondent was asked about his part in the purchase decision, about any differences of opinion within the company, and about the reasons for the decision to get a product in this general category, he was asked: "Regardless of who had the final authority, who, would you say, had the most influence on the decision to get a (product)?" Later in the interview, after the choice of a particular type of product and/or suppliers was discussed, he was asked a closely similar question: "Regardless of who had the final authority, who, would you say, had the most influence on the choice of which particular (product) to get?"

The most striking fact about the answers to these questions about influence is that the people involved in each decision do not agree very much about who had "most influence." For both types of decision, the number of persons named as most influential increases almost as fast as the number of informants increases, as Table 3 shows. Although the number of persons named as most influential, as a fraction

TABLE 3
Number of Persons Named As Having Most Influence in Relation to Number of Respondents*

A. Decision to Buy Product in General Category

(1) Number n of decisions	(2) Number of respondents† per decision	(3) Average number of persons named per decision	Column (3) Column (2)
7	2	1.43	.72
4	3	2.50	.83
7	4	2.86	.72
3	5	3.33	.67
4	6	3.50	.58
3	7	3.00	.43
0	8	—	—
2	9	5.50	.61

B. Decision about Specific Product to Buy

(1) Number n of decisions	(2) Number of respondents per decision	(3) Average number of persons named per decision	Column (3) Column (2)
5	2	1.80	.90
7	3	2.00	.67
4	4	2.75	.69
8	5	3.75	.75
0	6	—	—
2	7	3.00	.43
1	8	6.00	.75

* A few respondents named more than one person as most influential; in these cases, the total number of separate persons named was counted. A few respondents named a group or unit as most influential; this was counted as one "person." Names of persons outside the regular organization, e.g., "the customer," the (outside) architect, were counted when mentioned.

† Cases in which fewer than two persons answered the question about who had most influence are omitted from the table.

of number of informants, tends to drop as the number of informants increases, this drop is not large or consistent. Clearly, there is much disagreement among informants as to who had the most influence on specific decisions.

These differences in judgments about who is most influential may stem from a number of sources. First, persons who took some part in an organizational decision sometimes have varying amounts and kinds of information about the entire process by which the decision was made. Secondly, a few informants may have wished to inflate their own importance by naming themselves as most influential. However, this cannot be a large effect because the average number of persons naming themselves was 1.3 per decision (out of an average of 5.5 informants), both for decisions to buy and for decisions about what particular product to buy.

Several more fundamental reasons for differences in perceptions of influence have to do with the nature of the decision-making processes. The data on resolution of differences have already suggested that purchase decisions are usually made by mutual agreement among the interested parties. A review of the individual cases (see Patchen, 1969) indicates also that in most cases there was no single prime "decision-maker" but that instead the decision was made through a process of consensus and accommodation. One illustrative case is the decision by an engineering "job shop" to use a new type of steel for cross-rods in conveyors which they were manufacturing. Discussing this decision, the Superintendent of the Machine Shop said, "It's a combined effort between Engineers, Shop, and Purchasing." The Superintendent of Industrial Engineering added that "No one had the final say on it . . . all three decisions (Engineering, Purchasing, Manufacturing) were favorable."

In addition to the fact that the locus of decision-making is often diffuse, it also frequently happens that various people play different kinds of roles in the decision, often at different stages. For example, the decision by a manufacturing company to lease, and switch additional clerical work to, a larger computer involved persons in a variety of roles. The Plant Accountant at one of the major plants, informants said, "led the way" in pointing out the need for this computer. Several persons, including the corporate Manager of Computer Operations conducted an "economic feasibility study." The Chief Engineer was a central person in the discussions because much of the work would be done for his department's operation. After long study and discussion, formal reports were presented to the Plant Manager whose job was to evaluate the reports and to weigh differences of opinion. Then the Plant Manager decided, he said, that the "advantages outweighed the disadvantages." Finally, the Chief Engineer and

Plant Accountant had to "sell" the computer idea to the Controller at the Corporate level, who is in charge of Data Processing for the entire company. Reporting on a decision of this kind (which is much abbreviated here), it is small wonder that respondents will differ on whom they name as most influential in a decision.

CHARACTERISTICS OF INFLUENTIALS

A large majority of answers concerned characteristics of the influential (see Table 4). The most frequently mentioned characteristics are ones which have to do with the extent to which a person *will be affected* by the decision. Sometimes the explanation for influence was a general statement that someone would be affected. For example, in a company which makes musical instruments, the choice of a tractor truck was said by one informant to have been influenced most by the traffic supervisor. "He lives with the situation so he must have the choice," he said. Closely related is the somewhat more specific assertion that a certain person was influential in the decision concerning a purchase because the product would be used by him or by his department. For example, in describing the decision to use vanadium in the production of steel, the Superintendent of the mill involved named himself as most influential "because I had to use it in my open hearth."

In addition to being affected by virtue of having to use the product, a man may be affected in other ways by the decision. A variety of responsibilities, the meeting of which might be affected by the decision, were mentioned as reasons for great influence. These included a man's responsibility for the unit where the product was to be used; responsibility for the performance of the product; responsibility for outcomes (e.g., sales, profits) which may be affected by the purchase decision; and financial responsibility for the purchase. For example, in discussing the decision by a steel company to switch from using silico-manganese to ferro-manganese in the production process, the Assistant to the Works Manager named the Open Hearth Superintendent and himself as having been most influential in this decision. "We are the two people directly responsible for the product," he explained. In discussing the decision to buy a new printing press, the corporate Vice President in charge of purchasing named the manager of a new plant which would use the press as most influential; "Mr. B. has to run the plant at a profit," he explained. In another company, the Plant Engineer named the Sales Manager as having most influenced the decision to buy a new piercing press for manufacturing, saying, "He says he needs it and, if he can't get it, he won't fulfill sales." In each of these cases, the person or persons named as most influential did not have the formal authority to make the decision.

TABLE 4
Reasons Given As to Why Person Named As Influential Was Able to Exert Influence on Purchase Decision

| | Average Percent of All Responses* | | |
Reason Given for Influence	About Decision to Make Purchase of General Type (N = 33 Decisions)	About Decision to Make Specific Purchase (N = 32 Decisions)	About Both Decisions Combined (N = 33 Decisions)
I. Characteristics of influential			
A. Expertise			
General knowledge	7.8	10.9	9.4
Information on specific matter ...	4.1	10.3	5.6
Opinion respected due to expertise	2.6	0.0	1.9
Subtotal, expertise	14.5	21.2	16.9
B. Is affected by decision			
He (his dept.) uses product	6.1	10.1	8.5
He (his dept.) has need for product	5.8	1.0	3.5
He (his dept.) affected by decision	2.4	2.4	2.2
Responsible for unit where product used	5.1	1.3	3.2
Responsible for performance or output of product	2.8	3.8	3.4
Responsible for something (sales profits, etc.) affected by product	5.1	1.4	3.5
Has financial responsibility	0.0	0.4	0.2
Subtotal, affected by decision	27.3	20.4	24.5
C. Interest of person or his unit	1.6	1.7	1.9
D. Duties (responsibilities) include making choice of or recommending product	13.2	18.3	15.5
E. Duties include tasks (tests, specs, etc.) relevant to decision	4.3	5.7	5.7
F. Has authority to make decision	7.5	2.0	5.4
G. Responsibility or position: general, unspecified	5.7	3.8	4.7
H. Other characteristics (judgment; alertness; in position to get information)	0.8	1.0	0.9

TABLE 4 (concluded)

	About Decision to Make Purchase of General Type (N = 33 Decisions)	About Decision to Make Specific Purchase (N = 32 Decisions)	About Both Decisions Combined (N = 33 Decisions)
	*Average Percent of All Responses**		
Reason Given for Influence			
II. Activities of influential			
A. Information-gathering or technical			
Gathered or reviewed information	2.7	4.6	3.2
Did relevant technical work (tests, specifications, etc.)	2.5	2.6	2.3
Subtotal, information-gathering or technical	5.2	7.2	5.5
B. Prodded others to act			
Brought need to attention of others	4.8	1.6	3.1
Brought product to attention of others	0.6	0.4	0.5
Prodded others; pushed it; communicated much	3.6	2.0	3.1
Subtotal, prodded others	9.0	4.0	6.7
C. Other actions of influential			
Made recommendation, made decision, gave support to action, or other miscellaneous actions	3.5	5.1	4.0
Made threat or promise	0.0	0.0	0.0
III. Reasons influential had for his viewpoint	4.4	1.0	3.2
IV. Answer unclear	0.9	7.3	3.0
V. Other answers	2.4	1.1	1.8
All answers	100%	100%	100%

* For each purchase decision, the percentage of answers falling into each response category was tabulated. Then these percentages were averaged for all 33 decision cases. Each entry in the table represents the average percentage of answers falling in the particular category. One case is omitted with respect to reasons for influence about decision to make specific purchase, since no answers to this question are available in this case.

Another way in which a man may be affected by a decision is because he or his unit has need for a particular product or service. Such need as a basis for strong influence was mentioned particularly with respect to the general decision to buy a product in a certain category.

An example of need being a basis for influence is provided by the case of the decision by a manufacturing company to lease a large computer. The Chief Engineer was named as most influential in this decision by one respondent who explained, "Because he's the one that would require it for his department's operation."

For all cases, an average of 24.5 percent of all reasons given to explain a person's strong influence concerned the influential being affected by the decision in some way. Such reasons were somewhat more frequent with respect to the basic decision to buy a product in the general category than with respect to the decision about what specific product to buy.

Expertise

The second most frequently mentioned characteristics of influentials were ones bearing on their expertise (an average of 16.9 percent of all reasons given for influence). Sometimes this was general knowledge relevant to the decision; e.g., a vice president of engineering was said by one informant to have been most influential in the choice of a type of piercing press "because he knows presses—40 years experience." Sometimes it was information specifically about the decision to be made. For example, in another company, the manager of the Engineering and Control Department was named as having had most influence in the decision to buy a new printing press "because he analyzed it all and knows the most about all—price, specs, and everything about the whole deal." The data show also that expertise is an important basis of influence both in the basic decision to buy a product in some general category and in the decision about what specific product to get. However, expertise is more prominent as a basis of influence with respect to the latter type of more specific decision.

Responsibility for Decisions

Another type of characteristic mentioned with some frequency was a man's formal responsibility to recommend a product (an average of 15.5 percent of reasons given concerning both decisions) or to perform tasks which provide vital information for the decision (5.7 percent of reasons about both decisions). For example, a buyer in a musical instruments company was said by a respondent to have had the most influence in choosing a mold used for making organ parts. "That's how this company is operated and it's also his function," the respondent said. In most cases, such influence reflects a particular division of labor in the company. However, it appears rare for someone (e.g., a purchasing agent) to be delegated so much responsibility for purchase decisions of a given type that his recommendation will override the wishes of those who will use the product or be affected by it. Thus, in the case of the mold for organ parts just mentioned, other respondents (including the buyer himself) named several engineering personnel as most influential.

DISCUSSION

Bases of Influence

We turn now to a consideration of the implications of the substantive findings. The data from these cases fit well the description by recent theorists of organizational decision-making as a process of accommodation among a number of concerned individuals and units. When differences of opinion arose in these cases, they appear to have been resolved usually by a process of seeking consensus, in part through further information-seeking. Evidence of bargaining as a method of reaching a decision is rare. As March and Simon point out (March & Simon, 1958, p. 131), bargaining as a decision-making process has some potentially disruptive consequences, placing strains on the status and power systems in the organization. The present results support their speculation that organizations will tend to try to solve disputes by problem solving and persuasion. Of course, such techniques may not be successful in some circumstances, e.g., when common goals are weak and where each side is committed to a different solution.

With respect to the central question addressed by the study, that concerning the basis of influence, the data permit some conclusions about influence in these situations. Considering the five types of power distinguished by French and Raven, the data indicate first that coercive power and reward power are noticeable chiefly by their absence. Influence was never attributed to the characteristics of control over material sanctions, nor to activities involving use of such sanctions (e.g., threat, promise, punishment, reward). It is possible that some respondents were reluctant to talk about such modes of influence. It may be, too, that the possible use of sanctions lurks behind other characteristics or activities which were sometimes mentioned by respondents as reasons for influence. Still, the total absence of reference to sanctions suggests that their direct use was rare in these situations. Also apparently rare in these situations were referent power. Such a basis of power might be expected to be revealed in part by references to admirable personal characteristics of influentials, which might serve as a basis for identification. Alternatively, mention of the personal loyalty a man commanded might also reveal the presence of referent power. Such explanations of the basis of influence were almost totally absent.

Influence did appear to be due often to expert power. A man's expertise was frequently mentioned as the reason he was influential in a decision. Activities connected with expertise (e.g., running tests) were also mentioned sometimes. A second basis of power which was present was legitimate power. The responsibilities, duties, or formal authority which a man had, the characteristics of someone with legitimate power, were given with some frequency as reasons for influence.

What is most interesting in the data, however, are the reasons for influence which are given most often by respondents and which do not fit neatly into any of French and Raven's five categories. These explanations concern characteristics of influential persons which make them affected in some way by a decision. (Also relevant here are explanations of influence in terms of activities which are most likely to be carried out by those affected by the decision, e.g., bringing a need to the attention of others.) Why should being affected by, and thus having a stake in a decision, give one strong influence on the outcome? What is the basis of the power which is apparently exerted by such persons?

Part of the answer to this question probably lies in the fact that those who have the greatest stake in a decision are likely to bring their needs to the attention of others and may push their preferences. However, these factors alone do not seem to be the major ones involved. The comments of many persons focused not on the fact that those affected pushed their preferences but that others thought it appropriate (other things roughly equal) to defer to those preferences. The key to understanding the influence of those most affected by a decision is, I suggest, that these affected persons are likely to react to the decision in a way which *affects others*. And others know this.

First, if faced with too many contrary decisions on matters which directly affect him, a man's satisfaction and motivation on the job may be reduced. He may even leave the organization if he can. Knowing this, the superiors of those most affected by a decision may tend to defer to their wishes.

The peers of those most affected by a decision (e.g., those in other departments) may also have important reasons for deferring to those most concerned. The man most affected by a decision may react with anger toward a peer who opposes his wishes in this matter. He may reduce his necessary cooperation with this peer in the ordinary work interaction which occurs later. He may also be more inclined to oppose this peer on a later decision which affects the latter most directly. Knowing these things, the peer may feel it wise to defer to the wishes of the man most concerned in this instance.

From such individual motivations of superiors and peers, norms may grow which make it customary to grant strong influence to those most affected by a decision. (This is usually accompanied by a norm which specifies that strong influence will also be granted to those with formal responsibility for the decision.) The advantages of norms, as compared to direct influence attempts, have been discussed by Thibaut and Kelley (1959).

What is being asserted, then, is that those who are affected by a decision usually have resources (their cooperation at least) which are relevant to the needs of others. The power stemming from their stake in the decision rests not on the exercise of sanctions prior to the decision but on the fact that this stake provides them with motivation (known to others) to use these resources later. The use of these resources may depend upon the nature of the decision and upon who supported or opposed their preferences. If this interpretation of the present results is tenable, it suggests that an adequate conceptualization of the influence process must take account not only of the influential's control over resources but also of his motivations to use these resources. From this perspective, the characteristics which make certain persons influential include not only those which affect their control over resources but those (like being affected by a decision) that make credible their motivation to use the resources they possess. In parallel fashion, for the target of influence we need to consider not only his needs but also his perception of the likelihood that compliance with the influencer's request will cause the influencer to use his resources in a given way.

This discussion suggests that two columns might be added to make Table 1 more complete—one showing the readiness of the influencer to use the resources he controls and the other showing the target's perception of the likelihood that compliance will lead the influencer to take certain actions.

These general points concerning the will to use sanctions and the perceived likelihood of their use are not completely new ones. They are familiar, for example, to those concerned with deterrence in international affairs. But the importance of motivation to use resources has tended to be neglected in discussions of power in interpersonal and intraorganizational relationships.

Other Types of Decisions

The findings reported here are based on a very special type of decision (purchasing) in a particular type of organization (business firms). To what extent are these findings, especially those concerning the influence accorded to those with greatest stake, useful in understanding decision-making in other, sometimes more exciting, contexts.

We may note, first, some indications that the kinds of decision processes found in these settings are not unique.

In discussing his study of foreign policy decision-making in the American Government, Pruitt (1964) states that influence is based in part on the "importance of his position" to each participant. Though Pruitt does not indicate whether there were implicit norms to grant influence to those with most concern and stake, his research is consistent with the present study in showing an association between concern about the decision and influence.

Some observations by Bauer (1968, p. 17), based in part on research done by him and his associates, are also relevant. He says:

> In any ongoing institution, the ability to get important things done is dependent upon maintaining a reservoir of goodwill. The person who fights every issue as though it were vital exhausts his resources including, most especially, the patience and goodwill of those on whom he has to depend to get things done. Therefore, it should be considered neither surprising nor immoral that, when an issue is of low salience, the sensible individual may use it to build goodwill for the future, or pay off past obligations, by going along with some individual for whom the issue is of high salience. Bauer, Pool, and Dexter found many men in Congress treating foreign trade legislation in this way. On the other hand, business men for whom this was an issue of low salience were careful not to expend an excessive amount of their finite goodwill on it.

In Congressional decision-making as in business purchasing, then, influence on specific decisions often appears to be determined by informal norms which accord influence to those with greatest stake in, and concern about, the decision. However, it should not be expected that those who have a strong stake in a decision will be influential in all organizational settings. It seems likely that "stake" will be most important as a basis of influence in those situations where the continued cooperation of those with the stake is important for those with greater control over sanctions, and where such continued cooperation is not assured (e.g., subordinates have opportunities to go elsewhere). This is likely to be true in many different types of organizations, e.g., governmental, educational, voluntary. Many such organizations are likely to be concerned about creating a high level of harmony, cooperation, and motivation throughout the organization. Thus, as in the case of the business purchase decisions studied here, we would expect to find that those in authority often will be willing to grant strong influence to relatively low-rank persons (e.g., middle-level management) when these low-rank persons have a strong stake in the decisions in question.

On the other hand, there are some situations where those with greatest authority and greatest control over organizational sanctions (e.g., pay, promotion) are not greatly concerned about the continued cooperation of those persons with a strong stake in a decision. This may be because a high level of motivation is not required for such persons to do their jobs reasonably well (e.g., in routine jobs), because others in the organization are not much dependent on their help (situations of low interdependence), or because their opportunities to go elsewhere are limited. In such kinds of situations one might expect to find influence on decisions less often being enjoyed by those affected by the decision and more often by those in formal positions of authority and/or those able to use or threaten direct use of sanctions.

REFERENCES

Bachman, J., Bowers, D., & Marcus, P.   Bases of supervisory power: A comparative study in five organizational settings. In A. Tannenbaum (Ed.), *Control in organizations*. New York: McGraw-Hill, 1968.

Bauer, R.   The study of policy formation: An introduction. In R. Bauer & K. Gergen (Eds.), *The study of policy formation*. New York: Free Press, 1968.

French, J., Jr., & Raven, B.   The bases of social power. In D. Cartwright (Ed.), *Studies in social power*. Ann Arbor: Institute for Social Research, 1959.

Gergen, K.   Assessing the leverage points in the process of policy formation. In R. Bauer & K. Gergen (Eds.). *The study of policy formation*. New York: Free Press, 1968.

Hilsman, R.   The foreign-policy consensus: An interim research report. *Journal of Conflict Resolution*, 1959, *3*, 361–382.

Lawrence, P., & Lorsch, J.   Differentiation and integration in complex organizations. *Administrative Science Quarterly*, 1967, *12*, 1–47.

Lindblom, C. *The policy-making process*. Englewood Cliffs, N.J.: Prentice-Hall, 1968.

March, J., & Simon, H. *Organizations*. New York: Wiley, 1958.

Patchen, M.   Alternative questionnaire approaches to the measurement of influence in organizations. *American Journal of Sociology*, 1968, *69*, 41–52.

Patchen, M.   Case studies of decision-making in organizations: Purchase decisions in business firms. Ann Arbor: Survey Research Center, University of Michigan, 1969.

Pruitt, D.   Problem-solving in the department of state. Denver: Department of International Relations, Monograph Series in World Affairs, University of Denver, 1964.

Tannenbaum, A.   Control and effectiveness in a voluntary organization. *American Journal of Sociology*, 1961, *67*, 33–46.

Tannenbaum, A. (Ed.) *Control in organizations*. New York: McGraw-Hill, 1968.

Tannenbaum, A., & Kahn, R.　Organizational control structure: A general descriptive technique as applied to four local unions. *Human Relations,* 1957, *10,* 127–140.

Thibaut, J., & Kelley, H.　*The social psychology of groups.* New York: Wiley, 1959.

Thompson, J. D.　*Organizations in action.* New York: McGraw-Hill, 1967.

Weber, M.　*Theory of social and economic organization.* New York, Free Press, 1947.

23

The Abilene Paradox: The Management of Agreement*

JERRY B. HARVEY

The July afternoon in Coleman, Texas (population 5,607) was particularly hot—104 degrees as measured by the Walgreen's Rexall Ex-Lax temperature gauge. In addition, the wind was blowing fine-grained West Texas topsoil through the house. But the afternoon was still tolerable—even potentially enjoyable. There was a fan going on the back porch; there was cold lemonade; and finally, there was entertainment. Dominoes. Perfect for the conditions. The game required little more physical exertion than an occasional mumbled comment, "Shuffle 'em," and an unhurried movement of the arm to place the spots in the appropriate perspective on the table. All in all, it had the makings of an agreeable Sunday afternoon in Coleman—that is, it was until my father-in-law suddenly said, "Let's get in the car and go to Abilene and have dinner at the cafeteria."

I thought, "What, go to Abilene? Fifty-three miles? In this dust storm and heat? And in an unairconditioned 1958 Buick?"

But my wife chimed in with, "Sounds like a great idea. I'd like to go. How about you, Jerry?" Since my own preferences were obviously out of step with the rest I replied, "Sounds good to me," and added, "I just hope your mother wants to go."

"Of course I want to go," said my mother-in-law. "I haven't been to Abilene in a long time."

* Reprinted by permission of the publisher from *Organizational Dynamics* (Summer 1974). Copyright © by AMACOM, a division of American Management Associations.

So into the car and off to Abilene we went. My predictions were fulfilled. The heat was brutal. We were coated with a fine layer of dust that was cemented with perspiration by the time we arrived. The food at the cafeteria provided first-rate testimonial material for antacid commercials.

Some four hours and 106 miles later we returned to Coleman, hot and exhausted. We sat in front of the fan for a long time in silence. Then, both to be sociable and to break the silence, I said, "It was a great trip, wasn't it?"

No one spoke.

Finally my mother-in-law said, with some irritation, "Well, to tell the truth, I really didn't enjoy it much and would rather have stayed here. I just went along because the three of you were so enthusiastic about going. I wouldn't have gone if you all hadn't pressured me into it."

I couldn't believe it. "What do you mean 'you all'?" I said. "Don't put me in the 'you all' group. I was delighted to be doing what we were doing. I didn't want to go. I only went to satisfy the rest of you. You're the culprits."

My wife looked shocked. "Don't call me a culprit. You and Daddy and Mama were the ones who wanted to go. I just went along to be sociable and to keep you happy. I would have had to be crazy to want to go out in heat like that."

Her father entered the conversation abruptly. "Hell!" he said.

He proceeded to expand on what was already absolutely clear. "Listen, I never wanted to go to Abilene. I just thought you might be bored. You visit so seldom I wanted to be sure you enjoyed it. I would have preferred to play another game of dominoes and eat the leftovers in the icebox."

After the outburst of recrimination we all sat back in silence. Here we were, four reasonably sensible people who, of our own volition, had just taken a 106-mile trip across a godforsaken desert in a furnace-like temperature through a cloud-like dust storm to eat unpalatable food at a hole-in-the-wall cafeteria in Abilene, when none of us had really wanted to go. In fact, to be more accurate, we'd done just the opposite of what we wanted to do. The whole situation simply didn't make sense.

At least it didn't make sense at the time. But since that day in Coleman, I have observed, consulted with, and been a part of more than one organization that has been caught in the same situation. As a result, they have either taken a side-trip, or, occasionally, a terminal journey to Abilene, when Dallas or Houston or Tokyo was where they really wanted to go. And for most of those organizations, the negative consequences of such trips, measured in terms of both human misery and economic loss, have been much greater than for our little Abilene group.

This article is concerned with that paradox—the Abilene Paradox. Stated simply, it is as follows: Organizations frequently take actions in contradiction to what they really want to do and therefore defeat the very purposes they are trying to achieve. It also deals with a major corollary of the paradox, which is that *the inability to manage agreement is a major source of organization dysfunction*. Last, the article is designed to help members of organizations cope more effectively with the paradox's pernicious influence.

As a means of accomplishing the above, I shall: (1) describe the symptoms exhibited by organizations caught in the paradox; (2) describe, in summarized case-study examples, how they occur in a variety of organizations; (3) discuss the underlying causal dynamics; (4) indicate some of the implications of accepting this model for describing organizational behavior; (5) make recommendations for coping with the paradox; and, in conclusion, (6) relate the paradox to a broader existential issue.

Symptoms of the Paradox

The inability to manage agreement, not the inability to manage conflict, is the essential symptom that defines organizations caught in the web of the Abilene Paradox. That inability effectively to manage agreement is expressed by six specific subsymptoms, all of which were present in our family Abilene group.

1. Organization members agree privately, as individuals, as to the nature of the situation or problem facing the organization. For example, members of the Abilene group agreed that they were enjoying themselves sitting in front of the fan, sipping lemonade, and playing dominoes.

2. Organization members agree privately, as individuals, as to the steps that would be required to cope with the situation or problem they face. For members of the Abilene group "more of the same" was a solution that would have adequately satisfied their individual and collective desires.

3. Organization members fail to accurately communicate their desires and/or beliefs to one another. In fact, they do just the opposite and thereby lead one another into misperceiving the collective reality. Each member of the Abilene group, for example, communicated inaccurate data to other members of the organization. The data, in effect, said, "Yeah, it's a great idea. Let's go to Abilene," when in reality members of the organization individually and collectively preferred to stay in Coleman.

4. With such invalid and inaccurate information, organization members make collective decisions that lead them to take actions contrary to what they want to do, and thereby arrive at results that are counterproductive to the organization's intent and purposes. Thus, the Abilene group went to Abilene when it preferred to do something else.

5. As a result of taking actions that are counterproductive, organization members experience frustration, anger, irritation, and dissatisfaction with their organization. Consequently, they form subgroups with trusted acquaintances and blame other subgroups for the organization's dilemma. Frequently, they also blame authority figures and one another. Such phenomena were illustrated in the Abilene group by the "culprit" argument that occurred when we had returned to the comfort of the fan.

6. Finally, if organization members do not deal with the generic issue—the inability to manage agreement—the cycle repeats itself with greater intensity. The Abilene group, for a variety of reasons, the most important of which was that it became conscious of the process, did not reach that point.

To repeat, the Abilene Paradox reflects a failure to manage agreement. In fact, it is my contention that the inability to cope with (manage) agreement, rather than the inability to cope with (manage) conflict is the single most pressing issue of modern organizations.

Other Trips to Abilene

The Abilene Paradox is no respecter of individuals, organizations, or institutions. Following are descriptions of two other trips to Abilene that illustrate both the pervasiveness of the paradox and its underlying dynamics.

Case 1: The Boardroom.   The Ozyx Corporation is a relatively small industrial company that has embarked on a trip to Abilene. The president of Ozyx has hired a consultant to help discover the reasons for the poor profit picture of the company in general and the low morale and productivity of the R&D division in particular. During the process of investigation, the consultant becomes interested in a research project in which the company has invested a sizable proportion of its R&D budget.

When asked about the project by the consultant in the privacy of their offices, the president, the vice president for research, and the research manager each describes it as an idea that looked great on paper but will ultimately fail because of the unavailability of the technology required to make it work. Each of them also acknowledges that continued support of the project will create cash flow problems that will jeopardize the very existence of the total organization.

Furthermore, each individual indicates he has not told the others about his reservations. When asked why, the president says he can't reveal his "true" feelings because abandoning the project, which has been widely publicized, would make the company look bad in the press and, in addition, would probably cause his vice president's ulcer to kick up or perhaps even cause him to quit, "because he has staked his professional reputation on the project's success."

Similarly, the vice president for research says he can't let the president or the research manager know his reservations because the president is so committed to it that "I would probably get fired for insubordination if I questioned the project."

Finally, the research manager says he can't let the president or vice president know of his doubts about the project because of their extreme commitment to the project's success.

All indicate that, in meetings with one another, they try to maintain an optimistic façade so the others won't worry unduly about the project. The research director, in particular, admits to writing ambiguous progress reports so the president and the vice president can "interpret them to suit themselves." In fact, he says he tends to slant them to the "positive" side, "given how committed the brass are."

The scent of the Abilene trail wafts from a paneled conference room where the project research budget is being considered for the following fiscal year. In the meeting itself, praises are heaped on the questionable project and a unanimous decision is made to continue it for yet another year. Symbolically, the organization has boarded a bus to Abilene.

In fact, although the real issue of agreement was confronted approximately eight months after the bus departed, it was nearly too late. The organization failed to meet a payroll and underwent a two-year period of personnel cutbacks, retrenchments, and austerity. Morale suffered, the most competent technical personnel resigned, and the organization's prestige in the industry declined.

Case 2: The Watergate.

Apart from the grave question of who did what, Watergate presents America with the profound puzzle of why. What is it that led such a wide assortment of men, many of them high public officials, possibly including the President himself, either to instigate or to go along with and later try to hide a pattern of behavior that by now appears not only reprehensible, but stupid? (*The Washington Star and Daily News*, editorial, May 27, 1973.)

One possible answer to the editorial writer's question can be found by probing into the dynamics of the Abilene paradox. I shall let the reader reach his own conclusions, though, on the basis of the following excerpts from testimony before the Senate investigating committee on "The Watergate Affair."

In one exchange, Senator Howard Baker asked Herbert Porter, then a member of the White House staff, why he (Porter) found himself "in charge of or deeply involved in a dirty tricks operation of the campaign." In response, Porter indicated that he had had qualms about what he was doing, but that he ". . . was not one to stand up in a meeting and say that this should be stopped. . . . I kind of drifted along."

And when asked by Baker why he had "drifted along," Porter replied, "In all honesty, because of the fear of the group pressure that would ensue, of not being a team player," and ". . . I felt a deep sense of loyalty to him [the President] or was appealed to on that basis." (*The Washington Post*, June 8, 1973, p. 20.)

Jeb Magruder gave a similar response to a question posed by committee counsel Dash. Specifically, when asked about his, Mr. Dean's, and Mr. Mitchell's reactions to Mr. Liddy's proposal, which included bugging the Watergate, Mr. Magruder replied, "I think all three of us were appalled. The scope and size of the project were something that at least in my mind were not envisioned. I do not think it was in Mr. Mitchell's mind or Mr. Dean's, although I can't comment on their states of mind at that time."

Mr. Mitchell, in an understated way, which was his way of dealing with difficult problems like this, indicated that this was not an "acceptable project." (*The Washington Post*, June 15, 1973, p. A14.)

Later in his testimony Mr. Magruder said, ". . . I think I can honestly say that no one was particularly overwhelmed with the project. But I think we felt that this information could be useful, and Mr. Mitchell agreed to approve the project, and I then notified the parties of Mr. Mitchell's approval." (*The Washington Post*, June 15, 1973, p. A14.)

Although I obviously was not privy to the private conversations of the principal characters, the data seem to reflect the essential elements of the Abilene Paradox. First, they indicate agreement. Evidently, Mitchell, Porter, Dean, and Magruder agreed that the plan was inappropriate. ("I think I can honestly say that no one was particularly overwhelmed with the project.") Second, the data indicate that the principal figures then proceeded to implement the plan in contradiction to their shared agreement. Third, the data surrounding the case clearly indicate that the plan multiplied the organization's problems rather than solved them. And finally, the organization broke into subgroups with the various principals, such as the President, Mitchell, Porter, Dean, and Magruder, blaming one another for the dilemma in which they found themselves, and internecine warfare ensued.

In summary, it is possible that because of the inability of White House staff members to cope with the fact that they agreed, the organization took a trip to Abilene.

Analyzing the Paradox

The Abilene Paradox can be stated succinctly as follows: Organizations frequently take actions in contradiction to the data they have for dealing with problems and, as a result, compound their problems rather than solve them. Like all paradoxes, the Abilene Paradox deals with absurdity. On the surface, it makes little sense for organizations, whether they are couples or companies, bureaucracies or governments, to take actions that are diametrically opposed to the data they possess for solving crucial organizational problems. Such actions are particularly absurd since they tend to compound the very problems they are designed to solve and thereby defeat the purposes the organization is trying to achieve. However, as Robert Rapaport and others have so cogently expressed it, paradoxes are generally paradoxes only because they are based on a logic or rationale different from what we understand or expect.

Discovering that different logic not only destroys the paradoxical quality but also offers alternative ways for coping with similar situations. Therefore, part of the dilemma facing an Abilene-bound organization may be the lack of a map—a theory or model—that provides rationality to the paradox. The purpose of the following discussion is to provide such a map.

The map will be developed by examining the underlying psychological themes of the profit-making organization and the bureaucracy and it will include the following landmarks: (1) Action Anxiety; (2) Negative Fantasies; (3) Real Risk; (4) Separation Anxiety; and (5) the Psychological Reversal of Risk and Certainty. I hope that the discussion of such landmarks will provide harried organizations travelers with a new map that will assist them in arriving at where they really want to go and, in addition, will help them in assessing the risks that are an inevitable part of the journey.

Action Anxiety

Action anxiety provides the first landmark for locating roadways that bypass Abilene. The concept of action anxiety says that the reason organization members take actions in contradiction to their understanding of the organization's problems lies in the intense anxiety that is created as they think about acting in accordance with what they believe needs to be done. As a result, they opt to endure the professional and economic degradation of pursuing an unworkable research project or the consequences of participating in an illegal activity rather than act in a manner congruent with their beliefs. It is not that organization members do not know what needs to be done—they do know. For example, the various principals in the research organization cited *knew* they were working on a research project that had no real possibility of succeeding. And the central figures of the Watergate episode apparently *knew* that, for a variety of reasons, the plan to bug the Watergate did not make sense.

Such action anxiety experienced by the various protagonists may not make sense, but the dilemma is not a new one. In fact, it is very similar to the anxiety experienced by Hamlet, who expressed it most eloquently in the opening lines of his famous soliloquy:

> To be or not to be; that is the question:
> Whether 'tis nobler in the mind to suffer
> The slings and arrows of outrageous fortune
> Or to take arms against a sea of troubles
> And by opposing, end them? . . . (*Hamlet,* Act III, Scene II)

It is easy to translate Hamlet's anxious lament into that of the research manager of our R&D organization as he contemplates his report to the meeting of the budget committee. It might go something like this:

> To maintain my sense of integrity and self-worth or compromise it, that is the question. Whether 'tis nobler in the mind to suffer the ignominy that comes from managing a nonsensical research project, or the fear and anxiety that come from making a report the president and V.P. may not like to hear.

So, the anguish, procrastination, and counterproductive behavior of the research manager or members of the White House staff are not much different from those of Hamlet; all might ask with equal justification Hamlet's subsequent searching question of what it is that

> makes us rather bear those ills we have than fly to others we know not of. (*Hamlet,* Act III, Scene II)

In short, like the various Abilene protagonists, we are faced with a deeper question: Why does action anxiety occur?

Negative Fantasies

Part of the answer to that question may be found in the negative fantasies organization members have about acting in congruence with what they believe should be done.

Hamlet experienced such fantasies. Specifically, Hamlet's fantasies of the alternatives to current evils were more evils, and he didn't entertain the possibility that any action he might take could lead to an improvement in the situation. Hamlet's was not an unusual case, though. In fact, the "Hamlet syndrome" clearly occurred in both organizations previously described. All of the organization protagonists had negative fantasies about what would happen if they acted in accordance with what they believed needed to be done.

The various managers in the R&D organization foresaw loss of face, prestige, position, and even health as the outcome of confronting the issues about which they believed, incorrectly, that they disagreed. Similarly, members of the White House staff feared being made scapegoats, branded as disloyal, or ostracized as non-team players if they acted in accordance with their understanding of reality.

To sum up, action anxiety is supported by the negative fantasies that organization members have about what will happen as a consequence of their acting in accordance with their understanding of what is sensible. The negative fantasies, in turn, serve an important function for the persons who have them. Specifically, they provide the individual with an excuse that releases him psychologically, both in his own eyes and frequently in the eyes of others, from the responsibility of having to act to solve organization problems.

It is not sufficient, though, to stop with the explanation of negative fantasies as the basis for the inability of organizations to cope with agreement. We must look deeper and ask still other questions: What is the source of the negative fantasies? Why do they occur?

Real Risk

Risk is a reality of life, a condition of existence. John Kennedy articulated it in another way when he said at a news conference, "Life is unfair." By that I believe he meant we do not know, nor can we predict or control with certainty, either the events that impinge upon us or the outcomes of actions we undertake in response to those events.

Consequently, in the business environment, the research manager might find that confronting the president and the vice-president with the fact that the project was a "turkey" might result in his being fired. And Mr. Porter's saying that an illegal plan of surveillance should not be carried out could have caused his ostracism as a nonteam player. There are too many cases when confrontation of this sort has resulted in such consequences. The real question, though, is not, Are such fantasized consequences possible? but, Are such fantasized consequences likely?

Thus, real risk is an existential condition, and all actions do have consequences that, to paraphrase Hamlet, may be worse than the evils of the present. As a result of their unwillingness to accept existential risk as one of life's givens, however, people may opt to take their organizations to Abilene rather than run the risk, no matter how small, of ending up somewhere worse.

Again, though, one must ask, What is the real risk that underlies the decision to opt for Abilene? What is at the core of the paradox?

Fear of Separation

One is tempted to say that the core of the paradox lies in the individual's fear of the unknown. Actually, we do not fear what is unknown, but we are afraid of things we do know about. What do we know about that frightens us into such apparently inexplicable organizational behavior?

Separation, alienation, and loneliness are things we do know about—and fear. Both research and experience indicate that ostracism is one of the most powerful punishments that can be devised. Solitary confinement does not draw its coercive strength from physical deprivation. The evidence is overwhelming that we have a fundamental need to be connected, engaged, and related and a reciprocal need not to be separated or alone. Everyone of us, though, has experienced aloneness. From the time the umbilical cord was cut, we have experienced the real anguish of separation—broken friendships, divorces, deaths, and exclusions. C. P. Snow vividly described the tragic interplay between loneliness and connection:

> Each of us is alone; sometimes we escape from our solitariness, through love and affection or perhaps creative moments, but these triumphs of life are pools of light we make for ourselves while the edge of the road is black. Each of us dies alone.

That fear of taking risks that may result in our separation from others is at the core of the paradox. It finds expression in ways of which we may be unaware, and it is ultimately the cause of the self-defeating, collective deception that leads to self-destructive decisions within organizations.

Concretely, such fear of separation leads research committees to fund projects that none of its members want and, perhaps, White House staff members to engage in illegal activities that they don't really support.

The Psychological Reversal of Risk and Certainty

One piece of the map is still missing. It relates to the peculiar reversal that occurs in our thought processes as we try to cope with the Abilene Paradox. For example, we frequently fail to take action in an organizational setting because we fear that the actions we take may result in our separation from others, or, in the language of Mr. Porter, we are afraid of being tabbed as "disloyal" or are afraid of being ostracized as "non-team players." But therein lies a paradox within a paradox, because our very unwillingness to take such risks virtually ensures the separation and aloneness we so fear. In effect, we reverse "real existential risk" and "fantasied risk" and by doing so transform what is a probability statement into what, for all practical purposes, becomes a certainty.

Take the R&D organization described earlier. When the project fails, some people will get fired, demoted, or sentenced to the purgatory of a make-work job in an out-of-the-way office. For those who remain, the atmosphere of blame, distrust, suspicion, and backbiting that accompanies such failure will serve only to further alienate and separate those who remain.

The Watergate situation is similar. The principals evidently feared being ostracized as disloyal non-team players. When the illegality of the act surfaced, however, it was nearly inevitable that blaming, self-protective actions, and scapegoating would result in the very emotional separation from both the President and one another that the principals feared. Thus, by reversing real and fantasied risk, they had taken effective action to ensure the outcome they least desired.

One final question remains: Why do we make this peculiar reversal? I support the general thesis of Alvin Toffler and Philip Slater, who contend that our cultural emphasis on technology, competition, individualism, temporariness, and mobility has resulted in a population that has frequently experienced the terror of loneliness and seldom the satisfaction of engagement. Consequently, though we have learned of the reality of separation, we have not had the opportunity to learn the reciprocal skills of connection, with the result that, like the ancient dinosaurs, we are breeding organizations with self-destructive decision-making proclivities.

A Possible Abilene Bypass

Existential risk is inherent in living, so it is impossible to provide a map that meets the no-risk criterion, but it may be possible to describe the route in terms that make the landmarks understandable and that will clarify the risks involved. In order to do that, however, some commonly used terms such as victim, victimizer, collusion, responsibility, conflict, conformity, courage, confrontation, reality, and knowledge have to be redefined. In addition, we need to explore the relevance of the redefined concepts for bypassing or getting out of Abilene.

Victim and Victimizer. Blaming and fault-finding behavior is one of the basic symptoms of organizations that have found their way to Abilene, and the target of blame generally doesn't include the one who criticizes. Stated in different terms, executives begin to assign one another to roles of victims and victimizers. Ironic as it may seem, however, this assignment of roles is both irrelevant and dysfunctional, because once a business or a government fails to manage its agreement and arrives in Abilene, all its members are victims. Thus, arguments and accusations that identify victims and victimizers at best become symptoms of the paradox, and, at worst, drain energy from the problem-solving efforts required to redirect the organization along the route it really wants to take.

Collusion. A basic implication of the Abilene Paradox is that human problems of organization are reciprocal in nature. As Robert Tannenbaum has pointed out, you can't have an autocratic boss unless subordinates are willing to collude with his autocracy, and you can't have obsequious subordinates unless the boss is willing to collude with their obsequiousness.

Thus, in plain terms, each person in a self-defeating, Abilene-bound organization *colludes* with others, including peers, superiors, and subordinates, sometimes consciously and sometimes subconsciously, to create the dilemma in which the organization finds itself. To adopt a cliché of modern organization, "It takes a real team effort to go to Abilene." In that sense each person, in his own collusive manner, shares responsibility for the trip, so searching for a locus of blame outside onself serves no useful purpose for either the organization or the individual. It neither helps the organization handle its dilemma of unrecognized agreement nor does it provide psychological relief for the individual, because focusing on conflict when agreement is the issue is devoid of reality. In fact, it does just the opposite, for it causes the organization to focus on managing conflict when it should be focusing on managing agreement.

Responsibility for Problem-Solving Action. A second question is, Who is responsible for getting us out of this place? To that question is frequently appended a third one, generally rhetorical in nature, with "should" overtones, such as, Isn't it the boss (or the ranking government official) who is responsible for doing something about the situation?

The answer to that question is No.

The key to understanding the functionality of the No answer is the knowledge that, when the dynamics of the paradox are in operation, the authority figure—and others—are in unknowing agreement with one another concerning the organization's problems and the steps necessary to solve them. Consequently, the power to destroy the paradox's pernicious influence comes from confronting and speaking to the underlying reality of the situation, and not from one's hierarchical position within the organization. Therefore, any organization member who chooses to risk confronting that reality possesses the necessary leverage to release the organization from the paradox's grip.

In one situation, it may be a research director's saying, "I don't think this project can succeed." In another, it may be Jeb Magruder's response to this question by Senator Baker:

> If you were concerned because the action was known to you to be illegal, because you thought it improper or unethical, you thought the prospects for success were very meager, and you doubted the reliability of Mr. Liddy, what on earth would it have taken to decide against the plan?

Magruder's reply was brief and to the point:

> Not very much, sir. I am sure that if I had fought vigorously against it, I think any of us could have had the plan cancelled. (*Time*, June 25, 1973, p. 12.)

Reality, Knowledge, Confrontation. Accepting the paradox as a model describing certain kinds of organizational dilemmas also requires rethinking the nature of reality and knowledge, as they are generally described in organizations. In brief, the underlying dynamics of the paradox clearly indicate that organization members generally know more about issues confronting the organization than they don't know. The various principals attending the research budget meeting, for example, knew the research project was doomed to failure. And Jeb Magruder spoke as a true Abilener when he said, "We knew it was illegal, probably, inappropriate." (*The Washington Post*, June 15, 1973, p. A16.)

Given this concept of reality and its relationship to knowledge, confrontation becomes the process of facing issues squarely, openly, and directly in an effort to discover whether the nature of the underlying collective reality is agreement or conflict. Accepting such a definition of confrontation has an important implication for change agents interested in making organizations more effective. That is, organization change and effectiveness may be facilitated as much by confronting the organization with what it knows and agrees upon as by confronting it with what it doesn't know or disagrees about.

Real Conflict and Phony Conflict

Conflict is a part of any organization. Couples, R&D divisions, and White House staffs all engage in it. However, analysis of the Abilene Paradox opens up the possibility of two kinds of conflict—real and phony. On the surface, they look alike, but, like headaches, have different causes and therefore require different treatment.

Real conflict occurs when people have real differences. ("My reading of the research printouts says that we can make the project profitable." "I come to the opposite conclusion.") ("I suggest we 'bug' the Watergate." "I'm not in favor of it.")

Phony conflict, on the other hand, occurs when people agree on the actions they want to take, and then do the opposite. The resulting anger, frustration, and blaming behavior generally termed "conflict" are not based on real differences. Rather, they stem from the protective reactions that occur when a decision that no one believed in or was committed to in the first place goes sour. In fact, as a paradox within a paradox, such conflict is symptomatic of agreement!

Group Tyranny and Conformity

Understanding the dynamics of the Abilene Paradox also requires a "reorientation" in thinking about concepts such as "group tyranny"— the loss of the individual's distinctiveness in a group, and the impact of conformity pressures on individual behavior in organizations.

Group tyranny and its result, individual conformity, generally refer to the coercive effect of group pressures on individual behavior. Sometimes referred to as Group-think, it has been damned as the cause for everything from the lack of creativity in organizations ("A camel is a horse designed by a committee") to antisocial behavior in juveniles ("My Johnny is a good boy. He was just pressured into shoplifting by the kids he runs around with").

However, analysis of the dynamics underlying the Abilene Paradox opens up the possibility that individuals frequently perceive and feel as if they are experiencing the coercive organization conformity pressures when, in actuality, they are responding to the dynamics of mismanaged agreement. Conceptualizing, experiencing, and responding to such experiences as reflecting the tyrannical pressures of a group again serves an important psychological use for the individual: As was previously said, it releases him from the responsibility of taking action and thus becomes a defense against action. Thus, much behavior within an organization that heretofore has been conceptualized as reflecting the tyranny of conformity pressures is really an expression of collective anxiety and therefore must be reconceptualized as a defense against acting.

A well-known example of such faulty conceptualization comes to mind. It involves the heroic sheriff in the classic Western movies who stands alone in the jailhouse door and singlehandedly protects a suspected (and usually innocent) horsethief or murderer from the irrational, tyrannical forces of group behavior—that is, an armed lynch mob. Generally, as a part of the ritual, he threatens to blow off the head of anyone who takes a step toward the door. Few ever take the challenge, and the reason is not the sheriff's six-shooter. What good would one pistol be against an armed mob of several hundred people who *really* want to hang somebody? Thus, the gun in fact serves as a face-saving measure for people who don't wish to participate in a hanging anyway. ("We had to back off. The sheriff threatened to blow our heads off.")

The situation is one involving agreement management, for a careful investigator canvassing the crowd under conditions in which the anonymity of the interviewees' responses could be guaranteed would probably find: (1) that few of the individuals in the crowd really wanted to take part in the hanging; (2) that each person's participation came about because he perceived, falsely, that others wanted to do so; and (3) that each person was afraid that others in the crowd would ostracize or in some other way punish him if he did not go along.

Diagnosing the Paradox

Most individuals like quick solutions, "clean" solutions, "no risk" solutions to organization problems. Furthermore, they tend to prefer solutions based on mechanics and technology, rather than on attitudes of "being." Unfortunately, the underlying reality of the paradox makes it impossible to provide either no-risk solutions or action technologies divorced from existential attitudes and realities. I do, however, have two sets of suggestions for dealing with these situations. One set of suggestions relates to diagnosing the situation, the other to confronting it.

When faced with the possibility that the paradox is operating, one must first make a diagnosis of the situation, and the key to diagnosis is an answer to the question, Is the organization involved in a conflict-management or an agreement-management situation? As an organization member, I have found it relatively easy to make a preliminary diagnosis as to whether an organization is on the way to Abilene or is involved in legitimate, substantive conflict by responding to the Diagnostic Survey shown in the accompanying figure. If the answer to the first question is "not characteristic," the organization is probably not in Abilene or conflict. If the answer is "characteristic," the organization has a problem of either real or phony conflict, and the answers to the succeeding questions help to determine which it is.

In brief, for reasons that should be apparent from the theory discussed here, the more times "characteristic" is checked, the more likely the organization is on its way to Abilene. In practical terms, a process for managing agreement is called for. And finally, if the answer to the first question falls into the "characteristic" category and most of the other answers fall into the category "not characteristic," one may be relatively sure the organization is in a real conflict situation and some sort of conflict management intervention is in order.

Coping with the Paradox

Assuming a preliminary diagnosis leads one to believe he and/or his organization is on the way to Abilene, the individual may choose to actively confront the situation to determine directly whether the underlying reality is one of agreement or conflict. Although there are, perhaps, a number of ways to do it, I have found one way in particular to be effective—confrontation in a group setting. The basic approach involves gathering organization members who are key figures in the problem and its solution into a group setting. Working within the context of a group is important, because the dynamics of the Abilene Paradox involve collusion among group members; therefore, to try to solve the dilemma by working with individuals and small subgroups would involve further collusion with the dynamics leading up to the paradox.

The first step in the meeting is for the individual who "calls" it (that is, the confronter) to own up to his position first and be open to the feedback he gets. The owning up process lets the others know that he is concerned lest the organization may be making a decision contrary to the desires of any of its members. A statement like this demonstrates the beginning of such an approach:

> I want to talk with you about the research project. Although I have previously said things to the contrary, I frankly don't think it will work, and I am very anxious about it. I suspect others may feel the same, but I don't know. Anyway, I am concerned that I may end up misleading you and that we may end up misleading one another, and if we aren't careful, we may continue to work on a problem that none of us wants and that might even bankrupt us. That's why I need to know where the rest of you stand. I would appreciate any of your thoughts about the project. Do you think it can succeed?

What kinds of results can one expect if he decides to undertake the process of confrontation? I have found that the results can be divided into *two* categories, at the technical level and at the level of existential experience. Of the two, I have found that for the person who undertakes to initiate the process of confrontation, the existential experience takes precedence in his ultimate evaluation of the outcome of the action he takes.

ORGANIZATION DIAGNOSTIC SURVEY

Instructions: For each of the following statements please indicate whether it *is* or *is not* characteristic of your organization.

---

1. There is conflict in the organization.
2. Organization members feel frustrated, impotent, and unhappy when trying to deal with it. Many are looking for ways to escape. They may avoid meetings at which the conflict is discussed, they may be looking for other jobs, or they may spend as much time away from the office as possible by taking unneeded trips or vacation or sick leave.
3. Organization members place much of the blame for the dilemma on the boss or other groups. In "back room" conversations among friends the boss is termed incompetent, ineffective, "out of touch," or a candidate for early retirement. To his face, nothing is said, or at best, only oblique references are made concerning his role in the organization's problems. If the boss isn't blamed, some other group, division, or unit is seen as the cause of the trouble: "We would do fine if it were not for the damn fools in Division X."
4. Small subgroups of trusted friends and associates meet informally over coffee, lunch, and so on to discuss organizational problems. There is a lot of agreement among the members of these subgroups as to the cause of the troubles and the solutions that would be effective in solving them. Such conversations are frequently punctuated with statements beginning with, "We should do . . ."
5. In meetings where those same people meet with members from other subgroups to discuss the problem they "soften their positions," state them in ambiguous language, or even reverse them to suit the apparent positions taken by others.
6. After such meetings, members complain to trusted associates that they really didn't say what they wanted to say, but also provide a list of convincing reasons why the comments, suggestions, and reactions they wanted to make would have been impossible. Trusted associates commiserate and say the same was true for them.
7. Attempts to solve the problem do not seem to work. In fact, such attempts seem to add to the problem or make it worse.
8. Outside the organization individuals seem to get along better, be happier, and operate more effectively than they do within it.

The Technical Level. If one is correct in diagnosing the presence of the paradox, I have found the solution to the technical problem may be almost absurdly quick and simple, nearly on the order of this:

"Do you mean that you and I and the rest of us have been dragging along with a research project that none of us has thought would work?

It's crazy. I can't believe we would do it, but we did. Let's figure out how we can cancel it and get to doing something productive." In fact, the simplicity and quickness of the solution frequently don't seem possible to most of us, since we have been trained to believe that the solution to conflict requires a long, arduous process of debilitating problem solving.

Also, since existential risk is always present, it is possible that one's diagnosis is incorrect, and the process of confrontation lifts to the level of public examination real, substantive conflict, which may result in heated debate about technology, personalities, and/or administrative approaches. There is evidence that such debates, properly managed, can be the basis for creativity in organizational problem solving. There is also the possibility, however, that such debates cannot be managed, and, substantiating the concept of existential risk, the person who initiates the risk may get fired or ostracized. But that again leads to the necessity of evaluating the results of such confrontation at the existential level.

Existential Results. Evaluating the outcome of confrontation from an existential framework is quite different from evaluating it from a set of technical criteria. How do I reach this conclusion? Simply from interviewing a variety of people who have chosen to confront the paradox and listening to their responses. In short, for them, psychological success and failure apparently are divorced from what is traditionally accepted in organizations as criteria for success and failure.

For instance, some examples of success are described when people are asked, "What happened when you confronted the issue?" They may answer this way:

> I was told we had enough boat rockers in the organization, and I got fired. It hurt at first, but in retrospect it was the greatest day of my life. I've got another job and I'm delighted. I'm a free man.

Another description of success might be this:

> I said I don't think the research project can succeed and the others looked shocked and quickly agreed. The upshot of the whole deal is that I got a promotion and am now known as a "rising star." It was the high point of my career.

Similarly, those who fail to confront the paradox describe failure in terms divorced from technical results. For example, one may report:

> I didn't say anything and we rocked along until the whole thing exploded and Joe got fired. There is still a lot of tension in the organization, and we are still in trouble, but I got a good performance review last time. I still feel lousy about the whole thing, though.

From a different viewpoint, an individual may describe his sense of failure in these words.

> I knew I should have said something and I didn't. When the project failed, I was a convenient whipping boy. I got demoted; I still have a job, but my future here is definitely limited. In a way I deserve what I got, but it doesn't make it any easier to accept because of that.

Most important, the act of confrontation apparently provides intrinsic psychological satisfaction, regardless of the technological outcomes for those who attempt it. The real meaning of that existential experience, and its relevance to a wide variety of organizations, may lie, therefore, not in the scientific analysis of decision making but in the plight of Sisyphus. That is something the reader will have to decide for himself.

The Abilene Paradox and the Myth of Sisyphus

In essence, this paper proposes that there is an underlying organizational reality that includes both agreement and disagreement, cooperation and conflict. However, the decision to confront the possibility of organization agreement is all too difficult and rare, and its opposite, the decision to accept the evils of the present, is all too common. Yet those two decisions may reflect the essence of both our human potential and our human imperfectibility. Consequently, the choice to confront reality in the family, the church, the business, or the bureaucracy, though made only occasionally, may reflect those "peak experiences" that provide meaning to the valleys.

In many ways, they may reflect the experience of Sisyphus. As you may remember, Sisyphus was condemned by Pluto to a perpetuity of pushing a large stone to the top of a mountain, only to see it return to its original position when he released it. As Camus suggested in his revision of the myth, Sisyphus' task was absurd and totally devoid of meaning. For most of us, though, the lives we lead pushing papers or hubcaps are no less absurd, and in many ways we probably spend about as much time pushing rocks in our organizations as Sisyphus did in his.

Camus also points out, though, that on occasion as Sisyphus released his rock and watched it return to its resting place at the bottom of the hill, he was able to recognize the absurdity of his lot, and for brief periods of time, transcend it.

So it may be with confronting the Abilene Paradox. Confronting the absurd paradox of agreement may provide, through activity, what Sisyphus gained from his passive but conscious acceptance of his fate. Thus, through the process of active confrontation with reality, we may take respite from pushing our rocks on their endless journeys and, for brief moments, experience what C. P. Snow termed "the triumphs of life we make for ourselves" within those absurdities we call organizations.

SELECTED BIBLIOGRAPHY

Chris Argyris in *Intervention Theory and Method: A Behavioral Science View* (Addison-Wesley, 1970) gives an excellent description of the process of "owning up" and being "open," both of which are major skills required if one is to assist his organization in avoiding or leaving Abilene.

Albert Camus in *The Myth of Sisyphus and Other Essays* (Vintage Books, Random House, 1955) provides an existential viewpoint for coping with absurdity, of which the Abilene Paradox is a clear example.

Jerry B. Harvey and R. Albertson in "Neurotic Organizations: Symptoms, Causes and Treatment," Parts I and II, *Personnel Journal* (September and October 1971) provide a detailed example of a third-party intervention into an organization caught in a variety of agreement-management dilemmas.

Irving Janis in *Victims of Groupthink* (Houghton-Mifflin Co., 1972) offers an alternative viewpoint for understanding and dealing with many of the dilemmas described in "The Abilene Paradox." Specifically, many of the events that Janis describes as examples of conformity pressures (that is, group tyranny) I would conceptualize as mismanaged agreement.

In his *The Pursuit of Loneliness* (Beacon Press, 1970), Philip Slater contributes an in-depth description of the impact of the role of alienation, separation, and loneliness (a major contribution to the Abilene Paradox) in our culture.

Richard Walton in *Interpersonal Peacemaking: Confrontation and Third Party Consultation* (Addison-Wesley, 1969) describes a variety of approaches for dealing with conflict when it is real, rather than phony.

24

Nominal versus Interacting Group Processes for Committee Decision-Making Effectiveness*

ANDREW VAN DE VEN and ANDRE L. DELBECQ

It is clear that as the accumulation and fractionalization of knowledge increases, creative solutions to complex problems will increasingly involve group processes. This fact partly explains the proliferation of numerous committees in complex organizations. Although the *functions* of the committee have long been recognized in management literature, contemporary research is questioning the conventional *processes* followed in most committee meetings. The purpose of this paper is to review one portion of recent small-group research, that dealing with nominal versus interacting group processes, in order to provide a theoretical justification for greater structuring of behavior in selected decision phases of a committee's work.

Before reviewing related theoretical literature, however, a brief description of a nominal group is in order. Imagine a meeting room in which seven to ten individuals are sitting around a table in full view of each other. However, they are not speaking to each other. Instead, each individual is writing ideas on a pad of paper in front of him. At the end of 10 to 20 minutes, a very structured sharing of ideas takes place. Each individual in round-robin fashion provides one idea from his private list which is written on a flip-chart by a recorder in full view of other members. There is still no discussion, only the recording of privately generated ideas. This round-robin listing continues until each member indicates he has no further ideas to share. The output of this nominal process is the total idea set created by this structured process. Generally, spontaneous discussion then follows for a period (in the same fashion as an interacting group meeting) before nominal voting. Nominal voting simply means that the selection of priorities, rank-ordering, or rating (depending on the group's decision-rule) is

---

* From *Academy of Management Journal,* 1971, *14,* 203–212.

done by each individual privately, and the group decision is the pooled outcome of the individual votes.

This description is, admittedly, the variant of the nominal group process which the authors have fully described elsewhere (see footnote 2). Simpler processes which do not encompass the round-robin listing or any specific voting procedure are also often used by researchers. Therefore, in the following theoretical review we are not discriminating in terms of a particular nominal approach; rather, we are speaking of the differences between groups where people interact spontaneously as opposed to groups where people work as individuals and the group outcome is the pooled summary of their individual efforts.

We shall begin by examining small-group research relating process to creative problem solving.

RELATIONSHIP OF THE GROUP PROCESS TO CREATIVE PROBLEM SOLVING[1]

The past 15 years have seen a rapid growth of research interest in the comparative effectiveness of individuals versus groups, and nominal[2] versus interacting[3] group processes in decision-making situations which require subjects to generate information concerning a problem. Osborn, a major proponent of "brainstorming" techniques in problem solving, posited "the average person can think up twice as many ideas when working with a group than working alone" (34, pp. 228–229). When comparing the mean number of ideas produced by a group with the mean number of ideas produced by individuals, brainstorming groups were found to be superior to an equal number of individuals who were brainstorming independently (34, pp. 228–229;

[1] Creativity in group problem solving is defined as the reconceptualization of given information on a problem into multiple alternative solution combinations, and bringing a new idea or solution into being which has not existed before. See: J. C. Flanagan, "The Definition and Measurement of Ingenuity," in *Scientific Creativity: Its Recognition and Development*, ed. Taylor and Barron (New York: John Wiley & Sons, 1963); J. W. Haefle, *Creativity and Innovation* (New York: Reinhold, 1962); F. E. Fiedler, "Leader Attitude, Group Climate, and Group Creativity," *Journal of Abnormal and Social Psychology*, 65, 5 (1962); W. C. Schultz, "Creative Behavior: Training and Theory Development," *Personal Communication* (1963).

[2] The nominal group is defined as a group in which individuals work in the presence of others but do not verbally interact. Typically, some written output is obtained from each participant. The authors have fully described a nominal group format in "A Group Process Model for Problem Identification and Program Planning" forthcoming in *Journal of Applied Behavioral Science*.

[3] The interacting group is defined as a group in which all communication acts take place between members with minimal controls or formal structuring. A. L. Delbecq, "The World within the Span of Control: Managerial Behavior in Groups of Varied Size," *Business Horizons* (August 1968).

19, pp. 147–157). Further, brainstorming groups were found to be superior to conventional discussion groups in problem-solving situations (34, pp. 228–229; 4, pp. 1–29; 36, pp. 171–176). Taylor, Berry, and Block found interacting groups to be superior to individuals in problem-solving situations when comparing the performance of individuals working alone with that of a group in which the same individuals participate at another time (41, pp. 23–47). They state: "Such group superiority may very well account for the widespread impression that group participation does facilitate the production of ideas."

A different comparison of the same measure of group processes is the examination of nominal groups as opposed to brainstorming or interacting group performance in terms of (*a*) the mean number of unique ideas, (*b*) the mean total number of ideas, and (*c*) the quality of ideas produced. Based upon these three measures of performance, nominal groups have been found to be significantly superior to brainstorming groups in generating information relevant to a problem (42, pp. 23–47; 14, pp. 308–318; 7, pp. 205–210; 4, pp. 1–29; 5, pp. 51–55; 40; 44, pp. 338–341; 27).

Numerous researchers concur that "group participation when using brainstorming techiques inhibits creative thinking" (42, pp. 23–47; 14; 7, pp. 205–210; 4, pp. 1–29; 5, pp. 51–55). Even though brainstorming techniques attempt to eliminate criticism (34, p. 84), interacting groups still contain inhibitory influences which are not easily dissipated (14, p. 37). These individual inhibitions in interacting groups result in decreased quality of ideas generated in terms of creativity, originality, and practicality (8, pp. 159–163).

Tersely summarized, the nature of inhibiting influences which act to reduce the performance of interacting groups in problem solving seems to relate to the following causes:

1. A "focus" effect wherein interacting groups "fall into a rut" and pursue a single train of thought for long periods (42, pp. 23–47; 13, pp. 12–29).
2. The "self-weighting" effect, wherein an individual will participate in the group to the extent that he feels equally competent with others (26; 8, pp. 159–163).
3. The fact that covert judgments are made but are not expressed as overt criticisms (8, pp. 159–163).
4. The inevitable presence within most organizational groups of status incongruities, wherein low-status participants may be inhibited and "go along" with opinions expressed by high-status participants, even though they feel their opinions are better (43, pp. 314–318).
5. Group pressures for conformity and implied threat of sanctions from the more knowledgeable members (21, 10).

6. The influence of dominant personality-types upon the group (10).
7. The amount of time and effort spent by the group to maintain itself (10; 13, pp. 12–29). As orientation to maintain group interaction increases, quality of solutions decreases. (7).
8. A tendency to reach "speedy decisions" before all problem dimensions have been considered (30 pp. 278–283; 11).

As a result of these inhibitive factors, the latent resources of individual group members are often not brought to bear on problem solving. By contrast, nominal groups are successful in overcoming some of these difficulties, and we can now explore some of the factors which explain their greater effectiveness.

The nominal group process facilitates the generation of a larger number of relevant problem dimensions than conventional interacting groups and facilitates creative decision making. Causation seems to relate to a number of process characteristics of nominal groups. Nominal groups:

1. Stimulate creative tension by means of the presence of others, the silence, and the evidence of activity. This tension is important for individual commitment to search process. Thus, the social facilitation of the group setting is retained and amplified.[4]
2. Avoid evaluation or elaborating comments while problem dimensions are being generated (30, pp. 278–283).
3. Provide each individual time and opportunity to engage in reflection (search) and force participants to record their thoughts (13, pp. 12–29; 32, pp. 155–174; 25, pp. 640–647).
4. Avoid the dominance of group output by strong personality types (33).
5. Prevent premature closure to the alternative search process and decision making (30, pp. 278–283; 3, pp. 251–274).
6. Allow all participants to share in the opportunity for influencing the direction of group-decision outcome (37, pp. 310–325; 16, pp. 47–56).
7. Encourage the generation of minority opinions and ideas, which consequently are more likely to be voiced (32, pp. 155–174; 39, pp. 211–217).
8. Tolerate conflicting, incompatible ideas since all ideas are revealed in writing (12, pp. 199–213; 18, pp. 367–382; 43, pp. 314–318).
9. Alleviate "hidden agendas" or covert political group dynamics which are difficult to develop when writing (15, pp. 682–690).

---

[4] For a treatment of tension as a condition of change see G. W. Dalton, "Influence and Organizational Change," paper presented at the Conference on Organizational Behavior Models (Kent, Ohio: Kent State University, College of Business Administration, May 16, 1969).

10. Induce a sense of responsibility in the members to achieve group success (2, pp. 42–47).
11. Impose a burden upon all participants to work and produce their share in the necessary task (1; 12).
12. By means of written expression, induce a greater feeling of commitment and a greater sense of permanance than does spoken expression (25, pp. 640–647; 4, pp. 1–29).

OTHER PROCESS CHARACTERISTICS FACILITATING CREATIVITY

One of the critical process characteristics facilitating creativity is the separation of problems from solutions. Group problem-solving processes which separate ideation (problem-identification) from evaluation (solution getting) are superior to group processes which combine them (6, pp. 175–179; 30; 31, pp. 320–323; 29). "It appears to be a human tendency to seek solutions even before the problem is understood. This tendency to be "solution minded" seems to become stronger when there is anxiety over the nature of the decision" (30, pp. 278–283). Research indicates that the success of problem-solving groups in arriving at creative decisions is related to the proportion of time spent working on the problem (38, pp. 338–341). Nominal group activity generates significantly better ideas in the final third period of an individual's independent work than in the first two thirds of the period (35, pp. 171–176; 36). Thus, the number of alternative solutions and the quality of group performance can be increased by group process which (a) retards speedy decisions, and (b) causes the group to perceive the task with an attitude of "problem mindedness" as opposed to "solution mindedness" (32, pp. 155–174; 29). Nominal groups facilitate problem centeredness by task assignments which focus on problems and avoid solution generations.

Research also suggests that individuals in a group will hesitate to identify personal problem dimensions when dealing with tasks having social-emotional dimensions (11). Rather, participants in a group will tend to focus upon and disclose organizational, institutional, or conventionally accepted problem characteristics. When the social-emotional dimensions of a problem are important and need to be identified, a structured process of separating personal ("inside") from institutional or organizational ("outside") categories is helpful. Separate nominal group task assignments have been found to be a successful process for eliciting responses to these dual problem concerns.[5]

---

[5] For example, in a group meeting with elderly persons exploring services, "organizational or outside" problems such as cost of drugs, transportation, etc. were easily mentioned. Only when groups of elderly people were asked to separately list "personal" problems did areas such as fear of death, loneliness, preoccupation with sickness, feeling disliked by younger people, and other critical social-emotional issues come out.

Another characteristic of the nominal group process relates to the size and composition of the group. As the size of the group or committee increases, the superiority of the nominal group over the conventional brainstorming or interacting group increases in terms of total number of non-overlapping ideas produced (5, pp. 51–55). Nominal group processes can accommodate large numbers of participants without the dysfunctions of conventional discussion involving many participants.

Several studies have tested the effects of homogeneous or heterogeneous group composition on group problem-solving effectiveness. Heterogeneous groups, defined by low correlations in personality profiles and producing members with substantially different perspectives on a problem, were found to produce a higher proportion of high-quality, high-acceptance solutions than homogeneous groups (22, pp. 27–32; 24, pp. 273–291; 23). On the other hand, homogeneous groups were found to facilitate group performance because of less likelihood of interpersonal conflict and dominance of the group by one or a few (17, pp. 333–335; 20, pp. 276–284). The mixed results found in these studies suggest that there is value in using the heterogeneous group if its detrimental effects can be controlled. Given the composition of group membership, Bouchard (4, p. 6) suggests that structured group processes (such as nominal processes) can facilitate problem solving by: (a) specifying role requirements (41, pp. 190–196) and (b) structuring communication networks (28, pp. 38–50).

Thus, a number of research studies substantiate the superiority of nominal groups as compared to conventional brainstorming or interacting groups given judgmental tasks of problem and need identification or estimation. The research reported above indicates that interacting groups produce a smaller number of problem dimensions, fewer high-quality suggestions, and a smaller number of different kinds of solutions than groups in which members were constrained from interaction during the generation of critical problem variables.

THE ROLE OF INTERACTING GROUP PROCESSES IN PROBLEM SOLVING

The research, however, suggests that different phases of problem solving require different group process strategies. While the nominal group process is most effective for generating information and for fact-finding concerning a problem, interacting group processes stimulate individuals to consider other dimensions of a problem and help synthesize and evaluate alternative solution possibilities (44, pp. 38–341; 11). Further, interacting groups are functional in elaborating, modifying, and working toward a consensus when implementing solutions to problems (11).

Final choices made by groups after interaction are better than decisions based simply on the statistical pooling of individual judgments (19, pp. 147–157). The process by which group interaction is structured, however, is critical in reducing the detrimental effects of interacting groups, noted earlier, which inhibit individual judgments (11). Our experience indicates that one group interaction process which facilitates equal sharing of ideas by individuals is the "recorded round-robin" technique.[6] The recorded round-robin technique is a structured group process in which each individual in turn is given the opportunity to disclose one idea at a time to the group. A member in the group writes the idea on a flip chart in full view of the group. The idea is summarized exactly as the individual wishes. This process continues until all ideas are exhausted and is followed by spontaneous interaction. The round-robin process facilitates self-disclosure of ideas, even by less secure members who may hesitate to bring some problem dimensions before the group in the conventional interacting situation (9, pp. 47–74). Further, the recorded round-robin procedure of disclosing problem dimensions decreases argumentation over semantics and facilitates increased balance in participation (11). When interacting discussion follows the round-robin listing, clarification and synthesis occur naturally, furthermore having the total set of variables placed in writing before the group helps to avoid the loss of critical items.

Thus, when the task requirement of a group is fact finding or information generation, use of nominal group processes are suggested by the research. When the problem requires information synthesis, evaluation, or group consensus, interacting group processes are prescribed (11; 13, pp. 12–29; 30, pp. 278–283). In fact, some authors suggest that interacting groups should be used exclusively for sharing and evaluating information, but the generation of ideas or solutions is better accomplished by nominal group processes (13, pp. 12–29). Further, for effective problem solving, Maier and Hoffman (30, pp. 278–283) suggest that one meeting should be conducted for information generation, and another meeting for reaching a solution, in order to avoid group ambiguity about roles and process. (Of course, from a practical standpoint, group problem-solving processes must also consider: (a) the time factor, (b) the rationality of a solution, and (c) the behavioral consequences of implementing a solution following the decision (44, pp. 92–93).

---

[6] For a complete description of the use of the "recorded round-robin" technique, see Delbecq and Van de Ven, "A Group Process Model."

IMPLICATIONS FOR COMMITTEE
DECISION-MAKING EFFECTIVENESS

In summary, several guidelines for committee decision-making effectiveness can be inferred from the above review of small-group theory and research:

1. Management of the decision-making *process* within a committee or group is critical in affecting: *(a)* the content of interaction, *(b)* the distribution of interaction, *(c)* the affectional (emotional and expressive) overtones of interaction, and most important, *(d)* the quality of the decision outcome.
2. The common process of committee decision making is unstructured, face-to-face discussions. Numerous reasons have been stated regarding why the conventional interacting group inhibits, and more structured group processes facilitate, creative decision making. Thus, the adage, "two heads are better than one" depends upon the process whereby the two heads are joined.
3. When the phase of the problem is fact finding, or idea generation, the research suggests that a nominal group process be used. The superiority of the nominal group over the interacting group (or even the brainstorming group) is clearly substantiated in terms of generating a higher quality and quantity and a greater variety of ideas on fact-finding or idea-generating tasks. Further, our experience suggests that the nominal group is a time-saving process since it can be activated and concluded with greater rapidity than interacting group processes.
4. When the problem-solving phase requires information synthesis, evaluation, or working toward group consensus, the research suggests interacting group processes are functional. An interacting group process which decreases the inhibiting influences of unstructured interacting groups, yet incorporates discussion dynamics, is the "recorded round-robin" process followed by spontaneous interaction.
5. The dynamics of interacting groups often jeopardize the democratic ideal of equal influence through verbal voting procedures. To avoid the dominance by a limited few "leaders" in the final choice of priorities or decision components, nominal group voting is suggested.[7]
6. In general, we suggest that the optimal combination of processes for creative problem solving is: *(a)* use of nominal group processes for fact finding and idea generation in the first phase; *(b)* structured group interaction (such as the "recorded round-robin" tech-

---

[7] The authors are currently preparing a report of laboratory research showing the increased validity of subjective probability estimation using nominal voting procedures.

nique) followed by informal discussions for clarification and evaluation of information, during the second phase; and (c) nominal group voting for final independent individual judgments in the final phase.

It would appear from the above that those managers who call a committee meeting without attention to the problem phase and to structuring group processes may fail to stimulate the latent superiority of group judgment over isolated individual decisions.

REFERENCES

1. Bales, R. F. "The equilibrium problem in small groups. In T. Parsons, R. F. Bales, & E. A. Shils, *Working papers in the theory of action.* New York: Free Press, 1953.

2. Benne, K. D., & Sheats, P. Functional roles of group members: *Journal of Social Issues, 2,* 1948.

3. Bennett, E. B. Discussion, decision, commitment, and consensus in group decision. *Human Relations, 8,* 1955.

4. Bouchard, T. J., Jr. Personality, problem-solving procedure, and performance in small groups. *Journal of Applied Psychology Monograph, 53,* 1, part 2, February 1953.

5. ——, & Hare, M. Size, performance, and potential in brainstorming groups. *Journal of Applied Psychology, 54,* 1, February 1970.

6. Brilhart, J. K., & Jochem, L. M. Effects of different patterns on outcomes of problem-solving discussion. *Journal of Applied Psychology, 48,* 1964.

7. Campbell, J. P. Individual versus group problem-solving in an industrial sample. *Journal of Applied Psychology, 52,* 3, 1968.

8. Collaros, F. A., & Anderson, L. R. Effect of perceived expertness upon creativity of members of brainstorming groups. *Journal of Applied Psychology, 53,* 2, April 1969.

9. Culbert, S. A. Trainer self-disclosure and member growth in two T-groups. *Journal of Applied Behavioral Science, 4,* 1.

10. Dalkey, N. C., & O. Hilmer An experimental application of the Delphi method to the use of experts. *Management Science, 5,* 1963.

11. Delbecq, A. L., & Van de Ven, A. A group process model for problem identification and program planning. *Journal of Applied Behavioral Science* (forthcoming).

12. Deutsch, M. An experimental study of the effects of cooperation and competition on group process. *Human Relations, 2,* 1949.

13. Dunnette, M. D. Are meetings any good for solving problems? *Personnel Administration,* March–April 1964.

14. Dunnette, M., Campbell, J., & Jaastad, K. The effect of group participation on brainstorming effectiveness for two industrial samples. *Journal of Applied Psychology, 47,* 1, 1963.

15. Foureizos, N. T., Hutt, M. L., & Guetzkow, H. Measurement of self-oriented needs in discussion groups. *Journal of Abnormal and Social Psychology, 45,* 1950.

16. Goldman, M., Bolen, M., & Martin, R. Some conditions under which groups operate and how this affects their performance. *Journal of Social Psychology, 54,* 1961.

17. Grace, H. A. Conformance and performance. *Journal of Social Psychology, 40,* 1954.

18. Guetzkow, H., & Gry, J. An analysis of conflict in decision-making groups. *Human Relations, 7,* 1954.

19. Hall, E. J., Mouton, J. S. & Blake, R. R. Group problem-solving effectiveness under conditions of pooling versus interaction. *Journal of Social Psychology, 59,* 1963.

20. Haythorn, W. The influence of individual members on the characteristics of small groups. *Journal of Abnormal and Social Psychology, 48,* 1953.

21. Hoffman, L. R. Group problem-solving. In L. Berkowitz (Ed.), *Advances in experimental social psychology,* II. New York: Academic Press, 1965.

22. ———, Homogeneity of member personality and its effect on group problem-solving. *Journal of Abnormal and Social Psychology, 58,* 1959.

23. ———, and Maier, N. R. F. Quality and acceptance of problem solutions by members of homogeneous and heterogeneous groups. *Journal of Abnormal and Social Psychology, 62,* 1961.

24. ———, & Smith, G. G. Some factors affecting the behaviors of members of problem-solving groups. *Sociometry, 23,* 1960.

25. Horowitz, M. W., & Newman, J. B. Spoken and written expression: An experimental analysis. *Journal of abnormal and social psychology, 68,* 1964.

26. Kelly, H. H., & Thibaut, J. W. Experimental studies in group problem-solving and process. In G. Lindzey (Ed.), *Handbook of social psychology.* Reading, Mass.: Addison-Wesley, 1954.

27. Leader, A. Patterns in judgmental decision-making: Individual and group performance across tasks. Doctoral dissertation, Bloomington, Ind.: Indiana University, Graduate School of Business, 1963.

28. Leavitt, H. J. Some effects of certain communication patterns on group performance. *Journal of Abnormal and Social Psychology, 46,* 1951.

29. Maier, N. R. F. *The appraisal interview: Objectives, methods, and skills.* New York: Wiley, 1958.

30. ———, & Hoffman, L. R. Quality of first and second solution group problem-solving. *Journal of Applied Psychology, 44, 4,* 1960.

31. ———, & Maier, A. R. A. An experimental test of the effects of 'development' versus 'free' discussions on the quality of group decisions. *Journal of Applied Psychology, 4,* 1957.

32. ———, & Solem, A. R. The contribution of the discussion leader to the quality of group thinking. *Human Relations, 3,* 1952.

33.   ———, & Maier, A. R. A.   *Supervisory and executive development.* New York: Wiley, 1957.

34.   Osborn, A. F.   *Applied Imagination,* rev. ed. New York: Scribners, 1957.

35.   Parnes, J. S.   Effects of extended effort in creative problem-solving. *Journal of Educational Psychology, 52,* 1961.

36.   Parnes, J. S., & Meadow, A.   Effects of brain-storming instruction on creative problem-solving by trained and untrained subjects. *Journal of Educational Psychology, 50,* 1959.

37.   Pelz, D. C.   Some social factors related to performance in a research organization. *Administrative Science Quarterly,* 1956.

38.   Shaw, M. E.   Some effects of problem solution efficiency in different communication wills. *Journal of Experimental Psychology, 48,* 1954.

39.   Shukla, R. H.   The effects of training. Unpublished master's thesis, College of Engineering, University of Wisconsin, Madison, 1970.

40.   Speesman, J. C., & Moos, R. H.   Group compatibility and productivity. *Journal of Abnormal and Social Psychology, 65,* 1962.

41.   Taylor, D. W., Berry, P. C., & Block, C. H.   Does group participation when using brainstorming facilitate or inhibit active thinking? *Administrative Science Quarterly, 3,* 1958.

42.   Torrance, E. P.   Group decision-making and disagreement. *Social Forces, 35,* 1957.

43.   Vroom, V. H., Grant, L. D., & Cotton, T. S.   The consequences of social interaction in group problem-solving. *Journal of Applied Psychology, 53,* 4, August 1969.

44.   Zogona, S. V., Eillis, J. E., & MacKinnon, W. S.   Group effectiveness in creative problem-solving tasks: An examination of relevant variables. *Journal of Psychology, 62,* 1966.

section five

Leadership

Introduction

Upon leaders fall the not always enviable task of fusing organizational purpose with the drives of individuals and groups. Until about the middle of this century, the study of how leaders do this concerned itself almost totally with a search for personality traits that somehow combined to produce leadership. The meager and inconsistent findings from this approach gave way to an emphasis on leader behavior. A series of studies at the Ohio State University identified two broad dimensions of leader behavior, *consideration* (relationship-oriented behavior by the leader) and *initiating structure* (task-oriented behavior). Researchers and theorists then groped for the discovery of some optimal blend of these dimensions that would generally characterize effective leaders.

Alas, no such simple formula could be unearthed. The effects of consideration on performance, and the effects of initiating structure on both satisfaction and performance, were not at all consistent. Furthermore, no consistent effects could be ascribed to the manner or degree in which leaders involved subordinates in decision making.

Thus, the study of leadership within the context of work behavior has, in the past two decades, taken different directions. In the House and Mitchell article, we see the quest for a *contingency* theory. Such a theory would allow us to identify situational variables that render various forms of leader behavior more or less efficacious. A number of contingency theories have been offered up, but the "path-goal" theory described by House and Mitchell appears to hold the most promise for resolving conflicting findings, yet still affording a succinct and plausible statement of important relationships.

Kerr and Jermier find considerable heuristic value in the concept "substitutes for leadership." They view effective leadership as that which complements other sources of structure and rewards in the work situation. Where substitutes for these functions abound, much of leader behavior will be either redundant, neutralized, or resisted.

Miles notes that different motives may underlie what superficially seems to be the same leader style. Thus, leaders who involve subordinates in decision making may do so for the purpose of dissolving subordinate resistance or because of the felt need to use their expertise. Miles' discussion suggests that the inner purpose of the leader will determine whether the outward style has significance.

Shetty and Peery maintain that leadership is more than style, and at the executive level it is more than managerial skills. Leadership must be grounded in local texture: the requirements of survival in a particular technological or market niche, the personalities of the natives, and the traditions of the tribe. Intimate familiarity with these matters is acquired only over a long period of tenure in the firm. Shetty and Peery conclude that the transferability of CEO's and other top-level executives is quite limited.

Pfeffer urges us to consider a much more disturbing question: do we give leaders too much credit, as well as too much blame, for what happens to organizations? Pfeffer argues, on the one hand, that the latitude of action by leaders is limited by constraints. On the other hand, external forces neither controlled nor understood by leaders account for most of the variance in a firm's performance. Is leader effectiveness little more than a distortion of our perceptual process?

25
Path-Goal Theory of Leadership*

ROBERT J. HOUSE and TERENCE R. MITCHELL

An integrated body of conjecture by students of leadership, referred to as the "Path-Goal Theory of Leadership," is currently emerging. According to this theory, leaders are effective because of their impact on subordinates' motivation, ability to perform effectively, and satisfactions. The theory is called Path-Goal because its major concern is how the leader influences the subordinates' perceptions of their work goals, personal goals, and paths to goal attainment. The theory suggests that a leader's behavior is motivating or satisfying to the degree that the behavior increases subordinate goal attainment and clarifies the paths to these goals.

HISTORICAL FOUNDATIONS

The path-goal approach has its roots in a more general motivational theory called expectancy theory (Mitchell, 1974a). Briefly, expectancy theory states that an individual's attitudes (e.g., satisfaction with supervision or job satisfaction) or behavior (e.g., leader behavior or job effort) can be predicted from: (1) the degree to which the job, or behavior, is seen as leading to various outcomes called (expectancy) and (2) the evaluation of these outcomes called (valences). Thus, people are satisfied with their job if they think it leads to things that are highly valued, and they work hard if they believe that effort leads to things that are highly valued. This type of theoretical rationale can be used to predict a variety of phenomena related to leadership, such as why leaders behave the way they do (Nebeker & Mitchell, 1974) or it can help us to understand how leader behavior influences subordinate motivation.

This latter approach is the primary concern of this article. The implication for leadership is that subordinates are motivated by leader behavior to the extent that this behavior influences expectancies, e.g., goal paths and valences, e.g., goal attractiveness.

* From *Journal of Contemporary Business*, Autumn 1974, 81–97. Reprinted with permission.

Several writers have advanced specific hypotheses concerning how the leader affects the paths and the goals of subordinates (Evans, 1970; Hammer & Dachler, 1973; Dansereau et al., 1973; House, 1971; Mitchell, 1973; Graen et al., 1972a; House & Dessler, 1974). These writers focused on two issues: (1) how the leader affects subordinates' expectations that effort will lead to effective performance and valued rewards, and (2) how this expectation affects motivation to work hard and perform well.

While the state of theorizing about leadership in terms of subordinates' paths and goals is in its infancy, we believe it is promising for two reasons. First, it suggests effects of leader behavior that have not yet been investigated but which appear to be fruitful areas of inquiry. And, second, it suggests with some precision the situational factors on which the effects of leader behavior are contingent.

The initial theoretical work by Evans (1970, 1974) asserts that leaders will be effective by making rewards available to subordinates and by making these rewards contingent on the subordinates' accomplishment of specific goals. Evans argued that one of the strategic functions of the leader is to clarify for subordinates the kind of behavior that leads to goal accomplishment and valued rewards. This function might be referred to as path clarification. Evans also argued that the leader increases the rewards available to subordinates by being supportive toward subordinates, i.e., by being concerned about their status, welfare, and comfort. Leader supportiveness is in itself a reward that the leader has at his or her disposal, and the judicious use of this reward increases the motivation of subordinates.

Evans studied the relationship between the behavior of leaders and the subordinates' expectations that effort leads to rewards and also studied the resulting impact on ratings of the subordinates' performance. He found that when subordinates viewed leaders as being supportive (considerate of their needs) and when these superiors provided directions and guidance to the subordinates, there was a positive relationship between leadership behavior and subordinates' performance ratings.

However, leader behavior was only related to subordinates' performance when the leader's behavior also was related to the subordinates' expectations that their effort would result in desired rewards. Thus, Evans' findings suggest that the major impact of a leader on the performance of subordinates is clarifying the path to desired rewards and making such rewards contingent on effective performance.

Stimulated by this line of reasoning, House (1971) and House and Dessler (1974) advanced a more complex theory of the effects of leader behavior on the motivation of subordinates. The theory intends to explain the effects of four specific kinds of leader behavior on the following three subordinate attitudes or expectations: (1) the satisfaction of subordinates, (2) the subordinates' acceptance of the leader, and (3) the expectations of subordinates that effort will result in effective performance and that effective performance is the path to rewards. The four kinds of leader behavior included in the theory are: (1) directive leadership, (2) supportive leadership, (3) participative leadership, and (4) achievement-oriented leadership. Directive leadership is characterized by a leader who lets subordinates know what is expected of them, gives specific guidance as to what should be done and how it should be done, makes his or her part in the group understood, schedules work to be done, maintains definite standards of performance and asks that group members follow standard rules and regulations. Supportive leadership is characterized by a friendly and approachable leader who shows concern for the status, well-being and needs of subordinates. Such a leader does little things to make the work more pleasant, treats members as equals and is friendly and approachable. Participative leadership is characterized by a leader who consults with his subordinates, solicits their suggestions, and takes these suggestions seriously into consideration before making a decision. An achievement-oriented leader sets challenging goals, expects subordinates to perform at their highest level, continuously seeks improvement in performance *and* shows a high degree of confidence that the subordinates will assume responsibility, put forth effort, and accomplish challenging goals. This kind of leader constantly emphasizes excellence in performance and simultaneously displays confidence that subordinates will meet high standards of excellence.

A number of studies suggest that these different leadership styles can be shown by the same leader in various situations (House & Dessler, 1974; Stogdill, 1965; House, Velancy & Van der Krabben, unpublished). For example, a leader may show directiveness toward subordinates in some instances and be participative or supportive in other instances (Hill, 1974). Thus, the traditional method of characterizing a leader as either highly participative and supportive *or* highly directive is invalid; rather, it can be concluded that leaders vary in the particular fashion employed for supervising their subordinates. Also, the theory, in its present stage, is a tentative explanation of the effects of leader behavior—it is incomplete because it does not explain other kinds of leader behavior and does not explain the effects of the leader on factors other than subordinate acceptance, satisfaction, and expectations. However, the theory is stated so that additional variables may be included in it as new knowledge is made available.

PATH-GOAL THEORY

General Propositions

The first proposition of path-goal theory is that leader behavior is acceptable and satisfying to subordinates to the extent that the subordinates see such behavior as either an immediate source of satisfaction or as instrumental to future satisfaction.

The second proposition of this theory is that the leader's behavior will be motivational, i.e., increase effort, to the extent that (1) such behavior makes satisfaction of subordinates' needs contingent on effective performance and (2) such behavior complements the environment of subordinates by providing the coaching, guidance, support, and rewards necessary for effective performance.

These two propositions suggest that the leader's strategic functions are to enhance subordinates' motivation to perform, satisfaction with the job, and acceptance of the leader. From previous research on expectancy theory of motivation (House, Shapiro, & Wahba, 1974) it can be inferred that the strategic functions of the leader consist of: (1) recognizing and/or arousing subordinates' needs for outcomes over which the leader has some control, (2) increasing personal payoffs to subordinates for work-goal attainment, (3) making the path to those payoffs easier to travel by coaching and direction, (4) helping subordinates clarify expectancies, (5) reducing frustrating barriers, and (6) increasing the opportunities for personal satisfaction contingent on effective performance.

Stated less formally, the motivational functions of the leader consist of increasing the number and kinds of personal payoffs to subordinates for work-goal attainment, and making paths to these payoffs easier to travel by clarifying the paths, reducing road blocks and pitfalls, and increasing the opportunities for personal satisfaction en route.

Contingency Factors

Two classes of situational variables are asserted to be contingency factors. A contingency factor is a variable which moderates the relationship between two other variables such as leader behavior and subordinate satisfaction. For example, we might suggest that the degree of structure in the task moderates the relationship between the leaders' directive behavior and subordinates' job satisfaction. Figure 1 shows how such a relationship might look. Thus, subordinates are satisfied with directive behavior in an unstructured task and are satisfied with nondirective behavior in a structured task. Therefore,

FIGURE 1
Hypothetical Relationship between Directive Leadership and Subordinate Satisfaction with Task Structure As a Contingency Factor

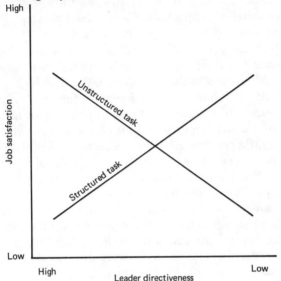

we say that the relationship between leader directiveness and subordinate satisfaction is contingent upon the structure of the task.

The two contingency variables are (*a*) personal characteristics of the subordinates and (*b*) the environmental pressures and demands with which the subordinates must cope in order to accomplish the work goals and to satisfy their needs. While other situational factors also may operate to determine the effects of leader behavior, they are not presently known.

With respect to the first class of contingency factors, the characteristics of subordinates, path-goal theory asserts that leader behavior will be acceptable to subordinates to the extent that the subordinates see such behavior as either an immediate source of satisfaction or as instrumental to future satisfaction. Subordinates' characteristics are hypothesized to partially determine this perception. For example, Runyon (1973) and Mitchell, Smyser, and Weed, (1974) show that the subordinate's score on a measure called Locus of Control moderates the relationship between participative leadership style and subordinate satisfaction. The Locus-of-Control measure reflects the degree to which an individual sees the environment as systematically responding to his or her behavior. People who believe that what happens to them occurs because of their behavior are called internals; people who believe that what happens to them occurs because of luck or chance are called externals. Mitchell et al. (1974) findings suggest that internals are more satisfied with a participative leadership style and externals are more satisfied with a directive style.

A second characteristic of subordinates on which the effects of leader behavior are contingent is subordinates' perception of their own ability with respect to their assigned tasks. The higher the degree of perceived ability relative to task demands, the less the subordinate will view leader directiveness and coaching behavior as acceptable. Where the subordinate's perceived ability is high, such behavior is likely to have little positive effect on the motivation of the subordinate and to be perceived as excessively close control. Thus, the acceptability of the leader's behavior is determined in part by the characteristics of the subordinates.

The second aspect of the situation, the environment of the subordinate, consists of those factors that are not within the control of the subordinate but which are important to need satisfaction or to ability to perform effectively. The theory asserts that effects of the leader's behavior on the psychological states of subordinates are contingent on other parts of the subordinates' environment that are relevant to subordinate motivation. Three broad classifications of contingency factors in the environment are:

1. The subordinates' tasks.
2. The formal authority system of the organization.
3. The primary work group.

Assessment of the environmental conditions makes it possible to predict the kind and amount of influence that specific leader behaviors will have on the motivation of subordinates. Any of the three environmental factors could act upon the subordinate in any of three ways: first, to serve as stimuli that motivate and direct the subordinate to perform necessary task operations; second, to constrain variability in behavior. Constraints may help the subordinate by clarifying expectancies that effort leads to rewards or by preventing the subordinate from experiencing conflict and confusion. Constraints also may be counterproductive to the extent that they restrict initiative or prevent increases in effort from being associated positively with rewards. Third, environmental factors may serve as rewards for achieving desired performance, e.g., it is possible for the subordinate to receive the necessary cues to do the job and the needed rewards for satisfaction from sources other than the leader, e.g., co-workers in the primary work group. Thus, the effect of the leader on subordinates' motivation will be a function of how deficient the environment is with respect to motivational stimuli, constraints, or rewards.

With respect to the environment, path-goal theory asserts that when goals and paths to desired goals are apparent because of the routine nature of the task, clear group norms or objective controls of the formal authority systems, attempts by the leader to clarify paths and goals will be both redundant and seen by subordinates as imposing unnecessary, close control. Although such control may increase performance by preventing soldiering or malingering, it also will result in decreased satisfaction (see Figure 1). Also with respect to the work environment, the theory asserts that the more dissatisfying the task, the more the subordinates will resent leader behavior directed at increasing productivity or enforcing compliance to organizational rules and procedures.

Finally, with respect to environmental variables the theory states that leader behavior will be motivational to the extent that it helps subordinates cope with environmental uncertainties, threats from others, or sources of frustration. Such leader behavior is predicted to increase subordinates' satisfaction with the job context and to be motivational to the extent that it increases the subordinates' expectations that their effort will lead to valued rewards.

These propositions and specification of situational contingencies provide a heuristic framework on which to base future research. Hopefully, this will lead to a more fully developed, explicitly formal theory of leadership.

Figure 2 presents a summary of the theory. It is hoped that these propositions, while admittedly tentative, will provide managers with some insights concerning the effects of their own leader behavior and that of others.

FIGURE 2
Summary of Path-Goal Relationships

Leader Behavior and Contingency Factors		Cause	Subordinate Attitudes and Behavior
1 Directive	1 Subordinate characteristics		1 Job satisfaction Job → rewards
	Authoritarianism	Personal	
2 Supportive	Locus of control	Influence > perceptions	
	Ability		2 Acceptance of leader
	2 Environmental factors		Leader → rewards
3 Achievement-oriented	The task		
	Formal authority system	Influence > Motivational stimuli	3 Motivational behavior Effort → performance
	Primary work group	Constraints	Performance → rewards
4 Participative		Rewards	

356 Section V. Leadership

EMPIRICAL SUPPORT

The theory has been tested in a limited number of studies which have generated considerable empirical support for our ideas and also suggested areas in which the theory requires revision. A brief review of these studies follows.

Leader Directiveness

Leader directiveness has a positive correlation with satisfaction and expectancies of subordinates who are engaged in ambiguous tasks and has a negative correlation with satisfaction and expectancies of subordinates engaged in clear tasks. These findings were predicted by the theory and have been replicated in seven organizations (House, 1971; House & Dessler, 1974; Szilagyi & Sims, 1974; Dermer, 1974). They suggest that when task demands are ambiguous or when the organization procedures, rules, and policies are not clear, a leader behaving in a directive manner complements the tasks and the organization by providing the necessary guidance and psychological structure for subordinates. However, when task demands are clear to subordinates, leader directiveness is seen more as a hindrance.

However, other studies have failed to confirm these findings (Weed, Mitchell, & Smyser, 1974; Dermer & Siegel, 1973; Schuler, 1973; Downey et al., 1974; Stinson & Johnson, 1974). A study by Dessler (1973) suggests a resolution to these conflicting findings—he found that for subordinates at the lower organizational levels of a manufacturing firm who were doing routine, repetitive, unambiguous tasks, directive leadership was preferred by closed-minded, dogmatic, authoritarian subordinates, and nondirective leadership was preferred by nonauthoritarian, open-minded subordinates. However, for subordinates at higher organizational levels doing nonroutine, ambiguous tasks, directive leadership was preferred for both authoritarian and nonauthoritarian subordinates. Thus, Dessler found that two contingency factors appear to operate simultaneously: subordinate task ambiguity and degree of subordinate authoritarianism. When measured in combination, the findings are as predicted by the theory; however, when the subordinate's personality is not taken into account, task ambiguity does not always operate as a contingency variable as predicted by the theory. House, Burill and Dessler (unpublished) recently found a similar interaction between subordinate authoritarianism and task ambiguity in a second manufacturing firm, thus adding confidence in Dessler's original findings.

Supportive Leadership

The theory hypothesizes that supportive leadership will have its most positive effect on subordinate satisfaction for subordinates who work on stressful, frustrating, or dissatisfying tasks. This hypothesis has been tested in ten samples of employees, (House, 1971; House & Dessler, 1974; Szilagyi & Sims, 1974; Stinson & Johnson, 1974; Schuler, 1973; Downey et al., 1974; Weed et al., 1974) and in only one of these studies was the hypothesis disconfirmed (Szilagyi & Sims, 1974). Despite some inconsistency in research on supportive leadership the evidence is sufficiently positive to suggest that managers should be alert to the critical need for supportive leadership under conditions where tasks are dissatisfying, frustrating, or stressful to subordinates.

Achievement-Oriented Leadership

The theory hypothesizes that achievement-oriented leadership will cause subordinates to strive for higher standards of performance and to have more confidence in the ability to meet challenging goals. A recent study by House, Valency and Van der Krabben provides a partial test of this hypothesis among white collar employees in service organizations. For subordinates performing ambiguous, nonrepetitive tasks, they found a positive relationship between the amount of achievement orientation of the leader and subordinates' expectancy that their effort would result in effective performance. Stated less technically, for subordinates performing ambiguous, nonrepetitive tasks, the higher the achievement orientation of the leader, the more the subordinates were confident that their efforts would pay off in effective performance. For subordinates performing moderately unambiguous, repetitive tasks, there was no significant relationship between achievement-oriented leadership and subordinate expectancies that their effort would lead to effective performance. This finding held in four separate organizations.

Two plausible interpretations may be used to explain these data. First, people who select ambiguous, nonrepetitive tasks may be different in personality from those who select a repetitive job and may, therefore, be more responsive to an achievement-oriented leader. A second explanation is that achievement orientation only affects expectancies in ambiguous situations because there is more flexibility and autonomy in such tasks. Therefore, subordinates in such tasks are more likely to be able to change in response to such leadership style. Neither of the above interpretations have been tested to date; however, additional research is currently under way to investigate these relationships.

Participative Leadership

In theorizing about the effects of participative leadership it is necessary to ask about the specific characteristics of both the subordinates and their situation that would cause participative leadership to be viewed as satisfying and instrumental to effective performance.

Mitchell (1973) recently described at least four ways in which a participative leadership style would impact on subordinate attitudes and behavior as predicted by expectancy theory. First, a participative climate should increase the clarity of organizational contingencies. Through participation in decision making, subordinates should learn what leads to what. From a path-goal viewpoint participation would lead to greater clarity of the paths to various goals. A second impact of participation would be that subordinates, hopefully, should select goals they highly value. If one participates in decisions about various goals, it makes sense that this individual would select goals he or she wants. Thus, participation would increase the correspondence between organization and subordinate goals. Third, we can see how participation would increase the control the individual has over what happens on the job. If our motivation is higher (based on the preceding two points), then having greater autonomy and ability to carry out our intentions should lead to increased effort and performance. Finally, under a participative system, pressure toward high performance should come from sources other than the leader or the organization. More specifically, when people participate in the decision process they become more ego-involved; the decisions made are in some part their own. Also, their peers know what is expected and the social pressure has a greater impact. Thus, motivation to perform well stems from internal and social factors as well as formal external ones.

A number of investigations prior to the above formulation supported the idea that participation appears to be helpful (Tosi, 1970; Sadler, 1970; Wexley et al., 1973), and Mitchell (1973) presents a number of recent studies that support the above four points. However, it is also true that we would expect the relationship between a participative style and subordinate behavior to be moderated by both the personality characteristics of the subordinate and the situational demands. Studies by Tannenbaum and Allport (1956) and Vroom (1959) have shown that subordinates who prefer autonomy and self-control respond more positively to participative leadership in terms of both satisfaction and performance than subordinates who do not have such preferences. Also, the studies mentioned earlier by Runyon (1973) and

Mitchell et al. (1974) showed that subordinates who were external in orientation were less satisfied with a participative style of leadership than were internal subordinates.

House and Dessler (1974) has also reviewed these studies in an attempt to explain the ways in which the situation or environment moderates the relationship between participation and subordinate attitudes and behavior. His analysis suggests that where participative leadership is positively related to satisfaction, regardless of the predispositions of subordinates, the tasks of the subjects appear to be ambiguous and ego-involving. In the studies in which the subjects' personalities or predispositions moderate the effect of participative leadership, the tasks of the subjects are inferred to be highly routine, and/or non–ego-involving tasks.

House reasoned from this analysis that the task may have an overriding effect on the relationship between leader participation and subordinate responses, and that individual predispositions or personality characteristics of subordinates may have an effect only under some tasks. It was assumed that when task demands are ambiguous, subordinates will have a need to reduce the ambiguity. Further, it was assumed that when task demands are ambiguous, participative problem-solving between the leader and the subordinate will result in more effective decisions than when the task demands are unambiguous. Finally, it was assumed that when the subordinates are ego-involved in their tasks they are more likely to want to have a say in the decisions that affect them. Given these assumptions, the following hypotheses were formulated to account for the conflicting findings reviewed above:

1.   When subjects are highly ego-involved in a decision or a task and the decision or task demands are ambiguous, participative leadership will have a positive effect on the satisfaction and motivation of the subordinate, *regardless* of the subordinate's predisposition toward self-control, authoritarianism, or need for independence.

2.   When subordinates are not ego-involved in their tasks and the task demands are clear, subordinates who are not authoritarian and who have high needs for independence and self-control will respond favorably to leader participation and their opposite personality types will respond less favorably.

These hypotheses were derived on the basis of path-goal theorizing, i.e., the rationale guiding the analysis of prior studies was that both task characteristics and characteristics of subordinates interact to determine the effect of a specific kind of leader behavior on the satisfaction, expectancies, and performance of subordinates. To date, one major investigation (Schuler, 1974) has supported some of these predictions in which personality variables, amount of participative leadership, task ambiguity, and job satisfaction were assessed for 324 employees of an industrial manufacturing organization. As expected, in nonrepetitive, ego-involving tasks, employees (regardless of their personality) were more satisfied under a participative style than a nonparticipative style. However, in repetitive tasks which were less ego-involving the amount of authoritarianism of subordinates moderated the relationship between leadership style and satisfaction. Specifically, low authoritarian subordinates were *more satisfied* under a participative style. These findings are exactly as the theory would predict, thus it has promise in reconciling a set of confusing and contradictory findings with respect to participative leadership.

SUMMARY AND CONCLUSIONS

We have attempted to describe what we believe is a useful theoretical framework for understanding the effect of leadership behavior on subordinate satisfaction and motivation. Most theorists today have moved away from the simplistic notions that all effective leaders have a certain set of personality traits or that the situation completely determines performance. Some researchers have presented rather complex attempts at matching certain types of leaders with certain types of situations, e.g., the articles written by Vroom and Fiedler on this issue. But, we believe that a path-goal approach goes one step further. It not only suggests what type of style may be most effective in a given situation—it also attempts to explain *why* it is most effective.

We are optimistic about the future outlook of leadership research. With the guidance of path-goal theorizing, future research is expected to unravel many confusing puzzles about the reasons for and the effects of leader behavior that have, heretofore, not been solved. However, we add a word of caution: the theory, and the research on it, are relatively new to the literature of organizational behavior. Consequently, path-goal theory is offered more as a tool for directing research and stimulating insight than as a proven guide for managerial action.

REFERENCES

Dansereau, F., Jr., Cashman, J., & Graen, G. Instrumentality theory and equity theory as complementary approaches in predicting the relationship of leadership and turnover among managers. *Organizational Behavior and Human Performance*, 1973, *10*, 184–200.

Dermer, J. D. Supervisory behavior and budget motivation. Unpublished manuscript, Working paper W. P. Sloan School of Management, Massachusetts Institute of Technology, Cambridge, Mass., 1974.

Dermer, J. D., & Siegel, J. P.   A test of path goal theory: Disconfirming evidence and a critique. Mimeograph. Faculty of Management Studies, University of Toronto, 1973.

Dessler, G.   An investigation of the path goal theory of leadership. Unpublished doctoral dissertation, Bernard M. Baruch College, City University of New York, 1973.

Downey, H. K., Sheridan, J. E., & Slocum, J. W., Jr.   Analysis of relationships among leader behavior, subordinate job performance and satisfaction: A path goal approach. Mimeographed, 1974.

Evans, M. G.   The effects of supervisory behavior on the path goal relationship. *Organization Behavior and Human Performance*, 1970, 55, 277–298.

Evans, M. G.   Extensions of a path goal theory of motivation. *Journal of Applied Psychology*, 1974, 59, 172–178.

Graen, G., Dansereau, F., Jr., & Minami, T.   Disfunctional leadership styles *Organization Behavior and Human Performance*, 1972a, 7, 216–236.

Graen, G., Dansereau, F., Jr., & Minami, T.   An empirical test of the man-in-the-middle hypothesis among executives in a hierarchical organization employing a unit analysis, *Organization Behavior and Human Performance*, 1972b, 8, 161–285.

Hammer, T. H., & Dachler, H. P.   The process of supervision in the context of motivation theory. Research Report No. 3, Department of Psychology, University of Maryland, 1973.

Hill, W. A., & Ruhe, J. A.   Attitudes and behavior of black and white supervisors in problem-solving groups, *Organization Behavior and Human Performance*, in press.

House, R. J.   A path goal theory of leader effectiveness, *Administrative Science Quarterly*, September 1971, 16(3) 321–338.

House, R. J., & Dessler, G. The path goal theory of leadership: Some post hoc and a priori tests. To appear in Hunt, J. G. (Ed.) *Contingency approaches to leadership*, Carbondale, Ill.: Southern Illinois University Press, 1974.

House, R. J., Shapiro, H. J., & Wahba, M. A.   Expectancy theory as a predictor of work behavior and attitude: A re-evaluation of empirical evidence. *Decision Sciences*, in press.

House, R. J., Valency, A., & Van der Krabben, R.   Some tests and extensions of the path goal theory of leadership (in preparation).

Mitchell, T. R.   Expectancy model of job satisfaction, occupational preference and effort: A theoretical, methodological and empirical appraisal. *Psychological Bulletin*, (in press), 1974.

Mitchell, T. R., Smyser, C. R., & Weed, S. E.   Locus of control: Supervision and work satisfaction. Unpublished, Technical Report No. 74–56, University of Washington, 1974.

Mitchell, T. R.   Motivation and participation: An integration, *Academy of Management Journal,* 1973, *16* (4), 160–679.

Nebeker, D. M., & Mitchell, T. R.   Leader behavior: An expectancy theory approach. *Organizational Behavior and Human Performance,* 1974.

Runyon, K. E.   Some interactions between personality variables and management styles. *Journal of Applied Psychology,* 1973, 57 (3), 288–294.

Sadler, J.   Leadership style, confidence in management and job satisfaction, *Journal of Applied Behavioral Sciences,* 1970, 6, 3–19.

Schuler, R. S.   A path goal theory of leadership: An empirical investigation. Doctoral dissertation, Michigan State University, East Lansing, Michigan, 1973.

Schuler, R. S.   Leader participation, task structure and subordinate authoritarianism. Mimeographed. Cleveland State University, 1974.

Stinson, J. E., & Johnson, T. W.   The path goal theory of leadership: A partial test and suggested refinement. *Proceedings,* 7th Annual Conference of the Mid-West, Division of the Academy of Management, Kent, Ohio, April 1974, 18–36.

Stogdill, R. M.   *Managers, employees, organization.* Bureau of Business Research, Division of Research, College of Commerce and Administration. The Ohio State University, 1965.

Szilagyi, A. D., & Sims, H. P.   An exploration of the path goal theory of leadership in a health care environment. *Academy of Management Journal* (in press).

Tannenbaum, A. S., & Allport, F. H.   Personality structure and group structure: An interpretive study of their relationship through an event-structure hypothesis. *Journal of Abnormal and Social Psychology,* 1956, 53, 272–280.

Tosi, H.   A re-examination of personality as a determinant of the effects of participation. *Personnel Psychology,* 1970, 23, 91–99.

Vroom, V. H.   Some personality determinants of the effects of participation, *Journal of Abnormal Social Psychology,* 1959, 59, 322–327.

Weed, S. E., Mitchell, T. R., & Smyser, C. R.   A test of House's path goal theory of leadership in an organizational setting. Paper presented at Western Psychological Association, 1974.

Wexley, K. N., Singh, J. P., & Yukl, J. A.   Subordinate personality as a moderator of the effects of participation in three types of appraisal interviews. *Journal of Applied Psychology,* 1973, 83, (1), 54–59.

26

Substitutes for Leadership: Their Meaning and Measurement*

STEVEN KERR and JOHN M. JERMIER

Current theories and models of leadership seek to explain the influence of the hierarchical superior upon the satisfaction and performance of subordinates. While disagreeing with one another in important respects, these theories and models share an implicit assumption that while the style of leadership likely to be effective may vary according to the situation, *some* leadership style will be effective *regardless* of the situation. It has been found, however, that certain individual, task, and organizational variables act as "substitutes for leadership," negating the hierarchical superior's ability to exert either positive or negative influence over subordinate attitudes and effectiveness. This paper identifies a number of such substitutes for leadership, presents scales of questionnaire items for their measurement, and reports some preliminary tests.

A number of theories and models of leadership exist, each seeking to most clearly identify and best explain the presumedly powerful effects of leader behavior or personality attributes upon the satisfaction and performance of hierarchical subordinates. These theories and models fail to agree in many respects, but have in common the fact that none of them systematically accounts for very much criterion variance. It is certainly true that data indicating strong superior-subordinate relationships have sometimes been reported. In numerous studies, however, conclusions have had to be based on statistical rather than practical significance, and hypothesis support has rested upon the researcher's ability to show that the trivially low correlations obtained were not the result of chance.

Current theories and models of leadership have something else in common: a conviction that hierarchical leadership is always important. Even situational approaches to leadership share the assumption that while the *style* of leadership likely to be effective will vary ac-

* From *Organizational Behavior and Human Performance* 22, (1978), pp. 375–403.

cording to the situation, *some* leadership style will *always* be effective *regardless* of the situation. Of course, the extent to which this assumption is explicated varies greatly, as does the degree to which each theory is dependent upon the assumption. Fairly explicit is the Vertical Dyad Linkage model developed by Graen and his associates (Graen, Dansereau, & Minami, 1972; Dansereau, Cashman, & Graen, 1973), which attributes importance to hierarchical leadership without concern for the situation. The Fiedler (1964, 1967) Contingency Model also makes the general assumption that hierarchical leadership is important in situations of low, medium, and high favorableness, though predictions about relationships between LPC and performance in Octants VI and VII are qualified (Fiedler & Chemers, 1974, p. 82). Most models of decision-centralization (e.g., Tannenbaum & Schmidt, 1958; Heller & Yukl, 1969; Vroom & Yetton, 1973; Bass & Valenzi, 1974) include among their leader decision-style alternatives one whereby subordinates attempt a solution by themselves, with minimal participation by the hierarchical superior. Even in such cases, however, the leader is responsible for initiating the method through delegation of the problem, and is usually described as providing (structuring) information.

The approach to leadership which is least dependent upon the assumption articulated above, and which comes closest to the conceptualization to be proposed in this paper, is the Path-Goal Theory (House, 1971; House & Mitchell, 1974). Under circumstances when both goals and paths to goals may be clear, House and Mitchell (1974) point out that "attempts by the leader to clarify paths and goals will be both redundant and seen by subordinates as imposing unnecessary, close control." They go on to predict that "although such control may increase performance by preventing soldiering or malingering, it will also result in decreased satisfaction."

This prediction is supported in part by conclusions drawn by Kerr, Schriesheim, Murphy, and Stogdill (1974) from their review of the consideration-initiating structure literature, and is at least somewhat consistent with results from a few recent studies. A most interesting and pertinent premise of the theory, however, is that even unnecessary and redundant leader behaviors will have an impact upon subordinate satisfaction, morale, motivation, performance, and acceptance of the leader (House & Mitchell, 1974; House & Dessler, 1974). While leader attempts to clarify paths and goals are therefore recognized by Path-Goal Theory to be unnecessary and redundant in certain situations, in no situation are they explicitly hypothesized by Path-Goal (or any other leadership theory) to be irrelevant.

This lack of recognition is unfortunate. As has already been mentioned, data from numerous studies collectively demonstrate that in many situations these leader behaviors *are* irrelevant, and hierarchical leadership (as operationalized in these studies) per se does not seem to matter. In fact, leadership variables so often account for very little criterion variance that a few writers have begun to argue that the leadership construct is sterile altogether, that "the concept of leadership itself has outlived its usefulness" (Miner, 1975, p. 200). This view is also unfortunate, however, and fails to take note of accurate predictions by leadership theorists even as such theorists fail to conceptually reconcile their inaccurate predictions.

What is clearly needed to resolve this dilemma is a conceptualization adequate to explain both the occasional successes and frequent failures of the various theories and models of leadership.

SUBSTITUTES FOR LEADERSHIP

A wide variety of individual, task, and organizational characteristics have been found to influence relationships between leader behavior and subordinate satisfaction, morale, and performance. Some of these variables (for example, job pressure and subordinate expectations of leader behavior) act primarily to influence which leadership style will best permit the hierarchical superior to motivate, direct, and control subordinates. The effect of others, however, is to act as "substitutes for leadership," tending to negate the leader's ability to either improve or impair subordinate satisfaction and performance.

Substitutes for leadership are apparently prominent in many different organizational settings, but their existence is not explicated in any of the dominant leadership theories. As a result, data describing formal superior-subordinate relationships are often obtained in situations where important substitutes exist. These data logically ought to be, and usually are, insignificant, and are useful primarily as a reminder that when leadership styles are studied in circumstances where the choice of style is irrelevant, the effect is to replace the potential power of the leadership construct with the unintentional comedy of the "Law of the instrument."[1]

What is needed, then, is a taxonomy of situations where we should not be studying "leadership" (in the formal hierarchical sense) at all. Development of such a taxonomy is still at an early stage, but Woodward (1973) and Miner (1975) have laid important groundwork through their classifications of control, and some effects of nonleader sources of clarity have been considered by Hunt (Note 2) and Hunt and Osborn (1975). Reviews of the leadership literature by House and

---

[1] Abraham Kaplan (1964, p. 28) has observed: "Give a small boy a hammer, and he will find that everything he encounters needs pounding."

Mitchell (1974) and Kerr et al. (1974) have also proved pertinent in this regard, and suggest that individual, task, and organizational characteristics of the kind outlined in Table 1 will help to determine whether or not hierarchical leadership is likely to matter.

Conceptual Domain of Substitutes for Leadership. Since Table 1 is derived from previously conducted studies, substitutes are only suggested for the two leader behavior styles which dominate the research literature. The substitutes construct probably has much wider applicability, however, perhaps to hierarchical leadership in general.

It is probably useful to clarify some of the characteristics listed in Table 1. "Professional orientation" is considered a potential substitute

TABLE 1
Substitutes for Leadership

Characteristic	Will Tend to Neutralize	
	Relationship-Oriented, Supportive, People-Centered Leadership: Consideration, Support, and Interaction Facilitation	Task-Oriented, Instrumental, Job-Centered Leadership: Initiating Structure, Goal Emphasis, and Work Facilitation
Of the subordinate		
1. Ability, experience, training, knowledge		X
2. Need for independence	X	X
3. "Professional" orientation	X	X
4. Indifference toward organizational rewards	X	X
Of the task		
5. Unambiguous and routine		X
6. Methodologically invariant		X
7. Provides its own feedback concerning accomplishment		X
8. Intrinsically satisfying	X	
Of the organization		
9. Formalization (explicit plans, goals, and areas of responsibility)		X
10. Inflexibility (rigid, unbending rules and procedures)		X
11. Highly specified and active advisory and staff functions		X
12. Closely knit, cohesive work groups	X	X
13. Organizational rewards not within the leader's control	X	X
14. Spatial distance between superior and subordinates	X	X

for leadership because employees with such an orientation typically cultivate horizontal rather than vertical relationships, give greater credence to peer review processes, however informal, than to hierarchical evaluations, and tend to develop important referents external to the employing organization (Filley, House, & Kerr, 1976). Clearly, such attitudes and behaviors can sharply reduce the influence of the hierarchical superior.

"Methodologically invariant" tasks may result from serial interdependence, from machine-paced operations, or from work methods which are highly standardized. In one study (House, Filley, & Kerr, 1971, p. 26), invariance was found to derive from a network of government contracts which "specified not only the performance requirements of the end product, but also many of the management practices and control techniques that the company must follow in carrying out the contract."

Invariant methodology relates to what Miner (1975) describes as the "push" of work. Tasks which are "intrinsically satisfying" (another potential substitute listed in Table 1) contribute in turn to the "pull" of work. Miner believes that for "task control" to be effective, a force comprised of both the push and pull of work must be developed. At least in theory, however, either type alone may act as a substitute for hierarchical leadership.

Performance feedback provided by the work itself is another characteristic of the task which potentially functions in place of the formal leader. It has been reported that employees with high growth-need strength in particular derive beneficial psychological states (internal motivation, general satisfaction, work effectiveness) from clear and direct knowledge of the results of performance (Hackman & Oldham, 1976; Oldham, 1976). Task-provided feedback is often: (1) the most immediate source of feedback given the infrequency of performance appraisal sessions (Hall & Lawler, 1969); (2) the most accurate source of feedback given the problems of measuring the performance of others (Campbell, Dunnette, Lawler, & Weick, 1970); and (3) the most self-evaluation evoking and intrinsically motivating source of feedback given the controlling and informational aspects of feedback from others (DeCharms, 1968; Deci, 1972, 1975; Greller & Herold, 1975). For these reasons, the formal leader's function as a provider of role structure through performance feedback may be insignificant by comparison.

Cohesive, interdependent work groups and active advisory and staff personnel also have the ability to render the formal leader's performance feedback function inconsequential. Inherent in mature group structures are stable performance norms and positional differentiation (Bales & Strodtbeck, 1951; Borgatta & Bales, 1953; Stogdill, 1959; Lott

& Lott, 1965; Zander, 1968). Task-relevant guidance and feedback from others may be provided directly by the formal leader, indirectly by the formal leader through the primary work group members, directly by the primary work group members, by staff personnel, or by the client. If the latter four instances prevail, the formal leader's role may be quite trivial. Cohesive work groups are, of course, important sources of affiliative need satisfaction.

Programming through impersonal modes has been reported to be the most frequent type of coordination strategy employed under conditions of low-to-medium task uncertainty and low task interdependence (Van de Ven, Delbecq, & Koenig, 1976). Thus, the existence of written work goals, guidelines, and groundrules (organizational formalization) and rigid rules and procedures (organizational inflexibility) may serve as substitutes for leader-provided coordination under certain conditions. Personal and group coordination modes involving the formal leader may become important only when less costly impersonal strategies are not suitable.

ELABORATION OF THE CONSTRUCT

Table 1 was designed to capsulize our present knowledge with respect to possible substitutes for hierarchical leadership. Since present knowledge is the product of past research, and since past research was primarily unconcerned with the topic, the table is probably oversimplified and incomplete in a number of respects. Rigorous elaboration of the substitutes construct must necessarily await additional research, but we would speculate that such research would show the following refinements to be important.

Distinguishing between "Substitutes" and "Neutralizers." A *neutralizer* is defined by Webster's as something which is able to "paralyze, destroy, or counteract the effectiveness of" something else. In the context of leadership, this term may be applied to characteristics which make it effectively *impossible* for relationship and/or task-oriented leadership to make a difference. Neutralizers are a type of moderator variable when uncorrelated with both predictors and the criterion, and act as suppressor variables when correlated with predictors but not the criterion (Zedeck, 1971; Wherry, 1946).

A *substitute* is defined to be "a person or thing acting or used in place of another." In context, this term may be used to describe characteristics which render relationship and/or task-oriented leadership not only impossible but also *unnecessary*.[2] Substitutes may be corre-

---

[2] This potentially important distinction was first pointed out by M. A. Von Glinow in a doctoral seminar.

lated with both predictors and the criterion, but tend to improve the validity coefficient when included in the predictor set. That is, they will not only tend to affect which leader behaviors (if any) are influential, but will also tend to impact upon the criterion variable.

The consequences of neutralizers and substitutes for previous research have probably been similar, since both act to reduce the impact of leader behaviors upon subordinate attitudes and performance. For this reason it is not too important that such summaries of previous research as Table 1 distinguish between them. Nevertheless, an important theoretical distinction does exist. It is that substitutes do, but neutralizers do not, provide a "person or thing acting or used in place of" the formal leader's negated influence. The effect of neutralizers is therefore to create an "influence vacuum," from which a variety of dysfunctions may emerge.

As an illustration of this point, look again at the characteristics outlined in Table 1. Since each characteristic has the capacity to counteract leader influence, all 14 may clearly be termed neutralizers. It is *not* clear, however, that all 14 are substitutes. For example, subordinates' perceived "ability, experience, training, and knowledge" tend to impair the leader's influence, but may or may not act as substitutes for leadership. It is known that individuals who are high in task-related self-esteem place high value upon nonhierarchical control systems which are consistent with a belief in the competence of people (Korman, 1970). The problem is that subordinate perceptions concerning ability and knowledge may not be accurate. Actual ability and knowledge may therefore act as a substitute, while false perceptions of competence and unfounded self-esteem may produce simply a neutralizing effect.

"Spatial distance," "subordinate indifference toward organizational rewards," and "organizational rewards not within the leader's control" are other examples of characteristics which do not render formal leadership unnecessary, but merely create circumstances in which effective leadership may be impossible. If rewards are clearly within the control of some other person this other person can probably act as a substitute for the formal leader, and no adverse consequences (except probably to the leader's morale) need result. When no one knows where control over rewards lies, however, or when rewards are linked rigidly to seniority or to other factors beyond anyone's control, or when rewards are perceived to be unattractive altogether, the resulting influence vacuum would almost inevitably be dysfunctional.

Distinguishing between Direct and Indirect Leader Behavior Effects. It is possible to conceptualize a *direct effect* of leadership as one which occurs when a subordinate is influenced by some leader behavior *in and of itself*. An *indirect effect* may be said to result when the subordinate is influenced by the *implications* of the behavior for some future consequence. Attempts by the leader to influence subordinates must always produce direct and/or indirect effects or, when strong substitutes for leadership exist, no effect.

This distinction between direct and indirect effects of leader behavior has received very little attention, but its importance to any discussion of leadership substitutes is considerable. For example, in their review of path-goal theory, House and Dessler (1974, p. 31) state that "subordinates with high needs for affiliation and social approval would see friendly, considerate leader behavior as an immediate source of satisfaction" (direct effect). As Table 1 suggests, it is conceivable that fellow group members could supply such subordinates with enough affiliation and social approval to eliminate dependence on the leader. With other subordinates, however, the key "may be not so much in terms of what the leader does but may be in terms of how it is *interpreted* by his members" (Graen et al., 1972, p. 235). Graen et al. concluded from their data that "consideration is interpreted as the leader's evaluation of the member's role behavior. . ." (p. 233). For these subordinates, therefore, consideration seems to have been influential primarily because of its perceived implications for the likelihood of receiving future rewards. In this case the effect is an indirect one, for which group member approval and affiliation probably cannot substitute.

In the same vein, we are told by House and Dessler (1974, pp. 31–32) that:

> Subordinates with high needs for achievement would be predicted to view leader behavior that clarifies path-goal relationships and provides goal-oriented feedback as satisfying. Subordinates with high needs for extrinsic rewards would be predicted to see leader directiveness or coaching behavior as instrumental to their satisfaction if such behavior helped them perform in such a manner as to gain recognition, promotion, security, or pay increases.

It is apparent from House and Dessler's remarks that the distinction between direct and indirect effects need not be limited to relationship-oriented behaviors. Such characteristics of the task as the fact that it "provides its own feedback" (listed in Table 1 as a potential substitute for task-oriented behavior) may provide achievement-oriented subordinates with immediate satisfaction (direct effect), but fail to negate the superior's ability to help subordinates perform so as to obtain future rewards (indirect effect). Conversely, subordinate experience and training may act as substitutes for the indirect effects of task-oriented leadership, by preventing the leader from improving subordinate performance, but may not offset the direct effects.

Identifying Other Characteristics and Other Leader Behaviors.
Any elaboration of the substitutes construct must necessarily include
the specification of other leader behaviors, and other characteristics
which may act as substitutes for leader behaviors. As was mentioned
earlier, most previous studies of leadership were concerned with only
two of its dimensions. This approach is intuitively indefensible.
Richer conceptualizations of the leadership process already exist, and
almost inevitably underscore the importance of additional leader activities. As these activities are delineated in future research, it is likely
that substitutes for them will also be identified.

Table 2 is offered as a guide to research. It portrays a state of increased sophistication of the substitutes construct, assuming future
development along lines suggested in this section. Substitutes would
be differentiated from neutralizers, and direct effects of leadership
empirically distinguished from indirect effects. The columns on the
right are intended to represent as-yet-unexplored leader behaviors,
and the dotted lines on the bottom indicate the presence of additional
characteristics which may act either as neutralizers, or as true substitutes for leadership.

Distinguishing between Cause and Effect in Leader Behavior.
Another area where the substitutes construct appears to have implications for leadership research concerns the question of causality. It is
now evident from a variety of laboratory experiments and longitudinal
field studies that leader behavior may result from as well as cause
subordinate attitudes and performance. It is possible to speculate
upon the effect that leadership substitutes would have on the relative
causal strength of superior- and subordinate-related variables. This
paper has tried to show that such substitutes act to reduce changes in
subordinates' attitudes and performance which are *caused* be leader
behaviors. On the other hand, there seems no reason why leadership
substitutes should prevent changes in leader behavior which *result*
from different levels of subordinate performance, satisfaction, and morale. The substitutes for leadership construct may therefore help to
explain why the direction of causality is sometimes predominantly
from leader behavior to subordinate outcomes, while at other times
the reverse is true.

*Specification of Interaction Effects among Substitutes and Neutral-
izers.* From the limited data obtained thus far, it is not possible to
differentiate at all among leadership substitutes and neutralizers in
terms of relative strength and predictive capability. We have received
some indication that the strength of a substitute, as measured by its
mean level, is not strongly related to its predictive power. Substitutes
for leadership as theoretically important as intrinsic satisfaction, for
example, apparently need only be present in moderate amounts.

TABLE 2
Substitutes for Leadership: A Theoretical Extension

Characteristic	Will Act as a Substitute for					
	Relationship-Oriented, Supportive, People-Centered Leadership (Consideration, Support, and Interaction Facilitation):		Task-Oriented, Instrumental, Job-Centered Leadership (Initiating Structure, Goal Emphasis, and Work Facilitation):		(Other Leader Behaviors . . .)	
	Directly	Indirectly	Directly	Indirectly	Directly	Indirectly
Substitutes						
Of the subordinate						
1. Ability			X	X	?	?
3. "Professional" orientation		X		X	?	?
Of the task						
5. Unambiguous and routine			X	X	?	?
7. Provides its own feedback concerning accomplishment			X		?	?
8. Intrinsically satisfying	X				?	?
Of the organization						
12. Closely knit, cohesive work groups	X		X	X	?	?
Neutralizers						
4. Indifference toward organizational rewards		X		X	?	?
13. Organizational rewards not within the leader's control		X		X	?	?

Other, less important substitutes and neutralizers, might have to be present to a tremendous degree before their effects might be felt. Clearly, the data reported in this study are insufficient to determine at what point a particular substitute becomes important, or at what point several substitutes, each fairly weak by itself, might combine to collectively impair hierarchical leader influence. Multiplicative functions involving information on the strength and predictive power of substitutes for leadership should be able to be specified as evidence accumulates.

CONCLUSIONS

The research literature provides abundant evidence that for organization members to maximize organizational and personal outcomes, they must be able to obtain both guidance and good feelings from their work settings. Guidance is usually offered in the form of role or task structuring, while good feelings may stem from "stroking" behaviors,[3] or may be derived from intrinsic satisfaction associated with the task itself.

The research literature does *not* suggest that guidance and good feelings must be provided by the hierarchical superior; it is only necessary that they somehow be provided. Certainly the formal leader represents a potential source of structuring and stroking behaviors, but many other organization members do too, and impersonal equivalents also exist. To the extent that other potential sources are deficient, the hierarchical superior is clearly in a position to play a dominant role. In these situations the opportunity for leader downward influence is great, and formal leadership ought to be important. To the extent that other sources provide structure and stroking in abundance, the hierarchical leader will have little chance to exert downward influence. In such cases it is of small value to gain entree to the organization, distribute leader behavior questionnaires to anything that moves, and later debate about which leadership theory best accounts for the pitifully small percentage of variance explained, while remaining uncurious about the large percentage unexplained.

Of course, few organizations would be expected to have leadership substitutes so strong as to totally overwhelm the leader, or so weak as to require subordinates to rely entirely on him. In most organizations it is likely that, as was true here, substitutes exist for some leader activities but not for others. Effective leadership might therefore be described as the ability to supply subordinates with needed guidance

---

[3] *Stroking* is used here, as in transactional analysis, to describe "any type of physical, oral, or visual recognition of one person by another" (Huse, 1975, p. 288).

and good feelings which are not being supplied by other sources. From this viewpoint it is inaccurate to inform leaders (say, in management development programs) that they are incompetent if they do not personally provide these things regardless of the situation. While it may (or may not) be necessary that the organization as a whole function in a "9–9" manner (Blake & Mouton, 1964), it clearly is unnecessary for the manager to behave in such a manner unless no substitutes for leader-provided guidance and good feelings exist.

Dubin (1976, p. 33) draws a nice distinction between "proving" and "improving" a theory, and points out that "if the purpose is to prove the adequacy of the theoretical model . . . data are likely to be collected for values on only those units incorporated in the theoretical model. This usually means that, either experimentally or by discarding data, attention in the empirical research is focused solely upon values measured on units incorporated in the theory."

In Dubin's terms, if we are really interested in improving rather than proving our various theories and models of leadership, a logical first step is that we stop assuming what really needs to be demonstrated empirically. The criticality of the leader's role in supplying necessary structure and stroking should be evaluated in the broader organizational context. Data pertaining to both leadership and possible substitutes for leadership (Table 1) should be obtained, and both main and interaction effects examined. A somewhat different use of information about substitutes for leadership would be as a "pre-screen," to assess the appropriateness of a potential sample for a hierarchical leadership study.

What this all adds up to is that, if we really want to know more about the sources and consequences of guidance and good feelings in organizations, we should be prepared to study these things *whether or not* they happen to be provided through hierarchical leadership. For those not so catholic, whose interest lies in the derivation and refinement of theories of formal leadership, a commitment should be made to the importance of developing and operationalizing a *true* situational theory of leadership, one which will explicitly limit its propositions and restrict its predictions *to those situations* where hierarchical leadership theoretically ought to make a difference.

REFERENCES

Bales, R., & Strodtbeck, F.   Phases in group problem solving. *Journal of Abnormal and Social Psychology*, 1951, **46**, 485–495.

Bass, B., & Valenzi, E.   Contingent aspects of effective management styles. In J. G. Hunt & L. L. Larson (Eds.), *Contingency approaches to leadership*. Carbondale: Southern Illinois Press, 1974.

Blake, R., & Mouton, J. *The managerial grid*. Houston: Gulf, 1964.

Borgatta, E., & Bales, R. Task and accumulation of experience as factors in the interaction of small groups. *Sociometry*, 1953, **16**, 239–252.

Campbell, J., Dunnette, E., Lawler, E., & Weick, K. *Managerial behavior, performance and effectiveness*. New York: McGraw-Hill, 1970.

Dansereau, F., Cashman, J., & Graen, G. Instrumentality theory and equity theory as complementary approaches in predicting the relationship of leadership and turnover among managers. *Organizational Behavior and Human Performance*, 1973, **10**, 184–200.

DeCharms, R. *Personal causation*. New York: Academic Press, 1968.

Deci, E. Intrinsic motivation, extrinsic reinforcement, and inequity. *Journal of Personality and Social Psychology*, 1972, **22**, 113–120.

Deci, E. *Intrinsic motivation*. New York: Plenum, 1975.

Dubin, R. Theory building in applied areas. In M. Dunnette (Ed.), *Handbook of industrial and organizational psychology*. Skokie, Ill.: Rand McNally,1976.

Fiedler, F. E. A contingency model of leadership effectiveness. In L. Berkowitz (Ed.), *Advances in experimental social psychology*. New York: Academic Press, 1964.

Fiedler, F. E. *A theory of leadership effectiveness*. New York: McGraw-Hill, 1967.

Fiedler, F. E., & Chemers, M. M. *Leadership and effective management*. Glenview, Ill.: Scott, Foresman, 1974.

Filley, A. C., House, R. J., & Kerr, S. *Managerial process and organizational behavior* (2nd ed.). Glenview, Ill.: Scott, Foresman, 1976.

Graen, G., Dansereau, F., Jr., & Minami, T. Dysfunctional leadership styles. *Organizational Behavior and Human Performance*, 1972, **7**, 216–236.

Greller, M., & Herold, D. Sources of feedback: A preliminary investigation. *Organizational Behavior and Human Performance*, 1975, **13**, 244–256.

Hackman, R., & Oldham, G. Motivation through the design of work: Test of a theory. *Organizational Behavior and Human Performance*, 1976, **16**, 250–279.

Hall, D., & Lawler, E. Unused potential in R and D labs. *Research Management*, 1969, **12**, 339–354.

Heller, F. A., & Yukl, G. Participation, managerial decision making, and situational variables. *Organizational Behavior and Human Performance*, 1969, **4**, 227–234.

House, R. J. A path-goal theory of leader effectiveness. *Administrative Science Quarterly*, 1971, **16**, 321–338.

House, R. J., & Dessler, G. The path-goal theory of leadership: Some post hoc and a priori tests. In J. G. Hunt & L. L. Larson (Eds.), *Contingency approaches to leadership*. Carbondale: Southern Illinois University Press, 1974.

House, R. J., Filley, A. C., & Kerr, S. Relation of leader consideration and initiating structure to R and D subordinates' satisfaction. *Administrative Science Quarterly*, 1971, **16**, 19–30.

House, R. J., & Mitchell, T. R. Path-goal theory of leadership. *Journal of Contemporary Business*, 1974, **3**, 81–97.

Hunt, J. G., & Osborn, R. N.   An adaptive-reactive theory of leadership: The role of macro variables in leadership research. In J. G. Hunt & L. L. Larson (Eds.), *Leadership frontiers*. Carbondale: Southern Illinois University Press, 1975.

Huse, E. F.   *Organization development and change*. St. Paul: West, 1975.

Kaplan, Abraham.   *The conduct of inquiry*. San Francisco: Chandler, 1964.

Kerr, S., Schriesheim, C., Murphy, C. J., & Stogdill, R. M.   Toward a contingency theory of leadership based upon the consideration and initiating structure literature. *Organizational Behavior and Human Performance*, 1974, **12**, 62–82.

Korman, A.   Toward a hypothesis of work behavior. *Journal of Applied Psychology*, 1970, **54**, 31–41.

Lott, A., & Lott, B.   Group cohesiveness as interpersonal attraction: A review of relationships with antecedent and consequent variables. *Psychological Bulletin*, 1965, **64**, 259–302.

Miner, J.   The uncertain future of the leadership concept: An overview. In J. G. Hunt & L. L. Larson (Eds.), *Leadership frontiers*. Carbondale: Southern Illinois Press, 1975.

Oldham, G.   Job characteristics and internal motivation: The moderating effect of interpersonal and individual variables. *Human Relations* 1976, **29**, 559–570.

Stogdill, R.   *Individual behavior and group achievement*. New York: Oxford University Press, 1959.

Tannenbaum, R., & Schmidt, W.   How to choose a leadership pattern. *Harvard Business Review*, 1958, **36**, 95–101.

Van de Ven, A., Delbecq, A., & Koenig, R.   Determinants of coordination modes within organizations. *American Sociological Review*, 1976, **41**, 322–338.

Vroom, V., & Yetton, P.   *Leadership and decision making*. Pittsburgh: University of Pittsburgh Press, 1973.

Wherry, R.   Test selection and suppressor variables. *Psychometrika*, 1946, **11**, 239–247.

Woodward, J.   Technology, material control, and organizational behavior. In A. Negandhi (Ed.), *Modern organization theory*. Kent: Kent State University, 1973.

Zander, A.   Group aspirations. In D. Cartwright & A. Zander (Eds.), *Group dynamics: Research and theory* (3d ed.), New York: Harper & Row, 1968.

Zedeck, S.   Problems with the use of "moderator" variables. *Psychological Bulletin*, 1971, **76**, 295–310.

REFERENCE NOTES

1.   Bish, J., & Schriesheim, C.   *An exploratory analysis of Form XII of The Ohio State Leadership Scales*. Paper presented at the National Academy of Management Conference, 1974.

2.   Hunt, J.   *Different nonleader clarity sources as alternatives to leadership*. Paper presented at the Eastern Academy of Management Conference, 1975.

3. Schriesheim, C. *The development and validation of instrumental and supportive leadership scales and their application to some tests of path-goal theory of leadership hypotheses.* Unpublished doctoral dissertation. The Ohio State University, 1978.
4. Wigdor, L. *Effectiveness of various management and organizational characteristics on employee satisfaction and performance as a function of the employee's need for job independence.* Unpublished doctoral dissertation, City University of New York, 1969.

27

Human Relations or Human Resources?*

RAYMOND E. MILES

The proselyting efforts of the advocates of participative management appear to have paid off. The typical modern manager, on paper at least, broadly endorses participation and rejects traditional, autocratic concepts of leadership and control as no longer acceptable or, perhaps, no longer legitimate.

However, while participation has apparently been well merchandised and widely purchased, there seems to be a great deal of confusion about what has been sold and what has been bought. Managers do not appear to have accepted a single, logically consistent concept of participation. In fact, there is reason to believe that managers have adopted two different theories or models of participation—one for themselves and one for their subordinates.

These statements reflect both my analysis of the development of the theory of participative management and my interpretation of managers' attitudes toward these concepts.

My views are based in part on a number of recent surveys of managers' beliefs and opinions. The most recent of these studies, which I conducted, was begun with a group of 215 middle and upper level managers in West Coast companies, and has been continued with a sample of over 300 administrators from public agencies.[1] This study was designed to clarify further certain aspects of managers' attitudes uncovered by earlier research under the direction of Dale Yoder of Stanford[2] and Profs. Mason Haire, Edwin Ghiselli, and Lyman Porter of the University of California, Berkeley.[3]

This series of studies involved the collection of questionnaire data on managers' opinions about people and on their attitudes toward various leadership policies and practices. Several thousand managers in all, both here and abroad, have participated.

This article is not intended to summarize all of the findings on managers' leadership attitudes available from these studies. Rather, my primary purpose is to construct a theoretical framework that may explain some of the principal dimensions of managers' views and some of the implications of their beliefs and opinions, drawing on the research simply to illustrate my views.

Participative Theories

While the suggestion that managers have accepted a two-sided approach to participation may be disturbing, it should not be too surprising. Management theorists have frequently failed to deal with participation in a thorough and consistent manner. Indeed, from an examination of their somewhat ambivalent treatment of this concept, it is possible to conclude that they have been selling two significantly different models of participative management.

One of the scholars' models, which we will designate the *human relations* model, closely resembles the concept of participation which managers appear to accept for use with their own subordinates.

The second, and not yet fully developed, theory, which I have labeled the *human resources* model, prescribes the sort of participative policies that managers would apparently like their superiors to follow.

---

[1] See Raymond E. Miles, "Conflicting Elements in Managerial Ideologies," *Industrial Relations,* October 1964, pp. 77–91. The subsequent research with public administrators is still being conducted, and reports have not yet been published.

[2] See Dale Yoder, "Management Theories as Managers See Them," *Personnel,* July–August 1962, pp. 25–30; "Management Policies for the Future," *Personnel Administration,* September–October 1962, pp. 11–14 ff.; Dale Yoder et al., "Managers' Theories of Management," *Journal of the Academy of Management,* September 1963, pp. 204–211.

[3] See Mason Haire, Edwin Ghiselli, and Lyman W. Porter, "Cultural Patterns in the Role of the Manager," *Industrial Relations,* February 1963, pp. 95–117, for a report on the Berkeley studies.

I shall develop and examine these two models, compare them with managers' expressed beliefs, and consider some of the implications of managers' dual allegiance to them.

Both the *human relations* and the *human resources* models have three basic components:

1. A set of assumptions about people's values and capabilities.
2. Certain prescriptions as to the amount and kind of participative policies and practices that managers should follow, in keeping with their assumptions about people.
3. A set of expectations with respect to the effects of participation on subordinate morale and performance.

This third component contains the model's explanation of how and why participation works—that is, the purpose of participation and how it accomplishes this purpose. In outline form, the models may be summarized as shown in Exhibit 1.

Human Relations Model

This approach is not new. As early as the 1920s, business spokesmen began to challenge the classical autocratic philosophy of man-

---

EXHIBIT 1
Two Models of Participative Leadership

Human Relations	*Human Resources*
Attitudes toward People	
1. People in our culture share a common set of needs—to belong, to be liked, to be respected.	1. In addition to sharing common needs for belonging and respect, most people in our culture desire to contribute effectively and creatively to the accomplishment of worthwhile objectives.
2. They desire individual recognition but, more than this, they want to feel a useful part of the company and their own work group or department.	2. The majority of our work force is capable of exercising far more initiative, responsibility, and creativity than their present jobs require or allow.
3. They will tend to cooperate willingly and comply with organizational goals if these important needs are fulfilled.	3. These capabilities represent untapped resources which are presently being wasted.
Kind and Amount of Participation	
1. The manager's basic task is to make each worker believe that he is a useful and important part of the department "team."	1. The manager's basic task is to create an environment in which his subordinates can contribute their full range of talents to the accomplishment of organizational goals. He must attempt to uncover and tap the creative resources of his subordinates.

EXHIBIT 1 *(concluded)*

Human Relations	Human Resources
2. The manager should be willing to explain his decisions and to discuss his subordinates' objections to his plans. On routine matters, he should encourage his subordinates to participate in planning and choosing among alternative solutions to problems.	2. The manager should allow, and encourage his subordinates to participate not only in routine decisions but in important matters as well. In fact, the more important a decision is to the manager's department, the greater should be his effort to tap the department's resources.
3. Within narrow limits, the work group or individual subordinates should be allowed to exercise self-direction and self-control in carrying out plans.	3. The manager should attempt to continually expand the areas over which his subordinates exercise self-direction and self-control as they develop and demonstrate greater insight and ability.

Expectations

1. Sharing information with subordinates and involving them in departmental decision making will help satisfy their basic needs for belonging and for individual recognition.	1. The overall quality of decision making and performance will improve as the manager makes use of the full range of experience, insight, and creative ability in his department.
2. Satisfying these needs will improve subordinate morale and reduce resistance to formal authority.	2. Subordinates will exercise responsible self-direction and self-control in the accomplishment of worthwhile objectives that they understand and have helped establish.
3. High employee morale and reduced resistance to formal authority may lead to improved departmental performance. It should at least reduce intradepartment friction and thus make the manager's job easier.	3. Subordinate satisfaction will increase as a by-product of improved performance and the opportunity to contribute creatively to this improvement.

Note: It may fairly be argued that what I call the *human relations* model is actually the product of popularization and misunderstanding of the work of pioneers in this field. Moreover, it is true that some of the early research and writings of the human relationists contain concepts which seem to fall within the framework of what I call the *human resources* model. Nevertheless, it is my opinion that while the early writers did not advocate the *human relations* model as presented here, their failure to emphasize certain of the *human resources* concepts left their work open to the misinterpretations which have occurred.

agement. The employee was no longer pictured as merely an appendage to a machine, seeking only economic rewards from his work. Managers were instructed to consider him as a "whole man" rather than as merely a bundle of skills and aptitudes.[4] They were urged to create a "sense of satisfaction" among their subordinates by showing interest in the employees' personal success and welfare. As Bendix notes, the "failure to treat workers as human beings came to be re-

---

[4] See Reinhard Bendix, *Work and Authority in Industry* (New York: John Wiley & Sons, 1956), pp. 287–340.

garded as the cause of low morale, poor craftsmanship, unresponsive-
ness, and confusion."[5]

The key element in the *human relations* approach is its basic objective of making organizational members *feel* a useful and important part
of the overall effort. This process is viewed as the means of accomplishing the ultimate goal of building a cooperative and compliant
work force. Participation, in this model, is a lubricant which oils away
resistance to formal authority. By discussing problems with his subordinates and acknowledging their individual needs and desires, the
manager hopes to build a cohesive work team that is willing and anxious to tangle with organizational problems.

One further clue to the way in which participation is viewed in this
approach is provided in Dubin's concept of "privilege pay."[6] The
manager "buys" cooperation by letting his subordinates in on departmental information and allowing them to discuss and state their
opinions on various departmental problems. He "pays a price" for
allowing his subordinates the privilege of participating in certain decisions and exercising some self-direction. In return he hopes to obtain
their cooperation in carrying out these and other decisions for the
accomplishment of departmental objectives.

Implicit in this model is the idea that it might actually be easier and
more efficient if the manager could merely make departmental decisions without bothering to involve his subordinates. However, as the
advocates of this model point out, there are two parts to any
decision—(1) the making of the decision and (2) the activities required
to carry it out. In many instances, this model suggests, the manager
might do better to "waste time" in discussing the problem with his
subordinates, and perhaps even to accept suggestions that he believes
may be less efficient, in order to get the decision carried out.

In sum, the *human relations* approach does not bring out the fact
that participation may be useful for its own sake. The possibility that
subordinates will, in fact, bring to light points which the manager may
have overlooked, if considered at all, tends to be mentioned only in
passing. This is treated as a potential side benefit which, while not
normally expected, may occasionally occur. Instead, the manager is
urged to adopt participative leadership policies as the least-cost
method of obtaining cooperation and getting his decisions accepted.

In many ways the *human relations* model represents only a slight
departure from traditional autocratic models of management. The

---

[5] Ibid., p. 294.

[6] Robert Dubin, *The World of Work* (Englewood Cliffs: N.J., Prentice-Hall, 1958),
pp. 243–244. It should be noted that Dubin treats the concept of privilege pay within a
framework which goes beyond the *human relations* approach and, in some respects, is
close to the *human resources* model.

method of achieving results is different, and employees are viewed in more humanistic terms, but the basic roles of the manager and his subordinates remain essentially the same. The ultimate goal sought in both the traditional and the *human relations* model is compliance with managerial authority.

Human Resources Model

This approach represents a dramatic departure from traditional concepts of management. Though not yet fully developed, it is emerging from the writings of McGregor, Likert, Haire, and others as a new and significant contribution to management thought.[7] The magnitude of its departure from previous models is illustrated first of all in its basic assumptions concerning people's values and abilities, which focus attention on all organization members as reservoirs of untapped resources. These resources include not only physical skills and energy, but also creative ability and the capacity for responsible, self-directed, self-controlled behavior. Given these assumptions about people, the manager's job cannot be viewed merely as one of giving direction and obtaining cooperation. Instead, his primary task becomes that of creating an environment in which the total resources of his department can be utilized.

The second point at which the *human resources* model differs dramatically from previous models is in its views on the purpose and goal of participation. In this model the manager does not share information, discuss departmental decisions, or encourage self-direction and self-control merely to improve subordinate satisfaction and morale. Rather, the purpose of these practices is to improve the decision making and total performance efficiency of the organization. The *human resources* model suggests that many decisions may actually be made more efficiently by those directly involved in and affected by the decisions.

Similarly, this model implies that control is often most efficiently exercised by those directly involved in the work in process, rather than by someone or some group removed from the actual point of operation. Moreover, the *human resources* model does not suggest that the manager allow participation only in routine decisions. Instead, it implies that the more important the decision, the greater is his *obligation* to encourage ideas and suggestions from his subordinates.

In the same vein, this model does not suggest that the manager

---

[7] See particularly Douglas McGregor, *The Human Side of Enterprise* (New York: McGraw-Hill, 1960); Rensis Likert, *New Patterns of Management* (New York: McGraw-Hill, 1961); and Mason Haire, "The Concept of Power and the Concept of Man," in *Social Science Approaches to Business Behavior*, ed. George Strother (Homewood, Ill.: The Dorsey Press, Inc., 1962), pp. 163–183.

allow his subordinates to exercise self-direction and self-control only when they are carrying out relatively unimportant assignments. In fact, it suggests that the area over which subordinates exercise self-direction and control should be continually broadened in keeping with their growing experience and ability.

The crucial point at which this model differs dramatically from other models is in its explanation of the causal relationship between satisfaction and performance. In the *human relations* approach improvement in subordinate satisfaction is viewed as an intervening variable which is the ultimate cause of improved performance. Diagrammatically, the causal relationship can be illustrated as in Exhibit 2.

In the *human resources* model the causal relationship between satisfaction and performance is viewed quite differently. Increased

EXHIBIT 2
Human Relations Model

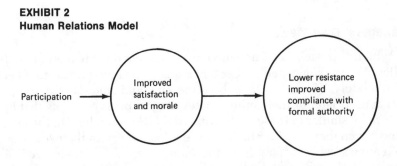

subordinate satisfaction is not pictured as the primary cause of improved performance; improvement results directly from creative contributions which subordinates make to departmental decision making, direction, and control. Subordinates' satisfaction is viewed instead as a by-product of the process—the result of their having made significant contributions to organizational success. In diagram form the *human resources* model can be illustrated as in Exhibit 3.

The *human resources* model does not deny a relationship between participation and morale. It suggests that subordinates' satisfaction may well increase as they play more and more meaningful roles in decision making and control. Moreover, the model recognizes that improvements in morale may not only set the stage for expanded participation, but create an atmosphere which supports creative problem solving. Nevertheless, this model rejects as unsupported the concept that the improvement of morale is a necessary or sufficient cause of improved decision making and control. Those improvements come directly from the full utilization of the organization's resources.

EXHIBIT 3
Human Resources Model

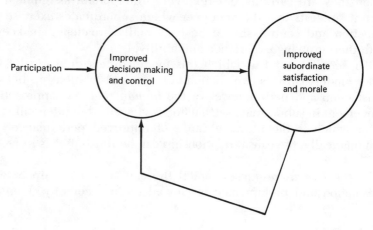

Managers' Own Views

Which approach to participative management do managers actually follow? It was suggested earlier that managers' views appear to reflect both models. When they talk about the kind and amount of participation appropriate for their subordinates, they express concepts that appear to be similar to those in the *human relations* model. On the other hand, when they consider their own relationships with their superiors, their views seem to flow from the *human resources* model. A brief review of the relevant findings suggests some of the bases for this interpretation.

Participation for Subordinates.   When we look at managers' views on the use of participative policies and practices with the subordinates who report to them, two points seem clear:

1.   Managers generally accept and endorse the use of participative concepts.
2.   However, they frequently doubt their subordinates' capacity for self-direction and self-control, and their ability to contribute creatively to departmental decision making.

In the Stanford studies, an overwhelming majority of managers indicated their agreement with statements emphasizing the desirability of subordinate participation in decision making.[8] In the Berkeley studies, a majority of the managers in each of 11 countries, including the United States, indicated their agreement with such concepts as sharing information with subordinates and increasing subordinate in-

---

[8] Yoder et al., "Managers' Theories of Management," pp. 204–211.

fluence and self-control.[9] Similarly, in my recent studies, managers overwhelmingly endorsed participative leadership policies.

On the other hand, while managers appear to have great faith in participative policies, they do not indicate such strong belief in their subordinates' capabilities. For example, the Berkeley group in their international study found that managers tended to have a "basic lack of confidence in others" and typically did not believe that capacity for leadership and initiative was widely distributed among subordinates.[10] In my own study, managers in every group to date have rated their subordinates and rank-and-file employees well below themselves, particularly on such important managerial traits as *responsibility, judgment,* and *initiative.*

But if managers do not expect creative, meaningful contributions from their subordinates, why do they advocate participative management? A reasonable answer seems to be that they advocate participative concepts as a means of improving subordinate morale and satisfaction. This interpretation gains support from my recent studies. Here, managers were asked to indicate their agreement or disagreement with statements predicting improved morale and satisfaction and statements predicting improved performance as the result of following various participative leadership policies. In connection with each of these policies, managers indicated consistently greater agreement with the predictions of improved morale than with the predictions of improved performance.

The fact that managers appear to have serious doubts about the values and capabilities of those reporting to them seems to rule out their acceptance of the *human resources* model for use with their subordinates. On the other hand, the fact that they do endorse participation and seem quite certain about its positive impact on morale suggests a close relationship between their views and those expressed in the *human relations* model. Moreover, the types of participative policies which managers most strongly advocate seem to support this interpretation.

In my research, managers indicate strongest agreement with policies that advocate sharing information and discussing objectives with subordinates. However, they tend to be somewhat less enamored with the policies which suggest increasing subordinate self-direction and self-control. This pattern of participation seems much closer to that of the *human relations* approach than to the pattern advocated in the *human resources* model.

Participation for Themselves.   When I examined managers' views

---

[9] Haire, Ghiselli, and Porter, "Cultural Patterns," pp. 95–117.
[10] Ibid.

toward their relationships with their own superiors, a much different pattern of responses became evident:

1. Managers in my studies tend to see little, if any, difference between their own capabilities and those of their superiors. In fact, they tend to rate themselves equal to, if not higher than, their superiors on such traits as *creativity, ingenuity, flexibility,* and *willingness to change.*
2. When asked to indicate at which levels in their organizations they feel each of the participative policies would be most appropriate, managers invariably feel most strongly that the full range of participative policies should be used by their own superiors.

More importantly, they also tend to be most certain that these participative policies will result in improved organizational performance *at their own level.*

Thus, when managers discuss the type of participative policies which their superiors should follow with managers at their own level, they appear to espouse the *human resources* model. They see themselves as reservoirs of creative resources. Moreover, the fact that they frequently view themselves as more flexible and willing to change than their superiors suggests that they feel their resources are frequently wasted. Correspondingly, they expect improvement in organizational performance to result from greater freedom for self-direction and self-control on their part.

Reasons behind Views

If the evidence of the current survey does represent managers' attitudes toward participative leadership, one serious question immediately comes to mind. How can managers desire one type of authority and control relationship with their superiors and at the same time advocate another type with their subordinates? A general answer, of course, is that this pattern of attitudes is just human nature. We tend not only to think more highly of ourselves than we do of others, but also to want more than we are willing to give. There are, however, other logical, more specific explanations for managers' reluctance to accept the *human resources* model for use with their subordinates.

In the first place, the *human relations* model has been around much longer, and an exceptionally good selling job has been done in its behalf. The causal relationship among participation, satisfaction, and performance, despite a lack of empirical validation, has become common wisdom. The *human resources* model, on the other hand, has not been as fully or systematically developed, and has not been the subject of as hard a sell. Managers may "feel" some of the concepts expressed in the *human resources* model and intuitively grasp some of their implications for their relationships with their superiors, but little pressure has been put on them to translate their attitudes into a systematic model for use with their subordinates.

A second explanation for managers' failure to accept the *human resources* model for use with their subordinates is that they are simply reluctant to "buy" a theory that challenges concepts to which they are deeply and emotionally attached. There is no question that the *human resources* model does attack a number of traditional management concepts. Two of the bedrock concepts that are directly challenged deal with: (1) the origins and applicability of management prerogatives, and (2) the source and limits of control.

The *human resources* model recognizes no definable, immutable set of management prerogatives. It does not accept the classical division between those who think and command and those who obey and perform. Instead, it argues that the solution to any given problem may arise from a variety of sources, and that to think of management (or any other group) as sufficient in and of itself to make all decisions is misleading and wasteful.

This approach does not directly challenge the "legal" right of management to command. It suggests, however, that there is a higher "law of the situation" that thoughtful managers will usually observe, deferring to expertise wherever it may be found. In this model the manager's basic obligation is not to the "management team" but to the accomplishment of departmental and organizational objectives. The criterion of success, therefore, is not the extent to which orders are carried out but the results obtained.

Admitting that he may not have all the answers is as difficult for the manager as for any of the rest of us. He has been taught to hide his deficiencies, not to advertise them. Holding on to information, maintaining close control, and reserving the right to make all decisions are ways by which the manager can ensure his importance. Further, many organizations have reinforced this type of behavior either (*a*) by failing to emphasize the manager's obligation to develop and utilize his human resources or (*b*) by failing to reward him when he does make this effort.

In the area of control the *human resources* model challenges the traditional concept that control is a scarce resource. In traditional theory there is presumed to be a virtually fixed amount of control. This fixed amount can be distributed in a variety of ways, but control given to one group must eventually be taken away from another. Given this concept, the manager is reluctant to allow his subordinates any real degree of self-control—what he gives up to them, he loses himself. In fact, it is frequently this basic fear of losing control which limits the amount of participation that managers are willing to allow.

The *human resources* model does not accept this lump-of-control theory. Instead, it argues that the manager increases his total control over the accomplishment of departmental objectives by encouraging self-control on the part of his subordinates. Control is thus an additive and an expanding phenomenon. Where subordinates are concerned with accomplishing goals and exercising self-direction and self-control, their combined efforts will far outweigh the results of the exercise of any amount of control by the manager.

Moreover, the fact that subordinates desire to exercise greater self-control does not mean that they reject the manager's legitimate concern for goal accomplishment. Rather, there is evidence that they in fact seek a partnership that will allow them to play a larger role, yet also will allow for a corresponding increase in management's control activity.[11]

In all, the fact that managers are reluctant to adopt a model which forces them to rethink, and perhaps restructure, their perceptions of their own roles and functions is not surprising. It is also not surprising that some writers in this field have hesitated to advocate a model which challenges such deeply held concepts. The *human relations* approach is easy to "buy," since it does not challenge the manager's basic role or status. It is correspondingly easy to sell, since it promises much and actually demands little. The *human resources* model, on the other hand, promises much but also demands a great deal from the manager. It requires that he undertake the responsibility of utilizing all the resources available to him—his own and those of his subordinates. It does not suggest that it will make his job easier; it only acknowledges his obligation to do a much better job.

Logical Implications

The nature of the evidence to date does not warrant any firm or sweeping conclusions. Nevertheless, it does suggest enough support for the interpretations made here to make it worthwhile, and perhaps imperative, to draw some logical implications from the fact that managers seem to have adopted two apparently conflicting attitudes regarding participative management.

The first implication, and the easiest one to draw, is that, given managers' present attitudes, the *human resources* model has little chance of ever gaining real acceptance as a guide to managers' relationships with their subordinates. Managers at every level view them-

---

[11] See Clagget C. Smith and Arnold Tannenbaum. "Organizational Control Structure: A Comparative-Analysis," *Human Relations*, November 1963, pp. 299–316.

selves as capable of greater self-direction and self-control, but apparently do not attribute such abilities to their subordinates. As long as managers throughout the organizational hierarchy remain unaware that the kind of participation *they* want and believe *they* are capable of handling is also the kind their subordinates want and feel they deserve, there would seem to be little hope for the *human resources* approach being actually put into practice.

A second, and somewhat more complex, implication of managers' current views is that real participation will seldom be found in modern organizations. Participation, in the *human relations* model, is viewed as an "ought" rather than a "must." The manager is under no basic obligation to seek out and develop talent, or to encourage and allow participation; it is something which he "probably should do" but not something for which he is made to feel truly responsible. Viewing participation in this fashion, the manager often junks it when problems arise or pressure builds up from above—the very times when it might be expected to produce the greatest gains.

A third implication, closely related to the second, is that the benefits which the *human resources* approach predicts from participative management will not accrue as long as managers cling to the *human relations* view. From the *human relations* model, a manager may draw a rule for decision making which says that he should allow only as much participation, self-direction, and self-control as is required to obtain cooperation and reduce resistance to formal authority. In the area of job enlargement, for example, the manager following the *human relations* model would be tempted to enlarge his subordinates' jobs just enough to improve morale and satisfaction, with little real concern for making full use of their abilities. This limited approach borders on pseudoparticipation and may be interpreted by subordinates as just another manipulative technique.

The *human resources* model, on the other hand, does not hold the manager to so limited a decision rule. In fact, it affirms that he is obligated to develop and encourage a continually expanding degree of responsible participation, self-direction, and self-control. The only limiting factors legitimate in this approach are the basic requirements of capacity to perform and the need for coordination. The manager following the *human resources* model would therefore continually expand subordinates' responsibility and self-direction up to the limits of their abilities, and/or to the point at which further expansion would produce a wasteful overlap among the responsibilities of members of his department. Even these limits, however, are far from absolute. The *human resources* model suggests that with subordinates' broadened abilities and expanded information, voluntary cooperation can erase much of the need for specific job boundaries.

A fourth and final implication can be drawn from managers' confused and conflicting attitudes toward participative management. Managers' attitudes, as suggested earlier, in part reflect the ambivalent and inconsistent treatment which scholars have given to participative leadership concepts, and are not likely to change until theorists firm up their own thinking.

Some Final Comments

It must be clear at this point that I feel that management scholars should focus their attention on developing and promoting the application of the *human resources* approach. While I cannot, at this stage, base my preference for the *human resources* model on solid empirical evidence, there is one strong argument for its potential usefulness. It is the fact that managers up and down the organizational hierarchy believe their superiors should follow this model.

Critics of the *human resources* approach have argued that (1) its costs outweigh its benefits because in its final form the *human resources* model prescribes management by committee at every level, which results in wasted effort and the inability to act in crisis situations; and (2) this approach is unsuitable for organizations or organizational groups whose members have neither the desire nor the ability to meet its challenge.

In answer to the first charge, this approach does imply a need for additional information flow to subordinates at all levels, and I admit that collecting and disseminating information increases costs.

However, information collected and *used* at lower levels may be less costly than information collected for use at upper levels that is subsequently ignored or misused. Further, and more important, the application of the *human resources* model does not require—in fact, would make unnecessary—committee-type sharing of routine departmental tasks.

This model would suggest that subordinates are generally willing to go along with their superiors' decisions on more or less routine matters, particularly when they are well informed and feel free to call important points to their bosses' attention. Moreover, this approach implies that many matters are to be delegated directly to one or more subordinates who, in most instances, will coordinate their own activities. At the same time, this model emphasizes that full and extended discussion by the whole department will be utilized where it can do the most good—on complex and important problems that demand the full talent and complete concern of the group. One could argue that under these circumstances crises should arise less often and consensus should be more quickly reached when they do arise.

There is no quick and easy answer to the second charge that the *human resources* model is more adaptable to and more easily applied with some groups than with others. Note, however, that it is the *human relations* approach, and not the *human resources* model, which promises quick and easy application. The latter cannot be put into full-blown practice overnight in any situation, particularly where subordinates have been conditioned by years of traditional or pseudoparticipative techniques of leadership. It involves a step-by-step procedure wherein the manager expands subordinates' responsibilities and participation in keeping with their developing abilities and concerns. High expectations and full support, coupled with an open recognition of the inevitability of occasional shortcomings, are required to achieve successful application.

Finally, there is a familiar ring to the critics' charge that many organization members are either unwilling or unable to contribute creatively, or to accept any real measure of responsibility. In fact, this charge brings us back once again to the heart of the conflict in managers' attitudes toward participation—their own view that subordinates are suited only for the *human relations* type of participation, while they themselves are well suited for the full range of participation suggested in the *human resources* model.

28
Are Top Executives Transferable across Companies?*

Y. K. SHETTY and NEWMAN S. PEERY, JR.

The chief executive officer (CEO) plays a crucial role in determining the efficiency of an enterprise. He is responsible for the proper use of company resources—human, technical, and material. His decisions, his power and his leadership have vital consequences for the company as a whole.

Management of a total enterprise demands different ways of thinking and the exercise of skills beyond those required for the management of a division or department. Companies are increasingly aware that they must select and develop effective CEOs. As yet, however, clearly established selection criteria that might make top executives

* From *Business Horizons*, June 1976, *19*, pp. 23–28. Copyright 1976 by the Foundation for the School of Business at Indiana University. Reprinted by permission.

transferable across companies and industries do not exist. This article examines the relationship between existing executive transfer patterns and the organizational performance criterion of profitability.

Views on Transferability

Two basic positions have been advanced about top executive transfers. One holds that all top executives perform the same major functions and use the same basic skills; hence, executives are readily transferable across companies and industries as well as from position to position. Some prominent individuals often cited as examples to substantiate this viewpoint include Robert McNamara, George Romney, McGeorge Bundy and Arjay Miller.

The second position is that top executives use fairly specialized skills, many of which are uniquely related to the industry and the environment of a specific job. Thus, executives are not readily transferable. Ernest Dale, after many years of management consulting experience, noted that ". . . there has been little transfer of management from one major sphere of administrative activity to another—from say, military organizations to business or vice versa. . . . There is even relatively little transfer of general managers from one industry to another. It is almost impossible to transfer in or out of some industries, or even in or out of some companies, and often for very good reasons. The knowledge required to fill a management position satisfactorily is not only managerial. Familiarity with technical matters, products, personalities and tradition, a type of knowledge that can be acquired only through long and painstaking experience in the actual situation, is also required in most cases."[1]

Many practicing managers express strong reservations about top executives switching industries. They do not think that a manager who lacks a basic knowledge of the firm's product line and markets can still be an effective manager. Furthermore, the experience of conglomerate firms in recent years provides some additional support for the non-transferability position. Generally speaking, conglomerate firms have performed poorly in recent years. It might be argued that this poor performance can be largely attributed to the lack of, or limited, cross-industry transferability of managerial skills. The issue of transferability is of increasing concern to companies seeking yardsticks by which to measure the performance of their top executives, as well as to others seeking guidelines for the selection and development of such executives.

---

[1] Ernest Dale, "Management Must be Made Accountable," *Harvard Business Review* (March–April 1960), p. 53.

A recent study by Donald L. Helmich found that when executives were selected from outside a former CEO's immediate circle within the firm, the results were more growth in sales, greater product diversification, and an increased number of added subsidiaries than when executives were selected from the former CEO's immediate group.[2] Though this suggests that some transferability of skills exists, the question remains whether a CEO selected from outside the organization would also perform well, and the relationship between outside transfers and profitability remains.

The study discussed in this article was designed to answer such questions as: To what degree are CEOs transferable across companies and industries? What is the relationship between chief executive transfer patterns and company performance? Are any dimensions of successful chief executive skills crucial in the transfer process? To what degree do top executive transfers reflect the particular contexts within which an organization functions?

Subjects of the study were 270 chief executives of companies included in *Business Week's* list of 368 large firms. Background information relating to the positions held prior to their current posts was collected for each executive. Mobility patterns were used as indicators of the transferability of their skills. Executives were subsequently classified according to whether they: (1) were associated with the same company for a number of years; (2) came from another company within the same industry, as indicated by identical Standard Industrial Classification (SIC) codes; (3) came from a company in a *similar* industry, as indicated by the two companies having at least the first digit of their SIC codes in common; or (4) came from a company in a completely unrelated industry, as indicated by completely different SIC codes.

Since the performance of a chief executive is closely related to the performance of the company itself, profitability and growth were used as measures of performance. Average return on invested capital for 1970–74 was the basic indicator of profitability. Sales growth for the same period was used as an indicator of growth. Data on return to invested capital, sales, number of employees, and so forth, were obtained from company financial statements and from *Moody's Industrial Manual* and *Standard & Poor's Register of Corporations, Directors and Executives.*

Patterns of Executive Transfers

Findings indicate that top executives do not transfer readily across companies and industries (see accompanying table). For example, of

---

[2] Donald L. Helmich, "Organizational Growth and Succession Patterns," *Academy of Management Journal* (December 1974), pp. 771–775.

Chief Executive Transfer Patterns

Sources of Executive Transfer	Number	Percent
Internal—same company	241	89.3
External—same industry	8	3.0
External—related industry	7	2.5
External—different industry	14	5.2
Total	270	100.0

the 270 chief executives in the study, 241 (89 percent) had previous positions with the same company. Only 29 firms (approximately 10 percent) had gone outside their organizations to recruit their chief executives. Of these 29 firms, 8 stayed within their industry group, 7 went to a related industry, and 14 ventured outside the industry.

A comparatively higher proportion of smaller companies (40,000 employees or less and sales of $3 billion or less) than larger ones recruited their top executive officers from outside the firm. As the size of the firm increases there is a higher percentage of executives who have worked up within the firm. A smaller company may not provide as much opportunity to gain broader experience required at the top level compared to a larger firm. Increasing size is also usually accompanied by a diversification of the company's product market, which in turn provides for broader experience in general management. The nature of the industry and the patterns of executive transfers showed no significant relationship.

Effect on Company Performance

The average incumbency for a chief executive officer is approximately six years. Of the 270 CEOs in the original sample, 110 had been appointed prior to 1970. To measure the relationship between transfer patterns and executive performance, data on the operations of those 110 firms between the years 1970–74 were collected.

Most executives averaged between 5–10 percent on their rates of return on invested capital regardless of whether they were recruited from within the same organization or not. Although 23 percent of the firms with inside CEOs achieved a return on invested capital in excess of 10 percent, only 1 of the 11 outside CEOs achieved a return on investment in excess of 10 percent and he was from a related industry. Similarly, only one of the firms with average sales growth in excess of 20 percent had a chief executive from outside the organization. Thus, given a choice between an inside and outside CEO, an inside seems to increase a firm's chances of high performance.

Case for Internal Selection

A number of interrelated reasons contribute to the strong bias in favor of internal selection of a CEO. First, firms seek to maintain a satisfactory level of performance and are likely to avoid unnecessary risks. Our results indicate that satisfactory performance is likely to be achieved by an inside CEO. An outside executive is not likely to significantly improve performance and may simply add another source of uncertainty. Second, most companies pursue systematic internal promotion programs as a matter of organizational policy. A well-planned system of internal promotion is an effective way to maintain a high degree of motivation among executives and create a sense of loyalty to the organization.

Another explanation is that companies may be trying to avoid the potential instability and discontinuities resulting from bringing in an outsider. When a company hires an outside man as chief executive, he generally brings with him his own people to fill top management positions. The result is an executive exodus. Research shows that the outside successor precipitates a greater number of strategic replacements and reassignments than does the inside successor.[3] Bringing in an outsider also means that the inside executives are passed over in the selection process, which may prompt their leaving the company.

An inside successor, by contrast, often has developed commitments to the current management group and is less likely to generate substantial uncertainty and instability. Continuity can be maintained. Coupled with this is the influence of the retiring chief executive in selecting his own successor. Most people think that corporate directors are responsible for selecting the chief executive. In reality, the chief executive most often recommends his successor and the board usually routinely approves the choice. Only when sluggish growth and slowing profits threaten the company are corporate boards likely to develop more interest in picking a new chief executive. When a company is doing well, directors tend to let the incumbent name his own man. In such cases, the top positions are usually filled by internal people.

Another constraint on the transferability of chief executives might be the need for personal information as a central part of the executive's job. A prior study of 190 managers found that they used personal sources of information far more than impersonal sources.[4] More recently, Henry Mintzberg found that executives rely heavily on face-

---

[3] Donald Helmich and Warren B. Brown, "Successor Type and Organizational Change in the Corporate Enterprise," *Administrative Science Quarterly* (September 1972), pp. 371–381.

[4] Francis Joseph Aguiler, *Scanning the Business Environment* (New York: Macmillan, 1967).

to-face contacts and personal information sources for most decisions.[5] An executive recruited from another company is not likely to have the personal information contacts in the organization and may therefore initially have to rely more on formal reports and official sources than would an executive promoted from within.

Case for External Selection

Some writers argue that external executive recruitment might be a source of external contacts who supply environmental information for an organization.[6] This suggests that the selection of an executive from another firm within the same industry could provide important inputs into the policy-making process. However, our data suggest that such inputs would be potentially less disruptive if they occurred at lower executive levels. The skills required at the top executive level may be highly specialized and unique to industries as well as to companies.

The Executive Skill Mix

Executive skill—an ability to translate knowledge into action—combines distinct areas of expertise.[7] It appears that the three most important skills are technical, organizational, and institutional.

Technical skills involve an understanding of, and proficiency in, relevant methods, processes, procedures, or techniques.

Organizational skills involve an ability to: structure organizational relationships, both physical and interpersonal; work effectively as a group member; coordinate others' activities; and see the organization as a whole.

Institutional skills involve an ability to define the overall goals of the organization by opportunistic surveillance of, and negotiation with, the environment and also insuring legitimization of the organization. It involves the relationship of an individual business to the industry, the community, and to the political, social, economic, and technical forces of the nation.

The relative importance of these skills varies with the organizational hierarchy. At the lower levels of management, technical skills are most important; at the intermediate levels, organizational skills are

---

[5] Henry Mintzberg, "A New Look at the Chief Executive's Job," *Organizational Dynamics* (Winter 1973), pp. 20–30.

[6] Jeffrey Pfeffer and H. Leblebici, "Executive Recruitment and the Development of Interfirm Organizations," *Administrative Science Quarterly* (December 1973), pp. 449–461.

[7] Robert Katz, "Skills of an Effective Administrator," *Harvard Business Review* (January-February 1955), pp. 33–42.

as important as technical skills; at the top level, both organizational and institutional skills are required, but the major requirement is for institutional skill.

Organizational skills are primarily concerned with the internal aspects of structure, coordination, mediation, and interpersonal relationships; and institutional skills are primarily concerned with creating organizational responses to a changing environment. Exercising institutional skills entails having an understanding of the external environment relevant to the company. Extensive knowledge about the industry in which the company operates is a crucial ingredient. To define realistically the overall goals of his company, a top executive must be continually engaged in opportunistic surveillance of and negotiation with the company's environment, and must strive for legitimization of the organization in its milieu.

Importance of Institutional Skills

Institutional skills are more important today than ever before; the chief executive has increasing responsibility for adjusting the company to its environment. Many top executives claim that besides managing internal affairs, they are more and more frequently called upon to arbitrate conflicting claims of workers, consumers, shareholders, environmentalists, and the government. Alonzo L. McDonald, Jr., managing partner of McKinsey and Co., the consulting firm, says, "Just a few years ago the CEO of a big company spent 10 percent of his time on external matters. Today the figure is generally 40 percent."[8]

If institutional skills are of primary importance to top executives, infrequent shifts across industries by CEOs and companies may indicate that different industries have particular economic, market, technical, and other characteristics, each of which calls for unique managerial strategies and skills. For example, it would be exceedingly difficult for an executive to transfer between an electronic industry and a consumer goods industry. The technology, markets, and general industrial environments of these industries differ drastically. Electronic industries put a premium on advancing the state of the art and on new technological achievements, and face an uncertain and variable market environment. In the consumer goods field, there is much less emphasis on research and development, and a greater concentration on low-cost mass production operations and on promotional advertising. Each industry requires unique managerial approaches and skills.

Our data suggest that the transferability of top executives is limited even between companies in the same industry. Different companies

---

[8] "Chief Executive Officer," *Business Week* (May 4, 1974), pp. 37–86.

within the same industry may have somewhat particular environments, each of which demands unique combinations of managerial
strategy and skills. This may be due to variations in size, ownership,
personalities, traditions and internal functioning characteristics. All of
the above factors—emphasis on maintaining internal promotion patterns, minimizing instability, the requirements of personal information, and uniqueness of industry and company environments—may be
operating in various combinations to limit transfers of executives
across companies and industries.

Implications for Management

This study suggests several alternatives for companies to help them
create more effective strategies for top executive selection and
development. Since internal recruitment of CEOs is more likely to
lead to higher performance, planned development of executive talent
should receive top priority. Companies should try to perfect meaningful programs that tag high-potential individuals early in their careers
so that they may be properly motivated and adequately rewarded
to remain with the organization. Then they may be appropriately
groomed for responsible top management spots.

Companies looking for catalysts from outside may do well to bring
in executives earlier in their careers at lower levels in the organization.
Such a strategy would provide an opportunity for the new executive to
familiarize himself with the firm. Also, this tactic would combine the
benefits of new ideas and familiarity with the company.

Finally, any top executive coming from outside would do well to
realize his inherent limitations. Decisions regarding transfer should
not be based on an assumption that homogeneity exists within any
industry. Organizational factors play a major role in influencing the
effectiveness of a top executive, and since these are minimally susceptible to change, the new executive needs to attempt to adapt to the key
factors of the new company.

Though the top executive is important to the success of a firm, the
most effective source of qualified executives has not been identified.
Some have argued that top managers are interchangeable across firms
and industries, and that managers can therefore switch jobs and perform effectively irrespective of industry. Others believe that top managers are unlikely to be successful unless they have a thorough understanding of the industry and its environment. This study indicates that
there seem to be serious constraints limiting the transferability of executives across companies as well as industries. Of those surveyed,

companies recruiting their chief executives internally performed much better than those that recruited from outside. This implies that executives promoted from within are aided by knowing the company, its traditions, personalities, and unique ways of functioning. In other words, knowing the "organizational culture" is a crucial factor in defining the effectiveness of a chief executive.

29

The Ambiguity of Leadership*

JEFFREY PFEFFER

Problems with the concept of leadership are addressed: (a) the ambiguity of its definition and measurement, (b) the issue of whether leadership affects organizational performance, and (c) the process of selecting leaders, which frequently emphasizes organizationally-irrelevant criteria. Leadership is a process of attributing causation to individual social actors. Study of leaders as symbols and of the process of attributing leadership might be productive.

Leadership has for some time been a major topic in social and organizational psychology. Underlying much of this research has been the assumption that leadership is causally related to organizational performance. Through an analysis of leadership styles, behaviors, or characteristics (depending on the theoretical perspective chosen), the argument has been made that more effective leaders can be selected or trained or, alternatively, the situation can be configured to provide for enhanced leader and organizational effectiveness.

Three problems with emphasis on leadership as a concept can be posed: (a) ambiguity in definition and measurement of the concept itself; (b) the question of whether leadership has discernible effects on organizational outcomes; and (c) the selection process in succession to leadership positions, which frequently uses organizationally irrelevant criteria and which has implications for normative theories of lead-

* From *Academy of Management Review* 2, no. 1, (1977), pp. 104–12. An earlier version of this paper was presented at the conference, Leadership: Where Else Can We Go?, Center for Creative Leadership, Greensboro, North Carolina, June 30–July 1, 1975.

ership. The argument here is that leadership is of interest primarily as a phenomenological construct. Leaders serve as symbols for representing personal causation of social events. How and why are such attributions of personal effects made? Instead of focusing on leadership and its effects, how do people make inferences about and react to phenomena labelled as leadership (5)?

THE AMBIGUITY OF THE CONCEPT

While there have been many studies of leadership, the dimensions and definition of the concept remain unclear. To treat leadership as a separate concept, it must be distinguished from other social influence phenomena. Hollander and Julian (24) and Bavelas (2) did not draw distinctions between leadership and other processes of social influence. A major point of the Hollander and Julian review was that leadership research might develop more rapidly if more general theories of social influence were incorporated. Calder (5) also argued that there is no unique content to the construct of leadership that is not subsumed under other, more general models of behavior.

Kochan, Schmidt, and DeCotiis (33) attempted to distinguish leadership from related concepts of authority and social power. In leadership, influence rights are voluntarily conferred. Power does not require goal compatibility—merely dependence—but leadership implies some congruence between the objectives of the leader and the led. These distinctions depend on the ability to distinguish voluntary from involuntary compliance and to assess goal compatibility. Goal statements may be retrospective inferences from action (46, 53) and problems of distinguishing voluntary from involuntary compliance also exist (32). Apparently there are few meaningful distinctions between leadership and other concepts of social influence. Thus, an understanding of the phenomena subsumed under the rubric of leadership may not require the construct of leadership (5).

While there is some agreement that leadership is related to social influence, more disagreement concerns the basic dimensions of leader behavior. Some have argued that there are two tasks to be accomplished in groups—maintenance of the group and performance of some task or activity—and thus leader behavior might be described along these two dimensions (1, 6, 8, 25). The dimensions emerging from the Ohio State leadership studies—consideration and initiating structure—may be seen as similar to the two components of group maintenance and task accomplishment (18).

Other dimensions of leadership behavior have also been proposed (4). Day and Hamblin (10) analyzed leadership in terms of the closeness and punitiveness of the supervision. Several authors have conceptualized leadership behavior in terms of the authority and discretion subordinates are permitted (23, 36, 51). Fiedler (14) analyzed leadership in terms of the least-preferred-co-worker scale (LPC), but the meaning and behavioral attributes of this dimension of leadership behavior remain controversial.

The proliferation of dimensions is partly a function of research strategies frequently employed. Factor analysis on a large number of items describing behavior has frequently been used. This procedure tends to produce as many factors as the analyst decides to find, and permits the development of a large number of possible factor structures. The resultant factors must be named and further imprecision is introduced. Deciding on a summative concept to represent a factor is inevitably a partly subjective process.

Literature assessing the effects of leadership tends to be equivocal. Sales (45) summarized leadership literature employing the authoritarian-democratic typology and concluded that effects on performance were small and inconsistent. Reviewing the literature on consideration and initiating structure dimensions, Korman (34) reported relatively small and inconsistent results, and Kerr and Schriesheim (30) reported more consistent effects of the two dimensions. Better results apparently emerge when moderating factors are taken into account, including subordinate personalities (50), and situational characteristics (23, 51). Kerr, et al. (31) list many moderating effects grouped under the headings of subordinate considerations, supervisor considerations, and task considerations. Even if each set of considerations consisted of only one factor (which it does not), an attempt to account for the effects of leader behavior would necessitate considering four-way interactions. While social reality is complex and contingent, it seems desirable to attempt to find more parsimonious explanations for the phenomena under study.

THE EFFECTS OF LEADERS

Hall asked a basic question about leadership: is there any evidence on the magnitude of the effects of leadership (17, p. 248)? Surprisingly, he could find little evidence. Given the resources that have been spent studying, selecting, and training leaders, one might expect that the question of whether or not leaders matter would have been addressed earlier (12).

There are at least three reasons why it might be argued that the observed effects of leaders on organizational outcomes would be small. First, those obtaining leadership positions are selected, and perhaps only certain, limited styles of behavior may be chosen. Second, once in the leadership position, the discretion and behavior of the leader are constrained. And third, leaders can typically affect only a few of the variables that may impact organizational performance.

Homogeneity of Leaders

Persons are selected to leadership positions. As a consequence of this selection process, the range of behaviors or characteristics exhibited by leaders is reduced, making it more problematic to empirically discover an effect of leadership. There are many types of constraints on the selection process. The attraction literature suggests that there is a tendency for persons to like those they perceive as similar (3). In critical decisions such as the selections of persons for leadership positions, compatible styles of behavior probably will be chosen.

Selection of persons is also constrained by the internal system of influence in the organization. As Zald (56) noted, succession is a critical decision, affected by political influence and by environmental contingencies faced by the organization. As Thompson (49) noted, leaders may be selected for their capacity to deal with various organizational contingencies. In a study of characteristics of hospital administrators, Pfeffer and Salancik (42) found a relationship between the hospital's context and the characteristics and tenure of the administrators. To the extent that the contingencies and power distribution within the organization remain stable, the abilities and behaviors of those selected into leadership positions will also remain stable.

Finally, the selection of persons to leadership positions is affected by a self-selection process. Organizations and roles have images, providing information about their character. Persons are likely to select themselves into organizations and roles based upon their preferences for the dimensions of the organizational and role characteristics as perceived through these images. The self-selection of persons would tend to work along with organizational selection to limit the range of abilities and behaviors in a given organizational role.

Such selection processes would tend to increase homogeneity more within a single organization than across organizations. Yet many studies of leadership effect at the work group level have compared groups within a single organization. If there comes to be a widely shared, socially constructed definition of leadership behaviors or characteristics which guides the selection process, then leadership activity may come to be defined similarly in various organizations, leading to the selection of only those who match the constructed image of a leader.

Constraints on Leader Behavior

Analyses of leadership have frequently presumed that leadership style or leader behavior was an independent variable that could be selected or trained at will to conform to what research would find to be optimal. Even theorists who took a more contingent view of appropriate leadership behavior generally assumed that with proper training, appropriate behavior could be produced (51). Fiedler (13), noting how hard it was to change behavior, suggested changing the situational characteristics rather than the person, but this was an unusual suggestion in the context of prevailing literature which suggested that leadership style was something to be strategically selected according to the variables of the particular leadership theory.

But the leader is embedded in a social system, which constrains behavior. The leader has a role set (27), in which members have expectations for appropriate behavior and persons make efforts to modify the leader's behavior. Pressures to conform to the expectations of peers, subordinates, and superiors are all relevant in determining actual behavior.

Leaders, even in high-level positions, have unilateral control over fewer resources and fewer policies than might be expected. Investment decisions may require approval of others, while hiring and promotion decisions may be accomplished by committees. Leader behavior is constrained by both the demands of others in the role set and by organizationally prescribed limitations on the sphere of activity and influence.

External Factors

Many factors that may affect organizational performance are outside a leader's control, even if he or she were to have complete discretion over major areas of organizational decisions. For example, consider the executive in a construction firm. Costs are largely determined by operation of commodities and labor markets; and demand is largely affected by interest rates, availability of mortgage money, and economic conditions which are affected by governmental policies over which the executive has little control. School superintendents have little control over birth rates and community economic development, both of which profoundly affect school system budgets. While the leader may react to contingencies as they arise, or may be a better or worse forecaster, in accounting for variation in organizational outcomes, he or she may account for relatively little compared to external factors.

Second, the leader's success or failure may be partly due to circumstances unique to the organization but still outside his or her control. Leader positions in organizations vary in terms of the strength and position of the organization. The choice of a new executive does not fundamentally alter a market and financial position that has developed over years and affects the leader's ability to make strategic changes and the likelihood that the organization will do well or poorly. Organizations have relatively enduring strengths and weaknesses. The choice of a particular leader for a particular position has limited impact on these capabilities.

Empirical Evidence

Two studies have assessed the effects of leadership changes in major positions in organizations. Lieberson and O'Connor (35) examined 167 business firms in 13 industries over a 20 year period, allocating variance in sales, profits, and profit margins to one of four sources: year (general economic conditions), industry, company effects, and effects of changes in the top executive position. They concluded that compared to other factors, administration had a limited effect on organizational outcomes.

Using a similar analytical procedure, Salancik and Pfeffer (44) examined the effects of mayors on city budgets for 30 U.S. cities. Data on expenditures by budget category were collected for 1951-1968. Variance in amount and proportion of expenditures was apportioned to the year, the city, or the mayor. The mayoral effect was relatively small, with the city accounting for most of the variance, although the mayor effect was larger for expenditure categories that were not as directly connected to important interest groups. Salancik and Pfeffer argued that the effects of the mayor were limited both by absence of power to control many of the expenditures and tax sources, and by construction of policies in response to demands from interests in the environment.

If leadership is defined as a strictly interpersonal phenomenon, the relevance of these two studies for the issue of leadership effects becomes problematic. But such a conceptualization seems unduly restrictive, and is certainly inconsistent with Selznick's (47) conceptualization of leadership as strategic management and decision making. If one cannot observe differences when leaders change, then what does it matter who occupies the positions or how they behave?

Pfeffer and Salancik (41) investigated the extent to which behaviors selected by first-line supervisors were constrained by expectations of others in their role set. Variance in task and social behaviors could be accounted for by role-set expectations, with adherence to various demands made by role-set participants a function of similarity and relative power. Lowin and Craig (37) experimentally demonstrated that leader behavior was determined by the subordinate's own behavior. Both studies illustrate that leader behaviors are responses to the demands of the social context.

The effect of leadership may vary depending upon level in the organizational hierarchy, while the appropriate activities and behaviors may also vary with organizational level (26, 40). For the most part, empirical studies of leadership have dealt with first-line supervisors or leaders with relatively low organizational status (17). If leadership has any impact, it should be more evident at higher organizational levels or where there is more discretion in decisions and activities.

THE PROCESS OF SELECTING LEADERS

Along with the suggestion that leadership may not account for much variance in organizational outcomes, it can be argued that merit or ability may not account for much variation in hiring and advancement of organizational personnel. These two ideas are related. If competence is hard to judge, or if leadership competence does not greatly affect organizational outcomes, then other, person-dependent criteria may be sufficient. Effective leadership styles may not predict career success when other variables such as social background are controlled.

Belief in the importance of leadership is frequently accompanied by belief that persons occupying leadership positions are selected and trained according to how well they can enhance the organization's performance. Belief in a leadership effect leads to development of a set of activities oriented toward enhancing leadership effectiveness. Simultaneously, persons managing their own careers are likely to place emphasis on activities and developing behaviors that will enhance their own leadership skills, assuming that such a strategy will facilitate advancement.

Research on the bases of hiring and promotion has been concentrated in examination of academic positions (e.g., 7, 19, 20). This is possibly the result of availability of relatively precise and unambiguous measures of performance, such as number of publications or citations. Evidence on criteria used in selecting and advancing personnel in industry is more indirect.

Studies have attempted to predict either the compensation or the attainment of general management positions of MBA students, using personality and other background information (21, 22, 54). There is some evidence that managerial success can be predicted by indicators of ability and motivation such as test scores and grades, but the amount of variance explained is typically quite small.

A second line of research has investigated characteristics and backgrounds of persons attaining leadership positions in major organizations in society. Domhoff (11), Mills (38), and Warner and Abbeglin (52) found a strong preponderance of persons with upper-class backgrounds occupying leadership positions. The implication of these findings is that studies of graduate success, including the success of MBA's, would explain more variance if the family background of the person were included.

A third line of inquiry uses a tracking model. The dynamic model developed is one in which access to elite universities is affected by social status (28) and, in turn, social status and attendance at elite universities affect later career outcomes (9, 43, 48, 55).

Unless one is willing to make the argument that attendance at elite universities or coming from an upper class background is perfectly correlated with merit, the evidence suggests that succession to leadership positions is not strictly based on meritocratic criteria. Such a conclusion is consistent with the inability of studies attempting to predict the success of MBA graduates to account for much variance, even when a variety of personality and ability factors are used.

Beliefs about the bases for social mobility are important for social stability. As long as persons believe that positions are allocated on meritocratic grounds, they are more likely to be satisfied with the social order and with their position in it. This satisfaction derives from the belief that occupational position results from application of fair and reasonable criteria, and that the opportunity exists for mobility if the person improves skills and performance.

If succession to leadership positions is determined by person-based criteria such as social origins or social connections (16), then efforts to enhance managerial effectiveness with the expectation that this will lead to career success divert attention from the processes of stratification actually operating within organizations. Leadership literature has been implicitly aimed at two audiences. Organizations were told how to become more effective, and persons were told what behaviors to acquire in order to become effective, and hence, advance in their careers. The possibility that neither organizational outcomes nor career success are related to leadership behaviors leaves leadership research facing issues of relevance and importance.

THE ATTRIBUTION OF LEADERSHIP

Kelley conceptualized the layman as:

> an applied scientist, that is, as a person concerned about applying his knowledge of causal relationships in order to *exercise control* of his world (29, p. 2).

Reviewing a series of studies dealing with the attributional process, he concluded that persons were not only interested in understanding their world correctly, but also in controlling it.

> The view here proposed is that attribution processes are to be understood not only as a means of providing the individual with a veridical view of his world, but as a means of encouraging and maintaining his effective exercise of control in that world (29, p. 22).

Controllable factors will have high salience as candidates for causal explanation, while a bias toward the more important causes may shift the attributional emphasis toward causes that are not controllable (29, p. 23). The study of attribution is a study of naive psychology—an examination of how persons make sense out of the events taking place around them.

If Kelley is correct that individuals will tend to develop attributions that give them a feeling of control, then emphasis on leadership may derive partially from a desire to believe in the effectiveness and importance of individual action, since individual action is more controllable than contextual variables. Lieberson and O'Connor (35) made essentially the same point in introducing their paper on the effects of top management changes on organizational performance. Given the desire for control and a feeling of personal effectiveness, organizational outcomes are more likely to be attributed to individual actions, regardless of their actual causes.

Leadership is attributed by observers. Social action has meaning only through a phenomenological process (46). The identification of certain organizational roles as leadership positions guides the construction of meaning in the direction of attributing effects to the actions of those positions. While Bavelas (2) argued that the functions of leadership, such as task accomplishment and group maintenance, are shared throughout the group, this fact provides no simple and potentially controllable focus for attributing causality. Rather, the identification of leadership positions provides a simpler and more readily changeable model of reality. When causality is lodged in one or a few persons rather than being a function of a complex set of interactions among all group members, changes can be made by replacing or influencing the occupant of the leadership position. Causes of organizational actions are readily identified in this simple causal structure.

Even if, empirically, leadership has little effect, and even if succession to leadership positions is not predicated on ability or performance, the belief in leadership effects and meritocratic succession provides a simple causal framework and a justification for the structure of the social collectivity. More importantly, the beliefs interpret social actions in terms that indicate potential for effective individual intervention or control. The personification of social causality serves too many uses to be easily overcome. Whether or not leader behavior actually influences performance or effectiveness, it is important because people believe it does.

One consequence of the attribution of causality to leaders and leadership is that leaders come to be symbols. Mintzberg (39), in his discussion of the roles of managers, wrote of the symbolic role, but more in terms of attendance at formal events and formally representing the organization. The symbolic role of leadership is more important than implied in such a description. The leader as a symbol provides a target for action when difficulties occur, serving as a scapegoat when things go wrong. Gamson and Scotch (15) noted that in baseball, the firing of the manager served a scapegoating purpose. One cannot fire the whole team, yet when performance is poor, something must be done. The firing of the manager conveys to the world and to the actors involved that success is the result of personal actions, and that steps can and will be taken to enhance organizational performance.

The attribution of causality to leadership may be reinforced by organizational actions, such as the inauguration process, the choice process, and providing the leader with symbols and ceremony. If leaders are chosen by using a random number table, persons are less likely to believe in their effects than if there is an elaborate search or selection process followed by an elaborate ceremony signifying the changing of control, and if the leader then has a variety of perquisites and symbols that distinguish him or her from the rest of the organization. Construction of the importance of leadership in a given social context is the outcome of various social processes, which can be empirically examined.

Since belief in the leadership effect provides a feeling of personal control, one might argue that efforts to increase the attribution of causality to leaders would occur more when it is more necessary and more problematic to attribute causality to controllable factors. Such an argument would lead to the hypothesis that the more the *context* actually effects organizational outcomes, the more efforts will be made to ensure attribution to *leadership*. When leaders really do have effects, it is less necessary to engage in rituals indicating their effects. Such rituals are more likely when there is uncertainty and unpredictability associated with the organization's operations. This results both from the desire to feel control in uncertain situations and from the fact that in ambiguous contexts, it is easier to attribute consequences to leadership without facing possible disconfirmation.

The leader is, in part, an actor. Through statements and actions, the leader attempts to reinforce the operation of an attribution process which tends to vest causality in that position in the social structure. Successful leaders, as perceived by members of the social system, are those who can separate themselves from organizational failures and associate themselves with organizational successes. Since the meaning of action is socially constructed, this involves manipulation of symbols to reinforce the desired process of attribution. For instance, if a manager knows that business in his or her division is about to improve because of the economic cycle, the leader may, nevertheless, write recommendations and undertake actions and changes that are highly visible and that will tend to identify his or her behavior closely with the division. A manager who perceives impending failure will attempt to associate the division and its policies and decisions with others, particularly persons in higher organizational positions, and to disassociate himself or herself from the division's performance, occasionally even transferring or moving to another organization.

CONCLUSION

The theme of this article has been that analysis of leadership and leadership processes must be contingent on the intent of the researcher. If the interest is in understanding the causality of social phenomena as reliably and accurately as possible, then the concept of leadership may be a poor place to begin. The issue of the effects of leadership is open to question. But examination of situational variables that accompany more or less leadership effect is a worthwhile task.

The more phenomenological analysis of leadership directs attention to the process by which social causality is attributed, and focuses on the distinction between causality as perceived by group members and causality as assessed by an outside observer. Leadership is associated with a set of myths reinforcing a social construction of meaning which legitimates leadership role occupants, provides belief in potential mobility for those not in leadership roles, and attributes social causality to leadership roles, thereby providing a belief in the effectiveness of individual control. In analyzing leadership, this mythology and the process by which such mythology is created and supported should be separated from analysis of leadership as a social influence process, operating within constraints.

REFERENCES

1. Bales, R. F. *Interaction Process Analysis: A Method for the Study of Small Groups* (Reading, Mass.: Addison-Wesley, 1950).
2. Bavelas, Alex. "Leadership: Man and Function," *Administrative Science Quarterly* 4 (1960), pp. 491–98.
3. Berscheid, Ellen, and Elaine Walster. *Interpersonal Attraction* (Reading, Mass.: Addison-Wesley, 1969).
4. Bowers, David G., and Stanley E. Seashore. "Predicting Organizational Effectiveness with a Four-Factor Theory of Leadership," *Administrative Science Quarterly* 11 (1966), pp. 238–63.
5. Calder, Bobby J. "An Attribution Theory of Leadership," in *New Directions in Organizational Behavior*, ed. B. Staw and G. Salancik (Chicago: St. Clair Press, 1976).

6. Cartwright, Dorwin C., and Alvin Zander. *Group Dynamics: Research and Theory*, 3d ed. (Evanston, Ill.: Row, Peterson, 1960).
7. Cole, Jonathan R., and Stephen Cole. *Social Stratification in Science* (Chicago: University of Chicago Press, 1973).
8. Collins, Barry E., and Harold Guetzkow. *A Social Psychology of Group Processes for Decision Making* (New York: Wiley, 1964).
9. Collins, Randall. "Functional and Conflict Theories of Stratification," *American Sociological Review* 36 (1971), pp. 1002–19.
10. Day, R. C., and R. L. Hamblin. "Some Effects of Close and Punitive Styles of Supervision," *American Journal of Sociology* 69 (1964), pp. 499–510.
11. Domhoff, G. William. *Who Rules America?* (Englewood Cliffs, N.J.: Prentice-Hall, 1967).
12. Dubin, Robert. "Supervision and Productivity: Empirical Findings and Theoretical Considerations," in *Leadership and Productivity*, ed. R. Dubin, G. C. Homans, F. C. Mann, and D. C. Miller (San Francisco: Chandler Publishing, 1965), pp. 1–50.
13. Fiedler, Fred E. "Engineering the Job to Fit the Manager," *Harvard Business Review* 43 (1965), pp. 115–22.
14. Fiedler, Fred E. *A Theory of Leadership Effectiveness* (New York: McGraw-Hill, 1967).
15. Gamson, William A., and Norman A. Scotch, "Scapegoating in Baseball," *American Journal of Sociology* 70 (1964), pp. 69–72.
16. Granovetter, Mark. *Getting a Job* (Cambridge, Mass.: Harvard University Press, 1974).
17. Hall, Richard H. *Organizations: Structure and Process* (Englewood Cliffs, N.J.: Prentice-Hall, 1972).
18. Halpin, A. W., and J. Winer. "A Factorial Study of the Leader Behavior Description Questionnaire," in *Leader Behavior: Its Description and Measurement*, ed. R. M. Stogdill and A. E. Coons (Columbus, Ohio: Bureau of Business Research, Ohio State University, 1957), pp. 39–51.
19. Hargens, L. L. "Patterns of Mobility of New Ph.D.'s among American Academic Institutions," *Sociology of Education* 42 (1969), pp. 18–37.
20. Hargens, L. L., and W. O. Hagstrom. "Sponsored and Contest Mobility of American Academic Scientists," *Sociology of Education*, 40 (1967), pp. 24–38.
21. Harrell, Thomas W. "High Earning MBA's," *Personnel Psychology* 25 (1972), pp. 523–30.
22. Harrell, Thomas W., and Margaret S. Harrell. "Predictors of Management Success." *Stanford University Graduate School of Business, Technical Report No. 3 to the Office of Naval Research.*
23. Heller, Frank, and Gary Yukl. "Participation, Managerial Decision Making, and Situational Variables," *Organizational Behavior and Human Performance* 4 (1969), pp. 227–41.
24. Hollander, Edwin P., and James W. Julian. "Contemporary Trends in the Analysis of Leadership Processes," *Psychological Bulletin* 71 (1969), pp. 387–97.

25. House, Robert J. "A Path Goal Theory of Leader Effectiveness," *Administrative Science Quarterly* 16 (1971), pp. 321–38.

26. Hunt, J. G. "Leadership-Style Effects at Two Managerial Levels in a Simulated Organization," *Administrative Science Quarterly* 16 (1971), pp. 476–85.

27. Kahn, R. L., D. M. Wolfe, R. P. Quinn, and J. D. Snoek. *Organizational Stress: Studies in Role Conflict and Ambiguity* (New York: Wiley, 1964).

28. Karabel, J., and A. W. Astin. "Social Class, Academic Ability, and College 'Quality'," *Social Forces* 53 (1975), pp. 381–98.

29. Kelley, Harold H. *Attribution in Social Interaction* (Morristown, N.J.: General Learning Press, 1971).

30. Kerr, Steven, and Chester Schriesheim. "Consideration, Initiating Structure and Organizational Criteria—An Update of Korman's 1966 Review," *Personnel Psychology* 27 (1974), pp. 555–68.

31. Kerr, S., C. Schriesheim, C. J. Murphy, and R. M. Stogdill, "Toward a Contingency Theory of Leadership Based Upon the Consideration and Initiating Structure Literature," *Organizational Behavior and Human Performance* 12 (1974), pp. 62–82.

32. Kiesler, C., and S. Kiesler. *Conformity* (Reading, Mass.: Addison-Wesley, 1969).

33. Kochan, T. A., S. M. Schmidt, and T. A. DeCotiis. "Superior-Subordinate Relations: Leadership and Headship," *Human Relations* 28 (1975), pp. 279–94.

34. Korman, A. K. "Consideration, Initiating Structure, and Organizational Criteria—A Review," *Personnel Psychology* 19 (1966), pp. 349–62.

35. Lieberson, Stanley, and James F. O'Connor. "Leadership and Organizational Performance: A Study of Large Corporations," *American Sociological Review* 37 (1972), pp. 117–30.

36. Lippitt, Ronald. "An Experimental Study of the Effect of Democratic and Authoritarian Group Atmospheres," *University of Iowa Studies in Child Welfare* 16 (1940), pp. 43–195.

37. Lowin, A., and J. R. Craig. "The Influence of Level of Performance on Managerial Style: An Experimental Object-Lesson in the Ambiguity of Correlational Data," *Organizational Behavior and Human Performance* 3 (1968), pp. 440–58.

38. Mills, C. Wright. "The American Business Elite: A Collective Portrait," in *Power, Politics, and People*, ed. C. W. Mills (New York: Oxford University Press, 1963), pp. 110–39.

39. Mintzberg, Henry. *The Nature of Managerial Work* (New York: Harper and Row, 1973).

40. Nealey, Stanley M., and Milton R. Blood. "Leadership Performance of Nursing Supervisors at Two Organizational Levels," *Journal of Applied Psychology* 52 (1968), pp. 414–42.

41. Pfeffer, Jeffrey, and Gerald R. Salancik. "Determinants of Supervisory Behavior: A Role Set Analysis," *Human Relations* 28 (1975), pp. 139–54.

42. Pfeffer, Jeffrey, and Gerald R. Salancik. "Organizational Context and the Characteristics and Tenure of Hospital Administrators," *Academy of Management Journal* 20 (1977).

43. Reed, R. H., and H. P. Miller. "Some Determinants of the Variation in Earnings per College Men," *Journal of Human Resources* 5 (1970), 117–90.

44. Salancik, Gerald R., and Jeffrey Pfeffer. "Constraints on Administrator Discretion: The Limited Influence of Mayors on City Budgets," *Urban Affairs Quarterly*, in press.

45. Sales, Stephen M. "Supervisory Style and Productivity: Review and Theory," *Personnel Psychology* 19 (1966), pp. 275–86.

46. Schutz, Alfred. *The Phenomenology of the Social World* (Evanston, Ill.: Northwestern University Press, 1967).

47. Selznick, P. *Leadership in Administration* (Evanston, Ill.: Row, Peterson, 1957).

48. Spaeth, J. L., and A. M. Greeley. *Recent Alumni and Higher Education* (New York: McGraw-Hill, 1970).

49. Thompson, James D. *Organizations in Action* (New York: McGraw-Hill, 1967).

50. Vroom, Victor H. "Some Personality Determinants of the Effects of Participation," *Journal of Abnormal and Social Psychology* 59 (1959), pp. 322–27.

51. Vroom, Victor H., and Phillip W. Yetton. *Leadership and Decision Making* (Pittsburgh: University of Pittsburgh Press, 1973).

52. Warner, W. L., and J. C. Abbeglin. *Big Business Leaders in America* (New York: Harper and Row, 1955).

53. Weick, Karl E. *The Social Psychology of Organizing* (Reading, Mass.: Addison-Wesley, 1969).

54. Weinstein, Alan G., and V. Srinivasan. "Predicting Managerial Success of Master of Business Administration (MBA) Graduates," *Journal of Applied Psychology* 59 (1974), pp. 207–12.

55. Wolfle, Dael. *The Uses of Talent* (Princeton: Princeton University Press, 1971).

56. Zald, Mayer N. "Who Shall Rule? A Political Analysis of Succession in a Large Welfare Organization," *Pacific Sociological Review* 8 (1965), pp. 52–60.

section six

Organizations: Structure, Environment, and Change

Introduction

We concluded the previous section with an article (by Jeffrey Pfeffer) which suggested that leaders—even at the highest levels of rank—receive too much credit and too much blame for what happens in organizations. To begin with, Pfeffer argued that leaders have little latitude for action because of internal constraints; and, furthermore, external forces largely determine the fortunes of organizations. In this section we examine more carefully the "big picture" of the internal structure of organizations, going beyond the level of individual or small group behavior, and we take due account of the external environmental forces that constrain organizational choice.

A selection from the work of Mariann Jelinek describes the various "basic conformations" or types of formal structure that may characterize organizations. To some extent, structure evolves through experience; yet to some extent, structure is also a matter of deliberate choice. In either case, structure depends on the stage of development of the organization, strategies for survival and growth, product line, and technology.

Miles, Snow, Meyer, and Coleman elaborate upon the importance of a proper fit between overall strategy and a corresponding structure. They proceed to identify three types of strategy-structure combinations, each effective in certain environments. A fourth type, the "Reactor," is predicted to fail precisely because of the absence of alignment between distinctive strategy and structure.

Galbraith approaches the issue of structure from the standpoint of the information-processing needs of an organization. These needs depend upon such factors as the diversity of product line, complexity of technology, and market uncertainties.

Organization Development (OD) is a term that has been used to describe efforts directed at changing an organization's "culture" or "climate." The intent of such efforts is to promote trust, openness, collaborative problem solving, team development, and constructive approaches to resolving conflict. Attainment of these ends should, in turn, enable an organization to adapt more effectively to the realities of its external environment. However, the charge has been made that OD practitioners, with all their good intentions, often fail in their efforts because of naivete about the politics of organizations. Cobb and Margulies respond to this criticism about OD and offer some prescriptions concerning the political posture of OD consultants.

Professor Tai K. Oh reports upon an approach to structure—by Japanese management—quite unlike any within the experience of U.S. firms. And abundant evidence in the newspapers and trade journals every day attests to the apparent success of this approach. Can U.S. firms expect to take such an approach with the same results? Oh suggests that Japanese business organization can neither be understood nor duplicated outside of a larger economic and cultural context. Thus, whatever we might wish for an array of choices of structure, that array is constrained by the values and institutions of the societal matrix.

30

Organization Structure: The Basic Conformations*

MARIANN JELINEK

A key issue in organization design is the choice of the main structural conformation. There are varieties of each form, and a range of possible styles within the forms. Nevertheless, the choice of one or another of the basic configurations is the selections of certain capabilities and benefits—and certain disadvantages and potential problems as well. The choice implies constraints of a fundamental nature.

What are the main options, and what are their associated constraints? What are the forms' strengths and weaknesses, and the trade-offs involved in choice of one as against another? These topics will be the subject of this paper. In passing, we shall also make reference to various dimensions of structure and other organizational factors, such as strategy and environment, which affect the organization designer's choice. We will deal with the basic organizational configurations as they evolved historically—although clearly no organization is compelled to repeat this historical sequence.

THE SIMPLE ORGANIZATION OR "AGENCY" FORM

The simple organization is one with little or no structure; it typically consists of the boss (owner, leader, or manager) and the employees or workers. An example would be a workshop in which a master craftperson supervised a number of apprentices or helpers. Direction or coordination is provided by personal supervision, and each worker acts as the *agent* or extension of the boss. More extensive examples would include most large organizations before the evolution of formal, bureaucratic means of organizing. For example, kings directed extensive establishments personally, and each subordinate's authority and

* This selection was specially written by Mariann Jelinek for inclusion in *Organizations by Design*, ed. Mariann Jelinek, Joseph A. Litterer, and Raymond E. Miles (Plano, Tex.: Business Publications, 1981), where it first appeared. © 1981, Mariann Jelinek.

power derived directly from a relationship with the king, whose agent the subordinate was. More modern examples of the larger sort are difficult to identify, with the possible exception of some religious, cult, or political groups. Here, too, the subordinates' power and authority derive directly from the leader; it is as agents of the leader, doing whatever is required, that the subordinates act. Typically, such a subordinate owes responsibility only to the leader personally, rather than for a position, and duties are defined by the leader's requests.

Many organizations begin as simple organizations. An entrepreneur with an idea hires others to assist in its realization. Typically, each employee does what the entrepreneur directs, and, particularly at initial stages, there is little or no formality. Anyone can be asked to do whatever needs doing, the work is the responsibility of all organization members, under the personal direction of the entrepreneur. As Mintzberg (1979) has pointed out, such organizations are flexible, but decidedly limited in their capacity to cope with complexity. They tend to operate simple technologies in simple environments, in order that needed coordination can take place through the leader—whose capacity to process information is necessarily limited.

DIVIDING THE WORK

Most organizations quickly become more formalized than the simple agency model. As an early step in formalization, work is explicitly divided. Thus the interest of Adam Smith (1776) and Charles Babbage (1832) in the steps or functions that went into pin making: formally dividing the work, and assigning different individuals responsibility for different parts, substitutes this structure for a portion of the control exercised by the leader in the agency or simple form. People no longer must be told what to do; instead they're assigned to do one specific portion of the work regularly. Their responsibility is limited to that portion of the work.

As Smith and Babbage noted, dividing the work permits significant advantages because it facilitates specialization. Among the results are increases in efficiency, speed, and expertise; reduced waste; less time to learn the job (because less must be learned, and more frequent repetition speeds the process); and less time lost in changing from one tool or operation to another. The same advantages accrue whether the work to be subdivided is pin making, assembling an automobile or refrigerator, teaching or engineering: specialization permits development of in-depth knowledge, experience, and facility *within a limited area*. Thus a large and complex task is often better accomplished by dividing it into smaller, more comprehensible pieces. In particular, where the range of skills required in a large task differ markedly, or where the strength or time requirements of different portions of the task differ, division of labor offers advantages.

The consequences of division of work are not wholly positive, however. Once the work is divided, people tend to orient themselves toward their portion of the work, rather than toward other portions, or toward the task as a whole. This orientation colors department members' perceptions, for instance, so that they quite naturally seek to make their own work easier and more meaningful, to acquire a larger share of resources, and to exercise more control over the flow of work to them and from them to others. Essentially, people behave in ways consistent with the structuring of tasks. Division of the work makes one portion of it central to them, and they proceed to behave in just that fashion—as if their portion of the work were central. These tendencies are called "suboptimization," the optimizing of a portion of the work, rather than the whole. They constitute one potentially dysfunctional consequence of dividing the work.

FUNCTIONAL FORM

The systematic division of work, typically reflected in departments, is fairly obvious. Somewhat less obvious is the basis for dividing it. How should the work be divided? There are numerous ways of dividing the work, and, given the potential consequences, the designer should choose knowledgeably from among the options. The basis on which work is divided will implicitly set the various departments' goals, and define members' perceptions. If we note that "function" means "a portion of the tasks or activities necessary" (Litterer, 1973), we will have a starting place. By functional form, we mean an organizational structure that divides the work among departments or units, each responsible for a portion of it. Some common bases for dividing work among functional departments would include (see Figures 1–5):

Business Function: Manufacturing, sales, personnel, R&D departments.

Managerial Function: Controller, planning, operations.

Technical Function or Process: Painting, welding, stamping, assembly.

Similar Tools or Techniques: Typing, operations research, computer center.

Time: Day shift, evening shift.

Shared Product or Purpose: Maintenance, editorial department, police.

Geographic Location: Kalamazoo plant, New England region.

Client Served: Consumer sales, government contracts, industrial equipment.

FIGURE 1
Functional Departments—Manufacturing Firm—Highly Centralized

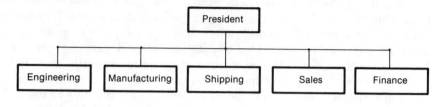

FIGURE 2
Functional Departments—School

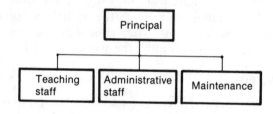

FIGURE 3
Functional Departments—Hospital

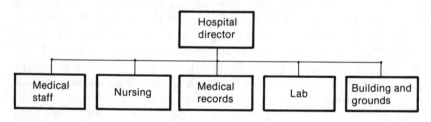

FIGURE 4A
Departments by Managerial Function and Process

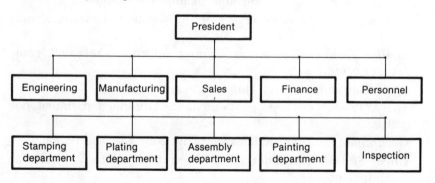

FIGURE 4B
Departments by Process—City Government

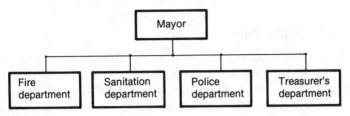

FIGURE 5
Departments by Clients Served

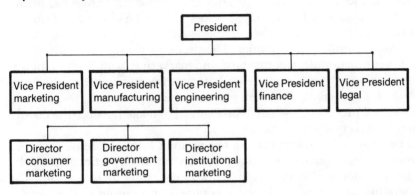

Some of these distinctions rest upon the activities of the manufacturing process, others on the output or client, still others on characteristics like time or location. It is important to note that the distinctions are not precise and mutually exclusive. Indeed, they are often used in combinations, particularly in more complex organizational forms. When someone refers to a "functional organization structure," she or he means an organization in which each department performs only a portion of the needed activities of the organization, with coordination occurring at top levels. It is often provided by the president (as in Figures 1, 4A and 4B, for instance)—making the functional form a logical successor to the agency organization, for the top manager still maintains a large amount of control. Functional organization identifies key aspects of the task, and clearly assigns responsibility for them. It permits and encourages specialization around these key tasks. Its disadvantages, beyond suboptimization, include potential difficulties in work flow between and among departments, and information overload as top managers become overwhelmed with too many coordinating decisions. This form of organization *specializes;* its main problem is *reintegration* of the specialized, differentiated activities.

DIVISIONAL STRUCTURE

While product departments were mentioned above, most typically product organization occurs in larger organizations that have evolved several distinctly different products or product lines. It usually implies product coordination at least one level *below* top management. Historically, the divisional structure evolved first at Du Pont and General Motors, to meet a specific set of needs. Du Pont, which was reorganized from a cluster of family-owned predecessor firms in 1902, was soon expanded further by acquisition into the largest explosives manufacturing company in the United States. Du Pont had some 31 factories producing three main product lines—dynamite, black powder, and smokeless military gunpowder. The products were sufficiently different in raw materials, manufacture, and marketing to multiply complexities further. A great many new administrative mechanisms—like uniform and systematic information on costs and revenues, and rational allocation procedures—had to be evolved to make possible the coordination of so many activities.

Because of the differences in the product lines, the basic structure selected was organization into three operating departments, one for each product line. Within each, a functional structure was set up. The operating departments shared a common accounting system, and a common system for evaluating unit performance (return on investment). Resources for investment were allocated from the top. It was clear from the outset, however, that running so large and so complex an organization would require more managerial capacity than just a single chief executive. To coordinate and manage the firm as a whole—in contrast to the individual departments within it—an executive committee made up of the operating department heads was formed. This structure explicitly recognized the need for both product line, or operating responsibilities, and for organizationwide, coordinative responsibilities. It was only thus, by explicitly monitoring and managing relationships among the product lines, that the company as a whole could avoid the inefficiencies that had plagued the predecessor companies. The explicit charge of the executive committee was to coordinate and integrate activities for the firm as a whole. (See Figure 6 for a simplified organization chart.) Over time, the distinction between product line operations and the overall management of the firm was more strongly drawn, and more clearly reflected in structure by ensuring that the operating department heads were not the majority membership of the executive committee. Instead, corporate-level executives were appointed. This separation of tasks allowed the company to concentrate on new products, to allocate investment among the competing activities of the various product lines rationally, and to attend to financing new capital for expansion.

FIGURE 6
Du Ponts Organization Prior to 1911 (much simplified)

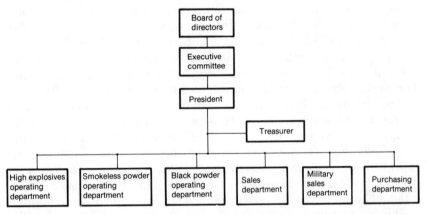

Source: Adapted from Alfred D. Chandler, Jr., and Stephen Salisbury, *Pierre S. Du Pont and the Making of the Modern Corporation* (New York: Harper & Row, 1976).

Du Pont's original structure made use of product-line form (the operating departments), functional departmentalization (within the main operating departments), and of staff as well as line managers. These innovations were essentially structural means to divide the work *of management*, distinguishing various product operations from corporate management, and from the specialized ancillary support functions not concerned directly with operations. By providing structural legitimacy for all of these functions, Du Pont's divisional structure achieved a high order of performance in a vastly more complex business situation than had existed before.

GENERAL MOTORS

General Motors, too, evolved a divisional structure in response to product-line differences. However, the genesis was different from Du Pont's. GM was founded by William C. Durant, who assembled it from widely diverse companies manufacturing everything from entire automobiles—such as Cadillac, Buick, Oakland, and even Cartercar—to components, tractors, an early refrigerator, and other things. Each had originally been an independent firm. There was no overall structure, to begin with, and no communication among different portions of the company. Aside from the name, the various factories shared little. In the absence of controls or coordination, the various lines competed with one another, not only for financial resources within the firm, but outside it, in the marketplace as well.

GM's product line, even after some eliminations, contained 10 car models and seven brands. All but two were losing money in 1921. Since the products competed directly (as smokeless powder and dynamite did not, at Du Pont), coordination was even more essential. The problem at GM was to retain the advantages of decentralized independence—which permitted each division to specialize itself to concentrate on a specific market niche—while coordinating the whole firm. The design problem was to combine centralized control on financial and policy matters (to coordinate among divisions) with decentralized operations (to ensure timely and adequate operating decisions). Under Durant, the executive committee had consisted of the heads of the operating divisions (much like Du Pont's first structure), and had exercised little or no control. After Durant's bankruptcy, the firm was reorganized with a new executive committee. The division heads were retained in an advisory capacity, but were not executive committee members. A central financial staff, answerable to the executive committee, directed accounting and reporting procedures to ensure complete and comparable data. The divisions and their products were reduced, streamlined, and positioned so that each division was responsible for a single product-line and a specific price range designated by the executive committee.

This basic structure reflected the philosophy of the company (see Figure 7): divisions should be autonomous and operate independently within broad policy boundaries laid down by the corporation. Policy should be a corporate responsibility, aimed at corporate coordination. The corporation would direct the reporting and accounting procedures, and would allocate financial resources. This philosophy, and this structure, continues to the present day with relatively little change. GM grew to be the largest producer of automobiles in the world with this structure.

ADMINISTRATIVE STRUCTURES

As organizations grew more complex, greater use was made of formal arrangements, written records and procedures, and explicit assignment of responsibilities. This formality offered many advantages, as Max Weber noted. Weber described a completely specified organization, which he called "bureaucracy" (from the French word for office, bureau). Weber's description was "an ideal type," or a model ab-

FIGURE 7
Simplified Organization Chart, General Motors, 1924

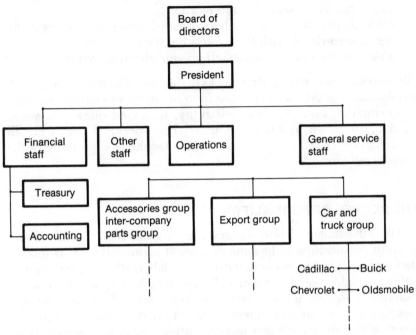

Source: Adapted from Alfred D. Chandler, Jr., and Stephen Salisbury, *Pierre S. Du Pont and the Making of the Modern Corporation* (New York: Harper & Row, 1976).

stracted from the compromises required in the real world. By ignoring such compromises, the ideal type highlights the characteristics of bureaucracy. A bureaucracy, according to Weber, was rules based, in stark contrast to the earlier agency forms based on the leader's preference. As a result, the bureaucratic form provided a notable advance in efficiency, reliability, and predictability. The chief characteristics of the bureaucracy were:

1. Tasks are assigned to specific organization units and members as official duties, attached to *positions* (not individuals).
2. Authority is hierarchical, with higher positions holding greater authority, responsibility, and control. Power is concentrated at the top.
3. Formal rules govern behavior, ensuring uniformity in order to facilitate coordination.
4. Organization membership is a full-time commitment, typically a career for life.

5. Training and expertise are the basis for recruitment. There is a high degree of specialization.
6. Promotion is by seniority and merit.
7. Official activities are carefully segregated from private life; people act in accordance with their roles, not their preferences.
8. Files record and summarize all organizational activities.

Weber was aware of some drawbacks to this sort of organization, but he emphasized the advantages of the form in contrast to earlier methods of organizing. Predictability, reliability, increased output, lessened friction, discretion, and reduced material and personal costs were all advantages he cited as deriving from the technical superiority of the bureaucratic form.

THE DEGREE OF FORMALITY

The advantages of bureaucracy are so great that virtually every modern organization is, to some degree, "bureaucratic." This formality may be limited to an explicit division of labor, allowing and encouraging specialization, for instance. It may even be required by law: for example, hospitals are required to hire only specialists (medical doctors and trained nurses and technicians) to perform medical services. Even in private enterprises manufacturing proprietary materials for profit, such degrees of formality as explicit and accurate records of costs and revenues, payments and taxes, inspections, and injuries are required. These are all examples of formality. Such measures as the number of specialist job categories, differing from one another so that incumbents are not immediately interchangeable, provide one indication of the degree of formality in an organization. Another measure is the degree to which procedures are specified in advance. If most activity within the organization is governed by protocol or procedure, and there is a set response to most situations, we can identify the organization as quite formal. Such organizations typically also have many levels of hierarchy, and require that situations that fall outside the set rules of operation be referred upward, to superiors. So, too, with conflict or differences between different departments or units. Such an organization is often referred to as "mechanistic" (Burns and Stalker, 1961) because it is expected to operate like a machine.

At its extreme, the "machine bureaucracy" centralizes power and decision making, reserving them to the top executive. At the extreme, such an organization is rigid and highly formal—everything is specified, and organization members are allowed virtually no discretion. The underlying assumption is that tasks, environment, and circumstances will always remain the same. Of course the extreme is far more rigid and specific than real-world organization structures would be.

Nevertheless, it is clear that a range of bureaucratization is possible. To the degree that an organization does rely on rules, specify the duties of members, rely on specialists and so on, it is bureaucratic. To the extent that decision making is delegated downward, initiative is permitted or encouraged, and informal arrangements vary the procedures, the organization is less bureaucratic. Virtually every organization of any size, public or private, is to some degree bureaucratic. This ubiquity testifies loudly to the advantages that Weber noted. These benefits are counterbalanced by costs—red tape, alienation, rigidity, inefficiency when rules fail to deal adequately with reality: in short, all that we imply by the stereotype "bureaucratic." The designer must recognize both costs and benefits.

In contrast to the highly bureaucratic, highly formal organization are informal or "organic" organizations (Burns and Stalker, 1961). These organizations rely on expertise and problem solving, rather than "the rules" or hierarchy, to accomplish tasks. People do what must be done, results matter more than rules, and tasks may frequently change, depending on the job at hand. Rather than relying on rules or procedures, such organizations may well rely on external training—as, for instance, when professional engineers, accountants, or architects are hired, then expected to work with relatively few formal rules. Instead, professional training and discretion are invoked. Of course, professional organizations are not the only organic organizations. Any organization that is relatively informal and operates in a flexible fashion may be identified as organic; professional organizations are merely one frequently encountered type of organic organization.

Organic, informal organization is very attractive, to most of us. Many of us like to imagine ourselves operating with few rules or constraints. We see ourselves as capable and responsible organization members, easily able to choose appropriate actions, and always in agreement with organizational goals. The difficulties of organic organizations are the obverse of those of bureaucracy: the informality and lack of rules that allows freedom of action also make for unpredictability; inefficiency, as people may "reinvent the wheel"; inconsistency, as decisions are made one way this week and another next. The lack of structure also fails to provide guidance for some who need direction. In short, organic organizations too have liabilities, and the designer must be aware of these as well as the undeniable advantages in choosing an appropriate degree of formality.

LINE AND STAFF

Bureaucracy, with its carefully delineated hierarchy of authority and control assumes that any higher organization member is more knowledgeable and has more responsibility than any lower member.

Increasing complexity—as at Du Pont and GM—quickly led to the recognition of several sorts of authority, however. While some executives were directly responsible for operations, if the organization as a whole was to be coordinated and run effectively, various administrative mechanisms had to be explicitly managed. Thus, for instance, accounting procedures and reporting systems had to be designed, managed, maintained, and their results interpreted. This was clearly a specialist activity, and just as clearly ancillary to the main activities of the firm. While essential to large-scale, complex operations, it was not part of operations. The solution was to divide the work—to specifically designate responsibility for the new technical requirements to specialists who held no other responsibility, while operating departments and members were designated as "line" activities. Organizationally, since support activity was all-pervasive yet not part of the central activity of manufacturing, these structural units were distinguished as "staff."

Staff units are specialized support activities which are traditionally expected to advise (but not to command) line managers and members. In current organizations, this exclusively "advisory" role frequently breaks down—especially where staff units must approve budgetary expenses, for instance. Nevertheless, the traditional model is still typically invoked. Staff units are usually responsible for the development of specialized expertise and technical data, longer range activities concerning the coordination of the firm as a whole, and the like. The advantages of separating staff activities is akin to that of specialization in general—it encourages the development of greater expertise in the designated area. The disadvantages are also related to specialization. Because the staff unit concentrates only on its specialty, which may be quite arcane and esoteric to other organization members, staff personnel may become cut off from organizational reality and from other organization members. Difficulties include getting staff recommendations accepted by line personnel, ensuring realistic staff recommendations, and resolving jurisdictional disputes between line and staff.

These difficulties, and the need for greater responsiveness to both the needs of external environmental segments and internal coordination led to the next organizational form, simultaneous organization.

SIMULTANEOUS FORMS

The functional and divisional organizational forms were designed with an eye to separating the work into distinct pieces, generally eliminating overlap, and assigning relatively clear responsibility for activities along whatever underlying dimension was selected. In contrast, *simultaneous* organizational forms, of which the most familiar is the matrix, seek to design along multiple dimensions at the same time. The aim is to gain the benefits of several sorts of specialization, several emphases for attention at once. In order to do so, simultaneous organizations arrange people according to two (or occasionally more) basic divisions of work.

Simultaneous organization evolved first under the Defense Department and received major impetus at NASA, the National Aeronautics and Space Administration, and in the aerospace industry. The typical predecessor arrangements were functional departmentalization, with coordination occurring at the top (as in Figure 1). This structure did serve to encourage needed specialization and technical expertise, by grouping technical specialists together. This grouping facilitated their communication with one another around work problems, thus providing a highly experienced technical resource pool. The structure was not adequate for coordinating the highly complex projects of aerospace work, however. The required communications across functional departments and technical specialties were not occurring smoothly, resulting in delays and increased costs. The design solution was to reorganize along both technical specialties and projects, simultaneously. Project teams, drawn from numerous departments as needed, worked together on a given project. Meanwhile, all project members were still members of their functional departments, with access to their resources of technical expertise. (See Figure 8.) Each project member was responsible both to the functional department head, and to the project head; both evaluated the member.

FIGURE 8
Matrix Organization in Manufacturing

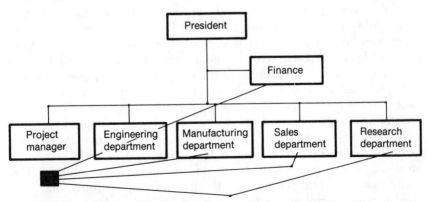

Note: Team members are drawn from various departments as needed, and report to *both* the project manager and their home department head.

Critical characteristics of the matrix form include simultaneous attention to two or more essential organizational tasks (here, the development and maintenance of specialized technical expertise, and the coordination of diverse specialists around a common temporary task). Functional departments are oriented toward the acquisition, maintenance, and development of specialized *resources*—people and equipment, for instance. Project teams are oriented toward the production of *output*. As a result, relationships, authority patterns, and evaluation all become highly complex and usually negotiated—because there are no clear and simple answers. The multiple dimensions of organization foster an ongoing tension—which can be highly creative, if appropriately balanced—between the underlying *resource* orientation and the desired *output* orientation.

The matrix form encourages a far more useful view of organizational realities, because it legitimates the sort of bargaining and negotiation that is essential when many goals—for instance, both output and resource goals—are to be met at once. It also encourages a general managerial viewpoint well down in the organization, where members see these alternate dimensions interacting and begin quite early in their careers to understand the trade-offs required.

Matrix forms, like functional and departmental forms, evolve in response to the problems around them, as managers seek new answers. In the case of the matrix, the first step was temporary teams, and temporary assignments. Later steps simply recognized that the organization faced an ongoing stream of such temporary projects. Thus while any individual project was temporary, another would take its place for firms involved in project work. For such organizations, a permanent project orientation (with projects changing) and a permanent functional organization (with appropriate resources maintained) were needed.

The advantage of simultaneous organizations like the matrix is their ability to maximize along several dimensions. Because project teams can be easily constituted and dissolved, the simultaneous form can be highly responsive to change as well. Because of this responsiveness, and because of the technical support the departmental structure provides, organization members often find they can "have their cake and eat it too," gaining benefits of motivation, involvement, and worthwhile participation. Disadvantages include substantial managerial overhead—particularly in the early stages (which may last for two or three years) while participants learn to negotiate and bargain instead of referring all conflicts up the hierarchy for resolution. The complexity and uncertainty of authority and responsibility lines can trouble some members, as can the need for high order interpersonal skills.

CONCLUSIONS

Choice among organizational forms is contingent upon many factors. No single form—functional, product or geographic division, combination, or simultaneous—is "best" for all circumstances. The best choice is the one that best balances the costs and benefits for maximum gain, in the context of clear thinking about present and future organizational needs. Critical organizational dimensions must be addressed, as must the organization's ability to bear the costs and tolerate the disadvantages of any particular form. Stability is economically efficient, but may impose heavy costs in terms of lost flexibility, creativity, and involvement. Innovative simultaneous organizations emphasize responsiveness, but may impose substantial costs in terms of duplication, inefficiencies, and sheer complexity. Not all people tolerate well an ambiguous structure that requires multiple reporting relationships and bargaining. Each of the major design options—simple organizations, organization by functional components, by product, by division, mixed forms, and simultaneous forms—meets a particular set of needs. Each emphasizes some strengths at the price of some weaknesses. Design is the art of balancing these factors to choose appropriately.

REFERENCES

Babbage, Charles. *On the Economy of Machinery and Manufacturers.* London: Charles Knight, 1832.

Burns, T., and G. M. Stalker. *The Management of Innovation.* London: Tavistock Publications, 1961.

Chandler, Alfred D. *Strategy and Structure.* Cambridge, Mass.: MIT Press, 1962.

Chandler, Alfred D., and Steven Salisbury. *Pierre S. Du Pont and the Making of the Modern Corporation.* New York: Harper & Row, 1977.

Jelinek, Mariann. "Organizational Design." In Don Hellriegel and John W. Slocum, Jr., *Organizational Behavior,* 2d ed. St. Paul: West Publishing Co., 1979, chap. 4.

Litterer, Joseph A. *The Analysis of Organizations,* 2d ed. New York: John Wiley & Sons, 1973.

Mintzberg, Henry. *The Structuring of Organizations.* Englewood Cliffs, N.J.: Prentice-Hall, 1979.

Sloan, Alfred P. *My Years at General Motors,* ed. John McDonald and Catherine Stevens. Garden City, N.Y.: Doubleday Anchor, 1972.

Smith, Adam. *The Wealth of Nations.* London: Straham and Candell, 1776.

31

Organizational Strategy, Structure, and Process*

RAYMOND E. MILES, CHARLES C. SNOW, ALAN D. MEYER, and HENRY J. COLEMAN, JR.

Organizational adaptation is a topic that has received only limited and fragmented theoretical treatment. Any attempt to examine organizational adaptation is difficult, since the process is highly complex and changeable. The proposed theoretical framework deals with alternative ways in which organizations define their product-market domains (strategy) and construct mechanisms (structures and processes) to pursue these strategies. The framework is based on interpretation of existing literature and continuing studies in four industries (college textbook publishing, electronics, food processing, and health care).

An organization is both an articulated purpose and an established mechanism for achieving it. Most organizations engage in an ongoing process of evaluating their purposes—questioning, verifying, and redefining the manner of interaction with their environments. Effective organizations carve out and maintain a viable market for their goods or services. Ineffective organizations fail this market-alignment task. Organizations also constantly modify and refine the mechanism by which they achieve their purposes—rearranging their structure of roles and relationships and their managerial processes. Efficient organizations establish mechanisms that complement their market strategy, but inefficient organizations struggle with these structural and process mechanisms.

For most organizations, the dynamic process of adjusting to environmental change and uncertainty—*of maintaining an effective alignment with the environment while managing internal interdependencies*—is enormously complex, encompassing myriad decisions and

---

* From *Academy of Management Review* 3, no. 3, (1978), pp. 546–62.

behaviors at several organization levels. But the complexity of the adjustment process can be penetrated: by searching for patterns in the behavior of organizations, one can describe and even predict the process of organizational adaptation. This article presents a theoretical framework that managers and students of management can use to analyze an organization as an integrated and dynamic whole—a model that takes into account the interrelationships among strategy, structure, and process. For a complete discussion of the theoretical framework and research studies, see (15). Specifically, the framework has two major elements: (*a*) a general model of the process of adaptation which specifies the major decisions needed by the organization to maintain an effective alignment with its environment and (*b*) an organizational typology which portrays different patterns of adaptive behavior used by organizations within a given industry or other grouping. But as several theorists have pointed out, organizations are limited in their choices of adaptive behavior to those which top management believes will allow the effective direction and control of human resources (4, 5, 6). Thus the theoretical framework to prevailing theories of management is also related. An increased understanding of the adaptive process, of how organizations move through it, and of the managerial requirements of different adjustment patterns can facilitate the difficult process of achieving an effective organization-environment equilibrium.

In the following sections, a typical example of organizational adaptation drawn from one of our empirical research studies is first presented. Second, a model of the adaptive process that arose from this research is described and discussed. In the third section, four alternative forms of adaptation exhibited by the organizations in our studies are described. Finally, the relationship between the organizational forms and currently available theories of management is discussed.

AN EXAMPLE OF ORGANIZATIONAL ADAPTATION

As an example of the problems associated with the adaptive process, consider the experience of a subsidiary of one of the companies in our studies.

> Porter Pump and Valve (PPV) is a semiautonomous division of a medium-sized equipment-manufacturing firm, which is in turn part of a large, highly diversified conglomerate. PPV manufactures a line of heavy-duty pumps and components for fluid-movement systems. The company does most of its own castings, makes many of its own parts, and maintains a complete stock of replacement parts. PPV also does special-order foundry work for other firms as its production schedule allows.

Until recently, Porter Pump and Valve had defined its business as providing quality products and service to a limited set of reliable customers. PPV's general manager, a first-rate engineer who spent much of his time in the machine shop and foundry, personified the company's image of quality and cost efficiency. In the mid-70s corporate management became concerned about both the speed and direction of PPV's growth. The management and staff at corporate headquarters began considering two new product and market opportunities, both in the energy field. Fluid-movement systems required for nuclear power generation provided one of these opportunities, and the development of novel techniques for petroleum exploration, well recovery, and fluid delivery provided the second. PPV had supplied some components to these markets in the past, but it was now clear that opportunities for the sale of entire systems or large-scale subsystems were growing rapidly.

PPV's initial moves toward these new opportunities were tentative. The general manager discovered that contract sales required extensive planning, field-contact work, and careful negotiations—activities not within his primary area of interest or experience. Finally, in an effort to foster more rapid movement into these new markets, executives in the parent organization transferred the general manager to a head-office position and moved into the top spot at PPV a manager with an extensive background in both sales and engineering and who was adept at large-scale contract negotiations.

Within a year of the changeover in general managers, PPV landed several lucrative contracts, and more appeared to be in the offing. The new business created by these contracts, however, placed heavy coordination demands on company management, and while the organization's technology (production and distribution system) has not been drastically revised over the past two years, workflow processes and the operational responsibilities of several managers have changed markedly. Materials control and scheduling, routine tasks in the past, are now complex activities, and managers of these operations meet regularly with the executive planning committee. Moreover, a rudimentary matrix structure has emerged in which various line managers undertake specific project responsibilities in addition to their regular duties. Key personnel additions have been made to the marketing department and more are planned, with particular emphasis on individuals who are capable of performing field planning and supervising and who can quickly bring new fluid systems to full operation. Budgets of some of the older departments are being cut back, and these funds are being diverted to the new areas of activity.

As illustrated, Porter Pump and Value experienced changes in its products and markets, in the technological processes needed to make new products and serve new markets, and in the administrative structure and processes required to plan, coordinate, and control the company's new operations. None of the usual perspectives which might be used to analyze such organizational changes—for example, economics, industrial engineering, marketing, or policy—appears to address all of the problems experienced by Porter Pump and Valve. Therefore, how can the adaptive process which occurred at PPV be described in its entirety?

THE ADAPTIVE CYCLE

We have developed a general model of the adaptive process which we call the *adaptive cycle*. Consistent with the strategic-choice approach to the study of organizations, the model parallels and expands ideas formulated by theorists such as Chandler (9), Child (10), Cyert and March (11), Drucker (12, 13), Thompson (18), and Weick (19, 20). Essentially, proponents of the strategic-choice perspective argue that organizational behavior is only partially preordained by environmental conditions and that the choices which top managers make are the critical determinants of organizational structure and process. Although these choices are numerous and complex, they can be viewed as three broad "problems" of organizational adaptation: the *entrepreneurial problem*, the *engineering problem,* and the *administrative problem*. In mature organizations, management must solve each of these problems simultaneously, but for explanatory purposes, these adaptive problems can be discussed as if they occurred sequentially.

The Entrepreneurial Problem

The adaptive cycle, though evident in all organizations, is perhaps most visible in new or rapidly growing organizations (and in organizations which recently have survived a major crisis). In a new organization, an entrepreneurial insight, perhaps only vaguely defined at first, must be developed into a concrete *definition of an organizational domain: a specific good or service and a target market or market segment*. In an ongoing organization, the entrepreneurial problem has an added dimension. Because the organization has already obtained a set of "solutions" to its engineering and administrative problems, its next attempt at an entrepreneurial "thrust" may be difficult. In the example of Porter Pump and Valve, the company's attempt to modify its products and markets was constrained by its present production process and by the fact that the general manager and his staff did not possess the needed marketing orientation.

In either a new or ongoing organization, the solution to the entrepreneurial problem is marked by management's acceptance of a particular product-market domain, and this acceptance becomes evident when management decides to commit resources to achieve objectives relative to the domain. In many organizations, external and internal commitment to the entrepreneurial solution is sought through the development and projection of an organizational "image" which defines both the organization's market and its orientation toward it (e.g., an emphasis on size, efficiency, or innovation).

Although we are suggesting that the engineering phase begins at this point, the need for further entrepreneurial activities clearly does not disappear. The entrepreneurial function remains a top-management responsibility, although as Bower (7) has described, the identification of a new opportunity and the initial impetus for movement toward it may originate at lower managerial levels.

The Engineering Problem

The engineering problem involves the creation of a system which *operationalizes management's solution to the entrepreneurial problem.* Such a system requires management to select an appropriate technology (input-transformation-output process) for producing and distributing chosen products or services and to form new information, communication, and control linkages (or modify existing linkages) to ensure proper operation of the technology.

As solutions to these problems are reached, initial implementation of the administrative system takes place. There is no assurance that the configuration of the organization, as it begins to emerge during this phase, will remain the same when the engineering problem finally has been solved. The actual form of the organization's structure will be determined during the administrative phase as management solidifies relations with the environment and establishes processes for coordinating and controlling internal operations. Referring again to Porter Pump and Valve, the company's redefinition of its domain required concomitant changes in its technology—from a pure mass-production technology to more of a unit or small-batch technology (21).

The Administrative Problem

The administrative problem, as described by most theories of management, is primarily that of reducing uncertainty within the organizational system, or, in terms of the present model, of rationalizing and stabilizing those activities which successfully solved problems faced by the organization during the entrepreneurial and engineering phases. Solving the administrative problem involves more than simply rationalizing the system already developed (uncertainty reduction); it also involves formulating and implementing those processes which will enable the organization to continue to evolve (innovation). This conception of the administrative problem, as a pivotal factor in the cycle of adaptation, deserves further elaboration.

Rationalization and Articulation. In the ideal organization, management would be equally adept at performing two somewhat conflicting functions: it would be able to create an administrative system (structure and processes) that could smoothly direct and monitor the organization's current activities without, at the same time, allowing the system to become so ingrained that future innovation activities are jeopardized. Such a perspective requires the administrative system to be viewed as both a *lagging* and *leading* variable in the process of adaptation. As a lagging variable, it must rationalize, through the development of appropriate structures and processes, strategic decisions made at previous points in the adjustment process. As a leading variable, the administrative system must facilitate the organization's future capacity to adapt by articulating and reinforcing the paths along which innovative activity can proceed. At Porter Pump and Valve, management modified its planning, coordination, and control processes substantially in order to pursue the company's newly chosen areas of business (the "lagging" aspect of administration). At the same time, key personnel were added to the marketing department; their duties included product development, market research, and technical consulting. These activities were designed to keep PPV at the forefront of new product and market opportunities (the "leading" aspect of administration).

THE STRATEGIC TYPOLOGY

If one accepts the adaptive cycle as valid, the question becomes: How do organizations move through the cycle? That is, using the language of our model, what strategies do organizations employ in solving their entrepreneurial, engineering, and administrative problems? Our research and interpretation of the literature show that there are essentially three *strategic types* of organizations: Defenders, Analyzers, and Prospectors. Each type has its own unique strategy for relating to its chosen market(s), and each has a particular configuration of technology, structure, and process that is consistent with its market strategy. A fourth type of organization encountered in our studies is called the Reactor. The Reactor is a form of strategic "failure" in that inconsistencies exist among its strategy, technology, structure, and process.

Although similar typologies of various aspects of organizational behavior are available (1, 2, 3, 15, 16, 17), our formulation specifies relationships among strategy, technology, structure, and process to the point where entire organizations can be viewed as integrated wholes in dynamic interaction with their environments. Any typology is unlikely to encompass every form of organizational behavior—the world of organizations is much too changeable and complex to permit such a claim. Nevertheless, every organization that we have observed appears, when compared to other organizations in its industry, to fit predominantly into one of the four categories, and its behavior is generally predictable given its typological classification. The "pure" form of each of these organization types is described below.

Defenders

The Defender (i.e., its top management) deliberately enacts and maintains an environment for which a stable form of organization is appropriate. Stability is chiefly achieved by the Defender's definition of, and solution to, its entrepreneurial problem. Defenders define their *entrepreneurial* problem as *how to seal off a portion of the total market in order to create a stable domain,* and they do so by producing only a limited set of products directed at a narrow segment of the total potential market. Within this limited domain, the Defender strives aggressively to prevent competitors from entering its "turf." Such behaviors include standard economic actions like competitive pricing or high-quality products, but Defenders also tend to ignore developments and trends outside of their domains, choosing instead to grow through market penetration and perhaps some limited product development. Over time, a true Defender is able to carve out and maintain a small niche within the industry which is difficult for competitors to penetrate.

Having chosen a narrow product-market domain, the Defender invests a great deal of resources in solving its *engineering* problem: *how to produce and distribute goods or services as efficiently as possible.* Typically, the Defender does so by developing a single core technology that is highly cost-efficient. Technological efficiency is central to the Defender's success since its domain has been deliberately created to absorb outputs on a predictable, continuous basis. Some Defenders extend technological efficiency to its limits through a process of vertical integration—incorporating each stage of production from raw materials supply to distribution of final output into the same organizational system.

Finally, the Defender's solution to its administrative problem is closely aligned with its solutions to the entrepreneurial and engineering problems. The Defender's *administrative* problem—*how to achieve strict control of the organization in order to ensure effi-*

ciency—is solved through a combination of structural and process mechanisms that can be generally described as "mechanistic" (8). These mechanisms include a top-management group heavily dominated by production and cost-control specialists, little or no scanning of the environment for new areas of opportunity, intensive planning oriented toward cost and other efficiency issues, functional structures characterized by extensive division of labor, centralized control, communications through formal hierarchical channels, and so on. Such an administrative system is ideally suited for generating and maintaining efficiency, and the key characteristic of stability is as apparent here as in the solution to the other two adaptive problems.

Pursued vigorously, the Defender strategy can be viable in most industries, although stable industries lend themselves to this type of organization more than turbulent industries (e.g., the relative lack of technological change in the food-processing industry generally favors the Defender strategy compared with the situation in the electronics industry). This particular form of organization is not without its potential risks. The Defender's *primary risk* is that of *ineffectiveness*— being unable to respond to a major shift in its market environment. The Defender relies on the continued viability of its single, narrow domain, and it receives a return on its large technological investment only if the major problems facing the organization continue to be of an engineering nature. If the Defender's market shifts dramatically, this type of organization has little capacity for locating and exploiting new areas of opportunity. In short, the Defender is perfectly capable of responding to today's world. To the extent that tomorrow's world is similar to today's, the Defender is ideally suited for its environment. Table 1 summarizes the Defender's salient characteristics and the major strengths and weaknesses inherent in this pattern of adaptation.

Prospectors

In many ways, Prospectors respond to their chosen environments in a manner that is almost the opposite of the Defender. In one sense, the Prospector is exactly like the Defender: there is a high degree of consistency among its solutions to the three problems of adaptation.

Generally speaking, the Prospector enacts an environment that is more dynamic than those of other types of organizations within the same industry. Unlike the Defender, whose success comes primarily from efficiently serving a stable domain, the Prospector's prime capability is that of finding and exploiting new product and market opportunities. For a Prospector, maintaining a reputation as an innovator in product and market development may be as important as, perhaps even more important than, high profitability. In fact, because of the

TABLE 1
Characteristics of the Defender

Entrepreneurial Problem	*Engineering Problem*	*Administrative Problem*
Problem:	*Problem:*	*Problem:*
How to "seal off" a portion of the total market to create a stable set of products and customers.	How to produce and distribute goods or services as efficiently as possible.	How to maintain strict control of the organization in order to ensure efficiency.
Solutions:	*Solutions:*	*Solutions:*
1. Narrow and stable domain. 2. Aggressive maintenance of domain (e.g., competitive pricing and excellent customer service). 3. Tendency to ignore developments outside of domain. 4. Cautious and incremental growth primarily through market penetration. 5. Some product development but closely related to current goods or services.	1. Cost-efficient technology. 2. Single core technology. 3. Tendency toward vertical integration. 4. Continuous improvements in technology to maintain efficiency.	1. Financial and production experts most powerful members of the dominant coalition; limited environmental scanning. 2. Tenure of dominant coalition is lengthy; promotions from within. 3. Planning is intensive, cost oriented, and completed before action is taken. 4. Tendency toward functional structure with extensive division of labor and high degree of formalization. 5. Centralized control and long-looped vertical information systems. 6. Simple coordination mechanisms and conflict resolved through hierarchical channels. 7. Organizational performance measured against previous years; reward system favors production and finance.
Costs and Benefits:	*Costs and Benefits:*	*Costs and Benefits:*
It is difficult for competitors to dislodge the organization from its small niche in the industry, but a major shift in the market could threaten survival.	Technological efficiency is central to organizational performance, but heavy investment in this area requires technological problems to remain familiar and predictable for lengthy periods of time.	Administrative system is ideally suited to maintain stability and efficiency but it is not well suited to locating and responding to new product or market opportunities.

Source: Raymond E. Miles and Charles C. Snow, *Organizational Strategy, Structure, and Process* (New York: McGraw-Hill, 1978), Table 3–1.

inevitable "failure rate" associated with sustained product and market innovation, Prospectors may find it difficult consistently to attain the profit levels of the more efficient Defender.

Defining its *entrepreneurial* problem as *how to locate and develop product and market opportunities*, the Prospector's domain is usually broad and in a continuous state of development. The systematic addition of new products or markets, frequently combined with retrenchment in other parts of the domain, gives the Prospector's products and markets an aura of fluidity uncharacteristic of the Defender. To locate new areas of opportunity, the Prospector must develop and maintain the capacity to survey a wide range of environmental conditions, trends, and events. This type of organization invests heavily in individuals and groups who scan the environment for potential opportunities. Because these scanning activities are not limited to the organization's current domain, Prospectors are frequently the creators of change in their respective industries. Change is one of the major tools used by the Prospector to gain an edge over competitors, so Prospector managers typically perceive more environmental change and uncertainty than managers of the Defender (or the other two organization types).

To serve its changing domain properly, the Prospector requires a good deal of flexibility in its technology and administrative system. Unlike the Defender, the Prospector's choice of products and markets is not limited to those which fall within the range of the organization's present technological capability. The Prospector's technology is contingent upon both the organization's current *and* future product mix: entrepreneurial activities always have primacy, and appropriate technologies are not selected or developed until late in the process of product development. Therefore, the Prospector's overall engineering problem is *how to avoid long-term commitments to a single type of technological process*, and the organization usually does so by creating multiple, prototypical technologies which have a low degree of routinization and mechanization.

Finally, the Prospector's *administrative* problem flows from its changing domain and flexible technologies: *how to facilitate rather than control organizational operations*. That is, the Prospector's administrative system must be able to deploy and coordinate resources among numerous decentralized units and projects rather than to plan and control the operations of the entire organization centrally. To accomplish overall facilitation and coordination, the Prospector's structure-process mechanisms must be "organic" (8). These mechanisms include a top-management group dominated by marketing and research and development experts, planning that is broad rather than intensive and oriented toward results not methods, product or project structures characterized by a low degree of formalization, decentralized control, lateral as well as vertical communications, and so on. In contrast to the Defender, the Prospector's descriptive catchword throughout its administrative as well as entrepreneurial and engineering solutions is "flexibility."

Of course, the Prospector strategy also has its costs. Although the Prospector's continuous exploration of change helps to protect it from a changing environment, this type of organization runs the *primary risk* of *low profitability and overextension of resources*. While the Prospector's technological flexibility permits a rapid response to a changing domain, complete efficiency cannot be obtained because of the presence of multiple technologies. Finally, the Prospector's administrative system is well suited to maintain flexibility, but it may, at least temporarily, underutilize or even misutilize physical, financial, and human resources. In short, the Prospector is effective—it can respond to the demands of tomorrow's world. To the extent that the world of tomorrow is similar to that of today, the Prospector cannot maximize profitability because of its inherent inefficiency. Table 2 summarizes the Prospector's salient characteristics and the major strengths and weaknesses associated with this pattern of adaptation.

TABLE 2
Characteristics of the Prospector

Entrepreneurial Problem	Engineering Problem	Administrative Problem
Problem:	*Problem:*	*Problem:*
How to locate and exploit new product and market opportunities.	How to avoid long-term commitments to a single technological process.	How to facilitate and coordinate numerous and diverse operations.
Solutions:	*Solutions:*	*Solutions:*
1. Broad and continuously developing domain.	1. Flexible, prototypical technologies.	1. Marketing and research and development experts most powerful members of the dominant coalition.
2. Monitors wide range of environmental conditions and events.	2. Multiple technologies.	
3. Creates change in the industry.	3. Low degree of routinization and mechanization; technology embedded in people.	2. Dominant coalition is large, diverse, and transitory; may include an inner circle.
4. Growth through product and market development.		3. Tenure of dominant coalition not always lengthy; key managers may be hired from outside as well as promoted from within.
5. Growth may occur in spurts.		4. Planning is comprehensive, problem oriented, and cannot be finalized before action is taken.

TABLE 2 (concluded)

Entrepreneurial Problem	Engineering Problem	Administrative Problem
		5. Tendency toward product structure with low division of labor and low degree of formalization.
		6. Decentralized control and short-looped horizontal information systems.
		7. Complex coordination mechanisms and conflict resolved through integrators.
		8. Organizational performance measured against important competitors; reward system favors marketing and research and development.
Costs and Benefits:	*Costs and Benefits:*	*Costs and Benefits:*
Product and market innovation protect the organization from a changing environment, but the organization runs the risk of low profitability and overextension of its resources.	Technological flexibility permits a rapid response to a changing domain, but the organization cannot develop maximum efficiency in its production and distribution system because of multiple technologies.	Administrative system is ideally suited to maintain flexibility and effectiveness but may underutilize and misutilize resources.

Source: Raymond E. Miles and Charles C. Snow, *Organizational Strategy, Structure, and Process* (New York: McGraw-Hill, 1978), Table 4–1.

Analyzers

Based on our research, the Defender and the Prospector seem to reside at opposite ends of a continuum of adjustment strategies. Between these two extremes, a third type of organization is called the Analyzer. The Analyzer is a unique combination of the Prospector and Defender types and represents a viable alternative to these other strategies. A true Analyzer is an organization that attempts to minimize risk while maximizing the opportunity for profit—that is, an experienced Analyzer combines the strengths of both the Prospector and the Defender into a single system. This strategy is difficult to pursue, particularly in industries characterized by rapid market and technological change, and thus the word that best describes the Analyzer's adaptive approach is "balance."

The Analyzer defines its *entrepreneurial* problem in terms similar to both the Prospector and the Defender: *how to locate and exploit new product and market opportunities while simultaneously maintaining a firm core of traditional products and customers*. The Analyzer's solution to the entrepreneurial problem is also a blend of the solutions preferred by the Prospector and the Defender: the Analyzer moves toward new products or new markets but only after their viability has been demonstrated. This periodic transformation of the Analyzer's domain is accomplished through imitation—only the most successful product or market innovations developed by prominent Prospectors are adopted. At the same time, the majority of the Analyzer's revenue is generated by a fairly stable set of products and customer or client groups—a Defender characteristic. Thus, the successful Analyzer must be able to respond quickly when following the lead of key Prospectors while at the same time maintaining operating efficiency in its stable product and market areas. To the extent that it is successful, the Analyzer can grow through market penetration as well as product and market development.

The duality evident in the Analyzer's domain is reflected in its *engineering* problem and solution. This type of organization must learn *how to achieve and protect an equilibrium between conflicting demands for technological flexibility and for technological stability*. This equilibrium is accomplished by partitioning production activities to form a dual technological core. The stable component of the Analyzer's technology bears a strong resemblance to the Defender's technology. It is functionally organized and exhibits high levels of standardization, routinization, and mechanization in an attempt to approach cost efficiency. The Analyzer's flexible technological component resembles the Prospector's technological orientation. In manufacturing organizations, it frequently includes a large group of applications engineers (or their equivalent) who are rotated among teams charged with the task of rapidly adapting new product designs to fit the Analyzer's existing stable technology.

The Analyzer's dual technological core thus reflects the engineering solutions of both the Prospector and the Defender, with the stable and flexible components integrated primarily by an influential applied research group. To the extent that this group is able to develop solutions that match the organization's existing technological capabilities with the new products desired by product managers, the Analyzer can enlarge its product line without incurring the Prospector's extensive research and development expenses.

The Analyzer's administrative problem, as well as its entrepreneurial and engineering problems, contains both Defender and Prospector characteristics. Generally speaking, the *administrative* problem of the Analyzer is *how to differentiate the organization's structure and processes to accommodate both stable and dynamic areas of operation.* The Analyzer typically solves this problem with some version of a matrix organization structure. Heads of key functional units, most notably engineering and production, unite with product managers (usually housed in the marketing department) to form a balanced dominant coalition similar to both the Defender and the Prospector. The product manager's influence is usually greater than the functional manager's since his or her task is to identify promising product-market innovations and to supervise their movement through applied engineering and into production in a smooth and timely manner. The presence of engineering and production in the dominant coalition is to represent the more stable domain and technology which are the foundations of the Analyzer's overall operations. The Analyzer's matrix structure is supported by intensive planning between the functional divisions of marketing and production, broad-gauge planning between the applied research group and the product managers for the development of new products, centralized control mechanisms in the functional divisions and decentralized control techniques in the product groups, and so on. In sum, the key characteristic of the Analyzer's administrative system is the proper differentiation of the organization's structure and processes to achieve a balance between the stable and dynamic areas of operation.

As is true for both the Defender and Prospector, the Analyzer strategy is not without its costs. The duality in the Analyzer's domain forces the organization to establish a dual technological core, and it requires management to operate fundamentally different planning, control, and reward systems simultaneously. Thus, the Analyzer's twin characteristics of stability and flexibility limit the organization's ability to move fully in either direction were the domain to shift dramatically. Consequently, the Analyzer's *primary risks* are both *inefficiency and ineffectiveness* if it does not maintain the necessary balance throughout its strategy-structure relationship. Table 3 summarizes the Analyzer's salient characteristics and the major strengths and weaknesses inherent in this pattern of adaptation.

Reactors

The Defender, the Prospector, and the Analyzer can all be proactive with respect to their environments, though each is proactive in a different way. At the extremes, Defenders continually attempt to develop greater efficiency in existing operations while Prospectors ex-

TABLE 3
Characteristics of the Analyzer

Entrepreneurial Problem	Engineering Problem	Administrative Problem
Problem:	*Problem:*	*Problem:*
How to locate and exploit new product and market opportunities while simultaneously maintaining a firm base of traditional products and customers.	How to be efficient in stable portions of the domain and flexible in changing portions.	How to differentiate the organization's structure and processes to accommodate both stable and dynamic areas of operation.
Solutions:	*Solutions:*	*Solutions:*
1. Hybrid domain that is both stable and changing.	1. Dual technological core (stable and flexible component).	1. Marketing and engineering most influential members of dominant coalition, followed closely by production.
2. Surveillance mechanisms mostly limited to marketing; some research and development.	2. Large and influential applied engineering group.	2. Intensive planning between marketing and production concerning stable portion of domain; comprehensive planning among marketing, engineering, and product managers concerning new products and markets.
3. Steady growth through market penetration and product-market development.	3. Moderate degree of technical rationality.	3. "Loose" matrix structure combining both functional divisions and product groups.
		4. Moderately centralized control system with vertical and horizontal feedback loops.
		5. Extremely complex and expensive coordination mechanisms; some conflict resolution through product managers, some through normal hierarchical channels.
		6. Performance appraisal based on both effectiveness and efficiency measures, most rewards to marketing and engineering.

TABLE 3 (concluded)

Entrepreneurial Problem	Engineering Problem	Administrative Problem
Costs and Benefits:	Costs and Benefits:	Costs and Benefits:
Low investment in research and development, combined with imitation of demonstrably successful products, minimizes risk, but domain must be optimally balanced at all times between stability and flexibility.	Dual technological core is able to serve a hybrid stable-changing domain, but the technology can never be completely effective or efficient.	Administrative system is ideally suited to balance stability and flexibility, but if this balance is lost, it may be difficult to restore equilibrium.

Source: Raymond E. Miles and Charles C. Snow, *Organizational Strategy, Structure, and Process* (New York: McGraw-Hill, 1978), Table 5–1.

plore environmental change in search of new opportunities. Over time, these action modes stabilize to form a pattern of response to environmental conditions that is both *consistent* and *stable.*

A fourth type of organization, the Reactor, exhibits a pattern of adjustment to its environment that is both *inconsistent* and *unstable;* this type lacks a set of response mechanisms which it can consistently put into effect when faced with a changing environment. As a consequence, Reactors exist in a state of almost perpetual instability. The Reactor's "adaptive" cycle usually consists of responding inappropriately to environmental change and uncertainty, performing poorly as a result, and then being reluctant to act aggressively in the future. Thus, the Reactor is a "residual" strategy, arising when one of the other three strategies is improperly pursued.

Although there are undoubtedly many reasons why organizations become Reactors, we have identified three. First, *top management may not have clearly articulated the organization's strategy.* For example, one company was headed by a one-man Prospector of immense personal skills. A first-rate architect, he led his firm through a rapid and successful growth period during which the company moved from the design and construction of suburban shopping centers, through the construction and management of apartment complexes, and into consulting with municipal agencies concerning urban planning problems. Within 10 years of its inception, the company was a loose but effective collection of semiautonomous units held together by this particular individual. When this individual was suddenly killed in a plane crash, the company was thrown into a strategic void. Because each separate unit of the company was successful, each was able to argue strongly for more emphasis on its particular domain and operations. Consequently, the new chief executive officer, caught between a number of conflicting but legitimate demands for resources, was unable to develop a unified, cohesive statement of the organization's strategy; thus, consistent and aggressive behavior was precluded.

A second and perhaps more common cause of organizational instability is that *management does not fully shape the organization's structure and processes to fit a chosen strategy.* Unless all of the domain, technological, and administrative decisions required to have an operational strategy are properly aligned, strategy is a mere statement, not an effective guide to behavior. One publishing company wished, in effect, to become an Analyzer—management had articulated a direction for the organization which involved operating in both stable and changing domains within the college textbook publishing industry. Although the organization was comprised of several key Defender and Prospector characteristics such as functional structures and decentralized control mechanisms, these structure-process features were not appropriately linked to the company's different domains. In one area where the firm wished to "prospect," for example, the designated unit had a functional structure and shared a large, almost mass-production technology with several other units, thereby making it difficult for the organization to respond to market opportunities quickly. Thus, this particular organization exhibited a weak link between its strategy and its structure-process characteristics.

The third cause of instability—and perhaps ultimate failure—is *a tendency for management to maintain the organization's current strategy-structure relationship despite overwhelming changes in environmental conditions.* Another organization in our studies, a food-processing company, had initially been an industry pioneer in both the processing and marketing of dried fruits and nuts. Gradually, the company settled into a Defender strategy and took vigorous steps to bolster this strategy, including limiting the domain to a narrow line of products, integrating backward into growing and harvesting, and assigning a controller to each of the company's major functional divisions as a means of keeping costs down. Within recent years, the company's market has become saturated, and profit margins have shrunk on most of the firm's products. In spite of its declining market, the organization has consistently clung to a Defender strategy and structure, even to the point of creating ad hoc cross-divisional committees whose sole purpose was to find ways of increasing efficiency further. At the moment, management recognizes that the organization is in trouble, but it is reluctant to make the drastic modifications required to attain a strategy and structure better suited to the changing market conditions.

Unless an organization exists in a "protected" environment such as a monopolistic or highly regulated industry, it cannot continue to behave as a Reactor indefinitely. Sooner or later, it must move toward one of the consistent and stable strategies of Defender, Analyzer, or Prospector.

MANAGEMENT THEORY LINKAGES TO ORGANIZATIONAL STRATEGY AND STRUCTURE

Organizations are limited in their choices of adaptive behavior to those which top management believes will allow the effective direction and control of human resources. Therefore, top executives' theories of management are an important factor in analyzing an organization's ability to adapt to its environment. Although our research is only in its preliminary stage, we have found some patterns in the relationship between management theory and organizational strategy and structure.

A theory of management has three basic components: (*a*) a set of assumptions about human attitudes and behaviors, (*b*) managerial policies and actions consistent with these assumptions, and (*c*) expectations about employee performance if these policies and actions are implemented (see Table 4). Theories of management are discussed in more detail in Miles (14).

During the latter part of the 19th century and the early decades of the 20th, mainstream management theory, as voiced by managers and by management scholars, conformed to what has been termed the *Traditional* model. Essentially, the Traditional model maintained that the capability for effective decision making was narrowly distributed in organizations, and this approach thus legitimized unilateral control of organizational systems by top management. According to this model, a select group of owner-managers was able to direct large numbers of employees by carefully standardizing and routinizing their work and by placing the planning function solely in the hands of top managers. Under this type of management system, employees could be expected to perform up to some minimum standard, but few would be likely to exhibit truly outstanding performance.

Beginning in the 20s, the Traditional model gradually began to give way to the *Human Relations* model. This model accepted the traditional notion that superior decision-making competence was narrowly distributed among the employee population but emphasized the universality of social needs for belonging and recognition. This model argued that impersonal treatment was the source of subordinate resistance to managerial directives, and adherents of this approach urged managers to employ devices to enhance organization members' feel-

TABLE 4
Theories of Management

Traditional Model	Human Relations Model	Human Resources Model
Assumptions	*Assumptions*	*Assumptions*
1. Work is inherently distasteful to most people. 2. What workers do is less important than what they earn for doing it. 3. Few want or can handle work which requires creativity, self-direction, or self-control.	1. People want to feel useful and important. 2. People desire to belong and to be recognized as individuals. 3. These needs are more important than money in motivating people to work.	1. Work is not inherently distasteful. People want to contribute to meaningful goals which they have helped establish. 2. Most people can exercise far more creative, responsible self-direction and self-control than their present jobs demand.
Policies	*Policies*	*Policies*
1. The manager's basic task is to closely supervise and control his (her) subordinates. 2. He (she) must break tasks down into simple, repetitive, easily learned operations. 3. He (she) must establish detailed work routines and procedures and enforce these firmly but fairly.	1. The manager's basic task is to make each worker feel useful and important. 2. He (she) should keep his (her) subordinates informed and listen to their objections to his (her) plans. 3. The manager should allow his (her) subordinate to exercise some self-direction and self-control on routine matters.	1. The manager's basic task is to make use of his (her) "untapped" human resources. 2. He (she) must create an environment in which all members may contribute to the limits of their ability. 3. He (she) must encourage full participation on important matters, continually broadening subordinate self-direction and control.
Expectations	*Expectations*	*Expectations*
1. People can tolerate work if the pay is decent and the boss is fair. 2. If tasks are simple enough and people are closely controlled, they will produce up to standard.	1. Sharing information with subordinates and involving them in routine decisions will satisfy their basic needs to belong and to feel important. 2. Satisfying these needs will improve morale and reduce resistance to formal authority—subordinates will willingly cooperate and produce.	1. Expanding subordinate influence, self-direction, and self-control will lead to direct improvements in organizational performance. 2. Work satisfaction may improve as a "by-product" of subordinates making full use of their resources.

Source: Raymond E. Miles, *Theories of Management* (New York: McGraw-Hill, 1975), Figure 3–1.

ings of involvement and importance in order to improve organizational performance. Suggestion systems, employee counseling, and even company unions had common parentage in this philosophy. The Depression and World War II both acted to delay the development and spread of the Human Relations model, and it was not until the late 40s and early 50s that it became the prime message put forth by managers and management scholars.

Beginning in the mid-50s, a third phase in the evolution of management theory began with the emergence of the *Human Resources* model which argued that the capacity for effective decision making in the pursuit of organizational objectives was widely dispersed and that most organization members represented untapped resources which, if properly managed, could considerably enhance organizational performance. The Human Resources approach viewed management's role not as that of a controller (however benevolent) but as that of a facilitator—removing the constraints that block organization members' search for ways to contribute meaningfully in their work roles. In recent years, some writers have questioned the extent to which the Human Resources model is applicable, arguing for a more "contingent" theory emphasizing variations in member capacity and motivation to contribute and the technological constraints associated with broadened self-direction and self-control. The Human Resources model probably still represents the leading edge of management theory, perhaps awaiting the formulation of a successor model.

Linking the Strategic Typology to Management Theory

Are there identifiable linkages between an organization's strategic type and the management theory of its dominant coalition? For example, do top executives in Defenders profess Traditional beliefs about management and those in Prospectors a Human Resources philosophy? The answer to this question is, in our opinion, a bit more complex than simply yes or no.

One of our studies investigated aspects of the relationship between organizational strategy-structure and management theory. Although the results are only tentative at this point, relatively clear patterns emerged. In general, Traditional and Human Relations managerial beliefs are more likely to be found in Defender and Reactor organizations, while Human Resources beliefs are more often associated with Analyzer and Prospector organizations. But this relationship appears to be *constrained in one direction;* it seems highly unlikely that a Traditional or Human Relations manager can function effectively as the head of a Prospector organization. The prescriptions of the Traditional model simply do not support the degree of decentralized decision making required to create and manage diversified organizations. It is quite possible for a Human Resources manager to lead a Defender organization. Of course, the organization's planning and control processes under such leadership would be less centralized than if the organization were managed according to the Traditional model. Using the Human Resources philosophy, heads of functional divisions might either participate in the planning and budgeting process, or they might simply be delegated considerable autonomy in operating their cost centers. (In Defender organizations operated according to the Human Resources philosophy, human capabilities are aimed primarily at cost efficiency rather than product development.)

The fit between management theory and the strategy, structure, and process characteristics of Analyzers is perhaps more complex than with any of the other types. Analyzers, as previously described, tend to remain cost efficient in the production of a limited line of goods or services while attempting to move as rapidly as possible into promising new areas opened up by Prospectors. Note that the organization structure of the Analyzer does not demand extensive, permanent delegation of decision-making authority to division managers. Most of the Analyzer's products or services can be produced in functionally structured divisions similar to those in Defender organizations. New products or services may be developed in separate divisions or departments created for that purpose and then integrated as quickly as possible into the permanent technology and structure. It seems likely to us, although our evidence is inconclusive, that various members of the dominant coalition in Analyzer organizations hold moderate but different managerial philosophies, that certain key executives believe it is their role to pay fairly close attention to detail while others appear to be more willing to delegate, for short periods, moderate amounts of autonomy necessary to bring new products or services on line rapidly. If these varying managerial philosophies are "mismatched" within the Analyzer's operating units—if, for example, Traditional managers are placed in charge of innovative subunits—then it is unlikely that a successful Analyzer strategy can be pursued.

Holding together a dominant coalition with mixed views concerning strategy and structure is not an easy task. It is difficult, for example, for managers engaged in new product or service development to function within planning, control, and reward systems established for more stable operations, so the Analyzer must be successfully differentiated into its stable and changing areas and managed accordingly. Note that experimentation in the analyzer is usually quite limited. The exploration and risk associated with major product or service breakthroughs are not present (as would be the case in a Prospector), and thus interdependencies within the system may be kept at a manageable level. Such would not be the case if Analyzers attempted to be both cost-efficient producers of stable products or services and active in a major way in new product and market development. Numerous organizations are today being led or forced into such a mixed strategy (multinational companies, certain forms of conglomerates, many organizations in high-technology industries, etc.), and their struggles may well produce a new organization type and demands for a supporting theory of management. Whatever form this new type of organization takes, however, clearly its management-theory requirements will closely parallel or extend those of the Human Resources model (15).

CONCLUSIONS

Our research represents an initial attempt: (*a*) to portray the major elements of organizational adaptation, (*b*) to describe patterns of behavior used by organizations in adjusting to their environments, and (*c*) to provide a language for discussing organizational behavior at the total-system level. Therefore, we have offered a theoretical framework composed of a model of the adaptive process (called the adaptive cycle) and four empirically determined means of moving through this process (the strategic typology). In addition, we have related this theoretical framework to available theories of management (Traditional, Human Relations, Human Resources). Effective organizational adaptation hinges on the ability of managers to not only envision and implement new organizational forms but also to direct and control people within them.

We believe that managers' ability to meet successfully environmental conditions of tomorrow revolves around their understanding of organizations as integrated and dynamic wholes. Hopefully, our framework offers a theory and language for promoting such an understanding.

REFERENCES

1. Anderson, Carl R., and Frank T. Paine. "Managerial Perceptions and Strategic Behavior," *Academy of Management Journal* 18 (1975), pp. 811–23.
2. Ansoff, H. Igor. *Corporate Strategy* (New York: McGraw-Hill, 1965).
3. Ansoff, H. Igor, and Richard Brandenburg, "A Language for Organizational Design," *Management Science* 17(1971), pp. B717–B731.
4. Ansoff, H. Igor, and John M. Stewart. "Strategies for a Technology-Based Business," *Harvard Business Review* 45 (1967), pp. 71–83.

5. Argyris, Chris. "On Organizations of the Future," *Administrative and Policy Study Series* 1, no. 03–006 (Beverly Hills, Calif.: Sage Publications, 1973).

6. Beer, Michael, and Stanley M. Davis. "Creating a Global Organization: Failures along the Way," *Columbia Journal of World Business*, 11 (1976), pp. 72–84.

7. Bower, Joseph L. *Managing the Resource Allocation Process* (Boston: Division of Research, Harvard Business School, 1970).

8. Burns, Tom, and G. M. Stalker. *The Management of Innovation* (London: Tavistock, 1961).

9. Chandler, Alfred D., Jr. *Strategy and Structure* (Garden City, N.Y.: Doubleday, 1962).

10. Child, John. "Organizational Structure, Environment, and Performance—The Role of Strategic Choice," *Sociology* 6 (1972), pp. 1–22.

11. Cyert, Richard, and James G. March. *A Behavioral Theory of the Firm* (Englewood Cliffs, N.J.: Prentice-Hall, 1963).

12. Drucker, Peter F. *The Practice of Management* (New York: Harper & Row, 1954).

13. Drucker, Peter F. *Management: Tasks, Responsibilities, Practices* (New York: Harper & Row, 1974).

14. Miles, Raymond E. *Theories of Management* (New York: McGraw-Hill, 1975).

15. Miles, Raymond E., and Charles C. Snow. *Organizational Strategy, Structure, and Process* (New York: McGraw-Hill, 1978).

16. Rogers, Everett M. *Communication of Innovations: A Cross-Cultural Approach*, 2d ed. (New York: Free Press, 1971).

17. Segal, Morley. "Organization and Environment: A Typology of Adaptability and Structure," *Public Administration Review* 35 (1974), pp. 212–20.

18. Thompson, James D. *Organizations in Action* (New York: McGraw-Hill, 1967).

19. Weick, Karl E. *The Social Psychology of Organizing* (Reading, Mass.: Addison-Wesley, 1969).

20. Weick, Karl E. "Enactment Processes in Organizations," in *New Directions in Organizational Behavior*, ed. Barry M. Staw and Gerald R. Salancik (Chicago: St. Clair, 1977), pp. 267–300.

21. Woodward, Joan. *Industrial Organization: Theory and Practice* (London: Oxford University Press, 1965).

32

Organization Design: An Information Processing View*

JAY R. GALBRAITH

THE INFORMATION PROCESSING MODEL

A basic proposition is that the greater the uncertainty of the task, the greater the amount of information that has to be processed between decision makers during the execution of the task. If the task is well understood prior to performing it, much of the activity can be preplanned. If it is not understood, then during the actual task execution more knowledge is acquired which leads to changes in resource allocations, schedules, and priorities. All these changes require information processing *during* task performance. Therefore *the greater the task uncertainty, the greater the amount of information that must be processed among decision makers during task execution in order to achieve a given level of performance.* The basic effect of uncertainty is to limit the ability of the organization to preplan or to make decisions about activities in advance of their execution. Therefore it is hypothesized that the observed variations in organizational forms are variations in the strategies of organizations (1) to increase their ability to preplan, (2) to increase their flexibility to adapt to their inability to preplan, or (3) to decrease the level of performance required for continued viability. Which strategy is chosen depends on the relative costs of the strategies. The function of the framework is to identify these strategies and their costs.

THE MECHANISTIC MODEL

This framework is best developed by keeping in mind a hypothetical organization. Assume it is large and employs a number of specialist groups and resources in providing the output. After the task has been divided into specialist subtasks, the problem is to integrate the sub-

---

* Reprinted from *Interfaces* 4, no. 3 (May 1974), pp. 28–36. Copyright © 1974, The Institute of Management Sciences.

tasks around the completion of the global task. This is the problem of organization design. The behaviors that occur in one subtask cannot be judged as good or bad per se. The behaviors are more effective or ineffective depending upon the behaviors of the other subtask performers. There is a design problem because the executors of the behaviors cannot communicate with all the roles with whom they are interdependent. Therefore the design problem is to create mechanisms that permit coordinated action across large numbers of interdependent roles. Each of these mechanisms, however, has a limited range over which it is effective at handling the information requirements necessary to coordinate the interdependent roles. As the amount of uncertainty increases, and therefore information processing increases, the organization must adopt integrating mechanisms which increase its information processing capabilities.

1. Coordination by Rules or Programs

For routine predictable tasks March and Simon have identified the use of rules or programs to coordinate behavior between interdependent subtasks [March and Simon, 1958, chap. 6]. To the extent that job related situations can be predicted in advance, and behaviors specified for these situations, programs allow an interdependent set of activities to be performed without the need for interunit communication. Each role occupant simply executes the behavior which is appropriate for the task-related situation with which he is faced.

2. Hierarchy

As the organization faces greater uncertainty its participants face situations for which they have no rules. At this point the hierarchy is employed on an exception basis. The recurring job situations are programmed with rules while infrequent situations are referred to that level in the hierarchy where a global perspective exists for all affected subunits. However, the hierarchy also has a limited range. As uncertainty increases the number of exceptions increases until the hierarchy becomes overloaded.

3. Coordination by Targets or Goals

As the uncertainty of the organization's task increases, coordination increasingly takes place by specifying outputs, goals or targets [March and Simon, 1958, p. 145]. Instead of specifying specific behaviors to be enacted, the organization undertakes processes to set goals to be achieved and the employees select the behaviors which lead to goal accomplishment. Planning reduces the amount of information processing in the hierarchy by increasing the amount of discretion exercised at lower levels. Like the use of rules, planning achieves integrated action and also eliminates the need for continuous communication among interdependent subunits as long as task performance stays within the planned task specifications, budget limits, and targeted completion dates. If it does not, the hierarchy is again employed on an exception basis.

The ability of an organization to coordinate interdependent tasks depends on its ability to compute meaningful subgoals to guide subunit action. When uncertainty increases because of introducing new products, entering new markets, or employing new technologies these subgoals are incorrect. The result is more exceptions, more information processing, and an overloaded hierarchy.

DESIGN STRATEGIES

The ability of an organization to successfully utilize coordination by goal setting, hierarchy, and rules depends on the combination of the frequency of exceptions and the capacity of the hierarchy to handle them. As the task uncertainty increases, the organization must again take organization design action. It can proceed in either of two general ways. First, it can act in two ways to reduce the amount of information that is processed. And second, the organization can act in two ways to increase its capacity to handle more information. The two methods for reducing the need for information and the two methods for increasing processing capacity are shown schematically in Figure 1. The effect of all these actions is to reduce the number of exceptional cases referred upward into the organization through hierarchical channels. The assumption is that the critical limiting factor of an organizational form is its ability to handle the nonroutine, consequential events that cannot be anticipated and planned for in advance. The nonprogrammed events place the greatest communication load on the organization.

1. Creation of Slack Resources

As the number of exceptions begin to overload the hierarchy, one response is to increase the planning targets so that fewer exceptions occur. For example, completion dates can be extended until the number of exceptions that occur are within the existing information processing capacity of the organization. This has been the practice in solving job shop scheduling problems [Pounds, 1963]. Job shops quote delivery times that are long enough to keep the scheduling

FIGURE 1
Organization Design Strategies

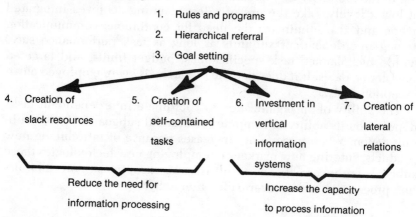

1. Rules and programs
2. Hierarchical referral
3. Goal setting

4. Creation of slack resources

5. Creation of self-contained tasks

6. Investment in vertical information systems

7. Creation of lateral relations

Reduce the need for information processing

Increase the capacity to process information

problem within the computational and information processing limits of the organization. Since every job shop has the same problem standard lead times evolve in the industry. Similarly budget targets could be raised, buffer inventories employed, etc. The greater the uncertainty, the greater the magnitude of the inventory, lead time, or budget needed to reduce an overload.

All of these examples have a similar effect. They represent the use of slack resources to reduce the amount of interdependence between subunits [March and Simon, 1958; Cyert and March, 1963]. This keeps the required amount of information within the capacity of the organization to process it. Information processing is reduced because an exception is less likely to occur and reduced interdependence means that fewer factors need to be considered simultaneously when an exception does occur.

The strategy of using slack resources has its costs. Relaxing budget targets has the obvious cost of requiring more budget. Increasing the time to completion date has the effect of delaying the customer. Inventories require the investment of capital funds which could be used elsewhere. Reduction of design optimization reduces the performance of the article being designed. Whether slack resources are used to reduce information or not depends on the relative cost of the other alternatives.

The design choices are: (1) among which factors to change (lead time, overtime, machine utilization, etc.) to create the slack and (2) by what amount should the factor be changed. Many operations research models are useful in choosing factors and amounts. The time-cost trade-off problem in project networks is a good example.

2. Creation of Self-Contained Tasks

The second method of reducing the amount of information processed is to change the subtask groupings from resource (input) based to output-based categories and give each group the resources it needs to supply the output. For example, the functional organization could be changed to product groups. Each group would have its own product engineers, process engineers, fabricating and assembly operations, and marketing activities. In other situations, groups can be created around product lines, geographical areas, projects, client groups, markets, etc., each of which would contain the input resources necessary for creation of the output.

The strategy of self-containment shifts the basis of the authority structure from one based on input, resource, skill, or occupational categories to one based on output or geographical categories. The shift reduces the amount of information processing through several mechanisms. First, it reduces the amount of output diversity faced by a single collection of resources. For example, a professional organization with multiple skill specialties providing service to three different client groups must schedule the use of these specialties across three demands for their services and determine priorities when conflicts occur. But, if the organization changed to three groups, one for each client category, each with its own full complement of specialists, the schedule conflicts across client groups disappears and there is no need to process information to determine priorities.

The second source of information reduction occurs through a reduced division of labor. The functional or resource specialized structure pools the demand for skills across all output categories. In the example above each client generates approximately one third of the demand for each skill. Since the division of labor is limited by the extent of the market, the division of labor must decrease as the demand decreases. In the professional organization, each client group may have generated a need for one third of a computer programmer. The functional organization would have hired one programmer and shared him across the groups. In the self-contained structure there is insufficient demand in each group for a programmer so the professionals must do their own programming. Specialization is reduced but there is no problem of scheduling the programmer's time across the three possible uses for it.

The cost of the self-containment strategy is the loss of resource specialization. In the example, the organization foregoes the benefit of a specialist in computer programming. If there is physical equipment, there is a loss of economies of scale. The professional organization would require three machines in the self-contained form but only a large time-shared machine in the functional form. But those resources which have large economies of scale or for which specialization is necessary may remain centralized. Thus, it is the degree of self-containment that is the variable. The greater the degree of uncertainty, other things equal, the greater the degree of self-containment.

The design choices are the basis for the self-contained structure and the number of resources to be contained in the groups. No groups are completely self-contained or they would not be part of the same organization. But one product divisionalized firm may have 8 to 15 functions in the division while another may have 12 of 15 in the divisions. Usually accounting, finance, and legal services are centralized and shared. Those functions which have economies of scale, require specialization, or are necessary for control remain centralized and not part of the self-contained group.

The first two strategies reduced the amount of information by lower performance standards and creating small autonomous groups to provide the output. Information is reduced because an exception is less likely to occur and fewer factors need to be considered when an exception does occur. The next two strategies accept the performance standards and division of labor as given and adapt the organization so as to process the new information which is created during task performance.

3. Investment in Vertical Information Systems

The organization can invest in mechanisms which allow it to process information acquired during task performance without overloading the hierarchical communication channels. The investment occurs according to the following logic. After the organization has created its plan or set of targets of inventories, labor utilization, budgets, and schedules, unanticipated events occur which generate exceptions requiring adjustments to the original plan. At some point when the number of exceptions becomes substantial, it is preferable to generate a new plan rather than make incremental changes with each exception. The issue is then how frequently should plans be revised—yearly, quarterly, or monthly? The greater the frequency of replanning the greater the resources, such as clerks, computer time, input-output devices, etc., required to process information about relevant factors.

The cost of information processing resources can be minimized if the language is formalized. Formalization of a decision-making language simply means that more information is transmitted with the same number of symbols. It is assumed that information processing resources are consumed in proportion to the number of symbols transmitted. The accounting system is an example of a formalized language.

Providing more information, more often, may simply overload the decision maker. Investment may be required to increase the capacity of the decision maker by employing computers, various man-machine combinations, assistants-to, etc. The cost of this strategy is the cost of the information processing resources consumed in transmitting and processing the data.

The design variables of this strategy are the decision frequency, the degree of formalization of language, and the type of decision mechanism which will make the choice. This strategy is usually operationalized by creating redundant information channels which transmit data from the point of origination upward in the hierarchy where the point of decision rests. If data are formalized and quantifiable, this strategy is effective. If the relevant data are qualitative and ambiguous, then it may prove easier to bring the decisions down to where the information exists.

4. Creation of Lateral Relationships

The last strategy is to employ selectively joint decision processes which cut across lines of authority. This strategy moves the level of decision making down in the organization to where the information exists but does so without reorganizing around self-contained groups. There are several types of lateral decision processes. Some processes are usually referred to as the informal organization. However, these informal processes do not always arise spontaneously out of the needs of the task. This is particularly true in multinational organizations in which participants are separated by physical barriers, language differences, and cultural differences. Under these circumstances lateral processes need to be designed. The lateral processes evolve as follows with increases in uncertainty.

Direct Contact. [Direct contact] between managers who share a problem. If a problem arises on the shop floor, the foreman can simply call the design engineer, and they can jointly agree upon a solution. From an information processing view, the joint decision prevents an upward referral and unloads the hierarchy.

Liaison Roles. When the volume of contacts between any two departments grows, it becomes economical to set up a specialized role to handle this communication. Liaison men are typical examples of specialized roles designed to facilitate communication between two interdependent departments and to bypass the long lines of communication involved in upward referral. Liaison roles arise at lower and middle levels of management.

Task Forces. Direct contact and liaison roles, like the integration mechanisms before them, have a limited range of usefulness. They work when two managers or functions are involved. When problems arise involving seven or eight departments, the decision-making capacity of direct contacts is exceeded. Then these problems must be referred upward. For uncertain, interdependent tasks such situations arise frequently. Task forces are a form of horizontal contact which is designed for problems of multiple departments.

The task force is made up of representatives from each of the affected departments. Some are full-time members, others may be part-time. The task force is a temporary group. It exists only as long as the problem remains. When a solution is reached, each participant returns to his normal tasks.

To the extent that they are successful, task forces remove problems from higher levels of the hierarchy. The decisions are made at lower levels in the organization. In order to guarantee integration, a group problem-solving approach is taken. Each affected subunit contributes a member and therefore provides the information necessary to judge the impact on all units.

Teams.   The next extension is to incorporate the group decision process into the permanent decision processes. That is, as certain decisions consistently arise, the task forces become permanent. These groups are labeled teams. There are many design issues concerned in team decision making such as at what level do they operate, who participates, etc. [Galbraith, 1973, chaps. 6 and 7]. One design decision is particularly critical. This is the choice of leadership. Sometimes a problem exists largely in one department so that the department manager is the leader. Sometimes the leadership passes from one manager to another. As a new product moves to the marketplace, the leader of the new product team is first the technical manager, followed by the production manager, and then the marketing manager. The result is that if the team cannot reach a consensus decision and the leader decides, the goals of the leader are consistent with the goals of the organization for the decision in question. But quite often obvious leaders cannot be found. Another mechanism must be introduced.

Integrating Roles.   The leadership issue is solved by creating a new role—an integrating role [Lawrence and Lorsch, 1967, chap. 3]. These roles carry the labels of product managers, program managers, project managers, unit managers (hospitals), materials managers, etc. After the role is created, the design problem is to create enough power in the role to influence the decision process. These roles have power even when no one reports directly to them. They have some power because they report to the general manager. But if they are selected so as to be unbiased with respect to the groups they integrate and to have technical competence, they have expert power. They collect information and equalize power differences due to preferential access to knowledge and information. The power equalization increases trust and the quality of the joint decision process. But power equalization occurs only if the integrating role is staffed with someone who can exercise expert power in the form of persuasion and informal influences rather than exert the power of rank or authority.

Managerial Linking Roles. As tasks become more uncertain, it is more difficult to exercise expert power. The role must get more power of the formal authority type in order to be effective at coordinating the joint decisions which occur at lower levels of the organization. This position power changes the nature of the role which for lack of a better name is labeled a managerial linking role. It is not like the integrating role because it possesses formal position power but is different from line managerial roles in that participants do not report to the linking manager. The power is added by the following successive changes:

a. The integrator receives approval power of budgets formulated in the departments to be integrated.
b. The planning and budgeting process starts with the integrator making his initiation in budgeting legitimate.
c. Linking manager receives the budget for the area of responsibility and buys resources from the specialist groups.

These mechanisms permit the manager to exercise influence even though no one works directly for him. The role is concerned with integration but exercises power through the formal power of the position. If this power is insufficient to integrate the subtasks and creation of self-contained groups is not feasible, there is one last step.

Matrix Organization. The last step is to create the dual authority relationship and the matrix organization [Galbraith, 1971]. At some point in the organization some roles have two superiors. The design issue is to select the locus of these roles. The result is a balance of power between the managerial linking roles and the normal line organization roles. Figure 2 depicts the pure matrix design.

The work of Lawrence and Lorsch is highly consistent with the assertions concerning lateral relations [Lawrence and Lorsch, 1967; Lorsch and Lawrence, 1968]. They compared the types of lateral relations undertaken by the most successful firm in three different industries. Their data are summarized in Table 1. The plastics firm has the greatest rate of new product introduction (uncertainty) and the greatest utilization of lateral processes. The container firm was also very successful but utilized only standard practices because its information processing task is much less formidable. Thus, the greater the uncertainty the lower the level of decision making and the integration is maintained by lateral relations.

FIGURE 2
A Pure Matrix Organization

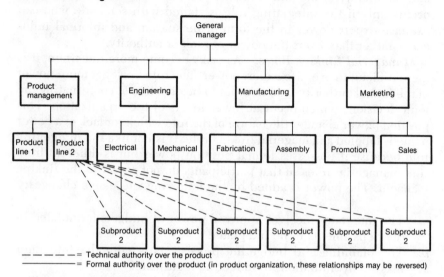

— — — — — = Technical authority over the product
————————— = Formal authority over the product (in product organization, these relationships may be reversed)

Table 1 points out the cost of using lateral relations. The plastics firm has 22 percent of its managers in integration roles. Thus, the greater the use of lateral relations the greater the managerial intensity. This cost must be balanced against the cost of slack resources, self-contained groups and information systems.

TABLE 1

	Plastics	Food	Container
Precent of new products in last ten years	35%	20%	0%
Integrating devices	Rules	Rules	Rules
	Hierarchy	Hierarchy	Hierarchy
	Planning	Planning	Planning
	Direct contact	Direct contact	Direct contact
	Teams at 3 levels	Task forces	
	Integrating department	Integrators	
Percent of integrators/ managers	22%	17%	0%

Adopted from Paul Lawrence and Jay Lorsch, *Organization and Environment* (Boston: Division of Research, Harvard Business School, 1967), pp. 86–138, and Jay Lorsch and Paul Lawrence, "Environmental Factors and Organization Integration." Paper read at the Annual Meeting of the American Sociological Association, August 27, 1968, Boston, Mass.

CHOICE OF STRATEGY

Each of the four strategies has been briefly presented. The organization can follow one or some combination of several if it chooses. It will choose that strategy which has the least cost in its environmental context. [For an example, see Galbraith, 1970]. However, what may be lost in all of the explanations is that the four strategies are hypothesized to be an exhaustive set of alternatives. That is, if the organization is faced with greater uncertainty due to technological change, higher performance standards due to increased competition, or diversifies its product line to reduce dependence, the amount of information processing is increased. *The organization must adopt at least one of the four strategies when faced with greater uncertainty.* If it does not consciously choose one of the four, then the first, reduced performance standards, will happen automatically. The task information requirements and the capacity of the organization to process information are always matched. If the organization does not consciously match them, reduced performance through budget overruns, schedule overruns will occur in order to bring about equality. Thus the organization should be planned and designed simultaneously with the planning of the strategy and resource allocations. But if the strategy involves introducing new products, entering new markets, etc., then some provision for increased information must be made. Not to decide is to decide, and it is to decide upon slack resources as the strategy to remove hierarchical overload.

There is probably a fifth strategy which is not articulated here. Instead of changing the organization in response to task uncertainty, the organization can operate on its environment to reduce uncertainty. The organization through strategic decisions, long-term contracts, coalitions, etc., can control its environment. But these maneuvers have costs also. They should be compared with costs of the four design strategies presented above.

SUMMARY

The purpose of this paper has been to explain why task uncertainty is related to organizational form. In so doing the cognitive limits theory of Herbert Simon was the guiding influence. As the consequences of cognitive limits were traced through the framework, various organization design strategies were articulated. The framework provides a basis for integrating organizational interventions, such as information systems and group problem solving, which have been treated separately before.

REFERENCES

Cyert, Richard, & James March. *The Behavioral Theory of the Firm.* Englewood Cliffs. N.J.: Prentice-Hall, 1963.

Galbraith, Jay. "Environmental and Technological Determinents of Organization Design: A Case Study." In *Studies in Organization Design*, ed. Paul Lawrence and Jay Lorsch. Homewood, Ill.: Richard D. Irwin, 1970.

Galbraith, Jay. "Designing Matrix Organizations." *Business Horizons*, 1971, pp. 29–40.

Galbraith, Jay. *Organization Design.* Reading, Mass.: Addison-Wesley Publishing, 1973.

Lawrence, Paul, & Jay Lorsch. *Organization and Environment.* Boston, Mass.: Division of Research, Harvard Business School, 1967.

Lorsch, Jay, & Paul Lawrence. "Environmental Factors and Organization Integration." Paper read at the Annual Meeting of the American Sociological Association, August 27, 1968, Boston, Mass.

March, James, & Herbert Simon. *Organizations.* New York: John Wiley & Sons, 1958.

Pounds, William. "The Scheduling Environment." In *Industrial Scheduling*, ed. Muth, John F., and Thompson, Gerald L. Englewood Cliffs, N.J.: Prentice-Hall, 1963.

Simon, Herbert. *Models of Man.* New York: John Wiley & Sons, 1957.

33

Organization Development: A Political Perspective*

ANTHONY T. COBB and NEWTON MARGULIES

It is now accepted that organizational politics exist in every organization and are involved in almost every facet of organizational life. Organizational politics are certainly involved in intervention programs. Despite these facts, organization development (OD) has been characterized as lacking any political sophistication whatsoever. In order to increase their success rate, OD consultants have been asked to become more politically involved in their intervention programs [Bennis, 1969; Pettigrew, 1975]. We argue here that OD has developed an unrecognized political orientation that aids OD consultants in the political arena and supports their intervention programs, and we explore the practical and ethical/value considerations of greater political involvement.

* From *Academy of Management Review* 6, no. 1 (1981), pp. 49–59. © 1981 by the Academy of Management 0363-7425

During the last several years the area of organizational politics (OP) has attracted the interest of social scientists and practitioners alike. In the field of organization development (OD), interest has focused on the use of OP in intervention programs. It is now generally recognized that such programs inevitably affect organizational politics and are affected by them [Bennis, 1969; Cobb, 1977; Pettigrew, 1975].

Despite this knowledge, the movement of OD into the study and use of OP has been cautious and conservative. At present, the interest OD displays in OP remains largely peripheral to what can be called its clinical or process orientation: one that relies on a relatively intimate client/consultant relationship to facilitate self-discovery, help, and renewal [Margulies & Raia, 1978, pp. 110–111]. There are a number of views regarding this level of OP interest. One extreme holds that any political orientation will necessarily divert attention from OD's clinical mission and inevitably subvert it. Another extreme view holds that OD consultants ought to assume a political activist role to ensure that program objectives are implemented. Both views maintain that OD has been devoid of any political orientation. The former maintains that this is how it should be, the latter that it must no longer remain so.

Our purposes in this article are two: First, we assert that, while OD is not politically sophisticated, neither is it devoid of a political orientation. OD has developed an unrecognized political orientation in many of its values and some aspects of its most frequently used technology. Although this political orientation is restricted in scope, it has proved useful in supporting OD's clinical objectives. We believe that the effectiveness of OD can be enhanced when professionals recognize, accept, and use this existing political orientation in the service of organizational change.

Our second purpose is to explore some of the ramifications of a greater level of political involvement in intervention programs. Although increased political involvement can aid the OD consultant and the host organization, so too can it do harm, particularly when it moves to the extreme of political activism.

To address these issues properly, a political perspective is developed first to view OD's past and its alternative political futures. This perspective provides focus for subsequent discussions.

A POLITICAL PERSPECTIVE

A political perspective with sufficient range to deal with the issues raised here can be developed by briefly addressing two topics. First, a definition of the term *organizational politics* is provided and, second, what can be called the political subsystem is described.

The Meaning of Organizational Politics

The literature provides many definitions of OP developed from a variety of perspectives. Mayes and Allen [1977] provide an adequate survey of these. In terms relevant to OD, organizational politics can be defined as *the use of power to modify or protect an organization's exchange structure.* An exchange structure is composed of an organization's resource distribution system and those who have formal authority to decide to what purposes resources will be used. An exchange structure in equilibrium represents the status quo and is "legitimate." Efforts to change the status quo, then, involve political action both on the part of those who challenge and those who seek to maintain it.

As seen in this light, OP per se is neither good nor bad. Actually, OP can either help or hinder the organization, depending on the processes used and the objectives sought. Even though it is easy for the OD consultant to become involved in politics, it is entirely another matter to have the sophistication to manage the use of OP productively.

The Political Subsystem

For convenience, the notion of a social subsystem [Guest, Hersey, & Blanchard, 1977] is used here to denote the subsystem about which the OD consultant is expert and in which he or she operates. This subsystem co-exists with many others, one of which can be labeled the political subsystem.

The political subsystem is composed of the sources, locations, and flow of power through the organization. The basic criterion of effectiveness within the subsystem is the extent to which sufficient power can be accumulated and transferred to those locations (i.e., individuals) in the organization to maintain productive operations, solve problems, and implement solutions. A political subsystem is efficient to the extent that power can be accumulated and transferred quickly and with precision.

A tenet of general systems theory is that subsystems interact with one another. Therefore, changes in either the social or political subsystem will produce changes in the other. The interactive relationship poses at least two basic problems to OD consultants concerned with organizational politics. The first is determining how support can be generated within the political subsystem to aid work within the social subsystem. The second is knowing what changes are necessary in the social subsystem to facilitate the development of an effective and efficient political subsystem.

POLITICAL ORIENTATIONS IN ORGANIZATION DEVELOPMENT

Because there is interaction between the social subsystem and the political subsystem, successful change in the former requires complementary and supportive changes in the latter. It is because OD is well aware of such subsystem interaction [Benne & Birnbaum, 1969; Leavitt, 1965] that there has been recent concern that OD consultants should become more politically sophisticated and active in order to increase intervention success [Burke, 1976; Pettigrew, 1975]. Yet, historically speaking, OD interventions on the whole have enjoyed a great deal of success. Given that OD consultants have traditionally displayed, at most, a minimal interest in OP, the issue must be raised of how they are able to survive at all, much less be successful. One reason may be just good fortune. Another may be that clients themselves come to see that political cooperation is necessary to protect their own self-interests. We will argue that there is still a third reason: OD has developed a largely unrecognized political orientation in addition to its clinical one and this political orientation complements the clinical one in producing successful interventions.

Where in OD does this political orientation lie? Even now, organization development does not appear to be an easily defined field or profession. For the purposes here, OD can be viewed as a profession built on a foundation composed of three basic interactive elements: its values, its technology, and its knowledge of the human side of organizations. If there is a political orientation in OD that helps guide the political behavior of consultants, then, it should reside in one or more of these elements.

The knowledge base of OD incorporates clinical concepts relevant to power, models of power, and even sources of power available to consultants for work in interventions [Huse, 1980, pp. 143–148]. Properly viewed, such concepts of power *can* form a foundation on which to build political theory and intervention strategy. Yet, even today the knowledge base of OD remains essentially lacking in political theory and models to help *guide* the consultant in terms of political intervention strategies [Beer, 1976; Bennis, 1969]. Therefore, if political assistance is given to the consultant, it must come from the value or technological base of the field. It is our view that it comes from both.

Political Support in the Value Based

For the purposes here, the value component of OD is viewed in structural terms. At its base lie fundamental philosophical or value orientations. These would include rationalism, pragmatism, existentialism [Friedlander, 1976], humanism, and democracy [Friedlander

& Brown, 1974]. These basic orientations, then, provide the context for the development of more specific values: values concerning intervention concepts, means, and end-states. Valued clinical *aims*, or end-states of intervention, include individual growth and increased organizational effectiveness with the capability of self-renewal [French, Bell, & Zawacki, 1978]. Valued *means* for reaching this end-state include confrontation, honesty, open communications, the movement toward power equalization, and collaboration. Concepts that support these valued means include beliefs in the goodness of people, Theory Y assumptions, and the potential and desire for growth by organizational members. Such historically entrenched values of OD, then, provide the general context here for discussion.

The OD consultant is an expert in creating a social environment within which the client system can achieve full utilization of its own human resources to solve its problems [French et al., 1978]. Basic to the full utilization of human resources are such necessary processes as collaboration and participation. Collaboration, however, requires that power be exchanged, shared, and pooled. Participation in decision making requires a "franchise" that comes only with the power to make inputs. Thus, if the consultant is to achieve collaboration and participation in the social subsystem, supportive changes must occur within the political subsystem to allow it. Some of these changes include the general reduction of power differentials between organizational members, the transfer of power to those who are to participate in decision making, and the removal of structural obstacles to the flow of power in the organization generally and between levels of authority in particular. The consultant is guided in these tasks by many of the values OD has developed.

The belief that power equalization should be used in interventions is a central concept in OD [Leavitt, 1965]. Strauss [1963, p. 41] stated, for example, that "the main thrust of the 'human relations movement' over the last 20 years has been toward . . . 'power equalization'." In the nearly 20 years since Strauss's observation, this general orientation has become valued in its own right and is reflected in a number of other values that focus on more specific political problems. This can be demonstrated by examining specific values oriented to the individual, superior/subordinate relations, and organization structures paralleling the micro, intermediate, and macro perspectives of the organization.

The Individual's Political Position. Participation raises the basic political issue of who should be given the right, and thus the power, to participate in decision making. On the level of the nation or state, for example, the extent of citizen participation is justified and supported by the assumptions made regarding the capabilities and traits of the polity (i.e., citizens).

The political position of organizational members is justified and supported as well by basic assumptions regarding workers. McGregor [1960] has articulated some of these assumptions. Theory X assumptions support a political structure in which power is centralized and participation removed from the rank and file. Theory Y assumptions support a political structure in which power is decentralized, justifying a wide base of participation. The clinical side of Theory Y assumptions focuses on the individual as a potential resource in problem solving. Theory Y also justifies the political necessity of transferring some measure of participatory power to the worker. Thus, although OD consultants may not recognize it, when they promote a clinical value orientation, coinciding with Theory Y, they are establishing as well some of the political subsystem changes needed to support their clinical aims.

Superior/Subordinate Relations.   Historically, one of OD's principal concerns has been with leadership style. In its clinical context, OD has tied leadership style to interactions among subordinates, satisfaction, and productivity [Lewin, Lippitt, & White, 1939]. In terms of organizational change, OD has recognized that changes on one level require "complementary and reinforcing changes in organizational levels above and below that level" [Benne & Birnbaum, 1969, p. 331]. It is not surprising, therefore, to see that OD has developed a value orientation to leader/subordinate relations that supports the power exchange required for collaboration and interlevel adjustments between subordinates and superiors. Authoritarian leadership removes power from subordinates, thereby suppressing participation, collaboration, and the upward flow of influence, whereas democratic leadership facilitates them. The fact that OD values democratic leadership produces changes not only in the social subsystem, but complementary and reinforcing changes in the political subsystem as well.

The Organization Structure.   In accordance with general systems theory, the structural subsystem [Guest et al., 1977] will affect the political subsystem. Although they did not address the political subsystem specifically, Burns and Stalker [1961] recognized this interactive effect. They noted that the rigid power structure of mechanistic organizations tends to hamper the power flow necessary for broad organizational problem solving. Organic organizations, on the other hand, facilitate problem solving by allowing an easier flow of power through the political subsystem to wherever it is needed.

The behavioral administrative structures articulated by Likert [1961, 1967] are relevant to this discussion. System 1 tends to impede, but System 4 tends to facilitate the flow of power through the political subsystem. As a result, System 4 facilitates broad organizational collaboration, participation, and communication in the establishment of goals and resource distribution.

Organization development values an organic System 4 administrative structure for a number of clinical reasons. When such a structure is adopted by the client, however, it promotes changes within the political subsystem. These political changes, in turn, facilitate work within the social subsystem.

The Practical and Political Utility of Values. Fundamentally, OD values a democratic workplace and the power equalization inherent in it. It was demonstrated above that this value orientation is manifest whether one takes a micro, intermediate, or macro perspective of the organization. Part of the reason OD may hold these values is that they are generally accepted in our society. Clinically speaking, they are valued because OD believes that they promote effective organizational performance and personal growth. One should not ignore, however, the political utility these values have in terms of the consultant's clinical objectives.

Consider the problems typically faced by the consultant and client system. They tend to be unstructured, complex, novel, and complicated. Evidence indicates that these types of problems are best solved by a broad-based participatory effort utilizing the resources of those best able to attend to them regardless of formal power position [Burns & Stalker, 1961; MacCrimmon & Taylor, 1976].

Such collaborative and participative efforts, however, require commensurate political subsystem support. Many OD values, some of which have been presented here, can be seen as helpful in promoting political support for clinical objectives.

Political Support in the Technological Base

The technological base of OD can be divided into two interdependent components. One includes the tools and techniques the consultant can use in intervention. The second includes the roles assumed by the consultant (e.g., facilitator, interviewer) and the operational know-how, expertise, or knowledge to use the tools, techniques, and roles available to the consultant. Political supports can be found in both components.

Tools and Techniques. The value OD gives to power equalization finds expression in some of its techniques as well. Laboratory training, for example, promotes a commitment to open and honest communications regarding interpersonal relations, organizational life, and diagnosis. But such a commitment "does inevitably imply some democratization [that] . . . may indeed undermine formal authority to a considerable degree" [E. Schein, 1972, p. 93]. Intervention techniques that include such components as these, then, serve to operationalize the political as well as clinical side of the democratic values held by OD consultants.

Other techniques appear to play a political part in integrating vested interests by facilitating actual change in the exchange structure. Techniques oriented toward roles provide a case in point. Organizational roles prescribe occupant behavior, areas of decision making, character of reporting relationships, legitimate power, and the like. In short, roles contain many components of the status quo exchange structure. Many role techniques, therefore, have a political side in that they intervene "directly in the relationship of power, authority, and influence" of role occupants and reciprocals [Harrison, 1978, p. 159]. When OD consultants facilitate change in such role components, then, they are working within both the social and political subsystems to accomplish their aims.

The political subsystem is also affected by a number of techniques oriented to "structural" or "work engineering." The negotiation of resource exchanges and integration of vested interests, for example, is a political subsystem change that occurs along with the institution of a management-by-objectives system. The clinical objectives of job enrichment include ownership of the task, increases in perceived task importance, and the like. To accomplish these objectives, however, "vertical loading" is required, whereby previous supervisory prerogatives are given to the subordinate.

Consultant Roles and Operational Knowledge. Consultants are called on to play a variety of roles when using their knowledge and techniques. The literature describes many of these roles; our focus here is on a distinctly political role that cuts across many others and is often ignored: the diplomatic role. The purpose of this role is to communicate the vested interests of one party to another in a language that can be fully understood. The diplomat then seeks to integrate these vested interests when possible and, when not, to reduce the friction caused by competition by negotiations, trade-offs, and the like.

In order to support the clinical objectives of intervention, the consultant often assumes one of at least two diplomatic roles. One might be called the "enfranchiser" role. The socio-organizational distance between higher level and lower level participants is often large. So, too, is the power differential within the political subsystem. In order to communicate and facilitate the integration of vested interests, the consultant often becomes a "communications channel" between the parties. For lower level participants, consultants become surrogate participants in decision making; for higher level decision makers they are representatives of the organizational citizenry.

The consultant often plays a diplomatic role horizontally in the organization as well. The consultant is frequently called on to mediate between organizational groups that are interdependent but have different vested interests, values, perceptions, and beliefs. Like Lawrence and Lorsch's integrator [1967], the consultant facilitates communication between parties by serving as a communications channel or by facilitating face-to-face interaction. By working with and between both groups, the consultant aids in the integration of their vested interests while focusing on their interaction process.

Whether moving vertically, horizontally, or obliquely in the organization, the OD consultant is in a unique position to carry the interests of one party to another. The parties can speak openly to the consultant, without fear of repercussions, and can be confident that the consultant is concerned about them as well as about the general welfare of the organization. This promotes the power generation and transfer necessary for effective political subsystem operation. Thus, the consultant plays the clinical role of communications channel and the political role of power channel at the same time for the same purpose: beneficial change in the social subsystem.

The Political Side of Organization Development

The more one explores OD, the more one can see its political side. It is true, however, that OD's clinical orientation remains paramount and that the political side plays a mostly unrecognized, supportive role. Evaluations made by Bennis [1969], Beer [1976], and Burke [1976] hold true today. Organization development has not come to fully appreciate the impact that OP has on change programs. Nor has OD developed the models, knowledge, and facts that represent a sophisticated political orientation.

Nevertheless, OD's brand of "political pacifism" should not be ignored. It needs to be further explored for at least three reasons. The first is to see if the direction it provides is appropriate for the various situations OD consultants encounter. Second, if OD is determined to become more politically active, a foundation for such growth may be found not only in the values and technology of OD but its knowledge base as well. Third, OD's present political orientation can serve as a reference point. As such, it is useful for exploring those issues involved in assuming a greater political role.

POLITICAL INVOLVEMENT: CONSIDERATIONS FOR ORGANIZATION DEVELOPMENT

The OD profession has been urged to become more politically oriented and active [Bennis, 1969; Burke, 1976; Pettigrew, 1975]. In this regard at least two questions need to be raised. First, what would be the utility of increased political intervention? Second, what would be the consequences in terms of OD's ethical/value base? Before these questions can be answered, just what is meant by "increased political involvement" needs to be explored.

A Continuum of Political Involvement

It is possible to describe the extent and character of OP involvement along a continuum. At the extremes lie "political pacifism" and "political activism." The midrange is represented by the "political moderate" position.

Political Pacifism. Political pacifism has been represented above. It includes a fundamental commitment to clinical rather than political intervention. While a political element does exist, it is minimal, generally unrecognized, and oriented to clinical support rather than being used as a means of change in its own right.

Political Moderation. The political moderate advocates the development of knowledge, models, and strategies to overcome political blindspots [Bennis, 1969; Harrison, 1978; Pettigrew, 1975]. The use of these, however, remains subordinate to, and strictly supportive of, work within the social subsystem. The political role played by the consultant is at most one of a "political facilitator" who seeks to establish a political climate supportive of clinically oriented change. Honesty, truth, collaboration, participation, and the like are still pursued. Political facilitation works to overcome the political impediments to these components of change. The clients operating within this climate work toward the establishment of a new status quo, *one chosen by them.*

Political Activism. Political activism advocates deep involvement in the political subsystem—at least as much as, if not more than, in the social subsystem. Here the consultant adopts the role of "political activist," of someone who has some vision of what the client system's condition ought to be. This vision is realized by politically overcoming resistance to it. In this sense, then, the political activist maintains that "the ends justify the means" and advocates such strategies as limiting and channeling communication for political purposes, the use of covert or hidden agendas, and the political use of intervention research [V. Schein, 1977]. Coercive politics may also be used. Damaging information gained in intervention, for example, might be used against those who stand in the way of the consultant [Pettigrew. 1975].

The Utility of Increased Political Involvement

It has been argued that increased political involvement will lead to greater chances of intervention success than that provided by the current approach of political pacifism. Because these arguments have been directly and indirectly stated in the literature [Bennis, 1969; Harrison, 1978; Pettigrew, 1975; V. Schein, 1977], they are only briefly reviewed here.

The moderate position takes due note of the evidence that supports the existence of OP and the political subsystem, and their effect on any change program [Bennis, 1969; Cyert & March, 1964; March, 1962; March & Simon, 1958; Thompson, 1967]. Ignoring this evidence creates a significant gap in the operational knowledge of OD and its approach to change. Furthermore, this knowledge gap makes it impossible to develop appropriate reactive and proactive strategies to support the clinical aims of the intervention program. Evidence can be cited demonstrating that once this gap is filled, political tools, techniques, and strategies can be developed to serve the clinical ends of the OD consultant [Harrison, 1978; Selznick, 1949]. Although individual studies are subject to criticism, the corpus of evidence represents a systematic approach with generally positive results across applications. As a whole, then, the evidence lends support to the moderate position.

Political activism builds on the arguments provided by the moderate position. Activists assume that not only are politics a fact of organizational life but that some powerful and sophisticated members of the client system use politics to protect and extend their own selfish interests. These are formidable "opponents." Political activism, say the activists, is the best way to deal with them, and they cite evidence indicating that activist techniques (e.g., political manipulation of communication, research information) have successfully overcome such "opponents" [Pettigrew, 1975; V. Schein, 1977]. Unfortunately, most of this "evidence" is anecdotal and lacking in empirical validation. Much more empirical work needs to be done to support the activist position.

Some Caveats Regarding Increased Political Involvement

With all the arguments made for increased political involvement on the part of OD consultants, there is a surprising lack of attention given to some of the problems that may emerge. These potential problems deserve attention.

Political Success Requires Political Sophistication. Consultants in OD are probably more politically sophisticated than they realize or may be willing to admit. Nevertheless, OD consultants are clinicians, not politicians. Their training may have prepared them for political pacifism but not activism. To urge political pacifists to use techniques employed by activists can invite disaster. Recently, a broader base of political training and knowledge has been offered to OD consultants [Huse, 1980, pp. 143–148; NTL, 1980]. Though consultants now have the opportunity to develop greater political sophistication, the cautious and conservative progress of OD into OP may well be justified on utilitarian grounds. Little, if any, sophistication is required to enter the political arena, but a great deal is required to work productively within it.

Political Reaction in the Client System. Largely ignored in arguments favoring political involvement are considerations of how the client system may react. Activists maintain, for example, that organizational "opponents" should be politically overcome. It must be remembered, however, that what is home ground to the opponent is foreign territory to the consultant. If opponents have any political sophistication, they will have identified and marshalled sources of power, formed long-standing alliances, and developed political strategies that have proven value in that particular system. One can expect such opponents to use their power and strategies when they perceive that their vested interests are attacked.

In addition, one needs to consider how the client system itself will react to political confrontation. It is one thing to be able to win a political confrontation; it is quite another to keep such confrontations from adversely affecting the political subsystem. Political pacifism seems to have evolved to minimize the danger of disruption. Political moderates, and activists in particular, need to carefully consider this aspect of political subsystem reactivity.

Reaction to the OD Profession. Perhaps the biggest concern related to increased political activity, particularly political activism, is how clients will react to OD itself. Since its beginning, OD has developed an image of being close to what Charles Perrow [1977] called "the forces of light." This image derives from the emphasis on such fundamental values as honesty, openness, collaboration, and a steadfast concern for everyone in the client system. This image has utilitarian value. OD technology, for example, requires cooperation, trust, and client confidence in the consultant. The OD image supports these qualities, and the consultant depends on this image.

The success that political activists have enjoyed may be partly based on this image as well. Limiting and channeling communication for political purposes, the use of hidden or covert agendas, and the political manipulation of intervention research strategies may be successful partly because clients don't expect OD consultants to behave in this manner. Thus, using the element of surprise, the activist can catch opponents unprepared to effectively resist.

Images can change. As the reputation of the activist consultant grows, clients will no longer be caught by surprise. They can be expected, rather, to take the initiative and attack the consultant first. At the very least, the activist will no longer enjoy the trust and cooperation of clients who are preparing for political confrontation.

This would be a relatively minor concern for OD as a profession if clients could be counted on *not* to generalize their perceptions of activist consultants—an unrealistic hope. If the OD profession suffers an image change reflecting political activism, the chances of success even for political pacifists are reduced.

Consider the following example: A nationally known consultant company conducted management audits for a major governmental unit in the Pacific Southwest. Following the audits, high-ranking officials were fired, in light of evidence gained in some of the audits. Word quickly spread that these audits were political covers with the hidden agenda of marshalling evidence to do away with preselected officials. Whether or not this rumor was correct, from that point forward the audits created a great deal of political turmoil. Perhaps the activist is prepared for this type of reaction. The issue, however, is whether OD as a profession can accept this type of image change.

Facilitation versus Activism.   Political moderates remain committed to the traditional clinical orientation of organization development. They argue that political facilitation of social change is not only compatible with this orientation but will increase chances of intervention success as well. They conclude, therefore, that OD ought to promote such political involvement on the part of its practitioners. Although there is evidence to support this position, a number of caveats must be kept in mind. First, OD must take care to see that consultants are properly prepared to assume the role of a political facilitator. Second, political facilitation must be exercised with due caution lest the client system overreact. Third, OD must recognize that it is all too easy to slip from the facilitator role into the activist role. The boundaries between them are often difficult to define, particularly in the hour-to-hour and day-to-day operation of an intervention program.

Political activists maintain that political facilitation is not enough to achieve intervention success in the face of determined political resistance. Greater rates of success can, however, be expected if the consultant uses whatever power politics are required to confront and remove such resistance. Political activism, however, carries with it not only the problems of negative client-system reaction, but also the problems of a negative image change for the OD profession as a whole.

On utilitarian grounds alone, OD is well advised to increase political involvement only with extreme caution and due deliberation. Beyond utilitarian considerations, OD consultants and the field as a whole should address as well the issue of how political involvement affects the value base of the profession.

Value Considerations

Political involvement, particularly as it approaches political activism, has consequences for the values of organization development. There has been a general lack of discussion regarding what these consequences may be, yet this is an important topic, because the distinctive character and practice of OD, as with any professional field, is based as much on its values as on its technology and knowledge [Margulies & Raia, 1978]. The value base plays an important role in the image of OD; the use of its technology, and in providing the context and objectives for intervention itself. The value base reflects the nature of the relationship between client and consultant and what constitutes acceptable consultant behavior. Clients depend on the value base of OD just as they do in any professional relationship. It has been argued above that consultants depend on it as well.

Political activism provides a good context for discussion. The sharp contrast between the values inherent in political activism and the traditional values of OD produces issues more easily discerned than when lesser levels of political involvement are addressed. At the same time, the issues raised by these contrasts provide some points of departure for addressing the more subtle issues of lesser forms of political involvement. The assertion that the ends justify the means, whether explicitly advocated [V. Schein, 1977] or implicitly assumed provides the focus for value considerations.

Can the Means and Ends Be Separated? In theory, it may be possible to separate one's objectives and the means used to achieve them. In practice, and particularly in OD, the means used appear more often than not to affect the ends attained. From a value perspective, an OD intervention program is successful if the organizational health of a client system is improved and if it has achieved or expanded its capacity for self-renewal [French et al., 1978]. These goals, in turn, are dependent on, and evolve from, the achievement of a host of other clinical objectives. Such objectives may well be displaced in an intervention program using the philosophy and techniques of political activism.

The displacement of clinical objectives can occur for a number of reasons. First, intense political activity often leads to the compromise of objectives for political expediency. One must consider the point at which such compromise becomes failure from a clinical perspective. Second, political activism, by its nature, fosters political activity in the client system of a similar character. Such activity can itself displace clinical goals. Moreover, the aftermath of political activism, with its tendency to produce win/lose conflict, can leave strains and tensions in the client system that drain energy from productive uses and future renewal. Finally, the capacity for self-renewal requires that the consultant teach those in the client system the concepts, methods, and values that will allow them to solve future as well as present problems [French et al., 1978]. One must consider, then, whether political activism teaches the client methods of self-renewal, or suspicion, distrust, and the fine art of political warfare.

Presuming the Ends That Justify the Means.   Political activism is literally presumptuous: the activist presumes to know the good ends that justify the means used to achieve them. Traditionally, however, the OD consultant leaves the configuration of the ends (i.e., desired condition) to the decision making of the clients. In fact, the end traditionally pursued by OD consultants is to help establish the means by which the client can effectively and efficiently pursue a new status quo. Thus, within OD the means and ends are often the same.

The political moderate position recognizes this. It seeks to work within the political subsystem to help establish the climate necessary to support such traditional change elements as honesty, openness, collaboration, and participation. There is no doubt that these elements are value laden. To the extent that political activism replaces these traditional elements with a conscious restriction of openness and a limitation of both collaboration and participation, it is replacing the valued ends of OD for the means to reach some other set of objectives. Thus OD must consider, for example, if political resistance is a form of participation to be confronted and worked through or confronted and wiped out for some vision of what ought to be. In so considering, OD must consider as well whether it will still value the welfare of individuals, even those frightened enough to resist.

On the Value of Conserving OD Values.   If OD itself is to remain dynamic, the profession must constantly undergo changes to meet the challenges it faces. To the extent that OD values have promoted political naiveté within the profession, they may need to change to guide action in the political arena. It should be recognized, however, that the value base has served OD well in the past. If some values are to change, perhaps this would be best accomplished conservatively with the objective of *guiding* political involvement to reach *clinical ends.* Certainly traditional values should not be casually tossed aside to allow for politically expedient behaviors.

CONCLUDING REMARKS

We have focused on an important aspect of the growing field of organization development—its movement into the study and use of organizational politics. The present political orientations in the field, largely operationalized by OD consultants themselves, have been generally ignored and in some cases rejected. One purpose of the foregoing discussion has been to establish, as clearly as possible, the existence of these orientations. Broader recognition of OD's political orientations and the further development of political knowledge and skills can aid both the OD consultant and the field.

Political involvement is not, however, without its problems, and our second purpose has been to explore some of the utilitarian and value problems that can arise from increased political intervention. By exploring OD's present political orientation and its future political alternatives, we obtain a more complete understanding of the roles, skills, and strategies available to the OD consultant. This understanding, in turn, can only enhance the field.

REFERENCES

Beer, M. On gaining influence and power for OD. *Journal of Applied Behavioral Sciences,* 1976, *12,* 45–51.

Beene, K., & Birnbaum, M. "Principles of changing." In W. G. Bennis, K. Benne, & R. Chin (Eds.), *The planning of change.* New York: Holt, Rinehart & Winston, 1969.

Bennis, W. G. Unresolved problems facing organization development. *Business Quarterly,* 1969, *34*(4), 80–84.

Berke, W. W. Organization development in transition. *Journal of Applied Behavioral Sciences,* 1976, *12,* 22–43.

Burns, T., & Stalker, G. M. *The management of innovation.* London: Tavistock, 1961.

Cobb, A. T. *Political planning and organizational innovation.* Paper presented at the annual meeting of the Academy of Management, Orlando, Florida, August 1977.

Cyert, R. M., & March, J. G. *A behavioral theory of the firm.* Englewood Cliffs, N.J.: Prentice-Hall, 1964.

French, W., Bell, C., & Zawacki, R. Mapping the territory. In W. French, C. Bell, & R. Zawacki (Eds.), *Organization development: Theory, practice, and research.* Plano, Tex.: Business Publications, 1978, 5–12.

Friedlander, F. OD reaches adolescence: An exploration of its underlying values. *Journal of Applied Behavioral Science,* 1976, *12,* 7–22.

Friedlander, F., & Brown, L. D. Organization development. In M. Rosenzweig & L. Porter (Eds.), *Annual review of psychology.* Palo Alto, Calif.: Annual Reviews, Inc., 1974, pp. 313–341.

Guest, R., Hersey, P., & Blanchard, D. *Organizational change through effective leadership.* Englewood Cliffs, N.J.: Prentice-Hall, 1977.

Harrison, R. When power conflicts trigger team spirit. In W. French, C. Bell, & R . Zawacki (Eds.), *Organization Development: Theory, Practice, and Research,* 1978, pp. 158–164.

Huse, E. F. *Organization development and change.* New York: West, 1980.

Lawrence, P., & Lorsch, J. *Organization and environment.* Boston: Harvard University Graduate School of Business Administration, 1967.

Leavitt, H. J. Applied organizational change in industry: Structural, technological, and humanistic approaches. In J. G. March (Ed.), *Handbook of organizations.* Skokie, Ill.: Rand McNally, 1965, pp. 1144–1170.

Lewin, K., Lippitt, R., & White, R. Patterns of aggressive behavior in experimentally created "social climates." *Journal of Social Psychology,* 1939, *10,* 271–299.

Likert, R. *New patterns of management.* New York: McGraw-Hill, 1961.

Likert, R. *The human organization: Its management and value.* New York: McGraw-Hill, 1967.

MacCrimmon, K., & Taylor, R. N. Decision making and problem solving. In M. Dunnette (Ed.), *Handbook of industrial and organizational psychology.* Skokie, Ill.: Rand McNally, 1976, pp. 1397–1453.

March, J. G. The business firm as a political coalition. *Journal of Politics,* 1962, *24,* 662–678.

March, J. G., & Simon, H. *Organizations.* New York: Wiley, 1958.

Margulies, N., & Raia, A. P. *Conceptual foundations of organizational development.* New York: McGraw-Hill, 1978.

Mayes, B. T., & Allen, R. Toward a definition of organizational politics. *Academy of Management Review,* 1977, *2,* 672–678.

McGregor, D. *The human side of enterprise.* New York: McGraw-Hill, 1960.

NTL Institute. *1980 programs.* Arlington, Va.: NTL Institute, 1980.

Perrow, C. The short and glorious history of organizational theory. In H. Tosi & W. C. Hamner (Eds.), *Organizational behavior and management.* Chicago: St. Clair, 1977, pp. 8–19.

Pettigrew, A. M. Toward a political theory of organizational intervention. *Human Relations,* 1975, *28,* 191–208.

Schein, E. *Organizational psychology.* Englewood Cliffs, N.J.: Prentice-Hall, 1972.

Schein, V. Political strategies for implementing changes. *Group & Organization Studies,* 1977, *2,* 42–48.

Selznick, P. *TVA and the grass roots.* Berkeley: University of California Press, 1949.

Strauss, G. Some notes on power-equalization. In H. J. Leavitt (Ed.), *The social science of organizations.* Englewood Cliffs, N.J.: Prentice-Hall, 1963.

Thompson, J. D. *Organizations in action.* New York: McGraw-Hill, 1967.

34
Japanese Management—A Critical Review*

TAI K. OH[1]

One must look beyond the behavioral aspects of the Japanese management system to the economic conditions which support the system to understand fully its contribution to Japan's economic recovery. Permanent employment (Nenko) has created a highly efficient dual wage and labor market system but it excludes two thirds of the Japanese labor force from its benefits.

The startling economic recovery of Japan since the end of World War II has been widely attributed to the effectiveness of Japanese management. American management scholars and practitioners have been particularly impressed with the way in which the permanent employment system, known as Nenko, gives employees job security and promotes strong corporate loyalty, high motivation, and group effectiveness while still maintaining the flexibility to meet fluctuations in demand for labor and new developments in technology. It has been seriously suggested that U.S. managers might apply some of the principles underlying the Nenko system (7).

The way in which Japanese cultural behavior patterns and value orientations have affected the organizational behavior characteristic of Nenko has been widely discussed in management literature and is fairly well understood (2, 3, 7, 20, 21, 25, 37). The dynamics of Nenko managerial behavior have been described, examined, and discussed in great detail, and Nenko management's role in Japan's remarkable economic achievements has been duly identified and properly appreci-

* From *Academy of Management Review* 1, no. 1, (1976), pp. 14–25.

[1] The author wishes to acknowledge the generous cooperation and support of Dean Jack W. Coleman of the School of Business Administration and Economics, California State University, Fullerton, in obtaining funds for the collection and acquisition of the data on which this article is based, both in Japan and in the U.S. The author also gratefully acknowledges the generous cooperation and support for this study from Professor Shunichiro Umetani, Japan Institute of Labor.

Portions of this paper were presented at the Thirty-Fifth Annual Meeting of the Academy of Management, New Orleans, Louisiana, August, 1975.

ated. But the time has now come to look beyond the behavioral aspects of the Japanese management system for a more complete set of answers to the question of how and why the system works so well.

There are several critical economic factors essential to the existence of the Japanese management system which might well be necessary preconditions for the successful application of Nenko principles to U.S. operations. Japan's economic history and the peculiar structure of its industrial sector and labor market bear a large measure of responsibility for the development of and continued effectiveness of the Nenko system. In exploring Japan's permanent employment system in its proper context as an interdependent part of the socioeconomic structure of Japanese industry, some unexamined social and economic costs of the system will receive long overdue attention. In this perspective, the applicability of Nenko principles to U.S. operations must be reconsidered.

THE NENKO SYSTEM—A BRIEF DESCRIPTION AND HISTORY

The Nenko system of management has attracted widespread discussion among American management scholars and practitioners ever since James Abegglen introduced the system to the United States (1).

The basic features of the system are simple: an employee enters a large firm after junior high, high school, or college graduation, receives in-company training, and remains an employee until retirement at age 55.

The practice of payment according to length of service reinforces and maintains the permanence of employment among the workers within a firm. Usually only young, recent graduates can afford to enter such a system at beginning wages, and older workers cannot afford the loss of earnings a change of employer would entail. As a result, interfirm mobility is severely limited, and the vast majority of employees in Nenko firms remain with the same employers, throughout their careers. This makes extensive in-company training a profitable investment, and ties to the employer are often further reinforced by the employee's acquisition of enterprise-specific skills.

Japanese employees have reacted to the permanence of employment under Nenko by developing the strong group loyalty and system of shared obligations, heavy dependence on powerful superiors, and intense competitive drive that have come to be associated with Japanese management in the minds of American businessmen and businesswomen. Among members of a Nenko group, who are associated more by location and situation than by any other common factor, such cohesiveness, coordination, and effectiveness is accomplished by several powerful behavioral control mechanisms—a rigid, hierarchical structure based on seniority; intense emotional involvement in the life of the group; early indoctrination into the group ethos; total fulfillment of security needs; and economic interdependence. Yet within the framework of this system, there are areas in which competition is intense and highly motivating. There is competition among different firms within an industry, competition among separate work groups within a single firm, and individual competition for promotion within classes of employees who join a firm in the same year. In the last case, precise measurement of individual performance in terms of work function is not very feasible in the Japanese corporate management system; other criteria such as flexibility, group support, and corporate loyalty are employed to determine promotability (24, 34).

One of the most widespread misconceptions about Nenko is that it pervades the management of Japanese industrial concerns. Actually, the Nenko system is seldom operative in any but the larger Japanese firms (which form only a tiny minority of all firms in Japanese industry) and applies to a minority of Japanese workers. According to an estimate made by Solomon Levine in the early 1960s, the Nenko system applies to less than 30 percent of the nonagricultural labor force (18). Unfortunately, this limitation of Nenko protection and benefits to a minority of Japanese workers appears to be essential to the continued survival of the Nenko system, and is probably its greatest cost to Japanese society.

The best foundation for understanding Nenko and its position in the socioeconomic system of Japanese industry today is a knowledge of its development from its inception to the present.

Nenko After World War I

Although the roots of Nenko can be traced back to the 1920s and even earlier (19, 26, 37), the Nenko system became firmly established consequent to World War I (28). During the boom which occurred at that time, Japanese industry expanded rapidly. The rapid growth of the factory system required an immediate expansion of the labor force, and so the need to recruit and retain large numbers of factory workers became a major concern of management. At the Mitsubishi-Nagasaki shipyard, for example,

> the ratio of resigning workers to staying workers was as high as 52.0 percent. The situation hit the machinery and metal industries so hard that they lost three fourths of their workers because the latter moved to other industries (27, pp. 145–146).

Japanese employers attacked the problem of employee turnover on two fronts, and the practices they initiated to deal with it can be easily recognized as basic elements of the Nenko system today. First, companies began to recruit labor directly from the farm population and educational institutions and to provide intra-enterprise training for several years. The result was usually workers with highly specialized skills useful only to a specific industry. This worked to reduce inter-firm mobility. Second, the principle of using length of service as the principal wage determinant was initiated to create a further barrier to separation. During the first half of their working life, employees under the Nenko system are underpaid for the work they have performed, so in order to collect all their rightful wages, they must work until retirement, during which time overpayment for work performed will compensate for prior underpayment (8). This delayed compensation adds a significant hidden value to beginning wages offered by Nenko employers.

Of course, length of service is not the only determinant of wage increases. The Japanese wage is a highly complex value composed of many allowances and benefits, few of which have any connection with individual work performance. The basic starting wage, determined by the labor market and the educational level of the new employee, is a minor part of the total wage. Numerous small allowances for commuting, housing, dependents, etc., are added according to employee need, but by far the most important determinant of wage increase is length of service. Rewards for individual performance account for a very small range of variation on the wage increase curve (16, 19, 30). Since age and length of service theoretically reflect degree of skill acquired through occupational progression, payment by length of service does not deviate too drastically from value of work performed. When regular workers are recruited upon graduation, whether from junior high school, high school or college, their training program increases their value to their firm as they progress through occupations with increasing skill requirements and become more proficient at their work (30).

These two management policies of highly specialized training and payment according to length of service were introduced effectively to meet the economic objective of preventing workers from moving to other places of employment. Employers tended to reinforce the permanence of employment in these firms by their reluctance to hire other than new school graduates, who represented a savings in wage costs and were the most adaptable to a system which values long-term commitments (26). Thus there tended to be little shopping around for labor on the open market or from other firms unless the supply of new graduates was nearly exhausted (19). As a behavioral consequence of these policies, Nenko workers came to be involved in a closed system which fostered a strong sense of loyalty to the firms for which they worked.

Although Japanese employers were careful to discourage interfirm mobility, they had not yet reached the point prior to World War II where they actually guaranteed continued employment to their workers until retirement. They practiced performance evaluation, and employees who performed poorly had to leave the enterprise because of explicit and implicit discrimination against them. During recessions, there was widespread discharge of employees.

This gave Japanese employers considerable control over their labor costs. Although individual wages increased with time, a group of employees hired during any particular year would decline in number as time went by, so that the total wage outlay for that group remained rather stable. Fujida's model, shown in Table 1, illustrates this wage pattern clearly.

TABLE 1
Model Wage Pattern for Employees Beginning Service with a Firm in the Same Year under the Pre-World War II Nenko System

Years of Employment	Number of Employees	Wage per Employee	Employer's Total Wage
10	1	10	10
9	2	9	18
8	3	8	24
7	4	7	28
6	5	6	30
5	6	5	30
4	7	4	28
3	8	3	24
2	9	2	18
1	10	1	10
			220

Source: Wakao Fujida. *Labor Organization and Activities* (*Rodo Kumiai no Soshiki to undo*) (Kyoto: Minerva, 1962), p. 278.

Nenko also worked behaviorally to keep wages down. Workers with the same length of service in a firm competed for increased wages by competing for retention, leaving the actual rate of wage increase unaffected. Nenko employers were limited in the area of wage increase since length-of-service, the main determinant of wages, is an inflexible factor. Therefore, emphasis was placed on increasing welfare benefits and rewards in order not to conflict with the wage and length of service status structure among workers (17, 18). The costs to the firm of such rewards and benefits are not easy to evaluate because until recently, few Japanese enterprises bothered with precise accounting of such benefits, considering them "social overhead." Such costs probably represent an asset to the firm because they involve substantial tax advantages. Investment in noncash welfare services is facilitated by generous government and bank loans, especially when real estate is involved, because it represents a good investment (4).

Nenko after World War II

One of the most significant developments in Japanese industry after World War II was the unionization of the big Japanese industries where Nenko is pervasive. This put an end to the old system of employee discharge. Nenko worker's employment with a company is now guaranteed until retirement at age 55, and companies no longer discharge them unless there are serious economic conditions endangering the existence of the firm. Employees are not laid off during ordinary recessions.

The resulting employment security has intensified cohesiveness and group consciousness among Nenko workers and has been an important factor in the stabilization which the large enterprises require for rational economic planning in the face of rapid technological change and economic growth. But if large Japanese industrial employers had not countered with certain restrictions on the Nenko system, their total wage payments would have gone out of control (8). Fujida's model, shown in Table 2, illustrates this dilemma. The solution was to limit the number of new Nenko recruits, as illustrated by Fujida in Table 3, and to compensate for the decrease in number of permanent employees by extensive use of temporary, subcontract, daily, and retired workers. This limited the number of permanent employees to a cyclically justifiable minimum (29) and set the pattern for what has come to be known as the dual wage structure and dual labor market of Japan. This pattern as it operates today will be examined in detail.

NENKO AND NON-NENKO FIRMS AND EMPLOYEES: A "DUAL" SYSTEM

Japanese industrial firms range in size from huge corporations with 1,000 or more employees to tiny household enterprises. The labor force employed in these firms is composed of permanent employees in big enterprises, retired workers, temporary workers, and subcontract and daily workers. The dual wage and labor market structure is formed by the interrelationships of these firms and employee groups.

TABLE 2
Hypothetical Model of Wage Pattern for Employees Beginning Service with a Firm in the Same Year under the Post World War II Nenko System with All Employees Being Given Guaranteed Employment

Years of Employment	Number of Employees	Wage per Employee	Employer's Total Wage
10	10	10	100
9	10	9	90
8	10	8	80
7	10	7	70
6	10	6	60
5	10	5	50
4	10	4	40
3	10	3	30
2	10	2	20
1	10	1	10
			550

Source: Wakao Fujida. *Labor Organization and Activities (Rodo Kumiai no Soshiki to undo)* (Kyoto: Minerva, 1962), p. 320.

Size Distribution of Industrial Firms

Large industrial firms with 300 or more employees, in which the Nenko system is in widespread use, account for less than 1 percent of the total number of firms enumerated, and this ratio has remained virtually unchanged for over a decade. Medium-small firms, in contrast, comprise over 99 percent of all the enterprises in Japanese industry (11, 1965, 1973).

Distribution of Labor Force by Size of Firm

From 1962 to 1970, a little over 25 percent of the labor force was employed by small firms of less than 20 employees, from 40 to 45 percent was employed by medium-sized firms of from 20 to 299 employees, and 30 to 33 percent was employed in firms of 300 or more employees (11, 1973). Since the Nenko system seldom applied to workers in medium-small enterprises, the statistics support Levine's estimate that only about a third of the labor force is employed in Nenko firms, and that Nenko coverage has not expanded significantly over the past decade.

TABLE 3
Model of Wage Pattern for Employees Beginning Service with a Firm in the Same Year under the Post-World War II Nenko System, with Limited Recruitment of Employees and Guaranteed Employment

Years of Employment	Number of Employees	Wage per Employee	Employer's Total Wage
10	5	10	50
9	5	9	45
8	5	8	40
7	5	7	35
6	5	6	30
5	5	5	25
4	5	4	20
3	5	3	15
2	5	2	10
1	5	1	5
			275

Source: Wakao Fujida. *Labor Organization and Activities (Rodo Kumiai no Soshiki to undo)* (Kyoto: Minerva, 1962), p. 321.

Wage and Benefit Differences by Size of Firm

Compensation paid by Japanese industry is of two kinds: standard wages and fringe benefits. There are substantial differences in both types of compensation by size of firm.

The Standard Wage and Its Determinants. The standard wage covers the minimum cost of living of the wage earner and is composed primarily of the basic wage, the hierarchy (length of service) allowance, and various family and living allowances. It is determined by such factors as education, length of service, performance evaluation, and cost of living. For regular workers who are hired directly from an educational institution without skill or experience, the level of education and the labor market determine the level of the starting wage. The average high school graduate, 16 years old, a juvenile and unskilled, receives no family allowance or hierarchical allowance but is paid as if still a member of an original family unit with no dependents. As a result, the starting wage is extremely low. In 1972, the monthly starting salary of college graduates was $179, for high school graduates $142, and for junior high graduates $114 (Y280 = $1.00) (13). The standard wage then increases primarily in relation to workers' length of service but also according to the needs of their age group, their education, and perhaps to a small degree their performance appraisal. The cost of living is also considered when the worker is the sole supporter of his or her family.

In the large firms where Nenko is in effect, there is a much stronger and more consistent correlation between wages and length of service than among small firms where Nenko is not practiced (10). Because job classification plays little or no role in the determination of wages in these firms, they usually evidence very little occupational structure (18). (Simple and unitary group participation in the achievement of work objectives is another reason for the absence of clearly differentiated occupational roles and structure (23).) There are some indications that length of service could become a somewhat less important wage determinant among Nenko firms in the future; large Japanese firms have talked increasingly of establishing some sort of job evaluation and merit rating system which would tie compensation directly to occupation and skill. Nevertheless, the basic structure of the Nenko system remains as yet one of permanent employees in large establishments who are paid largely on the basis of length of service (19).

Differentials in the Standard Wage by Size of Firm. There are substantial wage differences between large Nenko and small, non-Nenko firms in the Japanese manufacturing industry. In 1970, workers in medium-small industry still made slightly less than two thirds the wages of workers in large enterprises, and workers employed by firms with from one to three employees, who constitute 14 percent of all workers in the manufacturing industry (11, 1973), received wages little more than one tenth as high as the wages of workers in large enterprises (13).

From these statistics (summarized in Table 4), an outline of the dual wage structure of the Japanese labor market begins to emerge.

Prospects for Erosion of Wage Differentials. It has been suggested that, because of the labor shortage resulting from economic expansion and a low birth rate, the wage gap between large and small firms has begun to narrow (36). There has been considerable narrowing, but it seems to be confined largely to young workers. Since wage increases for workers in smaller firms do not keep pace with wage increases in large firms, the significance of the narrowing is limited. Overall, the trend does not appear strong enough to suggest that the dual wage structure will be phased out in the forseeable future (22).

Fringe Benefits

It is the practice of Japanese employers to make semiannual bonus payments based on workers' current wages. Table 5 shows the size of the bonuses paid to employees in the manufacturing industry by size of firm for 1960–1972 and reveals a clear positive correlation between size of firm and size of bonus (11, 1973).

TABLE 4
Selected Characteristics of Japanese Manufacturing Firms and Employees, by Size of Firm

Size of Firm by Number of Employees	Percent Distribution by Size, 1969	Percent Distribution of Workers, 1970	Wage Indices, 1970*
1-19		27.0	
1-3			13
4-9			47
10-19			63
20-299		40.0	
20-99			70
100-299			77
1-299	99.4	67.0	
300 or more	.6	33.0	100

* Wages of workers in firms of 300 or more employees = 100.
Source: Japan Medium-Small Enterprise Agency (Chusho Kigyo Cho), *White Paper on Medium-Small Enterprise* (1973), Appendixes 2, 6 and 10.

TABLE 5
Semiannual Bonuses Paid in the Japanese Manufacturing Industry, by Size of Firm, 1960–1972*

	Size of Firm (number of employees)		
Year	500 or more	100–499	30–99
1960	3.36	2.76	1.75
1962	3.52	3.01	2.02
1964	3.60	3.00	2.10
1966	3.62	3.20	2.22
1968	3.91	3.57	2.68
1970	4.40	4.02	3.04
1972	4.29	3.96	3.05

* In terms of monthly wage.
Source: Japan, Ministry of Labor, *White Paper on Labor (Rodo Hakusho)* (Tokyo, 1973), p. 393.

Another striking feature of firms under the Nenko system is their distinctly well-equipped welfare facilities for workers. Their welfare benefits include company dormitories, housing facilities, summer resorts, loans, and so on (1). In contrast, medium and small enterprises have few such welfare facilities. Retirement payments are another advantage enjoyed only by employees of large scale enterprises.

Other Differences

Employment in small enterprises has some other disadvantages not clearly shown by wage and benefit statistics alone. First, while wages in smaller firms are lower, the hours required to earn them are longer (13). Second, employment security is constantly jeopardized due to the fact that medium-small enterprises frequently go bankrupt while larger enterprises are not permitted to go bankrupt (5). Third, employment by small firms is relatively dangerous. According to a Japanese government report, "In the manufacturing industry, the accident rate among firms of 30–99 employees is 6 times higher than that of firms with 1,000 or more employees" (12, p. 30).

Temporary, Subcontract, Daily, and Retired Workers—Their Roles and Their Wages

Simplified methods of production made possible by technological change have enabled Japanese employers to rely to a great extent on workers other than their regular employees. The extensive use of temporary, subcontract, daily, and retired workers gives employers the needed labor force flexibility to deal with fluctuations in the economy. Unfortunately, little substantive data concerning these types of workers are available (35).

Temporary Workers. Temporary workers are hired by management for specific time periods when expansion of the work force is required by the business cycle. Most of the time they function as regular workers in terms of skills and work content, but they are paid less—often 50 percent less—than regular workers (21), and the wide variety of fringe benefits enjoyed by Nenko workers are not available to them (15). Their jobs are not guaranteed, since their tenure depends on the current business cycle.

The use of temporary workers has been a growing trend. Statistics on the automotive industry between 1954 and 1960 show that by 1961 the proportion of temporary workers among 11 firms had risen from 5.5 percent in 1954 to more than one third of the total work force (32).

Subcontract and Daily Workers. Frequently, big firms will contract with smaller firms to supply labor for them. The workers supplied by these firms have an even lower status and more casual attachment to their employers than temporary workers (19). Usually, they perform unskilled tasks, but occasionally are found doing the same work as permanently employed workers. Like temporary workers they receive no fringe benefits and depend on the business cycle for employment, but their compensation tends to be even lower than that of temporary workers. Table 6 shows the wage ratio between daily workers and regular workers[2] in the manufacturing industry by size of firm for 1966–1972. Subcontract workers are even more economical because management is not responsible for them directly and saves the expense of direct hiring. The utilization of these workers varies from industry to industry, but the shipbuilding industry utilizes especially large numbers of them.

TABLE 6
Wage Indices for Daily Workers in the Japanese Manufacturing Industry, by Size of Firm, 1960–1972

Year		Size of Firm		
	All Sizes	*500 or More Employees*	*100–499 Employees*	*30–99 Employees*
1960	45.0	37.0	50.5	57.1
1962	48.5	41.8	54.1	56.5
1964	50.5	40.5	54.1	64.1
1966	45.0	39.5	49.2	52.1
1968	44.5	38.7	45.9	56.3
1970	43.6	38.1	46.2	52.7
1972	41.9	35.0	46.6	49.7

Note: Wage of regular employees = 100.
Source: Japan, Ministry of Labor, *White Paper on Labor (Rodo Hakusho)* (Tokyo, 1973), p. 391.

Retired Workers.   Most Japanese firms, especially firms under the Nenko system, make retirement at age 55 mandatory (12). Since wages increase by length of service, this permits employers to terminate employees at the point at which their wages become excessively costly (19). The firms from which workers retire still consider them as a source of labor, often designating them as "special employees" and hiring them at reduced wages under yearly contracts. In this capacity they provide their employers with yet another source of labor force flexibility—one which is especially valuable since the special employees have acquired a lifetime of training in the skills required for work in those firms.

---

[2] Whether Nenko or non-Nenko can only be deduced approximately from these statistics by size of firm; i.e., regular workers in firms of 500 or more employees are usually under the Nenko system while those employed in firms of 30–99 employees are rarely if ever under the Nenko system. Regular employees of firms of 100–499 employees might be under the Nenko system.

Nenko retirement benefits beyond such supplementary employment are: (*a*) generous lump-sum retirement benefits based on the last monthly wage multiplied by the number of years of service, plus an additional factor that increases them by as much as 30 percent (33) and/or (*b*) in a small but growing number of cases, monthly pensions (19). Nevertheless the retirement years of the ordinary nonexecutive worker can be difficult, as public pension payments are severely inadequate ($65 per month at age 60) and access to company housing is cut off by compulsory retirement (33).

The Subcontracting System

There are many types of interfirm relationships involved in the subcontracting system in Japanese industry. In one type of subcontract arrangement, the master company invests directly in the smaller company and controls and regulates its management. In other cases, the arrangement may simply be that an independent smaller establishment delivers almost all of its output to the master company. The affiliates may produce component parts for completion in the large firm, or may manufacture finished products which are marketed in the master distribution system.

Subcontract relationships are often more than simple two-level arrangements. They frequently involve a pyramidal chain of relationships with a large master firm at the top subcontracting with a group of smaller firms who may in turn subcontract with a group of even smaller firms. In the automotive industry, there are 14 auto makers. Below those are 350 parts makers, and below the 350 parts makers are about 8,000 even smaller subcontract firms. Likewise, manufacturers of electrical parts contract out much of their minor cutting and initial assembly work to small firms and these small firms in turn subcontract some of their work to household enterprises (26).

This pyramidal structure of the manufacturing industry had its origins in the economic conditions peculiar to Japan at the beginning of its economic expansion period. Cheap surplus labor was widely available, but large Japanese firms lacked the capital necessary for accelerated industrialization. To make up for this lack of capital, they utilized the output of already established smaller enterprises whenever possible. Today there are several technological and other reasons for subcontracting. Not all subcontracting arrangements in the Japanese manufacturing industry are exploitative in nature. Nevertheless, some firms in the subcontracting system still do serve the purpose of providing large firms with a valuable cushion against fluctuations in the business cycle, enabling them to make higher profits by manufacturing goods at lower cost. Conversely, these types of small subcontract firms depend on the market provided by the larger firms and must resist the trend toward higher wages in order to produce at a price their larger partners are willing to pay (9, 19).

LABOR UNIONS AND THE NENKO SYSTEM

At present, union membership in Japan numbers about 12 million workers distributed among more than 56,000 unit unions (the closest equivalent to local unions in the United States) (19).

Japanese labor unions characteristically include manual as well as nonmanual workers and are organized on an enterprise basis. The enterprise-wide union typically includes all branches and plants of a single firm, whether production includes single or multiple lines and whether one or several industries are involved. The union usually reflects the structure of the enterprise entity (17).

Japanese unions are found primarily in the larger public and private enterprises. Nearly 70 percent of all organized workers are employed by firms with 500 or more employees, while firms with less than 30 employees account for less than one percent of all union membership. Only about 34.4 percent of the wage and salary earners eligible to become union members are organized (13). In other words, very few workers outside the Nenko system belong to a labor union.

Naturally, Japanese unions tend to resist changes which appear to threaten job security, wages, or benefits. Within the firms they represent, they have tended to resist the introduction of job evaluation and merit-rating systems which link compensation directly to occupational skills because they want to protect the middle-aged and older employees who benefit from the present system and are most likely to be hurt by the changes.

Because the system of payment by length of service still prevails in Nenko firms, there are substantial differences in reward between workers in their 20s and workers in their 40s regardless of the nature of their performance or the work they perform. This has given rise to some dissatisfactions and frustrations among younger workers. Management has tended to cultivate such natural grievances in order to prevent younger employees from unifying with older ones to oppose management (15).

Thus, unions, in protecting the wages and benefits of older Nenko workers, find themselves in the ironic position of siding with management in support of a policy which is intended to keep labor down. Since the benefits the unions have secured for their firms are supported to some degree by the dual wage structure, they also find themselves opposed to the betterment of wages, benefits, and security among unorganized workers in medium and small industries who suffer from the burden the dual wage structure imposes (16). Tsuru summarizes the dilemma of the Japanese labor movement:

> Here is a paradoxical situation of organized workers in large firms sharing in the productivity rise with the monopoly capitalists who tend to exploit their small subsidiary firms, which in turn can survive only by exploiting their non-union workers to the utmost (31, p. 96).

Thus the major effect of the Japanese labor movement appears to be to reinforce Nenko and the dual wage and labor market system.

SUMMARY AND CONCLUSIONS

Much has been said about the effectiveness and efficiency of Japanese management practices. On-the-job training, security, and employee loyalty and motivation have been particularly admired. Behaviorally speaking, the question of whether these practices would be compatible with American behavior patterns and value orientations should not be overlooked. Clearly the question of adapting Nenko principles to U.S. management operations is much larger and involves the possibility that a Nenko-type management system might require the stability of permanent employment, which seems to require for its existence a kind of supporting labor market and wage structure which does not exist in the United States. Japanese managerial effectiveness cannot be understood and probably cannot be duplicated outside the context of the Japanese industrial relations system.

Robert Cole's view of the Japanese and U.S. management systems as "generalized functional alternatives which are compatible with the demands of advanced industrial technologies" (6, p. 630) illustrates how U.S. and Japanese management function within the context of two radically different industrial relations systems. In the context of Cole's concept, the Japanese alternative to the demands of advanced industrial technology has been to place great value on employee commitment among key workers in large firms as a resource, and to encourage it by a system of deferred rewards combined with guaranteed lifetime employment, while maintaining a large pool of untenured and underpaid workers to deal with changing business conditions. The American alternative has been to provide flexibility to meet business fluctuations and the need for external sources of trained labor on short notice by maintaining high rates of interfirm mobility. The sacrifice has been in "high turnover rates, poor returns on training costs, high cost of recruitment and termination, and seemingly high levels of alienation" (6, p. 628).

In terms of the cost-benefit tradeoff involved, it seems unlikely that U.S. employees would welcome the Japanese system. One would not expect employees of medium-small firms in the United States to willingly accept the role and wages of their Japanese counterparts. Even though unemployment is quite high among U.S. youth, it seems unlikely that the beginning wages offered Japanese youth would appeal to them, especially when only a third could expect to receive Nenko-type wage increases and benefits as compensation. Furthermore, it is questionable whether U.S. employees would be willing to accept mandatory requirement at age 55, without an adequate pension, and then to work on yearly contracts at reduced wages until disability or death.

If the assertion is correct that the stability of permanent employment and all it entails is a necessary precondition for the successful adaptation of Nenko principles to U.S. management operations, American management scholars and practitioners who have been interested in such adaptation may want to take a long, careful second look at the idea.

REFERENCES

1. Abegglen, James. *The Japanese Factory* (Glencoe, Ill.: Free Press, 1958).
2. Abegglen, James C. *Management and Worker: The Japanese Solution* (Tokyo: Sophia University, 1973).
3. Bairy, Maurice. "Motivational Forces in Japanese Life," in Robert J. Ballon (Ed.), *The Japanese Employee* (Tokyo: Sophia University, 1969), chap. 2.
4. Ballon, Robert J. "Lifelong Remuneration System," in *The Japanese Employee*, ed. Robert J. Ballon (Tokyo: Sophia University, 1969), chap. 6.
5. Ballon, Robert J. "Participative Employment," in *The Japanese Employee*, ed. Robert J. Ballon (Tokyo: Sophia University, 1969), chap. 3.
6. Cole, Robert E. "Permanent Employment in Japan: Facts and Fantasies," *Industrial and Labor Relations Review*, 26, no. 1 (1972).
7. Drucker, Peter. "What We Can Learn From Japanese Management," *Harvard Business Review* 49, no. 2 (1971).
8. Fujida, Wakao. *Labor Union Organization and Activities (Rodo Kumiai no soshiki to undo)* (Kyoto: Minerva, 1962).
9. Ito, Taikichi. *The High Growth of the Japanese Economy and the Problems of Small Enterprises* (Tokyo: Keio University Institute of Management and Labour Studies, Reprint Series, March 1964).
10. Japan, Institute of Labor. *Japan Labor Statistics* (Tokyo: 1970).
11. Japan, Medium-Small Enterprise Agency (Chusho Kigyo Cho). *White Paper on Medium-Small Enterprise (Chusho Kigyo Hakusho)*, (Tokyo, 1965, 1973).
12. Japan, Ministry of Labor (Rodosho). *Analysis of Labor Economics (Rodo Keizai no Bunseki)* (Tokyo, 1969).
13. Japan, Ministry of Labor. *White Paper on Labor (Rodo Hakusho)* (Tokyo, 1973).

14. Johnson, Richard Tanner, & William G. Ouchi.   "Made in America (Under Japanese Management)," *Harvard Business Review* 52, no. 5 (1974).

15. Kato, Tsunefumi.   *Socialistic Salaryman (Shakaishugiteki Salaryman)* (Tokyo: Kobunsha, 1967).

16. Kawada, H.   "Japanese Industrial Relations System: A Model for Developing Nations." Paper prepared for the University of Wisconsin Seminar on Comparative Labor Movements, Washington, D.C., April 1967.

17. Levine, Solomon B.   *Industrial Relations in Postwar Japan* (Urbana: University of Illinois Press, 1958).

18. Levine, Solomon B.   "Labor Markets and Collective Bargaining in Japan," in *The State and Economic Enterprise in Japan,* ed. William Lockwood (Princeton, N.J.: Princeton University Press, 1965).

19. Levine, Solomon B., & Gerald G. Somers.   "Youth Employment and Wages in Japan." *IRRI Reprint No. 132* (Madison, Wisconsin: Industrial Relations Research Institute), reprinted from *Youth Unemployment and Minimum Wages* (1970), chap. 11.

20. Nakane, Chie.   *Japanese Society* (Berkeley: University of California Press, 1970).

21. Nakayama, Saburo.   "Management by Participation in Japan," *Management Japan* 6, no. 4, and 7, no. 1 (1973).

22. Oh, Tai K.   "Characteristics of the Japanese Labor Market" (unpublished ms.), 1966.

23. Oh, Tai K.   "Understanding Japanese Management" (California State University, Fullerton, 1975). Mimeographed.

24. Ratcliffe, Charles Tait.   "Japan's Employment System in the 1970's," in Mainichi Newspapers, *How to Succeed in Japan; a Guide for the Foreign Businessman* (Tokyo: Japan External Trade Organization (Jetro), 1974).

25. Shuichi, Kato.   "Reconstruction of the Japanese Group," *Japan Quarterly* 21 (January–March 1974).

26. Somers, Gerald G., & Masumi Tsuda.   "Job Vacancies and Structural Change in Japanese Labor Markets." Paper presented for the Conference on Job Vacancy Research, National Bureau of Economic Research, New York, Feb. 11–13, 1965.

27. Sumiya, Mikio.   *Social Impact of Industrialization in Japan* (Tokyo: Japanese National Commission for UNESCO, 1963).

28. Sumiya, Mikio.   "The Impact of Technological Change on Industrial Relations in Japan," in *The Changing Patterns of Industrial Relations: Proceedings of the International Conference on Industrial Relations,* Japan Institute of Labor (Tokyo, 1965).

29. Taira, Koji.   "Characteristics of Japanese Labor Markets," *Economic Development and Cultural Change* 10 (January 1962).

30. Tsuda, Masumi.   "Japanese Wage Structure and Its Significance for International Comparisons," *British Journal of Industrial Relations* (July 1965).

31. Tsuru, Shigeto.   "Survey of Economic Research in Postwar Japan; Major Issues of Theory and Public Policy Arising Out of Postwar Economic Problems," *American Economic Review* 54, no. 4, Pt. 2 suppl. (June 1964), 96–97.

32. Umetani, Shunichiro. "Statistics Prepared from a Lecture Given by Iwakoshi at the University of Tokyo." Nissan Motor Co., Ltd., 1972 (mimeographed).

33. Umetani, Schunichiro. "The Life of the Japanese Worker," *Japan Labor Bulletin* (January 1, 1974).

34. Umetani, Schunichiro. "Man and Organization in Japan," *Japan Labor Bulletin* (October 1, 1974).

35. Yamamoto, Kiyoshi. "Labor Market for Temporary and Subcontract Workers," in *Bunken Kenkyu, Nihon no rodo mondai*, ed. Rodomondai Bunken Kenkyukai (Tokyo, 1966).

36. Yamamura, Kozo. "Wage Structure and Economic Growth in Postwar Japan," *Industrial and Labor Relations Review* (October 1965).

37. Yoshino, M. Y. *Japan's Managerial System; Tradition and Innovation* (Cambridge, Mass.: MIT Press, 1968).